Principles of Perceptual
Learning and Development

THE CENTURY PSYCHOLOGY SERIES

Eleanor J. Gibson
Cornell University

Principles of Perceptual Learning and Development

PRENTICE-HALL, INC.
Englewood Cliffs, New Jersey

On the titlepage:

A kitten looking down at a visual cliff (see Chapter 12).

(From *Scientific American,* by William Vandivert.)

ISBN: 0-13-709618-6

Library of Congress Catalog Card Number: 72-77536

10 9 8 7 6 5 4 3 2 1

152.1
G448

Acknowledgments:

Pp. 4–5, 108–109, 119, 215. William James. *Principles of psychology.* New York: Holt, 1890. By permission of Holt, Rinehart and Winston.

Pp. 21–22. H. v. Helmholtz. *Handbook of physiological optics.* Vol. III. Tr. by J. P. C. Southall. New York: Optical Society of America.

P. 42. W. H. Ittleson. *Perception and transactional psychology.* In S. Koch (Ed.), *Psychology: A study of a science.* Vol. V. New York: McGraw-Hill, © 1962.

Pp. 203, 205. I. Kohler. The formation and transformation of the perceptual world. *Physiological issues.* Vol. III, No. 4, 1964. International Universities Press, Inc.

P. 215. *The Complete Poems of Emily Dickinson.* Ed. Thomas H. Johnson. Boston: Little Brown & Co., 1960.

P. 151. Marcel Proust. *Swann's Way.* Tr. by C. K. Scott Moncrieff. New York: Random House, 1934.

P. 391. Jean Piaget. *Les mécanismes perceptifs.* 1967.

Preface

This book was begun in 1959 at the Institute for Advanced Study in Princeton, New Jersey. Four chapters were completed when I began to realize the magnitude of the plan I hoped to follow and to feel some doubt of my possessing the wisdom and theoretical sophistication that it deserved. I put it to one side then, and proceeded to write papers which were relevant to my goal and would give me an opportunity to delve deeper into the literature and the theoretical dilemmas that were disturbing me (the problem of reinforcement in perceptual development, for instance). The papers included a chapter on perception in children for Mussen's *Handbook of Research Methods in Child Development;* a chapter on perceptual development for a NSSSE Yearbook on Child Psychology; a review of perceptual learning for *Annual Review of Psychology;* and two papers on the theory of perceptual learning for International Congresses of Psychology, which also got a hearing at various university colloquia in this country. These experiences strengthened my confidence in the usefulness of the hypotheses I was developing, and so I started the book afresh in 1964 at the Center for Advanced Study in the Behavioral Sciences. I made good progress that year and owe a debt of gratitude to my colleagues at the Center who read chapters and argued with me, and to the Center personnel who made writing so pleasant.

In a sense I have really been preparing to write this book all my professional life. My Ph.D. dissertation, done under Clark Hull at Yale, incorporated an S-R model of the kind fashionable at that time, but the Pavlovian concepts I chose to work with (differentiation and generalization) were capable of translation into the concepts of perception. Later I worked on perceptual learning under an Air Force contract; on effects of early experience on discrimination of form with R. D. Walk and with support from the National Science Foundation; on comparative studies of depth perception (the visual cliff) again with R. D. Walk and support from the National Science Foundation; and on a psychological and experimental analysis of reading skill with the support of the United States Office of Education and the National Institutes of Health. The latter project was a revelation to me in many ways. I began to learn something about the development of language and I learned that even basic research might be pushed in the direction of real educational problems.

v

Cornell University gave me a home for much of this time, although nepotism rules prevented my being on the professorial staff until three years ago. Perhaps this was a blessing in disguise, for it allowed me leisure to devote to my research and to the graduate students. To them I owe an incalculable debt. Herbert and Anne Pick, Thomas and Louise Tighe, Carol Bishop, Harry Osser, William Schiff, Tom Bower, Albert Yonas, Sharon Shepela, and Franklin Schapiro are a few of the ones who worked with me and influenced my thinking at least as much as I did theirs. I hope they will feel they have a share in this book and will not find it wanting.

Who do I hope will read this book? My colleagues who are interested in perceptual learning and development, of course. I hope it will be useful for advanced undergraduate courses, not only in psychology but also in child development and in education. I have had students from all three sources in my classes. I am sure that a merging of these three disciplines is necessary. It would be possible for a course in developmental psychology to use the first eight chapters and the last six, omitting the strictly experimental material and the two chapters on phylogenetic development and imprinting. The first eight chapters cover theories of perceptual learning, four of them devoted to my own theory. The next four emphasize the experimental approach to perceptual learning and are particularly appropriate for a class or seminar oriented toward research, since they bring out many problems in need of experimental attack. The rest of the book is developmental: two chapters concerned with a phylogenetic approach (here I am much in debt to the ethologists), and the last six with development of perception in the human child.

Finally, I must express my gratitude to the two people who really made it possible to complete this book. One is my husband, whose theoretical integrity and intrepidity and whose love for argument have surely raised the theoretical level of my thinking many degrees. I have thought of this book as beginning where his left off, and have taken for granted his ideas about perception. The reader may need to consult his books first. The other is Mrs. Carol Kannus, whose ability to decipher my ill-scrawled manuscript and put it into sensible, beautifully typed English is nothing short of miraculous.

E. J. G.

Ithaca, New York
February, 1969

Contents

Preface   v

1   Introduction: Towards a Definition and a Taxonomy of Perceptual Learning   1

2   Traditional Theories of Perceptual Learning and Development   19

3   Contemporary Theories of Perceptual Learning: Cognitive Theories   37

4   Contemporary Theories of Perceptual Learning: Response-oriented Theories   53

5   A Differentiation Theory of Perceptual Development   75

6   A Differentiation Theory of Perceptual Development: Principles and Mechanisms   95

7   Selective Factors in Perceptual Learning   119

8   Perceptual Learning and the Total Cognitive Process   145

9   The Improvement of Perceptual Skills with Practice   163

10   Perceptual Learning with Imposed Transformation of the Stimulus Array   193

11   Intermodal Transfer of Perceptual Learning   215

12   The Study of Perceptual Development by Means of Controlled Rearing   233

13   The Phylogenesis of Perception: Taxonomy and Trends   263

14   Imprinting as a Type of Perceptual Development   297

15   The Development of Perception in the
     Individual: Methodological Considerations   317

16   The Development of Perception in the
     Individual: Perceiving Objects   341

17   The Development of Perception in the
     Individual: Perceiving Space and Events   369

18   The Development of Perception in the
     Individual: Perceiving by Means of
     Representations   395

19   The Development of Perception in the
     Individual: Perceiving by Means of Symbols   419

20   Trends in Perceptual Development   445

References   473

Index   515

Principles of Perceptual
Learning and Development

1

Introduction:
Towards a Definition and a
Taxonomy of Perceptual Learning

NEW WINE IN AN OLD BOTTLE

If anyone at all acquainted with the psychological literature of the last fifty years were asked what problem was of most absorbing interest to American psychologists of this period, he would surely answer "Learning." The great names of the times—Thorndike, Watson, Hull, Tolman—reflect this preoccupation and awe us with their influence. With this went a strong bias about the genesis and development of behavior, an empirical bias. But there is more than one kind of learning, as Tolman (1949) pointed out in a famous address by this title eighteen years ago. Tolman cast a more tolerant eye on cognition than the predominantly S-R theorists of the times, and yet he left out of consideration the kind of learning I am going to write about: perceptual learning. It goes without saying that none of his rival theorists talked about it. They were concerned with how we learn to press a bar, choose the right turn in a maze, acquire fear or aggression, repeat a list of nonsense syllables, and maybe identify a concept that the experimenter had privately defined. Four years ago, when I told a friend in the mainstream of psychology that I was writing a book about perceptual learning, he answered, "How can you write a whole book about it?"

This attitude is surprising, because it was a theory of perceptual development that laid the foundation for all these learning theories. Bishop Berkeley (1709), the first of the associationists to proclaim that elementary sense impressions were welded together by association with images of past impressions to form meaningful perceptions, fostered a pattern for a theory that dies hard. Especially convincing, history has shown, was his insistence that vision, through association, gains its meaning from touch, and that any apparent equivalence of sensory information is the result of associative integration.

More modern learning theory, when it dealt with perception at all, tended to say that visual sensations gained meaning through association with

1

actions, which in turn provided feedback stimulation (little s's, self-produced stimulation, mediating stimuli) but the idea is fundamentally similar. In the early twentieth century it gained impetus from the functionalists of the time—Thorndlike, Dewey, Carr. In the thirties it was reinforced again by Hullian theory and by a few perception psychologists who (like Dewey) emphasized transactions with the environment.

But psychology in the fifties and the sixties has found a need for great changes. One force for change was the impact of information theory and its implications for perception. It became clear that one cannot speak of a stimulus, or a response; one must know the set of alternative stimuli and responses (if indeed one can ever speak of a single one). One must, furthermore, know the properties or features that define the set and differentiate its members; one must recognize that these may vary in utility for a task such as discrimination, identification, or recognition, and so perceptual strategies must be considered. But this is getting ahead.

Communication theory, which fathered information theory, also drew our attention to speech, the most interesting and characteristically human behavior, and the most neglected by psychologists. In attempting to apply methods and concepts of information theory to speech, it became clear that something was drastically wanting—the concept of structure (Miller, Galanter, & Pribram, 1960; Garner, 1962). The Gestalt psychologists had pointed this out with respect to perception, but it became somehow much more convincing when chaining concepts were shown to be insufficient even for a sequential behavior.

The third and even more shattering impact has come quite recently from the demonstration by neurophysiologists that a stimulus is not confined to a point on a receptor surface or an instant in time (Maturana et al., 1960; Hubel & Wiesel, 1962, 1963). To be effective, a stimulus requires change, and is therefore relational. The stimulus energy must contain information—inhomogeneity. The demonstration that single neural fibers in the optical system of a frog or a cat fire specifically for stimulus displays with relational features such as edge character, motion, convexity, and different angles of orientation must convince even the most stubborn believer in punctate stimulation that it is time for a change. And if an anaesthetized, uneducated kitten picks up relational features of its environment, however simple, only think of the complexity and order of structure of stimulus information that must be available to a mature, educated human adult.

And so the question of perceptual development comes again into its own. Nature does not turn out an infant with knowledge and strategies ready-made for perceiving the complexities of all the information in the stimulation coming from the world, its furniture and events, and the man-made information bombarding him as well. How are sets of things in the world sorted out and assembled? How does a child learn the way members of a set differ? How does he learn to utilize distinctive features within the set in relation to a task? Are higher orders of structure in the stimulus information picked up increasingly with development? What strategies of perceptual processing exist or are learned? A new look in learning theory is going to be needed to answer such questions. To understand how structure in stimulation is detected, I think we are going to have to substitute something for the compounding of elementary Ss and Rs and for the notion that association and reinforcement are necessary and sufficient to account for learning. I think we are going to have to work out a theory of perceptual learning, shaking off, if we need to, some of the old and respectable, but possibly timeworn formulae.

WHAT IS PERCEPTUAL LEARNING?

A definition at this point is premature, because this whole book is an attempt to define the problem and the field, so I shall make a very general functional one for a start. Because it is functional, it points to an interaction between the organism and the environment. Because we are talking about learning, it points to a modification of behavior. But because we are talking about perception, the modification is in the organism's ability to extract information from the stimulation in its environment, rather than in its ability to change something in the environment, or do something to it.

Perception, functionally speaking, is the process by which we obtain firsthand information about the world around us. It has a phenomenal aspect, the awareness of events presently occurring in the organism's immediate surroundings. It has also a responsive aspect; it entails discriminative, selective response to the stimuli in the immediate environment. Without discriminative response, there would be no correlation with ongoing events, or with qualitative and quantitative differences in stimuli. Stimulation is vast, varied, and potentially more informative than the organism's ability to register it, except in specially devised environments like ones used to study effects of sensory deprivation. Perception is selective by nature. Selectivity can even be demonstrated at birth in some species, as studies of innate releasing stimuli have shown. But the extent of selectivity at birth varies with species. In man a rather gross selectivity at birth becomes progressively refined with development and experience.

Perceptual learning then refers to an increase in the ability to extract information from the environment, as a result of experience and practice with stimulation coming from it. That the change should be in the direction of getting better information is a reasonable expectation, since man has evolved in the world and constantly interacts with it. Adaptive modification of perception should result in better correlation with the events and objects that are the sources of stimulation as well as an increase in the capacity to utilize potential stimulation.

This definition describes an end result, admittedly, rather than a process. I will jump ahead and say just one or two things about the process, as I see it. It is not a passive absorption, but an active process, in the sense of exploring and searching, for perception itself is active. A strong case has been made for this in "The Senses Considered as Perceptual Systems" (J. J. Gibson, 1966). We do not just see, we look; we do not just hear, we listen. Perceptual learning is self-regulating, in the sense that modification occurs without the necessity of external reinforcement. It is stimulus oriented, with a goal of extracting and reducing the information in stimulation. Discovery of distinctive features and structure in the world is fundamental in the achievement of this goal.

Modifications in the way the world is perceived refer to a learning process which can be studied in the laboratory. Methods and paradigms for experiments on perceptual learning are available just as they are for experiments on motor learning or conditioning. But perceptual modification goes on in development, too, and I have found it impossible to arrive at a theory without considering both learning and development. The developmental method, involving comparisons of an individual over his lifetime, gives us insights about the direction of modification that no short-term experiment could. Laboratory control of stimulation in the learning experiments makes it possible to test hypotheses derived from observations of development. The aim will be therefore to benefit from studying both.

EXAMPLES OF PERCEPTUAL LEARNING
AND DEVELOPMENT

William James, who always knew a good problem when he saw it, pointed out the importance of perceptual learning in a style so irresistible that it deserves quotation.

That "practice makes perfect" is notorious in the field of motor accomplishments. But motor accomplishments depend in part on sensory discrimination. Billiard-playing, rifle-shooting, tightrope-dancing demand the most delicate appreciation of minute disparities of sensation, as well as the power to make accurately graduated muscular response thereto. In the purely sensorial field we have the well-known virtuosity displayed by the professional buyers and testers of various kinds of goods. One man will distinguish by taste between the upper and lower half of a bottle of old Madeira. Another will recognize, by feeling the flour in a barrel, whether the wheat was grown in Iowa or Tennessee. The blind deaf mute, Laura Bridgman, has so improved her touch as to recognize, after a year's interval, the hand of a person who once had shaken hers; and her sister in misfortune, Julia Brace, is said to have been employed in the Hartford

Asylum to sort the linen of its multitudinous inmates, after it came from the wash, by her wonderfully educated sense of smell (James, 1890, Vol. I, p. 509).

Thinking about something substantive in one's own experience often helps pin down a problem. Let me describe what I heard as I woke up this morning, for it points to an everyday aspect of perceptual learning that is not so apparent in James's examples of sensory "virtuosity." In my window came a medley of sounds. They divided for me into two kinds. One was the sound of the neighbor's lawnmower. I knew that one. The rest was a conglomeration (for me) of many bird songs. Suddenly a new one was added to the conglomeration and I could pick it out from the rest—it was the mourning dove. I knew it, as I did the lawnmower. What does it mean to say that I knew it? An easy answer would be to say that I had identified it by learning the name for it. But that would be no answer, for it would not explain how I had differentiated that particular pattern of sound from the rest of the medley. An ornithologist could no doubt have separated out all the patterns and named them for me. I know the names, too; there are wrens, robins, cardinals, finches, and so on. But I cannot differentiate the songs. In the case of the mourning dove, the fact that I know the name is incidental. I could call it a paloma just as well and still recognize the pattern of its song. I can go with the ornithologist to his field laboratory and listen to the sounds from the marsh. The patterns of physical energy coming to his ears and mine are the same. But from this burst of sound impinging on the eardrum, he can detect patterns and invariants where I cannot. He can describe to me some of the qualities—"listen to that low rhythmical rumbling sound"; but I cannot hear them separated from the rest of the buzzes and whirs even when he tells me their characteristics. How has he learned to detect the critical features which make the pattern distinct from all the others? This question is a central problem for perceptual learning.

Another common example of perceptual modification which comes to most of us eventually is adaptation to spectacle wearing. Dramatic experiments with spectacles which distort the appearance of things such as reversing them up and down, or making them look curved or slanted have been performed in the laboratory, and habituation has then been shown to occur. But a more modest version of the same thing happens when we get a new pair of bifocals or sunglasses. Habits of looking must be adapted to the bifocals, and very quickly are. Areas of fuzziness where focus changes are very noticeable at first (and irritating). But they soon disappear. When one looks through the near focus at a wall five or six feet away, the wall bends. But this too is soon adapted to. Some people report great annoyance from seeing the rims of the spectacles at first, and after images of them when the spectacles are removed. In this case, the rims do not disappear; one can pay attention to them if he so desires even after years of wearing the spectacles. But some real adaptation occurs to slight distortions produced by the lenses. Is this perceptual learning? We shall consider it in detail in a later chapter, for it points to something important—that learning can be inhibitory, and involve suppression as well as detection.

Perceptual Learning in Industry and Defense

Studies of the acquisition of industrial skills have frequently made the point that the major learning is perceptual, rather than motor (Seymour, 1956). Grading of products such as cheese and cloth has been studied by industrial psychologists. Binns (1926, 1936) compared the performance of skilled wool graders with that of untrained persons. The trained judges could grade accurately by sight alone, without touching the material. This equivalence of two modalities for making a skilled judgment points to one of the most interesting problems in the area of perceptual learning, the development of cross-modal equivalence (the equivalence between two kinds of sensory information, such as visual and tactual).

An amusing and yet commercially important example of technical perceptual skill is chick sexing (Lunn, 1948). Dividing the pullets from the cockerels shortly after hatching permits the poultry raiser to concentrate on the most productive aspect of his business, but to distinguish the sexes at this stage is exceptionally difficult (see Fig. 1–1). Experts were brought from Japan in 1934 to teach the secrets of this skill to American poultrymen, and some sorters have since learned to achieve an accuracy as high as 99.5 percent, with great benefit to the producers. The art, as its practitioners regard it, requires proper manipulation of the chick and visual discrimination of very subtle differences. Some invariant relationship exists which permits the sexes to be distinguished, but abstraction of this invariant from the amazingly variable accompanying features, as the pictures show, is no simple matter.

Wine-tasting has produced so many anecdotes of esoteric lore that two Cornell psychologists were induced a few years ago to make a little experimental exploration of it. James Gibson and Richard Walk, provided with six varietal white wines of New York State by the Widmer Wine Company, performed two experiments with their classes, one in perception and one in learning. The class in perception did a psychophysical experiment, making same-different judgments and matching to a sample. The class in learning was given practice in discrimination and in identification. Needless to say, none of the students developed a fine palate in this short time, but several interesting facts emerged. Some wines are more distinctive than others—the more distinctive the wine, the easier it is to identify by name (to learn to give the right name when six kinds are randomly presented); discrimination improves with practice, but all

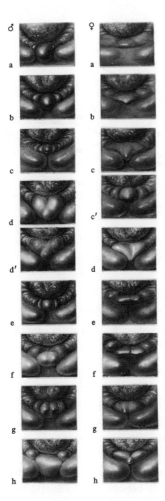

FIGURE 1–1. Variations in genital eminences of pullets and cockerels.

Differentiating the sex of newly hatched chicks is a perceptual skill that requires training and long practice. (From T. H. Canfield, Sex determination of day-old chicks, II. Type variations. *Poultry Science, 20:* 327–328, 1941.)

the improvement, in this case, showed up in the "same" judgments; identification also improves (see the learning curves in Fig. 1–2); just as much improvement in discrimination occurred when no correction was given for errors as when it was.

Not only industry presents real cases of perceptual learning; so do military occupations. Learning to land a plane requires perceptual skills of the highest degree: recognizing invariants in a flow pattern, for instance

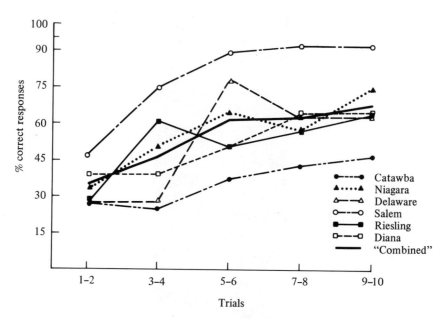

FIGURE 1–2.   Improvement with practice in identifying six varieties of white wine. (Data from R. D. Walk, unpublished.)

(see Gibson, Olum, & Rosenblatt, 1955). Reading maps and oscilloscopes requires perceptual training. A recent perceptual skill that has \been studied by psychologists is the interpretation of aerial photographs. The importance of this is evident; the Russian missile bases on Cuba were discovered by one clever man's detection of them in a photograph; they were hidden for nearly all observers of the photograph. The training for this skill becomes more specialized as new kinds of photography are developed, so that the picture resulting is not a natural one, but becomes to some extent coded. Distinctive features of natural military objectives such as bridges and hangars must be discovered and then matched to the corresponding features in the photograph.

　　Professional skills often require delicate use of an instrument designed to enhance perception. The physician's diagnostic aids, such as the stethoscope, the microscope, and the X-ray photograph, all demand training if the user is to discover relevant distinctive features of pattern and structure. Many of us recall our first biology class in high school and the baffling attempt to discover what was to be seen in the microscope. We can all sympathize with Thurber's description of his struggles to see what was there, his exultation when he finally saw something to draw, and the

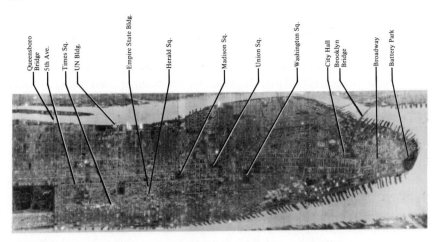

FIGURE 1–3.   Infrared photograph of Manhattan Island.

Identification of critical targets and distinctive features of a terrain in aerial photographs is a perceptual skill that becomes more specialized as new methods of photography are developed. (Photograph courtesy of H. R. B. Singer, Inc. and H. Leibowitz.)

ultimate shock when the teacher pointed out that he had drawn a picture of his own eyelashes. What subtle kind of learning goes on as the young would-be neurologist progresses from bare ability to discriminate gray matter from white to the discrimination and identification of cells from dozens of different areas of the nervous system?

Reading X-ray plates is a particularly interesting perceptual skill. M. Vernon (1957) called attention to an article in *Lancet* reporting a comparison of British and American specialists in reading chest radiographs (Johnson, 1955). The American readers called more of them positive for tuberculosis than did the British. They put more emphasis on minimal shadows because they had conducted extensive studies on minimal pulmonary lesions and learned the significance of very small, faint shadows. But in another study, the American readers picked out fewer films showing pneumoconiosis (a pulmonary disease to which coal miners are susceptible) than British readers, because the latter had been conducting extensive surveys on miners and were alert for minimal but relevant changes. Mere verbal description, however, has been found insufficient for training. Educational research with X-rays is now trying computerized methods, presenting the pictures on a scope and letting the learner indicate the critical features with a light pencil. The computer corrects the learner so that he can compare his selection of features with a trained selection.

Deprivation and Perceptual Development

As William James pointed out, blindness tends to engender the learning of unusual perceptual skills. It used to be thought that nature compensated in some way for the loss of vision by providing extraordinary sensory gifts of another kind, but now we know that these unusual powers are hard-won skills, learned of necessity. The so-called facial vision of the blind turns out, after long and careful research (Supa, Cotzin, & Dallenbach, 1944), to be auditory echolocation. Auditory feedback from sounds created by the observer, such as the sound of his footsteps or the tapping of a cane, is different depending on the objects surrounding the observer and on his location with respect to them. Discrimination of small binaural differences and differences in echo latencies (Ammons, Worchel, & Dallenbach, 1953) permits the skilled observer to locate obstacles in his path. Some animals, such as the bat, emit high-pitched sounds as they fly and direct themselves by the echo of the sound cast by obstacles. A man can operate a clicker or beeping instrument in a similar fashion and learn to differentiate the echoes (Griffin, 1958), but it turns out that most of the people who are highly trained and successful in avoiding obstacles by echolocation, like a blind boy who successfully rode a bicycle, make clicking sounds with their mouths or snap the fingers, providing their own sonar system.

Sonar operators at sea (see Fig. 1–4) frequently mistake the echoes returning from a school of large fish or a whale for those of a submarine, but they nevertheless learn to differentiate a large number of fish, as well as mines and other military objectives. Differences in size, surface texture, and density of the target may provide stimulus information for the discrimination and it is possible that shape does, too. Laboratory experiments have recently been conducted with both blind and seeing (but blindfolded) subjects, investigating their ability to discriminate distance, size, and texture of objects, with all sensory information except sound carefully controlled (Kellogg, 1962). Blind subjects who were unusually successful at locating a disc not only sent out their own sonar beams, but also oscillated their heads in a fashion referred to by Kellogg as "auditory scanning." One blind subject moved his head up and down as he sent out vocal signals, "as if he were trying to 'aim' the sound at the circumference of the disc in order to pinpoint the location of its edge (p. 402)." This is a remarkable and instructive case of skilled, active perceptual search. Kellogg found, too, that blinded subjects could distinguish between objects of the same size which were made of metal, wood, denim cloth, and velvet. They simply sounded different from one another. Sighted unpracticed subjects seldom performed above chance in this task.

Shape discrimination, by means of differential echo variables, has

FIGURE 1–4. Pilot lowering a sonar dome from his helicopter into the sea.

Echoic information from whales and submarines can be confused, but sonar operators learn to distinguish between many varieties of marine life. (John Dominis, *Life* Magazine © Time Inc.)

been studied by Rice (1967), who found four blind subjects capable of discriminating three metal targets of the same area but different shapes (circle, square, and triangle) with 80 percent accuracy. Auditory acuity must be normal or near normal in these subjects, but it is detection of changes in a sound that is critical, according to Rice. Echo detection in a soundproof chamber may not seem so hard a discrimination to learn, and it has been learned experimentally by a number of subjects. But in a noisy world, full of the sounds of traffic and other people, what a virtuoso it must be who can steer a bicycle by perceiving echoes!

Being deprived of sight, it seems, may lead an individual to learn to perceive and use systematically stimulus information that is potentially there for anyone to detect. It is auditory information as to the presence, location, size, shape, and even substance of a nearby object, and it substitutes for visual stimulation by supplying some of the same information about the world as vision does. Information about shape and texture is also given by touch to the blind man. But meanwhile he is living without visual experience. Does this mean that an individual blind from birth but by some means restored to sight would fail to discriminate and recognize familiar objects when they were first displayed to him visually? This question was put to John Locke by the philosopher Molyneux, and raises the interesting problem of transfer and equivalence between the modalities of sense. If a cube and a sphere had been differentiated tactually by the blind man, would they now be discriminably different to him when presented visually? Would he recognize them? We shall consider these questions in detail in a chapter on intermodal transfer. It is enough to point out here that this classic question of the philosophers was raised anew in recent years when a collection of cases of blind persons restored to sight through surgical removal of cataracts was published by von Senden (1960). The cases had been reported individually by surgeons over several centuries. Interesting as they are, they do not lead to an unequivocal answer to the question of intermodal transfer, or whether one must learn to see.

It seems clear from the cases reported by Senden that objects such as oranges and books are not recognized at first view, if one means by that identified by name. Senden reported that color alone is attended to at first, but that absolutely no attention is paid to contour. The same form in a different color, he says, is not recognized as the same object. When the book first appeared, many psychologists drew the conclusion that the human infant begins his visual life like the blind adult restored to sight, i.e., that he perceives the world at first as patches of color and only gradually integrates these separate elementary impressions into contours and structured forms. But the adult who has developed without access to visual stimulation is not the same organism as the infant who has immediate access to it; he has learned to substitute information from other modalities like sound and touch, and he has furthermore lost natural capacities that are present in the normal infant. We will consider in detail in a later chapter what can be learned about perceptual development from experimental studies of early sensory deprivation.

Perception of Permanent Properties of the World

One of the accomplishments of the human child, at least by the time he is of school age, is the recognition of many permanent properties of objects and many invariants of events. He perceives a ball coming toward him as the same ball, moving in a given direction, not as a new and larger object from instant to instant. When a toy falls on its side, presenting a different aspect to his view from the upright one it just had, he perceives it as the same toy, not a new one. When a ball rolls behind a chair and emerges on the other side, he is ready for it and perceives it as the same ball. Here in a nutshell is one of the most interesting questions of perceptual development: the development of perceived invariance.

Stimulation is constantly changing as an observer moves around the world, but the world and the objects in it have permanent properties. It is the permanent properties of the space we live in and the things in it that we need to perceive in order to behave adaptively. How is this possible when stimulation changes with every move of head, eyes, and body? Traditionally, psychologists have referred to this question as the "problem of perceptual constancy," splitting it up into problems of size constancy, shape constancy, color constancy, and so on. It has been assumed by many developmental psychologists that the child must learn to perceive invariant size, shape, and color, perhaps by association of temporally contiguous experiences, or by associating different visual impressions with some identical response which thus mediates constancy. Piaget (Piaget & Lambercier, 1951) has taught many psychologists to think of the development of the constancies as a process of intellectual construction.

We shall consider these questions in the chapters on perceptual development. I shall try to show then, in line with the concept of stimulus information adopted by J. J. Gibson (1966a and b), that since stimulation occurs over time, as well as over space, and has temporal as well as spatial structure, invariants are present in the stimulus transformations over time; and that it is pickup of these invariants that permits perception of the permanent properties of things.

PERCEPTION AND THE ENVIRONMENT

I am taking for granted, in penetrating into the questions of perceptual learning and development, some sophistication on the reader's part regarding the psychology of perception. But I must emphasize that my point of view about perception and the environment is not the conservative and traditional one. Like the ethologists, I think that understanding the adaptive relationship between behavior and the environment is our major goal, and that we must be concerned, therefore, with man's ecology, and not just stimulation considered as energy impinging on a receptor cell.

I assume with J. J. Gibson (1966) that there is structure in the world and structure in the stimulus, and that it is the structure in the stimulus—considered as a global array, not punctate—that constitutes information about the world. That there is structure in the world is self-evident to the physical scientist who uses elaborate tools and methods to discover it. The complex molecular structure of an enzyme containing more than a thousand atoms arranged in chains twisted, coiled, and cross-linked in intricate relationships has been described and even embodied in a solid model (New York *Times,* Jan. 22, 1967). The scientists who discovered this complex structure were indeed performing a job of intellectual construction involving more than perception, but the structure was there to be discovered, not purely imaginary. Perception deals with real structures, too: the ones in our immediate surroundings, from which stimulation emanates and travels to the sensory systems without intervening instrumentation and calculation.

To study perception, we must distinguish between the distal objects and surfaces of the world (the sources of stimulation) and the stimulation emanating from them that is proximal to the sensory systems. But perception is not of stimuli; it is of the distal objects and surfaces. Stimulation carries information about them, but only if it is examined over space and time. It is extraction of this information that characterizes perception; and it is increasing ability to extract this information that characterizes perceptual learning and development.

Gibson (1961) has proposed an ecological optics to deal with the variables of an optic array which carry information, in the sense of corresponding to environmental facts. These variables are not found in a ray of light at a given instant, but are found by analyzing structure, that is, boundaries, moving edges, transitions, gradients, and transformations over time. "Stimulus energy, unless it has structure, conveys no information. The natural structure of stimulation from the near environment conveys information directly. The structure of stimulation from representations conveys similar information, but indirectly. The structure of stimulation from socially coded or conventional signals conveys information still more indirectly (Gibson, 1966b, p. 245)."

I shall follow the distinctions made in the paragraph above, but I should point out at once that the information in the structure of stimulation is potential; it is not necessarily picked up by the organism exposed to it. There are levels of structure in stimulation; obvious, easy to perceive contrasts, but also higher order structures. A small child can pick up the pattern of "Three Blind Mice," but not that of a Shostakovich symphony. He discriminates visually simple linear order, but he has trouble perceiving the order in a set of graphic patterns where a common cluster of letters is repeated. The study of perceptual learning and perceptual development is primarily the effort to understand the increasing pickup of structure in stimulation.

Egon Brunswik (1956), like Gibson, stressed the importance of ecology, and the correspondence between the distal environment and perception, but he thought, as we shall see in an ensuing chapter, that the organism must learn by association to predict the distal events. Perceptual learning requires, in his view, the acquisition of knowledge of the relationships between proximal cues and distal events. Things in the environment are themselves associated, and perceptual learning consists of predicting these associations, becoming in "better and better agreement with the order in the environment (Björkman, 1966, p. 53)." An ecologically oriented view of perception like this is concerned with order in the environment and how it is "taken in," to use a term of Björkman's. But I think, as J. J. Gibson does, that this order is perceived directly, and not pieced together by associating the cue with the event. How indeed could the event be known prior to the association? Stimulus information must correspond with events, or we should never survive as a species or individuals.

A CLASSIFICATION OF WHAT IS TO BE PERCEIVED

A taxonomy or system of classification for ordering the knowledge we possess to date will greatly facilitate our study of perceptual development. I have found the most useful one, and the most natural one for me theoretically, to be an ecologically oriented one. A taxonomy which refers to the environment suits a functional, stimulus-oriented theory. Since it is the distal stimulus, in the end, in which perception is interested, the rubrics of my classification will be sources of stimulation: objects, space, events, representations of these, and coded sources of stimulation.

Objects

The world is full of things, to be approached and avoided, to be eaten or loved, to flee from or to fight against. The development of perception requires the discrimination of objects such as faces, food, toys, hot radiators, bottles that contain milk vs. bottles that contain medicine, and so on. Sets of objects, such as human faces, and the features that differentiate them must be attended to. The properties and variable dimensions of objects—their colors, texture, shape, and more complex structural variables like the ones that identify different vehicles, or animals, or plants —must be discriminated. Is there a learning process during development that makes this possible? We know that there must be a learning process involved in distinguishing two hundred kinds of mushrooms or in uniquely identifying wines by their year and vineyard of origin. When does this process begin in development?

Space

Objects and the organism exist in a spatial world with surfaces and gaps between them. Objects are outside the organism, in some relation of proximity to each other and to it. To secure them or avoid them, this relation must be appreciated; so must the ground of a terrestrial animal be perceived for locomotion toward or away from them. Whether or not man must learn to perceive space and its dimensions—near-far, right-left, up-down—is a question posed by philosophers long ago, and psychologists have unceasingly tried to invent experimental methods of answering the question. The experiments have ranged, in the stimulus-sources explored, from the largest dimensions to the smallest—from the judgment of distance of faraway aircraft to the minutest partitions of a Galton bar. They have included studies of obstacle avoidance by echolocation, and studies of avoidance of a visually perceived drop-off (by Richard Walk and E. J. Gibson; see frontispiece).

Events

The perception of events, happenings over time, is a sadly neglected topic in perception. One can think of only a few well-documented examples, like discrimination of the turning of a rigid object (Gibson & Gibson, 1957), studies of detection of an approaching object and impending collision (Schiff, 1965), and the observations of the ethologists that releasing stimuli often are provided by a patterned sequence of actions, such as the bird's courtship dance or the bee's dance indicating the whereabouts of food. There are also Michotte's (1963) beautiful experiments on the perception of causality, and on the phenomenal permanence of an object despite occlusion, and Johansson's (1950) studies of perceived motions in depth. But not many investigators have worked in this field.

The importance of event perception for perceptual development can hardly be overestimated. Watching an object come toward one or fall down, bringing the hands together or reaching out with the hand—these events provide an opportunity for the extracting of invariants. To perceive an event, some unity has to be detected over a temporal sequence of stimulation, and only extraction of some invariant rule or relation can give this. To what extent learning is involved in the perception of simple events, such as an object approaching, and more complex ones, such as the patterns of modern kinetic art, is a challenging question.

Representations

Two-dimensional drawings or pictures of things (unlike events) have been the commonest material of perception experiments. Representations of objects in photographs, representations of events in motion pictures, and reproductions of vibratory events in tape recordings give indirect information about the environment, but information nevertheless. Are pictures of things recognized and identified without learning? If so, how realistic must the picture be? Why is a cartoon or a caricature often as good for securing recognition as a high fidelity photograph? Do savages and young children have to learn that pictures are signs for things? How early do children recognize a picture as a picture? This question is relevant to space perception for, when a child does, he is distinguishing the plane of the picture from the space in the picture. There are intricate developmental problems here awaiting solution.

Coded Stimuli

Society provides its members with a class of stimulus sources which I shall refer to as coded. Examples are human speech, writing, and Morse code. They differ from representational sources, which are also man-made, because they are designed to correspond with some other set of events according to mapping rules which are more or less arbitrary. The correspondence may be of a very simple kind, such as Paul Revere's lanterns on Old North Church which signified how the British were coming: "One if by land and two if by sea." But most codes carry far more potential information than this, and furthermore have interesting internal structural properties—built-in rules or constraints relating classes of items. Here is the ideal case for studying development of the perception of structure. How do children learn to perceive the syntax of speech, the ordinal relations of numbers, and the spelling patterns of English orthography? Rules can be learned by verbal retention, if one means only parrotting them. But there is perceptual pickup of grammatical rules long before a child can tell you that a sentence has a subject and an object. Yet research on this most interesting of all psychological problems is still in its infancy.

PLAN OF THIS BOOK

Before getting on with the job, let me give a preview of what this book will try to do by explaining how it is organized. Like Gaul, it is divided into three parts. The first part is concerned with theories of perceptual learning.

I shall take up in Chapter 2 the traditional psychological theories. Then I shall consider the major contemporary theories, which seem to me to fall rather conveniently into categories of cognitively oriented, response-oriented, and stimulus-oriented theories. The last category includes my own ideas about perceptual learning and I have devoted four chapters to them. No doubt a rival theorist will think this excessive, but these ideas were, after all, the impetus for writing a book. Along with these theories I shall introduce experiments, when there are ones specifically designed to test or illustrate the position.

Since there is a large body of relevant experimental facts not necessarily derived from a theory, part two includes four chapters that are experimentally oriented. There are four major categories of perceptual learning experiments, and I have discussed paradigms and designs for each one, with numerous illustrations from existing experiments. I apologize to authors whose experiments I might have included but did not; each one of these chapters could have been a book in itself. I have tried to be critical in these chapters. They are not just summaries but are intended to evaluate the methods and point the way toward productive new research.

Part three is devoted to perceptual development, both phylogenetic and ontogenetic. Interest in perceptual development in children has increased enormously in the last few years, and so helped swell the content of this book. I found the classification that I have described particularly useful here. It is better than the sterile old headings of visual, auditory, and tactual perception, of color perception and form perception. The last chapter is an attempt to find and substantiate trends in perceptual development, and to reconcile these with my own principles of perceptual learning.

2

Traditional Theories of Perceptual Learning and Development

Perceptual learning, as a topic in the literature of experimental psychology, is new, stemming from the recent marriage of learning theory and to a lesser degree perception. The old marriage, the concept of perception as a function which develops by way of past experience, is as old as philosophy itself. When the British empiricists, beginning in the seventeenth century, elaborated the laws of association it was principally with the object of explaining perception. It could be said with some justice that the psychology of learning was born in the empiricists' attempts to explain man's perceptions of objects, space, and the relations between them. The epistemology of the philosophical empiricists does not seem to concern experimental psychologists of the present day, but the extent to which the vocabulary and concepts of these philosophers are ingrained in psychological terminology and thinking cannot be overstated. The roots of psychological problems and concepts are in their works.

THE NATIVISM-EMPIRICISM CONTROVERSY

A major intellectual controversy of all time is the opposition between nativist and empiricist tenets regarding the origins of knowledge. Both sides attempted to answer this question: where does our knowledge of the world, its spaces, objects, qualities, and properties come from? One solution was the notion that ideas of space and things were innate, prototypical, universal, and God given. The opposition to the nativist position was mustered in great strength by the British empiricists who sought to supplant it with the notion that knowledge arises from experience alone; and that experience comes only by way of the senses. Variations upon this argument can be traced through Hobbes, Berkeley, Hume, and the Mills with ever greater elaboration of theory (see Boring, 1942, chapter 1). Hochberg (1963) has reviewed as case studies a number of the problems which were argued, among them such questions as how distance, direction, and size are perceived; whether visual perceptions of distance and size are mediated by and dependent on habitual connections with touch; whether a man born blind but later given sight could distinguish by sight alone a sphere from a cube (the question Molyneux put to Locke).

Although the doctrine that all knowledge comes by way of the senses would not require such an assumption, it was generally argued by the empiricists that experience came originally as bits of punctiform and un-related sense data, which must be in some way combined. The doctrine of association was the result. As the linking force, by which meaningful percep-tions and complex ideas were composed, association supplied a means for going beyond simple, isolated sensations. The laws of association—con-tiguity, frequency, recency, and similarity—were debated by the British empiricists without agreement on the correct list. But it is interesting to recall in this day of behavior theory that the principle of associative frequency was introduced to account for man's cognitions, not his motor habits.

The controversy between the nativists and the empiricists, just before the theory of evolution made great changes in the concept of mental development, was summarized picturesquely by Warren (1921).

The debate between "nativists" and "empiricists" seemed to resolve itself into a question whether the "original constitution" with which each individual begins life is in the nature of *structure* (innate ideas, mental forms, etc.) or of *dynamic conditions* (laws of association, etc.). The nativists provided the newborn infant not with actual mental currency, but with drafts payable to bearer at sight; the associationists started him off in life with neither money nor drafts, but merely with an introduction to the bank, and compelled him to work his way to mental wealth according to the laws of associational economics (p. 118).

The effect of the concept of evolution was to make tenable an inter-mediate position, to bring biological influences into psychology, and to encourage comparative studies of development. Adaptation to the environ-ment was the primary concept of Darwinian biology, not only adaptation during an individual's lifetime but adaptation of the species as well. If the species has evolved adaptively, some endowment must be conferred by nature on the individual organism, on which the organism builds for him-self. The dichotomy of nativism versus empiricism gave way to the nature-nurture problem: what has nature conferred that nurture shapes further? It is safe to say that no twentieth-century psychologist believes in innate ideas, but most of the problems raised by the British empiricists persist. In the older scientific psychology, four contrasting positions stand out as theories of perceptual development and learning; they are unconscious inference, associated ideational context, functionalism, and Gestalt theory.

HELMHOLTZ AND UNCONSCIOUS INFERENCE

The great physicist Hermann von Helmholtz (1821–1894) interested himself not only in the physical problems of optics but in questions of visual perception, establishing a tradition for the scientist as well as the philosopher to examine the role of past experience in perception. In his *Physiological Optics* he wrote as a physicist, a physiologist, and a psychologist.

All perception, according to Helmholtz, has an element of inference which is wholly dependent on previous experiences. The inference is equivalent to a conclusion, but an unconscious one. The following passage regarding localization of a light source by interpreting (albeit unconsciously) the significance of its point of stimulation on the retina illustrates at once Helmholtz's concept of inference and its dependence on the accumulation of past experience.

Inasmuch as in an overwhelming majority of cases, whenever the parts of the retina in the outer corner of the eye are stimulated, it has been found to be due to external light coming into the eye from the direction of the bridge of the nose, the inference we make is that it is so in every new case whenever this part of the retina is stimulated; just as we assert that every single individual now living will die, because all previous experience has shown that all men who were formerly alive have died (*Physiological Optics*, Vol. III, p. 5).

Helmholtz recognized some organic, built-in substratum for perception which provided matter for inference, as the following passage shows:

As to the representation of space-relations, there certainly is something of this sort in the peripheral nerve terminals in the eye and to a certain extent in the tactile skin, but still only in a limited way; for the eye gives only perspective surface-images, and the hand reproduces the objective area on the surface of a body by shaping itself to it as congruently as possible. A direct image of a portion of space of three dimensions is not afforded either by the eye or by the hand. It is only by comparing the images in the two eyes, or by moving the body with respect to the hand, that the idea of solid bodies is obtained (p. 23).

How were these conclusions supposed to be performed? "Simply, of course, by the unconscious processes of association of ideas going on in the dark background of our memory (p. 26)." Testing and experimenting, however, were also noted as important in making accurate inferences about objects. A remark of Helmholtz's about children's experimentation with objects foreshadows Piaget:

They turn them constantly round and round, and touch them with the hands and the mouth, doing the same things over and over again day after day with the same objects, until their forms are impressed on them; in other words, until they get the various visual and tactile impressions made by observing and feeling the same objects on various sides (p. 31).

Empiricist though he was, Helmholtz felt forced to posit a "law of causation" as a law of thinking which is prior to all experience. "Generally," he said, "we can get no experience from natural objects unless the law of causation is already active in us. Therefore, it cannot be deduced first from experiences which we have had with natural objects (p. 32)." Here is a difficulty for all those theories of perception which would conceive of it as problem-solving (and there are many): the rules of inference must somehow first be provided.

The following statement makes clear his dependence upon man's nature as well as on sense data, and their unconscious interplay when a sense impression occurs:

The image at the time awakes the memory of everything like it experienced in previous visualizations, and likewise the recollection of everything regularly associated by special experiences with these former visual images, such as the number of steps we had to take to reach a man who appeared in the field of view to be of a certain size, etc. This kind of association of ideas is unconscious and involuntary, and is produced by a sort of blind force of nature, no matter if it occurs also according to the laws of our mental being; and hence it enters into our perceptions with all the external and compelling power of impressions that come to us from outside (p. 293).

Helmholtz, throughout the *Physiological Optics,* argued his empiricist point of view against Kantian theory and especially against the contemporary physiologist Hering. Kant held the opinion that space and time were categories of perception with which man was originally endowed. A number of German physiologists, following him, thought that perceived localization of points was immediately given by innate mechanisms characteristic of the stimulation of definite nerve fibers (Müller's local signs). Hering elaborated by assuming that the stimulation of an individual point on the retina produced three kinds of space sensation: an altitude value, an azimuth (breadth) value, and a depth value which was a bipolar quality for pairs of corresponding points. The emphasis on perception as compounded of sensations which were basically points of light was common to both Hering and Helmholtz. This has persisted in American psychology. Kant's intuitive categories, on the other hand, had some legitimate descendants in the Gestalt psychologists.

ASSOCIATION AND PERCEPTION IN AMERICAN PSYCHOLOGY

Titchener's Context Theory

With such examples from their contemporaries in philosophy and physiology, it is not surprising to find the late nineteenth-century psychologists typically espousing a perceptual theory based on meaningless sensations and the compounding of complex perceptions by some sort of accretion process. The best known of these theories was Titchener's context theory. He said, "No sensation means; a sensation simply goes on in various attributive ways. . . . All perceptions mean; they go on also in various attributive ways, but they go on meaningly (Titchener, Part II, 1919, p. 367)." Meaning, psychologically, was always context, the mental process which accrued to the sensory process. The accruing context was a constellation of ideas, or images of many kinds. Genetically, the sensory core was prior, the context was secondary. Introspective analysis of the ongoing psychological content was for Titchener the necessary and sufficient method of studying perception.

Sensation was always supplemented after birth. "General kinaesthetic supplements, derived from our experience of handling objects, are also exceedingly common: things looks heavy or light, sound heavy or light, precisely as they look or sound here or there, near or far (Titchener, 1919, p. 366)." The look of nearness or farness, hereness or thereness, needless to say, required processes supplemental to sensation.

Of all the forms of supplementation Titchener considered "kinaesthetic attitude" and words the most important.

The words that we read are both perception and context of perception; the auditory-kinaesthetic idea is the meaning of the visual symbols. And it is obvious that all sorts of sensory and marginal complexes receive their meaning from some mode of verbal representation: we understand a thing, place a thing, as soon as we have named it (p. 368).

Naming confers meaning—this is an old idea in psychology, like kinaesthetic supplements that give meaning to visual sensations.

William James

William James, a great eclectic psychologist, wrote about association, to be sure, but he departed from the traditional psychology of the empiricists by introducing many new concepts, one of them discrimination. He attributed this concept to Locke.

But Locke's descendants have been slow to enter into the path whose fruitfulness was thus pointed out by their master, and have so neglected the study of discrimination that one might almost say that the classic English psychologists have, as a school, hardly recognized it to exist. "Association" has proved itself in their hands the one all-absorbing power of the mind (James, Vol. I, p. 484).

James thought that psychology must "be writ *both* in synthetic and in analytic terms"; that "our original sensible totals are, on the one hand, subdivided by discriminative attention, and, on the other hand, united with other totals (p. 487)."

James thus foreshadowed not only the American functional psychology which owed so much to him, but also modern notions about the improvement of discrimination by practice. He considered this of equal importance with motor learning (cf. quotation in Chapter 1) and made a serious and original effort to explain it. His explanation did not call upon inference or the drawing of conclusions from past experiences, like Helmholtz, but appealed instead to active, unsubmerged processes.

In his chapter on "Discrimination and Comparison," James recognized two causes at work whenever practice improves discrimination. The first of these was an accretion hypothesis, but it was not aimed at explaining meaning, only at the refinement of distinctions between similar things. In his words,

First, the *terms* whose difference comes to be felt contract disparate associates and these help to drag them apart. . . . The effect of practice in increasing discrimination must then, in part, be due to the reinforcing effect, upon an original slight difference between the terms, of additional differences between the diverse associates which they severally affect (pp. 510–511).

His example was learning to distinguish claret from burgundy.

When we first drank claret we heard it called by that name, we were eating such and such a dinner, etc. Next time we drink it, a dim reminder of all these things chimes through us as we get the taste of the wine. When we try burgundy our first impression is that it is a kind of claret; but something falls short of full identification, and presently we hear it called burgundy. During the next few experiences, the discrimination may still be uncertain—"which," we ask ourselves, "of the two wines is this present specimen?" But at last the claret-flavor recalls pretty distinctly its own name, "claret," "that wine I drank at So-and-so's table," etc.; and the burgundy-flavor recalls the name burgundy and someone else's table.

James thought, in fact, that the names differed more than the flavors and helped to stretch the flavors farther apart.

James made it very clear that naming or identification could only stretch a difference when the difference was strong enough originally to keep the two terms from "calling up identical associates." He thought also that the above explanation was insufficient, and offered a second one. The second was that "the difference reminds us of larger differences of the same sort, and these help us to notice it (p. 510)." He gives as an example the reduction with practice of the two-point limen on the skin, and suggests that it is the "image of the doubleness" as it is felt in very easily distinguished places which helps detect it where otherwise it might have been missed. A dim doubleness, he thought, grew clear by being assimilated to the image of a distincter doubleness just previously felt. Both these ideas of James were to reappear in modern dress, as later chapters will show.

James also pointed out that personal interest was a sharpener of discrimination, acting, he thought, through directing attention to the distinction. This idea too has a familiar ring. It reappeared in the second quarter of the twentieth century as the so-called new look in perception.

American Functional Psychology

The notion that perception was supplemented by an accruing context of imagery resulting from earlier experience was supplanted in American psychology, beginning early in the 1900's, by a strong emphasis on response, and especially on localizing movements. Interest in perception was almost eclipsed by the impact of Behaviorism at this time, but Carr and his students at the University of Chicago kept some interest in space perception alive, strictly within the empiricist tradition. The following statement of Carr's is typical:

Like Stratton, we shall assume for each sense department a system of local signs. . . . We shall assume that these signs become *directly* associated by contiguity with localizing movements. These localizing movements may be movements of the eyes, the head, the body, or the hands and arms, or these movements may in time become symbolically represented by judgmental responses expressed in verbal terms (1935, pp. 28 ff.).

Stratton's experiment (1897) of wearing an inverting lens system in front of one eye with the other occluded (thus producing a 180° rotation of his visual field) and studying the ensuing perceptual changes was a challenge to the armchair theorizers, but its implications were not entirely clear. The title he chose, "Vision Without Inversion of the Retinal Image," suggests the confusion which could (and did) result as to the experiment's implications. Stratton reported that after wearing the device for some days locomotion became easy. He also suggested that visual objects might become reinverted in time so as to be seen right side up once more. Stratton concluded, in attempting to escape the ambiguity of the terminology, that upright vision, in the final analysis, was vision "in harmony with touch and motor experience." This harmonious relationship, the implication was, comes about through development of a system of learned localizing responses. The experimentally induced conflict between the visual and the motor system was indeed resolved in time and a new system for the visual guidance of locomotor and manipulative habits developed, but what this means for the genesis of space perception is still not clear after seventy years.

An experiment in Carr's laboratory by M. Wooster (1923) fore-shadowed a very popular trend in current research on perceptual learning. She had her subjects wear spectacles consisting of 40° prisms which deflected the apparent direction of all visual objects about 21° to the right. The subjects wore the spectacles for 20 minutes a day and were tested for development of adjustment of localizing responses to the novel visual-motor situation. They reached for a sounding buzzer mounted on an arc at arm's length in front of them. Slow and continual adjustment occurred (although error was never entirely eliminated).

On the basis of experiments such as these, Carr proposed a motor theory to account for the spatial relations obtaining between auditory, visual, and somaesthetic impressions of objects. He thought that visual, auditory, and somaesthetic impressions each constituted a sensory system with its own principles of internal spatial organization, unrelated to one another. They became spatially related only by virtue of their direct associative connection, by means of the same localizing response.

When two diverse sense objects are associated with different localizing responses, they are regarded as two different objects with separate locations. When two such sense objects are associated with the same localizing responses, that response will manipulate both impressions. The two impressions will thus have the same locality significance, and they will be regarded as two sensory attributes of a single object (p. 79).

This view that sensory impressions from different modalities are integrated by association with a common response is an early version of acquired equivalence of cues, to be considered in Chapter 4.

Perception in Developmental Psychology

Although child psychology flourished in the United States in the early twentieth century, few child psychologists were interested in problems of perceptual development. Insofar as textbooks in the area considered perceptual development at all, it was treated as sensory-motor development and appealed either to a motor theory like Carr's, or to an explanation based on an associative context of images like Titchener's. A quotation from Goodenough's *Developmental Psychology* (1934) illustrates a typical empiricist view:

Very early in life and without being aware that we are doing so, we learn to interpret this (binocular) difference in visual sensations in terms of tactual and muscular sensations we get from handling objects. . . . When we say the tree trunk *looks* rounded, we mean only that the visual sensation has the qualities that from infancy on we have learned to associate with objects that *feel rounded* (p. 138).

These sentences could almost have been written by Bishop Berkeley.

Now it should be remarked that one very powerful exception to the general empiricist trend existed in American child psychology. This exception was the emphasis placed on maturational processes by Arnold Gesell and his coworkers at Yale. Rather than experiment, they employed a longitudinal method of observation, looking for irreversible sequences in development. Gesell was not primarily interested in psychological controversies over the genesis of perception, but his book *Vision: Its Development in Infant and Child,* with Ilg and Bullis (1949), attempted to show the maturational trends and orderly stages of developing vision and had a wide influence. Although only directly observable motor processes were noted, a good many inferences about how the world looked were included. The aim of the book was to describe the changing action system and the visual world of the growing infant.

Here is an example of the kind of description which characterizes the book:

At *36 weeks,* he takes a cube and pushes another cube with the one in hand; or he brings one cube against the side of another cube. He differentiates the string attached to the ring and manipulates it exploitively. By such tokens he shows a recognition of the posture and relationship of two objects in space. He is just beginning to see them as solids and envelopes (p. 96).

At the same age, the infant is observed to thrust his hand part way into a cup and peer into it. The inference follows: "Optically speaking, his depth perception is still so meager that he has only a dim apprehension of container and contained (p. 96)."

According to Gesell, the visual world of the infant undergoes tridimensional differentiation by slow, progressive stages, dependent upon the elaboration of action systems. However questionable were the inferences about the infant's visual world and its growth, the inventories of emergence of eye movement types (pursuit, convergence, and so on) and changes in looking patterns were of factual interest and value. Evidence of rudimentary fixation a few hours after birth and its rapid extension and selectivity with growth, to give but one example, made it clear that basic components of vision are present in the human infant at birth and develop in successive phases of ever greater specificity and complexity. Not only prolongation of regard, but increased selectivity and capacity for cancelling out rival stimuli were noted by Gesell within the first few months of life. Observation of eye postures and looking in the very young infant have again become popular research techniques in the last few years and will be described in chapters 15 and 16.

LEARNING AND PERCEPTION IN
GESTALT PSYCHOLOGY

The rationalist and nativist line of thinking, deriving from Kant, had little impact on scientific psychology in the United States and England as compared with the empiricist line of thinking. But it did foreshadow the Gestalt psychology of the twentieth century. The Gestalt psychologists' emphasis on characteristics of the whole, upon a relational pattern which could not be explained as a sum of discrete and elementary sensory experiences (for instance, the melody which retains its identity despite transposition to another key), was clearly at odds with the structuralists' contention that complex perceptions consist of a sensory core with a context of associated images and ideas. So was their notion of depth as a primary characteristic of space perception at odds with the hypothesis that depth is built up by the association of localizing movements with elementary visual sensations, themselves depthless. Forces tending toward a best structure (e.g., the soap bubble) were assumed both in the physical world and in neural processes. An isomorphism between neural processes and perception was also assumed. Associative learning need have no useful role in perception if self-regulating processes of organization that result in one best structure are postulated. The question is, does any kind of learning have a useful role in perception?

In 1924, Koffka published the first edition of the *Growth of the Mind,* a Gestalt psychologist's view of how cognition develops. He conceived of the developmental process as one of articulation and differentiation, rather than as an accretion by association. The problem of perceptual development, for him, was "how a picture of the world as we know it gradually arises out of the primitive and diffuse configurations of early experience (1931, p. 380)."

He argued against the theory that the child's early perceptions are a chaos of simple but unconnected and meaningless sensations, pointing out that it is not simple stimuli which first attract the infant's attention and call forth some relatively differentiated response, but quite complex ones, such as the human voice.

The development of color vision as Koffka thought of it provides a good example of differentiation. There is first, he wrote, a distinction made only between color and noncolor; after this stage, " 'warm' and 'cold' configurations arise"; and then "differentiation takes place within the 'warm' and 'cold' colours, causing the four principal colours, red, yellow, green and blue to appear (p. 291)." The last step would be a differentiation leading to the appearance of the intermediate colors and, Koffka says, "though the development is essentially one of maturation, practice influences it very markedly (p. 292)."

For Koffka, maturation and learning were thus both involved in differentiation, but he rejected trial and error, and what he considered mechanistic explanations of learning. He combatted Thorndike's arguments for animal stupidity and argued that when the animal does learn, he reorganizes the situation in a meaningful way. Learning occurs, in many situations, when the field of perception undergoes a sudden and profound transformation. Köhler's well-known work on the *Mentality of Apes* (1925) contains innumerable examples of insightful learning traceable, in his opinion, to such a sudden reorganization of the perceptual field. The problems, typically, were of the roundabout kind; the animal's direct path to the objective was blocked, but a roundabout way (which could, however, be surveyed) was left open. The famous example of Sultan raking in the banana (beyond reach of his arm) with a stick is a case of solution or learning by means of "an alteration in the object of perception." The stick is suddenly perceived as a tool, rather than a mere stick. There is said to be closure; when the problem is solved, "everything in the perceptual situation depends upon the total configuration (Koffka, 1931, p. 223)." The process of learning is creative, involving articulation and redistribution of forces within the phenomenal field.

This example requires some comment. That primates do learn to rake in objects with sticks has been amply substantiated, and it is likewise accepted that the behavior is generally not ascribable to mere chance. When the behavior occurs suddenly, there does appear to be a kind of transformation of the perceptual process. But this is surely not an "alteration in the object of perception," as Koffka and Köhler said; it is, I think, detection of a property of the object previously (at least in the experimental situation) unnoticed.

Examples like the above one so impressed the Gestalt psychologists that their learning theory consisted, primarily, of the exploitation of insight, defined as reorganization of the perceptual field. The conception of perceptual learning in this book does not coincide with the conception of insight defined as perceptual reorganization. I am interested, rather, in the role of learning in perception. Examples like the above can be treated as cases of perceptual learning, and this is shown by Leeper's experiments on what he called "perceptual reorganization (1935)." Leeper pointed out that, for the Gestalt theorists, the importance of sensory reorganization in learning was stressed but the importance of learning for sensory reorganization was not recognized. He devised experiments, therefore, to investigate the role of learning in sensory reorganization.

One of Leeper's experiments employed incomplete figures, borrowed from Street (1931), like the one in Figure 2–1. They were exposed to groups of subjects under various conditions and with differing amounts of exposure. All the helps given the subjects—repetition, exposure of the complete picture from which the fragmentary one was taken, and knowl-

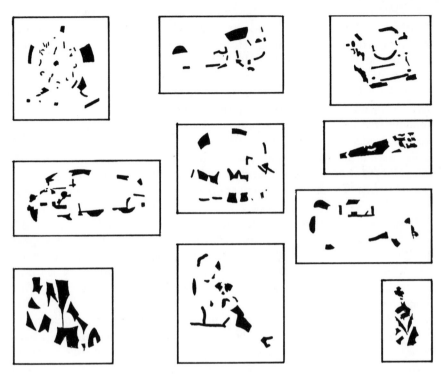

FIGURE 2–1. Figures from R. F. Street, used by Leeper (1935) in a demonstration of perceptual reorganization.

(Reprinted with the permission of the publisher from R. F. Street's *A Gestalt Completion Test: A Study of a Cross Section of Intellect— Teachers College Contributions to Education No. 481* [New York: Teachers College Press], copyright 1931, Teachers College, Columbia University.)

edge of the class to which the imperfectly portrayed object belonged— assisted in achieving the correct reorganization. Once achieved, it was retained. Leeper thought that "habit-derived organizations" were in conflict, in this situation, with "spontaneous organizing factors," but occasionally won out. The difficulty of assimilating past experience or habit, at least in the sense of associative principles, to a concept of dynamic self-distribution of forces is apparent in this interpretation.

In a second experiment, Leeper employed complete but ambiguous figures capable of two organizations (e.g., Boring's display entitled "My Wife and My Mother-in-law" shown in Fig. 2–2). Various groups of subjects were given different prior experiences: perceptual bias (a clear, unambiguous picture of one of the possible organizations), or verbal description of one of the alternatives. The effect of an unambiguous picture

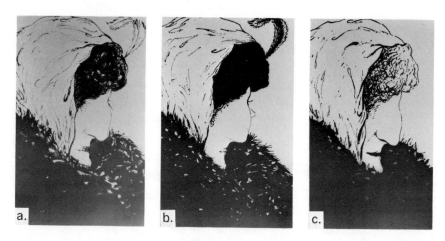

FIGURE 2–2. Ambiguous figures designed by Boring (1930) and used by Leeper (1935) in a demonstration of the effect of a prior perceptual experience on perceptual organization.

(Reprinted with the permission of the University of Illinois Press from E. G. Boring, *American Journal of Psychology, 42,* 1930, 444–445.)

on later perception of the ambiguous one was very strong, but the verbal description was not. Leeper concluded that his results justified the use of the term "habits of sensory organization," but on the whole, the evidence of habit here seems to be merely preservation of whatever organization was achieved. Ambiguous figures, carefully balanced between two alternatives, do not seem to the writer to be either common natural phenomena or ideal vehicles for the study of perceptual learning.

The view that learning defined as past experience had a role in perceptual organization in the articulation of a figure was attacked by Gottschaldt (1926) in an experiment which has often been interpreted as demonstrating that past experience has no effect on form perception. In fact, it is described in Koffka's *Principles of Gestalt Psychology* (1935) under the heading "Experimental Disproof of the Empiristic Theory." In Gottschaldt's experiment, the subjects were presented with simple line patterns (*a* patterns) projected on a screen for one second, and repeated after an interval with varying frequency. They were told to learn these figures so that they would remember them later and be able to draw them. After completing exposure of the *a* patterns, *b* patterns, which contained in each one an embedded *a* pattern, were shown for two seconds each (see Fig. 2–3). The subjects were told to describe the new patterns, mentioning anything that struck them. According to Koffka, if the empiristic theory

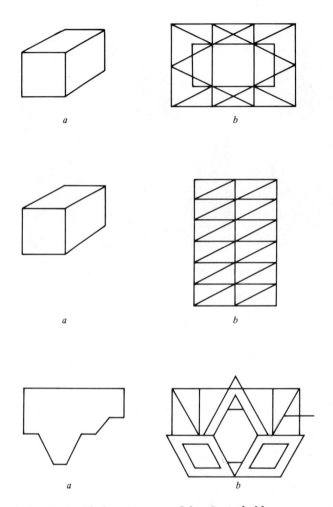

FIGURE 2–3. Embedded patterns used by Gottschaldt.

The subject's task was to find the *a* pattern on the left in the *b* pattern on the right. (From *A Source Book of Gestalt Psychology,* by William D. Ellis [London: Routledge & Kegan Paul, Ltd.; New York: Humanities Press, 1938].)

were right, "practice in seeing the *a* figure should make the *b* figure look like *a* plus something else (1935, p. 156)." Since 520 exposures of the *a* figures did not produce more spontaneous mentions of them in the *b* figures than did three exposures, Koffka concluded that the assumption was disproved. Perhaps the assumption as he worded it was, but the experiment by no means proves that learning does not alter or influence perception.

There are several reasons. The hypothesis, as stated by Koffka, is not the exact prediction of any theory; the responses obtained from the subjects (spontaneous remarks) do not prove that they did not see the experienced figures; and furthermore, years of previous experience with all these drawings and shapes could easily outweigh any practice within the experiment. These and other arguments produced a rash of repetitions of the Gottschaldt type of experiment (Braly, 1933; Djang, 1937; Henle, 1942; Hanawalt, 1942), and the results were generally interpreted as demonstrating some influence of past experience as an organizing factor. In Henle's experiment (1942), structural factors were said to be equated by using both letters or numbers and their respective mirror reversals as stimuli. Stimulation was impoverished by peripheral or by tachistoscopic exposure. The subjects drew what they saw. Because the letters and numbers in the familiar orientation were reproduced significantly more often than were the presumably less familiar reversals, past experience was inferred to influence perceptual recognition when structural forces were equal. Henle's experiment has been repeated recently (Robinson, Brown, & Hayes, 1964) with the additional use of a same-different judgment. The results obtained with an identification response were confirmed, but with the same-different judgment the results were not confirmed.

Zuckerman and Rock (1957) summarized these experiments dealing with what has been called the past experience issue in form perception, and concluded that strong structural factors could overcome the effects of familiarity. All the investigators pointed out the influence of set or selective attention in finding embedded forms. Hanawalt (1942) found not only that repetition of the same design was effective in locating such forms, but that practice yielded transfer to new designs. Amount of practice was the important factor. An attitude of search could not alone explain this transfer. The subjects learned, among other things, to look for distinctive parts of the embedded design in the whole complex.

What can be said about this prolonged and confusing controversy? The question of the effect of past experience in seeing a form on its present apprehension is a phenomenological way of putting the question; it raises many difficulties, both epistemological and experimental. It is not clear, as the hypothesis was stated by Gottschaldt and Koffka, whether the old experience must be always an exact repetition of the new one, nor how one can weigh its effects fairly when it is pitted against some presumably conflicting factor. Sometimes the structural factors of Gottschaldt provide an effective camouflage and sometimes they do not, so one cannot conclude that past experience in seeing the embedded figure is without effect; nor can much be specified about its mode of operation. We do not know whether or not it is literally the repeated experience itself that accomplishes something, since transfer to discovery of different embedded figures occurs. The problem will be reconsidered in a later chapter in the light of present-day theories.[1]

WERNER'S DIFFERENTIATION THEORY

Related to the Gestalt approach, but far more genetically slanted and unique in many ways, is Werner's developmental theory. It is described in his *Comparative Psychology of Mental Development,* the revised edition of which appeared in 1948. For Werner, the fundamental law of development was the increase of differentiation and hierarchical integration ("the development of biological forms is expressed in an *increasing differentiation* of parts or *hierarchization* [1961, p. 41]"). Werner traced this process through phylogenetic and ontogenetic development of the nervous system, but he did not stop with this application. This fundamental law of development, in his opinion, applied to perception, to motor activity, and in fact to "the *mental functions per se.*" He thought of developmental psychology as including not only development of the growing organism, but a comparative psychology of species, a psychology of primitive man, and the pathological conditions of the human adult which may be regressive. His key concepts in defining genetic levels of mentality were pairs of contrasting terms; syncretic-discrete, diffuse-articulated, indefinite-definite, rigid-flexible, labile-stable. Primitive organization he thought of as syncretic, relatively diffuse, rigid, indefinite, and labile.

Werner cited many examples drawn from lower organisms, young children, and primitive (archaic) people that exhibit syncretic, diffuse, and rigid perceptual organization. The examples, for the most part, are anecdotal. What he called *physiognomic* perception is a syncretic type of organization presumably characteristic of children and of the primitive world. The physiognomic quality is due to the high degree of fusion between person and thing, subject and object. "The average adult generally has a physiognomic experience only in his perception of other human beings, their faces and bodies. The child, on the other hand, frequently sees physiognomic qualities in all objects, animate or inanimate (p. 72)."

The somewhat epic quality of Werner's theory makes it difficult to test experimentally. There is no theoretical bridge, other than the descriptive terms syncretic, diffuse, etc., between the fundamental law of development and behavior. Werner's work did, however, include many experiments. The experimental data were often used to provide a phenomenological description of a developmental change, which had, for Werner, the function of explanation. A good example of this procedure is his discussion of the development of tonal sensitivity. Tonal discrimination, according to

[1] See Postman's (1963) discussion of this issue (pp. 66 ff), including his objection that the original Gottschaldt experiments were designed to prove the null hypothesis.

several investigators, increases up to age fourteen or so. How does this growing precision come about? Werner utilized the "genetic experimental method," as he terms it, with adult subjects to imitate and investigate the developmental process. His well-known experiments on "micro-melodies" were the result. Two tones separated by only a few vibrations, presented in succession, were at first not distinguishable ("ambiguous in quality"). But after repeated hearings, he said,

the "contour" of each tone becomes clearly defined and achieves a specific, fixed quality. The tones at first appear approximately on the same uncertain level, but after a time become perceptually separate. It is as if each tone were attempting to establish its self-subsistence and independence with respect to the other. The tonal interval actually *stretches out,* and the gap between the two tones widens. It may be safely proposed that in the ontogenetic development of tonal discrimination a process of subjective enlargement of the tonal distance must occur which is similar to that involved in our laboratory experiments (p. 102).

It seems almost philistine in the face of this clear and interesting description to suggest that phenomenological theorizing is not enough, and that a model specifying mechanisms or processes, constructs though they be, which could account for the stretching, would surely be of great interest. A few such models exist and will be considered in later chapters.

SUMMARY

The problem of perceptual development had a long history in philosophy before it became a matter of concern to psychologists. The nativism-empiricism controversy reached a peak of prominence among epistemologists between the seventeenth and nineteenth centuries. In this controversy, the British empiricists stand out as the most eloquent pleaders for the empiricist view, and their writings have left us a vast heritage of concepts which still tend to dominate learning theory in general, as well as theories of perceptual development. The laws of association, most often contiguity and frequency, were applied to perception—especially complex perceptions of things and space—since experience was assumed to originate as elementary, meaningless, formless sensory content.

In the late nineteenth century the controversy, taken up by psychologists as well as philosophers, was restated to some extent as a nature-nurture problem, but the empiricist position remained a stronghold. It was influenced greatly by the writings of Helmholtz, who introduced the notion of "unconscious inference"—an interpretation of incoming sense data in the light of earlier accumulated experience. The school of Titchener followed this path fairly closely, explaining complex perceptions as an accrual of imaginal content, derived from past experience, to a sensory core.

Two new movements in the early twentieth century—functionalism in the United States and Gestalt psychology in Germany—put a new face on the controversy. The functionalists were staunch empiricists, but for associated imagery they substituted associated movements—localizing movements, primarily, since their work in perception was generally confined to space perception.

The Gestalt psychologists, inheritors of the rational tradition of Kant, were interested in form and organization, and thought of any change in them as due to a dynamic redistribution of forces, both in the brain and, isomorphically, in perception. Rather than studying the contribution of learning to perception, they thought of learning as dependent on perceptual reorganization—a kind of reversal of the roles of learning and perception. Perceptual development was thought of as differentiation. Creative learning, that is, perceptual reorganization, was due not to experience but to self-redistribution of forces within the organism.

Child psychology in the United States at first showed little concern with perceptual development, though there was a strong movement toward making inventories of developing motor ability, including sense organ adjustments. Arnold Gesell, at Yale, pursued the method of longitudinal study of developmental patterns and emphasized the role of maturation. Heinz Werner, somewhat in the tradition of Gestalt psychology but primarily concerned with development, thought of development as differentiation and hierarchical integration, taking as his cases not only the child at various levels of growth, but animals, primitive man, and pathological regression. Past experience had a function in differentiation for Werner, but it was not one of the accrual of associative context, or the accumulation of matter for inference.

In the next chapter, some descendents in present-day psychology of the theory of unconscious inference and of associative accrual will be described.

3

Contemporary Theories of
Perceptual Learning:
Cognitive Theories

The traditional theories of perceptual learning, outlined in the last chapter, have many descendents today. Some of the theoretical biases which play a major role were derived from Helmholtz and the functionalists. Some, on the other hand, reflect the emphasis on response and reinforcement of the current S-R learning theories. In both cases, they can be categorized as enrichment theories, in the sense that something is thought to be added to preliminary registration of the environmentally produced stimulation, itself an elementary, meaningless, even punctate affair. The contribution of the perceiver has been thought to lie in various processes— hypotheses, inferences, probabilistic weighing of cues, distortion produced by affect and attitudes, new cues produced by his own responses—but always something is presumed to be added by way of a mediating process. The theories which have a cognitive emphasis will be considered in this chapter and the response-oriented theories in the following one.

PROBABILISTIC CUE-LEARNING

The functional psychology of Egon Brunswik [1] is original but it can be lineally traced to Helmholtz. Brunswik contended that the environment "presents itself as semierratic" and that therefore all functionally oriented psychology is "inherently probabilistic (Brunswik, 1955)." The perceiver's ecology is such that only partial information about objects is available to him, and this must be weighed in the light of his statistical knowledge of previous similar indices and their correlation with other environmental referents. The stimulus input is symptomatic of the world, where it points depending on a weighting only obtainable through accumulated experiences. In Brunswik's words, "the crucial point is that while God may not

[1] For a clear, comprehensive, and sympathetic exposition of Brunswik's position, see Postman and Tolman, 1959.

gamble, animals and humans do, and that they cannot help but to gamble in an ecology that is of essence only partly accessible to their foresight (1955b, p. 236)."

Perception and behavior are, in Brunswik's system, functions of the object which is the source of stimulation and which he refers to as "distal." But the stimulus does not specify the object, only some properties of it, and that with imperfect consistency. Thus, stimuli must be considered as cues which have only limited validity as indicators of objects. Since perception is of the distal object, the central problem is how the stimulus, itself proximal to the receptor surface, becomes an index to the distal thing. Brunswik was therefore especially interested in object constancy and its development. He assumed that constancy developed through experience and was subject to modification through training. Brunswik's students studied the constancy of size, color, and shape, as well as more esoteric forms such as the constancy of loudness and weight. Developmental trends (see Brunswik, 1956) for constancy of size, shape, and brightness were found to rise as a function of age, to reach a peak at about ten years of age, and then decline. The decline, Brunswik thought, reflected an analytic attitude which developed with maturity. Experiments by Klimp-finger (1933) suggested to him that distal and analytic attitudes were differentiated with experience and mediated the effects of practice on perceptual constancy.

The question for perceptual learning, following Brunswik's approach, is how the stimulus becomes a cue to the distal object which elicits it. The answer is that the stimulus must be assessed against an associatively acquired, mediating cue-family hierarchy. New cues, according to Brunswik, are incorporated through association by contiguity. A cue has greater or less validity in terms of the cue hierarchy which reflects previous sampling from the animal's environment. A high correlation between a cue and its environmental object would reflect high ecological validity; a high correlation between the cue and the perception would reflect perceptual learning; and both together would result in veridical perception.

Brunswik studied perceptual learning experimentally. His method was to examine the acquisition and use of artificial cues having different ratios of correlation with a criterion variable. He felt that perceptual learning required a "slow stamping-in" and was "surprisingly autonomous of explicit awareness (1955b, p. 241)." An experiment by Fieandt (Fieandt, 1936; Brunswik, 1956, pp. 124 ff.), who manipulated cues in a brightness constancy setup, illustrates the method. A disc shadowed by a concealed card was perceived as darker than its true shade, until the shadow caster was revealed to the subjects. By alternating the two conditions, a bit of the penumbra of the shadow was made noticeable; this came to act as a cue to the shadow, and this made the disc look brighter. The effect was weak, however, and was soon extinguished. The mere demonstration of the shadow and its accompanying penumbra falling on the disc did not permanently change the subject's perception; this result reinforced Brunswik's belief that perception is modified through a process of "submerged mediation," slow, laborious, without insight.

An experiment on cue learning by Brunswik and Herma (1951) introduced a merely probabilistic cue-and-referent relationship within an artificial miniature environment. The response induced was a judgment of successive weight contrast. Lifting a heavy weight is known to elicit an underestimation of weight in subsequent trials and lifting a light one, overestimation. In the experiment, the cue artificially paired with a heavy or light weight was presentation to the right or left hand. An additional cue, color of the object, was combined (tied) with it. Sequences of weight pairs were designed to present heavy weights more often to one hand (2/3 of the time) and much lighter weights to the other hand. In neutral trials both weights were heavy or both light to test for the development of an expectancy illusion in response to the arbitrary cue. Such an illusion did occur, reaching its maximum at the eleventh trial and then declining despite continued practice on the same schedule. The subjects' awareness of the cues was generally erroneous and seemed to be unrelated to performance, which, according to Brunswik, "underscored the unconscious component in perception (1956, p. 131)." But as regards the slow stamping-in, considerable doubt was cast, since there appeared to be an immediate effect in a number of subjects tested after a single practice trial (87.5 percent contrast performance).

While cue learning apparently occurred in these experiments, its generality as a principle of cognitive development has been questioned in several recent experiments. In an experiment on depth perception, Gibson, Gibson, Smith, and Flock (1959) isolated the cue of motion parallax from other possible depth cues. The observer saw only two transparent surfaces in a window moving at different velocities. If they were motionless, or moved at the same velocity, only one surface was seen. If they moved with different velocities, two separated surfaces were seen. The question was whether the amount of this separation would be perceived in accordance with the amount of velocity difference. The depth between the two surfaces could be varied, so as to vary the degree of differential velocity. If subjects were given full information about the stimulus conditions and then asked to make judgments of the relative depth of the two surfaces they could do so and achieved significant correlations between actual separation of the surfaces and the judged separation. However, only a minority of subjects reported that they had used the appearance of depth in making their estimates; the others reported relying on relative motion, or how far one passed the other. Since differential velocity is highly correlated in real life with other cues to differential depth such as relative size and relative disparity, it might have been expected that this conjunction would have already given an associative cue value to the differential motions in the experiment. But it did not. It was thought possible that a longer period of training with correction would increase the associative cue value for depth, and bring about a genuine appearance of depth. Two subjects were run on consecutive days with reinforcement, one for nine days and one for seven days. Twenty uncorrected trials were given each day, and then ten with correction. Their correlations improved rapidly from .20 and .30 to over .90. They were aware of velocity ratios and passing rate and deliberately tried to link them with depth positions. But the appearance of different depths was never induced by training. Furthermore, the slower moving surface sometimes appeared in front of the faster instead of behind it, as it should if the subject had been learning to see depth in the experiment. Thus the results do not support the theory of unconscious inference in perception or point to any process of conversion through cue learning of bidimensional impressions into perceptions of depth.[2]

Smedslund (1961) performed an experiment on the learning and utilization of probabilistic cues, employing inkblots composed of several components. Of four such components, two had cue validities of .66 and .68, the others none. The task was to guess the number on the back of the card. The subject looked at the card, guessed its number, and turned it over to check his guess. Of nine subjects, three showed fairly good learning and in fact discovered the cue in the first session. The others showed no learning at all after 1,100 and in some cases 4,800 stimulus presentations. Smedslund concluded that the data provided no trace of steadily accumulating probability learning without awareness.

Eriksen and Doroz (1963) presented subjects with ostensibly perceptual tasks in which extraneous but correlated cues were provided. A list of two-syllable nonsense items was rapidly exposed to the subjects, the instructions being to make a judgment of whether the word (which they could not easily identify) was pleasant or unpleasant. Actually, the items had the first or the last letter deleted and replaced by a dash, depending on whether the item was designated pleasant or unpleasant. The items were presented five times, in random order, and the subject's judgment corrected. Afterward, he was questioned about the basis for his judgment, the last question being a forced choice as to which position of the dash was contingent with pleasant and which with unpleasant. Analysis of the

---

[2] This is not to say that motion parallax in a natural environment does not yield information for depth. It did here, in the limited sense of causing a perception of one surface in front of another. But the absence of a continuous visible surface between the two display surfaces gave no information, via motion parallax, for the extent of ground or depth between the two. Even with prolonged training with correction, the relative velocities of these two boundary surfaces alone, however reliable as cues to this artificial situation, did not cause a perception of the extent of depth between the two.

results revealed that those subjects who had detected the cue and could report on it showed cue learning in the sense of above-chance performance. A number of these subjects spontaneously verbalized their awareness during the course of the experiment. But the subjects who were unable to verbalize the nature of the cue did not learn.

A second experiment was designed in the manner of the Brunswik and Herma experiment to determine whether an extrinsic cue (color), highly correlated with another referent (length of line), would distort perception in a test series where lines were actually of equal length. Again, the subjects were interrogated after the test series. More responses were given in the direction of the illusion by the subjects who became aware of the contingent relation between color and line length during the training (about 30 percent) than by the unaware group or by a control group. The experimenters concluded that human adults are rather insensitive to contingencies in their environment, and that there was no evidence in either experiment that subjects unaware of a cue had learned it or utilized it in making their judgments.

Brunswik's contention that perception is a probabilistic process, based on associative cue contingencies of which we are unaware, is not affirmed by these experiments. It is thus not a plausible basis for a general theory of perception or perceptual learning. Yet the possibility remains that there exist cases where cue contingencies have some effect on perception, even without awareness of the contingent value. One thinks of the horse Clever Hans responding to subtle movements of his master. But of course it was his master who was unaware of them. Perhaps Hans had computed the probabilities.

TRANSACTIONALISM

Brunswik's emphasis on real objects contrasts with the subjectivism of the self-styled Transactionalists, notably Ames, Cantril, and Ittelson, who emphasized the privacy of each individual's perceptual world. Yet their views are similar to Brunswik's in their Helmholtzian lineage, the notion that perception is dependent on unconscious inference from accumulated past experience.

Perceptions for the Transactionalists are determined for each individual by his purposes, his values, and his life history. Perception is externally oriented but that is because when we perceive, we "externalize certain aspects of our experience and thereby create for ourselves our own world of things and of people, of sights and sounds, of taste and touches (Ittelson, 1962, p. 677)." Out of transactions with the environment, a pattern of unconscious assumptions is built, and the total of these constitutes the individual's world, quite possibly a false one, as the following paragraph illustrates.

Any present perceptual experience consists of a total complex of significance. All previous experiences have been similarly composed. Through the course of experiencing, certain significances are found by the perceiver to have high probabilities of being related to each other. Other relationships have a low probability of occurring. The probabilities, high or low, are in turn weighted in terms of the relevance of the unique situations in which they have occurred to the large purposes and values of the experiencing person. All this is accomplished through a largely unconscious process and results in a set of *assumptions* or weighted averages of previous experiences which are brought to the present occasion and play a principal role in determining how the occasion is experienced. For each of us the sum total of these assumptions can be said to constitute our *assumptive world*. The assumptive world of any particular individual at any particular time determines his perceptions, that is, provides him with predictions of probable significances. His assumptive world is, therefore, in a very real sense the only world that he knows (Ittelson, 1962, p. 678).

The statement about weighting of probabilities sounds similar to Brunswik, but it differs profoundly in its emphasis on the importance to the individual of any particular experience and a personal evaluative influence in determining weighting. Furthermore, Brunswik was concerned with perception of the distal object and the importance of ecology, and insisted therefore on what he termed "representative design" of experiments and representative sampling within the ecology. The Transactionalists had no such concern. They chose highly unrepresentative and ambiguous situations for experiment, so as to show that perception can be illusory and rests on assumptions peculiar to individuals and cultures. A series of demonstrations devised by Adelbert Ames (see Ittelson, 1952) generally involved presenting a visual display in a dark surround, viewed with only one eye and with a motionless head, hardly a representative sampling of the environment.

Object constancy is of interest to the Transactionalists, as well as to Brunswik, but here too personal values are assumed to have a determining role. Ittelson defines constancy behavior as

the attempt of the individual to create and maintain a world which deviates as little as possible from the world which he has experienced in the past, which is the only world he knows, and which offers him the best possible chance of acting effectively and continuing to experience the particular satisfactions which he seeks out of living (Ittelson, 1951, p. 292).

The difficulty of predicting from such a theory is self-evident. It is especially manifest in some of the Ames demonstrations, such as the distorted room. The room, built to present under special monocular viewing conditions a proximal image equivalent to that produced by a normal room, does indeed look normal, while two people or faces stationed at the angles of maximal distortion look abnormal in size. But why should they, according to the constancy hypothesis just quoted? One might predict from the individual's attempts to maintain a world such as he has experienced in the past that they ought to maintain perceptual constancy at least to the extent of preventing the grotesque appearance of a dwarf and a giant.

Since perceptions are modifiable, being dependent on assumptions deriving from past experience and weighted by personal factors, a theory of perceptual learning is required. Kilpatrick (1954), after working with the monocular distorted room designed by Ames, stated that learning played a role in visual space perception and that two different learning processes could be distinguished. One process he called "reorganizational learning," in which an unconscious reweighting of visual cues was said to occur. The example was an alteration in an observer's perception of a monocular distorted room, consequent upon touching parts of the room with a wand. What was learned was "a new way of organizing into a whole the complex of previously established cue-percept relationships (Kilpatrick, 1954, p. 363)." The second process he called "formative learning," an "actual learned alteration in the way in which a given stimulus pattern is perceived." This process he thought explained how perceptions were constructed in the first place. Formative learning occurred, he stated, in visual space perception. It was assumed to be slow, continuous, and transferable. It is not clear how the two processes differ in any fundamental way, except that reorganizational learning was thought to depend on giveaway cues, that is, on minor defects in construction of the room which were not at first noticed.

An experiment carried out by Kilpatrick will illustrate the type of experimental situation and the research on perceptual learning characteristic of this school. Three miniature rooms were constructed so as to be monocularly equivalent from a fixed station point, two of them distorted and one normal (a 4×4 ft. cubical room; see Fig. 3–1). One of the distorted rooms was constructed so that it was actually larger on the left than on the right (L), and the other so that it was larger at the top than at the bottom (T). The rooms were set up in a large dark room and each was illuminated only from inside. A head rest for the subject insured his placing the eye at the exact spot so that the perspective projection of each room would yield the same proximal stimulation. At the outset, therefore, all three rooms would presumably have the same appearance. The subject was moved from room to room in a rolling chair by the experimenter. The learning sessions were conducted at the L room and consisted of throwing balls at a luminous spot in different locations on the back wall, and also of tracing the outline of the back wall with a wand. Half of the subjects performed these actions themselves and half watched the experimenter perform them. There were four learning sessions, with reports on the

FIGURE 3–1.   Two versions of monocular distorted rooms, based on a 4 × 4-foot cubical reference room.

> When viewed with one eye at the prescribed viewpoint (the chin in the hollow place on the horizontal crossbar) the rooms are perceived as like the cubic shape of the reference room. When the observer practiced tracing the outline or touching parts of the distorted room with a wand, his perception was found to be altered. (From I. F. P. Kilpatrick, *Explorations in Transactional Psychology* [New York: New York University Press, 1961].)

appearance of one of the rooms after each. The hypothesis tested in the experiment was that if formative learning were involved, there should be transfer from learning in the room L to room T. Room T should be seen as normal no longer but, at least to some degree, as being shaped like room L (presumably whatever room L looked like after training).

The results of the experiment showed modifications in the appearance of the L room in the direction of the true shape of the room. These modifications in appearance were said to carry over, at least to some degree, to the other two rooms so that they then looked somewhat more like the L room. The results were similar for the subjects who threw the ball themselves and for the passive learning subjects. The process which results in this sort of transfer of appearance is thought by Kilpatrick to be "the one on which the expansion and development of our perceptual world depends (1954, p. 369)." If the results of this experiment can be extended to such a generalization it is hard to see how veridical perception could be sufficiently frequent to prevent an enormous accident rate. The question arises under just what conditions transfer would be expected, a point on which the theory is not explicit.

Weiner (1956) performed a similar experiment with two distorted rooms, and found, after a long period of variegated looking (with inserted moving objects, two eyes, etc.), that the room took on the appearance of its objective shape and then, for one subject at least, tended to transfer its appearance briefly to the other distorted room. Weiner pointed out that this effect is not as surprising as it sounds, since the proximal stimulus for the two rooms was, in fact, identical. He states that the subject had developed a "preferred percept," a perceptual stereotype which was adaptive in the first situation but not in the second. He stressed the role of conflict and "openness to new hypotheses" in perceptual learning.

The striking thing about these experiments to the writer is their extreme "unrepresentativeness," to use Brunswik's term. How often do we observe without either binocular parallax or head movement parallax? A mere movement of the head will make the distorted room manifest. The ambiguity of viewing two different scenes elaborately constructed with geometrical nicety to present equivalent stimuli for a single eye is rare and exceptional; it is probably safe to say that this situation never occurs in nature. The subject's perception changed toward veridicality when stimulus information was made available from touching or viewing with two eyes. It is unjustifiable to generalize from the peephole situation to a normal situation where stimulus information about the size and distance of the walls of a room is given with considerably redundancy.

According to Ittelson, perceptual validation occurs by way of experiencing the consequences of action, which provides a check of the perceptual hypothesis on which the action was based. The difficulty of testing this theory is much greater than is the case with Brunswik's, since the causal variables assigned a role in learning include personal values, purposes, and even unconscious attitudes. Ittelson's list of experimental variables (1962, pp. 680 ff.) includes an astonishing variety of levels, most of them not experimentally manipulable: the external object, relating impingements, physiological excitation, awareness, unconscious aspects, psychological processes (sets, assumptions, values, purpose, weighted averages, etc.), and action. In short, the theory assumes that perception is learned, but does not include a clearly formulated theory of learning.

JUDGMENTAL AND PROBLEM-SOLVING THEORIES

In a review of research on perceptual learning, Drever (1960) classified the theories into four types, one of which he called judgmental or "ratiomorphic," in which perception is regarded as analogous to thinking. He included Brunswik and the Transactional psychologists in this class, but it seems worth separating them, in spite of some similarities, from those theories which place a heavy emphasis on concepts and categories as determiners of perception. The latter theories emphasize not only hypotheses derived from past experience but also the problem-solving, inferential nature of perception. Sensory input comes as meaningless sensations which are assigned or matched to a schema, a concept, or a category. The sensations are interpreted in terms of it, and can be filled in or completed by it.

The Schema Theory of Bartlett and Vernon

The notion of a schema, borrowed from Head and greatly extended in its application (see Oldfield & Zangwill, 1942) was first given prominence in the explanation of remembering and perception by Bartlett (1932). The schema was a kind of organized model, a classification of past experiences, one of its functions being to mediate the perception of objects in the environment. Building the schema was an active process of construction. Bartlett's own research dealt principally with remembering, but M. D. Vernon elaborated on the function of the schema in perception (see Vernon, 1954, 1955). In her words,

Thus we may postulate that every act of perception consists of the extremely exact registration, in the receptor areas of the cortex, of even the minutest qualities and variations in the sensory patterns conveyed to them; followed by a combination and integration of certain of these qualities resulting in a new construction—a percept which is not isolated, but exists as a part of a systematic categorization of experience in concepts and schemata (1954, pp. 14 ff.).

Naming occurs often in perception, and may facilitate pigeonholing the sensory input into appropriate categories. The sequence begins with recording the data and organizing them in schemata, and the schemata in turn direct subsequent perceptual activities (see Vernon, 1957).

The schemata operating in perception perform two functions, according to Vernon. They tell the observer what to expect, what sensory data to select from the total input, and secondly they tell him how to deal with these data; "how to classify, understand, and name them, and draw from them the inferences that give the meaning to the percepts (1955, p. 186)." The prime argument for these functions of the schema is the consistency and continuity of perception, which suggest to Vernon that the observer's knowledge of the world must be a factor in sorting and classifying events.

Vernon sought evidence for this view by presenting to observers for tachistoscopic viewing, ambiguous, unfamiliar, or bizarre pictures. The observer was not told what to expect, but was asked to identify or describe the presented material. When the observer was hesitant or inaccurate in his identification and description, the performance was contrasted with perception in everyday circumstances, and the inference drawn that no schemata were available into which the percepts could be fitted. In one experiment (1957) subjects were presented with strange modern paintings, very briefly exposed, and asked to identify them. Three examples were selected which the subjects failed to identify and were presented again a week later, mixed with a new set. On the second occasion, a majority of the previously exposed pictures were recognized promptly as ones that had been presented before. It seems contrary to Vernon's argument that failure to identify the pictures did not prevent the subject from recognizing them on the second presentation and discriminating them from other similar material.

Perceptual learning is assumed by Vernon, not discussed as such; the infant is said to acquire gradually the means of constructing his percepts of the external world. Perceptual learning, then, must be the acquiring of schemata. This process involves integration of experiences from different modalities through association by simultaneity of occurrence (Vernon, 1954). Vernon, following Piaget, considers that manipulation and experimentation with objects is essential in this learning. Except for the mention of association by simultaneity, no learning theory is specified.

Piaget

In view of the long series of experimental studies of perceptual development performed or sponsored by Piaget, and published in the *Archives de Psychologie,* it would seem fitting to devote many pages to an exposition of his work on perceptual learning. However, my review here will be brief, and I shall save the research for the appropriate sections on development of perception in the child. The fact is that Piaget has not committed himself to one theory of perceptual learning. One gathers from some of his work that perceptions involve inference of a quasi-rational kind from sensory information, but on the other hand, Piaget draws a sharp distinction between perception and truly rational or intellectual processes which obey the rules of logic. Cognitive development is a kind of interweaving of these latter processes with perception.[3]

Briefly, then, Piaget's view of perceptual development includes two rather distinct theoretical concepts. Basically, perception depends on sensory information which must be structured in some way by the observer, and his view is thus similar to that of Bartlett and Vernon. Development of a schema is vital to this construction. There is also the hint, in some of his writings, of a motor copy theory similar to that discussed in the next chapter.

Perception for Piaget involves assimilation of sensory input to a

[3] Several recent reviews of Piaget's views on perception and cognitive development are now available (see Wohlwill, 1962; Piaget, 1963; and Flavell, 1963).

schema and often, ensuing upon this, accommodation of the schema to the specific object. Thus, acquisition of schemata must be the fundamental process of perceptual learning. Perception is also probabilistic and subject to distortion, although the thought processes (at least at maturity) are not. The schema for Piaget is a sensory-motor plan, a cognitive structure referring to a class of action systems relating recurrent situations to a disposition to act in a characteristic way. It is categorical in the sense that there are similar action sequences forming a class which defines the schema. Repetition of situations is essential for schema formation, since the assimilation of similar situations strengthens (nourishes) the schema. Assimilatory activity engenders the schema, but it is not a mere accumulation since it is the product of continuous activity. A schema becomes more generalized, as more objects are assimilated to it. Differentiation can also occur, dividing a very general schema into subordinate ones.

In a rare discussion of perceptual learning as such, Piaget suggested that there were two kinds of perceptual modification (Piaget, 1960). One was a gradual equilibration, in the sense of progressive compensation for errors and distortion, produced by active exploration and putting things into relation. The other was increasing generalized assimilation, schematization. The schemata resulting from repetition have the effect, furthermore, of directing exploration. And finally, Piaget stated that the perceptual activities involved in perceptual learning are not themselves autonomous but are increasingly directed by the active operation of intelligence.

Throughout his work, Piaget has emphasized the role of activity and motor processes as distinguished from passive perception. The importance of exploratory activity in perception, and especially in its development, is often remarked. Examples of progress in skilled exploratory handling movements and of skilled ocular exploration are frequent. There is the suggestion that these exploratory activities are fundamental to schema formation, and there is the hint that adequate perception of forms and objects develops as a kind of copy of motor exploration by hand or eye. How seriously one can take the suggestion that perception of form is indeed a motor copy is hard to say, since the active intelligence enters in, at some point, and the lines between percept, schema, and concept are hard to draw. For the young infant, the object is "merely a sensory image at the disposal of actions (1954, p. 117)." The objective shape is constructed through movements governed by the child's actions. Objects become localized in space as they acquire permanent dimensions (constancy). Perceptual space may then be transformed as movements guided by vision become systematized, and consequently react back on it. As the sensory-motor schemata are built, so percepts change, and virtual relations between the schema and earlier or contingent perceptions become determining. The role of the motor copy in perceptual learning appears to be indirect, by way of the schema to which the percept is assimilated.

VARIETY

SIGNALS	EXAMPLES
-ing	The doctor the x-rays Jogging ev
-ed	Troubled b Tiny, unbou
, noun,	Anita, my
-ly	Anxiously
to	To get goo
from before into during in to with at inside	From the h

153.3

e husky
weather-wo

Bruner

The opinion that perceptions are a product of categorizing and inference is set forth eloquently by Bruner (1957). Problem-solving and inference are a model for perception, which is arrived at by a series of hypotheses, by trial and check, and by matching to a category. As cognitive development proceeds, perception is less and less dependent on immediately present stimulation and more and more dependent on the now-formed categories. Perception, says Bruner, involves an act of categorization. There are defining or criterial attributes, called cues, in the stimulus input which are used in "inferring the categorial identity of a perceived object," a process "as much a feature of perception as the sensory stuff from which percepts are made (1957, p. 123)." A theory of perception, according to Bruner, needs a mechanism capable of inference and categorizing as much as does a theory of cognition. All perceptual experience, he assumes, is "necessarily the end product of a categorization process (p. 124)."

Perceptual learning must then depend on the construction of a system of categories to which the stimulus input can be matched, that is, on "the learning of appropriate modes of coding the environment in terms of its object character, connectedness, or redundancy, and then in allocating stimulus inputs to appropriate categorial coding systems (1957, p. 127)."

As the learning progresses, categories become more prolific and more available, with the result that the input necessary for categorizing tends to become minimal; the stimulation may be fragmentary but the percept can be filled in by the category. The perceiver is in a state of greater readiness. The process of decision pursued in matching the stimulus input to a category is a sequential one, characterized by several states. First there is primitive categorization, in the sense of perceptual isolation of an object or event; second, there is a search for cues. The search is normally unconscious, especially if there is a good fit between the specifications of the category and the impinging cues. Third, there is a confirmation check, and then a confirmation completion, by which cue searching is terminated. These stages sound remarkably like Dewey's (1910) stages of problem solution and surely justify labeling the account a problem-solving theory of perceptual learning, although a variety of different metaphors are appealed to.

Bruner's theory leaves considerable room for idiosyncratic and non-veridical perception. The observer's perceptual readiness (meaning presumably his repertory of categories and their differential availability) must match the probability of occurrence of events going on in his world if his perception is to be veridical. It is not surprising, therefore, that Bruner underscored the dependence of perception on personality variables and attitudinal factors (Bruner, 1951)). The hypotheses which the observer applies in his search for cues might, presumably, reflect his personal needs, values, and personality patterns; the problem of validating the categories related to his needs would be very difficult. The accessibility of his categories is somehow dictated by his need states—a notion which had much to do with the so-called new look research in perception.

Aside from the new look experiments, which will be considered in Chapter 7, an example of the type of experiment designed to demonstrate that perception is a process of cue searching, inference, and matching is Potter's study of perceptual recognition (see Chapter 5 in Bruner et al., 1966). Colored photographs of familiar scenes or objects such as a fire hydrant were presented badly out of focus, with successive adjustments of the focus. The subjects guessed what the object was as the picture gradually came into focus. This procedure was said to result in a series of hypotheses as to how the stimulus input could be matched against a category. The behavior may perhaps be typical of the perceptual process in recognition, but it is equally likely that the behavior is a product of the experimental procedure and has no generality as a model of perception. The instructions were to guess or to try to figure out what the picture was of. The non-representativeness of the situation seems to me to be underlined by Bruner and Potter's (1964) finding that exposure to a substandard visual display interferes with its subsequent recognition.

Is this theory of the perceptual process assumed to account for discrimination as well as recognition? Apropos of this question, Postman says "The essential feature of treatments of perception as an inferential process is the assumption that the final judgment or discrimination is mediated by learned responses to proximal cues. . . . In fact, in the context of these analyses the terms *discrimination, judgment,* and *categorization* tend to be used interchangeably (Postman, 1963, pp. 47 ff.)."

That categorization is the same thing as discrimination, or that it can account for it, is highly unlikely, both by definition and in fact. The process of grouping into categories puts the emphasis on equivalences, common features. But discrimination puts the emphasis on differences. A paper by Bruner, Miller, and Zimmerman (1955) admits this point, raising the question of what is involved when identification or recognition improves with practice and suggesting that two aspects of recognition must be distinguished, discriminative skill and discriminative matching, the latter defined as a process of sorting the stimulus inputs into appropriate categories. Discriminative skill is not explained by a model of perception as a cue-inference-categorizing process.

Discrimination by matching to a prototype is characteristic of a number of template-matching models for recognition of patterns by machines. Rosenblatt (1958), for example, designed a model called the perceptron, which operates by comparing new stimulus patterns with previously recorded prototypes and then placing them in appropriate classes. The perceptron was said to be capable of learning new perceptual concepts, by dividing the environment into stimulus classes. An essential feature of such systems is the overlooking of differences. An illustration of how pattern classes might be built up with human subjects is provided in an experiment by Uhr, Vossler, and Uleman (1962), in which variations and distortions of patterns were presented and the subjects were asked to respond to them with proper names. The procedure simulated a computer program designed for machine recognition. A template-matching model of recognition is clearly not dealing with how improvement in discrimination occurs, a problem that we shall come to in the next chapter.

SUMMARY

During the past two decades, perceptual learning has come into prominence in psychology and a number of theoretical viewpoints have emerged. Of these, most can be described as enrichment theories, in the sense that perception is thought of as beginning with elementary sensory processes which are supplemented by other processes. Some of these theories are cognitively oriented, since the mediating processes are described in cognitive terminology, such as inferences, hypotheses, or problem-solving. These theories are descendents of Helmholtz's notion of unconscious inference in perception, but each has certain emphases or terms of its own which distinguish it.

Brunswik's theory of probabilistic cue learning in perception assumes that perception is always of the distal object, but that man's environment is such that it provides only uncertain information in the stimuli reaching the sense organs. These stimuli become cues or indicators of the real distal object and must be assessed against a cue-family hierarchy which gives the probable validity of the cue. Inferences are made of a sort essentially like those in gambling, using the store of previous experiences when the cue and the referent have been associated. Cue learning by association is the essential mechanism of perceptual learning for Brunswik.

The Transactionalist view of perception, with Ames, Cantril, and Ittelson as its principal proponents, is similar to Brunswik's view in its emphasis on unconscious inference from previous experience, but is subjectively oriented. The individual lives in his own world of assumptions, which may be illusory, and which determines his perceptions. The subjective evaluation of impinging stimulation is thought to be directed not only by previous experiences leading to weighted assumptions but also by personal values and attitudes.

The remaining theories described in this chapter place greater emphasis on the constructive and problem-solving nature of perception. The schema theory of Bartlett and Vernon looks at perception as a constructive process. Schemata, essentially conceptualizations of past experience, are constructed as the individual develops and these serve to mediate perception. Meaningless sensations are interpreted in terms of schemata. Perceptual learning in this theory is the construction of schemata.

Piaget has also made use of the schema and thinks of perception as an active, constructive process. However, Piaget makes a sharp distinction between perception and logical intellectual processes. Perception involves assimilation of the sensory input to a schema, so that acquisition of schemata is a fundamental process in perceptual learning. So is equilibration, putting things into relation by active exploratory processes. But schemata direct exploration as they become available. Furthermore, perceptual activities become less autonomous as development proceeds, and are increasingly directed by intellectual processes.

For Bruner, problem-solving is the model for perception. Perception is achieved by a sequence of operations including hypotheses, trial and check, and matching to a category. Perception always involves an act of categorization. Cues in the stimulus input are used to infer categories. Perceptual learning, therefore, must involve the formation of categories and the allocation of each stimulus input to the appropriate category. The hypotheses which direct the search for the right category may, for Bruner, reflect the personal needs and values of the observer.

These five theories have not, on the whole, led to many experiments on perceptual learning as such. Because the mediating processes are thought to be on the inside, to be inferential and unconscious, the theories are hard to test, with the possible exception of Brunswik's. Demonstrations which point to the role of assumptions or inferences have been frequent, but the generality and representativeness of such demonstrations for perception and for perceptual learning can be questioned.

4

Contemporary Theories of Perceptual Learning: Response-oriented Theories

The theories described in the last chapter were characterized by the term enrichment because perceptual development was viewed as a process of supplementing the sensory input with hypotheses or inferences. Another group of theories of perceptual development may also be classified as enrichment theories, but the supplementary processes are thought of as responses instead of conceptual or inferential processes. These response-oriented theories assume that association is the essential mechanism of integration, usually Pavlovian conditioning of stimuli to responses. The theories subdivide into two classes, those which consider perception derived from and isomorphic with a motor copy of objects and events, and those which consider perception as discrimination supplemented by response mediation. Motor copy theories will be considered first, since they bear some resemblance to the schema theories considered in the last chapter. The motor copy is a kind of representation of an external event, like the schema, albeit an integration of responses instead of images. The notion is not new, for Alexander Bain explained the perception of shape thus: "It depends upon the course given to the movements in following the outline of a material body. Thus we acquire a movement corresponding to a straight line, to a ring, an oval, etc. This is purely muscular (Bain, 1855, pp. 244–45)."

MOTOR COPY THEORIES

The Soviet Theory of Perception

Perception has been given considerable attention by psychologists in the Soviet Union during the past two decades. The leader in theory construction has been Leontiev; other psychologists, especially Zaporozhets, have contributed experiments and theoretical elaboration. The theory is materialistic, externally oriented, and genetic, as the following quotation bears witness:

The factor of decisive importance for the whole process of cognition, from sensation onwards, is practice. It is through practice that we test the accuracy of our images, ánd separate the true from the false. The classics of Marxism-Leninism provide detailed proofs of the proposition that, in practical activity, we use things in conformity with their real properties (Ananiev, 1957).

The conditioned reflex is considered the basic mechanism of integration and development of perception. Internal mental processes, including perception, are considered transformations of processes which initially occurred as actions upon external objects. According to Leontiev (1957), manipulation of objects with the hands is the first stage in the development of object perception, followed by tracing movements with the eyes. In the next stage, the process progressively loses the character of an external action toward objects, but the structure of the process remains the same, reproducing that of the corresponding external operations. The final stage consists of an abbreviation of the whole process, which becomes automatic and is transformed into a "dynamic stereotype." The stereotype is a reflection of the external world, based on action. Leontiev, in an opening address to the Eighteenth International Congress of Psychology in Moscow in 1966, termed this the "reflection theory"; perception constructs a likeness of the world through action.

Zaporozhets (1960) in an address titled "On the Reflectory Origin of Visual Perception of Objects" divided actions into two classes, executive and orienting. The classification is derived from Pavlov, executive movements being classical conditioned reflexes and orienting movements being exploratory reflexes. The orienting actions have the special function of mediating the perception of external objects and events. Under difficult conditions of perception (Sokolov, 1957), they are intensified, and executive action of the organism is postponed until the properties of the new stimulus are ascertained. More specifically, their role is to form a copy of the object, reproducing its features so as to yield a likeness. In the process of development, Zaporozhets said, gradual changes in the orienting movements occur. He described experiments undertaken in his laboratory to investigate the ontogenesis of orienting movements of the hand and the eye, with the purpose of demonstrating that copying movements ("conditioned orienting reactions") led to formation of an image of an object.

Development of the perception of an object, according to Zaporozhets, is an interaction between orienting movements of the hand and the eye. At an early stage of infancy unconditioned orienting movements of the eye that are imperfect take place. But later the hand teaches the eye by making contact with the object and tracing its contours. As the eye begins to follow the hand, its orienting movements correspond more and more with the shape of the perceived figure. Later the eye performs the orienting function independently, and finally begins to anticipate and direct the orienting function of the hand. Visual perception, in essence, is a reduced orienting movement, but it is also formed on the basis of practical activity and only gradually attains relative independence and achieves ideal forms.

Pick (1963) has summarized some of the experiments resulting from this theory. For example, in one experiment, unfamiliar visual figures were presented tachistoscopically to adults, and it was found that recognition was difficult without eye movements, although familiar figures could be recognized. The inference made was that some kind of reproduction or transformation of a motor copy had already been learned for the familiar figure, but was unavailable for the unfamiliar one. In another experiment with adults, lights were flashed on a screen in succession. The subjects followed the lights with eye movements and, when the sequence was repeated, anticipatory eye movements became conditioned. Gradually, the eye movements dropped out with repetition. The suggestion was that exploratory movements (orienting reflexes) play a crucial role in a new and unfamiliar situation, or when a difficult differentiation is required.

Ontogenetic experiments with children are obviously important for a motor copy theory. Experiments by Zinchenko and his coworkers demonstrate the importance of exploratory eye movements, but are not convincing as to the importance of copying. (See Zaporozhets, 1965). Preschool children were presented with two-dimensional unfamiliar forms in a matching task. The child looked at one for ten seconds and then matched it from a group of three. Three-year-old children matched at little better than a chance level, and eye movement recording showed no evidence of following around the contours. The children's eye movements were saccadic and fixations fell within the contour lines. But performance was better in the four-to-five age group, and their eye movements were said to be related to contour. Only similar figures were confused. The older children made no errors, moved their eyes around the contours, and paused on salient parts of the figures. The implication was drawn that feedback from eye movements which trace the figure is necessary for recognition.

The same figures used in the previous task were presented in another experiment in a format suitable for tactual exploration. The child was given a standard to explore tactually, and then chose the figure from a group of three by tactual search alone. The task was too difficult for the three year olds to perform at all and was still very difficult at seven years. Exploratory hand movements, slow and clumsy at four, changed with age. In the older children, contour-tracing was apparent and salient features were compared. The development of tactual search thus appeared to parallel development of visual search, but it was later in maturing. These results do not confirm the notion that the hand teaches the eye or that touch provides the basis for visual form perception.

The Soviet psychologists have elaborated their theory to cover auditory perception as well, emphasizing the role of feedback from articulatory responses or even from other kinds of response correlated in an experimental situation with some aspect of auditory stimulation. Pick (1963) reports experiments of Leontiev's in which subjects, presented with two tones, were asked to reproduce them vocally before making a judgment of which tone was higher in pitch. Difference thresholds were found to be lower when judgments were accompanied by vocal intonation. Correlations between ability to vocalize and pitch discrimination were high. When a subject had a narrow zone of accurate vocalization over the whole pitch range, his discrimination thresholds for pitch were found to be lower within this zone than outside it. These results are consistent, at least, with the hypothesis that a link is established between feedback from the articulatory musculature and the acoustic stimuli, and that a subject learns to discriminate by reproducing what he hears vocally on the basis of this kinesthetic feedback. The hypothesis, a kind of auditory motor copy theory, is similar to one described by Liberman, Cooper et al. (1962). With practice, the articulatory activity presumably becomes implicit.

In another experiment reported by Pick, Leontiev provided motor training along with discrimination of different tones, but the feedback introduced was from hand pressure. The subject pressed a lever to produce graded strength of pressure which he was to associate with a pitch continuum. He was corrected for his pressure responses. The subjects were said to have improved in pitch discrimination. This experiment did not involve a reproduction of the tonal stimulus itself, and therefore is not really an example of reflecting or creating a likeness of the physical stimulus. The subjects may have been learning the concept of a scale.

On first thought, the motor copy theory may seem to have an appealing and plausible simplicity. But on further consideration, a number of serious criticisms are apparent. First, the apparent parsimony of the theory is illusory, for early unconditioned orienting movements must be assumed as well as conditioned ones. For example, learning to follow a contour with movements of the eye is said to yield a percept of form. But the eye must be following something in its first explorations of the contour. How is the contour seen? Are there formless sensations at this stage? If so, how does the eye get from one contour point to the next in the sequence? A second criticism concerns the inferences from results of the experiments. Supposing that a correlation between contours of objects and exploratory movements does exist at some stage of development, no causal relationship has been proved of the kind required by the copy theory. One cannot logically conclude that the movements are the necessary cause of the perception of form. Finally, the question arises as to the generality of the theory. How would it explain perceptions other than those of form and scale? How would it treat, for example, the perception of color differences? It is hard to give serious consideration to a literal version of the motor copy theory.

J. G. Taylor

A theory of perception as the by-product of the acquisition of conditioned responses has been expounded by J. G. Taylor (1962). Taylor's theory is not based on the Marxian epistemology of the Soviet theory, and hence does not dwell on the notion that perception reflects the external material world by way of action upon it. But he supposes that responses such as approaching and manipulating objects and matching a tone by singing it underlie perception. Each response, he thinks, is mediated by a complex system of neural links, and perception is defined as the simultaneous activity of many of these links, "as determined by the properties of the environment at the moment (Taylor, 1960)." His book is an attempt to derive perceptual phenomena from S-R assumptions similar to those of Clark Hull, based on conditioning principles. The following quotation gives the flavor of Taylor's thinking:

> The essence of the behavioural theory is that perception is a state of multiple simultaneous readiness for actions directed to the objects in the environment that are acting on the receptor organs at any one moment. The actions in question have been acquired by the individual in the course of his life and have been determined by the reinforcing contingencies in the environment in which he grew up. What determines the content of perception is not the properties of the sensory transducers that are operated on by stimulus energies from the environment, but the properties of the behaviour conditioned to those stimulus energies; and the character of this behaviour in turn is determined by the needs of the organism and the relevance, to those needs, of the properties of the objects and substances in the environment that are responsible for the stimulus energies (Taylor, 1965, p. 1).

He cites evidence from experiments with distorting prism spectacles as corroboration of his theory. He reasoned that if opportunity to correct one sort of behavioral error while wearing the prisms results in the restoration of normal perception while perceptual distortion of other kinds remains, the inference can be drawn that perceptual development depends on the acquisition of specific responses. The experiments on adaptation to distortions produced by prism spectacles are now very numerous and their interpretation is by no means simple or unequivocal. They will be considered in a later chapter.

Hebb

A theory of perceptual development propounded by D. O. Hebb is similar to the Soviet theory in hypothesizing that form perception is generated by a copying process, but differs in that it is not couched in terms of conditioned responses. Hebb firmly rejects the notion that acquisition of specific overt responses to stimulus objects is the basis of perceptual integration (Hebb, 1962). His theory does assume integration through repetition and association, but the elements being integrated are neural processes. There is still the suggestion of a motor copy, however, since eye movements are thought by Hebb to produce neural excitations which in turn set up a reverberating circuit in the brain and give rise to a perception of form.

In his statement of how perceptual organization is learned, Hebb postulates a primitive figure-ground organization in the infant's vision. This is a "low-level property of identifiability" but it increases radically with repeated exposure. Progress from the primitive figure-ground organization to the finished perception is the major concern of the theory. Sensory processes are thought of as quite separate from perceptual processes, which depend upon mediation and learning. Color, for example, is sensory, but form must be integrated.

The mechanism of form integration is the cell assembly which grows by lowering synaptic resistance between cells. Cells which are repeatedly active at the same time become associated. A reverberatory activity thus takes place within the assembly. The growth of the assembly Hebb thought to be a slow process involving recruitment of new elements. The elements from which more complex perceptions develop include the line and the angle. The eye seeks out angles and follows lines, so as to provide the excitation of cells in sequence. To quote Hebb, "If line and angle are the bricks from which form perceptions are built, the primitive unity of the figure might be regarded as mortar, and eye movement as the hand of the builder (1949, p. 83)." Perception of a triangle is thus a complex integration. Fixation on one corner of a triangle leads to eye movements in the direction of the other corners present in peripheral vision. Integration of neural impulses proceeds with repeated fixation on the three corners. Further complexities of growth of cell assemblies and superordinate assemblies are brought in to account for constancy over changes of size and transformations of the triangle's shape. The finished superordinate assembly Hebb thinks of as lying outside sensory cortical projection areas, thus providing a basis for his distinction between sensation and perception.

From this description of Hebb's ingenious model, a few of its essential properties stand out. It is a representational theory of perception, like the schema theories and the Soviet motor copy theory. Although it is a neuropsychological theory, it also depends on responses because, as Hebb says, "motor learning got a foot inside the door through the emphasis on eye movements (1949, p. 107)." Finally, it most emphatically asserts the learned character of perception, except for the "primitive unity of figure."

How to make an experimental test of this model has presented an interesting problem. Hebb, in his book, cited as supporting evidence the damaging effects of depriving the young of early visual experience with the method of experimental dark-rearing of animals and with the occasional natural experiment of congenital cataract in man. These damaging effects will be considered in Chapter 12, but two reservations must be pointed out here. The results themselves present some contradictions and cannot be interpreted simply as proving that all visual perception is learned. Moreover, although they provide evidence of learning in visual perception, it is not necessarily evidence for Hebb's theory of learning but only evidence that learning occurs. As we have seen, and as the rest of this book will confirm, perceptual learning has not gone unnoticed and serious attempts exist to explain it in other ways.

If the fact of perceptual learning as such cannot be considered specific evidence for Hebb's theory, what can be said for it? Two kinds of prediction from the theory have led to experiments. One is the proposition that eye movements trace figure contours, with some causal relation to perceptual development. As has already been pointed out it cannot be assumed, even when tracing movements are demonstrated, that they play a causal role in the perceiving of forms. A number of experiments in Hebb's laboratory have examined tachistoscopic perception of words by skilled readers, with the assumption that reading does not train all parts of the retina in the same way, due to conventions of scanning from left to right (or right to left in some other cultures). Results of these experiments (see, for instance, Mishkin & Forgays, 1952, and a summary of experiments in Howard & Templeton, 1966, pp. 301 ff.) do find differential efficiency of recognition for material exposed to the right or the left of the fovea and the results in general support the influence of scanning habits in reading, but they are interpretable by other models than Hebb's.

A technique for holding an image fixed on a given portion of the retina, so as to prevent the slight eye tremor which appears to be essential for normal vision, has lent itself to a test of some predictions of Hebb's concept of the cell assembly. Research with these stabilized retinal images has shown that parts of the image or all of it may disappear with continued constant stimulation of the same receptors. If a complex image disappears by fragmentation, Hebb's theory would predict that parts such as lines and angles (the building blocks) would remain or disappear as intact elements. Experimental observations by Pritchard, Heron, and Hebb (1960) with the stabilized image technique provided some interesting examples of fragmentation in the disappearance of parts of patterns such as triangles, squares, circles, and other more complex outline figures. A single line tended to act as a unit (to appear or disappear as a whole) with breaks at the point of intersection with another line. Lines making up a triangle or square acted independently, except that activity of parallel lines was correlated. So far the data are in harmony with the theory but another result, that angles (corners) did not act as perceptual elements, was contradictory. Good figures, in the Gestalt psychologists' sense, such as circles, were relatively stable, but even circles sometimes fragmented, leaving short segments of curves. The conclusion drawn was that perceptual elements (straight lines and short curved segments) existed in their own right and that the more complex wholes, such as squares, are made up of simpler parts.

An experiment by Eagle and Klein (1962) replicated some of the same stimulus conditions but obtained rather different results. They found that angles persisted when squares and triangles were presented, whereas straight lines fragmented, or disappeared in a shorter time. Curved lines tended to persist as compared with jagged ones. Meaningful displays, such as letters and words, were more stable than less meaningful ones, a result also found by Pritchard et al. This research must be viewed with some reservations at the present time, since there is a possibility that fragmentation could be the result of apparatus problems, such as slippage of the contact lens worn during the experiment. Contradictory results could be explained in such a fashion. They could even be due to idiosyncratic factors, since the discomforts of the technique are such that the number of subjects, as well as of targets sampled, has been small. Experiments with prolonged fixation of luminous designs in a dark room (McKinney, 1963), without special apparatus, may provide some confirmation.

Hebb's theory at the moment presents a good many difficulties, as he himself has pointed out. Leaving aside the neurological problems, there are questions of its generality as a model for perception and perceptual development. It is restricted, so far at least, to the explanation of visual perception alone. Furthermore, its handling of comparative data seems less than satisfactory. Hebb recognizes species differences, of course, and considered in his book the relationship of learning to phylogenetic level. The hypothesis is offered that the lower the animal in the evolutionary tree, the more mature its level of efficiency of learning at birth. Going up the phylogenetic scale, the slower is the rate of learning at infancy. This may be true, though the proposition is not self-evident and supporting evidence is wanting. But it is a fact that dark-reared rats and newborn chicks and goats respond selectively to visual depth differences without any learning. The evidence for this capacity was found in investigations with the visual cliff, which requires discrimination of depth at an edge (see Chapter 12). Some kind of registration of contours and edges must have been possible. Furthermore, eye movements of the kind assumed to play a role in Hebb's theory are not possessed by all animals that perceive visual form adequately. One must conclude, therefore, that integration of cell assemblies might be a mechanism for development of form perception in some animals, but that it cannot be in all.

DISCRIMINATION THEORIES

When Gibson and Gibson contrasted enrichment theories with a differentiation or specificity theory of perceptual learning in 1955, they were answered by Postman (1955), who objected to the distinction. His thesis, in part, was that the kind of enrichment hypothesis exemplified by the addition of images to sense data is no longer of interest to contemporary associationists, and that the argument for a differentiation theory must be evaluated against the psychological and physiological associationism of present-day behavior theory. In Postman's opinion, perceptual learning should be defined by changes in stimulus-response relationships under controlled conditions of practice. The appropriate classes of response would be discriminative responses of the kind obtained in conventional psychophysical experiments, or discrimination learning experiments.

Note that the learning of overt discriminative responses is not the same mechanism as copying the stimulus, for no likeness between the response and the stimulation or the distal object is assumed. It is the response itself, whatever it may be, that is supposed to give discriminability. Since the response gives rise to new stimulation, it is possible to think of response-produced stimulation as being added to the original stimulation. I shall refer to this hypothesis as additive mediation.

The development of discriminative responses has been a concern of behaviorists, and especially conditioned response theorists from the beginning. Pavlov (1927) invented the method of contrast for producing differentiated conditioned responses. As every schoolboy knows, a dog that had learned to salivate at the sight of a circle would also salivate at the sight of an ellipse. He called this stimulus generalization. But if the circle and the ellipse were then presented one at a time, the circle always followed by food but the ellipse never, the animal eventually learned to salivate to the circle only. Was this a case of perceptual learning, in the sense that the dog's ability to discriminate was improved? Pavlov's experiment does not tell us. The dog may only have learned to attach different responses to similar shapes which he was perfectly capable of discriminating in the first place. We do not know, even if it was an improved discrimination, whether he could at this point transfer the discrimination if he were required to make other responses to the two shapes. It is the implications of this experiment that separate the psychologists who talk about differentiated perceptions from those who talk about discriminative responses. Discriminative responses are useful in measuring improved differentiation of perception, but as Wohlwill (1958) pointed out, a transfer test with different responses is necessary if we wish to ascertain whether perceptual learning really occurred.

The Predifferentiation Experiment

In 1940, I proposed that such transfer of discrimination (permanent reduction of generalization) should occur for the learning of a list whose stimulus items had originally generalized. If differentiation has once been achieved in a list of paired associates, there should be facilitation when a new list, pairing these items with different responses, is presented for learning. I referred to the items as "predifferentiated" (Gibson, 1940, p. 222), and experiments with such a transfer design have since been referred to as "predifferentiation experiments" (cf. Arnoult, 1957). The language of this hypothesis was couched in terminology borrowed from the conditioned response experiment, but my reasoning was not. I expected that the discrimination would transfer, because I thought that perceptual learning had occurred—that the stimuli had really become more discriminable, not that they had merely been associated with different responses. If one were concerned only with responses, one might expect interference by the first response when a new one must be attached to the same stimulus.

Let us consider briefly some examples of the predifferentiation experiment, before returning to the response-oriented discrimination theories of perceptual learning. I think of the predifferentiation experiment as a challenge to the Pavlovian assumption that discriminative responses constitute discrimination. Also, these experiments provide the reasons for the controls introduced in the later experimental paradigms designed to demonstrate the role of responses and response-produced mediation.

An experiment by Dibble (1948) studied the effect of opportunities for predifferentiation on learning verbal responses to a set of nonsense figures (scribbles) which were very similar to one another. Three groups of subjects were compared on a paired associates learning task. Group C, the control group, had no prior experience with the scribbles. Group E_D was given the figures, printed on cards, one at a time, and asked to draw reproductions of them, spending a minute on each drawing. Group E_I was given the cards in a pack, and told to lay them out so that all were visible, then pick up each one and compare it with the others, looking for distinguishing features for each one, and checking a second time to make sure that the search had elicited a unique feature or combination of features for each. The time for the search was limited to ten minutes (two minutes less than Group E_D). When the trials to learn the list of paired associates to a criterion of one perfect trial were compared for the three groups, Group

E_I was significantly superior to the other two groups. Group E_D was not significantly faster than the control group in trials to reach the criterion. Generalization (intralist confusion) errors were significantly reduced for Group E_I compared to both other groups. It seems clear from this experiment that prior differentiation of stimulus items can carry over to a learning task, but it is also apparent that what goes on during the opportunity for differentiation makes a difference. Drawing a reproduction did not help significantly.

In a second example, the precise stimulus-response relationships in the predifferentiation practice were carefully manipulated. Gagné and Baker (1950) had subjects perform a discriminative-motor task with four manual responses (hitting one of four switches on a horizontal panel) in response to four lights. The lights were arranged in two pairs, separated by 7½ inches. One of each pair was green, one red. The responses were arranged in pairs also, so that position and color discriminations were required for the subject to press the correct switch. The total task, involving all four S-R relationships, was presented to a control group without preliminary practice. A second group was given prior practice with color discrimination only. A third group had practice with position discrimination only. The measure used for comparison was mean response time in successive ten-trial stages on the total task. Response time was significantly shorter for both experimental groups. The question is, was this reduction specific to the practiced lights alone, or did it extend to the other pair of stimulus lights? There was, in fact, transfer to the other pair measured by both response time and error reduction. Since this transfer could not be accounted for on the basis of having increased the speed of specific responses made to specific stimuli, the conclusion was drawn that practice in discriminating lights varying in color or position resulted in a transferable reduction of generalization tendencies.

In both these experiments, discrimination practice with a set of stimulus objects transferred in spite of the fact that new responses or new stimulus-response relationships were involved in the second stage. The positive transfer appears to be attributable to increased differentiation among the stimulus objects.

Acquired Distinctiveness of Cues

How could the so-called predifferentiation experiments be interpreted by a behavior theorist who wished to restrict his theorizing to a stimulus-response-association model? In 1941 Miller and Dollard elaborated a hypothesis which they referred to as "acquired distinctiveness of cues." Stimuli, according to this hypothesis, may become more distinct from one another by being associated with distinctive responses which thereafter generate new stimuli compounded with the original ones. This process does not imply that new cues or distinctive features are found in the original stimuli themselves, but rather that distinctive cues are added by the response, i.e., stimulus discriminability is dependent on response discriminability. The nature of the response is all important, since common responses will lead to acquired equivalence. The hypothesis was stated by Miller as follows:

> According to stimulus-response theory, learning to respond with highly distinctive names to similar stimulus situations should tend to lessen the generalization of other responses from one of these situations to another since the stimuli produced by responding with the distinctive name will tend to increase the differences in the stimulus patterns of the two situations. Increased differentiation based on this mechanism has been called acquired distinctiveness of cues.
>
> On the other hand, if the individual learns to respond to two quite different situations with the same verbal response, the stimuli produced by this response will be a common element mediating an increased amount of generalization from one situation to the other. This has been called acquired equivalence of cues, or secondary generalization (Miller, 1948, p. 174).

Note that the term cue is substituted for stimulus (properly speaking, stimulus object) with the implication that it is more specific than the original stimulation, not just more. This implication is not justified theoretically, but I suspect that it has been responsible in part for the attractiveness of the theory.

EXPERIMENTS WITH LABELS.   A large number of experiments have been performed to test Miller's proposition that distinctive labels learned to stimuli will lessen generalization of other responses to these stimuli. Some of the experiments simply test the facilitating effect of the label; some compare its effect with other kinds of opportunities for predifferentiation such as observation; and some investigate the influence of characteristics of the label itself.

An experiment by Rossman and Goss (1951) is representative of the first group. Their subjects first learned verbal responses and then motor responses (pushing a lever) to a number of highly similar nonsense forms. There were four groups given different amounts of practice on the verbal task. The group which learned the verbal responses to mastery performed better than the groups with less practice. The subjects reported that they looked for identifying features of the forms to help them discriminate, so facilitation of the group which performed best was not necessarily due to the responses and the cues they produced.

More recent experiments have generally included a variety of control groups in an effort to isolate the effect of response-produced mediation. One by Goss (1953) compared the effect of different kinds of training with four intensities of white light as stimuli upon transfer to a subsequent motor task. One group learned verbal responses (nonsense syllables) to the lights; one observed and tried to discriminate the lights; one merely observed them; and one had no preliminary exposure to the lights. All three groups with some kind of preliminary practice excelled the control group in the motor task. Goss argued that the observation groups might have applied their own verbal labels, but it is equally possible that cues produced by labels had no causal role. Another experiment (Goss & Greenfield, 1958) was similar but included a wider variety of predifferentiation groups (different degrees of mastery of verbal responses, etc.). A group which merely looked, with no instructions to discriminate, showed no transfer, but all the other groups did, those receiving verbal training being superior. However, a later experiment by Smith and Goss (1955) found no advantage for a group which learned labels to a set of stimuli in pretraining over a group which saw and discriminated the stimuli. Both these groups were superior in Stage II discrimination learning to a control group which was simply shown the stimuli. Other experiments by Arnoult (1956) and by Vanderplas and Garvin (1959) found no facilitation from learning labels in a later task requiring discrimination. Vanderplas (1963) suggests that the relation between the tasks employed in the two stages of predifferentiation experiments may have contributed to the muddle of apparently contradictory results.

A further cause for concern in these experiments is the question of what is going on when the subject is observing. An experiment by Cantor (1955) compared the performance of children in a simple discrimination task (learning which of two pictured faces would be rewarded after choosing between them) following the learning of names for the faces or simply pointing to various features of them at the experimenter's request. Learning names for the faces was associated with faster choice of the correct picture in the second task. But there is no reason to believe that pointing to noses, eyes, etc., in both pictures would lead the subject to search for differences between the faces. Norcross and Spiker (1957) sought to remedy this situation by requiring the subjects to say "same" or "different" when pairs of faces were presented. The subjects again performed better after learning names. But it is still uncertain that equal attention to differences was paid during same-different judgments, which require a lower level of attention to exactly what the distinguishing features are, than does the task of assigning a specific name to each one. The latter task requires detection of some uniquely identifying aspect of each of the stimuli, and so, in this experiment, did the criterion task of Stage II.

A number of experiments with children involving pretraining with verbal responses have been summarized by Cantor (1965). Typically, the child learned labels (generally nonsense syllables) to each of a small number of stimulus objects (e.g., pictured faces) and then learned to make different motor responses (usually pushing buttons) to the objects. The learning situation was like paired associates or a successive discrimination problem. In these experiments the group that learned labels usually performed better on the second learning task than a control group. But, as Cantor points out, the stimulus objects were always discriminable in the first place, so it is not at all certain that they actually became more distinctive. It may be, as Spiker (1963) suggested, that the label simply gave the subject a handy means of rehearsal between trials while he was learning the second set of responses.

A third question raised in these experiments concerns the nature of the labels learned by subjects in Stage I. According to Miller, the labels should be highly distinctive in order to increase the differences between the stimulus patterns of the two situations. Several experimenters (Jeffrey, 1953; Murdock, 1958) have suggested that verbal responses are more distinctive than motor, and have found transfer results compatible with the hypothesis, but degree of distinctiveness is not commensurable in the two cases. Norcross (1958) tried to attack this problem directly by having her subjects learn a pair of very similar names to two stimulus patterns and a pair of different ones to two others. In Stage II of her experiment, the subjects performed better with the dissimilarly named stimulus patterns. It is possible in this setup that the highly similar responses were producing interference, rather than the different ones facilitation. In other experiments, similar labels were just as facilitating as different ones. Cantor (1965), discussing experiments by Guerjoy and by Reese, suggested that degree of learning should be a causal factor, and that similar responses themselves had to be differentiated before they could serve as distinctive labels. This process could be a kind of infinite regression!

A more direct test of the hypothesis that distinctive labels are the necessary condition for positive transfer in Stage II is provided by some experiments which compared the effect of learning the same labels for some of the stimuli with the effect of learning different labels for each one. Robinson (1955) compared four groups of subjects on a criterion task (Stage II) of discriminating fingerprints by a same-different judgment. One group learned distinctive names for the ten prints during Stage I pretraining; another group learned one name for five of the prints and a second name for the other five; a third group made successive comparisons judging whether the prints were the same or different; and the fourth had no pretraining. The three groups with pretraining all showed facilitation compared to the control group, but did not differ significantly from one another. According to the acquired distinctiveness hypothesis, the group which learned ten distinctive names should certainly have performed better on the criterion task than the group which learned the same names for a number of prints.

Similar results were obtained by Hake and Eriksen (1955) in an experiment in which subjects learned to apply two, four, or eight labels (letters of the alphabet) to a set of sixteen similar, unfamiliar patterns (five points of light selected at random from a 5 × 5 matrix). Following this task, the subjects learned new labels (two, four, or eight) to the same patterns. According to the acquired-distinctiveness hypothesis, the use of a very small number of labels in original learning should have reduced the distinctiveness of the light patterns and led to poorer performance in the second learning task, compared to the groups that learned more labels. But this was not the case. Hake and Eriksen concluded that the perceptual gain resulting from a labeling task was due to the subject's having to make a decision about the patterns on each trial, rather than to the label itself, because the task required the subject to search for aspects of the patterns by which they could be discriminated. In a second experiment, Hake and Eriksen (1956) studied the effect of prior practice in using certain labels before associating them with forms later to be recognized. The prior use of the labels (letters of the alphabet) made the learning task easier, but there was no group effect on the criterion task (recognition) on the number of labels used, or prior experience with the labels. Thus, increased skill in pairing responses with the forms was not accompanied by increased pattern differentiation. Within-subject correlations suggested, however, that increased skill in the use of verbal labels, with a large set of practiced responses, might lead to denotative use of the labels for organizing and identifying the stimulus aspects differentiated by practice. In other words, two processes might go on when well-practiced labels are available: differentiation of the set of stimulus patterns, and identification by means of the labels of the critical distinguishing aspects of the patterns.

The results of the above experiments were confirmed in an experiment by De Rivera (1959) who, like Robinson, used fingerprints as stimuli. In Task I, four groups of subjects learned responses (letters) to the prints, but two of the groups (A and B) learned a different response for each print, while the other groups (C and D) learned one response for five of the prints and another for the other five. Of the first two groups, one received 16 practice trials (B), one only eight (A). The second two groups had eight practice trials but had different instructions. One (C) was told that there were no common characteristics among the five prints named by the same letter, and to learn the response to each print individually; the other (D) was told to look for something common to the prints having the same response. Task II was the same for all groups, learning number responses to each of the prints. Performance on the second task was equally good for groups A and C, although Group C learned only two responses in Stage I. This outcome, like the experiments of Robinson, and Hake and Eriksen, suggests that the labels played no role except to force the subject to search for discriminable aspects of the prints. Group B, with more practice trials, performed better, but subjects who reported using the letters as mediating responses had no advantage. Group D, which looked for common features of the prints having the same response, made significantly more errors in Task II than Group C. Search for distinguishing features of the individual stimuli appears, thus, to have been a crucial factor in transfer of stimulus differentiation. This conclusion was substantiated by the subjects, who reported using distinguishing features such as one print having a loop in the center.

An experiment by Hendrickson and Muehl (1962) provides further evidence that distinctiveness of a pretrained response is not necessary for stimulus differentiation. The study compared three groups of kindergarten children in learning names for the letters b and d. One group, called the Attention-Consistent Motor Group, had pretraining in attending to the directional difference between the two letters and making consistent motor responses (pushing a handle with the left hand to d and with the right hand to b). Arrows below the letters pointed to the left and right; the arrow on the subject's left always pointed left for a left motor response and the opposite for an arrow pointing right. A second group, called the Attention-Inconsistent Motor Group, differed only in the placement of the arrows in relation to the motor response. Half the arrows pointed inward and half outward. The subject found the arrow that pointed the same way as the letter (sometimes on his left and sometimes on his right) and pushed the handle with the hand on the side of that arrow. Thus the motor responses to the two letters were inconsistent, half with the left hand and half with the right for each letter. A third group (control) had irrelevant pretraining, matching color stimuli. The transfer task was learning names to the two letters. The group with inconsistent motor training made fewer correct responses in pretraining than the group with consistent motor training but, nevertheless, the two groups did not differ significantly by any measure on the transfer task, though they both excelled the control group.

In the labeling experiments considered so far, the labels to be learned were irrelevant with respect to the stimulus. According to the hypothesis of acquired distinctiveness, any label should be adequate as long as it is distinctive. The weight of the evidence leads us to conclude that it is not necessary that the associated label be distinctive, but it might matter whether the response is relevant. If a label points to some distinctive feature of the stimulus object, will it be more effective than a neutral one? In the Hendrickson and Muehl experiment, both experimental groups had to match the direction of the arrow in relation to the letter. Being forced to make this relevant observation was undoubtedly important. Several experiments suggest that relevant labels are effective in facilitating discrimination.

An experiment by Pfafflin (1960) compared the effect of learning relevant or irrelevant labels to forms with the effect of observation of the forms on a later discrimination task. (The subject pressed one of two buttons for each form.) The forms were of three different degrees of meaningfulness. When the decreases in errors following pretraining were compared, significant facilitation occurred only when pretraining had been by observation or by learning relevant labels. Forms which differed in meaningfulness were affected differently by the three kinds of pretraining. Learning relevant labels to forms low in meaning was advantageous, probably because they helped the subject select distinctive features of the forms. Discrimination learning with highly meaningful forms was facilitated by observation more than by learning a label in pretraining. These results are not predictable from the hypothesis of acquired distinctiveness of cues as stated by Miller, since it would appear that it is not addition of response-produced cues to the stimulus complex which is important, but rather attention to distinguishing features of the stimulus itself. A similar conclusion follows from experiments of Campbell and Freeman (1955), Smith and Means (1961), and Segal (1964).

Experiments purportedly testing acquired distinctiveness have sometimes used relevant labels without comparison with irrelevant labels. In these experiments, random shapes like those of Vanderplas and Garvin (see Fig. 4–1) were the stimulus material. Names that were suggested by the shapes were assigned to them (e.g., arrow, crab, bird). In an experiment by Ranken (1963), pretraining with the shapes was followed by a recognition task (learning to recognize all the shapes correctly). In Stage I, the control group was shown the shapes without labels and told "not to use words in any way." The experimental group was given the names with the shapes and told to use them. In Stage II, a sample shape was shown the subject and withdrawn. Then he was required to select it from the entire set. The control subjects were told again at the beginning of this task not to use words in remembering the sample for recognition. The group given labels surpassed the control group in recognition learning. Both the suggestive labels and the instructions might have helped them.

Experiments with random shapes and relevant labels by Ellis and his colleagues will be described below, since they included equivalence training.

ACQUIRED EQUIVALENCE. Miller's statement of the acquired distinctiveness hypothesis was logically extended to the other side of the coin, acquired equivalence. If two different stimuli come to be responded to with the same response, there should be mediation leading to increased generalization. In three of the experiments described above (Robinson, Hake & Eriksen, De Rivera), such an effect would have been predicted, but occurred in only one case, i.e., the group in De Rivera's experiment which was told to look for common characteristics of the stimuli given the same label. Let us consider some other experiments which bear on the acquired equivalence hypothesis.

An experiment by Ellis, Bessemer, Devine, and Trafton (1962) tested both acquired distinctiveness and acquired equivalence of cues for a recognition task with tactile shapes (six-point random shapes cut from vinyl tile). There were three conditions of pretraining: learning relevant labels, one to

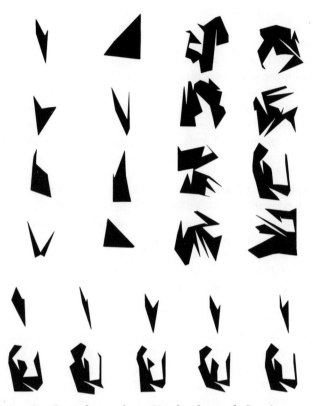

FIGURE 4–1.   Random shapes from Vanderplas and Garvin.

The shapes were constructed by the method of Attneave and Arnoult (1956) and have been used in many studies of shape discrimination and recognition, such as those of Ellis and Muller (1964). In the top four rows are a number of multivariate shapes used in an original learning task. In the bottom two rows are two sets of shapes prepared for an ensuing recognition task. One of the set of five is a prototype; the others are variations on the prototype. The subject must judge whether the practiced prototype is present in the set, and if so which one it is. (From J. M. Vanderplas & E. A. Garvin, Complexity, association value, and practice as factors in shape recognition following paired-associates training. *Journal of Experimental Psychology,* 1959, *57,* 157.)

each of a set of prototype shapes; learning one relevant label to half the shapes, and another to the other half; and observation by tactile inspection. The recognition task was selecting each prototype shape from a group of shapes which were variations on the prototype (see Fig. 4–1). The group which learned a unique label for each prototype did not perform better on the recognition task than the observation group (a result replicated in a similar experiment by Ellis, Feugue, Long, & Pegram, 1964). The group which learned only two labels was poorer at recognition, probably because the subjects disregarded all features of the shapes except the one suggested by the label. The experiment cannot be considered a test of acquired equivalence, as Miller stated the hypothesis, because the shapes given the same label (wide or narrow) were actually similar to begin with.

Ellis and Muller (1964) performed a similar experiment with visually presented random shapes, including the same three pretraining groups. There were also two levels of complexity of shape (6-pointed and 24-pointed shapes). When the shapes were simple, the observation group made more correct selections of the prototypes than the other two groups. When the shapes were complex, the group which learned different relevant labels for each one performed better on recognition if they had up to eight practice trials, but not with 16. With so many trials, the observation group would have time to locate the distinguishing features without the hint provided by the labels. The equivalence group was somewhat poorer than the other two groups. Again, the experiment cannot be considered a test of acquired equivalence, as Miller stated the hypothesis, due to preexisting similarity (width) of the shapes which were given the same label, and the tendency for the equivalence group to disregard other dimensions of difference. When a subject is asked to classify stimulus shapes on the basis of a feature actually present, other features are irrelevant and, as experiments in later chapters will describe (cf. especially Yonas & Gibson, 1967), they are not attended to.

The same criticism with respect to the test of acquired equivalence applies to an experiment by Katz (1963). Three groups of subjects (children) were shown four geometric forms. One group (DL) learned a separate label for each of the forms; one (CL) learned a common label for two forms and another common label for the other two. A third group was shown the figures without labels. The learning groups were given 150 trials. Afterward there followed a perceptual task (same-different judgments with a tachistoscopic exposure of pairs of the forms) and then a discrimination task (learning which of three of the forms concealed a prize). The three groups differed as to the number of same responses assigned to pairs of forms which had been given common labels in group CL, group CL making most errors. Group CL also made more errors in the discrimination task of confusing the two stimuli for which they had learned a common label. But on looking at the forms which were used in the experiment, it is clear that any pair of two have some feature in common which the other two do not share in like value. One can group the four forms into two classes by looking only at the bottoms, for instance, or only at the lower left corners. When such a dimension already exists and produces perceptual equivalence of one pair as against another, can one say that the label and its response-produced cue are the cause of increased generalization? It seems at least equally plausible that the children learned to pay attention only to that aspect of the forms which permitted most economical division into two categories.

Other experiments have found negative evidence as regards acquired equivalence. Liberman, Harris, Kinney, and Lane (1961) measured discriminability of acoustic differences within and between phoneme boundaries, and compared the data with comparable acoustic differences in sounds not perceived as speech. Discrimination was considerably better across the phoneme boundary than in the middle of a phoneme category. The control stimuli revealed no increase in discriminability in the region corresponding to the boundary, so that sharpening of acuity at the phoneme boundary must have been a product of learning. But higher thresholds were not found within the phoneme boundaries, relative to the controls, as acquired equivalence due to attachment of phoneme labels would require.

In another linguistic study, comparing deaf and hearing children on a word-discrimination task, Putnam, Iscoe, and Young (1962) found that words which had the same sign in sign language were not more difficult for deaf children to discriminate than words having different signs, as acquired-equivalence hypotheses would predict.

Equivalence experience was the major variable in an unusual experiment by Donderi and Kane (1965). They had subjects learn common responses (letters) during pretraining to pairs of nonidentical stimuli presented tachistoscopically, and then presented triplets of stimuli for prolonged fixation in a dark room. Common-response stimulus pairs (within the triplet) tended to disappear together, as identical stimulus pairs have been shown to do with a stabilized retinal image (Replogle, 1962). Interpretation of this phenomenon as acquired equivalence does not follow, however, because in another experiment the same effect was obtained without learning a common response. During pretraining, the subject was instructed to report the presence or absence of a given pair of lines in a tachistoscopic presentation, making a "yes" judgment when they appeared. The lines were a pair taken from a group of three arranged radially around a fixation point. The other two pairs were presented for the "no" judgment (each pair equally often). When the whole radial figure was presented for fixation, the pair whose presence or absence was reported on was linked most frequently in appearance or disappearance. Attention to that pair must have caused it to be grouped as a unit.

Grice (1965) has made a direct attack on the role of response-produced mediating cues in a series of generalization experiments. The general procedure involved pairing a conditioned stimulus with an air puff to the eye. Two negative stimuli (never reinforced by the air puff) were presented in a differential conditioning setup. The subjects also made two instructed manual or verbal reactions to the three stimuli. One of these reactions was common to the CS and one of the negative stimuli. One was made only to the second negative stimulus. Evidence for a mediational effect, an addition of stimuli to produce greater equivalence or greater difference, should show up in an asymmetrical generalization function for the two negative stimuli. In some cases, where the response was overt, an asymmetrical function occurred. But when the response was implicit the mediation effect never occurred. Even when the asymmetrical function occurred, the time relations which produced the predicted results were not in harmony with the theory. Grice concluded that his experiments produced little or no support for the response-produced cue theory. In the hypothesis of acquired equivalence or distinctiveness, the learned responses assumed to produce the mediating cues must be implicit in the transfer situation, but direct evidence of such an effect failed to appear.

What Is Discriminated?

In this review of the evidence regarding predifferentiation and its effects on later discrimination or discrimination learning, there seem to be no clear cases of experiments where response-produced cues, either distinctive or equivalent, have to be called upon to explain the results. Attention to distinctive features of the stimulus objects themselves or neglect of them seems, on the other hand, to be a reasonable alternative hypothesis. A stimulus-oriented discrimination theory, therefore, appears more promising than a response-oriented one. Such a theory would hold that something about the stimulus object itself is discriminated during Stage I of the predifferentiation experiments, something actually present in the stimulus information and not added by stimulation elicited by a learned response. This theory will be described in the chapters to follow.

SUMMARY

This chapter and the previous one have considered a number of contemporary theories of perceptual learning. The theories can be classified in several ways as similar and different. Fig. 4–2 has the theories arranged to show two major dimensions of difference and overlapping. The columns group the theories according to the psychological status of their principal concepts; whether they are cognitively oriented (one could say judgmentally), whether they are response oriented, or whether oriented to information in stimulation. The rows group the theories according to the kind of process which is considered the key to understanding perceptual change in development and in learning. Of the cognitively oriented theories, most assume an inferential process as the basic concept. The cognitive

Psychological Status of Main Concept

		Cognitively Oriented	Response-Oriented	Stimulus-Oriented
Type of Learning Process	Inference	Theories assuming unconscious inference or problem-solving		
	Formation of a Representation	Schema Theories	Motor Copy Theories	
	Improvement of Discrimination		Additive Mediation Theories	Differentiation Theory

FIGURE 4–2.   A classification of theories of perceptual learning.

schema theories may include inference, but emphasize principally the construction of a conceptual or imaginal representation of external objects and events. The response-oriented theories divide into two kinds, one of which, the motor copy theory, resembles schema theories in positing construction of a representation which underlies perception, the representation, however, deriving from motor activity. The other type of response-oriented theory thinks of perceptual development as an improvement in discrimination, the improvement occurring by way of associated responses which produce added stimulation. The last type of theory I have called stimulus oriented, because it considers perceptual development to be an improvement in discrimination of information which is actually present in stimulation. Differentiation of perception occurs as response to aspects of information in the stimulation becomes more selective and specific.

5

A Differentiation Theory of
Perceptual Development

Surely I can have no conception of Theaetetus until your snub-nosedness has left an impression on my mind different from the snubnosedness of all others whom I have ever seen, and until your other peculiarities have a like distinctness; and so when I meet you tomorrow the right opinion will be recalled. . . . Right opinion implies knowledge of differences.

Plato, *Theaetetus*

We have examined a number of theories which were advanced to account for the changes in perception dependent on development and learning. Most of these theories are enrichment theories, in that they account for the change in terms of some addition or accrual to the sensory input received from points of stimulation. The kind of enrichment is not the same in all theories; it may be probabilistic inference, response feedback, fill-in from a schema, or the formation of motor or neural copies. But all have in common the assumption that a difference exists between sensations, which are bare and meaningless, and perceptions, which arise when sensations are integrated and supplemented with information derived from some other source than the stimulus.

Instead of assuming that stimuli can give rise only to meager sensations, let us now consider the opposite assumption: that the environment is rich in varied and complex potential stimulus information, capable of giving rise to diverse, meaningful, complex perceptions. Let us suppose that there is information in stimuli to be picked up by a sensitive, exploring organism.

In the normal environment there is always more information than the organism is capable of registering. There is a limit to the attentive powers of even the best educated human perceiver. But he is also limited with respect to the complex variables of stimulation by his stage of development and his education. Perception in man's rich environment begins as only crudely differentiated and grossly selective. But as perception develops the organism comes to detect properties of stimulation not previously detected even though they may have been present. With growth and continued exposure to the world of stimulation, perception becomes better differentiated and more precise.

In the second chapter, two theories of perceptual development were considered that emphasized differentiation, Koffka's and Werner's. The theory to be proposed now is similar to these in its emphasis on differentiation, but it differs profoundly in other ways. Koffka's Gestalt theory assumed a process of neural organization, a dynamic self-distribution of neural forces, as the key explanatory concept. All learning was perceptual reorganization, but learning not so considered had no role in developing perception. I shall try to show that learning does have a role and not in the sense of organization. The principal difference between Koffka's view and this one is an emphasis on the correspondence which develops between variables of stimulation and perception, increasing both with maturation and with special opportunities for learning. The emphasis on increasing correspondence with stimulus variables also constitutes a major difference between this view and Werner's. Werner had another goal which I have not attempted to pursue—to delineate phenomenologically contrasting stages of maturation in perception.

A satisfactory learning theory requires two levels of elaboration. First, it is essential to spell out what is learned; that is, to demonstrate that a change actually takes place, and what, exactly, is the nature of the change. Learning of the kind referred to as classical conditioning, for instance, is demonstrated by comparing the power of an originally neutral stimulus to evoke a given response before and after pairing it with another stimulus which reliably evokes that response. What is learned is a change in the probability of the stimulus for evoking the particular response.

The second essential of a satisfactory theory is an elaboration of the principles for learning. Here explanatory processes at several levels are sometimes inferred. At a psychological level, association has often been appealed to as an explanatory mechanism, a process binding the response to the stimulus or one idea to another. At a physiological level, neural processes may be inferred. With the advent of computers, there has emerged a source of principles neither psychological nor physiological, a mathematical model of a sequence of operations which leads to a modification of the kind described.

Curiously enough, perceptual learning has received more attention by way of explanation than by way of description. The schema, the learned mediating responses, and the inferences operating at an unconscious level, all of which we considered in the last chapter, are inferred explanatory processes. But what is learned has, on the whole, been neglected.

WHAT IS LEARNED IN PERCEPTUAL LEARNING?

In an earlier discussion of perceptual learning (Gibson & Gibson, 1955), the view to be presented was called the specificity theory. Let us consider the reasons for choosing this term. Perceptual learning was defined as an increase in the ability of an organism to get information from its environment, as a result of practice with the array of stimulation provided by the environment. This definition implies that there are potential variables of stimuli which are not differentiated within the mass of impinging stimulation, but which may be, given the proper conditions of exposure and practice. As they are differentiated, the resulting perceptions become more specific with respect to stimulation, that is, in greater correspondence with it. There is a change in what the organism can respond to. The change is not acquisition or substitution of a new response to stimulation previously responded to in some other way, but is rather responding in any discriminating way to a variable of stimulation not responded to previously. The criterion of perceptual learning is thus an increase in specificity. What is learned can be described as detection of properties, patterns, and distinctive features.

Increase in Specificity

Some examples of increase in specificity of response to a set of stimuli will make the nature of the modification clear. An experiment by Gibson and Gibson (1955) made use of a set of 18 scribbles. They differed from a standard scribble along three dimensions of variation: number of coils, degree of compression, and orientation (right-left reversal). These scribbles were designed to be relatively indistinguishable at the outset of training. Twelve other drawings, designed to be easily distinguishable from each other and the first set of 18 were also prepared (see Figs. 5–1 and 5–2). The latter 12 drawings differed from one another along many dimensions. All the items were printed photographically on 2 × 4-inch cards, and made up in a pack which included four replicas of the standard scribble (see Fig. 5–1, center).

The task of the subjects was to recognize the standard item whenever it appeared in the pack of cards. The subject was first shown the standard for five seconds and told that some of the items in the pack would be exactly like it. He was to select those items which were exact copies. The experimenter showed him the cards, one at a time in random order, each with a three-second exposure. When he saw one which he recognized as

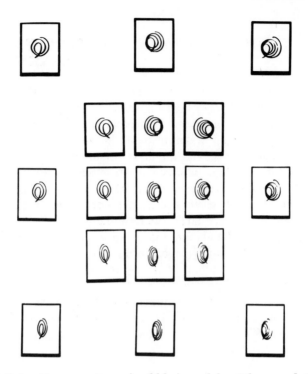

FIGURE 5–1. Nonsense items (scribbles) used by Gibson and Gibson.

These items differed in three dimensions of variation. The standard item is a four-coil scribble in the center. The others vary from it in number of coils, horizontal compression or stretching, and orientation (right-left reversal). (From J. J. Gibson & E. J. Gibson, Perceptual learning: Differential or enrichment? *Psychological Review,* 1955, *62,* 36.)

the standard, he reported "that's the one," "that's the same," or "that's the one I saw first." He was not told whether or not his judgment was correct.

When the experimenter had taken the subject through the whole pack once, the standard figure was presented a second time, and identified as such. Then a fresh pack in a different order was run through, in the same manner. This procedure was continued until the subject made only the four correct identifications in a single run through the series.

The subjects of the experiment included three age groups: twelve adults, ten older children (8½ to 11 years), and ten younger children (6 to 8 years).

Learning in this experiment was taken to be an increase in the specificity of the recognition of the standard item, or, in other words, a decrease in the size of the class of drawings which elicited the response of "same." The results, in fact, showed that the class of undifferentiated

FIGURE 5–2. Nonsense items differing in many dimensions of variation.

(From J. J. Gibson & E. J. Gibson, Perceptual learning: Differential or enrichment? *Psychological Review*, 1955, *62*, 36.)

items was reduced with repetition. For the three age groups, the class of items that was undifferentiated at the start differed greatly. For adults, the class of items responded to as "same" at the outset was small (M = 3.0). It was reduced to one, the standard alone, after an average of three runs. The older children started with a mean of 7.9 undifferentiated items and achieved perfect recognition after an average of 4.7 runs. The younger children started with a mean of 13.4 undifferentiated items, and only two finally succeeded in achieving perfect recognition. The class of undifferentiated items decreased to 3.9, on the average, after 6.7 runs. (Runs were stopped for these children when they became too tired or inattentive to continue.)

It was clear that errors of recognition were not random from an analysis which showed that the number of errors depended on the number of stimulus variables by which an item differed from the standard. If it differed by only one feature, such as compression, errors were significantly greater than if it differed by two, and so on.

This experiment exemplifies the kind of learning in which specificity of response to a standard item increases with repeated practice consisting of exposure to that stimulus and others originally undistinguishable from it.

One can also describe what has happened as a decrease in generalization (confusion) and an increase in the ability to differentiate the standard from the set of other items presented. The subjects did not learn to make a new response to this item; they responded with "same" from the beginning. But they learned to apply this response to one unique item in the set, or (with the youngest children) to a much smaller set of items. Neither was the training merely effective in reducing a response bias (saying "same"), for the word "same" was progressively restricted to only the appropriate item, the one identifiable with the standard.

As the subjects went through the trials, they made spontaneous comments describing characteristics of the figures. These comments were recorded, and it is noteworthy that many of them included adjectives describing the difference between the standard and other item, such as "too thin," "rounder," and the like. These relational responses showed a significant tendency to increase as the experiment progressed. Could one say, then, that differentiation is achieved because verbal differentiating responses were being learned to the nonsame items? No, since these responses were never taught the subjects, but were produced spontaneously as the experiment progressed and as the subject was simply confronted with the varying items. Furthermore, the youngest children in many cases made progressively more correct recognitions without producing adjectives for the variable dimensions. Finally, these verbal qualifying responses were not specific to any particular item. It seems certain, therefore, that they did not have a causal role in the achievement of specificity, but were correlated, when they appeared, with discovery of a critical dimension of difference.

Many other examples of increase in specificity are afforded by psychological experiments in which the subject's variable error decreases as the experiment progresses. In an experiment with lifted weights, the experimenter may present the subject with pairs of weights, asking him to decide whether the second weight is heavier or lighter than the first. The amount of difference between the weights of a pair is varied, so that the subject may at first make consistently accurate responses only to the larger differences. If repeated judging results in a significantly increased consistency of correct responses to the smaller differences, his specificity of response to the variable of weight difference has increased. Urban (1913) and Fernberger (1916) studied the effect of progressive practice in lifting weights, using a constant method without correction of errors. Precision increased and the interval of uncertainty decreased.

A particularly interesting example of increased specificity is Werner's (1940) experiment with "micro-melodies," referred to in Chapter 2. Not only were the subjects able, after considerable listening practice, to hear differences in tonal quality which they could not discriminate previously; they were able to perceive melodies created with these very small intervals, as evidenced by their ability to recognize them under transposition. The possibility of explaining the increased differentiation as due to association of new responses of any kind seems thus ruled out.

Detection of Properties and Patterns

What is learned in perceptual learning is not fully described with the demonstration of progressive specificity. Increased specificity is in a sense a criterion of learning. Achievement of specificity involves the detection of properties and patterns not previously responded to. Detection of properties was illustrated in the scribble experiment, as the subjects discovered the dimensions of difference. It would be hard to overemphasize the importance for perceptual learning of the discovery of invariant properties which are in correspondence with physical variables. The term "extraction" will be applied to this process, for the property may be buried, as it were, in a welter of impinging stimulation.

The perceiving of a particular bird song described in Chapter 1 is a case of extraction of relational properties of a high order. Here is a pattern with a characteristic rhythm and melody, varying to some extent with the individual bird, but maintaining more than enough invariant structure for the naturalist to hear it unerringly as unique. Or similarly, an instrument in an orchestra can be picked out and heard as distinct by the expert, though the task would be difficult if not impossible for the untutored amateur. In this case the melodic pattern over time is not invariant, but a bundle of acoustic properties unique to the instrument is.

An interesting example of the effect of learning on the perception of melodic patterns is available in the experiments of R. Francès (1958). Short melodies were recorded on tape and presented to subjects, each one followed by either a musical transposition or an imitation which only approximated transposition. The subjects were asked to distinguish whether or not the item was a true transposition. The stimulus variables were tonality and rhythm. The subjects included musicians and nonmusicians. There were significant differences depending on musical education: musicians perceived a transposition more accurately than nonmusicians. In another experiment, subjects with various degrees of musical training listened to a bithematic work after being informed of the number of themes and the plan of the work. During a first playing, the subjects were to discover the themes of the work; during a second playing, they tried to point out each theme and its variations whenever they appeared. There was a highly significant increase in correct recognitions of themes and variations depending upon musical training, and a decrease in confusions of themes. In a third experiment, Francès studied the effect of training on polyphonic perception. Three groups of subjects, with different amounts of musical training, were presented with fugues. The theme of the fugue, a given tone sequence, occurred from time to time in different pitches, while other patterns were played simultaneously. The subjects were first given pretraining with the theme of the fugue, and then heard the fugue as a whole. The task was to report the theme of the fugue immediately each time it occurred. A second test followed the first. Several different fugues were used. Correct recognitions increased with musical training of the subjects, and the differences persisted through the second test. Speed of recognition was also greater for trained subjects. A rhythmic and melodic pattern can thus be abstracted from its background of auditory stimulation more readily as a result of training in listening to such patterns.

Detection of Distinctive Features

Complex objects in real life can seldom be differentiated on the basis of single properties which render them unique. They are apt to be uniquely identifiable only by virtue of a bundle of properties. They are differentiated (and thereby identified) by their distinctive features. These features are not constructed by the mind but are discovered by the perceiver. When he is exposed to a new set of objects, what he learns are the distinctive features of each object and of the set. Distinctive features are relational, having contrasts or different values within a set. There may be many such features, some shared by certain members of a set, some by others, so that each member must be distinguishable from the others by its bundle of features. This bundle of distinctive features constitutes a potential higher order structure. Whether it is perceived as such, or whether there is perceptual analysis of features, is a question we shall return to.

Consider first a very simple example of exposure to a new set of objects. A psychologist arrives at an animal behavior station which has available for experimentation a large herd of goats. He is not familiar with goats. He plans his experiment and selects his subjects from a card file giving each animal's age, history, and so on. Now he must find his animals in the herd. They are tagged, but examining tiny ear tags of sixty animals is a lengthy process, so he must learn to recognize the animals by more obvious characteristics. After all, the goats appear to be able to distinguish one another. The goats, at first, look to him almost identical except for one or two characteristics, such as large or small, which are by themselves quite inadequate. But after a few months' acquaintance, he can spot his goat in the herd at a moment's notice and even from a fair distance. Furthermore, it is not only this goat which he has learned to recognize. He can enroll a new subject and find him, now, without a three-month or even a three-day warm-up. He has learned the distinctive features of goats and can recognize a new pattern of features with very little practice.

The first application of a system of distinctive features by psychologists was in an experiment carried out by Gagné and Gibson for the Air Force in 1944. Their subjects were military trainees from six classes in aircraft recognition in a preflight school. The men were obliged to learn to distinguish and identify some forty different makes of airplanes. They were trained with photographic slides and tested with semirealistic motion picture shots. The classes were equated by a pretest for recognition proficiency and equal numbers of slides were used for both control and experimental groups, with equal time and the same instructors. But in one group, instruction emphasized the total form of each plane without analysis of the form whereas in the other group a standard set of distinctive features was emphasized for each plane. The best results were secured by teaching distinctive features such as a tapered wing, a short nose, or a beer-bottle fuselage. There was a unique cluster of such features for each plane. It was not necessary that a full description or picture of each be memorized, but only that the feature pattern making it different from the others be detected. It was in fact concluded that no features should be emphasized unless they served to distinguish one plane from another.

DISTINCTIVE FEATURES OF PHONEMES.   A system of distinctive features for distinguishing units of speech, the phonemes, has been worked out in such explicit detail by Roman Jakobson that it may serve as a kind of model for attempts to specify distinguishing properties of other sets of objects and events.[1] Jakobson and Halle (1956) enumerated a set of twelve distinctive features for phonemes such that any phoneme is distinguishable from any other by its bundle of attributes. All of the features have a plus and minus value, that is, form a binary opposition. The opposition may define polar qualities of the same dimension, or the presence or absence of a certain quality. The twelve features are sufficient to give unique bundles for all the phonemes in all languages.

The unique bundle for each phoneme can be represented in a feature chart, such as Cherry's (see Fig. 5–3). By comparing the pattern of pluses and minuses for the phonemes, the uniqueness of any phoneme can be demonstrated. The feature chart does not describe elements for constructing the sounds. As Cherry puts it, the feature table "does not tell us precise sounds; rather it represents a cipher which describes the minimal distinctions between phonemes (Cherry, 1957, p. 94)." The emphasis on difference, rather than reference, is underlined in a statement of Jakobson and Halle (p. 11), "Whatever distinctive feature we tackle, *the denotation*

---

[1] I do not attribute this suggestion to Jakobson, for he has hinted (Jakobson, 1967) that he considers a description by distinctive features inappropriate for stimulation that is simultaneously presented, such as that for a picture. But we do not know that the information is processed simultaneously; and if it is, feature analysis may nevertheless be necessary for differentiation.

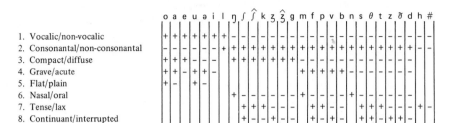

FIGURE 5–3.   Chart of distinctive features of English phonemes from Cherry (1957).

The pattern follows that of Jakobson and Halle (1956). (Reprinted from *On Human Communication* by Colin Cherry, by permission of The MIT Press, Cambridge, Massachusetts, copyright 1965, by The Massachusetts Institute of Technology.)

is always identical. . . . All phonemes denote nothing but mere otherness." The minimal distinction is one feature opposition between phonemes, but a pair may differ by a number of features. The number of feature differences thus provides a potential scale for predicting confusability.

The choice of these features is empirical, based on linguists' experience of languages and their phonemic structures. But there are other objective criteria of choice. The list must provide a unique pattern for each phoneme, and the properties chosen must be relational and invariant under certain transformations (different voices, shouting, whispering, etc.). "A distinctive feature is a *relational* property, so that the 'minimum same' of a feature in its combination with various other concurrent or successive features lies in the essentially identical *relation* between the two opposite alternatives (Jakobson & Halle, p. 14)."

As Cherry says, this feature description of phonemes constitutes a set of rules which the speaker must obey even though he is unaware of them (as he surely is). That these rules are psychological as well as logical ones is supported by the results of an experiment by Brown and Hildum (1956). If phonemes are distinguished from one another by differences in their feature patterns, it should follow that the smaller the number of feature oppositions between two phonemes, the greater should be their confusability under conditions of impoverishment or noise. Subjects were played a recording of triple-phoneme syllables (e.g., "prol"). They wrote in phonetic transcription, or pronounced, what they heard. The results were analyzed for mistaken identifications. The mistakes involving a change in a single phoneme were then classified according to the number of significant feature changes when compared to the syllables actually recorded. More than half the errors could be classified as a change in only one feature. Most of the others involved a change in only two. Errors in fact tended to be minimal as regards feature changes, so that the "distinctive features appear to provide dimensions for the description of the perceptual similarity of English phonemes (Brown & Hildum, p. 419)."

Confirmation of these results was obtained by Tikofsky and McInish (1968) with seven-year-old children as subjects and errors of discrimination as the criterion. The subject responded "same" or "different" after a pair of words or syllables had been presented. The pair was identical, or else differed in the initial consonant by one to five feature contrasts. Most of the confusion errors occurred when there was only one feature difference. It is especially interesting that errors were not equally distributed over different types of feature contrast. Two contrasting pairs accounted for most of the errors, so it follows that the contrasts should be differentially weighted as to ease of discriminability, and perhaps for priority of learning and processing.

Jakobson's distinctive feature theory of phoneme differentiation is of particular interest to developmental psychologists, because it has a built-in developmental hypothesis. In speaking and perceiving, features develop by differentiation in a progressively ordered, hierarchical fashion. There is a stratified splitting of categories, beginning with the consonant-vowel contrast (closed-open). The optimal consonant and the optimal vowel establish the elementary phonemic frame. Both constituents of this syllable may next be split into distinctive alternatives, the nasal-oral opposition for the consonant, and the grave-acute for the vowel. The oral category then differentiates into continuous-discontinuous, and so on. Evidence for this pattern of development by gradual binary fission is available in a few case histories of individual children. It will be considered later in more detail. Suffice it here to mention two findings. Scvachkin (cited by Tikofsky et al.) showed with Russian children that discrimination of phonemes improved with age, and that the earliest discriminations occurred between phoneme pairs having the greatest number of distinctive feature differences. Ruth Weir's study (1962) of the presleep soliloquies of her two-year-old son revealed a stage in the progress toward mature phonemic production in which some of the sound features were already well learned, but others had not yet reached a contrastive function. She noted, for instance, that

the original five point vowel triangle can still be reduced further to a three point triangle . . . the same as given by Jakobson and Halle as the first vocalic split, opposing the single compact /A/ to the diffuse and grave /U/ and the diffuse and acute /I/, or in our articulatory terminology, the preservation of only two features: high versus low, and front versus back (p. 43).

One other line of evidence coming from the study of aphasia makes the assumption that the developmental sequence is influential in determining the order of loss of features with dissolution. Jakobson and Halle note that the disintegration of the sound pattern exhibits a "time order of great regularity" and that "aphasic regression has proved to be a mirror of the child's acquisition of speech sounds; it shows the child's development in reverse (p. 57)."

That distinctive features of phonemes are learned, in any case, seems incontrovertible. For one thing, although there is overlapping from one language to another, there is variation. For another, research at the Haskins laboratory (Liberman et al., 1957) has provided experimental evidence to show that the boundaries between phonemes along some physically continuous dimensions are learned. This learning occurs very early in life, and since phonemes denote nothing ("mere otherness," as Jakobson & Halle said), it is hard to see how the process could be anything but discriminative. The course of development of phonemic feature differences argues against the statement that "discrimination of symbols must be an associative process (Postman, in Koch, p. 65)." The denotation of symbols may well be associative but not their discrimination.

DISTINCTIVE FEATURES OF GRAPHEMES.   Can a set of distinctive features for graphemes (alphabetic letters) comparable to the set for phonemes be specified so as to provide a unique cluster for each one? This task is not easy as is shown by Figure 5–4. The perceiver of cursive writing as distinguished from letterpress must allow not only for specific transformations produced by changes in the light and by the position and distance of the text, but also for many free variations depending on individual handwriting. The perceiver of print must allow for differences in typeface. The set of features for cursive writing and for print must be different. Nevertheless in both kinds of writing certain constancies must be preserved. If we could specify the invariants and demonstrate that they really function in the visual discrimination of letters, a big step would be taken in generalizing the notion of distinctive features to other objects of perception. A developmental study of the discrimination of letterlike forms showed that discrimination of such forms improves from four years to eight (see Chapter 16). What, actually, is it that is learned? Gibson, Osser, Schiff, and Smith (1963) analyzed a set of graphemes (simplified Roman capitals), and prepared a list of distinctive features for such letters. The list was then used as the basis for predictions of confusion between one letter and another, and an error matrix of confusions was obtained to test the predictions.

In selecting a list of features, the experimenter's intuition is the principal generator, but it can be assisted by evidence from experimental literature and by meeting certain criteria. A number of possible feature lists was drawn up and revised in the light of the following criteria: 1) the features had to be critical ones, present in some members of the set but not

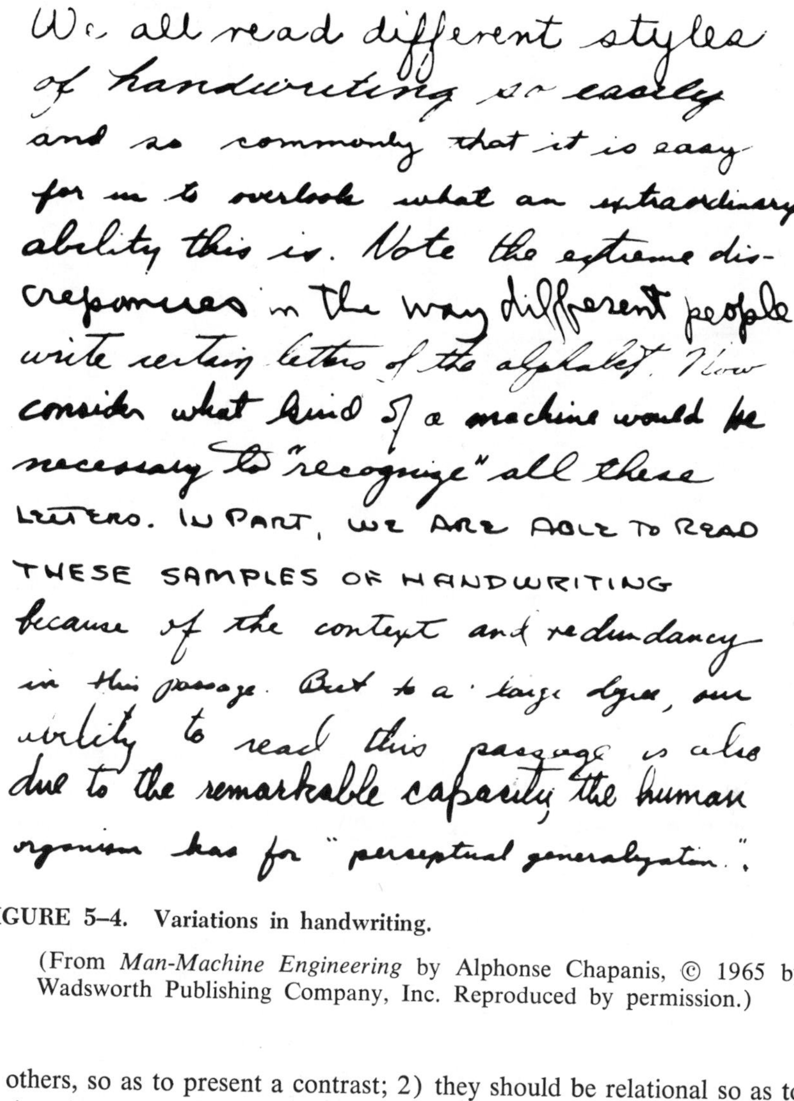

We all read different styles of handwriting so easily and so commonly that it is easy for us to overlook what an extraordinary ability this is. Note the extreme dis-crepancies in the way different people write certain letters of the alphabet. Now consider what kind of a machine would be necessary to "recognize" all these LETTERS. IN PART, WE ARE ABLE TO READ THESE SAMPLES OF HANDWRITING because of the context and redundancy in this passage. But to a large degree, our ability to read this passage is also due to the remarkable capacity the human organism has for "perceptual generalization."

FIGURE 5-4. Variations in handwriting.

(From *Man-Machine Engineering* by Alphonse Chapanis, © 1965 by Wadsworth Publishing Company, Inc. Reproduced by permission.)

in others, so as to present a contrast; 2) they should be relational so as to be invariant under brightness, size, and perspective transformations; 3) they should yield a unique pattern for each grapheme; and 4) the list should be reasonably economical. Economy is not a primary criterion, but there should certainly be fewer properties than letters.[2]

The feature list in Figure 5-5 was one of two chosen for test against an error matrix. The chart is filled in to show a plus for each feature present in each letter. Each feature in the chart is or is not a characteristic of each

---

[2] This is not generally true of property-list systems for machine recognition of letters (see Selfridge & Neisser, 1960; and Uhr, 1963, for instance).

Features	A	E	F	H	I	L	T	K	M	N	V	W	X	Y	Z	B	C	D	G	J	O	P	R	Q	S	U
Straight																										
horizontal	+	+	+	+		+	+								+											
vertical		+	+	+	+	+	+	+	+	+				+		+		+				+	+			
diagonal /	+							+	+		+	+	+	+	+								+	+		
diagonal \	+							+	+	+	+	+	+	+									+	+		
Curve																										
closed																+		+			+	+	+	+		
open V																				+						+
open H																	+		+						+	
Intersection	+	+	+	+			+	+					+			+						+	+	+		
Redundancy																										
cyclic change		+							+			+				+										+
symmetry	+	+		+	+		+	+	+	+	+	+	+	+		+	+	+			+					+
Discontinuity																										
vertical	+		+	+	+		+	+	+	+						+						+	+			
horizontal		+	+			+	+										+									

FIGURE 5–5. Chart of distinctive features for a set of graphemes.

of the 26 graphemes. Consider the letter A. One asks is there a straight line? Yes. If so, is there a horizontal line? Yes. Is there a diagonal to the right? Yes. To the left? Yes. Is there a curve? No. Is there intersection? Yes. And so on. The feature pattern is unique for each letter. The decision about features for each letter may proceed sequentially in an orderly progression, but there is not in this list a perfect hierarchy with progressive splitting. To define such a hierarchy is difficult, since the list of potential features for a writing system is presumably large and varies to some extent from one alphabet and type font to another. Not all possible features are represented in the roman capitals analyzed, yet those unrepresented are certainly potentially perceptible.

The features in the chart were not picked at random, but on the basis of a rationale. Take, first, the curve-straight distinction. Neurophysiological research with frogs (Maturana, Lettvin, McCulloch, & Pitts, 1960) showed that straight edges and curves projected on the retina evoked differential firing of nerve fibers. Other evidence from research with cats (Hubel & Wiesel, 1962) suggests that the orientation of a line in a receptor field (e.g., horizontal, vertical, diagonal) is responded to differentially by specific cortical fibers. Thus there is evidence at a physiological level that straight lines, curved lines, horizontals, verticals, and diagonals are abstracted and responded to as features of patterns.

The closed-open distinction for curves was considered a basic potential feature, since research on the development of form discrimination (Gibson, Gibson, Pick, & Osser, 1962) showed that this difference was discriminated very early. Research by Piaget and Inhelder (1956) on the discrimination of topological differences in forms also found this difference ontogenetically primitive. Intersection is another topological characteristic which, according to Piaget, is distinguished very early.

The features labeled redundancy (symmetry and cyclic change) are less obvious choices. The cyclic change feature was suggested by the stabilized retinal image work of Pritchard, Heron, and Hebb (1960) which showed that parallels act as units in appearing and disappearing. That it is a potential contrastive feature can be seen in comparing a V and a W.

Discontinuity makes sense as a feature if one assumes a scanning process which proceeds vertically downward or horizontally from left to right. Discontinuity would result if a line that is being scanned terminates. Theories of shape discrimination by means of analysis in terms of horizontal and vertical scans have received considerable attention recently (see, for instance, Sutherland, 1963). However, discontinuity is a reasonable topological feature without assuming a scanning process. Recent research by Hubel and Wiesel (1965) found that certain cortical cells fired if the narrow end or tip of a rectangular bar were moved into the receptor field of the cell, suggesting differential neural response to termination of a line or edge.

Having achieved a feature list which could specify roman capital letters, how can we find out whether the list selected is really being utilized in discrimination? The best test we could conceive was to compare the number of feature differences between pairs of letters with the number of confusions which children actually make between them.

An error matrix was obtained for this test from a large group of four-year-old children who did not yet read. A simple matching judgment was required of them since matching letters is easy for a child to comprehend. One letter was presented as the standard, followed by a multiple-choice set of six letters (one of them the standard). They were printed horizontally across a strip of paper. Each set was randomly selected, with the restriction that every letter appeared an equal number of times in the choice sets for every standard. Counterbalancing of choice sets and position in the set as well as order of standard assured freedom of bias from order effects, with equal opportunities for every letter to be mistaken for every other.

The confusion errors obtained from this experiment were subsequently correlated with the percent of features pairs of letters had in common. One correlation was obtained for each letter of the alphabet. In order to provide a kind of yardstick for evaluating the correlations, a spatial overlap measure was correlated with the errors as well.[3] The number of significant correlations between confusion errors and features shared was twelve, greater than chance expectation. There were eight significant correlations between errors and the overlap measures (and four in the wrong direction).

[3] The overlap measures were taken from a Ramo-Wooldridge report (1961). Letters were superimposed on a standardized matrix and amount of contour overlap measured.

This result increased our confidence in the feature list, but suggested that further work on it was needed. Our measure, percent of features shared, might not be the best. For instance, there might be a weighting of features for relative uniqueness or discriminability, as appears to be the case for phoneme features.

A second test of the feature list was provided by a multidimensional analysis of the confusion matrix.[4] If the features chosen are actually used in discrimination, one would expect them to be reflected in the dimensions resulting from analysis of the matrix. A three-dimensional solution of the matrix yielded two dimensions which were clearly and readily identifiable as 1) straight-curve and 2) relative diagonality. The third dimension was hard to label, except perhaps as complexity. Within the plots representing this dimension, the closed letters clustered in a small area, with the open characters removed toward the perimeter. At least several of the feature contrasts, curve-straight, and diagonality were thus confirmed, and to some extent the open-closed distinction.

New data for a confusion matrix were obtained recently by Albert Yonas and myself. The subject responded with a "same" or "different" judgment to a pair of letters presented simultaneously. He pressed a switch to initiate a trial, causing the projected letter-pair to appear on a small screen in front of him. He then pressed a button to indicate his judgment and caused a timer to stop, giving us his reaction time as well as a measure of errors. Nine letters were drawn from the alphabet (C, E, F, G, M, N, P, R, W). They were all paired with one another, and with themselves. The subjects in this experiment were college sophomores and seven-year-old children. We were interested in the confusability of the different pairs; would we confirm results from the earlier experiment? The nine letters were selected, therefore, to sample the range from the earlier experiment—pairs we predicted to be highly confusable and others to be very low in confusability. We also used the same type-form in preparing slides of the letters.

The latency and error data correlated well, and the high- and low-confusion pairs were on the whole as predicted. The letters P and R were most often confused by adults and had the longest latency; E and F, M and N, C and G, and M and W followed, in that order. Pairs which never elicited an error were G and M and G and N, and latencies for these judgments were among the shortest (over 100 ms. less than P and R). The children's results followed a similar pattern, but M and N and M and W had longer mean latencies than P and R (indicating the same major confusion we had found with four year olds). Diagonals are low in discriminability for children, even at seven years when they have learned the alphabet. The curve-straight distinction, on the other hand, is a highly discriminable one. For example, P and F, which overlap to a high degree

4 This analysis was carried out for us by Dr. Warren Torgerson.

and are rather similar in global shape, were almost never confused and were responded to as different with a very low mean latency by both adults and children. The children's latencies were all very much longer than adults', indicating the importance of practice in differentiating letters.

These data are encouraging for a distinctive feature theory of letter discrimination, especially since a proximity analysis again yielded curve-straight and diagonality as high-priority feature contrasts. We would like to be able to answer some questions about how the features are used for perceptual differentiation. We thought that a comparison of the same and the different judgments might tell us something about this. Is there analysis of the letter shapes to the extent that every feature is compared, possibly one at a time in sequence, before a decision of "same" or "different" is made? If that were the case, the latency for a pair differing in many features should be short, for a contrast should be found quickly and permit a decision of "different." A pair differing in only one feature should have a long latency, since nearly the whole set of features might have to be compared before a difference was found. An identical pair should have the longest latency, since all features would have to be compared.

That this simple model will not suffice is clear from our data. It is partly supported, in that the "different" judgments varied consistently from very slow to very quick depending on number and kind of feature differences. But the mean latency for "same" judgments was not longer than that for "different" judgments. It was, in fact, slightly shorter (though not shorter than the shortest "different" judgments). It may be that some high-order feature of the pair taken as a whole—some overall structure, for instance symmetry—is searched for first in a simultaneous presentation. If symmetry were present, a "same" judgment could occur very quickly.

It is obvious that much more thinking and research will be necessary before we can say how the perceptual process uses distinctive features for discrimination. We will consider further the question of how learned differentiations are achieved in the next chapter.

COMPUTER MODELS FOR PATTERN RECOGNITION

In discussing the distinctive features of graphic characters, I had occasion to mention computer models for pattern recognition. These models do not necessarily attempt to simulate learning, but they have implications for what is learned. Their success or lack of it is, by analogy, relevant to a psychological theory of what is learned.

Minsky (1961), in writing about models for visual pattern recognition by machines, classified them into two types: one, models that match the objects against standards or prototypes, and two, models that use property lists. In the first, identification takes place by a normalization and template-matching process. The unknown figure is first normalized (transformed in one or more specified fashions) and then compared as a whole with templates of prototypes; by means of some measure of matching (e.g., overlap), the best fitting template is chosen. The template-matching scheme is limited if the class of equivalence transformations is large; and also because for each pattern, the system has to be presented with a prototype. This method is clearly no analogue for the differentiation theory proposed in this chapter, but it appears to have a good deal in common with schema theories which hypothesize a process of matching input to preformed categories.

The second method is to some extent analogous to differentiation of distinctive features. The property-list method subjects each object to a sequence of tests, detecting in each test some property or characteristic of importance. The properties may be abstract, and should be invariant under commonly encountered equivalence transformations (e.g., size and position changes for recognition of visual patterns). The trick for these systems is to get the right property list. Human ingenuity seems to be, so far, the best generator of the list; though statistical techniques (e.g., a random net system, such as the perceptron, Rosenblatt, 1958, 1962) have been tried for generating sets of appropriate properties.

Uhr (1960, 1963) has given considerable attention to computer simulations of pattern recognition as models for form perception. In discussing the first class of programs, he said "simple-minded and fallible as this type of template or atomistic-matching approach may be, it is certainly a model for perception. In fact it is close to the classical associationist model, with occasional modulations of sophistication (1960, p. 179)." He calls "analytic" the methods which can be described as "abstracting from combinations of basic units particular features or qualities of importance, for identifying rather more abstract and complex things like edges, ends, curves, angles, and slopes (p. 179)."

With the template-maching methods, it is the template or prototype which must be available (learned) for the stimulus that is to be recognized to be matched to it. For the analytic or property-list methods, it is the properties, or detecting operations (e.g., is there a curve?) which must be available (learned) for a set of items, such as letters of the alphabet, to be recognized. The computer programs, so far, can help us very little in deciding how either templates or features might be learned. To quote Selfridge and Neisser: "The most important learning process, of all is untouched: No current program can generate test features of its own. The effectiveness of all of them is forever restricted by the ingenuity or arbitrariness of their programmers (1960, p. 68)." Still, good tips on what these features might be for recognition of alphanumeric characters, plane shapes, and so on may be found by looking at the relative success of different programs, and they may be examined for convergence with the results of confusion matrices such as the ones obtained in our laboratory.

A program by Feigenbaum and Simon called EPAM (Elementary Perceiving and Memorizing Machine) considers perception in relation to ensuing more complex behavior such as reading, memorizing, or drawing (Feigenbaum & Simon, 1962, 1963). The first step in the program is discriminating the items or stimulus objects presented. Two learning processes are postulated, a discrimination learning process and an image-building process. When a stimulus object is presented, it is sorted through a discrimination net (see Fig. 5–6). At each node of the net, some feature of the stimulus is noticed, and the branch for that characteristic is followed to the next node. At terminal nodes, an image may be presented which can be compared to any stimulus sorted to the terminal node. If the two are similar in the features compared, the stimulus has been recognized. The image-building (familiarization) process occurs when the stimulus has been sorted to a terminal which has no image. The familiarization process copies the stimulus (or part of it) and stores this as an initial

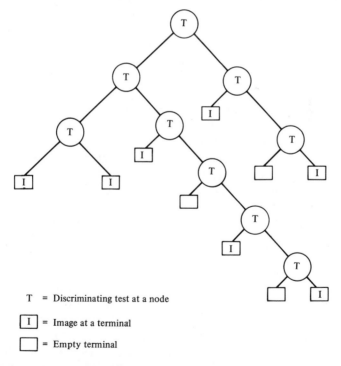

T = Discriminating test at a node

I = Image at a terminal

= Empty terminal

FIGURE 5–6. A typical EPAM discrimination net.

(From E. A. Feigenbaum & H. A. Simon, Performance of a reading task by an elementary perceiving and memorizing program. *Behavioral Science*, 1963, *8*, 72–76.)

image at the terminal. But if there is an image at the terminal, and any positive difference is detected between the stimulus and the image, discrimination learning takes place. The differences detected are used to construct a new test: the previous terminal node becomes a branch node, new branches are added to the discrimination net, and initial images are attached to the branches. The image has a special role in this model because it permits learning to proceed when a pair of stimuli to be discriminated are not presented simultaneously. For paired associate learning, no new associational process is postulated; rather, the S-R pair is assumed to be associated by familiarization and learning to discriminate the pair as a unit.

The potential distinctive features (as well as the noticing order or priority of features) which can be used as tests in the discrimination net are not generated by this program, but are already coded in the computer. Thus, the features themselves are postulated and we still have the problem of accounting for detection of invariant and useful attributes in the first place. But this program does suggest how a set of features sufficient for distinguishing a class of objects, such as the letters of the alphabet, might be ordered so as to achieve recognition. It also suggests the way in which an image of an object may be related, in a kind of cognitive flow chart, to prior perceptual processing, a problem to which we shall return.

SUMMARY

This chapter introduced a differentiation theory of perceptual learning. The term differentiation is not itself intended to be a hypothetical explanatory construct, but only to point to what it is that is learned in perceptual learning. The learned modification is in what is responded to. The modification can be characterized, generally speaking, as increasing specificity of correspondence between stimulus information provided by the environment and the organism's perception of it.

The kind of stimulus information that is increasingly picked up as learning and development proceed can be described in several ways. There may be reduced generalization and increasing precision of response to fine differences along a stimulus dimension. There may be detection of invariant relations and structure previously not responded to. Experiments showing the effect of training or practice in detection of patterns (such as melodies) and relational properties of stimuli were cited as examples. There may be detection of patterns of distinctive features of a set of stimulus objects or events. Distinctive features of phonemes and graphemes were examined in detail as examples of learned differentiation of features. Two types of computer models for pattern recognition were described as they bear on the problem of what is learned.

6

A Differentiation Theory of Perceptual Development: Principles and Mechanisms

"When a red ivory ball, seen for the first time, has been withdrawn, it will leave a mental representation of itself, in which all that it simultaneously gave us will indistinguishably coexist. Let a white ball succeed to it; now, and not before, will an attribute detach itself, and the color, *by force of contrast, be shaken out into the foreground. Let the white ball be replaced by an egg, and this new difference will bring the* form *into notice from its previous slumber, and thus that which began by being simply an object cut out from the surrounding scene becomes for us first a* red *object, than a* red round *object, and so on."*

Martineau, *Essays Philosophical and Theological*

In the previous chapter, it was argued that the change which takes place in perceptual development and learning is one of differentiation. A closer correspondence between the sources of stimulation and perception is achieved; this can be described as detection of properties, patterns, and distinctive features not previously registered. The next step is to proceed to the statement of principles. Having described what perceptual learning is, how might it be achieved? Two ways of proceeding are available: 1) formulation and test of predictions from assumptions about what is learned, and 2) postulation of hypothetical psychological mechanisms. They will be discussed as they bear on the foregoing analysis of perceptual development as differentiation.

PREDICTIONS FROM ASSUMPTIONS ABOUT WHAT IS LEARNED

The goal of any learning theory is by and large the attainment of principles that can be used for prediction of the course of learning and for application if one should want to steer its course. It is possible, from the preceding analysis of what is learned, to make certain testable predictions. They can be roughly divided into two classes, ones relating to discrimination-learning experiments, and ones relating to the discrimination process after perceptual learning has taken place.

Predictions for Discrimination Learning

Experiments which include practice or training in the improvement of perception are of major interest, since they have to do with the course of learning and the way in which it may be influenced. They are not easy to perform, however, because adult subjects have had years of previous experience with judging differences and learning distinctive features of common objects. It is necessary to find novel material or else to perform experiments with young children. Nevertheless, several testable propositions about the learning process follow from the definitions and analysis of what is learned.

LEARNING DIMENSIONS OF DIFFERENCE AS DISTINGUISHED FROM LEARNING PROTOTYPES. In a multidiscrimination-learning task, the subject learns by discovering the differences between members of the set of stimuli presented for discrimination. He should then be able to transfer them to new members of the set. The differential properties need not be dimensions, in the sense of being continuous, but must be relational properties which provide at least one contrast within the set.

An experiment by Anne D. Pick (1965) compared two hypotheses for learning visual discrimination of forms. The first was that improvement depends on learning how the forms differ; the second was that it depends on learning prototypes or images of each form. The method was to train the subjects (kindergarten children) to discriminate between standard forms and specified transformations of them. Afterward, three tests were made for transfer of learning which attempted to separate experimentally the learning of prototypes and the learning of differences.

The forms were visually presented and were designed to be like letters, though they were not actual letters (see Fig. 6–1). Transformations involving changes from line to curve (two degrees), reversal, rotation, perspective change, and a size change were prepared for each standard form. These were the critical dimensions of difference, six in all. The child performed a matching task, judging whether a standard was the same or different from a transformation, and was corrected for errors until he was able to match perfectly. In the transfer task, the child again judged whether a transformation was the same or different from its standard, but the forms were changed so as to create three different transfer groups.

For one group (EI) the children were given the same standards in

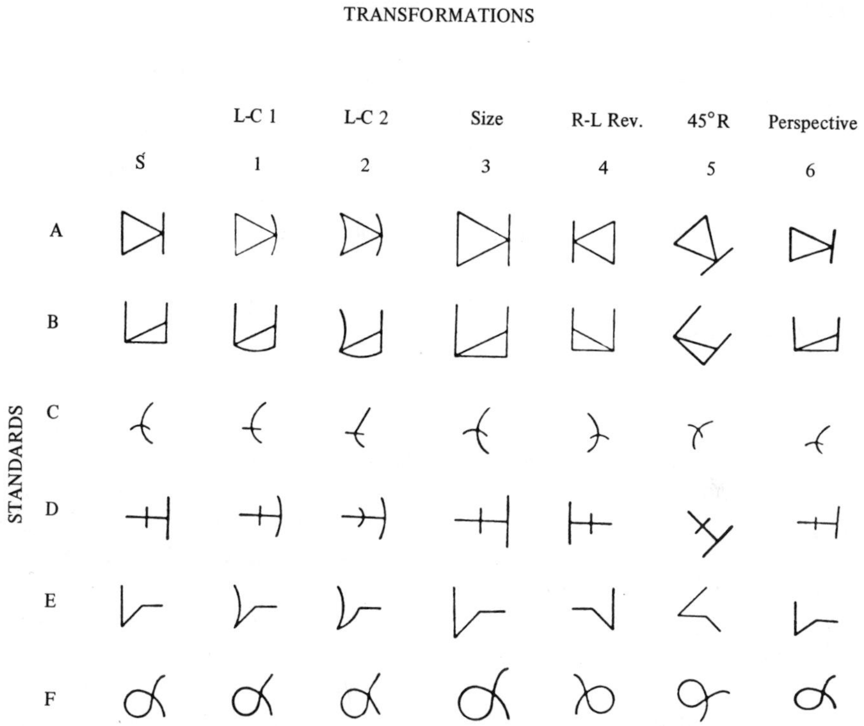

TRANSFORMATIONS

FIGURE 6–1. **Six standard forms (column S on the left) and six transformations of each of them.**

(From Anne D. Pick, Improvement of visual and tactual form discrimination. *Journal of Experimental Psychology,* 1965, *69,* 333.)

the transfer task as in the training task, but new transformations. If improvement had depended on forming a prototype of the standard and matching against it, this group should show high transfer. Another group (EII) was given new standards in the transfer trials, but the transformations of these standards were the same dimensions of difference as those in the training session. If learning had depended on discovering the dimensions by which the standards and their transformations differed, this group should show high transfer. In the third group (C), both new standards and new transformations appeared in the transfer task.

The results are shown in Table 6–1. The number of confusion errors are compared for the three groups. The groups are all significantly different from one another. The control group, which had both new standards and new transformations, made most errors, as would be expected. Group EII, which had new forms but familiar types of transformations, made fewest errors. The hypothesis is thus supported that learning the

TABLE 6-1

Errors Made in Transfer by Groups with Three Types of Pretraining

Group	Errors
EI (same standards, different transformations)	69
EII (different standards, same transformations)	39
C (different standards, different transformations)	101

From Anne D. Pick, Improvement of visual and tactual form discrimination. *Journal of Experimental Psychology*, 1965, *69*, 331-339.

dimensions of difference is important for improvement in discrimination of visual forms. Since Group EI, which had familiar standards but new transformations, was superior to the control group, it appears that learning of prototypes also occurred, but the fact that Group EII was best suggests that learning of a prototype was not the sole or the essential process in improvement of discrimination.

In order to extend the generality of this finding, Pick repeated the experiment with tactual discrimination. The stimulus forms were raised lines, metal reproductions of the material used in the previous experiment. The subjects (first-grade children) were blindfolded and explored the forms with their fingers, making a successive comparison of standard and transformation. The results differed somewhat from those of the first experiment. Groups EI and EII were both superior to the control group, but equally so. Pick thought that this result might be related to the successive method of comparison here; the subject had to retain some sort of memory image of the standard in order to judge whether the comparison form was the same or not. Prototype learning would thus be useful.

To check this interpretation, a third experiment was run with simultaneous tactual comparison (the subject explored the standard and comparison forms together, one with each hand). The results of this experiment fully supported the hypothesis that dimensions of difference are learned and transfer to new discriminations, for EII was superior to both other groups and EI was no better than the control group. Presumably EI's superiority to the control group in the first experiment with visual discrimination had to do with the partially successive nature of the comparison, for the subjects had to look back and forth from one form to the other.

The proposition is supported, then, that in multidiscrimination learning, the subject improves by detecting the dimensions of difference between the stimuli presented. That an image of some sort may be formed, as well, is likely. It has a role, it seems, when retention over time is required. Perhaps the role is that of making possible the detection of the distinctive features of the absent comparison item. It is highly probable that it has a role in production, too, as in drawing a particular form. It would seem that distinctive features are necessary and sufficient for discrimination, but that a structured image is also necessary for other tasks.

EMPHASIS ON DISTINCTIVE FEATURES. Discrimination learning should be facilitated when distinctive-feature differences (or differential properties) are emphasized in training. The experiment on aircraft recognition by Gagné and Gibson (Chapter 5) is direct evidence for this proposition. Other experiments bear on it, though not as directly, since differences in distinctive features have seldom been analyzed. Some of the experiments on stimulus predifferentiation and acquired distinctiveness undoubtedly owe their positive results to this principle, however unintended. The experiments with relevant labels learned to visual forms in a pretraining condition are examples (see Chapter 4). Presumably the relevant labels indicated some distinctive feature or feature pattern of the forms which facilitated discrimination in a transfer test.

An experiment by Trabasso (1963) studied the role of emphasis of relevant features in a concept-learning experiment. Flower patterns were the material. Angle of leaf was the relevant dimension and it was emphasized in various ways in different experimental groups (by holding constant irrelevant dimensions, by exaggerating the angle, by adding color as a redundant variable, and so on). The experimental groups learned faster than the control group and transferred use of the relevant feature perfectly to a new, harder problem.

CONTRAST. Learning of differential properties should be facilitated by providing examples of contrasts along a dimension so as to define and assist isolation of the critical variable property. Graduated contrasts should be particularly effective for isolating a continuous relational property.

Pavlov's (1927) method of contrasts for establishing differential conditioned reflexes suggests the importance of the principle. Pavlov found that establishment of a conditioned reflex to a particular stimulus brought with it generalization of the conditioned response to similar stimuli. Differentiation could however be achieved, and the method finally adopted in his laboratory for establishment of a fine discrimination involved presentation of contrasting stimuli, beginning with broad differences and working toward finer ones. In Pavlov's words:

The question can now be discussed as to how the specialization of the conditioned reflex, or, in other words, the discrimination of external agencies, arises. Formerly we were inclined to think that this effect could be obtained by two different methods: the first method consisted in repeating the definite conditioned stimulus a great many times always accompanied by reinforcement, and the second method consisted in contrasting the single definite conditioned stimulus, which was always accompanied by reinforcement, with different neighboring stimuli which were never reinforced. At present, however, we are inclined to regard this second method as more probably the only efficacious one, since it was observed that no absolute differentiation was ever obtained by use of the first method, even though the stimulus was repeated with reinforcement over a thousand times. On the other hand, it was found that contrast by even a single unreinforced application of an allied stimulus, or by a number of single unreinforced applications of different members of a series of allied stimuli at infrequent intervals of days or weeks, led to a rapid development of differentiation (Pavlov, 1927, p. 117).

Another bit of positive evidence for this proposition comes from the controversy over the continuity-discontinuity issue in discrimination learning. Haire (1939), in arguing for hypotheses as against continuity, cited an experiment with a string-pulling discrimination in which a big increase in weight differential caused an immediate jump to a choice of "lighter" from a choice based on a position habit.

Lawrence's (1952) experiment with four types of training for rats that were learning to discriminate two grays is especially apt. One group received all its training on the two-test stimuli, a pair of grays relatively close in brightness value. A second group received its first thirty training trials on a pair of grays far apart in brightness and then was shifted to the test pair. A third group had a gradual transition from the far-apart pair through two progressively closer pairs to the test pair. A fourth group received its first fifty trials with one member of the test pair and a gray two steps removed, and then was shifted to the test pair. Figure 6–2 shows the learning curves for the four groups. The group trained entirely on the test pair showed the smallest improvement (drop in errors). The gradual-transition group performed the most accurately on the trials with the test pair. Efficiency of learning the discrimination was greater for all the three groups trained on an easy discrimination before shifting to the difficult one, and was best when the preliminary training consisted of a gradual transition to the test pair. In interpreting these results, Lawrence concluded that an important factor in discrimination learning "is the necessity for the animal to isolate functionally the relevant stimulus dimension from all the other background and irrelevant cues (p. 516)."

Predictions for Efficiency of Discrimination Following Learning of Distinctive Features

Several predictions can be made about discrimination performance when there has been opportunity for previous learning of distinctive features for the set of objects or events utilized. These are not principles having to do

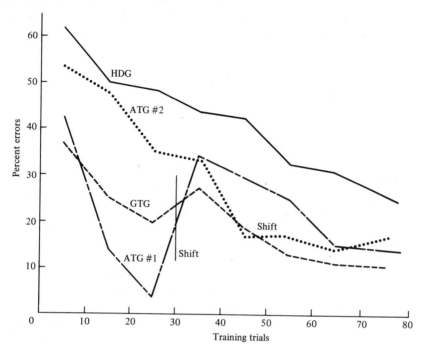

FIGURE 6–2. Learning curves for various types of discrimination training.

Group HDG was trained throughout the entire 80 trials on the test stimuli. Group ATG #1 received its first 30 training trials on a pair of grays far apart in brightness and then was shifted to the test pair. Group ATG #2 received its first 50 trials on one member of the test pair and a gray two steps removed, and was then shifted to the test pair. Group GTG was a gradual transition group. It began training on the pair of grays that was far apart and progressed through closer pairs to the test pair. All three groups that began with a greater contrast than the test pair learned faster and achieved greater accuracy than did group HDG. (From D. Lawrence, The transfer of discrimination along a continuum. *Journal of Comparative and Physiological Psychology*, 1952, *45*, 514.)

with discovering the distinctive features, but concern expectations for transfer. They serve as a testable check on the assumptions made so far, and also provide useful principles for instructional displays.

MAXIMAL DIFFERENCES. Discrimination should be best when feature differences between pairs of stimuli are maximal, and poorest when they are minimal.

The ideal experimental test of this prediction is the confusion matrix, given a set of distinctive features so that relative difference between items can be scaled. The work described in the last chapter correlating distinctive feature differences between graphemes with a confusion matrix is an attempt to test the prediction. The Brown and Hildum experiment, which found that most confusions in reproducing syllables depended on a one-feature difference, is another test with a positive outcome (see Chapter 5).

ENHANCEMENT. Discrimination should be facilitated when distinctive features are enhanced in a stimulus display.

Enhancement can occur in several ways, one of them being exaggeration. A cartoon drawing is one method of providing exaggeration of distinctive features, and caricatures have been used for this purpose by journalists as long as newspapers have existed. Caricatures of newsworthy persons seem to convey at a glance their unique and critical feature pattern, omitting the nonessentials. While common sense supports this observation, it might be challenged. It could be argued that a high-fidelity photograph would be just as useful as a caricature, or more so, for efficient perception of an object. Ryan and Schwartz (1956) answered this challenge. They compared the accuracy of discriminative judgments of the same objects in four modes of presentation—photographs, shaded drawings, line drawings (tracings of outlines of the photographs), and cartoons (see Fig. 6–4). The representations were presented tachistoscopically, using an ascending method of limits to obtain a threshold. The test was not the naming of the object; instead the subject had to specify its relative position (e.g., finger position in the hand illustrated). Significant differences were found: the

FIGURE 6–3. Caricature of Bertrand Russell by Low.

Low described caricature as an art of "calculated emphasis," an "evolutionary process of simplification, a kind of survival-of-the-most-significant." What the caricaturist wants to know is "in what particulars a man is like himself and no one else. His points of difference, not similarity of type." (Caricature by david low by arrangement with the Trustees and the London Evening Standard.)

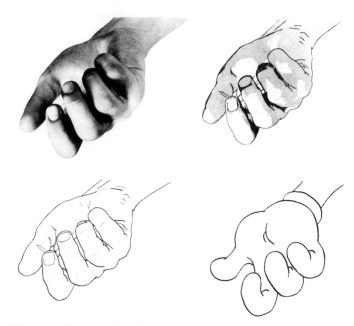

FIGURE 6–4. Four modes of representation after Ryan and Schwarz (1956).

A photograph, a shaded drawing, a line drawing, and a cartoon of a hand posture were compared for discriminability. The cartoons were easiest to perceive. (Photograph and drawings courtesy of Dr. T. A. Ryan.)

cartoons were perceived in the shortest time, while the outline drawings took longest, with photographs and shaded drawings about equal and between the others.

Fraisse and Elkin (1963) performed a somewhat similar experiment with four modes of presentation: the real object, a photograph, an outline drawing, and an accented drawing. (This latter mode of representation was not exactly a caricature but it did emphasize the essential features, with much heavier lines for certain features than the outline drawing.) A set of eight common objects was prepared in this way. They were presented tachistoscopically, and the subjects were asked to recognize and name the object presented. The subjects included four age groups, approximately seven through twenty-two years. Recognition threshold decreased with age, but the order of recognition was consistent: accented drawings were most easily perceived, real objects next most, photographs next, and outline drawings least. These results, on the whole, corroborate Ryan and Schwartz, but some difficulties of control are apparent, since brightness contrast was greater in the accented drawings and could have played a decisive role in the comparison with outline drawings. The superiority of the accented drawing over the photograph and object itself is, in any case, an important finding.

An interesting experiment with cartoons specially constructed to exaggerate a differential dimension was performed by Gardner and Wallach (1965). They were interested in the hypothesis of certain ethologists (see Tinbergen, 1953) that animals respond strongly to supernormal cases of critical stimulus dimensions of objects serving as releasers of instincts. They constructed silhouettes of human heads varying in babyishness, using two parameters of variation that differentiated with minimal overlap between babies and adults. The differentiating parameters were length of head at five axes and distance to the farthest anterior point on the chin (the baby's head, in contrast to the adult's, is wide and his chin small). A series of heads were constructed with exaggerated values at the extremes. Pairs of heads were then presented to subjects, with the instruction to select the more babyish of each pair. Each of the distorted superbaby figures was judged as more babyish than the accurate representation of the standard baby.

Enhancement of distinctive features in a stimulus display can also be promoted by maximizing the number of possible feature contrasts. When the potential number of feature contrasts is maximally displayed, discrimination should be facilitated. An experiment by Vurpillot and Brault (1959) illustrates the point. They presented familiar objects (little houses, cups, dolls) on a turntable which was then rotated so that the subject saw the object from all angles. Afterward, he was shown eight photographs of the object, in varying orientations, and asked to choose the one most like the object. The subjects were children from five through nine years old.

The children's choices were by no means random and certain features of the objects played a determining role in the child's selection from the photographs (the cup's handle, the doll's face, windows of the house). By nine years, three-quarter views (showing more than one side) were chosen over photographs showing only one side, marking an age trend toward choosing the most informative picture, the experimenters thought.

Enhancement of distinctive features may also be accomplished by elimination of nondistinctive features. Cartoons make use of this method as well as exaggeration of critical features. Removal of interfering or nondistinguishing stimulus variables makes easier the discrimination of the essential ones. An everyday example is static on the radio. When it is tuned out, speech patterns or melodies are more easily distinguished. This principle can be reversed. By adding static or confusing stimuli, distinctive patterns and features may be covered up or lost. Experiments with embedded figures are pertinent examples. An interesting fact in this connection is the possibility of the individual learning to ignore the irrelevant stimuli.

An experiment by Gollin (1960) provides evidence of progressive development with age in ignoring the effect of irrelevant elements in pattern perception. He compared performance on two versions of a tactual discrimination test. Patterns were constructed by hammering metal tacks into sheets of plywood. In task A, a pattern such as a triangle was presented for comparison with an identical one, or a slightly different one, and the subject was asked to make a judgment of "same" or "different." The patterns were placed within curtained boxes and the subject explored them, one at a time, with his hand. In task B, interfering tacks of a larger size were distributed within or outside the pattern in one member of each pair. The subject was told to disregard the larger tacks while making the same-different judgment. For both children and adults, the patterns free of interfering tacks were more accurately matched, but the difference between the A task and the B task was greater for children, who were less able to disregard the spatially distributed interferents. Furthermore, experience with the A task before proceeding to the B task facilitated adults, compared with a control group, but this effect was not apparent with children. In a second experiment (1961), two age groups of children were run, as well as adults. The results indicated a progressive increase with age in the ability to profit from training in segregating and matching the patterns under interfering conditions.

FAMILIARITY OF FEATURES. New objects belonging to a class of objects having very familiar distinctive features should be more easily discriminated from one another than an equivalent set of objects from an unfamiliar class.

This proposition follows from the assumption that objects are distinguished by unique bundles of distinctive features, the features being defined for a set of objects in such a way as to make use of contrasts and provide unique patterns. Previously unencountered members of a class should be discriminable from others if the differences which are critical for the class have been learned. Pick's experiment, described above, shows that critical dimensions of difference are learned and do transfer to new items. We should be able, then, to show that items which are structurally equivalent are nevertheless more or less easily discriminated and recognized depending on familiarity with differences that are critical for the set.

An opportunity for testing this proposition was afforded by a set of visual patterns devised by J. J. Gibson. These patterns are drawn so as to represent profiles of faces, simplified and somewhat caricatured, when they are in an upright orientation. When they are rotated 90°, they no longer appear to be faces, but look more like a kind of handwriting (see Fig. 6–5). In the face orientation they are characterized by familiar distinctive features, that is, the forehead, eye, nose, mouth, and chin. In the other orientation they are without such familiar features, since the curves and cusps of the line do not constitute the letters of cursive writing in any alphabet (although they perhaps resemble the Arabic). It is assumed that

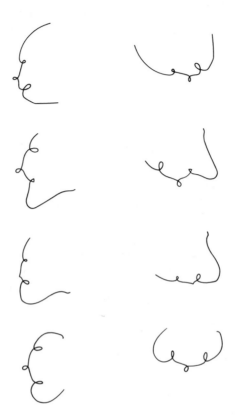

FIGURE 6–5. Cartoon drawings which resemble profiles of faces in one orientation but are like writing in another.

(From Eleanor J. Gibson, Perceptual development. *Child Psychology,* ed. H. W. Stevenson. Sixty-second Yearbook of the National Society for the Study of Education. Chicago: Distributed by University of Chicago Press, 1963, p. 173.)

two different orientations of the same tracing make it different with respect to the frame of the tracing, and thus potentially different with respect to what it represents. The effect of orientation on form in line drawings is admittedly a puzzle, but this assumption seems safe.[1]

An experiment of the writer's [2] compared the upright and the rotated items for recognizability. Twelve items were selected, four which differed greatly from one another (shown in Fig. 6–5), and eight others, two of which differed only slightly from each of the first four.

[1] For the complexities of orientation in form perception, see Howard and Templeton (1966), chapters 12 and 13.
[2] The subjects were run by Mrs. Rima Lesser.

Subjects were assigned to either the writing or the profile group. In the profile group they were told they would see some faces; in the writing group they were told they would see some secret writing. One pattern was then presented alone for ten seconds in a small window, and the subject was instructed to observe it carefully so that he would recognize it again. Then all twelve patterns were presented, in random order, for recognition. The subject was told to look for the same pattern he had seen and to point it out to the experimenter. After going through the twelve patterns, the experimenter went on to another trial, presenting another pattern as a standard, with similar instructions, until each of the original four patterns had appeared as a standard.

There were three age groups of subjects, college students from a psychology course, children from a kindergarten, and children from the third grade in a public school.

The results are summarized in Table 6–2. Recognition errors decreased with age for both types of pattern. But errors were greater for the

TABLE 6–2

Errors in Recognition of Profiles and Writing

	N	Type	Mean Total Errors	Sig. Diff.*
Adults	12	Pro	3.16	p < .01
	12	Wri	6.18	
Third Grade	15	Pro	6.47	p = .07
	15	Wri	11.13	
Kindergarten	15	Pro	12.60	p = .05
	15	Wri	16.85	

* Mann-Whitney U test.

patterns in the writing orientation for all age groups. There is some indication that the difference was more pronounced with age. While this trend is not strong enough to be accepted with great confidence, it suggests that the children are not more adept at physiognomic perception than the adults, as has sometimes been maintained. This would be expected if the distinctive features of faces are learned (and perhaps especially of faces represented by line drawings).

These results point to another fact about distinctive features. Stimulus variables that specify distinctive features for one class of objects, like faces, may be irrelevant variables for another class. Perspective transformations, for instance, are irrelevant for writing, but they are information for spatial location. One can write with blue ink or black ink or red ink, and the color is irrelevant for discriminating letters. But it may be information about the writer or the side of the ledger. Discovering distinctive features for a class involves differentiating relevant from irrelevant variables, the relevant ones being ones that have contrasts within the class.

MECHANISMS OF PERCEPTUAL LEARNING

The predictions above, which followed from the hypotheses in the last chapter about what is learned, turn out to have support in experimental evidence. Now I would like to speculate about processes which may bring about the kind of modification described. Since I have questioned the sufficiency of association with a new response as an explanatory concept for perceptual learning, a search is in order for others. Three possibilities will be proposed. They follow intuitively, if not in a strict logical sense, from the analysis of what is learned.

Abstraction

The importance of the discovery of dimensions of difference was emphasized in the evidence discussed above. A distinctive feature of a letter, for instance, may be a contrastive relation such as straight-curved, or upright-oblique. Such a relation is invariant under many kinds of change (e.g., size, color). In Lawrence's experiment, for another example, the dimension of "lighter than" was the invariant relationship.

I believe the process by which the critical dimension is discovered is abstraction, an ancient and respectable concept which deserves its place in the description of perceptual development. Abstraction occurs when an invariant relation is discovered over a number of varying objects or events. The relation must literally be extracted from the confrontation by nonidentical pairs or cases presenting a contrast, or from cases embedded in different contexts. This process is not necessarily a conscious search. Abstraction at a perceptual level has been assumed before, by Werner, for instance, and by William James. James thought that the process of abstraction was a function of the diversity of other properties present with it in stimulation.

What is associated now with one thing and now with another tends to become dissociated from either, and to grow into an object of abstract contemplation by the mind. One might call this the *law of dissociation by varying concomitants*. . . . *Why* the repetition of the character in combination with different wholes will cause it thus to break up its adhesion with any one of them, and roll out, as it were, alone upon the table of consciousness, is a little of a mystery. One might suppose the nerve-processes of the various concomitants to neutralize or inhibit each other more or less and to leave the process of the common term alone distinctly active (James, 1890, Vol. 1, pp. 508–509).

I am not sure (nor was James) that varying concomitants alone guarantee abstraction, because it is generally a contrast—a relational difference, or a direction of difference—that must be dissociated from varying concomitants. But James's use of the term "dissociation" makes it clear how far this concept is from "association." The relation is separated out from a complex, extracted from it, rather than added on.

An experiment by Turnure and Wallach (1965) attempted to test James's hypothesis. They prepared a number of line figures which contained one of two target shapes embedded in a larger drawing. The context drawing surrounding the target varied in each case in a number of ways. In several tasks of a concept-formation type, such as classifying, a subject was presented with five examples of one target embedded in different contexts, and with five of the other always embedded in the same context. When the subjects were shown the target figures alone afterward and asked whether they recognized either or both, they chose the one with varying context most often. In this experiment, the discovery of an invariant embedded feature was required for classification when it occurred in varied contexts, but no analysis was necessary when the context was also invariant.

In discrimination tasks where several stimulus dimensions are varied but only one dimension (a contrast like black-white) is chosen for reinforcement, adding more irrelevant dimensions does not make learning the immediate task easier. However, in the long run it may facilitate abstraction of the relevant dimension, since it has been shown to facilitate learning the reversed discrimination, such as shifting the reinforcement from black to white (Fritz, 1966). Quick transfer in a reversal shift is a plausible indication that the relevant dimension of contrast has been abstracted from the total complex of stimulation.

Variation of absolute values along a dimension isolates an invariant relation. For example, in Lawrence's experiment, the animal was brought quickly to respond to the light-dark relationship by a progression of stimulus pairs which retained the invariant relation while constantly changing the absolute values. The only property which remained stable, and therefore isolable, was light-dark.

The transposition experiment is a classical demonstration of learning a relationship at a simple level. Transposition has been demonstrated with numerous animals in a discrimination-learning setup, using only one pair of stimuli which vary on the selected dimension for training, and another pair for the transfer trial. This is a primitive and limiting case for the condition of abstraction, since only one contrast pair is usually presented.

Köhler (1918) demonstrated that a pair of hens, for example, trained to peck at grains on the darker of two gray backgrounds, would continue to peck at the darker when a new pair was presented, the originally darker square now being lighter.

The experiment requires nonconfounding of other possible variables, such as position, for the critical relation to emerge. A first step in establishing perception of a relation which can be transposed might be practice in responding to the critical difference with other dimensions held constant. But a second step in establishing perception of a relation involves abstraction of the critical relationship with other dimensions of stimulation varying as well, but never in perfect correlation.

For example, if one set out to teach a young child to discriminate pure weight, pairs of objects contrasting in mass only (alike in size, shape, color, and texture) would be presented for the first stage of practice. But real abstraction of the weight relationship as such would require a second stage of practice in which the other dimensions vary but do not covary with mass.

Phoneme discrimination must progress in some such way, for the essential contrasts come to be detected despite differences in pitch, loudness, speed, and other vocal attributes. Similarly, in the discrimination of letters written by different hands, one man's tilt may be another man's upright, but the tilt-upright contrast is relational and invariant with respect to the other features and must be detected as such if the letters are to be read.

Can one say that differences are stimulus information? One can, if perceptual learning does in fact consist of responding to variables present in stimulation but not previously responded to. An interesting behavioral experiment in this connection was performed by Honig and Day (1962). They used a derived dimension, as they termed it, one defined by the relationship between stimuli, in a generalization experiment with pigeons. The pigeons were trained to peck at one key when a pair of identical colors was displayed, and at another key when the colors differed in wavelength by a difference of 40 μ. The difference pair had continually varying wavelengths up and down the spectrum but maintained the 40 μ difference during training. After the pigeons had learned to make specific responses to the identical pair and to the difference pair, two sessions of generalization testing were given. Stimulus pairs were drawn from the training range so as to provide differences varying from 0 to 70 μ. There was an orderly and appropriate shift in the distribution of responses for the different differences between 0 and 40 μ. A continuum of stimulus difference thus "functioned as a stimulus dimension in a manner similar to the physical continua usually used to obtain generalization gradients (p. 30)."

The experiment just cited dealt with abstraction of a relation or contrast existing in a single physical dimension of wavelength. But pattern abstraction or multidimensional contrast also occurs. The melody of the bird song is an example. Is there information in this kind of stimulus for an abstracted pattern? Studies of speech units represented on the sound spectrograph led scientists at the Haskins Laboratory to investigate what the critical features of the patterns on the spectrograph might be (Cooper, Liberman, & Borst, 1951). For any given speech sound, repeated spectrographic records showed many variations due, presumably, to irrelevant free variants of speakers. To quote the authors, "By examining numerous spectrograms of the same sounds, spoken by many persons and in a variety of contexts, an investigator can arrive at a description of the acoustic features common to all of the samples, and in this way make progress toward defining the so-called invariants of speech (p. 318)." In order to validate the selection of invariants by this process, an instrument called the pattern playback was constructed which reconverted spectrograms into sound, either as they were originally recorded, or after modification, or after a synthetic reconstruction. The playback could operate from a spectrogram painted by hand, or partially painted out so as to delete presumed irrelevant details. The features on the original spectrograms which were most prominent could be copied and played back to test for intelligibility. The success of this technique implies that the critical invariant pattern is abstracted by individual hearers, independent of absolute stimulus values, and that the invariant aspect is information in its own right.

Filtering

There is another side to the coin in considering the abstraction of relations from the total stimulus input. The irrelevant randomly varying stimuli are filtered out. Idiosyncratic variations are ignored. The ignoring of rival stimuli when a hearer is listening to a single voice in a group situation (the cocktail party phenomenon) is a familiar example of filtering.

Ignoring noncritical stimulation appears, in fact, to be a second important process in perceptual learning, reciprocal to abstracting out. Its role is shown in experiments with embedded figures, where practice seems to lower the threshold for seeing the contour of a design despite camouflaging lines present in the display. Figures similar to those of Gottschaldt (see Chapter 2) are used in such studies. Francès (1963) has performed an experiment on what he termed learning of perceptual segregation. He wished to test the hypothesis that discovery of hidden patterns depends primarily on filtering out the noisy stimulation, and that this discovery is affected by certain kinds of practice. Specifically, he asked whether practice in a kind of filtering activity would influence the process of segregation, and whether the influence would be confined to the same type of camouflage used in the practice items, or would transfer to other types.

His experiment included four groups: 1) a control group which performed only a test series involving segregation of seven sample figures from different camouflaged backgrounds (figures taken from Gottschaldt); 2) an experimental group which was given preliminary practice in segregating the figures from twenty-two different camouflaged backgrounds; 3) a group which practiced tracing, copying, and drawing from memory the figures without camouflage; 4) a group which had preliminary practice in segregation with extremely different material (different figures, all figures located on the same grid, orientation and size varied from sample; see Fig. 6–6).

The results showed a highly significant effect of practice in segregation (Group 2), which persisted throughout the entire test. (The test was divided into four phases and grew more difficult with each phase.) Memorizing the figures (Group 3) was also effective in improving performance in the test series, but only if the practice included drawing from memory and extended over a longer time than had the practice in Group 2. Shorter practice without drawing from memory was only effective in easy phases of the test. No facilitation was produced by practice in Group 4. It appeared probable that certain spatial attitudes generated by the practice material for Group 4 carried over and interfered with the test task where they did not apply.

The subjects in this task searched for features of the figure to be segregated, but at the same time profited from practice in ignoring the nonessential and interfering aspects of the total field of stimulation. That such a process occurs in ordinary perceptual learning and in the child's perceptual development is strongly suggested by these experiments, although they may be unrepresentative insofar as camouflage does not typify real-life situations.

To what extent is extraction of a figure from a mass of confusing visual context comparable to auditory perception of a single spoken message in a context of others? Broadbent (1958) summarized a large number of experiments on selective listening to speech, and examined the conditions which facilitate the ignoring of a voice or a message. These were spatial separation, difference in voice quality, relevance or irrelevance of the message, and others. The fact that speech is sequential makes it unlike a visual stimulus display, but a filter mechanism, perhaps of the kind proposed by Broadbent, may be needed for both kinds of perception. The filter is supposed to be set to pass certain features of stimulation but not others. To quote Broadbent, "The relation of figure and ground in visual perception is clearly similar to that between selected and rejected speech messages: in both cases the former is reacted to in detail, while the latter receives only a general and undifferentiated response (p. 60)."

What could be the nature of the process which suppresses some part of the input? Broadbent eschewed detailed physiological speculations, and

FIGURE 6–6. Embedded figures used by Francès.

Practice in segregating several target figures from a large page like this did not transfer to finding single embedded figures of the type first used by Gottschaldt. (From *Psychologie Française*, 1963, *8*, 20, reproduced with the permission of the publishers.)

looked instead for the experimental conditions of efficient filtering. From the principles he found, he constructed what he called an information-flow diagram. This suggests that a nervous system is a network of a particular type, containing a filter between the sensory and the temporary storage mechanism on the one hand, and the channel which passes the messages on

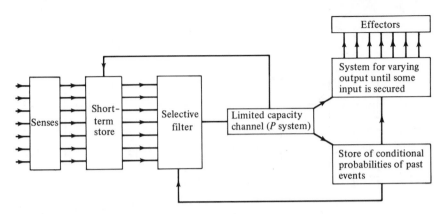

FIGURE 6–7. A possible information-flow diagram including a selective filter, as conceived by Broadbent (1957).

(From D. Broadbent, *Perception and Communication,* New York: Pergamon Press, Inc., 1958, p. 299.)

to the effector systems on the other hand (see Fig. 6–7). The filter mechanism is central rather than peripheral. What happens to the material which does not pass the filter is not clear from this model. Broadbent (1957) is reluctant to postulate an inhibitory mechanism. Other work (see Deutsch & Deutsch, 1963; Treisman, 1964) suggests that some mechanism for attenuation exists. An inhibitory mechanism of the kind localized by Hernandez-Peon et al. (1956) in the reticular system to explain reduction of sensory messages in one channel when activity is strong in another channel is not easy to conceive for segregation of figures from irrelevant context. It may be that different levels of neural functioning are involved in the inhibition of sensory qualities as distinguished from the segregation of patterns.

It is safest to avoid speculation about a mechanism until more knowledge is available about segregation in patterned stimulus input. Untouched territory awaits the psychologist who is willing to tackle the problem of passing over irrelevant visual input in the extracting of a pattern. The problem is especially interesting for developmental psychologists, since the ability to ignore irrelevant stimuli may be an important aspect of perceptual development, and we shall return to it.

Peripheral Mechanisms of Attention

In the foregoing paragraphs on filtering attention has been conceived as a central process which selects or rejects from the stimulus input. The rejected material in a sense gets into the nervous system, although it is damped at some stage. In the case of the embedded figures, for instance, the camouflaging lines are not made to disappear. The subject sees them and could make some sort of report about them. He can often say something about the voices he is not listening to at the cocktail party. But there is another way of conceiving attention which must now be considered. There are the exploratory sense organ adjustments, sometimes called observing responses.

The exploratory activity of the visual system includes fixating the eyes, scanning, and head turning. Such adjustments are obviously instrumental in selective perception. Exploratory activity is typical of all the sensory systems. Listening involves turning the head toward a sound source, smelling involves sniffing the air, tasting involves rolling food or liquid over the tongue, and touching involves palpating with the fingers. These exploratory systems are treated in detail by Gibson (1966) and need not be described further here. Their selective function is obvious; they expose the receptors to chosen aspects of potential stimulation. It also seems likely that practice in exploring the flowing array of available stimulation will facilitate the discovery of the critical properties of objects in the world.

Selective attention of the peripheral kind can be quite specific, as witness the case of so-called observing responses in the learning of a discrimination problem in the laboratory. The hypothesis of observing responses has been emphasized and investigated by a number of psychologists (Wyckoff, 1952; Atkinson, 1961). In these investigations, the probability of a subject's making a given observing response is generally assumed to be determined by reinforcement. Atkinson's model assumes that, if an observing response occurs and leads to the selection of a stimulus which elicits a reinforced response, the subject will tend to repeat that observing response on the next trial. If the observing response occurs and leads to the selection of a stimulus which elicits an incorrect discrimination response, the subject will tend not to repeat that observing response. In an experiment designed to test his model, Atkinson's results led him to conclude that, for the type of discrimination problem considered, asymptotic behavior could be predicted in terms of the postulated relations between reinforcement schedules, observing responses, and discrimination responses. The discrimination task was set up so that two overt and mutually exclusive observing responses were available, as prearranged by the experimenter (pressing either of two keys). Pressing a key caused one or another light to go on, giving potential differential information about the response to be reinforced.

House and Zeaman (1962) made use of the concept of observing response in explaining shifts from one dimension to another in discrimination learning, assuming that an observing response is learned for a dimension such as color. It is impossible to specify the particular response for color in such a case, although the evidence that the subject has learned to pay attention to a given dimension is convincing. They also assume, however, that a specific observing response is reinforced and that its learning follows the rules of operant conditioning. Theories which hypothesize the mediation of observing responses in discrimination learning, even though couched in S-R reinforcement terms, are not enrichment theories, because they do not assume that stimuli arising from the response process enhance discrimination by becoming themselves the effective stimuli. The mediating response, rather, functions as a selective mechanism which gets the system centered on the relevant stimulus variables. Tighe and Tighe (1966, pp. 360 ff.) term them subtractive as opposed to additive theories. The hypothesis of observing responses seems to me to be a way of preserving the rubrics of stimulus-response psychology without acknowledging or talking about perception, especially when no overt response can be pointed to.

Specific observing responses of the kind postulated by Wyckoff, Atkinson, and House and Zeaman, controlled by reinforcement contingencies, may have a role in perceptual learning, but they do not help explain the development of skilled systematic exploratory activity. I agree with Piaget (1963) that this is crucial for perceptual development, as will appear in later chapters. In the next chapter we shall consider in detail how exploratory activity is directed and what factors play a role in selectivity of perception.

SUMMARY

This chapter has sought for principles underlying perceptual learning. Six propositions followed from the assumptions about what is learned. Three had to do with discrimination learning, and were concerned with differences in distinctive features and dimensions of difference when stimulus objects are presented for discrimination learning. The first stated that in a multi-discrimination-learning task, the subject learns by discovering the dimensions of difference between members of the set of stimuli presented, and will afterwards be able to transfer them to new members of the set. The second held that learning should be facilitated when distinctive features are emphasized in training. The third held that learning of differences should be facilitated by providing graded examples of contrasts along a dimension so as to define and permit isolation of the critical variable.

The other three propositions predicted discrimination performance, assuming that previous learning of distinctive features has taken place. The first stated that discrimination will be optimal when feature differences between pairs of stimuli are maximal, and poorest when they are minimal. The second stated that discrimination should be best when distinctive features are enhanced in a stimulus display. The third stated that new stimuli belonging to a class of objects having familiar distinctive features should be more easily discriminated from one another than an equivalent set of stimuli without familiar distinctive features.

Three processes were suggested as basic for perceptual differentiation. These were abstraction of differential properties of stimuli, filtering out of irrelevant variables of stimulation, and selective attention of the kind described as exploratory activity of sense organs. These three processes are thought to operate together in producing the kind of modification referred to as perceptual learning.

7

Selective Factors in
Perceptual Learning

Such an empiricist writer as Mr. Spencer, for example, regards the creature as absolutely passive clay, upon which 'experience' rains down. The clay will be impressed most deeply where the drops fall thickest, and so the final shape of the mind is moulded. . . . If such an account were true, a race of dogs bred for generations, say in the Vatican, with characters of visual shape, sculptured in marble, presented to their eyes, in every variety of form and combination, ought to discriminate before long the finest shades of these peculiar characters. In a word, they ought to become, if time were given, accomplished connoisseurs *of sculpture. Anyone may judge of the probability of this consummation.*

William James, 1890, Vol. 1, p. 403.

It has been argued that what is learned in perceptual learning are distinctive features, invariant relationships, and patterns; that these are available in stimulation; that they must, therefore, be extracted from the total stimulus flux. The processes which are relevant for extraction include orienting responses of the sense organs; abstraction of relations and invariants; and filtering relevant features from irrelevant stimulation.

It is clear from this account that perception is not passive reception. It is active search. From the welter of stimulation constantly impinging on the sensory surfaces of an organism, there must be selection. Perception is furthermore adaptive and regulatory. It focuses on wanted stimulation and rejects the rest. When one considers the rain of stimulation at any one instant, and the factor by which this is increased when temporal sequences of stimuli are included, it seems nothing short of miraculous that we pick up information at all. The miracle has gone unheralded for a long time, because we fell into the error of speaking of the stimulus, as if such a thing as a stimulus ever existed. James's "blooming, buzzing confusion" was an apter description of what might be expected from the stimulus situation. And yet, with this manifold energy pouring on the receptors, we do take information from our environment. I see the windowsill and the winter landscape outside; I see the yellow pages of notes and outlines pinned up beside me; I read a page; I hear the clock ticking; I feel the warmth of the radiator; but I don't perceive all these things at once, though the information for all of them is available.

So perception actively selects and rejects. The search process is adaptive, and I think it is self-regulatory. From too much available information, it extracts what is salient. From confusion and uncertainty, order, differentiation, and economy are achieved.

If a search process goes on in perception, and if it is adaptive, what directs it and what terminates it? In other words, what is the selective mechanism? We are interested not only in current filtering of input, but in the changes in selection over time. What reinforces the selective process so that a permanent change results? For decades the answer to the reinforcement question has centered around homeostatic regulation of the organism's metabolic needs, and in particular, reduction of drives. In a typical laboratory study of learning, the experimenter creates a drive, such as hunger or thirst, and then selects out the behavior he wants by appropriate manipulation of reinforcement. Reinforcement is external, comes from the environment, and the behavior reinforced is instrumentally related to it. When he does not use hunger or thirst, in a verbal learning experiment for instance, the experimenter gives the subject specific knowledge of results—"right" or "wrong," or a red light flashing, or a marble rolling out of a dispenser.

Reinforcement in this meaning of the term simply will not work with perceptual learning. Perceptual learning in lifelike situations is typically self-regulated and not externally reinforced. Perceptual differentiation of distinctive features of objects and sounds is not instrumental in securing food or water like pressing a bar in a Skinner box. It is adaptive, but it does not change the environment. Even if there were an experimenter around to provide reinforcement, there is no observable response for him to choose to control.

The problem for this chapter is the mechanism for initiating and terminating perceptual search. I shall propose in the following pages that the direction of the search is determined by the task and by cognitive motives. Its termination, with resulting perceptual change, can be effected by external reinforcement and knowledge of results, but primarily reinforcement is internal, and is epitomized by the term "reduction of uncertainty."

In what follows I am making two assumptions that should be explicit. One is that we can talk about perception as a function. In the previous chapters, I devoted much space to perceptual content, to what the end product of perceptual learning is like. But now we are going to consider perceptual functioning, the activity that characterizes perception as a process. Second, I am assuming that cognitive strategy is economical. The notion of behavioral economy as adaptive is ancient. I need only remind the reader of the law of least effort, or of the child taking the shortest path to the goal of highest valence. The argument is self-evident here. Perceptual activity searches the environment in the service of adaptive, economical action. Locating the path perceptually saves one from stumbling. Perceiving the cliff edge can save a climb up again or even save life.

THE DIRECTION OF PERCEPTUAL SEARCH

Perception is action, but it is exploratory action, not executive action in the sense of manipulating the environment. Exploration is directed and becomes increasingly directed with development. We speak of the directive aspect of perception as attention. We are not now asking what the effects of attention are, or how it is implemented by posture and sense-organ adjustment, but rather how exploratory ranging over the world of stimulation is guided. The range of stimulation may emanate from printed characters on a page to be scanned, from a ski slope to be traversed, or from the cries and laughter of a noisy playground where one must find one's child.

The Task

Many years ago in the history of psychology a small revolution was produced by demonstrations of the effect on perception of the task assigned the subject, the *Aufgabe*. Everyone is familiar with the classic examples of the effects of the assigned task on the response to the stimulus display. If I give you two digits placed one above the other, you can add them, or subtract them, or multiply them; the stimulus display on the page is the same, but what you do with them depends on the task I set you. It is enough to be reminded of the classical experiment, for it is simple and the results are obvious and easily confirmed.

Külpe demonstrated in 1904 that a tachistoscopic presentation of syllables printed in letters of different colors may result in different perceptions depending on the instructions given the subject. If the task given was to count the letters, he might be totally unable to report on the colors or their spatial arrangement; if he was told to notice the colors, he would be uncertain of the other features irrelevant to the instructions. Later years saw this experiment questioned, not for its repeatability, but for its interpretation. Was the effect actually due to perception or to memory? Experiments by Chapman (1932) and by Lawrence and Coles (1954) compared the effects of telling the subject what to report on before stimulus presentation and immediately afterward. The argument went that only the prior instruction should be effective if the effect was on perception. But a similar effect occurred under certain conditions with postpresentation instructions, so it was argued that the influence of the task-set was on memory—what is reported on first is favored. The argument does not take account, however, of a major result of several experiments—that some of the information goes unregistered, and cannot be retrieved even with immediate interrogation. Preinstructed items have been shown to be favored, even when the order of reporting is controlled (Wilcocks, 1925; Harris & Haber, 1963; Egeth & Smith, 1967).[1] Thus the tachistoscopic experiments in Külpe's tradition do show that instructions about what information to extract influence what is perceived or what on the other hand goes unnoticed.

The effect of the given task on the strategy of perception can be observed in experiments where different perceptual tasks such as discrimination, identification, or categorization can be compared. An analysis makes it clear how different the perceptual processes might be. Discrimination of two stimulus displays, with the requirement to say only whether or not they are different, can be accomplished by the detection of a single feature difference, and the rest of the display can be disregarded. Processing by features would thus be economical perceptual strategy, and would be optimal if the most distinctive feature—the one shared by fewest members of the stimulus set—were searched for first. Identification on the other hand requires selection of a label that fits the pattern or total bundle of features as distinct from the total bundle of every other. Processing by features would be optimal if the search began with the feature that came closest to splitting the set into a fifty-fifty distribution. But processing the total pattern, if higher order structure is present and can be detected, would be the best strategy.

A comparison of predictions for discrimination as opposed to identification on the basis of optimal strategies that differ for the two tasks was made by Bower (1965). In a matching task, a subject was presented with all the possible pairs drawn from a presentation set and asked to judge whether they were "same" or "different." In the identification task, the members of the set were presented singly and the subject required to select immediately afterward a previously learned identifying response to each one. Different predictions for a confusion matrix (for which errors between items should be most frequent) were made for the two tasks, on the basis of optimal strategies, assuming that sequential tests of distinctive features occur in both discrimination and identification. The stimuli differed in a controlled fashion, so that frequency of occurrence within the set of a given distinctive feature was known. For discrimination (matching), probability

---

[1] See Egeth (1967) for a summary of this controversy.

of a confusion error should be monotonically related to the frequency of a single feature by which two items differ, the least frequent feature having the greatest task utility for differentiation, and vice versa. Distribution of errors in matching yielded the predicted function in Bower's experiment. For identification (selecting the right response), Bower argued, the probability of an error should be least when a distinguishing feature's frequency is at fifty percent, since it divides the set evenly. Distribution of errors in the identification task yielded a curvilinear function, as predicted, with confusion errors fewest when stimuli differed by a feature with fifty percent frequency in the set. The results thus support the notion that differential appropriate strategies of noticing take place in discrimination and identification tasks with the same stimulus items. Bower's stimulus items were random dot patterns of 15 dots. The displays were very unfamiliar and possessed no easy-to-grasp higher order relations. If higher order structural variables were detectable, it is likely that a different task analysis, not assuming sequential processing of individual features, should be made.

Other perceptual tasks also permit differential predictions on the basis of perceptual strategy. Munsinger and Kessen (1966b) have demonstrated the role of the task assigned in an experiment employing random, closed shapes of different numbers of independent turns (five, ten, fifteen, and twenty turns). Instructions for one task were to estimate the number of turns when a shape was exposed tachistoscopically for a brief interval (200 ms.). The subjects were told the four categories (number of turns) and instructed to use only these four in responding. Accuracy of estimation was inversely related to level of variability of the shapes, less information being transmitted for figures with a larger number of turns. In a second task, subjects were presented with 24 random shapes at exposure durations of eight seconds and asked to learn category names for them, in a paired associates procedure. In this task, there was a curvilinear relation between transmitted information and number of turns in the figures. Names were learned better for figures of five and forty turns than for figures of ten and twenty turns. Variability in the figure is apparently processed differently in the two tasks. The five-turn figures have an advantage in both tasks, because their relative simplicity permits relatively easy perception of their overall angularity, a structural feature characterizing the whole shape. Beyond that, perception of relative angularity as a single feature is difficult with a very short exposure. With longer exposures, idiosyncratic features of individual shapes can be singled out, and the forty-turn shapes have an advantage because there are more ways in which they can differ distinctively. Parameters within the same set of stimulus materials can thus have a different effect depending on the task and the kind of exploratory activity it permits.

Further experiments could be cited. The reader is referred to

Garner (1962) for a discussion of the varying effects of kinds and amount of stimulus redundancy depending on the task. It seems clear that the task assigned interacts with stimulus information to effect strategies of perceiving as well as what is perceived. But we do not generally live in the laboratory and have tasks assigned us by an experimenter. What directs and drives perception outside an experimental situation?

Intrinsic Cognitive Motivation

Despite the long reign of S-R reinforcement theory and the focus of Freudian psychology on personal hidden motives, a few voices have reminded us over the years that the need to detect what goes on in the world around us is a strong motive in its own right. James, speaking of Helmholtz's "law of inattention," said "Helmholtz's law is that we leave all impressions unnoticed which are valueless to us as signs by which to *discriminate things* (Vol. 1, p. 456)." The implication is that we are set to discriminate things. Oddly enough, the behaviorists who insisted that all the important motives were metabolic tissue needs forgot something that Pavlov, their own prophet, had told us. An animal that has been conditioned to differentiate two stimuli, and then becomes unable to do so as they are made more similar, suffers a nervous breakdown. Making difficult discriminations is uncomfortable. Consider the behavior of a dog, taught to differentiate between a circle and an ellipse, when the difference between the two was progressively decreased until the diameters of the ellipse reached the ratio of eight to nine.

After three weeks of work upon this differentiation not only did the discrimination fail to improve, but it became considerably worse, and finally disappeared altogether. At the same time the whole behaviour of the animal underwent an abrupt change. The hitherto quiet dog began to squeal in its stand, kept wriggling about, tore off with its teeth the apparatus for mechanical stimulation of the skin, and bit through tubes connecting the animal's room with the observer, a behaviour which had never happened before. On being taken into the experimental room the dog now barked violently, which was also contrary to its usual custom; in short it presented all the symptoms of a condition of acute neurosis (Pavlov, 1927, p. 291).

The emphasis on purely physiological drives as motives began to decline shortly after the Second World War. A leader in this movement was Robert S. Woodworth, who presented a famous paper at the first meeting of the American Psychological Association following the war. The paper, entitled "Reinforcement of Perception," had as its thesis that

perception is always driven by a direct inherent motive which might be called the will to perceive. Whatever ulterior motives may be present from time to time, this direct perceptual motive is always present in any use of the senses

. . . to see, to hear—to see clearly, to hear distinctly—to make out what it is one is seeing or hearing—moment by moment, such concrete immediate motives dominate the life of relation with the environment (Woodworth, 1947, p. 123).

This view of the motivation of perceptual activity was soon afterward strengthened by the demonstration of what Harlow and his students called "environmental incentives." In a typical experiment, Harlow et al. (1950) presented monkeys with mechanical puzzles to be taken apart. The puzzles remained in the animals' living cages for 12 days, and were reset at intervals. At the end of this period, the monkeys were observed in test periods with the assembled puzzle. All of them performed successfully at once, but other monkeys who had had no opportunity to practice taking the puzzle apart were unable to do so in the test period. An "externally elicited drive," the authors thought, accounted for manipulation of the puzzle, and performance of the act itself provided an intrinsic reward. Even more to the point are experiments of Butler's (1953, 1954). Butler showed that discrimination learning occurred in monkeys when the only reward was an opportunity for visual perception. The monkey, during testing, was placed in a box provided with stimulus cards for discrimination

FIGURE 7–1. Monkey peering through window at a toy train.

The moving train and other monkeys were strong visual incentives. (From R. A. Butler, Incentive conditions which influence visual exploration. *Journal of Experimental Psychology*, 1954, *48*, 20.)

learning. If the subject pushed the correct card a window opened, allowing him a view of the room outside the box for a thirty-second period. The window afforded a view of the laboratory and the experimenter. In another experiment, Butler compared the behavior of monkeys when they were permitted to see different things. The open window afforded a view, on different occasions, of another monkey, a continually moving toy train (see Fig. 7–1), an array of food, and the empty room. The act of looking out was most frequent for the condition with another monkey present, and least for the empty room. In another experiment, Butler and Woolpy (1963) showed the importance for the monkeys of a clearly focused array. A picture that was in clear focus was consistently preferred to a blurred one, surely what Woodworth would have predicted.

Experiments rather similar to Butler's have been performed on children by Friedlander (1962). He studied the effect of what he called "cognitive reinforcers" on an operant response. It is gratifying to know that human children as well as monkeys will work to look at pictures, and that they prefer a slide from a Disney cartoon to a fuzzy circle of white light!

In recent years, intrinsic or cognitive motives have been stressed by a number of psychologists, although they differ in the terminology employed. Hunt (1963) has written of motivation "inherent in information processing and action." He thinks of incongruity, or dissonance between the incoming information and some cognitive state of the organism like an expectation, as producing arousal and directing activity. Berlyne (1966) wrote of exploration and curiosity as motives. He divided exploratory responses into two types. In one case, "when an animal is disturbed by a lack of information, and thus left a prey to uncertainty and conflict," it resorts to specific exploratory responses. In the other case, the animal seeks out stimulation that offers an "optimum amount of novelty, surprisingness, complexity, change, or variety." The latter type Berlyne termed "diversive exploration" and he investigated it in a number of experiments. In a typical one, a succession of patterns was made available by an automatic projector and a subject could look at each one for as long as he wished before pressing the switch for the next one. Figure 7–2 shows some of the patterns and the ways in which they varied (number of independent turns or components, symmetry, random vs. ordered, etc.). Berlyne refers to these as "complexity" variables. Exploration time, he reported, reached a peak and then declined as complexity became extreme. Specific exploratory responses result from an unpleasant degree of subjective uncertainty, according to Berlyne, and he believes that the termination of uncertainty will reinforce an instrumental response.

I agree with Berlyne that subjective uncertainty is an important motive and that it initiates exploratory activity and search. But I do not think that only responses are reinforced by reduction of uncertainty; I think

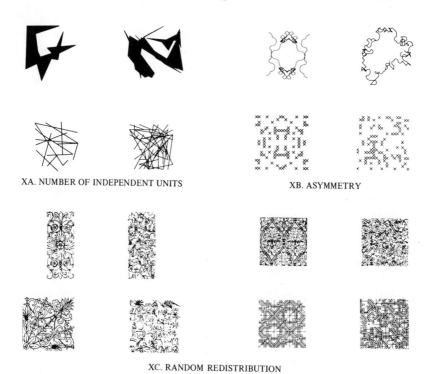

XA. NUMBER OF INDEPENDENT UNITS   XB. ASYMMETRY

XC. RANDOM REDISTRIBUTION

FIGURE 7–2. Patterns presenting various complexity variables, used for experiments in selective looking.

(From D. E. Berlyne, Curiosity and exploration. *Science,* 1966, *153,* 25–33. Copyright © 1966 by the American Association for the Advancement of Science.)

that what was selected in perception is affirmed and becomes part of the organism's permanent repertory of potential detectable features, invariants, and structures of the environment. I will return to this point later.

What Berlyne terms "diversive" exploratory behavior seems to be related to what happens in experiments on so-called sensory deprivation. I do not think these experiments are directly concerned with perceptual learning, but they are of some interest to us as further evidence that getting information from the environment is intrinsically rewarding, not secondarily so. The first experiments on prolonged sensory deprivation in human subjects were concerned with possible psychopathological consequences of such deprivation (e.g., Bexton, Heron, & Scott, 1954), but later work has been directed more toward the motivational aspects of deprivation. Jones (1967), in a paper entitled "Information Deprivation in Humans," put forth the thesis that "information deprivation generates a drive-variable," a kind of "stimulus hunger," and that deprived subjects will, if allowed, introduce varied stimulation. He reported experiments in which subjects were left for ten hours in a homogeneous, constant environment, that is an unlighted, relatively soundproof room. Apparatus was available to the subject for switching on light flashes in bursts of 24 at 1 sec. intervals. The switches on the subject's control panel permitted him to select from different sequences with relative information values of .00, .33, .67, and 1.00. The flashes were of two colors (red and green) and the information value was calculated with respect to the determination of the color sequence (an information value of 1.00 was a completely random determination of color, while a value of .00 was all flashes of the same color). A fifth switch provided simple alternation of the two colors. Results showed that the subject's choices were an increasing linear function of the information values associated with the flash sequences.

These experiments involve no perceptual learning. The situation is one where there is a contrived poverty of information, ecologically unrepresentative. The normal environment is full of events, and the corresponding stimuli, furthermore, are linked together in complex ways, in a "causal texture," to borrow Brunswik's metaphor. The environmental stimulation can present what some theorists term an "information overload," but the "causal texture" is a kind of structure, which, if detected, reduces the overload. It is this kind of indeterminate sequence that drives an organism to search the stimulus flux for invariants. It may be that the adult who lives in the same old familiar monotonous environment no longer does much perceptual learning. The infant and the person exposed to a changing environment must learn in order to maintain an adaptive relationship with their world.

There is something paradoxical about the question on which this experiment turns, that is, does the subject enjoy his uncertainty, and seek an unpredictable environment? This is exactly the opposite of the view I have been defending—that we seek clarity, that we search for structure, and that we look for the "causal texture" of the environment. It is essential to remember that the experimental situation was a thoroughly artificial one. A subject who lies on his back in a dark room (for 96 hours in one experiment) must be bored, to say the least. He has no task except to turn on switches as he chooses. Nothing he does has any importance except perhaps that the experimenter might be pleased if he takes a maximum sample of the entertainment provided; if so, he should select the ever-changing sequences. The impressive thing to me is that the subject apparently became acquainted with the random sequence when it was repeated. A so-called random sequence does have a structure, although it is much more complex than an alternation of red and green.

Another point to remember about Jones's experiment is the special meaning of the term "information" that he employs. The word has a common-sense meaning that is not at all the same as that of uncertainty or unpredictability. The ordinary meaning of "information" is in the sense of information about something. Egger and Miller, for example, use it in this sense when they speak of the "information hypothesis" of reinforcement (Egger & Miller, 1962, 1963). *"Any* cue," they say, "acquires reinforcing properties only when it provides information about a primary reward (1963, p. 132)." In experiments with rats, they found that a stimulus which regularly preceded reinforcement, as in simple conditioning, acquired secondary reinforcing properties. When it was made redundant by introducing other predictors, it was not significantly stronger as a secondary reinforcer than a control stimulus. The stimulus which predicts uniquely the advent of some event of adaptive significance—food in this case—is termed by Egger and Miller the "informative stimulus."

I am reminded by this experiment of a point which Howard Liddell liked to make about the Pavlovian conditioning experiment. There are, he said, two things the animal has to learn in this situation, and they are both perceptual learning. First he asks, "What is it?" when the conditioned stimulus appears. The animal's investigatory reflex shows that he does so. Second he asks, "What happens next?" This question clearly has to do with the predictive value of the CS or, as Miller and Egger put it, the informativeness of the stimulus. I differ with their opinion that getting information about an event is only a secondary reward. I think it is a primary reward, but I agree that a reduction of subjective uncertainty, not an increase of it, explains learning. Uncertainty, according to Garner, is "potential information," and "information is obtained by a reduction of uncertainty (Garner, 1962, p. 7)." Reduction of uncertainty in perception is thus consonant with obtaining information.

Let us be clear about where the information exists. First of all, it exists in the environment, in available stimulation. It is not so many unrelated bits, but contains "causal texture," which may or may not be picked up by the perceiver. The perceiver takes from the available stimulation what he can, up to his maximal capacity. When the information that he is able to pick up in a given situation increases, perceptual learning has occurred. This can happen because the organism, by noting distinctive features of objects and invariants of events (e.g., the bell always precedes food), reduces the amount of information that has to be processed by the brain so that as a result it can handle more of the total input, or (as I think) get more of the external available information.

Personal Attitudes, Autistic Factors, and Cultural Bias

About twenty years ago a fashion was launched in the psychology of perception known as the new look. It escaped from the presumably barren literature of psychophysics and sensory psychology and brought into perception a new set of problems stemming from psychoanalysis and the study of motivation. The idiosyncratic influence of individual attitudes and wants on perception was considered to be so strong that perception was thought of as a way of studying personality. The Rorschach test was an important forerunner of the new look. If what people see in inkblots enables the psychologist to diagnose their personality disorders, then everyday perception of ordinary people must be colored by their attitudes and motives, and their perceptions must reflect their personalities, the argument went. The literature that stemmed from this theory is enormous and a few examples must suffice. It is only tangentially relevant to the serious problems of perceptual learning. People's attitudes have an important role in directing their attention, but that does not answer the question of how learning comes about.

A good sample of work in this area is presented in a collection of essays called *Perception: An Approach to Personality* (Blake & Ramsey, 1951). The essays have titles such as "The Personal World Through Perception" (G. Klein) and "Unconscious Processes and Perception" (J. G. Miller). The diagnosis of personality was attempted by correlating supposed dimensions of personality with scores on perceptual tests based on the Gottschaldt figures, on susceptibility to autokinetic movement, on optical illusions, on the phi phenomenon, and others. Klein, for instance, studied the personality dimension of "tolerance vs. resistance to the unstable" in relation to the phi phenomenon, flicker fusion, and reports of movement in the Rorschach test. Form-bound people were said to be uncomfortable when they face instability; to show "constricted apparent movement ranges," lowered flicker-fusion thresholds, and an "intolerance for the unstable or equivocal." These people, it was suggested, may be clinically describable as "rigid, pedantic, compulsive persons (Blake & Ramsey, p. 344)." Else Frenkel-Brunswik (1949), similarly, sought to relate "tolerance of ambiguity" as a personality trait to tolerance of perceptual ambiguity, using laboratory tests of figure-ground reversal in ambiguous figures. Such analogies are interesting, but the problems of validity and reliability of the two dimensions being correlated are very serious ones, and any generalizations must be judged with extreme caution.

A more plausible case can be made for the selective influence of personal values on what is attended to. One cannot look in two directions at the same time, and what I choose to look at will not be the same as what you choose to look at. In a theater before the play begins, I observe the gowns and jewelry of the women around me but my husband has not seen even the handsome necklace of the woman directly in front of him. He can tell me a great deal about the construction of the ceiling, however. The point is so obvious that experiments are not needed to convince us of its truth. But an extension of the principle was made by the new look perceptionists when they argued that personal values not only orient perception, but actually distort it. The argument has some bearing on perceptual learning. I distrust the generalization that perception is typically distorted, because I think the biological need for clear discrimination is so great that evolution would have weeded out such a tendency.

Let us consider, briefly, two experiments purporting to demonstrate perceptual distortions, one illustrating the tendency to see what one wants to see, and the other the tendency not to see what one does not want to see. The first is the famous coin-size experiment of Bruner and Goodman (1947). Coins presented for size judgment to school children tended to be overestimated, and the overestimation was found to be related not only to the value of the coin, but to need. Poor children had a stronger tendency to overestimate size than rich children. Much controversy and cross fire was generated by this experiment. The numerous replications (or attempted ones) introduced elaborate controls and resulted in considerable methodological refinement but no resolution of the issue, the experimental findings being equivocal. It has never been clear, in any case, why a valued object should appear larger than it is.[2]

The experiments on not seeing what is noxious, threatening, or taboo, dubbed by Bruner and Postman (1947) "perceptual defense," have generated even more heat than the first experiment, but the resolution of the issue is just as far off. The typical experiment is that of presenting tachistoscopically taboo words randomly interspersed between neutral words. The threshold of perception is found to be higher for the socially improper items (McGinnies, 1949). As Bruner and Postman picturesquely put it: "These phenomena suggest to the guileless investigator the image of the superego peering through a Judas eye, scanning incoming percepts in order to decide which shall be permitted into consciousness (1949, p. 25)." Many counterinvestigators were not so guileless, however, and cries of "response bias" and "unequal frequency" were heard. They contended that the observer did perceive the dirty words but did not care to report them to the experimenter, or else that such words were so infrequently read that the observer was unpracticed in perceiving them. It was found that instructions and word frequency did indeed make a difference. The paradoxical nature of the finding (what was left of it) is still bothersome. In order to suppress a perception, must not the item first be recognized?

So-called autistic perception includes both perceptual defense and wishful perceiving. It is perception (if one should call it that) which is dominated by the person's affective state. Inner feelings and needs

---

[2] Nunally (1964) suggests that an organism tends to "amplify stimulation" from an object having reward value—he comes closer, his pupils dilate, etc. But would it therefore look bigger?

rather than stimulus information are said to control the perception. If so, something maladaptive is going on. Autism has been treated at length in a book on perceptual development by Solley and Murphy (1960), who comment thus: "Affect is part and parcel of the matrix of early experience and it is only through the impact of society's negative reinforcement of autistic perceptions that veridical perception is ever achieved, even in part (p. 78)." I do not share this view, for I think that veridical perception is adaptive. The individual does not have to be punished for misperception by society; he is punished for it by barking his shins or missing his plane.

The influence of culture on perception, however, is worth considering. The habits and attitudes characteristic of one's culture do surely have a selective effect in determining what one attends to. Is a Bushman more likely to scan a newspaper or examine animal tracks? Experiments are not necessary to convince us of the channeling of attention by culture.

Experiments purporting to show not just the channeling of attention by culture but the biasing of perception have been conducted by psychologists of the Transactional school (see Chapter 3). The argument runs that one's material environment is biased by containing typically some particular kind of furnishings such as all round huts and no angular, cornered houses (cf. Allport & Pettigrew, 1957). This bias weights the subject's experience so that he is inclined to see round things to the exclusion of angular ones. The argument sounds to me like James's example of the dogs raised in the Vatican, taking for granted that the environment and its furnishings are "dripped in" like rain, passively leaving their record, which deepens with every repeated shower.

The idea that perception is inference from habits built up through repeated impressions characteristic of a given material environment is discussed at length in a cross-cultural study of perceptual illusions by Segall, Campbell, and Herskovits (1966): "If human groups differ in their visual inference tendencies, it is because their visual environments differ (p. 78)." They suggest that one should be able to point to ecological differences and then relate them to perceptual inference differences. That differences in ecology should influence perception is reasonable, for a man's repertory of discriminated distinctive features is bound to depend on the objects and events that he has available to discriminate, the invariants that he has had an opportunity to discover. But that is not the same as passive weighting.

I have been trying to show that perception is an active search process and to say what it is that initiates and directs the search. Now I turn to the other aspect of the question: what terminates the search? This is the most interesting question of all, for what terminates the search decides what is retained as part of the organism's permanent repertory.

THE TERMINATION OF PERCEPTUAL SEARCH

What terminates the exploratory activity of perception? We are not interested in the mere cessation of ongoing activity, but in what is perceived when a search is terminated. What is satisfactory for perception and can be identified with its modification?

The answer to the last question where behavior is concerned has traditionally been reinforcement. Reinforcement has usually been conceived as reduction of some need state of the organism. Theories of operant learning, to be sure, have not always appealed to need reduction, but they have nevertheless considered reinforcers to be something applied externally by the experimenter: food pellets, water, release from painful stimulation, candy, and with human subjects praise, or faint murmurs of approval. Operant behavior followed by such reinforcement can be shown to increase in probability and this is thought by many learning psychologists to be the model for all learning. It is undoubtedly true that the responses of a subject can be controlled in this way by an experimenter, but I shall argue that experimenter control by reward or punishment is not a necessary condition for perceptual learning.

There must be some analogous principle for the reinforcement of perception. If reward and punishment do not govern perceptual learning, what does? Does knowledge of results, that is, being told whether or not one is correct at the end of an experimental trial? We shall first consider the relevant experiments with reward and punishment, and then go on to those concerned with knowledge of results.

Reward and Punishment

A number of experiments have attempted to demonstrate the effectiveness of rewards or punishments introduced by the experimenter for modification of perception.[3] The earliest of these experiments, and a

prototype of many later experiments, was performed by Schafer and Murphy (1943). An ambiguous figure, which could be perceived as either of two faces in profile, was the test display (see Fig. 7–3). Each profile was also available as a separate drawing. When one of the profiles was presented to the subject it was always accompanied by coins; when the other was presented, coins were retracted. After a series of such presentations, the ambiguous figure was shown. The subjects tended to report first

[3] Reviews of many of these can be found in Solley and Murphy (1960), in their chapters on the effect of rewards and punishments on perception.

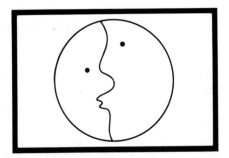

FIGURE 7–3. An ambiguous test figure which can be seen as either of two profiles.

(From R. Shafer & G. Murphy, The role of autism in a visual figure-ground relationship. *Journal of Experimental Psychology,* 1943, *32,* 336–337.)

the face which had been rewarded. The result was said to demonstrate autistic perception. This experiment was criticized on many grounds and was repeated by others with added controls (Rock & Fleck, 1950; Jackson, 1954; Solley & Long, 1958; Santos & Garvin, 1962). Some of these repetitions did not find autistic effects. In the one last cited, four comparisons of differently treated groups were made: reward vs. no-reward, punishment vs. no-punishment, reward and punishment, and a reward-punishment control group, in which rewards and punishments were assigned in a random manner to both faces. Punishment refers to withdrawal of coins. In only one condition, the punishment–no-punishment group, was there a difference in response to the test figure. The punished face was reported less often than the neutral one. Santos and Garvin conclude, "It is apparent that the Schafer-Murphy effect is not as general as might have originally been expected."

Supposing that a preference is actually demonstrated for the rewarded profile, what are we to conclude? Is this result really a modification of perception, or is it merely a change in the probability of a reporting response, a change in response bias? How would a child (or an adult, for that matter) interpret the procedure of being given a nickel whenever a certain profile was shown, but having one taken away whenever another was shown? Surely many subjects would infer that one face was supposed to be chosen. Solley and Long (1958) attempted to control for this possibility by having the subjects guess which face was going to be shown before seeing the test figure, and proving that there was no correlation between the guess and the report. In this experiment, however, the reported perceptions did not coincide with the reward-punishment prediction, the results being as often against the prediction as for it. The added instructions seem only to have obscured what was going on.

The outcome of these experiments is only confusion. It is pertinent to remind ourselves of Tolman's distinction between learning and performance; it is unlikely that the subjects were learning anything with respect to the ambiguous pair of profiles. The supposition is borne out by an experiment (Beatty, Dameron, & Greene, 1959) in which a different measure was used, the threshold for correct identification of a profile. No difference was found between the profile receiving money reward and that accompanied by withdrawal of money.

What would happen if the punishment in these experiments were really noxious and not merely the withdrawal of coins already presented by the experimenter? Smith and Hochberg (1954) employed profiles and an ambiguous test figure, as in the foregoing experiments, but associated one of the two profiles with an electric shock. The nonshocked face was reported more frequently in the test series. However, in another experiment (Pustell, 1957), shock-associated figures were seen as clearest in a test period. One can make a post hoc explanation by supposing that shock caused the figure to stand out. Mangan (1959, 1961) found that the results in this situation varied with the intensity of the shock; weak or medium shock served as an emphasizer, while strong shock had the opposite effect. But in either case, it is very unlikely that the subject learned to see something that he could not or did not see before.

Let us consider just one more experiment where an aversive stimulus was presented with a drawn figure in a training series and where the judgment used for a criterion measure was less susceptible to the charge of response bias. Hochberg and Brooks (1958) presented subjects with four polygonal figures, displayed three times each for ten seconds. Two of them were accompanied by bursts of unpleasant sound coming over earphones, described as a "chalk-on-blackboard screech." In a test period, 16 test patterns were presented, in each of which one of the four training figures had been embedded. They were presented with progressively increasing back lighting (making the embedded figure more visible) until the subject found the training figure. A majority of the subjects had higher recognition thresholds for the punished figures. But a plausible interpretation of these results would be that the screeches were distracting and so the opportunity to observe during training was not as great for the punished figures. The subject had to notice their distinctive features so as to recognize them later under conditions of concealment, but the opportunity for discovering these was unequal.

A similar interpretation of the many studies of the perception of size of objects as dependent on their values was suggested by McCurdy, who said, "departures from accurate size estimation which have been taken to favor the hypothesis that increase of value induces phenomenal magnification might better be interpreted as the result of the interference of expansive emotional states with meticulous adjustments (1956, p. 167)."

That the effect of reward on discrimination in animals is not to alter ability to discriminate, but only to change response probabilities is suggested by an experiment with pigeons (Boneau, Holland, & Baker, 1965). The performance of pigeons in discriminating colors was examined on trials before and after they had occasionally received reward for pecking when light of a given wavelength was displayed. Immediately after a reward, the birds showed increased probability of response to an unrewarded wavelength. But ability to discriminate was not changed for, by two trials later, the birds were differentiating between wavelengths 1 millimicron apart. These experimenters concluded that there was no change in ability of the pigeon to respond differentially to very similar wavelengths as a consequence of reward, but that the bird's tendency to peck, whatever the wavelength, was increased.

The conclusion from these experiments is that reward and punishment undoubtedly influence behavior, but it is very doubtful if they play an important role in perceptual learning, and certainly they do not play a necessary role.

Knowledge of Results

In most laboratory learning experiments, and in schoolroom learning as well, reinforcement does not involve concrete rewards and punishments, but some kind of informational feedback. The experimenter says "right" or "wrong," and the teacher corrects the pupil. Is it knowledge given by the tutor that selects the modification in perceptual learning? A number of perceptual experiments are available in which knowledge of results has been compared with practice unaccompanied by such knowledge.

Certain experiments of Thorndike's (1932) requiring absolute judgments of visual length of line, of the area of a form, of kinesthetic length, and of pressure on the skin seemed to show the need for knowledge of results if the estimate were to improve with practice. In one experiment, for example, the subject estimated the length in centimeters of strips of white paper from 3 to 27 cm. long. Practice consisted of making repeated judgments followed by the words "right" or "wrong." All the subjects improved from a pretest to a posttest. Thorndike compared these results with practice when the experimenter said nothing, and concluded that knowledge was essential for improvement. Later work has shown, however, that although knowledge given by the experimenter has the effect of correcting a constant error in the estimates, and does so rapidly, mere repetition without such information is effective in lowering the variable error. Seashore and Bavelas (1941), examining Thorndike's own data in a line-drawing experiment, found that repeated practice without correction resulted in more and more consistent approximation to a standard judgment, although the standard might be off by a constant amount. Baker and Young (1960), giving correction with a similar task, found that the sign of the constant error was learned very early in training, whereas subsequent practice brought about gradual reduction of variable error.

That correction effects a reduction in constant error was shown by Gibson and Bergman (1954), when subjects estimated the distances in yards of targets in a field. The shift occurred within the first few training trials. The subjects got an anchor for the scale of yards and after that correction had little effect. Eriksen (1958) studied the effect of correction on absolute judgments of brightness, of size, and with several multidimensional series (e.g., size-brightness, size-brightness-hue). Correction with practice made a difference when learning curves were plotted on the basis of error, including the constant error. But when the data were treated in terms of information transmitted (the consistency of the judgments, regardless of absolute error), there was no significant difference between correction and noncorrection. Practice increased the specificity of the judgments under both conditions. Eriksen concluded that correction contributes primarily to the "choice of response" and only secondarily to the subject's ability to discriminate among the stimuli. Its effect is on the numbers used by the subject, rather than on what is perceived. Wohlwill (1964), in an experiment on distance bisection, gave subjects training with correction. While the correction reduced an initial bias in the judgments, the effect was ephemeral and had little transfer value to distances different from those used in the training.

Along with this evidence that correction operates primarily on the words used by the subjects, we need to consider experiments where purely perceptual modification seems to have occurred without benefit of an experimenter's intervention. The information coming from one's own performance must be determining in this case. It would be available to the subject himself whatever the experimenter does. An interesting experimental situation where practice resulted in improved perception without correction by the experimenter is the task of setting oneself to the postural vertical in a chair which has been tilted laterally (Solley, 1956; Pearson & Hauty, 1959, 1960). A blindfolded observer, by pressing buttons on either arm of the chair, could drive it slowly to the right or left until he felt perfectly upright. Accuracy increased over a series of trials even though the subject was never told either the magnitude or direction of his errors. Pearson and Hauty then compared the improvement under three conditions. In one, the subject was given visual information about his position after each trial by means of an illuminated pointer and dial in front of him. In another, he was given a postural anchor; that is, he was returned to the vertical position after each trial. In the third, he was given no information about errors. Improvement occurred in all three conditions.

In the last condition, it was found that alternation of right and left in passing through the vertical favored zeroing in on the feeling of the upright and resulted in progressive reduction of errors; this procedure seemed to give the subject unique proprioceptive information, a kind of intrinsic perceptual differentiation permitting him to check his last setting.

The feedback from overt action, that is from gross bodily movements as well as from exploratory and searching movements of a sensory system, is held to be essential for perceptual development and learning by many psychologists. For example, we considered in an earlier chapter the motor copy theory of perceptual development popular among Russian psychologists, according to which the world is mirrored by actions which make copies of it. Another example is a theory popular with many American psychologists and expressed most often by Richard Held (1963). It holds that perceptual development requires "movement-produced sensory feedback." Evidence for this position has been adduced mainly from experiments on perceptual adaptation to a rearranged or distorted visual stimulus array, such as that produced by a wedge prism worn in front of an eye (see Chapter 10 for a discussion of these experiments). The notion of reafference or feedback stimulation resulting from self-produced movements of the organism is taken from von Holst (1954). Passive movements such as being conveyed in a vehicle or having one's arm moved by the experimenter are thought to be ineffective for perceptual learning or development. The reason is that the feedback from the subject's movement has to be matched against an internal copy of the commanded movement. In von Holst's terms, the reafferent signal has to be compared with the efferent signal.

An experiment designed to test this view was performed by Held and Bossom (1961). The subjects wore spectacles made of wedge prisms oriented so as to displace their visual fields laterally. Half of the subjects walked about while viewing the apparently displaced environment, initiating their own movements. The other half were moved about passively in wheelchairs so that they viewed the same environment but did not initiate the movements. The active subjects made initial errors of localizing objects in the real world, but these were substantially reduced after an hour of walking about. The passive subjects did not show a significant degree of improvement in localizing.

The interpretation of this experiment has been disputed. One argument is that the active subject simply gets more information about the nature of the optical displacement produced by the prisms. It has also been argued (Weinstein et al., 1964; Howard et al., 1965) that other sources of information than those from active movement could permit the subject to detect the optical displacement and should also permit adaptation to take place. The sense of one's own body, if it allows perception of the changed relation between the seen and the felt position of a limb, should be such a source, and there is evidence for this interpretation (Harris, 1963; Wallach, Kravitz, & Lindauer, 1963). I will argue in Chapter 10 that the essential condition for perceptual adaptation in these experiments is an opportunity for the subject to detect what I call multimodal stimulus invariants. Movement should facilitate such detection. But as far as our present question goes, we can certainly conclude that modification of perception in prism experiments is spontaneous and does not require extrinsic correction or reward or punishment given by an experimenter.

Visual discrimination and recognition have, been shown to improve with practice without benefit of correction by an experimenter. One example will suffice here. Munsinger (1965) showed children and adults random shapes of different levels of complexity. The shapes (closed figures) were constructed so as to contain five or twenty independent turns (angles or corners). There were four sets of four of these random shapes. One shape was shown the subject briefly by means of a tachistoscope. A set of four was in front of him, and he was to pick from among them the one he had seen. There were twenty trials per day for each set for four days. The subject was not told whether he was correct or not, but accuracy of recognition rose from the first day to the fourth; accuracy increased for both children and adults, for both levels of complexity, most for the five-turn shapes. The subject could gradually pick out distinguishing features of the more complex shapes and look for these. For the five-turn shapes, he might with practice detect an overall structural characteristic that permitted easy discrimination of one shape from the three accompanying it on the recognition chart.

One further point remains about perceptual learning in contrast to response learning where external reinforcement is a factor. When reinforcement is withdrawn in the typical response learning situation, extinction occurs. But extinction does not seem to occur in perceptual learning. Many years ago (Gibson, 1940), I attempted to make a stimulus response analysis of paired associate learning by way of Pavlovian principles of conditioning. The principles I chose were generalization and differential inhibition. The idea was that the stimulus members of a list generalized with one another initially, and that differential inhibition of the generalization was effected during practice through reinforcement by knowledge of results. Getting the response associated was a second stage, following the stimulus differentiation. As generalization increased, more confusion of responses would be expected and the list should be harder to learn. This prediction was indeed fulfilled (Gibson, 1942). But the analogy to conditioned response learning was imperfect. In Pavlovian conditioning, differential inhibition is said to dissipate in the manner of extinction after reinforcement is withdrawn. But differentiation did not extinguish in my experiment. There was no evidence of spontaneous recovery of generalization, which would require unequal forgetting for high- and low-generalization lists. I would now say that differentiation of the stimulus items (learning to tell them apart) depends on discovering the distinctive features of the set and does not depend on correction of erroneous responses. Some responses were forgotten after 24 hours, but the stimuli were still distinguishable. The point is that perceptual learning is not response learning, and the selection of distinctive features in perceptual learning is not dependent on differential reinforcement given by the experimenter.

Reduction of Uncertainty

We are now facing the central question: what is the selective principle of perceptual learning? It should be clear that it is inside, and that it is self-regulated and automatic. I will maintain that the selective principle can be understood if two things are kept in mind: first, that the stimulation continually impinging on the sense organs is full of information; and second, that the organism extracts information from this stimulation when perception occurs. That is retained which reduces uncertainty. Detection of information about invariant relations reduces subjective uncertainty. It even reduces information, in the technical sense of the communication theorists.

As I pointed out earlier in the chapter (see reference to Egger and Miller, p. 129), the term "information" has two meanings, so that use of the term sometimes leads to apparent paradoxes. Getting information about something—discovering the invariant properties of an object, for instance—reduces subjective uncertainty. Perceptual learning can also be thought of as reducing uncertainty in the sense of the number of alternatives to be cognized, by filtering the irrelevant and detecting invariant relations. This latter is close to the technical meaning of information. I do not believe there is a contradiction in saying that reduction of uncertainty occurs in both senses of the term. The exploratory action of the sense organs eliminates a lot of the potential input, and more important, the action of the nervous system in processing what gets to the receptors is to extract the invariants so that a great mass of the input (what might be called sensations) has no effect on perception.

Consider in relation to this concept what is learned: distinctive features, invariants, and structure. They are the epitome of the reduction of uncertainty. Out of a mass of stimulus properties emanating from a set of objects, the perceiving organism learns to choose only those necessary for distinguishing between the objects. To go back to the example of aircraft recognition (Chapter 5), it will be remembered that both the results of experiment and the introspections of subjects bore out the conclusion that only the critical differences should be emphasized for effective discrimination—an obvious reduction of the input to be processed.

Consider the invariants in the perception of events. When a car drives toward you its projected size or proximal stimulus keeps increasing, microsecond by microsecond. But you do not see an infinite number of cars of larger and larger size. There is an invariant aspect of the stimulation, a rule relating two properties of the stimulus over time which can be discovered and attended to, and which has manifest utility for the reduction of uncertainty.

The case for detection of structural variables as having utility for reduction of uncertainty is clearest of all. Structure provides the basis for chunking, processing many bits of information as a unit (Miller, 1956). In later chapters, I shall discuss the development of perception of structural variables, the higher order relations between features. The human infant attends early to certain features of the human face, but he learns after six or seven months to differentiate whole faces from one another, and eventually even isolates and discriminates facial expressions which are invariant over different faces. Development of perception of language and learning to read are cases where structure—order in the system—provides the basis for processing larger units and thus reducing the information.

After I had written these pages I heard a paper at the International Congress of Psychology delivered by V. P. Zinchenko of Moscow (Zinchenko, 1966). I had read some of his work before, and thought of him as belonging to the motor copy tradition of Russian psychology. Nevertheless, the theory expressed sounded very close to what I am saying. Zinchenko discussed object recognition, suggesting that it begins with a stage of "acquaintance," which discovers and selects "informative content adequate to the task." It goes on to a stage of "collating" the "given alphabet of the objects." To quote him,

The process of collating is radically reduced at the expense of eliminating excessive and redundant information, selecting critical and basic features, and transforming groups of separate features into structural "unit" ones. The identification of objects by such consolidated "unit" (specific) features is very rational, as the process of collating several features is replaced by collating one feature. . . . At the expense of organizing separate features into structures, the speed of processing information by the observer increases, the time of identification and response is reduced, the operative memory of the observer is unloaded, and more favorable conditions are created for anticipating and predicting as compared with the action at the previous level. . . . Overcoming the redundance of external stimulation, the developing system of perceptual actions brings information to the form more adequate to be taken into account in one's behavior (Zinchenko, pp. 70–71).

Zinchenko believes that the perceptual system, unaided by more complex processes, such as thinking and imagination, transforms input so as to render further processing of information more adaptive, and that it does so autonomously. He believes that perceptual "manipulations" are similar to transformations which took place earlier in practical action, such as rotating or straightening up. The analogy with practical action may be only a halfhearted one, however, for in defining a perceptual action, Zinchenko says (p. 64): "A perceptual action is a specific self-regulating process of search and processing of information, determined by the tasks of a living system, possessing a feedback mechanism and adapting to the specific features of the investigated object." This does not sound like a definition of practical or executive action (another Russian term), and in fact I was amazed at the closeness of its agreement with my own views.

It should be clear, however, that I do not think that the invariant over time, or the perceived structure, is integrated or pieced together by associating moment-to-moment snapshots or elements. Rather, the invariant and the structure are present in the stimulus flux; the active perceiver who explores and searches the environment may find and extract them. The infant of three months or so spends a great deal of time watching his hands; he brings them together, he moves them away from and then toward himself, he rotates them. This is the most useful activity for detecting invariants over time; so good that Piaget (Piaget & Inhelder, 1956) has even suggested that the child is experimenting so as to learn the geometry of space.

I think, therefore, that perceptual learning is taking out from the total stimulus information whatever is invariant about the world, whether it be a distinctive feature or a rule. Things are associated, to be sure; they are already associated in the world when they are contiguous with one another spatially or temporally. Noticing the relationship is information-reducing, whereas processing each sensation separately and associating one with another would be the opposite.

An Illustrative Experiment

I have been arguing that perception is active and adaptive, and that perceptual learning is self-regulated and progresses toward reduction of uncertainty in processing stimulus information. Then, in any perceptual task, we should expect the subject to shift his strategy toward the optimal one for the task and, when opportunity for practice is given, we should expect the information processed to be reduced over time. An experiment by Yonas and Gibson (1967) confirms these expectations and provides a concrete illustration of the rather abstract notions set forth in the preceding paragraphs.

The task chosen was disjunctive reaction time. The subject sat before a small screen where the stimulus display was projected and had his hand on a lever which could be moved either to the right or the left. The stimuli were a set of nine letters, of which one or more were identified as belong-

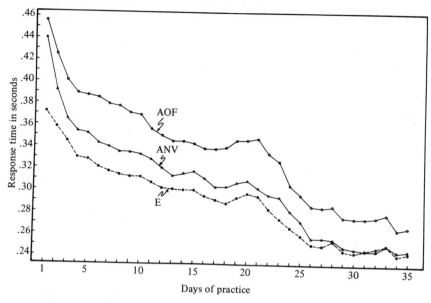

FIGURE 7–4. Practice curve for a long-term subject in a disjunctive reaction-time experiment by Yonas and Gibson.

Latency declined with practice in all three conditions, but most in condition ANV, where it was possible to differentiate a positive from a negative set of stimuli on the basis of a single distinctive feature.

ing to the positive set, requiring a unidirectional lever response. All the others belonged to the negative set, and were to be responded to by a push of the lever in the opposite direction.[4] The subject initiated the display by pressing a switch held in his left hand, at the same time starting a clock. The stimulus letter appeared projected on the screen and he moved the lever as fast as possible to the appropriate side. The positive stimuli were lettered beside the switch on the correct side, so that the subject did not have to remember this relationship.

There were three conditions in the experiment. In one (I), only one letter was assigned to the positive set. In a second (II), three letters were assigned to it. In a third (III), three letters were again assigned, but they were so chosen that a single distinctive feature (a diagonal) would serve to distinguish them from all the letters of the negative set. The total set of letters was identical for the three conditions.

We expected, on the basis of Sternberg's research, that latencies would be shorter when there was only one letter in the positive set. We expected,

[4] The task was suggested to us by experiments of Sternberg (1967).

on the basis of our own hypotheses, that the two conditions with three letters in the positive set would have equal latencies at first, but that with practice, latencies for Condition III should drop, approaching the practice curve for Condition I. The predictions were confirmed. Over five blocks of 27 trials each, latencies dropped for all three conditions. The curve for Condition I was lower than the other two. The curves for Conditions II and III started at the same point, but the curve for Condition III fell more rapidly. One subject, run for more than thirty days, reached an asymptote of practice, and the curve for Condition III did in fact fall to the level of Condition I. Condition II did not (see Fig. 7–4).

A few subjects noticed the single distinguishing feature, but most never did, and the times were much too fast for an intervening self-instruction. There appeared rather to be an automatic change in perceptual processing, reducing the information processed to the minimum distinctive feature. There was no differential reward involved, only self-regulatory processes within the subject.

SUMMARY

In the preceding chapters, the differentiation theory of perceptual learning was introduced and contrasted with an enrichment theory. It holds that perception does not develop by supplementing the stimulation, or by associating responses with it, but rather by differentiation of stimulation already rich in information. It is not "going beyond the information given," to use Bruner's words (1957), but consists rather in learning to extract the information in the available stimulation that has not already been detected and utilized. What is learned are distinctive feature, invariants, and higher orders of both, which I referred to as structure. The mechanism of perceptual learning is not association, but filtering and abstraction. The process is an active one, involving exploration and search. The search is directed by the task and by intrinsic cognitive motives. The need to get information from the environment is as strong as to get food from it, and obviously useful for survival. The search is terminated not by externally provided rewards and punishments, but by internal reduction of uncertainty. The products of the search have the property of reducing the information to be processed. Perception is thus active, adaptive, and self-regulated.

8

Perceptual Learning and the Total Cognitive Process

Perceptual learning has been considered, so far, without much reference to other cognitive processes such as remembering, attaining concepts, and using language. Now I want to examine the place of perceptual learning in the total cognitive process and to clarify its interaction with other processes. This is a large order, and one chapter cannot fill it in detail. But the relation of perceptual learning to memorial representation, to productive activity ensuing upon it, to concepts, and to language will be briefly considered with the aim of showing their interrelations in the total cognitive process.

RECOGNITION

The term discrimination usually implies a process of simultaneous or nearly simultaneous comparison and choice. Yet we can learn to perceive the similarities and differences among objects even when they are not simultaneously projected in a stimulus array. The term recognition implies the judgment that this object is the same as one perceived before. As we learn to recognize that an object is the same one we saw before, we also learn to distinguish it from a rather similar one previously presented. The simultaneous comparison is no doubt the simplest for differentiation of two stimulus objects and the discovery of contrasts and feature differences must begin in this way. Comparison of a present object with one which is no longer in the immediate environment is a costlier process.

Consider the scribble experiment described in Chapter 5. The subjects were shown a standard scribble, which was then removed. Afterward, a series of other scribbles, varying in one or more dimensions, were presented along with a few duplicates for recognition. If the deviating scribbles were presented simultaneously with the standard, the adult subjects could distinguish them at once (though the younger children could not always do so). But recognition of sameness required a mean of three repetitions of the series, even for adult subjects.

Why should recognition, in the sense of detecting sameness to or difference from an absent object, require more exposure or more repetitions than simultaneous comparison? The usual answer is that a storage process has become necessary. What is stored or represented has been called by various terms, such as "image" and "schema." Image is a reasonable term if there is literally a representation of a particular object. Feigenbaum and Simon (1963), whose model for perceiving and learning was described briefly in Chapter 6, spoke of an image of a previously presented stimulus which could be compared feature by feature with a present one as it was sorted through a discrimination net. Recall also Pick's experiment (see Chapter 6, p. 98) in which the opportunity to utilize a representation of a particular standard shape was compared with the opportunity to utilize learned dimensions of difference (kinds of transformation of the shape). The representation was valuable, it appeared, to the extent that the comparison shape was temporally separated from the standard.

An unanalyzed copy (template) has sometimes been thought of as stored and matched in a holistic fashion to current input in the recognition process. Since I believe that perceptual learning involves differentiation of distinctive features, I believe that comparison with anything remembered requires more than a representation which is a mere copy. I think that recognition of objects over temporal separation requires that their distinguishing properties be articulated. Woodworth (1938), in discussing memory for form in a famous chapter of his *Experimental Psychology,* cited much evidence to show that learning of an unfamiliar figure depends on analysis of it. Analysis implies attention to distinctive properties.

A nice example of a memory image in the above sense is provided by research on aircraft recognition by Gagné and Gibson (1947). Members of a class of aviation trainees were given extended practice in recognizing a number of different makes of aircraft by repeated presentations of projected slides of the aircraft, with identification and correction. Characteristics of the plane shapes were pointed out by the instructor, but there was no emphasis on learning these features (as there had been in the experiment reported in Chapter 5). At the end of thirty hours of instruction, each student was asked to draw three views of each of eight planes. The size of each drawing was kept constant by marks which fixed the length and wingspan, but not the shape or proportions. Composite drawings were then constructed for each view of each plane. The shape of the composite was finally compared with the real plane shape by superimposing the composite drawing over the outline of the silhouette of the aircraft, using a photographic enlarger to bring the outlines to the same size.

Inspection of the composite drawing and the superposed plane silhouette (see Fig. 8–1) reveal, first, that the planes were differentiated from one another, and were not representations of a generalized airplane. The drawings were specific to a given plane. On the other hand, there were consistent differences between the composite drawing and the actual shape of the aircraft's silhouette. These constant errors were not such as to cause misidentification of the plane, but were in fact exaggerations of

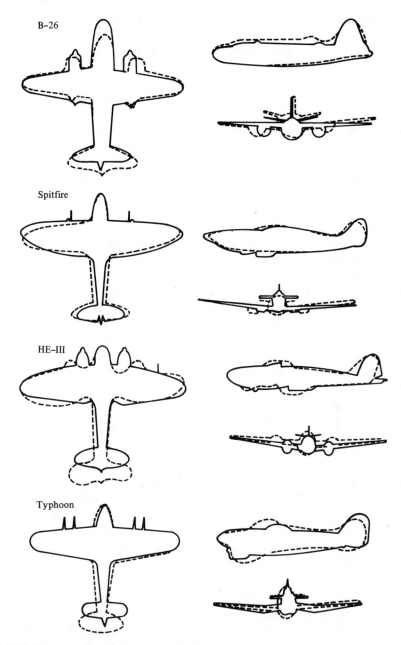

FIGURE 8–1. Composite remembered shapes of aircraft as compared with their real shapes, after Gagné.

(From J. J. Gibson [Ed.], *Motion Picture Testing and Research*. Report No. 7, Army Air Forces Aviation Psychology Program Research Reports, 1947, pp. 142–143.)

those features which made one plane distinguishable from others, so that the composites are in a sense caricatures. It seems, therefore, that memory images or schematic representations of the aircraft were indeed based on distinctive features detected while looking for differences.

PRODUCTION

The evidence from the composite drawings of aircraft suggests that distinctive features learned in the course of discriminating differences play a role in production as well as in the formation of memory representations. Other evidence comes from children's responses to simple forms when their behavior in discriminating is compared to copying such shapes as triangles and circles. Maccoby and Bee (1965), discussing the lag between perceiving and performing, suggest that copying a figure requires that its attributes be differentiated and that the more attributes of a figure a child has differentiated, the more accurate his drawing will be. The average child differentiates a circle, square, and triangle well enough to place each one accurately in a form board by two years of age, but it is common knowledge that he is not able to copy them accurately until much later. Copying a circle is placed in the Stanford-Binet test at three years, a square at four years, and a diamond at seven years. That the child has, however, perceived some distinguishing features of the more difficult figures is clear from his attempts before a good drawing can be produced. A characteristic error in drawing the square and the diamond is to exaggerate the corners, producing figures with ears (see Fig. 8–2). The error is sometimes said to result from an incapacity to perceive part-whole relationships, but it is corrected with practice, and correct recognition precedes correct drawing (Kaspar & Schulman, 1964).

The fact that a child of five who can draw a square quite acceptably may nevertheless be unable to draw a diamond has long been a puzzle. Why should drawing diagonals present a problem? Research by Rudel and Teuber (1963) showed that the child has difficulty in discriminating oblique lines from one another, compared to verticals and horizontals. It is not surprising then that producing an adequate diamond is a later achievement than drawing a square.

Further evidence of the lag between the ability to differentiate visual patterns and the ability to produce them, and evidence of the role of distinctive figural properties in production, is available in a paper by Gollin (1960). Gollin had children copy simple line drawings. On the day following the copying, they were given a matching test. The standard figure was presented, along with the child's copy and three others, one of which was an exact reproduction. Even in those cases where the child's own copy was poor, he chose the exact match. Furthermore, the poor drawings in many cases did include the distinctive features of the line drawings, albeit ill-organized or exaggerated. An eight-pointed star, for instance, was

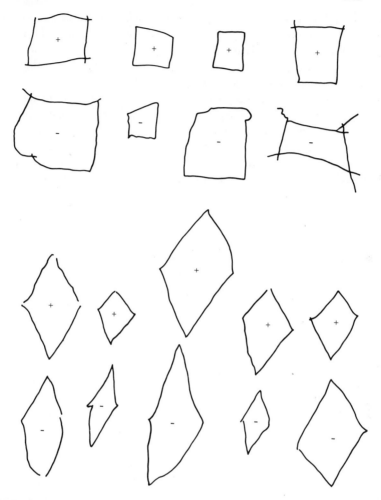

FIGURE 8–2. Drawings of squares and diamonds taken from the Stanford-Binet scoring manual.

The pluses (considered marginal passes) are contrasted with the minuses (failures), which often exaggerate corners by adding ears or other appendages. (From L. M. Terman & M. A. Merrill, *Measuring Intelligence,* Boston: Houghton Mifflin, 1937, pp. 220, 231.)

reproduced as a closed contour with points; but there were too many points —an exaggeration of the most prominent characteristic of the figure.

Experience in discriminating distinctive features of objects is thus a prerequisite not only for a representation adequate for comparison with absent objects, but also for reproducing them, even when the task is one of copying from a model. Piaget and Inhelder (1956) have emphasized the lag in development of representation as compared with perception, but have placed no stress on the role of distinguishing features in the development of representation. They stress, rather, the abstraction of shape, suggesting that it "is abstracted from the subject's own movements rather than from the object which occasions them." They also state that there is "an effort at composition based on the differentiated elements themselves," and that this process of composition is the "real mainspring in the abstraction of shape, p. 73)." Despite the emphasis on synthesis rather than analysis, their discussion of children's drawings is consistent with my point that differentiation of features shapes the memorial representation, and it also yields evidence that abstraction of distinguishing features precedes formation of an adequate memory image. Figure 8–3 from Piaget and

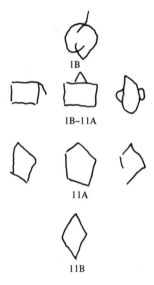

FIGURE 8–3.   Steps in the development of drawing a diamond.

(From J. Piaget & B. Inhelder, *The Child's Conception of Space* [London: Routledge & Kegan Paul, Ltd.; New York: Humanities Press, 1956].)

Inhelder illustrates developmental stages in the drawing of a diamond. They describe the stages as follows:

At substage IB the rhombus (diamond) is little more than a closed curve, after having been confused with the wandering open lines by which the children of substage IA distinguish shapes from spontaneously produced scribbles. But occasionally in substage IB the rough oval representing the rhombus is provided with a threadlike appendage denoting an acute angle. At the level midway between substages IB and IIA the rhombus acquires angles and straight sides though the slope of these cannot be controlled. Thus it is confused either with the square and rectangles or else with the triangle. Nevertheless, the acute angles together with the inclinations they govern are suggested in various ways, such as by lengths of straight line running from one corner of the square at an angle of 45°, or a triangle (beaks, hats, etc.) placed over the square. Alternatively, the obtuse angles may be indicated by means of little triangles or even curves (ears, etc.) on two sides of the square or rectangle (p. 75).

That an adequate representation is required for drawing, even when a standard is present for copying, is emphasized throughout; drawing implies for them the construction of an image, a transition from perception.

This view is reflected, to some extent, in the writing of Soviet psychologists. The following passage from Elkonin (1957, p. 56) presents the view that an internal image is constructed, but points out also that attention to distinctive features is basically involved: "It is also, presumably, on the basis of the orienting reflex that the child develops connections between those different properties of one and the same object which underlie formation of the image, and between the properties of an object and the means of action with it."

Memory images have been discussed so far only with reference to the visual system. There are memories for other sensory systems, too, and the course of development is presumably parallel to that for vision. A child discriminates phonemes of his own language before he can produce them accurately (Berko & Brown, 1961). It is far simpler to make a judgment of "same" or "different" for two simple melodies heard in immediate succession than it is to make the same judgment after a longer interval, and hardest of all to reproduce one or the other of them. In the case of the melody, we are a long way from being able to give an account in terms of distinctive features. That a pattern is abstracted is evident from the fact that a melody can be recognized when it is transposed in various ways, and it must be differentiated in some sense for recognition and reproduction to be possible. Sometimes literature affords us a better description than science. Note the following passage from Marcel Proust:

And so, hardly had the delicious sensation, which Swann had experienced, died away, before his memory had furnished him with an immediate transcript, summary, it is true, and provisional, but one on which he had kept his eyes fixed while the playing continued, so effectively that, when the same impression suddenly returned, it was no longer uncapturable. He was able to picture to himself its extent, its symmetrical arrangement, its notation, the strength of its expression; he had before him that definite object which was no longer pure music, but rather design, architecture, thought, and which allowed the actual music to be recalled. This time he had distinguished, quite clearly, a phrase which emerged for a few moments from the waves of sound (*Swann's Way,* p. 160, in *Remembrance of Things Past,* translated by C. K. Scott Moncrieff, 1934).

My conclusions so far are three. First, that some sort of memorial representation of the distinguishing and invariant features of a stimulus object or event is involved in differentiation of it from other objects or events in its absence. Second, that this representation is based on prior discovery of distinctive features of the object, or abstraction of invariant features of a pattern. Discrimination is thus prior to recognition. And third, that both discrimination and representation are prior to production. In other words, perceptual learning—discovery of distinguishing features and extraction of invariant patterns and relations—is a requisite for all the three processes, discrimination, recognition, and production, and the processes form a kind of cognitive hierarchy.

IMAGE, SCHEMA, AND CONCEPT

In the preceding pages I suggested that a memorial representation of an absent object may be involved in recognition. What sort of construct is this? It is not a mere copy in the sense of an immediate memory image. Perceptual learning is involved in its formation, for distinctive features must be abstracted through a differencing process, and an invariant pattern must be abstracted from the flow of enveloping and ensuing variously transformed stimuli.

Is this representation what Piaget terms a "schema"? It is a plan in a sense, since there must be a map of some sort, and a plan for action coordinated with it in the case of production. The plan for production contains the abstracted pattern and the articulated features, which may in the process of differentiation have been exaggerated. Piaget has used the term "schema" to refer to a sort of sensory-motor plan. The following sentences reveal his emphasis on the motor aspect: "the image is an internalized act of imitation, a copy or transfer, not of the object as such, but of the motor response required to bring action to bear upon the object. Thus, what the image furnishes, to a far greater degree than perception, is a *schema* of action (1956, p. 294)." The emphasis on action, in itself, is not inconsistent with the construct I have in mind, but the notion that the image is a copy of the action is. In the first place, it makes the action prior to the image, which creates some logical problems (especially since copying a geometric figure has been said to depend on the image). That exploratory activity is important in detecting properties of objects is surely true, but this need not imply that the activity itself is copied in an image. In the second place, the schema in Piaget's usage places no stress on its derivation from the discovery of distinctive features and pattern invariants, but such a derivation, it seems clear, is basic for the differentiated representation which serves for recognition. Piaget's hypothesis of assimilation of the perceptual process to the schema seems to imply, also, a kind of leveling or central tendency effect.

Other usages of the term "schema" imply, even more than Piaget's, a central tendency analogous to a composite photograph. Oldfield (1954) in writing of the convenience of the schema as a hypothesis for memory storage, emphasized its "generalized form." Bartlett (1932), who more than anyone is responsible for the hypothesis of a schema for remembering, emphasized alteration of the schema in the direction of conventionalization after the perceptual process and prior to recall. Such an alteration may occur, but we are concerned at this point with the role of perceptual learning in development of a memory image. The part played by "dominant details," which become articulated in Bartlett's notion of a schema, sounds closer to the discovery of distinctive features and their incorporation in the representation.

Attneave (1957), like Oldfield, spoke of a schema as a "representation of the central tendency or communality of the class of objects in question (1957, p. 81)." He familiarized subjects with "prototype" forms and then variants of them were presented as stimulus items in paired associates learning. Familiarization did more good when the same parts of the figure were subsequently varied than when different parts were varied. Attneave interpreted this as follows: "When an S who has become familiar with the prototype sees the first of the variations, his attention is drawn to those parts of the figure which differ from the prototype, and a set with respect to *where to look* for distinguishing characteristics is thereby established (p. 86)." His view is therefore not as different from mine, as the central-tendency notion implies. Subjects did make use of distinguishing features, and practice that permitted their differentiation was most effective. Attneave concluded that there is no reason why the term "schema" should not be extended to include the "whole system of class parameters."

The point can be raised that there are cognitive events which are highly generalized and nonspecific, many stages removed from the perceptual process. Of course this is true. Concepts involve not only abstraction of distinguishing features, as do the more concrete representations, but they may be class concepts or categories of very great generality and no specific reference (e.g., negative numbers). Common features of a group of objects may be abstracted to form a class concept, and there can even be concepts of classes of classes. The process of abstraction in the latter case no longer directly involves perceptual learning, since the material for abstraction is not in the immediate environment. There is a dimension of less to greater generality in passing from imaginal representations to class concepts. My concept of a tree is very general; my concept of an olive tree less so; and my image of the Russian olive tree in front of the house is highly specific. It has distinctive features which permit it to be differentiated from any other olive tree.

The discussion has implied so far that the distinctive features (as well as the abstraction of invariant patterns) are discovered in the course of perceptual learning, and that these processes are prior to forming a representation and a more generalized concept. This I think is true. But it is also true that a representation, once it is available, is itself useful in perceptual learning, and so on occasion is the more generalized concept. There is a feedback loop to a new discrimination process. Identification of the Russian olive tree is a good illustration. I had never seen a Russian olive tree and did not know there was one in the yard. But when some Boy Scouts rang the doorbell of my temporary residence and asked to see the Russian olive tree, it was quite easy to differentiate it from the other trees, because it passed the tests of an olive tree: its characteristic shape, gray-green foliage, and so on. The differences from other olive trees were detectable, but so were the features of an olive tree. The concept of the olive tree provided the "discrimination net," to use Feigenbaum and Simon's term, and the differences between the actual tree and the more generalized image yielded a newly differentiated perception. Thus the imaginal representation transfers to new discriminations and permits perceptual learning by providing the opportunity both for matching and for detection of differences.

Production, such as copying a diamond or a letter of the alphabet, or imitating an utterance, or repeating a tone has also been shown to depend on abstracting distinctive features and pattern invariants. And again, there can be shown to be a feedback loop to new perceptions. Production provides an opportunity for monitoring and self-check. As soon as it becomes possible, the child can compare his production with the event or object copied, and a new differencing process is possible. Correction of features or a gradual zeroing-in helps abstract a dimension and extract the invariant aspects of the pattern, recalling the analogy of the pattern playback.

Examples of the helpfulness of production in refining discrimination are available in the psychological literature. Experiments in training children to improve pitch in several cases required the subjects to sing the tones compared, with apparent success. Wyatt (1945) achieved excellent results by providing her subjects with double feedback, hearing the tone produced and also seeing the results on an oscilloscope, which permitted correction of the tone when it drifted. Pick (1963) has summarized Soviet experiments that found improvement of pitch discrimination related to motor feedback not only from vocal intonation but also from strength of scaled hand pressure. The latter case is complicated, since it suggests the involvement of both a conceptual scale and an opportunity for monitoring production so as to isolate tonal invariants. But it is clear that once an approximate production is possible, perceptual learning can be speeded by the resulting feedback of information and the new differencing process which the feedback permits.

THE ROLE OF VERBAL LABELS

That language is a mediating cue which confers distinctiveness on originally confounded, ambiguous, or indistinguishable stimuli has often been proposed. Proponents of the acquired distinctiveness or additive mediation theory have found the notion of verbal mediators especially attractive (see Chapter 4, pp. 64 ff.). If we decide against the additive mediation hypothesis in favor of the hypothesis that perceptual learning occurs through discovery of distinctive features and invariant patterns already present in stimulation, what role, if any, does the verbal label have in perceptual learning?

Language as a Facilitating Factor in Perceptual Learning

It is certainly true that verbal labels can be learned for objects, properties of objects, and concepts. But there is an important question of priority. Which comes first, the perception of the object as unique and the property as critical, or the name for it? It seems obvious to me that perception of objects and their features is prior in the developmental process to learning names for them. In the case of representation, the verbal label follows, normally, the differentiation of objects and their attributes. The child distinguishes faces from other objects long before he learns a word for face, and he learns the distinctive features of faces long before he can give verbal descriptions of noses as sharp or blunt, eyes as blue or brown, chins as protruding or receding, brows as high or low. He discriminates the phonemes of his own language, most assuredly, without having any verbal labels to attach to them, since in fact he can discriminate many of them before he can produce them. He can certainly produce them before he can name them—how many of us could label them?

Yet there comes a time in the long course of human cognitive development when words have been learned for a number of objects and for many of their properties. When words have been added to the cognitive repertory perceptual learning can be facilitated by them. This can happen in two ways: one, by drawing attention to previously unnoticed features when an educational instrument is at hand to point them out; and two, by increasing the efficiency of remembering, when an absent standard must be compared with a present stimulus. New objects can sometimes be characterized economically by previously learned labels (I note Woodworth's [1938] observation that a new form can often be conveniently remembered by cataloguing it with a familiar label and then a notation of departure from the exact label, a so-called schema with correction, such as "square with a notch in it").

Consider two experiments described earlier, the scribble experiment and the profile experiment. Both of these experiments were conducted by a recognition procedure. In the scribble experiment, the subject had to discover the dimensions of difference by which a number of scribbles deviated from a standard one, so as to recognize the standard as the same when it reappeared and so as to differentiate it from the others. The older subjects often spontaneously named these properties. The names, if they were correctly available, could be combined to characterize the standard and could facilitate remembering its distinctive features and comparing them with the other scribbles. Such a process undoubtedly accounted to some extent for the difference between the age groups. In the profile experiment, the features which differentiated figures could be fairly readily specified by labels when they were in their physiognomic position and again, this could have helped in holding on to a standard in its absence (rehearsing it, in fact). They might have had a selective role in guiding discrimination, also, since the subject could direct himself to compare chins, noses, and other features of faces.

Differentiating features must be noticed before they can be labeled. But after labels can be matched to features, they can exert a selective role in perceiving. The superior value of relevant labels to irrelevant ones in the acquired-distinctiveness experiments is only to be expected, for the role of the label is not to add a distinctive feature, but to point to one (see Chapter 4). The acquired-equivalence experiments become clearer as well. If common labels are learned to objects so as to call attention to certain features which they share, these features will be sought out in observing the objects and potential differences will go unnoticed. If a subject is forced to learn that half the shapes presented to him are wide and the other half narrow, regardless of their other features, the wide ones will be more confusable with other similar wide shapes than if he had observed the shapes while looking for their unique properties (see Ellis et al., 1964).

The question of priority arises for concepts and language, as well as for perception and language. In a recent paper on concepts, Kendler (1964) presented the view that a child, in acquiring a concept, has acquired "some implicit response, usually, although not necessarily, verbal in nature (p. 230)." According to his mediational view, concept acquisition is an associative process and concepts function as both cues and responses. Developmental differences Kendler thinks will be discovered to be localized in "response capabilities (p. 231)," which he categorizes primarily (three out of four ways) as dependent on language development, its increasing complexity, and its integration with other behavior.

In an earlier paper, Kendler stated that in concept learning of the kind he was investigating, the adult human subject abstracted the important features of the stimuli to which he was consistently responding and that it was to the cue properties of this implicit (mediated) response that the correct response (presumably verbal) was associated (Kendler, Glucksberg, & Keston, 1961). Though stated in S-R terms, this view is somewhat closer to the writer's.

An interesting view on the relation of language to the formation of concepts was expressed by Lenneberg (1962). In discussing the question of concept-language priority, he stated that children learn to use words following a relatively universal maturational schedule because they can match a word given them to a concept only when the concept has become available. In arguing for the priority of the concept, Lenneberg pointed out that congenitally deaf children, literally without language until five or six years of age, nevertheless show evidence of complex inferences and concepts.

Experiments by Furth (1961) provide convincing evidence that this is true. Furth proposed that cognitive capacity develops with experience, whether or not spoken language is part of the child's experience, and that the role of language is therefore extrinsic; that language may increase the efficiency of problem solution but not determine it. To investigate this hypothesis, he compared deaf and hearing children on several concept learning tasks. Three concepts, "sameness," "symmetry," and "opposition," were to be learned. They were chosen because different predictions could be made for the three. "Sameness" should be familiar, and perhaps equally so, to the two groups, since deaf children have a gesture for this idea, even though they have no word. "Symmetry" is unfamiliar, and probably equally so, to both, since hearing children seldom have this concept before the age of twelve. "Opposition" is a familiar concept to hearing children beyond six years, but not to deaf children. The three concept tasks were learned by groups of deaf and hearing children ranging from seven to twelve years old. Results for the "sameness" and "symmetry" concepts showed no superiority of the hearing children; in fact, there was a difference in favor of the deaf children on the symmetry task. On the "opposition" task, the hearing children were superior. The superiority of the hearing children in learning an "opposition" concept confirms the hypothesis that language can facilitate concept learning; the fact that these children knew words for long-short, big-little, and so on, helped in forming correct oppositive judgments for the dimensions used in the task (size, volume, length, number, brightness, position, and texture). But that language is not a necessary prerequisite for development of an abstract concept is clear from the outcome in the "symmetry" and "sameness" tasks, and from the fact that a majority of the deaf subjects did learn the "opposition" concept in spite of their verbal poverty.

One can, furthermore, point to cases of conceptual behavior in animals incapable of speech. The "oddity" concept can be learned by monkeys and transferred from one problem to another (see Harlow, 1951). Robinson (1955) has shown that chimpanzees can learn a concept of "sameness." And Weinstein (1941) was able to train monkeys in color categorization so successfully that they matched for color even when size, form, brightness, and saturation of the samples were varied from trial to trial. It seems reasonable to conclude, then, that language can exert an influence on both perception and conceptual behavior but that learning in either case does not depend on it.

The Whorfian Hypothesis

Linguists and psychologists have long been influenced in their thinking by a fact called to their attention by Benjamin Whorf, that one language is not necessarily directly translatable or mappable into another. Social psychologists have sometimes been led to the hypothesis that the concepts and even the percepts of men in a given culture are determined by the language of that culture. Such an hypothesis implies a theory of perceptual learning, that it is determined by the verbal environment. To quote Whorf, "We dissect nature along lines laid down by our native languages (Whorf, 1961, p. 464)."

To what extent is it true that perception is differentiated according to the categories laid down by language? Because the Eskimo has a larger vocabulary of terms indicating different qualities of snow than does the average man of another culture, can it be inferred that the Eskimo discriminates differences in snow with greater precision? The fact that a man does not have words for several kinds of snow does not in itself demonstrate that he is unable to perceive differences between them. That words may direct us to look for and discover features which we might not otherwise notice is, on the other hand, entirely likely.

Brown and Lenneberg (1954) reported experimental data relevant to the proposition that language (lexical) differences are indicative of cognitive differences. They chose hues (Munsell colors) and secured, first, codability indices of 24 colors. The codability index included five measures (length of naming responses, reaction time of naming, consistency of naming, etc). A factor analysis of the data indicated a general factor, codability, which might be described as consistent nameability, since degree of agreement between subjects had the highest factor loading. A discriminability score was also calculated for each of the colors from perceptual distance data between colors (taken from the Newhall, Nickerson, and Judd charts). The discriminability score gave a color's distinctiveness from the colors surrounding it. There was a negligible correlation (.074) between codability and distinctiveness of the colors. The colors were then presented to new subjects in a series of recognition tests. Four groups of subjects were asked to recognize colors under four conditions by pointing to a color on a chart including all 24. The conditions varied the number of colors presented at once for recognition, and the time between first presentation and recognition judgment. The latter variable was included because the subjects indicated that they named the color when it was first exposed, before the recognition test, and it was predicted that codability would increase in importance as the interval was lengthened. For Group A, only one color was exposed at a time with a 7 sec. interval before recognition. For Group B, four colors were exposed with a 7 sec. interval. For Group C, four colors were exposed with a 30 sec. interval. For Group D, four colors were exposed with a 3 min. interval. Table 8–1 gives the correlations between codability, discriminability, and recognition for the four groups. The figures tend to confirm the expectation that codability increases in importance as the interval between exposure and recognition is lengthened, at least when the influence of discriminability is held constant. It is interesting to note that, overall, discriminability predicts recognition better than codability. Language differences (codability) are related, it seems, to ability to recognize a color when memory is taxed by increasing

TABLE 8–1

Correlations between Codability (C), Discriminability (D), and Recognition (R) Under Four Conditions of Recognition

Group	C with R	R with D	C with R, D constant
A	.248	.540*	.248
B	.411	.460*	.426*
C	.415	.503*	.438*
D	.487*	.505*	.523*

* $p \leqq .05$

From R. W. Brown & E. H. Lenneberg, A Study in language and cognition. *Journal of Abnormal Social Psychology*, 1954, *54*, 454–462.

the number of colors to be recognized and by lengthening delay between exposure and recognition. Discriminability of the color outweighs the codability factor when the delay is short, and it is just as significantly related to recognition with long delays.

In a recent experiment, Lenneberg (1961) investigated the effect of a color label, suggested to the subject by the experimenter, on later recognition of the color. No bias toward the experimenter's label was found. Lenneberg concluded that naming habits of long standing furnished convenient anchorage points for color recognition when memory was involved, and that these habits resisted ephemeral influence. In the same paper, Lenneberg reported an investigation of the potential effect of color-naming habits on simultaneous discrimination of colors; that is, whether differential limens for hues are influenced by our naming habits. Since the Zuni language has naming frequency peaks for colors which contrast with those of English, Zuni subjects were compared with Anglo-American ones, with the prediction that there should be contrasting stretching and shrinking for the two populations in certain regions of the color space. The hypothesis was not confirmed, leading to the conclusion that hue discrimination is not affected by naming habits when color stimuli are matched under conditions of simultaneous presentation.

The influence of language on perception in these studies has thus been demonstrated under certain conditions which impose demands on memory. The writer has found no experimental evidence to support the more general hypothesis that man perceptually dissects nature along lines laid down by his native language. It is unlikely that perceptual learning is appreciably distorted by language categories, though it is likely that it can be facilitated by calling attention, verbally, to distinctive features of things.

SUMMARY OF INTERRELATIONS IN THE TOTAL COGNITIVE PROCESS

The developmental interrelationships of the cognitive processes considered in this chapter are summarized in Figure 8–4, which shows a developmental progression from one cognitive achievement to another, and feedback loops from processes achieved later to processes that began earlier. These loops (dotted lines) indicate potential subsequent refinement and facilitation of the processes available earlier by those achieved later. That is, while the chart suggests a developmental progression reading from the top down, it also contains the implication that later appearing processes, such as naming, may react on and contribute to further perceptual learning once they have become part of the organism's repertory of activities. In later chapters developmental evidence will be introduced. Here the purpose is to sketch the pattern of interrelationship of cognitive processes.

At the top of the chart is undifferentiated general responsiveness to stimulation, present to a limited extent even in the unborn foetus. Following this step is gross selective response to stimulus differences, present in the neonate, and demonstrable by techniques such as habituation and presentation of novel stimuli (cf. Chapter 15). Up to this point, we see no evidence of learning, but from birth on, learning and growth can proceed together. A few weeks after birth, it can be demonstrated that certain sounds and objects are differentiated from the background stimulation and attended to selectively (for instance, faces).

Following primitive separation of an object or event from the stimulus flow, perception differentiates in two ways. One, features which distinguish an object or event from others are abstracted (e.g., properties distinguishing one face from another, one voice from another, and so on) and progressively more economical processing of features is achieved. The second path of perceptual learning is the extraction of invariants of events and progressive

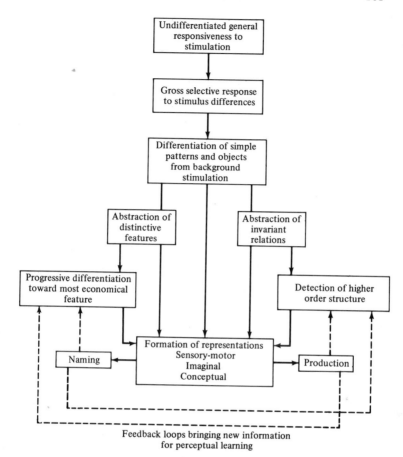

FIGURE 8–4. Developmental interrelations of cognitive processes.

pickup of higher order structure. Differentiation of sequential stimulus information, such as speech and writing, prominently embodies both.

Perceptual learning begins before permanent representations of things, patterns, and sequences can be developed. Some kinds of representation may be prior to others; for instance, a sensory-motor schema, in Piaget's sense, and a concrete image would be prior to an abstract concept. The representation, in turn, precedes the ability to produce a copy and to attach verbal labels. But when production and naming are possible, these activities can speed up further perceptual learning by providing information for monitoring and check, and by calling attention to distinctive features and higher order relations. They may help especially in the learning of distinctive features and structure of very complex sets of objects and coded stimuli such as speech and writing.

9

The Improvement of
Perceptual Skills with Practice

In the next four chapters, emphasis will be shifted from theory to the laboratory. We shall consider first a large body of experiments with human subjects that provide training for the improvement of perceptual judgments, in the traditional manner of learning experiments. I described these experiments at length in an earlier article (Gibson, 1953), so I shall choose examples to illustrate important subclasses of them. These classes are based on the kind of perceptual judgment used as the criterion measure.

The operations of measurement and the controls required for studying perceptual learning in the laboratory include those for any perception experiment. The stimulus array must be controlled and described and an indicator response of some kind must be available. Since we are asking whether perception changes in the direction of increasing correspondence to stimulus information, it is important to specify quantitatively or by accurate and relevant description what is present in the stimulation. We are interested not only in unidimensional stimulation, for which quantification is fairly easily secured, but even more in multidimensional stimulus arrays, such as the kind elicited by a face, or the sounds of human speech. The problem of quantification is therefore very difficult. Yet, the experimenter must, by whatever technical means he can command, have a better and more precise description of the stimuli than his subject is likely to achieve. Success in devising good experiments on perceptual learning depends in large measure on invention of methods of describing complex stimulus properties and invariants of stimulation.

On the other side of the equation, it is equally important to devise methods of measuring the relative selectivity of the subject's receptive capacities. It is not the shaping of the response that we are interested in but the nature and refinement of an organism's appreciation of stimulus variation. Diagnosing this ability from his behavior without confounding it with motor or verbal skill demands caution. On the other hand, we must not make a Type II error, and dismiss as merely motor and verbal learning all learned behavior in which manipulation and speech are involved. It would be such an error to state, for instance, that since we learn to differentiate the song patterns of thrushes and chickadees at the same time that we learn the birds' names, the learning must be purely verbal. One way of minimizing this difficulty in experiments on perceptual learning is to restrict responses to ones that are already in the subject's repertory and are also equally available.

The psychophysical methods were devised for the purpose of studying human sensitivity to dimensional aspects of stimulation, such as a frequency continuum, and they have been adapted, in recent years, to the study of more complex properties as well. The relevant behavior is always a choice in relation to the presented stimulation, indicated by the terms "detection," "discrimination," "recognition," and "identification." Clarification of these terms has been sought by a number of psychologists in recent years (Bush, Galanter, & Luce, 1963; Englund & Lundberg, 1963). While these tasks define different experimental operations and require different judgments, they all yield information about the extent to which the subject's judgments are or are not specific to stimulus variation. They are relevant procedures, therefore, for revealing a change in specificity of perception to stimulation. We will consider experiments on detection, discrimination, recognition, and identification in that order.

DETECTION EXPERIMENTS

A detection experiment is one in which the presence or absence of some aspect of stimulation is indicated by the subject. The aspect selected for detection might be a tone or a flash of light or a pressure on the skin or some more complex feature of patterned stimulation such as a break in a Landolt ring. The indicator response may be verbal—a "yes" or "no"— or it could be nonverbal, such as a pigeon pecking or not pecking. Experiments on the absolute threshold with human subjects are of this type. If trials in the experiment are repeated so as to give the subject practice, his threshold can be compared at the beginning and at the end, and the experiment qualifies as one on perceptual learning.

Signal detection experiments are in the tradition of older experiments on the absolute threshold, or lower limit, of sensitivity. They may be complicated by presenting the signal in a noisy background or, on the other hand, under impoverished conditions, such as low illumination or a very high rate of speed. Experiments requiring detection of a visual target range from those concerned with simple acuity to those concerned with complex forms, and perceptual learning has been demonstrated in all cases.

The Effect of Practice on Acuity Judgments

VISUAL ACUITY. Some conventional measures of visual acuity are the resolution of parallel lines, E charts, and the Landolt ring test. Practice of various types can yield differences in the score obtained on all these tasks. Wilcox (1936) found that the threshold for visual resolution of a pair of parallel bars presented at different light intensities became lower and less variable with practice. One subject, who practiced systematically over a period of ten days lowered his threshold to one-fourth the original value. He thought the improvement had to do with adopting a different criterion of doubleness. McFadden (1940) performed experiments with parallel bars presented at different distances. Improvement consisted in the subject's being able to resolve the test object at distances more remote from the eye. As the subjects watched the test object brought toward them, they noted that it appeared to go through a series of figural transformations, and came to recognize in this series signs of the onset of resolution. Thus it would appear, in this case, too, that improvement is related to a new criterion or distinguishing feature signalling doubleness.

A study by Shvarts (1957) used an E chart (ш , m , Ǝ , or E) with illumination which could be progressively lowered. The threshold was defined by the minimal illumination at which the subject could detect the orientation of the E. Repetition without knowledge of results increased sensitivity; repetition with verbal reinforcement and shock for wrong responses increased it more (though shock produced marked irregularity); subjects given a level of achievement to aim for increased most of all. Two things seem to be happening here. Reinforcement, exhortation, and punishment probably served to lower the subject's criterion of when to respond, the level of confidence that he would accept for having detected the target's orientation. This kind of change is not properly speaking perceptual learning. But there was also, Shvarts reported, a change in the signs by which the critical feature was recognized. "There are," he said, "probably 'zones' of sensitivity, connected with the perception of particular features of the stimulus." The critical features by which orientation was detected changed as illumination was lowered. Considering the difference in procedures, this report supports very well the learning of a new critical feature for doubleness in the resolution of a pair of lines.

Bruce and Low (1951) reported improvement of acuity measured by noting a break in a Landolt ring after practice in recognition of tachistoscopically exposed aircraft photographs. The same kind of practice was said to improve peripheral visual acuity for detecting a break in the ring (Low, 1946a and b). It is not clear what was happening here; probably a rather general change in the subject's observing habits, or a lowered criterion for response since there could not be any specific perceptual learning.

THE TWO-POINT LIMEN ON THE SKIN. Observing that the stimulation of two adjacent points on the skin is two instead of one is a judgment similar to the visual resolution of parallel bars. In this experiment the separation which permits the judgment of twoness can likewise be drastically reduced with practice. Volkmann obtained this result in an experiment in 1858. He also provided the earliest learning curve I know of, and the first demonstration of bilateral transfer of learning. The graph (Fig. 9–1) shows the effect of practice in Volkmann's experiment. Practice was given on the tip of the left middle finger, and it transferred to the symmetrical area on the other hand. But, as the crosshatched bars on the

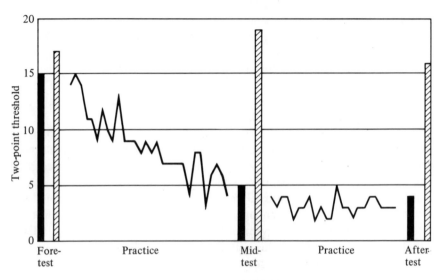

FIGURE 9–1. The effect of practice on the two-point threshold and its transfer.

> The tip of the left middle finger received the practice. Fore-, mid- and aftertests were given the right middle finger (black bars) and the volar surface of the left forearm (crosshatched bars). The percent of errors (shown on ordinate) decreased for the practiced finger and for the symmetrical unpracticed one, but not for the forearm. (After Robert S. Woodworth, *Experimental Psychology,* New York: Holt, Rinehart and Winston, Inc., 1938; data from Volkmann, A. W. Über den Einfluss der Uebung, *Leipzig Berichte Math.-phys. Classe,* 1858, *10,* 38–39; reprinted with permission of Holt, Rinehart & Winston, Inc.)

graph show, the improvement did not transfer to the forearm. Other experiments have confirmed Volkmann's results (Dresslar, 1894; Tawney, 1897; Mukherjee, 1933) and have also suggested how to interpret them. Boring (1920) pointed out that practice was effective when the subject learned to choose a different but stricter criterion of doubleness. Many experimenters have reported that a separation too small to feel like two points does nevertheless have a distinctive perceptible quality that is different from one, and the subject learns to detect this and use it as a cue for doubleness. Practice with correction enhances this learning because it teaches the subject that the distinctive quality he has come to detect can be used as a criterion for twoness. The limen is reduced, not by setting a lower criterion as acceptable for the judgment, but by learning to use a different one.

The Effect of Practice on Absolute Thresholds

Experiments on the upper or lower limits of sensitivity are similar to what are nowadays called detection experiments. The absolute threshold for sensing salt in solution, for instance, would require only a judgment of "yes" for its presence. It has been questioned whether these thresholds are really absolute (cf., for instance, Swets, 1961), since they are susceptible to change as a function of motivation, sequential effects, adaptation level, and practice. Isolating the effects of these factors is not easy; most experimental procedures tend to confound them. Blackwell (1953) conducted experiments on the absolute threshold for detection of a luminous spot in an empty field, running the same subjects for a very long period of practice. Thresholds were lowered over this period, and the introduction of rewards lowered them further.

An experiment by Zwislocki et al. (1958) is a good example of the effects of both practice and motivation on the absolute auditory threshold. The subjects had six practice sessions during which they listened to a 100 cps tone (presented continuously over an earphone) that rose or sank in intensity. They were instructed to try to detect the faintest signal possible. They pressed a control key in one direction which caused the sound to decrease in intensity as soon as they could hear a tone, and pressed the key in the other direction which caused the sound to increase in intensity when they could no longer hear it. With this ingenious method, the threshold could be determined by plotting the curve of rising and falling intensity. There was a significant improvement in threshold from session to session. During a single session, the threshold had some tendency to rise; probably, the experimenters thought, because of boredom and dwindling attention. This deterioration was eliminated in a group of subjects given increased payoff for bettering a previous day's threshold. The reinforcement thus enhanced the effect due to experience alone. When pretraining was given on a 1,000 cycle tone and then the subject was switched to a 100 cycle tone, there was no transfer of threshold improvement, so the effect of practice was quite specific: the subject was learning to detect "a particular sound in a background of physiological noise."

In order to see whether improvement was dependent on the tracking method used, practice was given a new group of subjects with a different method. Discrete tone bursts were presented singly or in pairs on a random schedule, and the subject judged whether one or two bursts had been presented. A light signalled the test interval and the subject was forced to make a choice. He was paid for a correct choice and forfeited the same amount if he was wrong. Over eight practice sessions, the percentage of correct choices increased significantly for all subjects, so the authors concluded that the improved thresholds were not due to a change in the listener's criterion of confidence, which might have been possible with the tracking method, and that during practice "more sensitive discrimination clues were learned."

Changes in absolute thresholds for detecting odors were studied by Engen (1960). He used a forced-choice method of limits. The subject was presented on each trial with a rack of four test tubes, each containing a clear liquid but only one also containing a highly diluted odorant. The subject had to select one and was told after his judgment which was the correct tube. Thresholds were lowered with practice, more for some odorants than others. Experienced subjects who showed large practice effects reported that they had discovered that an odor had two distinct thresholds. One was the threshold for the typical quality associated with the odorant, e.g., a "quality like banana oil." But there was a much lower concentration of the odorant at which the subject smelled an odor not identified by such a specific association but still noticeably different from that of the diluent. When practiced subjects were given instructions to adopt an attitude of selecting the tube "which seemed different in any way whatever," not one of attending to a particular quality, there was a marked decrease in threshold. With some odorants the more general criterion was likely to be adopted spontaneously because the odor was not unique or easily remembered and these odorants showed the largest effect of practice. Here practice permits learning, for the subject discovers a perceptible feature to be critical for a "yes" judgment, and it also allows him to change his criterion of discrimination from the original one with an associated name. It is important to keep effects due to a change in subjective criterion of confidence separated from those due to discovery of a new critical feature for discrimination, and the forced-choice method is valuable for this reason.

Detection of Complex Targets

While it is interesting to find that the apparent limit of sensitivity to a unidimensional variable is not really a limit and can be lowered with practice, there is much more opportunity to study what happens in perceptual learning when targets and background vary multidimensionally. Detection methods are appropriate for studying complex target detection and may also have interesting applications to real-life target detection under normal conditions and under noisy ones, such as a camouflaged background.

SEARCH TASKS. Search tasks are especially appropriate for studying the effects of practice on discovery of an assigned target. An old favorite was the cancellation task; the subject had to scan over a page of pied type, or mixed letters, and to cancel all the k's, or all the t's, or a combination of letters (see Woodworth, 1938, p. 194). This task was remodelled and studied in a number of experiments by Neisser (1963, 1964). A subject was asked to scan a list, usually consisting of fifty items, to find a specified target item. Each item in the list was, typically, a string of letters printed in a horizontal line. It might be a randomly selected string, or chosen by some rule, or the letters might make a word. In a list of random items, the subject might be instructed to find a single letter, k, which appeared only once in the list. The typed list was inserted behind a window which was illuminated at the beginning of search when the subject pressed a switch. The switch also started an electric timer. The subject scanned down the list, searching for his target, and released the switch to stop the timer when he found it. Over a series of such lists, the target was placed randomly at different positions in the list. Search time increased, of course, as the item was placed farther down in the list. The time could be plotted against position so as to yield a slope which indicated the increase in time for each new item scanned, giving a measure of time per item.

An interesting finding of experiments with this task is the great increase in scanning rate with continued practice. The subject learns to search with amazing efficiency for those distinguishing features which allow him to detect the target, and to ignore the others. Typically, after considerable practice, he may be unable to say in what context of letters the target letter was embedded. Whatever his perceptual strategy for ordinary letter identification may be, it changes with the requirements of this task. As Neisser put it, "with repeated scans they discover the perceptual operations that seem to be minimally sufficient for the problem (Neisser, 1964, p. 96)." The subject need not identify the k (for instance) as he would if he named it to himself. He need only discover the minimal bundle of features, such as curves, diagonals, or intersections which are not shared by the context letters.

If this is the case, one would expect that embedding the target in a context of letters that share distinctive features with it would slow down the scanning rate, and this is indeed true (Gibson & Yonas, 1966). One could also predict, if the subject is really not identifying the target letter, that a context of letters with acoustic similarity to it would not hamper the scanning rate, and this too is true (Kaplan et al., 1966). It is furthermore true that spoken letters acoustically similar to the target and coming in over earphones do not interfere with scanning rate (Gibson & Yonas, 1966). The subject, then, is not reading the letter in question but is only detecting a small set of critical distinguishing features. The perceptual learning of this optimal set is a striking result of the experiment.

Neisser (Neisser et al., 1963) was interested in the question whether the subject scans for several features at once in parallel, or whether features are tested sequentially, in some hierarchy. He accordingly compared time to scan for a single target with time to scan for several targets at once. A search for two targets at once (for either one or the other) did not take longer than a search for one (corroborated by Gibson & Yonas, 1966a). Searching for four or more targets did, but extended practice was so effective that after about two weeks, ten targets could be scanned for at once as rapidly as one. Figure 9–2 shows the learning curves for scanning for one, five, and ten targets at once.

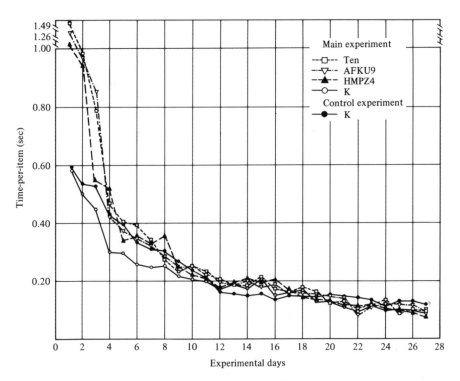

FIGURE 9–2. Learning curves showing the effect of practice on searching for multiple targets simultaneously.

(From U. Neisser, R. Novick, & R. Lazar. Searching for ten targets simultaneously. *Perceptual and Motor Skills*, 1963, *17*, 959.)

Neisser felt that the results indicated the occurrence of "parallel processing" for multiple features instead of "sequential processing," but this interpretation leaves unexplained what it is that these subjects were learning. What is it that effects such astonishing improvement? It seems to me that even in the case of multiple targets, the subjects must be learning to narrow down the search to a minimal set of features that distinguish the target set from context. How the critical information contained in ten randomly chosen letters can be condensed or filtered so as to detect any one of them very swiftly in a background of other letters is a puzzle here. It is hard to understand exactly what structure could permit processing by some higher order or finely filtered variable, but this still appears to be the most reasonable interpretation. That the learning is not merely the result of some very general learning set is suggested by the fact that the rate of scanning goes up as the number of targets is increased if the targets are changed from trial to trial (Kaplan & Carvellas, 1965).[1] Furthermore, as scanning speed increased in Neisser's experiment so did errors, and the errors seemed to be specific to particular visual configurations; several subjects, according to Neisser, would miss the same target in the same list, as if they had "evolved a particular system of stimulus analysis," one which was highly economical but not 100 percent guaranteed for detection. Neisser speaks of a "multi-level" perceptual system, one in which an observer "can decide there is no K in a given line without actually identifying the letters," as contrasted with his fully identifying one when asked to read it. I am not sure that "level" is the best word, but the observation confirms my own that there are different kinds of perceptual tasks or judgments with different optimal strategies.

FINDING EMBEDDED FIGURES. A still more complex detection task is one in which subjects are asked to detect a target design in a background which has been constructed to mask or camouflage it. The task was devised by Gottschaldt (1926), who was interested in defending the Gestalt psychologists' position that experience was not effective in organizing the perception of a form (see Chapter 2). He found that repeated perception of a simple design did not, in itself, result in a subject's spontaneously noting it when it was masked in a complex design. But instructions to search for it were effective. Later research (Hanawalt, 1942) showed not only that practice was effective when the same designs were repeated but also that there was transfer of practice to searching for new designs. Strategies are developed with practice which greatly improve the search. Hanawalt noted that the subjects learned to look for "essential parts" of the simple target designs; they also learned, when searching for it in the complex figure, to "switch dimensions," to try to see it in three dimensions if the target did not appear when it was viewed as two, or vice versa.

A very elegant experiment on the effects of practice in detection of embedded figures was performed by Kolers (Kolers, 1960; Kolers & Zink,

---

[1] It is not clear, however, that subjects had reached an asymptote of practice in this experiment; probably not.

1962), using a forced-choice detection method. The forms, both the simple
ones and the complex ones in which they were embedded, were geometrical patterns systematically constructed by selecting points from a
table of random numbers and joining them with lines (a method adapted
from Attneave & Arnoult, 1956). For the simple figures, five points were
chosen and connected to make pentagons. Four such figures were constructed in this way. All the points for these four figures were placed on
three different matrices and connected in three different ways. One of the
simple figures, the basic figure, was represented in all three complex ones.
The figures were drawn on cards with the four simple ones in the bottom
row and the three complex ones above (see Fig. 9–3; here the simple figures
are in rows 1 and 3, the complex ones in rows 2 and 4). The subject had to
choose from the four in the bottom row the basic figure which appeared
in all three figures in the upper row. A card was presented tachistoscopically
to a subject in a viewing box. Each card was presented 25 times or more

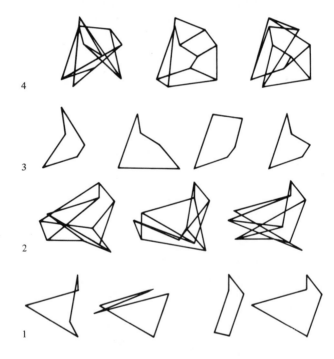

FIGURE 9–3. Two items from an embedded figures test employing a forced-
choice detection method.

One of the figures in row 1 can be found in all three figures in row 2 and
one of the figures in row 3 can be found in all three figures in row 4.
(From P. A. Kolers, Some aspects of problem-solving: I. Methods and
materials. WADD Technical Report 60-2, Project 7183, Task No. 71618,
1960, Wright-Patterson Air Force Base, Ohio, p. 2.)

and the subject required to call out his best judgment of the basic card each time. The subject's choice was not corrected. The criterion of a successful detection was ten consecutive correct responses beyond the fifteenth trial, and the score assigned was the first trial of the successful run of ten.

The probability of a correct response increased in a very regular fashion as trials on a given problem progressed, in itself a most interesting kind of perceptual learning, since the subject was not told whether he was right or wrong. This learning was specific to the problem. But as the subjects went on from problem to problem, some learning transferred. Correct detections were made sooner and the criterion was reached earlier; there was improvement with practice in both the number of correct detections and the speed of achieving them. Figure 9–4 shows the effects of practice for both specific problems and over problems, the total practice time

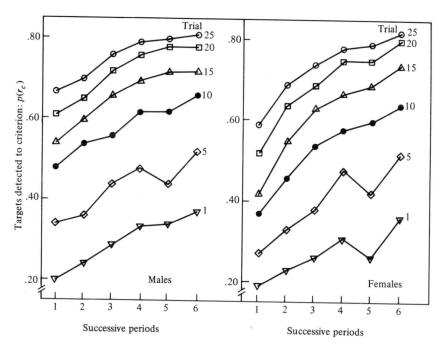

FIGURE 9–4. Two effects of practice on correct detection.

The parameter is the trial number, so comparison of the curves 1–25 demonstrates improvement in correct detection as trials on a given problem increase. Successive periods of practice are plotted on the abscissa, so the upward trend of all the curves shows improvement over problems as practice progresses. (From P. A. Kolers & D. L. Zink, Some aspects of problem-solving: Sequential analysis of the detection of embedded patterns. Tech. Doc. Reports No. AMRL-TDR-62-148, Project No. 7183. Task No. 718303, 1962, Wright-Patterson Air Force Base, p. 8.)

divided into six periods (about 16 problems per period). The number of targets detected to criterion rises over the period for all trial numbers (means of trials 1, 5, 10, 15, and 25 are plotted). This is the general practice effect over trials. Comparison of the number of targets correctly detected at different trials from 1 to 25 also rises consistently for all periods of practice. This is the learning that is specific to a problem.

Here we have two kinds of perceptual learning beautifully illustrated. Specific learning for a problem ran in a predictable sequence, Kolers found. In about 50 percent of all cases with at least one error, the subjects made a specific error before detecting the target correctly. The alternatives most similar to the target were, not surprisingly, mistaken for them most often. Actively trying to separate pentagons from the complex figures and to compare them with the bottom row was reported by the better subjects, and it would seem that adopting some such strategy and improving on it would account for learning over problems. Active search is thus important for improvement in this task, but it is not scanning in the sense of eye movements of contour tracing, since the displays were presented for only 500 msec. When performance of the poorer subjects was compared with that of the better ones sequentially over trials, they tended to make the same errors, but the poorer subjects often detected the correct target without recognizing that they had detected it. Knowing oneself when something is seen correctly is evidence for a self-regulatory mechanism in perceptual learning. Discovery of invariance of distinctive features of structure over the set can ring a bell in the successful subject.

DISCRIMINATION EXPERIMENTS

The term "discrimination" is used, in a general sense, to refer to any noticing of differences. But a discrimination experiment involves a noticing of differences between two (or more) stimuli presented simultaneously or in immediate succession. Immediate succession is intended to mean succession within a time interval short enough so that the chance of new interpolated stimuli is negligible. The indicator response in a discrimination experiment is not unique to each of the stimuli presented, but requires only the indication of difference. Judgments of "same" or "different," or, if the stimuli lie on a continuum, "more" or "less," are examples of such a response. An experimenter may present a pair of weights to a subject and ask him to indicate which is heavier. The one which is heavier on one trial will not be so on another trial, if it is paired with a still heavier weight, so the response "heavier" is not specific to a given weight. The pairs of weights presented will be arranged so that any one is as often lighter as it is heavier.

If perceptual learning occurs in a discrimination experiment, the specificity of a subject's response to differences between stimuli is increased. His variable error or interval of unce tainty is lowered. But it is very important to remember that this increase in specificity, a narrowing of the difference which can be noticed, is not the same thing as acquiring by association a specific response, because the response itself is not specific to a given stimulus. The change is similar to a decrease in what is called generalization between one stimulus and another in the literature of conditioning. I am using the term "generalization" as the inverse of "discrimination," making a clear distinction between "primary generalization," which I consider to be a failure to discriminate, and "secondary generalization," which implies ability to discriminate, since it is conceptual (see Gibson, 1959). Perceptual learning refers to a decrease in the first type only.[2]

---

[2] The meaning of "generalization" has been a matter of dispute for some years. The Pavlovian generalization experiment, designed for work with animals, left open the interpretation of generalization. The animal was conditioned to respond to a given stimulus and then other stimuli were applied, usually other values on the same continuum. If these stimuli were not reinforced as was the conditioned one (Pavlov's method of contrasts) the class of stimuli which elicited the conditioned response began to narrow. The ambiguity of the term "generalization" rose partly from the difficulty that the animal, during this procedure, might be learning his instructions. Generalized responses were not necessarily due to an inability to respond to differences between stimuli. Apparent discrepancies in the extent and range of generalization rose from variations in the time of measuring it, before or after introducing differential reinforcement (cf. Hovland, 1949; Littman, 1949).

When a set to discriminate is clearly present, generalization and the extent of psychophysical correspondence found in a discriminability function should be the same. That they are, in fact, for human subjects is probably the case if we accept a verbally instructed judgment with the method of single stimuli as analogous to the operation commonly used to study generalization. The question was investigated in an experiment by Kalish (1958). He used wavelength as the stimulus continuum. A plastic disc illuminated by monochromatic light provided the source. One wavelength (e.g., 600 μ) was selected as the standard. There were eight variable wavelengths above and below the standard. The subject was shown the standard color and asked to keep it in mind so he could identify it. He was to depress a telegraph key when this specific color appeared, but not when any other appeared. All nine stimuli were presented six times in random order. Response to a stimulus other than the standard was regarded as an instance of generalization. The shape of the gradients obtained by Kalish conformed to predictions made from the discriminability function for wavelength, leading him to conclude that "the inverse relationship between generalization and discriminability was confirmed."

Failure to confirm the inverse relationship between generalization and discriminability in experiments with animals (Guttman, 1963) is not particularly surprising, considering the difficulty of establishing a set to discriminate. One may wonder, however, why conditioning experiments with human subjects have not always found a neat correspondence between psychophysical measures of discriminability and the generalization gradient. One key to this apparent puzzle lies in a statement of Lashley and Wade (1946). They attacked the concept of generalization of a conditioned response as a "pseudo" one; they said "a test for irradiation (generalization) may give the appearance of a gradient of habit strength when it is actually measuring dis-

Lowered Differential Limens

Psychophysical experiments on the judgment of relative differences test sensitivity to small differences along a dimension such as pitch or weight; the differential limen is the smallest difference that can be consistently discriminated. A number of experiments (for example with lifted weights) have demonstrated that practice may have the effect of lowering a differential threshold. Urban (1913) studied the effect of progressive practice on lifting weights, using a constant method and giving no correction of errors. With practice, the coefficient of precision increased and the interval of uncertainty grew smaller. Fernberger (1916) repeated the experiment, with the same results. A more recent experiment (Björkman & Ottander, 1959) had two subjects practice over five days, again lifting weights with a constant method and with no knowledge of results given by the experimenter. There was a considerable reduction in the DL—roughly half the value at the end of the training period compared with the beginning. Knowledge of results provided by the experimenter is evidently not essential for improvement in the precision of this judgment.

The effect of training on relative discrimination of pitch has received much attention. The earlier literature was summarized in a monograph by Wyatt (1945), who made further interesting experiments herself. She tried various methods of training, including singing (listening to an oscillator tone and attempting to reproduce it) accompanied by visual feedback via a chromatic stroboscope. The subject could see whether or not the tone he produced was correct and, if not, what the magnitude and direction

---

criminative thresholds under distraction." It seems to be a fact that generalization has usually been measured under conditions of distraction with human subjects, for example, where shock was the reinforcer for a conditioned galvanic skin response or a blast of air to the cornea for a blink. Distraction introduced by a speed set has been present also in reaction time experiments with human subjects in which false reactions were counted as cases of generalization (e.g., Gibson, 1939; Brown, Bilodeau, & Baron, 1951).

By the term "primary generalization" I mean the extent to which stimulus presentations are responded to as if they were the same, when there is a set to discriminate (even though with animals such a set must be inferred). There seems to be no reason for confining the term's applicability to a conditioning situation. A bird which retrieves and broods a china egg is exhibiting generalization. Because the equivalence of the china egg to the bird's own is unlearned, the term "primary generalization" is appropriate. The distinction between "primary generalization" and "secondary generalization" was made by Hull (1943). Dollard and Miller also distinguished between innate stimulus generalization and learned secondary generalization. Secondary generalization refers to acquired equivalence of stimuli of the kind which exists between words having a common meaning (semantic generalization). Secondary generalization has also been referred to as mediated generalization.

of his error was. If the pattern drifted on the visual display, he could try to maneuver it back. Wyatt concluded that the pitch discrimination of initially pitch deficient adults could be improved. It is not clear from her experiments what factors, such as feedback, were important, since the training was designed to be remedial and was adjusted to the individual needs of the subject.

Recent research on relative judgments of pitch has concentrated on isolating the effects of different methods of practice. Baker and Osgood (1954) investigated discrimination transfer along a pitch continuum. Three groups of subjects were trained with pairs of tones differing only in frequency. All were given the same amount of corrected practice following a pretest, but the method of practice varied. One group was trained only on the test series. A second was trained on a series of easy-to-discriminate pairs and then shifted to the difficult test series. A third began training with the easy series and approached the test series by gradual steps. All were compared with a control group having no practice before the posttest. Only the group trained with a gradual transition from larger to smaller differences achieved a significant improvement. It may be that gradually increasing difficulty of the discrimination helps define some hitherto unnoticed aspect of the difference relation which can then come to serve as a distinctive or criterial feature for the judgment.

An experiment by Heimer and Tatz (1966) used four different experimental groups. Training was given at either of two different standard frequencies in subgroups with and without correction of their judgments. All the subjects practiced for five days. The tone pairs, recorded on tape, were sounded against a background of white noise. The subject recorded H or L (higher or lower) on an answer sheet. When correction was given, the subject heard the correct response spoken over the tape at the end of a 6 sec. interval after the pair of tones had been presented. Practice in this experiment resulted in lowered DL's for all groups. The groups which received knowledge of results had slightly lower DL's throughout than their counterpart groups, but the difference was not significant at the 5 percent level. Perhaps the most interesting result of this experiment is what happened on a test for transfer. Groups trained with a standard tone of 3,000 cps were tested for transfer to a standard tone of 800 cps, and vice versa. Compared to appropriate control groups with a very small amount of practice on the task, with the same standard, there was no transfer of the practice effect. Whatever the subjects were learning it was specific to the difference judgment at the given standard frequency.

It seems to be the fact that, unless practice is with progressively smaller differences in frequency, improvement in discrimination of a small frequency difference is specific to the particular frequency level experienced in practice. What does this fact show? It proves at least that the modification is not a matter of motivation, or a change of the subjective standard of confidence or a general warm-up effect for the task of discriminating tones. Similarly, Zwislocki et al. (1958) found that practice lowered the absolute threshold for detecting a tone, but that when practice was given on a tone of 1,000 cps, there was no transfer to a tone of 100 cps. Perhaps this means that even instances of stimulation within a presumably unidmensional continuum have the properties of events—features that can be detected over and above the supposedly inherent quality of pure pitch. The transients of a 1,000 cycle tone, or the step in pitch when two tones are presented in immediate succession, are events with properties that are quite specific and that can be detected better with active listening.

It also seems to be the fact that correction given by the experimenter is not essential for improvement of pitch discrimination; in at least one experiment it was of no value in facilitating improvement (Campbell & Small, 1963). Apparently the subject must experience a change, he must hear in a different way, and practice with progressively smaller differences helps. An experiment with an entirely different kind of stimulation, requiring visual discrimination of two circles differing in size, is instructive in this connection (Englund & Lundberg, 1963). Subjects improved with repetition in judging which of two circles was larger, without correction. Thinking that the effect might be due to extraneous factors such as acquaintance with the experimental setup, the authors substituted repeated judgments with pairs of equal circles. But from this experiment no improvement in discrimination resulted. Presumably, therefore, some kind of change in the subject's own perception of inequality seems to be essential. In an experiment giving subjects practice with lifted weights, Bevan and Saugstad (1955) found that practice with very small differences was not as effective for improvement as practice with larger differences. The latter permitted the subject, at least part of the time, to perceive something new about the difference relation. A very wide range of differences over the whole continuum, however, did not bring about increased precision, and this suggested again that what is learned in these experiments is specific. Transfer of perceptual learning should be more prominent where the stimulus displays to be compared are more complex and potentially share a number of distinctive features, like those described in the following paragraphs.

Improved Discrimination of Complex Stimuli

The discrimination of two multidimensional stimulus displays as same or different is relatively easy when they are presented simultaneously and clearly. It can improve with practice, however, if the material chosen is unfamiliar and if the indicator response reflects ease of discrimination precisely enough. Robinson (1955) gave subjects practice in making same-different judgments of finger prints, items that were quite unfamiliar to them.

My own observation as a subject during this experiment was that the similar and initially confusable finger prints became much more visibly different after making a number of same-different comparisons. Practice with simultaneous comparison transferred to another measure, recognition, again using judgments of same and different. What the subject was doing here was learning the distinctive features of fingerprints, hitherto unknown to him.

Pick's experiment, described in Chapter 6, gave children practice in making same-different comparisons with artificial graphic forms. The children learned to correct errors in discriminating them, and showed transfer to new forms as a result of the opportunity to learn the dimensions on which they differed.

RECOGNITION EXPERIMENTS

In Chapter 8, I discussed recognition and the fact that discrimination of samenesses and differences between objects can be learned when the stimuli in question are not present simultaneously or in immediate succession. If a subject is shown a set of stimulus items and asked later to pick out the ones he has seen from a larger set including items he has not seen, he is said to recognize an item when he says correctly "that is an old one." The experiment is similar to the discrimination experiment in that only two indicator responses are made use of. The subject says "old" or "new," as he would say "same" or "different," "greater" or "less."

Examples of experiments using recognition have already been described, notably the scribble experiment of Gibson and Gibson (see Chapter 5), and some of the predifferentiation experiments cited in Chapter 4, in which a subject had to pick an old item from a new set of confusable ones after some kind of pretraining. The latter experiments showed that practice tested by recognition might or might not be effective, depending on what the subject was set to learn during the practice. The effect of practice on later recognition of a stimulus item is obviously going to depend very much on the context of items out of which it must be recognized. If they are all similar to it the practice, to be effective, must have had to do with its distinctive features relative to the set, not with the common features of the set.

Fitts et al. (1956) studied the effect of context and other factors characterizing individual items as they interacted with practice on a recognition task. The figures (metric figures) were constructed within a 4×4 or 8×8 matrix by filling in columns to different heights. These heights were chosen either by a random sampling procedure, or by sampling with specified constraints so as to produce some degree of relative redundancy. The constrained figures were produced by sampling without replacement, so that only a fraction as many could be generated as by random sampling. For each figure several reproductions were constructed so as to include asymmetrical, single- or double-contoured, and symmetrical versions.

The recognition task employed a sorting board on which were arranged six rows of eight figures each. A copy of the test figure appeared in each row, randomly embedded among the context figures. Finding the six replications of the test figure constituted one trial. The subjects were given practice with all the types of figures. Constrained figures took longer to recognize than random ones—they looked more similar to one another. In a second run, the subjects were tested again with the same figures presented in four different orientations. There was a significant improvement in recognition time. Learning proceeded at differential rates for different classes of figures: there was greater improvement for vertically oriented figures than for horizontal ones, and more for bilaterally symmetrical than asymmetrical ones. It was concluded that the subjects learned to use different types of cues for recognizing different types of figures and that rate of learning varies in such a task with the type of cue available.

The histogram-like figures of this experiment are impossible to identify by any specific label, and are highly confusable. Perceptual learning with a recognition judgment occurred however, and without any correction by the experimenter. Learning to recognize histogram figures has also been demonstrated by Edmonds, Mueller, and Evans (1966), and Evans (1966), and Edmonds and Mueller (1968). In their experiments, knowledge of results given by the experimenter did not result in greater learning than when the subject was given no knowledge.

IDENTIFICATION EXPERIMENTS

An identification experiment differs from a detection, a discrimination, or a recognition experiment in that a unique response is required of the subject for each item presented. This procedure is called by Bush, Galanter, and Luce (1963) a "complete identification experiment." There must be established a one-to-one correspondence between a set of items and a set of responses. The responses required may be names, as when a child learns names for the letters of the alphabet. But they need not be names. They can be such indicator responses as pressing a button on a display panel, or they can be speaking a number. When a subject is asked to make absolute judgments of pitch, or to estimate distances in yards, he must respond with a number, and this is a case of identification.

In these experiments a subject who succeeds in giving the correct responses is clearly demonstrating his ability to discriminate between the items. He is doing more than that, however, since he is producing a unique response for each item. The method presents difficulties for studying perceptual learning since two kinds of learning will be going on at once if the set of responses was not previously known to the subject. To demonstrate that perceptual learning as such has occurred during an identification experiment, some other index than the identifying responses themselves is needed. What indices can be used? A discrimination test before and after the identification learning is possible. A demonstration of positive transfer to a learning situation where the responses have been changed is another possibility (see Wohlwill, 1958). For example, in a paired associates learning experiment (Gibson, 1941), subjects learned nonsense syllables to each of a set of visual forms. Following this task, they learned a new set of syllables to the set of forms. The number of confusion errors between forms was lower by more than 70 percent in the second learning task than in the first, suggesting that differentiation of the forms had been learned during the first task and had carried over to the second. Some of the predifferentiation experiments described in Chapter 4 are of this type.

An identification experiment where the subject is asked to make absolute judgments with reference to a scale of some kind avoids the confounding of perceptual improvement with response learning. The adult subject does not have to learn the responses in such an experiment if they are numbers in a series. Not only does he know the set of responses available, he has them already ordered. The task is to produce the appropriate number for each item in the stimulus continuum. Let us consider some of these experiments for what they may reveal about perceptual learning.

Absolute Estimation on a Single Dimension

Absolute estimations of magnitude along a dimension of stimulation such as brightness, loudness, hue, or pitch are apt to be limited in precision. There is reason to think, as Miller pointed out (1956), that when stimuli differ in only one respect we cannot identify more than six or seven of them correctly. But anecdote would have it that improvement is possible. Clerks of various trades become very accurate (we suppose) in judging the weight of articles sold by the pound; a violinist may have absolute pitch.

Whether the naming of absolute pitches can be improved with practice has been the subject of several experiments. Wedell (1934), for example, gave subjects progressive practice identifying tones by vibration rate, represented at appropriate points on a chart. Error was considerably reduced by training. All the subjects learned to identify nine tones without error, but when the series was longer (13 or more tones) no one mastered it in the number of trials given.

Early experiments have been criticized on the grounds that ordered practice and corrected trials closely following one another rendered the judgments actually relative. Terman (1965) attempted to improve on earlier procedures by giving randomized trials and distraction (sweeps of loud and soft tones similar to a fire-siren pattern) between trials. Tapes were programmed for use with a teaching machine. An answer-and-correction sequence was followed. The subjects used a musical nomenclature which referred to pitch name and octave height. Practice was given in weekly one-hour sessions. Ten of the eleven subjects improved. Accuracy was greatest at the extremes of the stimulus continuum. Generalization of pitch names, as would be expected, was most often close to the defined stimulus frequency. If errors were scored literally by the defined stimulus frequency, the level of performance achieved was not impressive, but if correct responses were counted as within three half-steps of the defined frequency, plus octave errors, scores of 84 percent or better were achieved. Evaluation of performance depends on how the scale is cut up, of course, but it seems that some improvement occurred.

Absolute judgments of odor intensities can be improved with practice, Engen (1961) has found. Twelve sets of stimuli were prepared, with different odorants and different dilution series (percentages of concentration). The response was assigning a rank order of intensity among five stimuli. Three observers practiced for seven weeks, and yielded a nice classical learning curve (see Fig. 9–5). When performance was measured

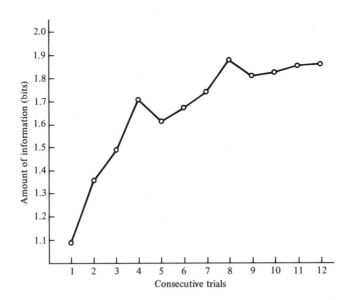

FIGURE 9–5. The effects of practice on absolute judgments of odor intensity measured by amount of information transmitted in 12 consecutive trials by 3 observers.

(From T. Engen, Identification of odors. *American Perfumer,* 1961, *76,* 43–47.)

by amount of information transmitted, efficiency rose from 1.1 bits to 1.85 (about four categories). A well-practiced observer was tested with a larger number of stimulus categories, but there was no improvement from presenting more than five alternative stimuli. Many more odor qualities could be identified (about 16) than intensities.

CONSTANT AND VARIABLE ERRORS. When judgments of magnitude are made along a continuum of stimulus variation, the observer can make two different kinds of error, a constant error and a variable error, and both may be improved with practice. He is said to make a constant error when all of his response values are too high or too low for the stimulus series. He overestimates or underestimates consistently. His variable error, on the other hand, does not depend on the anchoring of the response scale but refers instead to the precision with which he fits the numbers of his response scale to the different values of the stimulus continuum. There will be a range of stimulus values which he cannot consistently distinguish. This inconsistency, the variable error, may be reduced with practice, resulting in greater precision of correspondence between the S and the R set. The diagram in Figure 9–6 shows the two types of error and reduction in the errors after training.

An experiment by Gibson and Bergman (1954) illustrates the effect of practice on the two kinds of error. The task was to make estimates in yards of stretches of distance over the ground measured from the subject to targets scattered over a large empty field (see Fig. 9–7). The subjects were enlistees in the Air Force, taking basic training. They were divided into two groups which were given identical pretests and posttests, each test consisting of 18 judgments of widely varying distance stretches. Between the pretest and posttest one group estimated ninety other distances, none of which was included in the tests, and had their errors corrected by the experimenter. The other group spent the same time interval taking an unrelated paper and pencil test.

The estimates in both the pretest and the posttest showed constant errors and variable errors. For the group which was given intervening corrected practice both kinds of error were reduced. Constant errors, whether of underestimation or overestimation, shifted toward a better anchoring of the whole scale (see Fig. 9–8). The shift in constant error occurred very quickly after only a few corrections. The control group showed no change in constant error from pretest to posttest. The variable error was reduced in both groups, that is, judgments became more consistent within the scale. This kind of improvement therefore did not depend on correction.

Can we say that perceptual learning occurred here? The decrease in constant error found in the experimental group might be the result of an adjusted conceptual scale of yards. However, the reduction in variable error, which did not depend on correction but only on the repeated com-

Reduction of variable error

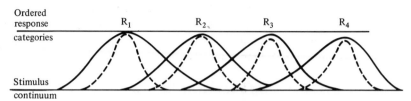

Each solid distribution indicates the range of stimuli which
might elicit a given response before training; each broken
one indicates the range which might elicit the response after
a hypothetical process of differentiation produced by training.

Reduction of constant error

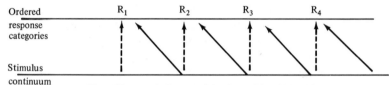

The solid arrows indicate an S-R relationship which might
exist before training; the broken arrows, a relationship
which might exist after hypothetical correction of a constant error.

FIGURE 9–6. A schematic comparison of the reduction of constant and variable error with practice.

(From E. J. Gibson, Improvement in perceptual judgments as a function of controlled practice or training. *Psychological Bulletin,* 1953, *50,* 424.)

paring and estimating of distance stretches, cannot be interpreted as an adjustment of a conceptual scale. Each stretch of distance estimated was always a new one, with a different magnitude from all previous stretches, so that no bias toward a set of numerical responses could be built in by practice. Reduction of the variable error in such an experiment seems therefore to be a genuine case of perceptual learning, a narrowing within the stimulus continuum of the range of values eliciting a given response. The perception of distance became more precise.

Absolute Judgments of Multivariate Stimuli

Absolute judgments of stimulus items varying in more than one dimension have been found to permit greater transmission of information than judgments with a unidimensional variable (Eriksen & Hake, 1955; Eriksen, 1958; Garner, 1963). Is there a limit even here to the amount of informa-

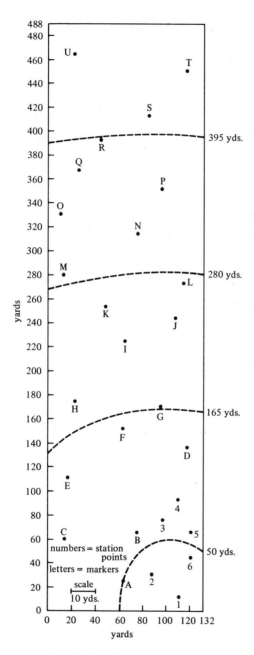

FIGURE 9–7. Map of a field with station points (1 through 6) and targets (A through U) laid out for distance estimation.

(From E. J. Gibson & R. Bergman, The effect of training on absolute estimation of distance over the ground. *Journal of Experimental Psychology*, 1954, *48*, 475.)

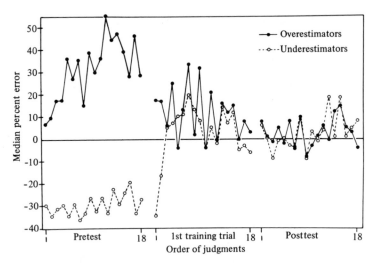

Median percent error for over- and underestimating O's (45 airmen)
in single trials of pretest, 1st training trial, and posttest.

FIGURE 9–8.   Changes in constant error as a function of training.

(From E. J. Gibson & R. Bergman, The effect of training on absolute
estimation of distance over the ground. *Journal of Experimental Psychology*, 1954, 48, 480.)

tion transmitted from the environment to the perceiver, and does training
raise the limit? Let us consider first combinations of stimulus variables
which are easily dimensionalized and can therefore be ranked or categorized in a way that does not involve learning new response names.

Color identification is such a case. More colors can be identified if
the samples vary in several dimensions instead of only on hue or only in
brightness, but even so absolute identification is limited. The number of
identifiable colors is said to be 15 or less (e.g., Halsey & Chapanis, 1951).
An experiment by Hanes and Rhoades (1959) sought to determine whether
significant improvement in this respect could be obtained with extended
practice. One subject studied color chips of the Munsell 21-chart Student
Set for several hours each day over a period of five months. The chips were
arranged in twenty constant-hue charts and one hue-value-chroma chart
(hue-brightness-saturation), with the chips of each hue chart separated
by one step in Munsell value and two steps in Munsell chroma. The number
of different chips was 465. The subject identified (or tried to identify)
each by the appropriate symbol in the Munsell notation. She selected her
own method for study. Tests were conducted with randomized presentation
of chips. When it became apparent that chips in the constant-hue charts
were too closely spaced for her to attain high accuracy, alternate chips were

withdrawn. Later, study was confined to 12 hues, with alternate chips. By elimination, the subject finally reached a set of fifty chips, all of which she could correctly identify. The observer's selection was her own. It is interesting that for one hue chart, blue-green, only one chip remained. It was concluded that the number of absolutely identifiable colors can be increased through practice. But a test after three and one-half months showed a decrease in the ability to identify with an increase in errors of about 25 percent. The errors showed tendencies to drift toward anchor points, that is, errors for colors of low saturation were in the direction of even lower saturation, while those of high saturation were in the direction of higher. Structure for multidimensional stimuli of this type, as I would put it, is given primarily by the system of classification. The anchors of the system are easily lost and the possibility of discovering higher order structure is limited.

Several experiments have been performed with multidimensional sound stimuli applying computerized teaching-machine techniques. In one by Swets, Millman, Fletcher, and Green (1962) the sound stimuli varied along four or five dimensions (frequency, amplitude, interruption rate, duty cycle, and duration), and had two to five values on each. The subject identified the sound presented by listing the value assumed by each dimension, that is, by a four- or five-digit number. A number of training procedures were compared: one was a standard, passive, procedure in which the subject pressed a space bar on his typewriter to initiate a trial and the computer identified a sound for him by typing a five-digit number and playing it; other procedures were conditions with overt response and various elaborate kinds of correction and reinforcement. The standard condition, with no overt response, no correction, and no reinforcement, led to the highest average of correct responses. The condition with most elaborate feedback and highest probability of reinforcement led to the lowest percentage of correct responses.

Swets and his collaborators (Swets et al., 1966) tried this experiment again with even more sophisticated computer appanages. The sounds varied along the same five dimensions. The subject was allowed to choose among instructional procedures, which included communicating with the computer via a cathode ray tube with a ten-inch display screen and a light pen. Values for each dimension of a sound were indicated visually on a matrix by the subject and then corrected. This elaboration of training procedure resulted in no increase in information transmitted. Comparison of different training procedures and sequences again indicated that simple observation of the sound and its identification was best, uncluttered by all the special paraphernalia and routines.

Learning thus takes place with stimuli varying on several dimensions; the subject learns about the dimensions, and when he must code the stimulus on several uncorrelated dimensions to identify it, he learns to analyze the dimensions within the complex. But reinforcement and overt correction of responses evidently play no crucial role in this kind of learning.

Identification of Complex Multivariate Stimuli

Objects in the world are always multivariate, and the ways in which they vary are often not dimensional. The isolated discrimination of small differences along a single dimension, or even along several dimensions as in the experiments above, is an exercise that is required only in a laboratory. Real objects and events such as human faces and human voices vary in many ways. Some ways are dimensional, like the loudness of a voice, but loudness is not what makes a voice unique and identifiable. What makes a face or a voice attributable to just one owner is a set of features. We can all identify a large number of faces and voices. It does not make sense to talk about bits of information transmitted in these perceptions; what are the bits and how would one count them? Furthermore, there does not seem to be an upper limit to the information transmitted as there is for sounds carefully varied in steps along five dimensions. What makes the difference?

The difference seems to be that real objects have structure as well as dimensional differences. We pick up a higher order of variable. It is hard to specify what this is, but it may be some kind of relation between features which is treated as a unit. For example, there is the physiognomic character by which a face is identified as distinct from all other faces. A face consists of forehead, eyes, nose, mouth, and chin, together with hair, cheekbones, ears, and dozens of other features for which no names exist. But it is perceived as one face, by adults at least.

Learning to identify complex patterns has received much study in the laboratory—for instance, learning names for nonsense forms. But since these experiments usually confound response learning with stimulus discrimination, they have not taught us very much about what we are now interested in. Learning to identify letters of the alphabet or the items of the Morse code for the alphabet can be studied experimentally, and these are real-life items even if they are man-made. We know surprisingly little about how a child learns to identify letters, despite its being an everyday occurrence. Perhaps that is why. We have often been told that a child confuses letters which are mirror images of one another, but we know little else except that getting 26 names successfully assigned to 26 graphic patterns is a hard task for most five year olds. The names bear no inherent relation to the patterns, and they must themselves be discriminated. Some are confusable within rhyming groups, such as A, K, and J. These sound similarities, as well as graphic similarities, may be a source of error for children in learning to identify letters.

The learning of Morse code, perhaps because it is of economic and military value, has received considerable study. It might tell us something about perceptual learning, since the responses are already learned and one source of confounding is thus eliminated. Usually it is studied as a paired associates task with concern for the formation of associations. The interesting questions of how the signals come to be heard as unique, and of how groups of signals eventually become heard as units rather than sequences of signals, are only beginning to be answered. Morse code signals that are similar are subject to errors of generalization (Keller & Taubman, 1943; Spragg, 1943; Keller & Schoenfeld, 1944). But similar sounding letter names (such as A and K), upon a reexamination of Keller and Taubman's data, seldom or never appear to be a source of confusion, for they are already differentiated and seem to have no effect on learning to differentiate the signals. There is no advantage for eventual differentiation in putting very similar signals close together in practice (Taylor, 1943; Rothkopf, 1958). Learners can discriminate signals that come much too fast for verbal description ("three dots and a dash") so verbal description is not a factor in differentiation (Rothkopf, 1958). Just listening to code items coming at operational speed, even without making overt responses, greatly facilitates learning the code (Allan, 1957, 1958; Barch & Levine, 1965). Delayed reinforcement (knowledge of results by presentation of the letter names, or of the message after hearing 15 to 30 characters at a time, or of messages lasting 5 to 12 minutes) is just as beneficial if not more so as immediate knowledge of results (Taylor, 1943). Hence immediate corrective feedback from an experimenter is not essential for improvement in item differentiation. Neither is it for learning to perceive the higher order structure in connected messages (Bryan & Harter, 1899), for the experienced receiver learns this on his own without any special intervention by the experimenter, who does not know while practice goes on what units the learner may be cutting out in receiving messages.

A proximity analysis of the errors made in learning Morse code (Shepard, 1963) reveals some interesting facts about properties of these dot-and-dash items which serve as distinctive features for differentiation at different stages of learning. In the earliest stage, analyzing data of Rothkopf (1957) obtained with same-different judgments, Shepard found that the two dimensions which served mainly for differentiation were length (number of elements) and heterogeneity (variety of elements). During intermediate stages of learning, analyzing data from Keller and Taubman (1943) and Plotkin (1943), Shepard found a different picture. The subjects now made frequent confusions of pattern—errors of reflection (e.g., . - - for - - .) and of complementarity (e.g., - . . - for . - - .). The learners were picking up internal structure, which they had not originally done. Finally, Shepard found at a still later stage of skill, analyzing data from Seashore and Kurtz (1944), that the subject had differentiated completely the inner structure of the items. Errors of reflection and complementarity had dropped out and the remaining errors were confusions between items having essentially the same structure but differing only in the length of a run of consecutive dots or dashes (e.g., - . . . . for - . . .). Shepherd attributes these terminal errors to a physiological limit, because the subjects were now receiving at a very fast rate. It might also be that they were progressing to higher units than the single item and were occasionally collapsing the structural unit or extending it, while retaining appreciation of the distinctive pattern. In any case, this beautiful analysis tells us for the first time in Morse code research something about progressive differentiation of structure.

Categorical Identification and Disjunctive Reaction Time

One does not think of categorical identification as having much to do with perceptual learning, and yet it can throw light on the subject, as recent experiments have shown. It would seem, superficially, that practice in categorizing should lead only to more generalized, less specific perceptions and thus result in the opposite of perceptual learning. But it is also possible that members assigned to a category actually share, potentially, some feature —either a minimal distinctive one or some higher order one—that distinguishes the category from other categories. If this is picked up with practice and processed without verbal intervention, perceptual learning has taken place.

Experiments on acquired equivalence which are interpreted as demonstrating additive mediation by a learned common response (the category name) can often be interpreted this way. A number of random shapes, for which one category name is to be learned, may actually share some distinguishing feature as contrasted with those assigned to another set. When the subject discovers such a feature, he has enormously reduced the amount of information that has to be handled in a perceptual process.

At the end of Chapter 7, I described an experiment by Yonas and Gibson (1967), in which the task was disjunctive reaction time and the stimuli (letters) were divided into two categories for response. In a condition where the positive set of three letters shared one feature which distinguished all three from the negative set, reaction time was significantly decreased with practice, compared to a condition where no single distinctive feature permitted such an economical process. This is a case of perceptual learning in categorical identification. Response equivalence (additive mediation) could not explain it, for responses were the same in the two conditions, whereas one showed greater improvement than the other.

An experiment by Rabbitt (1967) confirms our results, measuring latency of sorting into categories. Three packs of cards were made up, half containing the letter C, and half containing the letter O. On any card, one of these letters was embedded among seven other letters. In Pack One, C and O were embedded in a set of irrelevant letters containing no curved lines (A, E, F, H, I, K, and L). This was also true in Pack Two (irrelevant letters were M, N, T, V, W, X, and Y). In the Pack Three, the irrelevant letters all contained curves (B, D, G, J, P, Q, and S). The subjects began practice with either Pack One or Pack Two. Transfer was then tested by switching Pack One subjects to either Pack Two or Pack Three, and by switching Pack Two subjects to Pack One or Pack Three. There was marked decrement on transfer from either Pack One or Pack Two to Pack Three. The subject had learned to sort by discriminating only the minimal distinctive features which were appropriate for Packs One and Two, but they were not appropriate for Pack Three. Search time was lowered with practice in this task and the transfer findings indicate that what was learned —a reduced set of distinctive features—was specific to the task.

There is no external reinforcement or correction in these experiments. The subject is not told when he is going faster, or when he makes an error. The perceptual learning that takes place is automatic, self-regulated, and highly functional in reducing the information processed.

SUMMARY

This chapter considered experimental methods of investigating the effects of practice on perception. Does practice yield improvement? What are the kinds of improvement and what are the significant parameters of such experiments?

The methods were classified into four types of task: detection, discrimination, recognition, and identification. We can answer the first question unequivocally: practice yields improvement. It is adaptive, for thresholds are lowered, both constant and variable errors are reduced, and specificity of perception to stimulus variation is increased.

Methods of practice, kinds of stimulus variation, reinforcement, and correction all interact with the task (and each other) in these experiments. It makes a difference whether the stimulation is varied on a single dimension, or several, or is not describable dimensionally. For example, progressive practice may be of value for unidimensional variation but it is doubtful that it is otherwise. Correction is of value in changing a constant error, but one cannot but be impressed with the evidence that perceptual learning requires mainly the kind of reinforcement that self-knowledge—feedback from one's own performance—alone provides. Objects in the real world are multivariate, so many of these experiments have slight ecological validity, but they provide the proof that perceptual learning occurs, and that it can be studied without confounding by response learning.

10

Perceptual Learning with Imposed Transformation of the Stimulus Array

The World Thru 20-Diopter Prisms, Base Left
(After Wearing Them for Four Weeks)

The tipping floor and leering wall glare
And grasp, in league. Aggressive stairs approach
And pounce, looming chairs reach out to tear.
All stretches, shrinks, and flaming stains encroach.

With cunning steps I foil the league, with skill
The stairs subdue. From bolder feet the chairs retreat.
With steady view the stretchy rubbers still,
My confident gaze the glowing colors greet.

The bulges tease, the urchin dips appeal.
Two circling frames this fetching world enclose.
A euphoric cosmos the twin black frogs reveal.
The glowing world weighs gaily on my nose.

So vision is blurred, distorted, teased, reformed.
Can all the trusted standards be transformed?

Jean Gibson

In the preceding chapters, I have discussed the learning of distinctive features of objects, the detection of relational information which suffices to differentiate things and even symbols. Little has been said, so far, about an equally important kind of perceptual learning, the learning of invariant aspects of events. In this chapter I shall consider a class of experiments which appear to yield insights about this kind of perceptual learning. These are experiments with imposed transformations of the stimulus array.

An observer is provided with an instrument interposed between his sensory system and the world. A pair of spectacles is such an instrument.

But in these experiments the instrument has the effect of biasing the stimulus information that reaches the sense organ. The world itself is not changed, but the observer's relation to the information in stimulation is changed. The experiments ask whether and how he adjusts himself to this change. His adjustment is often referred to as adaptation to "distortion" or to "rearrangement" (Held, 1962). Experiments have been performed with a variety of transformations. We shall examine some representative ones, asking whether they shed any light on perceptual learning and development.

As with the experiments previously discussed, the first question to put is "what is learned?" It is not something new about the world. In fact, the distinctive features of things, like faces and alphabetic forms, and the relations between them stay the same. The observer must learn a new rule for the relationship between himself and the world of objects. Movement of the observer discloses the shift of information and new invariants must be discovered (or old ones recalibrated) for adaptation to the transformed array to take place.

It is essential to distinguish, in the first place, between two kinds of biased stimulus array, only one of which seems properly classified as a learning situation. Gibson discovered (1932) that prolonged inspection of a constantly biased visual display, such as a tilted or a curved line, would result in a phenomenal reduction of the tilt or curvature. He thought of it as a kind of normalization process. When the tilt or curve was replaced with an upright or a straight line, a negative aftereffect occurred; the line appeared tilted or curved in the opposite direction. This result was referred to by Gibson as "adaptation," since the resulting aftereffects follow the pattern of sensory adaptation to color, brightness, and temperature. He actually called it "adaptation-with-negative aftereffect" (1937). But the biasing here is found in a constant, isolated display and is not the same as an instrumentally imposed transformation which the subject must, so to speak, carry around with him and apply to all the objects and events which he may encounter. Perceptual adaptation to spectacle-wearing is a radically different phenomenon from sensory adaptation to curvature or tilt.

Looking through one's own spectacles is a familiar experience. When one puts on a pair of glasses with a new prescription, the world at first looks noticeably different: letters at reading distance, for instance, may appear larger and clearer. Our previously developed discriminative habits, such as differentiating the letters, are perfectly preserved, however, and unfamiliar irrelevant aspects, such as odd spectacle frames, are soon habituated to.

But these spectacles are not heavily biased. In fact they are supposed to correct one's vision. What happens if an observer goes around the world, exposing himself to any number of spatial encounters and objects, looking through spectacles which alter the pattern of light coming into the eye so as to impose curvature, tilt, reversal, displacement, or some combination of these transforms?

This is not the same case as a stationary biased display, because the array is not constant. Consider prismatic spectacles (Kohler, 1964). The observer moves his eyes behind the spectacles, and as he moves himself around the world (actually his head) he is confronted with objects and spaces differentially curved, and tilted to the right or the left. But the transform biases consistently. Relational information is perfectly preserved, if the transformed array, however biased, is correlated in a one-to-one fashion with the normal one. As Gibson (in Kohler, 1964) remarked of the Innsbruck experiments with distorting spectacles: "The implication is that light delivered by the spectacles to the eyes still carried information about the environment, but in an altered form. The information had not been destroyed, but only biased (p. 8)."

A feature of the spectacle-wearing experiment is that the meaning of things is unchanged. Houses are still perceived as houses, obstacles as obstacles, curbs as curbs, and so on. Much of the world is the same as before. Kohler (1964) reported, for instance, "When I wore the spectacles in the movies, they did not bother me in the least bit."

Thus positive transfer is clearly manifested when a transformation is imposed on the optic array to the eye. But a discrepancy appears when the head is moved. Rigid objects and surfaces appear to be elastic and to undergo disconcerting motions that correspond to movements of the head. The invariant relationship between head movement and the visual feedback that formerly served to guide action in space and time is no longer the same invariant. How much and what kind of adjustment occurs, and in what sense is it learning? [1]

EXPERIMENTS WITH DISPLACING OR TRANSFORMING OPTICAL SYSTEMS

The spectacle experiments, as they will be called, have investigated many kinds of systematic alteration, including left-right reversal, up-down reversal, inversion (reversal of both up-down and left-right), changes produced by wedge prisms, half prisms, and colored spectacles. The nature of the alteration imposed by the optical instrument determines, of course, the distortions or changes perceived when an observer first puts on the spectacles, some of them being much more complex than others. In all cases so far reported where the change was systematic and continuously imposed, some adaptation occurred and was followed, when the instrument was removed, by aftereffects in the opposite direction. The aftereffects can be used as a measure of the degree of perceptual compensation that has taken

[1] No attempt will be made to summarize the rapidly growing body of literature in this area. See Smith and Smith (1962) for a summary of earlier literature; Kohler (1964) for a summary of much of the Innsbruck work; Howard and Templeton (1966); and Rock (1966) for recent as well as earlier work.

place. Many interesting questions can be asked about these adjustments. What is it that adjusts, perception or motor response or both? When input is altered to the visual system, are intermodal effects observed? What is the locus of the habituation, peripheral or central? Is it contingent on other events, either internal or external, or is it absolute for a given receptor area? How fast does habituation occur, how lasting is it, and is it faster another time, as we should expect if learning is involved?

Inversion

Stratton's experiment of 70 years ago remains one of the most interesting to read, for he was concerned with the perceptual changes that occurred, and he presented a wealth of introspective observations which have mostly held up under replication. Stratton wore a lens system mounted in a tube in front of one eye, with the other eye occluded. Its effect was to reverse right to left and invert up and down. In his first experiment Stratton wore the lens system for parts of three days, blindfolding himself when the instrument was not in place. He attempted to move around and follow a normal routine, though he stayed indoors.

With this radical transformation of the visual array, not only are the visual spatial relations inverted as they might be in a double-mirror drawing situation; but also, since the instrument is mounted before the observer's eye, his relationship to things about him is changed in an abnormal way when his head turns. It is his own movement that brings about a perceptual discrepancy between impinging external stimulation and that arising from receptors in his muscles and joints. Visual perception of his limbs is altered, and since he feels them at the same time, movement produces a peculiar out-of-phase effect in what is normally a unified multimodel input system; there is a felt conflict between visual and proprioceptive input. As Stratton expressed it, ". . . the parts of my body were felt to be where they would have appeared had the instrument been removed; they were seen to be in another position." Or, again, "As to the uprightness or inversion of things, the general feeling was that the seen room was upside down; the body of the observer, represented in pre-experimental terms, was felt as standard and as having an upright position." But as experience and activity in the new situation continued, this standard lost its force. "When I looked out over a wide landscape, the position in which I felt my body to be and the position of the scene before me were surely discordant and unnatural. Yet I could not, as I had the day before, take either the one or the other unreservedly as standard. It seemed as if an abnormal position of my body in viewing things might just as well account for the facts as would an inversion of the scene."

Walking toward an object or reaching for it resulted in misdirected locomotion and failures to grasp. The visual effects of his own movement included a further anomaly of great interest; as he moved his head, he saw the world swinging round him, instead of maintaining constancy as it normally would.

In this experiment, and in a later repetition of it over a longer period, Stratton found himself gradually adjusting to the conflicts produced by the inverted array. Locomotion between obstacles improved, reaching movements were aimed correctly, and the swinging of the world with head movements was suppressed. A feeling of harmony between sight and felt movements began to be restored. Sounds, such as tapping with a pencil, were heard as issuing from their appropriate visual location (when the pencil was watched). People and objects in his surroundings began to look real, rather than incongruously reversed. Did they come to look right side up? This is not clear from Stratton's account; it is only clear that inter-sensory harmony was reestablished and that feelings of incongruity lessened, especially, he thought, when he was engaged in action.

It was repeatedly noticed in the course of the experiment that the total experience was much more harmonious during active movements of my body than when I inactively looked out upon the scene. This becomes intelligible when one sees how such movements gave additional vivacity to the new visual experience and to all that was in harmony with it, and tended to suppress those images of the body which did not accord with the new relations (p. 479, 1897b).

In an early stage of adjustment, Stratton reported that there was a double representation of the felt position of a limb being viewed. But progressively, and especially during activity, the older representation weakened. "During active operations on the visual surroundings, however, the older image of my body became, in many cases without my willing it, weaker than the new, and at times faded completely away (p. 358, 1897a)." The suppression of the conflicting, original felt limb position seems to have become nearly complete. "And in walking, when hands and feet rhythmically made their appearance in the visual field, the old representation, except perhaps for some faint inharmonious sensations in the back, was fully expelled without employing any device of will or of attention whatever (p. 469, 1897b)." The observations suggest very strongly that perceptual adjustment took place, at least in part, by means of suppressing the conflictful input from one system.

When the lenticular tube was removed on the eighth day, and a tube without lenses mounted in its place, aftereffects presented themselves, creating a new discordance between visually perceived directions and those perceived through the tactual and proprioceptive receptor systems. Furthermore, head and body movements were accompanied once more by apparent swinging of the environment round him.

What happened as the observer adjusted himself to the biased array? Can one say that perceptual learning occurred? An observation supporting this statement is the transfer that Stratton noted from his first experiment to the second later one. He made no measurements of accuracy of aiming or reaching, but he noted upon assuming the glasses a second time:

The scene before me was often reconstructed in the form it would have had in normal vision; and yet this translation was not carried to such an extent as at the beginning of the first experiment. The scene was now accepted more as it was immediately presented. Objects of sight had more reality in them—had more the character of "things," and less that of phantoms—than when the earlier trial began (p. 345, 1897a).

Stratton thought the explanation of his adjustment lay in a learned correspondence of local signs between touch and sight. He made the assumption that "a system of correspondence exists whereby a sign in one sense comes to be connected with and to suggest a particular sign in the other sense (p. 471, 1897b)." This explanation—a reintegration of associative connections between one local sign and another—may seem plausible at first glance but its inadequacy will become clear in later experiments from the Innsbruck laboratory. It is interesting that Stratton himself, as a result of his experiment, gave up the notion that the detection of visual direction depends on eye movements or head movements. He concluded:

Nor, on the other hand, are the visual directions made known to us and determined through our perceiving the "absolute," or pure motor, direction of the movements which alter the line of sight. The facts all go to show that the direction of movements of the head or eyes is not judged on purely muscular evidence, independently of the simultaneous changes in vision itself. . . . This will no doubt seem a hard saying to those who have been pinning their faith more and more on the unimpeachable witness of muscular sensations. It certainly makes the eye-movement doctrine of visual directions of little practical assistance for understanding the harmony between sight and touch (pp. 480–81, 1897b).

Following Stratton, several other investigators repeated his experiments, but with different lens systems and very different observations of the observer's adjustments. Ewert (1930), like Stratton, studied vision with complete inversion of the field, but he used a binocular optical system. The visual field was about 35° in extent, and the binocular system altered conditions for perceiving stereoscopic depth as well as direction. Descriptions of the subject's behavior were studied, with objective tests confined to laboratory situations, instead of the subject's observations of the everyday perceptual world. Ewert's subjects, over a period of 14 to 16 days, improved in accuracy on a series of overt localizing tasks, in fact on all tasks except one involving distance discrimination. The improvement was interpreted as due to the growth of new sensory-motor habits, but there were also references to inhibition of "sense-data from those receptors which may serve as distractors."

Experiments similar to Ewert's were carried out by Peterson and Peterson (1938) and by Snyder and Pronko (1952) and Snyder and Snyder (1957), the latter again emphasizing laboratory tests of motor adjustment rather than perceptual change. Both these experiments reported data on retention of motor adjustments to the lenses after a long period (eight months in the Peterson experiment and two years in the Snyder). There was excellent retention in both cases of motor performance with inverted vision. Both interpreted these results to mean that adaptation to visual inversion was attributable to the learning of highly specific responses. But it will be noted that Stratton reported a general carryover of a perceptual change which is not easily assimilated to such a view.

The most ambitious program of experiments following Stratton was begun in the Innsbruck laboratory by Erismann in 1928 and continued by Kohler and his colleagues (Kohler, 1951, 1964). A number of different optical systems were devised, some giving an up-down reversal and some a right-left reversal, but not an inversion as in the foregoing studies. In these experiments the subject generally wore the optical devices for a fairly long period, went about his daily routine, and made detailed notes of changing perceptual experiences, as Stratton had done. Interest centered less on measurements of eye-hand and other visual-motor coordinations than on perceptual reports, and an effort was made to keep the subject in his everyday world rather than simply in the laboratory.

An up-down reversing mirror worn on the head in the manner of an eyeshade was devised by Erismann and worn by several subjects for six days or longer. The subjects, like Stratton, recovered from the first behavioral disruption and adjusted their overt behavior so well that they managed to fence, bicycle, and ski. Changes in the visual direction perceived were reported to take place more slowly, however, and some very bizarre phenomena apparently occurred during this period. One subject reported that two adjacent heads, one upright and the other upside down, were both perceived as upright. In another case, the subject first saw an object as reversed, but, upon reaching for it and touching it, claimed that the perception turned right side up. Gravitational pull was influential in righting the appearance of an object or landscape. Kohler (1964) reported that for one subject, after five days, "perceptual errors hardly ever occurred"; and for another, "Correct veridical vision was achieved by subject M. after wearing the experimental spectacles for nine days."

Adaptation to right-left reversal (without up-down reversal) was observed in two subjects wearing spectacles devised by Kohler in the form of a pair of right-angle prisms mounted in goggles. This device permitted overlapping views of a field 33° by 25°, and had the secondary effect of reversing binocular disparity information. The depth perception of two rods seen through a window appeared reversed and in fact remained so, without correction, throughout the long experiment. There was, of course, much other depth information unaffected by a right-left reversal, for instance, motion parallax and perspective. One subject wore the spectacles for more than five weeks and Kohler himself wore them for more than three weeks. The adaptation in this experiment did not appear to be consistent; perception of left-right in the visual field varied from situation to situation, and with the subject's attention and attitudes (Kottenhoff, 1957a and b). Yet the subject who wore the spectacles longest achieved almost completely veridical perceptions, including reading "reversed" letters like b and d.

Lateral Displacement with Prisms

The first observations on the perceptual effects of looking through wedge prisms, with base to one side so as to produce a lateral displacement of the field of view, appear to be those discussed in Helmholtz (1924). The first systematic experiment with measurement of their effects was conducted by Wooster in 1923 using prisms which displaced the visual field about 20° to the right. Like many psychologists of the day (especially in Carr's laboratory where she was a student) she was primarily interested in measuring sensory-motor adjustments such as eye-hand coordination. These adjustments occurred even though her subjects wore the prisms for only twenty minutes a day for ten days. Localization of objects by reaching improved under various conditions of correction, and showed savings after a long period of time.

Wooster concluded that the new coordinations were simply a matter of sensory-motor learning. She was not concerned with perceptual change. But several years later, adaptation to prismatic spectacles was studied in relation to perception by Gibson (1933), and by Kohler at the Innsbruck laboratory (1951). Today, reports of experiments with prismatic spectacles are being published at a phenomenal rate. It is too soon to attempt a summary of this literature; I will only describe what happens perceptually when wedge prisms are first put on, what kinds of adaptation occur, and what appear to be some important conditions for adaptation.

When a base-left prism is placed before an eye looking straight forward, with eye and head fixed, a number of distortions are apparent in the visual field. These include an overall displacement to the right of the light rays entering the eye (the degree of displacement depending on the angle of the prism); an apparent curvature of all vertical straight lines in the world; and illusory colored fringes along vertical edges. True right angles are seen as acute or obtuse. Depending on the angle of regard there is differential image displacement, so that head movement from side to side results in a sort of moving compression of the object regarded, while up

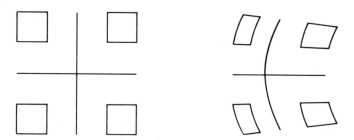

FIGURE 10–1. On the left is a standard display of two perpendicular axes and squares within their four quadrants; on the right is the same display as it would look seen through a prism.

(From I. Kohler, The formation and transformation of the perceptual world. *Psychological Issues,* Int. Univ. Press, 1964, *III*, 4, 56.)

and down movement results in apparent tilting of horizontal edges, a kind of rocking movement of things. The general appearance of the world, with head movement, has been described as "rubbery." It is no longer rigid. The photographs in Figure 10–2 show the differentially distorted appearance of a building seen through a prism (base right) with head turned right, left, up, or down.

Adaptation to prism-produced distortion occurs. For example, the apparent curves tend to straighten out and this is followed by a negative aftereffect of curvature when the spectacles are removed (Gibson, 1933). The color fringes also tend to disappear, to be followed by fringes of opposite color when the world is looked at without prisms. But the most remarkable kind of adaptation perhaps is that to the changing distortions accompanying head movement. The rubbery motions of the world tend to disappear, and then to reappear in the opposite direction when the light rays come straight to the eye.

Adaptation to different types of prism distortion varies with the type of distortion and with the time of exposure. Pick and Hay (1964) have provided data for several of these observed distortions after three days and after 42 days of wearing prisms. The prisms caused an 11° displacement of the visual field and were worn during all waking hours. The tests employed were assessments of the perceptual changes, not of the motor corrections. Results with the most sensitive tests are presented in Table 10–1, expressed as percent adaptation. It will be noted that nearly complete adaptation was found only for kinaesthetic localization of a visual target. To measure this performance, the observer was asked to touch a visual target without seeing the results of his aim. The least adaptation was achieved for the differential displacements produced by head movements, especially compression and expansion with side-to-side head movement. The loss of rigidity of objects, and hence of size constancy, is a formidable

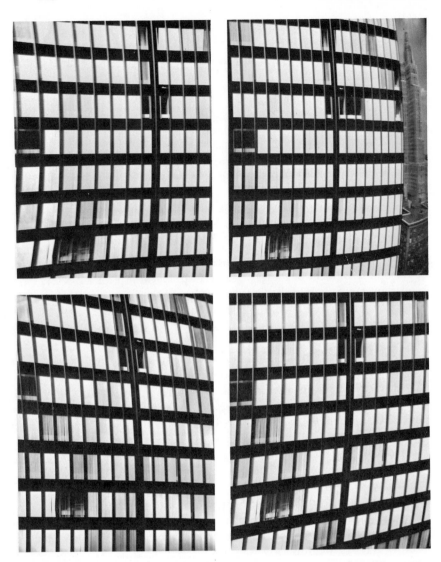

FIGURE 10–2. Distorted appearance of a building seen through a prism (base right) with the head turned to the right, left, up, or down (Kohler, 1962).

(From *Scientific American,* by William Vandivert.)

loss; yet, with time and experience, adaptation to the prismatic displacement conditional on differential head and eye posture began to take place.

Kohler himself was particularly interested in what he called "conditional" adaptation, followed by situational aftereffects. In a truly heroic experiment, Kohler wore 15° and finally 20° prisms for 124 days, and it

TABLE 10–1

Perceptual Adaptation of 3- and 42-Day Subjects to Various Prismatic Distortions

Distortion	Percent Adaptation 3 days	42 days
1. Overall horizontal displacement		
a. Visual localization of auditory target	44.6	
b. Kinaesthetic localization of visual target	85.8	90.1
2. Curvature of vertical lines	11.2	30.0
3. Color fringes at vertical edges	16.5	33.9
4. Differential displacement		
a. Tilting of horizontal lines with up-down head movement	8.4	14.6
b. Compression and expansion of fixated target with side-to-side head movement	0.8	9.8
c. Convergence of horizontal lines above and below eye level	Not tested	51.5

From H. L. Pick & J. C. Hay, Adaptation to prismatic distortion. *Psychonomic Science*, 1964, *1*, 199–200.

was then that these situational aftereffects were first observed. Kohler's own words state his discovery clearly:

It is known that the deflection of rays by a prism is minimum when the subject is looking through the center of the prism. As soon as the subject deviates from this line of vision, either horizontally or vertically, the distortions increase: angles become even more acute or obtuse, and lines which were close to being perpendicular or horizontal now appear markedly slanted. Furthermore, the quality of the perceptual alteration depends on the direction in which the subject's line of vision deviates. Thus, the same object appears thin when viewed through one side of the prism, and broadened when viewed through the other side, objectively horizontal or vertical lines are displaced one way when seen from below and another way when seen from above. And all this takes place for the same retinal area, the center of normal accurate vision. The question therefore arises: what are the aftereffects of so many different and contrasting sensory influences?

The situational aftereffect provides the answer; it is an aftereffect whose characteristics depend on particular conditions, in this case on the direction of the line of vision. Thus, the separation between two poles was decreased when looked at from the left, and increased when looked at from the right! Earlier, during the wearing of spectacles, the reverse had occurred. In other words, what we have here is a special kind of negative aftereffect: it occurs only when the total situation is the same as the one in which the prism-induced alterations originally occurred. This principle is applicable to all other aftereffects as well: those involving deformations, obliquities, apparent movements, etc. (Kohler, 1964, p. 39).

The impressive fact which we can infer from these observations, and many similar ones, is the organism's remarkable ability to extract multimodal conditional invariants from the stimulus flux, and to develop gradually highly differentiated perceptual responses to them. It is this fact which inclines me to feel that we are dealing, in prism adaptation, with a true case of perceptual learning, a progressive change under the transformed situation toward more highly differentiated perception.

Other experiments of Kohler's illustrate the point. He served as subject, again, in an experiment of fifty days duration in which he wore binocular half prisms. His upward regard had to pass through a 10° prism, but his downward regard looked through clear glass. He reports that during this time his vision became differentially adapted to the two conditions. And after removal of the spectacles, depending on the direction of his gaze, the same stimulus objects gave rise to specific negative aftereffects with one line of regard but not with another. Kohler referred to this as a "conditioned" aftereffect, because it depended on the "facilitating or inhibiting action of the subject's eye-head position as a new contributing factor." These tied aftereffects were apparent especially in visual orientation and perception of movement.

Pick and Hay (1966) and Hay and Pick (1966) referred to these results as "gaze-contingent adaptation." They were able to replicate many of Kohler's observations, though the magnitude of the effect was less. They were also able to show interocular transfer of adaptation to gaze-contingent distortions, implying central involvement in the process of adaptation (Pick, Hay, & Willoughby, 1966). Descriptively what the subject has done is to extract, over a period of exposure and practice, an invariant, conditional stimulus, with both visual and kinaesthetic-vestibular components. Eye movements, head movements, and retinal area stimulated are none of them alone sufficient to explain the specificity of perception which, after a long period, is differentiated from what originally appeared as a stretching, shearing, inconstant flux.

Colored Spectacles

Wishing to follow up his discovery of these conditional aftereffects, Kohler and his students put them to a severe test by the experiment of wearing spectacles of which the left halves were colored blue and the right halves yellow. One subject wore these for twenty days, another for sixty. As the subject looked to the left, everything appeared blue, but when he looked to the right, everything appeared yellow. When the spectacles were removed, it was reported that a negative aftereffect appeared, contingent on the direction in which the subject was looking. In other words, the same retinal receptors were differentially adapted. The subject "had the impression that objects to his left were bathed in warm yellowish candlelight, while objects to his right tended to take on colder colors," and the illusion moved with the subject's head movement (as the spectacles had), but not with eye movements. The replicability of this effect has been questioned, however (Harrington, 1965; and McCollough, 1965).

The conditional adaptation to color has been demonstrated in another way, the case of adaptation to the color fringes produced by prisms. The colors lie along vertical edges where a sharp brightness contrast exists. But the colors are different, depending on whether the lighter field is on the right or the left of the boundary; with base-right prisms, an edge with white to the left is bordered with yellow-red; but an edge with white to the right is bordered with blue. These borders of color are adapted to rather quickly and effectively. Then, when the glasses are removed, the opposite color fringes appear as an aftereffect. The same area on the retina, depending on whether the bright side of the border is to the right or left, will respond specifically, in the opposite fashion, to the adaptation. As Kohler put it,

> The subject looking at the world through prisms that have their bases facing to the right unconsciously learns a new rule: The boundary between a dark field on the left and a light field on the right always has a fringe of blue; when the dark field lies to the right of the light field, the fringe is always yellow. We must assume that the total adaptation process requires simultaneous adjustment to these two conditions (Kohler, 1962, p. 68).

This result was successfully replicated by Hay, Pick, and Rosser (1963). It now seems doubtful, however, that a learning process is involved since there is no interocular transfer for adaptation to chromatic fringes, as there is for gaze-contingent distortions (Pick, Hay, & Willoughby, 1966).

Minification and Magnification

Adaptation to looking through a minifying or magnifying optical device has been studied in several experiments. Because the visual angle is altered, things look nearer or farther, or larger or smaller, depending on conditions and on the attitude of the observer. Foley (1965) employed a lens system and observed the effect of both magnification and minification. There was an alteration in the apparent distance of objects, but not in their apparent size. Size-constancy judgments were not affected. Changes were reported, after several experiences of wearing the lenses, in absolute estimates of distance magnitudes, which may indicate adaptation to the altered apparent distance. The subjects wore the lenses for six hours on successive days, with normal vision intervening, so that judgmental effects rather than a perceptual shift may have been operating. Knowledge of the transformation and deliberate compensation could easily play a role.

Wallach and Kravitz (1965) used minifying lenses to study what Wallach termed "constancy of visual direction." The visual field is optically displaced with head movement in such a way that the world appears to swing instead of to remain stationary or constant—a parallel to the swinging effect found in experiments with inverting lenses and reversing prisms. Wallach and Kravitz measured adaptation to the swinging effect and found that after six hours of wearing the minifying device while following a normal daily routine the subjects achieved 50 percent of full adaptation.

An evenly distributed transformation of the entire visual field, such as magnification or minification, apparently preserves the relational information so perfectly that very rapid adaptation takes place. Even the swinging effect is adjusted to more rapidly than with prisms, where the nature of the transformation changes with eye and head movement. Detection of the transformation is easily achieved, and that might go a long way to explain the rapid compensation.

EXPERIMENTS WITH ENHANCED BINOCULAR DISPARITY

Wallach and his collaborators have performed a series of studies (Wallach & Moore, 1963; Wallach & Karsh, 1963a and b) in which one of the cues for perceived depth was altered so as to misrepresent the objective situation and contradict other visual information about depth. Retinal disparity was brought into conflict with motion perspective ("kinetic depth effect," in Wallach's terminology). The latter is known to be a strong, high-priority depth cue. The conflict was not brought about by the observer's own movement, as in the foregoing experiments, since he did not wear an instrument and carry it around with him in the world. The conflict was produced by the experimenter in the visual display that the subject had to observe. A mirror arrangement called a telestereoscope was used to increase retinal disparity in the two images of an object by increasing the interocular distance. Apparent depth is enhanced by this increase but now, when a three-dimensional wire form is viewed through the telestereoscope as it rotates around a vertical axis, information from disparity and motion perspective are at odds, and the wire form appears to distort as it rotates. Different cross sections go through different phases of expansion and contraction simultaneously depending on their orientation to lines of sight.

In a typical experiment, a subject began by viewing a stationary wire cube through the telestereoscope and making an estimate of its depth by adjusting a metal rod. Then, still looking through the telestereoscope, he watched the cube rotate for ten minutes. After this training period, as Wallach termed it, the subject made a new estimate of the cube's depth. The result of the experiment was that the enhanced depth estimate made before rotation was reduced significantly after watching the cube rotate for ten minutes. The rubbery distortion of the cube during rotation was followed, when viewed without the telestereoscope, by the opposite distortion, and normal retinal disparity was found to give rise to reduced depth. Effects of the training transferred to a different wire form, but in diminished degree.

Other experiments gave the subjects practice with a reduced interocular distance, so that they experienced diminished perceived depth when viewing the stationary cube. If compensation occurred with this condition, it should lead to increased stereoscopic depth, and to a slight degree it did.

If one considers this modification of depth perception to be learning (as Wallach does), it is interesting to ask how lasting it is. Experiments in which the subject sat with his eyes closed after viewing through the telestereoscope revealed a decrement of 73 percent of the original effect after 12 minutes. It did persist, but was not permanent. Further experiments led Wallach to conclude also that his training effect was cumulative and increased with length of the training period.

What happens to modify the subject's perception as he views the rotating wire form through the telestereoscope? A control experiment indicated that discrimination of the information provided by motion perspective was not modified. It would seem, therefore, that the nonvalidity of the stereoscopic information is somehow detected while viewing the rubbery deformations, and that this information is rather quickly recalibrated, or suppressed.

Wallach has argued that the adaptation-like effects found with the telestereoscope are best interpreted as the result of cue discrepancy. The change in stereoscopic depth perception occurs because, when the wire figure is rotated, two "different processes of depth perception pertaining to the same form take place simultaneously and cause conflicting results (p. 430, Wallach & Karsh, 1963a)." The result, he believes, is a tendency to reduce the perceptual discrepancy by modifying one of the two perceptual processes. Proof of the involvement of the kinetic depth effect, as opposed to mere rotation, is the evidence adduced to support this view. Earlier studies of the kinetic depth effect showed that certain wire figures were effective and sufficient to give a good depth effect, while others were not, even when rotated. Wallach and Karsh found that stereoscopic depth was modified to a significantly greater extent when viewing the wire forms that produced the best kinetic depth. They argued that it was thus not simply the distortion of the wire form under rotation that mattered, but the conflict of the two depth cues. Why it is the stereoscopic cue that is modified in the direction of veridicality is not fully explained by this notion. But at least it is clear from these experiments that feedback from action is not involved in the stereoscopic modification, since the subject remains inactive all the while he is looking through the telestereoscope. Information about cue validity must be provided by perspective changes as the wire form rotates. That the cue of binocular disparity is very easily suppressed and in many people unstable is a common observation, and its fast deterioration with disuse was further demonstrated by Wallach and Karsh (1963b), so the competing information would presumably not need to be exceptionally impressive for recalibration or suppression of the invalid stereoscopic cue to take place.

EXPERIMENTS WITH DISPLACED AUDITORY STIMULATION

Experiments analogous to those with displacing optical systems have been performed with the auditory modality, setting up a conflict between the information in these modalities. Pseudophones can be led into the subject's ears in such a way as to displace the normal interaural relations, with one ear artificially leading the other. Since auditory localization depends on minute binaural differences in time and intensity of the stimulation from a given sound source, a false lead of one ear should cause a displacement in localization of the source of a sound and a discrepancy with other information about the source, such as visual information. The question arises whether compensatory shifts will develop with prolonged exposure to displaced auditory stimulation.

Early experiments by P. T. Young (1928) and by Willey, Inglis, and Pearce (1937) with a reversal of auditory stimuli to the two ears (180° rotation around the vertical axis of the head) failed to find compensatory shifts of auditory localization, except when the subject was looking at a sound source. Then it was generally accurately localized in accord with the untransformed visual stimulation. Held (1955), working with a less radical shift, had his subjects wear electronic pseudophones which led with one ear so as to produce a rotational displacement of 22° of the aural axis. The subjects in one experiment wore the pseudophones for seven hours, going about in their normal surroundings and following their routine. Measurements of auditory localization of sound sources were taken before and after wearing the instrument.

The subjects of this experiment did demonstrate shifts of localization of about 10°, which tended to correct for the error produced by displacement of the aural axis. The subjects also reported that there appeared to be two sources of the same sound. A second experiment was conducted with rigid control of the subject's movements and the sound sources to which he was exposed, in an attempt to relate the shifts to the exact conditions of the new proprioceptive-auditory relations. Held concluded that auditory directional localization depends on an invariant relational stimulus that is a combination of binaural time difference with translational displacement of the head or body; and that shifts in localization after wearing pseudophones were due to the new invariant stimulus combinations to which the subject had been exposed. Compromises with the old relations, or separation of two possible localizing responses, the old and the new, could result.

Held argued that repeated combinations of a certain direction of head translation with a given time difference would lead to learned localizing responses—new ones in his experiment with atypical stimulation. He argued also that normal sound-localization is acquired in this way in the course of development—that is, by each time difference being frequently combined with a given head movement unique to the direction of the source producing the time difference. Is each instance a separate learning process? I shall return to this question, for I think that an invariant is differentiated that provides a rule for a multimodal system.

THE INTERPRETATION OF ADAPTATION TO SPATIALLY TRANSFORMED STIMULUS ARRAYS

How do we account for the phenomena of adaptation to prisms and other displacing devices? What do the facts of compensatory adjustment and highly specialized situational aftereffects mean? The facts have been included in this book because they represent perceptual modifications which seem, in some cases at least, to be learning. Furthermore, it has been argued by many of the psychologists whose work has been described (e.g., Kohler, Wallach, Held, Taylor) that the process of adjustment to spatial transforms is the way the system developed in the individual from the outset; in short, that the experiments are ways of studying perceptual development. As Kohler put it:

One can start with something completely formed and then restructure it by forcing it to change and adapt itself to opposite circumstances. The primary factors of prior experience, practice, and habit, as well as their interrelationship, will then manifest themselves in the resistances that are encountered in such a procedure. Much that has been built up in the course of life can only be discovered and disentangled in the context of the rehabituation experiment (Kohler, 1964, p. 148).

This point of view cannot be accepted without qualification. We are not studying an original developmental process in the rehabituation experiment, for we are dealing with a transfer situation instead; there is positive transfer of discrimination of distinctive features and properties of objects (whenever a systematic transformation is imposed), and there is negative transfer produced by input discrepant with old habits. Yet it is not unreasonable to suppose that the learning process in the two cases should have something in common. What could this be?

My view is that the goal of the learning and what is learned are in one important respect similar, both in development and in rehabituation. The goal of spatial perception is the search for invariants, for a world with constancy and rigidity. In the infant, head movements, eye movements, reaching movements, and eventually locomotor movements accompany exploratory looking and aiming at a target. A target can be seen only, or can also be grasped, or can be stepped on. From the flux of inputs, both visual and proprioceptive,[2] an invariant multimodal stimulus relationship is gradually extracted and comes to monitor activity. There can even be conscious search for this multimodal monitoring stimulation. I remember this well when learning to dive; the combination of looking, number of paces, force of spring, and head and arm position had to feel exactly right (and always the same) in order to hit the board and the water properly. What an amazingly complex input! But until this invariant pattern was differentiated, the action was ill-directed, the goal frustrated.

How is this similar to learning in the rehabituation experiments? I think it is because the conflict produced by displacement of one sensory system forces a search for new invariants. This search may be successful soon or later, depending on what kind of a transform of the original stimulus array has been imposed, and how the subject explores the new array. Learning the nature of the transform may be facilitating. The classical mirror-drawing experiments always found facilitation from insight into the nature of the reversal (Bray, 1928; Siipola, 1935). But something more still had to be learned.

Knowledge of the transformation does not, alone, suppress the old habits and disclose the new invariant of multimodal stimulation which alone can make the world rigid, constant, and therefore feasible for locomotion and action. This relational stimulation must be extracted from combined sensory input and feedback. The process has two aspects, I think; one a positive process of extracting or isolating the relational pattern that leads to stability, and the other an inhibitory process of suppressing irrelevant, shifting, discrepant input. The discrepant input is informative as to the nature of the transformation, as are errors, but it is not the discrepancy or the errors themselves which give the new relational pattern.

Movement is an important aspect of the subject's exploratory behavior in achieving compensation for it provides part of the essential information. To quote Held, "We have concluded that movement-produced visual stimulation is essential for the development of these forms of behavior. Apparently, movement with its accompanying change in visual stimulation allows the organism to take advantage of certain invariances entailed in its relation with a stable environment (Held, 1964, p. 3)." Passive movement is less likely to do this, since the person must know that he is moving, and how

[2] For a theoretical discussion of proprioception and its meaning with respect to vision, kinaesthesis, and feedback, see Gibson (1966).

he is moving, for the world to become stable rather than to appear itself to move.

Held has argued that it is the efferent aspect of active movement which makes it superior to passive movement in development of adaptation to visual displacement. Held and Hein (1958) found that passive movement of a hand viewed through prisms did not lead to improvement in pointing to a target, whereas active (self-initiated) movement of the hand did. Held and Bossom (1961) found that egocentric localization of the body with respect to a visual target after wearing prisms was compensated for when the subject walked about on his own, but not when he was pushed passively in a wheelchair. The field of view was restricted to the central 60°, so that the wheeled subject presumably could not see the point of contact of his wheels with the ground. In this case, there appears to be very little information available that he was moving, rather than the world. It seems clear from these experiments that compensation with prisms ordinarily involves combined visual, haptic, and vestibular information; that is, knowledge from the body, through motion, as to where it is in relation to the world. Self-initiated movement is obviously a good means of obtaining the latter kind of stimulus information as it changes in relation to visual stimulation, thus revealing the new invariant which yields a constant and rigid world.

Howard, Craske, and Templeton (1965) have argued that afferent stimulation from the world may be sufficient for development of compensation if it affords, through discrepant stimulation, information about the distortion. They had subjects look through mirrors which displaced the optic array two inches to the left. The subjects fixated a lighted target, with the head clamped in a head rest. A rod 14 inches from the subject was brought toward him till it hit him on the lips. It appeared, through the mirror, that it would hit his face two inches to the left of the lips. Twenty practice trials under this condition led to some compensation of pointing in the expected direction, although only afferent stimulation had been given. Here is a case where the transformation produced no discrepancy of curvature, or rocking motion with changing head posture. Detection of the transformation is given rather simply by the discordant stimulation, and a rule or simple shift is sufficient to produce at least a small amount of compensation. This is not the same case as the one where movement of the head wearing prisms causes a shift in degree of tilt or compression.

Perplexing facts have turned up in the recent literature of prism research, generally having to do with the exclusion of part of the input from some sensory system by such means as covering one eye, putting a box over the body, shutting off the view of one arm, or holding the head rigid in a bite board. Anomalies such as lack of transfer from one hand to the other (Harris, 1963; Hamilton, 1964) may then occur. I think what is happening here is the breaking up or disunifying of what is ordinarily a unified multimodal system of stimulus invariants, so that a complete harmonious transfer becomes impossible.

Normally there are stimulus invariants over whole systems, combining sight of the body and limbs, proprioception from feeling them, from head turning, and from reaching. But when the head is held rigid with a bite board, or the limbs concealed, these relational invariants over many systems are no longer available for consistent transfer over the total system, and the compensation has to be piecemeal rather than generalized along the appropriate continua. The monitoring of action depends on unique stimulation from an interlocking combination of information from the world and from the body. For example, a man can reach for a target with his head tilted to one side. This is an abnormal position, but he feels it listing, the eye position compensates, and so do the slants in the world change their angles. Relational invariants remain, in spite of change of absolute stimulation.

When one looks through prisms, discrepancies occur, but new invariants can be detected and should hold over the interlocking system. That is, if the head must rotate to a certain degree in order to see a target ahead, so must the reach and the step conform in their adjustment. Since the system has previously been a unified one, with continuity of subsystems and correlation between them, each new act should not have to be separately relearned. But putting part of the system out of action necessarily prevents good transfer. I might be able to dive without error after wearing prisms for a while; but systematic transfer would be very difficult if I were forced to wear a stiff collar at the same time I was being exposed to the changed visual array.

This point of view runs counter to the view of Stratton that specific new localizing movements are learned for each new instance of rearranged stimulation. It is also counter to the theories of some present-day psychologists, chief among them Taylor (1962). He believes that adaptation to spectacle-wearing represents learning of specific new conditioned responses to particular situations of rearranged stimulation. He bases his argument on experiments in which he wore prisms discontinuously but always at the same time of day and in the same setting, and found evidence of adaptation within that setting rather than a general change. I would argue that conditional adaptation is possible, but that it demonstrates further differentiation; not that there cannot be learning of a new invariant rule relating two systems.

SUMMARY

When transforming spectacles such as prisms are placed over the eyes, visual information about objects in the world is unchanged as regards their essential properties and distinctive features. Things which could be differentiated before, such as faces, or furniture, or even written symbols, can still be differentiated from one another, so that the meaning and identifiability of things is not lost.

But the location of things in regard to one's own position in space is shifted. Again, as long as a consistent transformation is imposed, all is not lost, and reasonably rapid compensation for the shift develops. To the extent that the transformation changes with eye, head, and body posture, the compensation becomes more exacting because it is conditional on a number of stimulus variables, a multimodal complex. The related stimulus events which monitor an action, such as walking toward something, include visual and haptic components, with moment-to-moment feedback adding to the complex. It is this kind of stimulus invariant which maintains constancy and rigidity of the world and the things in it. Compensation for a transformed array requires discovery of new invariants.

Conceivably, knowing the nature of the transformation, a verbal admonishment could simply be applied. This might work with something like magnification or a simple translation; you just allow for everything looking nearer than it is, or two inches to the right. But we know that the process of adaptation is by no means so cognitive. Verbal self-admonitions can no doubt be given, but a real perceptual shift takes place as well. For such a shift to occur when head and eye postures complicate the new relation of the person to a transformed array, exploratory looking and moving toward objects and surfaces are probably essential for detection of the multimodal stimulus invariants. Things *look* different and *feel* different as this occurs because the effective stimulation to which the person is now responding is different. The process of learning to respond to a new effective invariant stimulus may be a dual one, requiring suppression of discordant stimulation as well as isolation of the critical invariant. Exploration and filtering are key processes in extraction of invariants. The result is properly termed perceptual learning, because specificity is increased.

11

Intermodal Transfer
of Perceptual Learning

A cornerstone of the earlier enrichment theories of perceptual learning was the conviction that some modes of sensory experience are dependent on others for their meaning and that the senses, originally separate and specific, are integrated in the course of development (see references to Carr and Stratton in Chapter 2). Similar qualities are supposed to have become similar through common associates. Furthermore, a growing body of psychological research is coming to be classified as cross-modal transfer, and the term "transfer" carries with it the implication that this is a learning problem.

That there are relationships between the sensory systems is obvious; intersensory similarity is responsible for much of poetic metaphor. Emily Dickinson, for example, invokes similarities between three modes of experience in the following stanza:

> There's a certain slant of light
> On winter afternoons,
> That oppresses, like the weight
> Of cathedral tunes.

Psychologists, too, have long been fascinated by the similarity of qualities across modalities. In William James's words:

All sorts of analogies obtain between the spheres of sensibility. Why are "sweet" and "soft" used so synonymously in most languages? And why are both these adjectives applied to objects of so many sensible kinds? Rough sounds, heavy smells, hard lights, cold colors, are other examples. Nor does it follow from analogies such as these that the sensations compared need be composite and have some of their parts identical (James, 1890, Vol. 1, p. 209).

It does not necessarily follow, either, that sensations or qualities indigenous to one modality are transferred to another by virtue of being associated by contiguity; there is no proof that ice looks cold, for instance, because it feels cold and the coldness in the past has got associated with the visual sensations. The question is, how can we state the problem so as not to be taken in by an apparently obvious but possibly false answer?

Cross-modal transfer was first pointed out as relevant to perceptual learning by Molyneux, in a letter to John Locke. He asked, in a famous query:

> Suppose a man born blind, and now adult, and taught by his touch to distinguish between a cube and a sphere of the same metal. Suppose then the cube and sphere were placed on a table, and the blind man made to see: query, whether by his sight, before he touched them, could he distinguish and tell which was the globe and which the cube? . . . The acute and judicious proposer answers: not. For though he has obtained the experience of how the globe, how the cube, affects his touch, yet he has not yet attained the experience that what affects his touch so or so, must affect his sight, so or so. . . .

John Locke agreed with Molyneux, as did later Bishop Berkeley, who thought that visual qualities were necessarily associated with tactual qualities, and in fact got their meaning thereby. It is thus understandable that there should be tremendous interest in the rare available reports of blind men restored to sight by surgery. Cases of congenital cataract have occasionally been treated successfully later in life. A number of such cases, some of them centuries old, were collected in 1932 by von Senden, and have since had great influence on psychologists' opinions about visual development and especially cross-modal transfer. Hebb (1949) felt that they gave us considerable insight into visual development, which he concluded to be a slow learning process dependent in part on eye movements. But interpretations have differed. Von Senden's cases often permit contradictory conclusions, depending on the wording of the observations and the kind of observations made.

A few years ago, Gregory and Wallace (1963), psychologists at Cambridge University, presented observations on a case of restored sight which they had opportunity to observe at firsthand. The patient lost his sight at about ten months of age and was well over fifty when successful surgery was undergone. Though one cannot draw conclusions from this case about the nature of very early visual development, there are interesting observations on cross-modal transfer. Despite the fact that he had depended mainly on touch for recognizing objects, after the operation the patient soon learned to name visually perceived objects around him. Two observations are of particular interest. The experimenters found that he could recognize, without training, any letter in upper case type, though not in lower case. He had learned capital letters by touch. They had been inscribed on blocks and taught at the school for the blind, but lower case letters had not. Furthermore, when he was given the Ishihara test for color vision, he read all the numbers (the colored figures to be discriminated from the background) correctly. The examiners felt that these achievements were very strong evidence of transfer from earlier tactile experience.

All the observations on this case suggested that there are some common features for tactual and visual experience, and that transfer occurred when visual stimulation for these features was newly presented. For letters and numbers such is the case; curve-straight, diagonals, angles, and terminal endings are features that serve to differentiate the set of shapes in both departments of sense. But for other visual experiences, there was no immediate recognition. He did not recognize water in a Kodachrome transparency, for instance, and he was unable to differentiate facial expressions. The latter, in fact, gave him difficulty for months after the operation. Evidently, the distinctive features and invariants which permit fine differentiation of facial expressions are subtle and not easily learned, particularly for one who has lived a long life without any habits of visual attention. When the patient drew pictures—a house, a man, a tool—they were, in a sense, caricatures of features available to touch. The characteristic tactile features were present but exaggerated—corners, curves, straight lines, sharp vs. blunt terminals—well represented and perfectly recognizable, but always features accessible and useful for discrimination by touch as well as vision. He seemed, as Gregory and Wallace put it, to touch the salient features with his eyes. In the case of the numbers in the Ishihara test, he could not have recognized the numbers by scanning from dot to dot because he could not know what color was relevant until after the figure was differentiated; he must have processed the patterns of dots in larger structural units.

Some cross-modal transfer thus clearly takes place. On what processes could it depend? Two radically opposed theories have been argued, with minor variations. The first, taking for granted the doctrine of the specific energies of nerves, assumes that the sensory modes of experience are natively separate and unique, and that any intermodal similarities are the result of interpretation through association. From this view, cross-modal transfer in the case described by Gregory would have to be ascribable to associations built up between vision and touch during the patient's first ten months of life before he lost his sight, though of course the associations would be nonspecific since he was not taught letters or numbers at that time. Verbal mediation might later somehow be invoked.

The opposite point of view emphasizes what is called the "unity of the senses." Hayek (1952) wrote of the unitary character of the sensory order as follows:

One main point about this order is that, in spite of its division into the different modalities, it is still a unitary order, in the sense that any two events belonging to it may in certain definite ways resemble each other or differ from each other. Any colour and any smell, any tone and any temperature, or any tactual sensations such as smoothness or wetness and any experience of shape or rhythm may yet have something in common, or be at least in some sense akin to or in contrast with one another. . . .

This means that qualities of different modalities may vary along similar or parallel directions or dimensions, or that the same kinds of differences can occur in different modalities. . . .

There exist apparently certain intermodal or intersensory attributes, and with regard to some of the terms which we use for them, such as strong or weak, mild or mellow, tingling or sharp, we are often not immediately aware to which sense modality they originally belong (Hayek, pp. 19 ff.).

As befits this point of view, Hayek believed that the ordering of sensory qualities is purely relational, a matter of differences or contrasts.

The most colorful exponent of the unity of the senses was von Hornbostel. He emphasized the redundancy, as well as the similarity of experience, as witness his celebrated statement, "It matters little through which sense I realize that in the dark I have blundered into a pig-sty (Ellis, 1938, p. 210)." In addition to similarities and redundancies between modalities he emphasized the differentiation of modalities in evolution and ontogeny. Remarking the similarities between sensed vibration on the skin and hearing (later so elegently demonstrated by von Békésy, 1957, 1959), he said:

The "hearing" of the skin, in spite of its relation to that of the ears, seems to call for quotation marks, because it is at the same time related to the pressure-sense. In this double relation of the vibration-sensation, we still feel in our own bodies how an originally single sense splits into two, which only become independent of one another in the course of evolution (Ellis, 1938, p. 211).

Another concept introduced by von Hornbostel was "super-sensuous sense-perceptions." Movement, he pointed out, can be seen, heard, or felt on the skin; in fact, as we know from the phi phenomenon, it can be sensed without even taking place. This concept is related to what Michotte has called "amodal perception."

In a number of demonstrations, Michotte and his students (Michotte, Thines, & Crabbé, 1964) observed and recounted descriptions of perceptual details which have no visual sensations to correspond, but are rather, he thought, determined by the total stimulation. These experiences he called "amodal." One example he cited is the filling in of the blind spot in the visual field. If a subject is presented with a cross in such a way as to project its center on the blind spot of the retina, and its arms on sensitive areas, a complete cross is reported despite discontinuity of excitation of the receptor surface. Another example is Michotte's screening effect; one rectangle partially occluded by another but yet perceived as complete, though behind it. A third example is the tunnel effect; a moving form briefly hidden, so that there is an interval of invisibility, and then revealed. Observers report that the phenomenal object continues to exist and to move in the tunnel. Michotte conceived of these amodal perceptions (amodal because there is perception without sensation) as filling in, according to Gestalt laws of organization. But it may be, I believe, that when amodal perception occurs, the distinctive features are actually present (as in the case of the cross); the essential stimulus information is there and what is filled in perceptually is redundant. A gap in the cross would be perceived only when the property of termination could be differentiated. It could not be perceived in this example since there is no stimulus information for it.

I shall borrow Michotte's term amodal, though not his interpretation of amodal perception. I mean the term to suggest that there is information in stimulation which is not tied to specific sensations but is rather invariant over them. Many distinctive features of objects and events are of this kind (corners, motions, temporal patterns, and transitions). Information for them may be extracted from more than one kind of sensory experience.[1] Perhaps all cross-modal similarity is really amodal in this sense. In that case might not cross-modal transfer be explained on the basis of amodal identities, higher order properties of stimulation which are not sensation specific? But before we can consider whether cross-modal transfer is really transfer of learning, and if so, what it is that is learned, some distinctions between several types of intermodal relations must be drawn.

CLASSIFICATION OF INTERMODAL RELATIONS [2]

Similarity of qualities of different modes has already been mentioned. We need, however, to remind ourselves that these similarities do not necessarily require an explanation based on association. How would association explain the similarity of an oppressive weight and an oppressive cathedral tune?

Intermodal redundancy is a different case. A fire can be seen, heard, felt, smelled, and so on. An automobile can be seen, heard, and touched. The experiences are not necessarily similar, in spite of their opportunity for association. An associationistic doctrine might lead one to expect that the car should look like it sounds, but this is seldom claimed to be a fact.

An amodal property is not an intermodal relationship, strictly speaking. I mean by it higher order relational stimulation which is not specific to a modality. Intensive dimensions might be an example, but featural properties, such as sharpness, bluntness, and jerkiness, are elicited by stimulation as well, and are common to several modes. A jerky movement can be seen and it can be felt; a jerky rhythm can be heard. Jerkiness is therefore not a sensation-based property, but information for it is nevertheless present in stimulation; it is not simply in the mind of the perceiver.

Cross-modal transfer carries the implication that some discrimination

[1] For a discussion of information-based perception in contrast to sensation-based perception see Gibson (1966), especially pp. 204 ff. and 266 ff.

[2] For a scholarly analysis and classification of the interrelations of the sensory systems in perception, see Ryan (1940).

has been learned by presentation in one modality and that the discrimination can be made, without specific practice, when the objects to be discriminated are presented in a different modality. Gregory's patient who could read capital letters when they had been discriminated previously only by touch is an example.

What we shall be concerned with are cross-modal similarity, or equivalence of stimulation, and cross-modal transfer of discrimination. The two phenomena can be distinguished operationally. Cross-modal similarity is demonstrated by matching for equivalence. This can be done with a scaling technique, that is, stimuli presented in one modality can be used to scale stimuli along a dimension in another. But matching can also be observed when the same objects are sources of stimulation for two modalities. Cross-modal transfer is demonstrated experimentally with a transfer design. That is, a training series is followed by a test series presented to a different modality; performance on the test is then compared with an identical control test without previous practice. Experiments on these phenomena will be examined to discover whether cross-modal equivalence and transfer can be demonstrated experimentally and if so, under what conditions.

OBSERVATIONS ON CROSS-MODAL EQUIVALENCE

The degree of accuracy with which an extent or an intensity can be matched across modalities is an old problem, and there is considerable evidence that the judgment can be made with fair accuracy. Piéron (1922) studied matching of lengths between vision and kinaesthesis. A visual estimate of length and a passive kinaesthetic estimate (an imposed movement of the arm) could both be translated into a graphic representation of the length perceived with equal precision. Later studies comparing cross-sensory matching of extents by sight and touch with intrasensory matching have sometimes found cross matches that are good (Kelvin, 1954), but sometimes that are less accurate than intrasensory ones (Kelvin & Mulik, 1958). The question is whether or not the same information is somehow involved in cross-modal comparisons of extent.

It has been shown to be possible to scale magnitudes by matching apparent intensities across two modalities. Stevens, Mack, and Stevens (1960) had subjects produce, on a hand dynamometer, forces that matched subjectively the apparent intensity of various stimulus levels of electric shock, of white light, of white noise, of a 1,000-cycle tone, and of vibration applied to the fingertip. Both extent and intensity may then conceivably be amodal properties, providing the same kind of information in many sensory channels.

Magnitude, it may seem, is a rather simple property. It may also be objected that the subject is not making direct cross-modal matches, but instead is matching both experiences to some mediating judgmental scale with learned numerical properties. It is important to ask, therefore, whether cross-modal equivalence obtains for relational properties of a higher order such as patterns and rhythms. Gebhard and Mowbray (1959) asked subjects to match rates of visual flicker and auditory flutter. Rates of intermittent white light were to be matched to rates of intermittent white noise. Cross-sensory matching under these conditions was considerably less accurate than intrasensory matching. The authors suggest that discrimination of rate by the ear is much more similar to such discrimination by the skin than by the eye. Matching of visual and auditory rhythms, as distinguished from frequency rates, also gave little evidence of equivalence (Cole, Chorover, & Ettlinger, 1961).

Temporal patterns do not seem, therefore, to be identical to the eye and the ear. But pattern equivalence between hearing and seeing does seem to be demonstrable in another way. The sound spectograph is an instrument which converts speech or other sounds into a visual pattern. Time, in the auditory pattern, is transformed to the horizontal dimension of the visual array, while pitch becomes the vertical dimension. The spectographic transformation preserves certain pattern features of the acoustic event. The visible display can, at least in some cases, be matched appropriately to one of a set of sounds. Professor Thorpe of Cambridge University once told me that visual study of the appropriate spectograms was very useful to his students in learning to discriminate and identify bird songs. Cooper, Liberman, and Borst (1960) constructed an instrument called a pattern playback which reconverts spectograms into sounds. It is possible, with this instrument, to make an artificial spectogram and play it back. There may be conversion, then, from patterned visual information to patterned acoustic information and vice versa. Cooper et al. suggested that there is an important similarity between visual and auditory pattern features in the sense that stimulus changes which do or do not destroy the pattern in one modality would correspondingly destroy it or not in the other. There are, they thought, "functional similarities between vision and audition at a presumably high level of perception (p. 322)."

Kinney (1961) used the sound spectrograph and pattern playback in an attempt to test the hypothesis. She studied the effect of two variables on temporal discrimination in auditory patterns and on spatial discrimination in visual ones. The variables were type of pattern (the manner in which components were combined) and the degree of separation between components. Effects of the variables were parallel to some extent. Temporal discrimination in auditory patterns and spatial discrimination in visual patterns were better with near frequencies or close vertical elements, as predicted. One pattern variable (repetition) had a parallel effect but another (symmetry) did not appear to. More research should be done on this problem with other techniques, because study of Morse code errors (see Chapter 9) demonstrated that structural features like reflection and complementarity were detected with practice and, like their counterparts in visual patterns, caused confusion.

Certain properties are modality specific as color is to vision. Other properties are not. Pattern symmetry is not, since it can be seen and felt. It might appear superficially more effective for visual identification than for tactual. Walk (1965), comparing vision and touch, found that symmetrical forms were more easily differentiated than asymmetrical ones in a visually presented learning condition, but not in a tactual one. This finding could be due to the method of exploring the stimulus object tactually, which was presumably sequential in the experiment considered. When a cutout form is scanned tactually, with the finger moving round its contour, the kinaesthetic sequence will not be symmetrical, even though the form is. But if both hands scan at once, beginning at an apex on the axis of symmetry and proceeding in opposite directions, the sequence from muscles and joints would be symmetrical, and parallel effects in touch and vision might then be expected.

That some parallel properties exist for discrimination of auditory and visual patterns is confirmed in an experiment by Baker and Alluisi (1962). Visual metric figures constructed by filling in varying heights of columns on a square matrix [3] were matched cross-modally to auditory sequences, with pitch being substituted for column height in the visual figures, and time being substituted for the horizontal dimension. Levels of constraint and complexity (evaluated by information measures) were varied in parallel fashion in the two sets of figures. The subject listened to an auditory sequence and matched it to one of a set of the visual figures. When the results were compared with an all visual matching task using the same figures the error rate was similar, and the mean response times were nearly identical. Furthermore, in both conditions response time was longer to constrained figures and to more complex figures. The authors concluded that a "single, general, form-perceptive mechanism" was involved in both.

It is interesting that experiments which ask for cross-modal matching of rates or rhythm with only a time variable have found (so far) scant evidence for equivalence, while experiments with higher order figural properties have. In discussing their results, Baker and Alluisi point out that use of a constraining rule in generating figures results in sets of figures of greater homogeneity and fewer distinctive features per figure, making them difficult to identify. They go on to say that discriminations are made on the basis of distinctive details, and that all the information in the figure is not processed. I would say that these distinctive features are probably two-dimensional invariants of the stimulus which stand out to make a pattern

---

[3] See the description of research on recognition of metric figures in Chapter 9.

unique either visually or auditorily. As we saw in Chapter 9, it is easier to learn to identify multidimensional stimulus objects. Multidimensional invariant properties provide structure that reduces perceptual processing; these properties are more likely than a unidimensional variation to be amodal and thus constitute common distinctive features for several modalities.

Active exploration and search for invariant properties is also more likely to occur when more than one dimension of variation is provided in the discriminanda to be compared. The importance of active, exploratory perception is especially evident in touch (see Gibson, 1962). Comparisons of discrimination of objects by touch and sight, and cross-modal equivalences between them have been made by a number of experimenters. One will serve as an example here. Rudel and Teuber (1964) employed a set of five blocks of different shapes (square, sphere, cylinder, pyramid, and cone), painted black, smooth, and mounted on sticks (see Fig. 11–1).

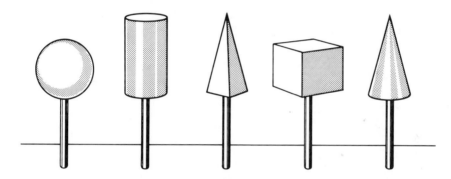

FIGURE 11–1. Solid geometrical shapes used by Rudel and Teuber for a study of intra- and intermodal matching.

(From R. G. Rudel & H. L. Teuber, Cross-modal transfer of shape discrimination by children. *Neuropsychologia*, 1964, *2*, 2. Reprinted by permission of Pergamon Press, Inc.)

Children between three and six years old served as subjects. One of the blocks was presented to the subject for feeling by touch or seeing by vision. After its withdrawal, the subject examined all five successively, trying to find a match for the standard. The blocks were presented for matching either visually or tactually, so there were four conditions of the experiment: visual presentation of standard followed by visual matching; visual presentation followed by tactual matching; tactual presentation followed by visual matching; and tactual presentation followed by tactual matching. Each subject took part in only one series. The task was too difficult for the three year olds because of the successive presentation, so two conditions of simultaneous presentation were arranged for them (visual-visual and tactual-visual). Successful matches were most frequent on the visual-visual series and least on the tactual-tactual. The cross-modal comparisons were in between (more than 80 percent correct for the five year olds). For the three year olds, the visual-visual comparisons were more accurate, but the tactual-visual were considerably better than chance.

A second series was run with four unfamiliar, profile-like shapes (see Fig. 11–2) and one prism-shaped block. Matching proved to be difficult (except for the distinctive prism) but the five year olds matched better than chance in all conditions; visual-visual and visual-tactual were equally good (55 percent correct matches). The older children sometimes tried to verbalize distinctive features (e.g., "This one's pointed on top"), but the words did not appear obviously related to success or failure. Equivalence across modalities, it seems, may be as perceptible as equivalence within one modality. The authors remarked, "There is some common aspect of perceptual activity which permits one to utilize information from within a sensory channel or from several channels in such a way that invariant properties of objects are extracted (Rudel and Teuber, p. 6)."

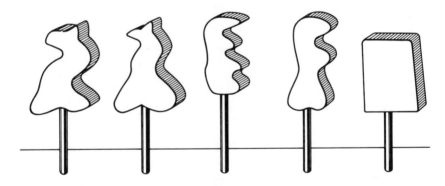

FIGURE 11–2. **Four unfamiliar irregularly shaped blocks and a flattened pyramid.**

> This was a difficult series for young children whether matching was intra- or intermodal. (From R. G. Rudel & H. L. Teuber, Crossmodal transfer of shape discrimination by children. *Neuropsychologia*, 1964, *2*, 2. Reprinted by permission of Pergamon Press, Inc.)

OBSERVATIONS ON CROSS-MODAL TRANSFER

Findings of equivalence like the ones just reported are sometimes held to be explainable by earlier learned association of the two modes of experience—either direct association with one another, or associations with a common verbal mediator. For this reason, transfer experiments, with discrimination learning preceding the tests for transfer in a different modality, may provide some significant observations because the discrimination learning can be controlled. If discrimination between a set of objects is originally impossible by, say, visual inspection, but becomes possible after tactual exploration, the inference of direct equivalence rather than mediated transfer is plausible, provided the training prevented tactual-visual association and somehow controlled verbal mediation. It could then be argued that what was learned during discrimination learning were distinctive features which were not modality specific. While none of the available experiments are entirely conclusive on this point, some of them are worth examining.

Two criteria must be met for the experiment to be useful. The material to be discriminated must be unfamiliar, so that differentiation has to be learned, and opportunities for learning specific mediating responses should be excluded. An experiment by Gaydos (1956) has often been quoted and its materials replicated in other experiments. Gaydos prepared 12 shapes cut from masonite. They were approximately two inches across at the largest dimension and some were unconventional, though several were very close to conventional shapes, such as a circle, an ellipse, and a square. Each shape was given a man's name (Art, Bill, etc.) which the subjects were required to associate with it. Half the subjects learned first to identify the shapes by sight and half by touch. Afterward they learned to identify them by the other modality. One group thus served as a control for the other. The subjects were adults. In both groups significant transfer occurred, with greater transfer from touch to vision.

Gaydos reported that verbalization influenced the learning and that certain shapes were associated with common geometric figures. His material makes such labeling almost inevitable. One cannot generalize from his conditions to unfamiliar material and infer that verbal mediation is a necessary condition for cross-modal transfer.

A transfer experiment by Holmgren, Arnoult, and Manning (1966) used stimulus materials less easily labeled. They were auditory patterns (four tones played in a sequence and recorded on tape, chosen so as to be rare in Occidental music), and the same tonal patterns were transformed to a visual display by means of an oscilloscope. In one experimental condition the subjects learned nonsense syllable responses to the auditory patterns in a first task, followed by the visual patterns paired with the same syllables in a second task. In the other experimental condition, the subjects began with the same task but the visual patterns were reassigned to the syllables in the second task. Control groups with no training on the tone patterns but equal training on different auditory stimuli (spoken letters) took more trials to criterion on Task II than subjects in the first condition and less than those in the second, demonstrating significant positive transfer in one case and negative in the other. Patterning common to the auditory and visual sequences seems to have been an effective amodal equivalent.

Experiments in which specific responses must be memorized are hard to interpret because so much of the variance in the results may be caused by the response learning and interact in some way with other variables. Some experiments by Caviness (1964) avoided this difficulty and employed genuinely unfamiliar material. Ten solid plastic objects (free forms) were especially designed by a sculptor (see Fig. 11–3). They were approximately

FIGURE 11–3. Free sculptured forms used by Caviness in a study of intermodal equivalence and transfer.

(Photograph by courtesy of J. J. Gibson.)

equal in size and weight. The rear half of each was convex, and the front bore five protuberances around a central hump. They could not be distinguished by counting anything and they were not readily describable in words. Cross-modal matching (feeling one of the ten objects and then choosing it from the set of ten by sight) was found possible, with about 89 percent accuracy. In a transfer experiment, Caviness presented two of the objects, successively, for either visual or tactual comparison. The subject judged whether they were the same or different. After twenty judgments made tactually, one group of subjects made twenty comparisons visually. The other group followed the opposite order. Errors were reduced in the second twenty judgments for both groups, using the other as a control (47 percent and 42 percent transfer). In another experiment, visual-visual and tactual-tactual groups comparable to those just described were run. Significantly fewer errors were made in the visual-visual condition than in the cross-modal ones, but not in the tactual-tactual. Caviness speculated that the cross-modal transfer found in his experiment could be explained by cross-modal equivalence. The subject cannot be prevented from encoding to words the features he distinguishes and the words are convenient memorial devices. But for transfer to occur, as in this experiment, stimulation from touch and vision must specify the same property in order to be codeable to the same word.

Comparable solid nonsense ceramic objects were used in an experiment by Björkman, Garvill, and Molander (1965), again with visual or tactual presentation. The instructions were varied for two conditions of original training, by telling the subjects in one condition that the objects they were learning to identify tactually (or visually) were going to have to be identified by the other mode later. One might expect this instruction to cause the subjects to pay special attention to aspects of the stimulus objects which would be equivalent in the other condition. Actually, significant transfer (about 60 percent) was found in both conditions but the specially motivated group was superior when visual training preceded tactual. These authors also found that increasing the distinctiveness of a modality-specific stimulus property (such as color) reduced cross-modal transfer. It is possible, therefore, to attend selectively to a modality-specific or, on the other hand, a nonsensory, amodal feature of a stimulus object. Experimental conditions may raise or lower the difficulty of attending to relevant amodal features, but only when it is reasonably easy to do so can cross-modal transfer be expected. Differences in distinctiveness of modality-specific and nonspecific properties and active exploration or attention to them may explain conflicting results in the literature of intermodal effects.

Printed and raised letter-like forms were used by Pick, Pick, and Thomas (1966) in a cross-modal transfer experiment. First-grade children learned to discriminate standard forms and particular transformations either visually or by touching. Then they were tested for transfer on the other condition. Subgroups received one of two kinds of training-test treatments, one which permitted transfer on the basis of transformation type and one which permitted transfer on the basis of a specific standard (see the description of the experiment by Pick, 1965, in Chapter 6). The groups that could use learned dimensions of difference (transformation type) for transfer both showed cross-modal transfer. Transfer in the other case was equivocal, occurring only under certain conditions of task difficulty. The forms in this experiment had no names and no specific responses were learned to them. Yet, distinctive differences specified by kinds of trans-formation were picked up and transferred. I think this experiment under-lines the need for and the potential value of further research on what it is that can be transferred intermodally.

Rudel and Teuber (1963) studied the decrement of the Müller-Lyer illusion with both visual and haptic presentation and with practice in one modality preceding practice in the other. There was significant transfer of the decrement to the settings made in the second modality, greater from touch to vision than from vision to touch. This is a particularly interesting case of transfer, because the practice gave the subject no knowledge of results; he did not know how he was doing. It seemed most unlikely from the subjects' comments that verbal mediation occurred, since they were unaware of the progressive diminution of the illusion.

THE EXPLANATION OF INTERMODAL EQUIVALENCE AND TRANSFER

At the beginning of this chapter two opposed views of intermodal transfer were contrasted, one stemming from the doctrine of the specific energies of nerves and the other from the concept of the unity of the senses. Having examined a fair amount of evidence that intermodal equivalence and inter-modal transfer do in fact occur (though our knowledge of the conditions for their occurrence is at present slight), let us return to the issue of how they are to be interpreted.

The separatist view takes several forms. In its simplest form, it merely states that sensory modalities are originally separate and specific, but dur-ing development are integrated. Birch and Lefford (1963) recently voiced strong support of this view, citing as evidence their experiment in which developmental curves for intermodal matching were presented. Three kinds of matches were made by children from five to eleven: visual-haptic (haptic meaning to them active, exploratory touching), visual-kinaesthetic (kinaes-thetic meaning to them passive stimulation with the arm and hand being moved by the experimenter), and haptic-kinaesthetic. Correct matches in-creased with age in all three conditions. But this improvement does not permit the inference that intersensory integration is responsible. We know that intramodal matching improves with age, too. Children improve, de-velopmentally, in extracting invariant features and higher order structural properties however the objects or events to be matched or identified are presented, as I shall show in later chapters.

A more specific version of a sensory integration theory is espoused by a number of Russian psychologists, following Leontiev. Pick (1964) has summarized the theory and described a number of experiments deriving from it. The theory is a motor copy theory (see Chapter 4), proposing that perception mirrors the world by making a reproduction of the physical object. Some of the experiments observed movements of the hands and fingers in exploring an object manually in order to identify it. The form of the exploratory movements was said to be determined by the shape of the object, with pauses at apex angles and a trajectory of movements corresponding to the shape. It was thought to be stimulation fed back from these movements that yielded the perception of specific objects. Tactual perception was considered more primitive than vision, giving rise to the notion that the hand teaches the eye. Zinchenko (see Pick, 1964, and Pick, Pick, and Klein, 1967), following up this idea, performed cross-modal experiments with children aged three to seven. The material was adapted from Gaydos (1956). Errors decreased with age, and improvement was interpreted as due to changes in hand and eye movements which presumably came to conform more closely to the contour. Errors decreased in visual-visual matching and in tactual-tactual matching as well as in cross-modal matching. Tactual-tactual matching was poorer than visual-visual, so the presumed dependence of vision on touch, here that the hand teaches the eye, was not supported.

The ancient notion that vision gains its meaning from touch, that the ball looks round because it feels round, has lost ground in all the work on cross-modal equivalence. It is true that both spatial order (and therefore spatial relations) and temporal order (and therefore temporal relations) are available to vision and to the skin. But a wider panorama of space and objects is available to vision. This means, I think, that greater complexity of structure and higher levels of constraint (rules within rules, so to speak) are possible to detect in visual displays. The fact that such relations are grasped (as they surely often are) is certainly not caused by association with touch. If further evidence for this point is needed, studies of the early blind (Drever, 1955; Axelrod, 1959) make it very clear that their deprivation of sight has sore consequences in the development of their appreciation of relationships such as identity, similarity, and difference. Insofar as there is intermodal facilitation for the detection of amodal relations, it is probably the other way around.

A mediation theory of cross-modal transfer that has always enjoyed a number of backers asserts that transfer is carried verbally (the same mediation theory that is often assumed to underlie intramodal transposition, as we shall see). Increase in transfer with age is cited as evidence, as is the failure of several experimenters (Ettlinger, 1960; and Burton & Ettlinger, 1960) to find cross-modal transfer with animals. But other experimenters (Stepien & Cordeau, 1960; Wilson & Shaffer, 1963) have obtained positive results with animals, and although verbalization may well increase transfer in children, there appears to be evidence that it is not essential. Blank and

Bridger (1964) compared two tasks, which they called cross-modal concepts and cross-modal equivalence with the expectation that verbalization would be necessary for one but not for the other. For cross-modal equivalence, they gave children (three to six years old) a series of seven two-choice discrimination problems. The child explored an object haptically, and then was asked to discriminate visually which of two objects he had just felt. The objects were familiar shapes such as cylinders and triangles. The four and five year olds performed better than chance, but could not verbalize the reasons for a correct choice. In the other task the child had to discover the concept of succession, one vs. two events (two light flashes and two sounds). No child solved the problem without verbalizing the concept either spontaneously or after questioning. The opposite was not true, however. A group informed of the solution to one problem did not necessarily show transfer to the next. In sum, it is often possible that some sort of translation rule could be formulated and applied, but there are also cases of cross-modal transfer where this does not happen. Two events must specify the same property to be codeable to the same word, unless the word has been specifically learned previously to each one.

One other mediation theory of cross-modal transfer, Piaget's, is based on the finding of increased transfer with age. A representative schema for an object is built up, he thinks, by systematic exploratory activity (see Chapter 3). There is progressive development of exploratory handling, with increasing search for significant features. The sensory-motor schema is a kind of referent common to two modalities, making cross-modal transfer possible. "Thus the whole trend of events appears to suggest that the power to imagine the shapes visually, when they are perceived through the sense of touch alone, is an expression of the sensorimotor schema involved in their perception (Piaget & Inhelder, 1956, p. 41)."

The concept of a schema which is common to two modalities is difficult to put to a test, though it has a good deal of appeal. But I find much more appeal and greater theoretical simplicity in the hypothesis that an amodal invariant in stimulation is responsible for cross-modal transfer. That is to say, stimulus information is not necessarily modality specific. Such information is always relational. The relation may be an amodal one, such as movement from here to there, which can be seen, felt, and heard. Distinctive features of objects and invariant features of events may be amodal, nonspecific, and insofar as they are, there can be cross-modal equivalence and transfer. Relations may be of many orders. Superordinate ones may be harder to detect than subordinate ones. It is not unreasonable to suppose that, developmentally, the detection of superordinate amodal relations occurs later rather than earlier and that cross-modal transfer as a consequence increases with age. Evidence that the more abstract amodal properties are higher order and are picked up later is unfortunately scarce.

I shall return to the subject in later chapters on perceptual development in children.

SUMMARY

In this chapter, I distinguished between three kinds of intermodal relation: intermodal similarity, defined by matching for equivalence; intermodal or, as it is usually called, cross-modal transfer, defined by transfer of discrimination learning across modalities; and amodal perceptual properties, which are not really intermodal at all. Amodal properties are present in stimulation and potentially perceptible, but they are not modality specific. They give information which is in the light or the sound or the vibrations but which is relational. Blue is modality specific; jerkiness is amodal. Various types of transformation over time, or over comparison of contrasting features in different instances of stimulation can be abstract or nonspecific. Change from straightness to curviness, or from smoothness to roughness are examples.

Experiments demonstrating cross-modal equivalence and cross-modal transfer were presented and some of the conditions for their occurrence pointed out. But research is badly needed on the latter point. We know little about just what conditions underlie such transfer and what ones do not.

Theories offered in explanation of intermodal effects relevant to perceptual learning were examined. Roughly, they fall into two groups, integration or mediation theories, and theories emphasizing the unity of the senses. Integration theories cite developmental data as evidence and propose that cross-modal equivalence and transfer are achievements that are learned in the course of development. But discovery of invariant stimulus relations and transformations may underlie perceptual development, both intramodal and intermodal. I have suggested that intermodal effects are the result of the pickup of invariant amodal stimulus information; that such information is of a high order in stimulation and is responded to increasingly in the course of development. If cross-modal transfer of discrimination turns out to be dependent on invariant features common to several modes of stimulation, then the term "transfer" becomes inappropriate and research should be focused, not on mediating responses, but on how detection of higher order relational properties of stimulation develops.

12

The Study of
Perceptual Development
by Means of Controlled Rearing

The experimental paradigms considered in the last three chapters have to do with perceptual learning in laboratory experiments. These are, for the most part, short-term experiments and one is often plagued by the doubt that they may not be telling us much about what goes on in perceptual development. The perfect experiment which controls all perceptual experience, beginning at birth, has been the ideal of theorists interested in the genesis of perception; particularly the ones who were bothered about the relative contributions of nature and nurture.

Such an experiment is crucial if one is convinced that early experience is vital in development and outweighs what happens later. The notion of critical periods in development has been taken over from the ethologists' work on imprinting, and has also been stressed by Hebb (1949). It requires methods of controlling the environment in very early infancy. How important is exposure to a complete world of stimulation for perception to develop normally? How pervasive are the effects of being deprived of the normal environment? Can early experience be stepped up so as to hasten perceptual development?

Experiments with controlled rearing can be divided roughly into two kinds: ones which deprive the young organism of some kind of stimulation which its species customarily enjoys, and ones which introduce extra stimulation or some special kind of experience. The latter has often been referred to as enrichment, but will here be called augmentation. The effects of early deprivation or augmentation on the development of intelligence have long been of interest. An impoverished environment cannot be deliberately introduced into an experiment with human children, but it exists in institutions such as orphanages, and its effects have been compared with those of a presumably normal environment, and with a presumably enriched environment such as that provided by a nursery school or a superior home. Fowler (1967) summarized a large number of studies of the effect of providing children with special opportunity for perceptual, motor, or

language activity. The best known system of supplementing early opportunities for learning is Montessori's (1912). Her program included perceptual exercises such as training with colors, motor exercises, and very
early instruction in reading. The system was introduced as an educational
innovation, rather than an experiment, and no formal measures of progress
were made as compared with a control group.

All these studies are necessarily ill-controlled; they do not explain
the process of development, but lead only to the general impression that
deprivation is bad and augmentation is good. Perhaps experiments on controlled rearing with animals can tell us more about the process of perceptual development; it will depend on how well the conditions of rearing
are controlled and how effective the testing conditions are. Understanding
will also depend on a sophisticated interpretation of the results. Exactly
what is the experimental animal deprived of? How is the nature of the
deprivation related to the criterion test? Is the effect of the deprivation
only to prevent certain experiences, or has it pathological consequences?
What is meant by augmenting or enriching the environment? Some of the
early experiments with visual deprivation were badly misinterpreted through
failure to realize that reducing the optical stimulation in an environment
may have special consequences, since being reared in the dark not only
precludes visual experience, it also may cause atrophy of the visual system
or failure of parts of the system to mature. Or it may substitute the learning
of habits controlled by another sensory system and so interfere with later
visual discrimination in a lighted environment. It is common knowledge
that sensory deficiency in man, such as blindness or deafness, may have
emotional consequences; and practically all histories of restored sight in
blind-born individuals stress the emotional upset accompanying restoration (Senden, 1960; Gregory & Wallace, 1963). The same consequences
appear in dark-reared rats when they are brought into the light (Gibson,
Walk, & Tighe, 1959). It is less common knowledge that pathological
conditions may develop which compete with normal development when normal stimulation is reintroduced. Riesen (1961) points out, for instance,
that primates reared in diffuse light develop spontaneous eye movements
(nystagmus) in the absence of visual objects to fixate. When targets for
fixation are later introduced, these binocularly uncoordinated eye movements interfere with development of normal binocular coordination.

Solomon and Lessac (1968) have criticized the design of deprivation
experiments, pointing out the inadequacy of the customary two-group design. Typically, one group of animals is deprived of some kind of environmental stimulation, more or less specified, while another group leads a
normal life in the usual laboratory environment. When both groups are
tested on a criterion task at the end of the period of deprivation, the normally reared group may appear superior, and it is then inferred that the

cause of its superiority is learning gained through exposure to the stimulation not presented to the other animals. Experience, presumably, permitted the control group to forge ahead and to develop normally, while the deprived group, lacking experience, fell behind and must needs catch up. But Solomon and Lessac point out that an equally good explanation could be in terms of deterioration of capacities in the deprived group. Therefore, one should determine whether the deprived group has the capacity in question before deprivation is begun. But the pretest and posttest design may bias the results because of experience gained during the pretest. They propose, therefore, a four-group experimental design. One group, prior to deprivation, is pretested for capacities operating at the start of the experiment; another group, prior to normal treatment, is also pretested. Two other groups, one destined for deprivation and one for normal rearing, are not pretested. All receive the same posttests. One can deduce, then, what the performance of the deprived group would have been without deprivation by observing how it compared with the control group at posttest, and with a group like itself at beginning and end. The deprived group may stay as it was in the beginning or it may deteriorate. The same sort of design should be applied to enrichment experiments, since it is possible that the favored group is really remaining static while the control group has deteriorated.

An experiment by Hubel and Wiesel (1963) illustrates the need to assess capacity before introducing biased rearing. They compared the distribution of retinal receptive fields in the striate cortex of adult r ;mally reared cats and of very young inexperienced kittens. Since light deprivation in the cat had been found to have an adverse influence on visual discrimination when the animal is returned to light, they surmised that stimulation—visual experience—might be necessary for development of the specifically responding receptive fields. But except for a certain general sluggishness, receptive fields in two visually deprived kittens (8 and 16 days old) strongly resembled those of mature cats in their responses to patterned stimuli. Visual experience is thus not necessary for the organization and development of striate nerve cells and their functional connections. But they found that prolonged rearing without patterned light did cause them to deteriorate. Lack of stimulation may lead not simply to a failure in forming neural connections, but on the other hand to the disruption of connections that were there originally.

Representative experiments will be discussed below under the rubrics of deprivation and augmentation. In both cases, the environmental intervention can be general or it can be specific. I have also introduced a third rubric which I will call biased rearing, a condition in which the environment is not impoverished or augmented, but changed so as to be unrepresentative for the species.

DEPRIVATION

General Impoverishment of Stimulation

Growing up in isolation, or in a generally impoverished environment has been suspected for centuries to be a cause of dull wittedness and maladaptive behavior. Psychologists were made particularly aware of the notion by Spitz's work. He coined the term "hospitalism" to describe a syndrome resulting from bare, drab surroundings in the early months of life, plus absence of maternal care. Infants reared in an institutional environment, in homogeneously colored surroundings, in a sheet-walled crib, and with only the ceiling to stare at, had a low level of informative stimulation to start life with. Moreover, in certain institutions, they were given only necessary care and feeding by a nurse, that is, a minimum of social stimulation. These infants were highly susceptible to disease, showed pathological behavior of various sorts, were apathetic, and dropped steadily on a developmental index. Spitz attributed the largest part of this unhappy picture to the second factor, the absence of maternal warmth and attention. "We do not think," he said, "that it is the lack of perceptual stimulation *in general* that counts in their deprivation. We believe that they suffer because their perceptual world is emptied of human partners . . . (Spitz, 1945)."

Disagreement with Spitz's view has been frequent; other investigators have argued that perceptual deprivation alone might be responsible for the intellectual manifestations of retardation. Dennis (1960) described similar conditions in an Iranian institution, and similar results of retardation in an ensuing test situation. Dennis thought that the stimulus deprivation and the absence of learning opportunities similar to the test situation were sufficient to explain the results. He reported that supplementary experience similar to the test situation brought about a significant gain in behavioral development in deprived infants (Dennis & Sayegh, 1965).

These studies made no attempt to diagnose the effects of the deprivation on perceptual development per se. A number of studies of dogs reared from birth in isolation from social contacts and in a restricted environment takes us a little farther, since tests were conducted experimentally under controlled conditions. The studies, carried out by McGill psychologists, are typified in one by Thompson and Heron (1954). Twenty-six Scottish terriers, genetically very similar, were divided into a control group and three experimental groups. The control dogs were raised as pets, while the experimental animals were raised in severely restricted, moderately restricted, or slightly restricted conditions. The severely restricted animals were raised in complete isolation in empty boxes with solid walls. The moderately and slightly restricted conditions involved cages. The period of restriction lasted from weaning to seven or ten months. At the end of this period, the restricted animals, as contrasted with the control dogs, were hyperactive and galloped about, although at first they showed poor sensory-motor coordination. This hyperactivity in restricted subjects has been noted by other investigators and is sometimes attributed to stimulation hunger. It appears superficially contradictory to the apathy and lack of perceptual curiosity often noted in descriptions of institutionally reared children. However, this activity may be a purely motoric thing, unrelated to the exploratory activity which characterizes perception.

The McGill dogs were given a number of "intelligence" tests: orientation tests, barrier tests, delayed reaction, and the Hebb-Williams maze. On all tests, the performance of the restricted animals was inferior to that of the control animals. In attempting to define the exact nature of the deficit suffered by the restricted dogs, Thompson and Heron describe it as a "lack of ability to discriminate relevant from irrelevant aspects of the environment," and a disturbance in attentional processes which showed up especially on the delayed-reaction test. They attribute the principal cause of this deficit to the lack of early perceptual experience, rather than to limitation of motor activity. If there is a stimulus hunger in the dog reared under severe restriction, but no experience in filtering out the irrelevant stimuli, then selective attention might reasonably be expected to be deficient. If this plausible interpretation turns out to be right, the detrimental effect of the deprivation is on attention—the exploratory, selective side of perception—and is not due to a lack of specific neural connections or cell assemblies like those posited by Hebb (1949) to account for perceptual content, such as the perception of a given form.

Melzack (1962) also emphasized the interpretation that apparent deficits in visual discrimination following restricted rearing are not due to a deficit in pattern perception but rather to the combination of a high level of arousal (distraction produced by the unfamiliar environment) and a difficulty in attending selectively to relevant properties of the discriminanda. He reared dogs in a restricted environment, but one which nevertheless contained visible corners and edges, so that pattern vision was possible. The dogs' ensuing difficulty in learning a light-dark discrimination as compared to control dogs was due, Melzack thought, "to inability to select relevant patterns from the total sensory input (because of the level of arousal) rather than to absence of pattern perception *per se* (p. 979)."

Another motivational factor proposed as an explanation of intellectual retardation following deprivation is the fear of so-called novel objects. Precocial animals (those that are precocious, or ready for life at birth) that have been imprinted on the mother during the first day of life, tend to develop fear responses to novel objects soon afterward. Perhaps it is true that a young animal reared in restricted circumstances will show a heightened fear of strange objects when the environment is made more complex at a later time. The reasoning here is not very profound, but it is a possible factor responsible for the behavior of animals reared in darkness or diffuse light after introduction to the complex array of an illuminated world. An investigation of the effects of environmental restriction upon the chimpanzee's responsiveness to objects was carried out by Menzel, Davenport, and Rogers (1963). They compared a group of wild-born chimpanzees exposed to a variety of people and objects with a laboratory-born restricted group. There were various degrees of restriction, with the maximally restricted group reared singly in bare cubicles. These animals never saw anything outside their cages. When they were about two years old tests were conducted with a number of objects, both in their rearing cages and in a special observation cubicle. The test situation was free; the objects were movable and could be manipulated; there was a large assortment of things ranging from toys to live animals enclosed in a plastic box. They were presented one at a time, and the chimpanzee's behavior was observed and recorded. Grasping or touching was significantly more frequent in the wild-born group. Stereotyped behavior such as rocking and swaying was characteristic of the restricted group. The investigators concluded that the restricted animals were retarded in their tendency to approach and manipulate objects, but were not lacking in discriminatory ability. Timidity was exhibited at the beginning of testing but in a matter of weeks grasping and manipulation increased and became adapted specifically to the object.

Rearing in a barren unchanging environment does appear from these studies to have an effect on perceptual development. But the effect is not so much a deficit due to the absence of specific experiences as it is maladaption of attention, and of perceptual motivation. All the terms used to describe the effect reflect this suggestion: apathy and lack of curiosity; stimulus hunger; timidity and lack of responsiveness to objects; and inability to filter the irrelevant from the critical when faced with a more complex environment.

Deprivation of Light and Pattern

These results of general restriction do not tell us much about development of the perception of the objects, edges, and spaces of the world. A number of experiments have studied the effect of depriving an individual of light, however, with a variety of animals as subjects. In these experiments there is manipulation of both independent and dependent variables. Light may be prevented entirely from entering the eye, or the light entering the eye may be made diffuse, so there is no patterned stimulation. A homogeneous field of light imposes stimulation on the retina, but it carries no information. It could make an important difference for development whether the organism is deprived of total stimulation as opposed to stimulation that carries information. Furthermore, either of these conditions may be applied to only one eye. As for dependent variables, the experimenter may choose to measure perception of spatial variables, or differentiation of objects and features of objects such as shape or color. The choice of both independent and dependent variable may affect the results. We shall consider first the effects of binocular deprivation, and then monocular deprivation.

BINOCULAR DEPRIVATION. Well-controlled experiments with dark-reared animals began with an experiment of Lashley and Russell in 1934. They reared rats in the dark for 100 days and then compared their accuracy of jumping to a stand placed at different distances with the accuracy of rats reared in the light. Force of jump was correlated with distance of the target platform, between 20 and 40 centimeters away. This measure was thought of as an index of depth discrimination. From the third day after beginning practice with the jumping stand, the dark-reared as well as the light-reared animals exhibited a high correlation between force of jump and distance of the landing platform. If experience in the light was needed, not much appeared to be required for gauging depth quite accurately.

Performance with the jumping stand does require some training, however, so light deprivation was not complete in Lashley and Russell's experiment. For this reason, Walk, Gibson, and Tighe (1957) tested dark-reared rats on a visual cliff which yields an index of depth perception that requires no training (see Fig. 12–1). Rats reared in the dark for thirty days or ninety days chose the shallow side of the cliff rather than the deep side, like their light-reared littermates. Nealy and Edwards (1960) confirmed these results. But an experiment of Nealy and Riley (1963) found that rats reared in the dark until they were ten months old no longer discriminated depth in this way when first brought into the light. After a month in the light, however, depth discrimination did appear. Discrimination of edge depth, as indicated by avoidance of a simulated cliff, is thus present in a rat despite dark-rearing, if the light deprivation is not carried on too long. But after some five or six months in darkness impairment begins to occur.

Form discrimination in the dark-reared rat also seems comparable to that in the light-reared animal, although the limit to which it can be carried without damage is not known. Hebb (1937) found that dark-reared rats segregated a figure from the ground at first vision; that is, seemed to perceive it as a unit distinct from its background. They could also generalize discrimination of a form such as a triangle over changes of size, brightness, and position, like normally reared rats. Hooded rats reared in the dark for ninety days were found by Gibson, Walk, and Tighe

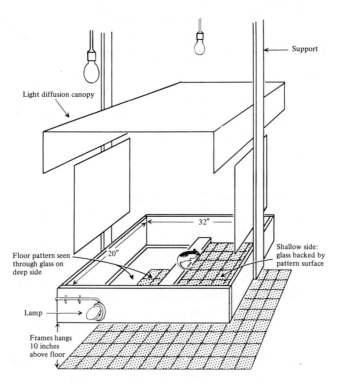

FIGURE 12–1. Drawing of a visual cliff.

The visual cliff is a simulated drop-off, designed so that an animal placed
on a center board is presented with a very shallow drop-off on one side
and an apparently deep one on the other. If he leaves the center board,
he must move either to the shallow or the deep side. If other cues to
differential depth of the two sides are controlled (tactual cues, echolocation, brightness, and odors, for instance) and if animals of a given
species preponderantly favor the shallow side over a series of trials, it
can be inferred that the preference indicates presence of the ability to
discriminate the difference visually. The drawing illustrates a cliff designed for rats. The floors of both the shallow and the deep sides are
covered with the same textured material. The center board is raised
slightly above both. At the floor level of the shallow side, a large sheet
of glass extends from the center board in both directions. The purpose
of the glass is to equate tactual and sound stimuli on the two sides. The
height of the center board is usually raised above the glass to correspond
with an animal's size, so that he will tend to look in both directions before moving off. The textured floor of the deep side, below the glass, can
be lowered to various depths in order to determine thresholds. Ideally,
lighting of the cliff should be from below so as to control brightness and
reflections from the glass. Textures used on the floors can be varied so
as to study the effect of size of elements, texture density, or homogeneous
as compared to nonhomogeneous surfaces. (From R. D. Walk & E. J.
Gibson, A comparative and analytical study of visual depth perception.
Psychological Monographs, 1961, *75*, 7. Copyright 1961 by the American
Psychological Association, and reproduced by permission.)

(1959) to be at no disadvantage in learning a form discrimination, although they were much shyer than normally reared littermates.

Development in a lighted environment affording patterned retinal images is thus not necessary for the rat to discriminate depth or form. What happens to cause the eventual impairment of visual discrimination in the dark-reared rat? It cannot be simply the lack of visual experience, for that is just as lacking at ninety days as it is at nine months. It must be something occurring, not something lacking. It could be degeneration of structures in the visual system, increasing with increasing length of deprivation. Or it could be a progressive strengthening of interfering habits, an increasing dependence on the monitoring of behavior and the exploring of the environment by sensory information of another kind than visual. Or it could be an increasing tendency to arousal and emotionality when the introduction to a lighted environment takes place.

It should be noted that rats are nocturnal animals whose ancestors have lived in low illumination for millions of years. Perhaps they are biologically used to the dark. What about diurnal birds? Studies with birds are of special interest since a number of species such as the chick are precocious in both visual and motor activity and can be shown to discriminate depth and shape immediately after hatching (Fantz, 1957; Walk & Gibson, 1961). Tucker (1957) reared chicks from hatching to ten weeks under four different conditions: I, in total darkness; II, both eyes covered with a translucent hood so that only diffuse light was experienced; III, a translucent hood over one eye; and IV, with normal binocular vision in a lighted environment. At ten weeks, all chicks were trained on a triangle-circle discrimination. Chicks in groups I and II were very significantly poorer than those in groups III and IV, which were similar to one another. Group I was poorer than Group II; only two chicks reached criterion, and two developed cataract, suggesting that deprivation of light as such is injurious over and above the effects of patterned light deprivation. But the chicks reared with binocular diffuse light were clearly inferior. Not only were their scores relatively poor on the training problem, but like the total darkness group, they did not recognize grains of food by pecking on first exposure, as normal chicks do soon after hatching, and after developing the ability to peck at grains in the food box they still could not peck at grains in other places. Both groups I and II showed other losses such as nystagmus and forced head torsion when one eye was covered. We know from Fantz (1957) that a discrimination is possible between triangles and circles (revealed by a preference for circles) in two-day-old dark-reared chicks. It is therefore indicated that the abnormalities in Tucker's chicks were not primarily due to the absence of opportunities for visual learning during the period of deprivation, in the usual sense of the term learning. The maintaining of the chicks' ability to perceive, let alone the improving of this ability, evidently depends on the availability of the stimulus information in light, and particularly in patterned light.

An experiment with a less visually precocious bird, the ring dove, was carried out by Siegel (1953). He reared his experimental group in plastic hoods which covered the birds' eyes and allowed only diffuse light to enter. The hoods were fitted before the doves' eyes opened, and were worn for eight to twelve weeks until testing commenced. A triangle-circle discrimination was learned faster by a normally reared control group than by the experimental group. Siegel attributed the difference to the visual inexperience of the experimental animals, but exactly how lack of visual experience hampered them was not explained. Perhaps the birds needed to learn to pay attention to visual information instead of the kind they were obliged to rely on before. It appears that it was not failure to form specific neural connections that made them slower, for Siegel found in a further experiment (1953b) that birds reared with diffuse light and then trained to perform the discrimination monocularly showed some transfer of the discrimination to the untrained eye. Since the deprived birds did learn the discrimination, and rapidly developed visually monitored pecking responses and spatial orientation, there was also no evidence for a critical period of stimulation in early infancy.

Failure of visually guided spatial behavior after dark-rearing, followed by rapid development of the behavior, is a characteristic result of many experiments. Kittens reared in the dark for four weeks (Walk & Gibson, 1961) initially showed no depth discrimination on the visual cliff, but the discrimination improved rapidly when the kittens were brought into a lighted environment (see Fig. 12-2). This is particularly interesting, because a stimulus-response explanation of the ensuing development would predict no improvement in cliff avoidance; since the kittens had walked over the glass on both sides of the apparatus without falling there was no differential reinforcement for choosing one side over the other.

A study of the effects of different durations of dark-rearing on monkey infants was carried out by Fantz (1965, 1967). The infants were kept in the dark for periods varying from one to eleven weeks. Tests of fixation preference with pairs of objects differing in size, color, and pattern were given at intervals during the deprivation period as well as after removal to a lighted nursery. Changes in what they looked at were related to length of deprivation. Infants with less than eight weeks in the dark all preferred patterned to plain surfaces, but with prolonged deprivation there was an increasing tendency to prefer the display with color rather than the display with pattern. Differential attention to solid or projecting objects over flat surfaces tended to increase with time spent in a lighted environment, but this preference decreased with time spent in the dark (see Fig. 12-3). The longer deprived infants did not cease to develop preferences, but developed abnormally, as the shift toward a preference for plain color and larger size indicates. These subjects did not develop a preference for patterned over plain displays even after 16 weeks of postdeprivation testing.

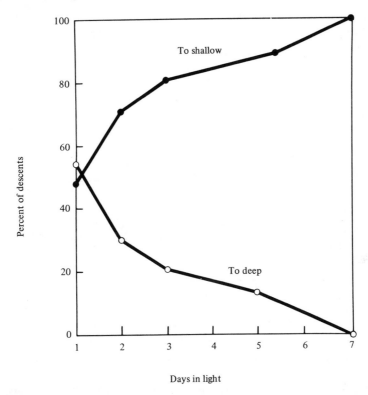

FIGURE 12–2. The development of avoidance of a visual cliff by dark-reared kittens as a function of days in the light.

(From R. D. Walk & E. J. Gibson. A comparative and analytical study of visual depth perception. *Psychological Monographs,* 1961, *75,* 37. Copyright 1961 by the American Psychological Association, and reproduced by permission.)

Tests of depth perception and obstacle avoidance bore out the finding that length of deprivation was important, but indicated ensuing improvement of the perception. Monkey infants kept in darkness for less than one month avoided the visual cliff after a few days or less of visual experience, while the longer deprived subjects required many days. A test of orientation in an obstacle field gave similar results; avoidance of obstacles was good after a short period of experience for most animals, but the longest deprived animals required several weeks of experience for consistent avoidance.

Some effects of visual deprivation were still apparent in tests of discrimination learning when the monkeys were 15 months old. The animals kept longest in the dark solved significantly fewer problems than the others. Study of the characteristics of the objects to be discriminated and the problems that were failed indicated that these subjects had not developed habits

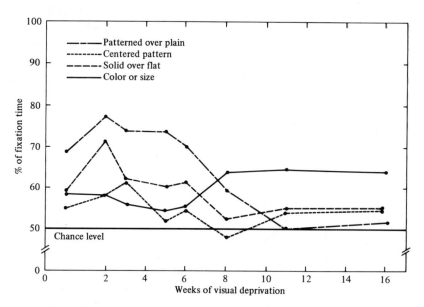

FIGURE 12–3. Differences in visual preferences of monkey infants following different lengths of visual deprivation from birth.

(From R. L. Fantz, Visual perception and experience in early infancy: A look at the hidden side of behavior development. From H. W. Stevenson, et al. [Eds.], *Early Behavior: Comparative and Developmental Approaches.* New York: Wiley, 1967, p. 209.)

of visual attention to object qualities of the discriminanda, the qualities of greatest ecological value, such as texture, shape, and sculptural features. It was not that the animals were blind. But the long deprivation, Fantz concluded, caused a loss of selective attention to patterns and to palpable criterial features of objects. These monkeys evidently had not learned the normal repertory of distinctive features of objects, failed to attend to them, and hence failed the problem.

Deficits have also been found in monkeys, when diffuse light was the only stimulation available (Riesen, Ramsay, & Wilson, 1964). Monkeys reared from birth to twenty or sixty days of age with diffusing eye covers were found to have low visual acuity when first tested at these ages with an optikinetic apparatus. But less than two weeks of limited patterned light experience was sufficient for most of the animals to recover normal acuity. Avoidance of the visual cliff was observed after eleven to twenty days of patterned light. Wilson and Riesen (1966) found no difference in trials required to learn a visual discrimination (black vs. white, triangle vs. circle, horizontal vs. vertical) in monkeys reared till sixty days with diffused light as compared with those so reared till only twenty days. Performance on visual discrimination tasks improved with experience in the light for both groups. Riesen felt that improvement was general, not specific to a training situation. Pattern and intensity discriminations, and transposition of a brightness discrimination to new pairs were learned faster as the duration of normal visual stimulation increased.

It seems certain that there are species differences in the amount of perceptual deficit as a result of light deprivation. Riesen's (1947) report of rearing two chimpanzees in darkness from birth to 16 months claimed striking deficits in perception. The results at first convinced the psychological world that lack of early visual experience literally resulted in blindness. The results were said to "require changes in current theories of learning and perception." Visual recognition of objects was slow in developing, as was learning to avoid approaching objects that delivered an electric shock. Oculomotor disturbances were prominent. But later histological examinations discovered that atrophy of the retinas had occurred. Such a high degree of degeneration was not found in similarly reared rats or cats, but some degeneration was found even in these animals (Rasch, Swift, Riesen, & Chow, 1961).

It is possible that the measures of visual discriminatory ability were insufficiently precise in the above experiments to reveal subtle differences due to learning. Finding really specific differences might give a clue to an appropriate model of perceptual learning. Ganz and Riesen (1962) examined the generalization gradient to hue in dark-reared monkeys. These monkeys' only visual experience was in the testing situation. They were trained to press a key to a light stimulus of a given wavelength, and then were given generalization tests with other wavelengths differing from the original in a graded series. The result was that the hue-naive group generalized with a flat slope (no gradient) on the first day of testing for generalization, and there was a progressive steepening of slope thereafter with continued testing, the slope eventually exceeding that of the experienced group. The experienced group exhibited a very moderate gradient which did not change. Since the deprived animals' visual experience was confined entirely to the experimental stimulus differences, a plausible interpretation of these results might be that differentiation increased as opportunity was provided to examine the range of wavelengths included in the tests, and progressed beyond that of the normally reared animals because this was the only variation in their visual experience, one to which they were very attentive.

Generalization to line patterns was the criterion examined by Ganz and Wilson (1967), the subjects being infant monkeys exposed only to diffused light, and controls reared in the usual visual environment. The questions raised were whether there would be innate transfer of the discrimination, and whether the transfer would take place when contour-following eye movements were prevented (the latter condition being designed to provide a test of Hebb's theory). The monkeys were trained to discriminate a horizontal from a vertical line, using a stabilized image technique in presenting the lines so that the subject could not follow the contour of the line with eye movements. During training, the animals wore contact lenses on which a pattern was projected. Transfer after learning was tested to fragmented lines, smaller figures, lines with reversed brightness relationships, and lines positioned on different retinal areas than those used in training. The main finding was that visually naive and visually experienced subjects transferred in the same way. There were differences among the transfer situations (e.g., perfect transfer to smaller sizes, little transfer to transposed brightness relationships), but no differences between the two groups were discernible. The authors concluded that there was an "innate line-recognition mechanism," not dependent on following contours with the eyes.

These experiments at present yield few straightforward conclusions. The duration of light deprivation, and whether it is light as such or patterned light makes a difference, since longer deprivation in the first case leads to neural degeneration. In both cases it may lead to other confounding factors, especially competing habits of attention. There is little evidence for critical periods of visual development, or for the necessity of acquiring specific neural connections in order to make possible form discrimination. Yet perceptual development after exposure to a visual world does in some sense occur.

MONOCULAR DEPRIVATION. If the development of visual form perception depends on visual experience, one might surmise that interocular transfer would only occur if the two eyes have had simultaneous stimulation with patterned light. Hebb (1949) implies, in discussing the development of "superordinate perceptions," that cell assemblies, the basis for superordinate integration, must be bilaterally developed if the eyes are to be equivalent in yielding the same perception (pp. 96 ff.). Monocular deprivation might thus be expected to prevent binocular equivalence. An experiment was designed to test this prediction by Riesen, Kurke, and Mellinger (1953). Kittens were reared in the dark until 14 weeks and then given 30 minutes of light daily, with patterned light to one eye but only diffused light to the other. At 17 to 20 weeks the kittens began learning a visual discrimination with the eye that had been exposed to patterned light. After mastery of the discrimination, the diffusing cover was placed over the trained eye, the untrained eye was uncovered, and a test was made for the discrimination. None of the experimental animals could discriminate with the previously unused eye. But two pet cats raised in a normally lighted visible environment could transfer a discrimination from the trained to the untrained eye, as would be expected.

The interpretation of these results is not at all obvious. Can one conclude that bilateral transfer of a habit from one eye to the other depends on previous visual learning in both eyes? For a number of reasons, no. In the first place, the deprived kittens were very slow at learning the first discrimination and showed evidence of marked visual unresponsiveness. Although transfer following learning was not immediate, it was accomplished quickly, with a saving as high as 90 percent in one case. Also, as the authors pointed out, the deprived kittens might have learned to suppress vision in the occluded eye. And, as later research by Hubel and Wiesel (1965) suggests, there might have been degeneration of cells operative in transfer, since cells normally fired binocularly from a given receptive field lose this function with deprivation of binocular stimulation.

Conclusive evidence that binocular visual experience is not necessary for achieving functional equivalence of the two eyes was provided later by Chow and Nissen (1955), who reared infant chimpanzees with patterned light to one eye and diffused light to the other, as in the above experiment, and compared their interocular transfer with a chimpanzee reared with patterned-light stimulation to each eye separately, that is, one eye at a time was exposed to patterned light for an hour and a half each day. The animals reared with only diffuse light to one eye confirmed the findings of Riesen et al.; transfer of a learned discrimination to the naive eye was not immediate, though there was a large saving in relearning. But the animal given exposure to patterned light in each eye separately exhibited immediate transfer of two learned discriminations. Chow and Nissen concluded that some patterned light experience, either monocular or binocular, was necessary for functional interocular equivalence, and that a central mechanism was involved.

We can go further and assert that transferability of pattern perception for the two eyes does not depend on previous experience of patterned light for each, together or separately, on the basis of an experiment by Myers and McCleary (1964). They reared cats with visual experience of diffuse light only (to both eyes). When the kittens were 30 to 35 weeks old, monocular training was given on a visual discrimination (cross vs. circle). The response was a conditioned leg flexion. Shock followed the negative stimulus if the animal did not flex. When a high criterion of learning was reached, transfer to the untrained eye was tested, and was found as good as for normally reared animals from a natural, lighted environment. Original learning was slower for the deprived animals, but transfer was immediately present.

The so-called interocular transfer experiments remind us that conclusions from deprivation experiments must be cautious because of species differences. But similar evidence as to functional equivalence of the two eyes exists for a nonmammalian species. McCleary and Longfellow (1961) studied interocular transfer of a learned visual discrimination in the goldfish. No artificial occlusion of an eye was necessary, since the objects to be discriminated were presented only to one eye, on one side, and the fish sees half the world with one eye and the other half with the other. After the fish had learned to distinguish a pair of forms presented in the field of view of one eye they were presented in the field of the other. There was immediate transfer when the untrained eye was tested, although the two retinae could never have been simultaneously stimulated by the same array.

Restriction of Motility and Sensory Feedback

A strict behaviorist would challenge interpretations of some of the preceding experiments on the grounds that deprivation of sensory experience was not what mattered, but rather the lack of opportunity to form S-R links, such as learned coordinations, between visual-spatial stimuli and motor responses of orienting and reaching. Riesen and Aarons (1959) performed an experiment in which kittens were reared either with only diffused light (one hour a day) which they experienced in a restraining holder, or else with normal visual exposure (one hour a day) also experienced in a restraining holder. After 14 weeks, they were given training on a problem requiring discrimination of a slowly rotating cross from a stationary cross. The crosses were projected from behind on translucent doors. The cat had to walk to the correct door and push it open. None of the animals learned the discrimination, whereas control animals reared in light and without restraint of movement did. The experimental animals were able, however, to learn a visual intensity discrimination.

Something very subtle may be missing in the restrained animals in this experiment; that is, the inability to differentiate objectively produced visual motion from motion of an image on the retina produced by the animal's own movement during locomotion (see Riesen, 1961). The cats who were given a look at the world an hour a day, but could not themselves move in relation to it, may have lost or failed to develop this discrimination. Information for the differentiation of the two kinds of movement rests on proprioceptive feedback from self-induced movement. During the discrimination training, the feedback was present but apparent motion of the actually stationary cross may have been confused with real motion of the moving cross owing to inability to connect the feedback with the motion in the former case.

Meyers (1964) attempted to check this explanation by using the indicator response (leg flexion) employed by Meyers and McCleary (1964). The animal was immobile in this case and its head was in a stock, so there could be no apparent motion of the stationary figure induced by the animal's own movement. Cats were reared with one hour of binocular patterned vision per day, while restrained. The rest of the time they lived in the dark.

Training was begun on the discrimination of motion at 29 weeks. The experimental animals achieved criterion on this task just as fast as normally reared control animals. Meyers concluded that the discrimination of motion was possible here because the animal was restrained during training as well as during early visual exposure, making retinal motion of the projected stationary stimulus impossible.

Held (1965) has gone much further in the emphasis on correlated sensory feedback resulting from self-initiated movement. He believes that lack of visual stimulation correlated with movement will result in failure of development of all visually guided spatial behavior. He follows von Holst (1954) in the belief that there is a unique kind of neural excitation ("re-afference") [1] following sensory stimulation consequent on movements initiated by the sensing animal itself and that "stimulus variation concurrent with and systematically dependent upon self-produced movement" is essential for perceptual development.

An experiment by Held and Hein (1963) was designed to test this proposition. The subjects were kittens, reared in the dark except for three hours daily for a few weeks before testing. The kittens were paired, and were given their daily light exposure in a compartment with cylindrical walls painted in stripes. Inside the cylinder, one kitten was free to walk about as he chose. He was harnessed to a lever from which a gondola was suspended at the other end in which the second kitten rode (see Fig. 12–4). The second kitten was restrained in the gondola with a neck yoke and body clamp. He was moved passively about in the cylinder as the active kitten walked around. His exposure to visual stimulation was thus presumably equivalent, except that it was uncorrelated with any movements of his own. Motion in the visual display would result from change in his own position but without proprioceptive information about his movement. He could, in fact, move his feet about inside the gondola, but this movement of course would result in no change of scene. He would be unable to tell, in short, whether his position in space was changing or whether the world was moving.

After some weeks of this exposure, tests of visually guided behavior were given: visual placing of the paw on approach to a surface, the visual cliff, and eye blink to an approaching object. The active kitten exhibited normal visual-spatial behavior in all these tests but the passively exposed kittens did not. After two days of freedom in an illuminated room, however, they displayed visually guided paw placement, and appropriate differentiation on the visual cliff.

Does this finding prove that visual stimulation concurrent with and dependent on self-produced movement is essential for development of the perceptual differentiation demanded in the tests? It well may, but it could

[1] See Chapter 10 for a discussion of reafference in adaptation to spatially transformed stimulation.

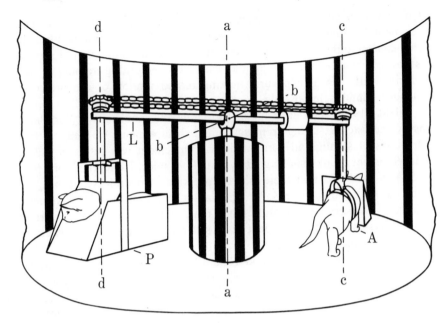

FIGURE 12–4.   The kitten carrousel.

Apparatus used by Held and Hein for equating motion and consequent visual feedback for an actively moving (A) and a passively moving (P) subject. (From R. Held & A. Hein, Movement produced stimulation in the development of visually guided behavior. *Journal of Comparative and Physiological Psychology,* 1963, *56,* 873.)

also mean that the passive kitten learned something else during its daily exposure to light; that its own movements within the gondola were unrelated to all the perceived motion of the world. It is conceivable that the passive kittens did perceptually differentiate the two sides, but did not at first know where their own movements would take them.

Other experiments of Held and his collaborators have further investigated visually guided behavior and confirm the importance of vision accompanied by reafference for accurately directed reaching to a visually presented target. But the target itself is attended to and recognized without relation to this. An experiment by Held and Bauer (1967) investigated reaching in infant monkeys that had been reared in an apparatus which prevented them from seeing their own limbs, although the limbs could be moved at will, and in fact, two monkeys were conditioned to extend an arm (hidden from them) when a nursing bottle was presented. After 34 days, an arm was exposed and tests of visually guided reaching were begun. Sight of the bottle elicited arm extension, but the reach was terminated as soon as the hand entered the monkey's view, and the monkey gazed intently at its hand, while moving it about. Reaching for objects was inaccurate, but became more precise as hand-watching subsided and glancing between hand and target began. Development of visually directed reaching, Held and Bauer concluded, required viewing the moving hand, but visual attention to objects and exploratory eye movements develop without any dependence on this.

Experiments with kittens prevented from seeing their paws by a large collar worn around the neck confirmed these conclusions (Hein & Held, 1967). The cats could see the world and locomote freely for six hours a day but they could not see their limbs. When the collars were removed, the cats were tested for presence of the visual placing response and also for visually directed reaching. In the placing test, the cats did show extension of the forepaws when they were brought close to a visible surface. However, when the surface was not solid but slatted, they aimed the paw at the air between the slats as often as at the slats. Visually elicited extension thus developed without sight of the forelimbs, but accurate placing required practice while viewing the limbs.

Conclusion

Experiments designed to examine the effect of light deprivation during early rearing, which looked so promising 25 years ago as a means of answering the nature-nurture question, and again 15 years ago as a means of testing such theories of perceptual development as Hebb's, have not on the whole fulfilled these promises. They have raised more questions than they answered. Raising new questions is not a bad thing, however, and we have gained some sophistication in rephrasing the old ones. We no longer ask "is perception learned or is it innate?" It is clear that an organism at birth has some perceptual capacities (varying in kind with the species) that are ready to go, and that ensuing interaction with an environment will modify them. The nature of the stimulus information from that environment will make a difference in the development, but the difference is not easily predicted.

When we think about these predictions, we have, in the back of our minds, a concept of the normal environment in which an organism is adapted to develop. A departure from this norm deprives the organism of typical stimulation and this results in organic degeneration, emotional maladjustment, the supplanting of behavior controlled by one kind of sensory information with behavior controlled by another, and the failure of the usual differentiations to develop. Is this normal environment a myth? I do not think so, for evolution depends on interaction of a species with its particular niche in the world. But living organisms also adapt individually to what is there, even when it is extraordinary, and that fact was forgotten by interpreters of the early deprivation research and the anecdotes of accidental deprivation.

The deprivation studies have not given us many clues to the nature of perceptual learning, except in a negative way. Specific learning to perceive a particular form or pattern by contour tracing is not the necessary condition for discrimination. Visual-motor coordinations, to develop adaptively, need opportunities for visual-motor practice, but that does not necessarily mean that a motor theory of all visual development is indicated, or that development is a matter of associations between the visual input and response. Let us turn now to the augmentation experiments and see whether they are more enlightening.

AUGMENTATION

Enhancement of the Normal Stimulus Environment

As we noted, Hebb's theorizing has been responsible for a series of experiments aimed to reveal the role of experience in perceptual development. The experimenter can subtract experience from, or add it to a normal environment. What happens if the stimulus environment is enhanced in the opportunities for obtaining perceptual experience? I am using enhancement to mean a nonspecific increase in complexity, with no attempt to define the actual experiences. Experiments at McGill University by Hymovitch (1952) and by Forgays and Forgays (1952) compared rats reared in the usual cages with others reared in open spaces that they were free to explore, including alleys, inclined runways, apertures, and even playthings. It was a kind of Operation Headstart for rats. When the rats were mature they were tested in the Hebb-Williams maze, which was considered a problem-solving test of intelligence. The rats reared in a free environment performed better than cage-reared animals; when playthings were added they performed still better. These investigators concluded that the superior performance was due to early perceptual experience gained from the wider sensory environment. No direct test of perceptual capacities was made; only maze performance was tested.

Forgus (1954, 1955) performed several experiments in the same tradition by increasing the complexity of the environment with sundry objects, but he did introduce some more specific tests. Moreover, some of his rats could only look at the supernumerary objects; they could not approach them so as to obtain tactual and haptic information. These animals were found to be actually superior to those permitted direct contact with the object-filled environment when tested with a form discrimination problem and on a T maze having visual aids to help differentiate the turns. They were presumably superior because they had learned to pay attention to visible properties of the environment. The direct-contact animals, however, performed better when tests on a maze were conducted in the dark. Since a repetition of this experiment by Walk (1958) failed to replicate the results, one must reserve judgment about the precise effects of the enriched environment on perceptual development. The unspecified nature of the enhanced sensory stimulation makes analysis difficult. We do not know just what the stimulus information was. Some of the reports of free-environment experiments have claimed that there is a critical period, early in life, when and only when the enhanced stimulation is effective (e.g., Forgays & Read, 1962), but since it is not clear just how it is effective, this conclusion must be viewed with skepticism, at least as regards perceptual development.

The introduction of massive stimulation in an otherwise impoverished environment has been attempted with human infants, with some indication that exploratory behavior and visual attention are facilitated. White and Held (1966) reported experiments with infants born and reared in an institution, with what are described as barren and homogeneous surroundings. A group of infants who was simply given twenty minutes a day of extra handling was later more visually attentive than a control group. "Attentive" was defined as "the state in which the infant's eyes are more than half open, its direction of gaze shifting at least once within any thirty-second period." Still another group was given the extra handling along with increased mobility (three times a day they were turned to the prone position) and the crib liners were removed so that the room could be seen; moreover from day 37 to day 124 they were provided with a special visual surrounding that included a multicolored stabile suspended above the crib; they also had color-printed crib-sheets. During the first five weeks in this visually complex environment the infants exhibited less visual exploratory behavior than the controls, and they cried oftener! Perhaps massive stimulation can be too massive. But after two and a half months the stabile began to be swiped at with the hand, and visually directed reaching developed faster than in the controls. By three and a half months, the augmented group exceeded in visual attentiveness. An interesting feature of the behavior of this group was a decrease in hand regard as compared with the control group; this is a characteristic activity around two months of age which probably serves multiple functions since it provides opportunity both for development of space perception and of visually directed manipulating and reaching.

White and Held (1966) gave still another group modified enrichment. At 37 days, pacifiers were mounted on the crib rails (see Fig. 12–5),

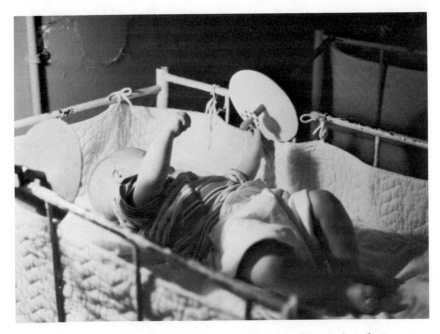

FIGURE 12–5.   Infant reaching for pacifier mounted on crib rail.

(From B. L. White & R. Held, Plasticity of sensorimotor development in the human infant, in *The Causes of Behavior II: Readings in Child Development and Educational Psychology,* ed. J. F. Rosenblith and W. Allinsmith, p. 67. Copyright © 1966 by Allyn and Bacon, Inc., Boston. Reprinted by permission of the publisher.)

colored in a red and white pattern against a white background. At 68 days, a stabile was provided, as in the previous study. These infants developed sustained hand regard at about 46 days, at the same time as control infants. The achievement of skilled reaching, however, came earlier than it did in the controls, and they showed more consistent visual attention than the controls (see Fig. 12–6). Nevertheless, the group showed a reduction in visual attentiveness, as did the control group, around the age of 100 days. The authors wrote with admirable candor: "It would appear that some uncontrolled variable is interacting with our various attempts at modifying the function." It does seem clear that providing accessible targets for the hands such as the pacifiers, instead of restricting the infant to the seeing and feeling of the empty hands, is an aid to the development of visually guided reaching. This condition is one which a normal environment would usually provide. On the whole, these experiments provide little evidence to show that the slogan for speeding perceptual development is simply "the more the better."

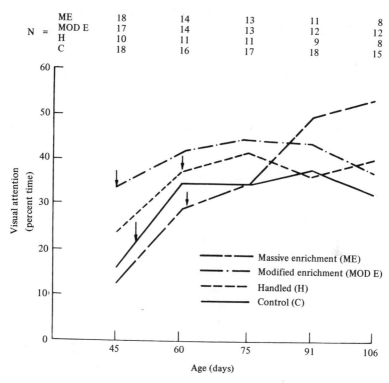

FIGURE 12–6. The development of visual attention in infants raised in four types of environment.

(From B. L. White & R. Held, Plasticity of sensorimotor development in the human infant, in *The Causes of Behavior II: Readings in Child Development and Educational Psychology,* ed. J. F. Rosenblith and W. Allinsmith, p. 68. Copyright © 1966 by Allyn and Bacon, Inc., Boston. Reprinted by permission of the publisher.)

Specific Augmentation

PROGRESSIVE TRAINING OF HUMAN INFANTS. Perhaps a more specific type of augmentation, followed by tests closely related to the type of environmental intervention, would yield more definite results. An interesting study of form discrimination in infants by Ling (1941) is relevant in this respect, though it was not aimed at the question. It involved prolonged training of a group of infants on a planned program of form discriminations, yielding evidence for development of what we have since come to call a learning set to discriminate forms, and to recognize them under transformations.

Infants between six and twelve months old were Ling's subjects. They came to the laboratory regularly three times a week and progressed from one discrimination problem to another. The baby was propped in a crib with a display board in front of him. On this board were displayed, on a given trial, two differently shaped bright yellow blocks, for instance, a circle and a cross. One block was fastened to the board and could not be removed. The other could be grasped and carried to the mouth; it provided reinforcement since it was sweetened.

Each child was taken through five series of discrimination problems. The first series had four problems: circle vs. cross, circle vs. triangle, circle vs. square, and circle vs. oval. After successive mastery of these, the child progressed to a second series of five problems in each of which one of the forms was rotated (e.g., square turned to diamond); then a third series in which there were size transformations; a fourth in which there was an increase in the number of negative stimulus blocks present during the choice; and a fifth in which the positive-negative forms were reversed.

There were, of course, individual differences, but 26 babies completed the whole series of problems and showed evidence of more and more rapid learning as the experiment continued, as well as transposition with rotation and change of size.[2] An exception to the trend of more rapid learning as the experiment continued occurred in Series V, reversal learning. The first reversal problem caused an abrupt increase in the mean number of trials to criterion; the subjects were "at first profoundly disturbed when the positive stimulus was abruptly made negative." However, the infants readjusted themselves to the new situation and the number of trials required in the ensuing problems fell to its previous level (see Fig. 12–7). Some subjects succeeded almost instantaneously in abstracting the changed relationship, though some were more stereotyped. As Ling remarks, the results show an unexpected degree of plasticity. This is all the more striking in view of the many experiments of the last decade on reversal learning in which older children (five to six years) frequently showed considerable difficulty in reversing the positive-negative relationship. The infants in this experiment do seem to have gained something general from their continued training.

What have they gained from this unusual learning program? Ling reported that in the beginning visual regard was momentary and intermittent, usually directed to one block at a time. As the infants grew older their attention increased "both in span and duration" and visual regard was coordinated, the two blocks being regarded simultaneously or, when five blocks were presented at once, the blocks were regarded systematically in sequence. These attentional changes might have developed, of course, without any special discrimination training. In a second experiment, Ling compared 12 of the subjects from Experiment I with an untrained control group

[2] Ling comments that "even at these very early age levels, there is a 'form constancy' which is of a very elementary perceptual nature (p. 20)."

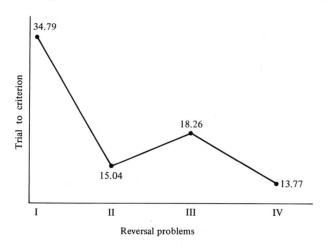

FIGURE 12–7. Interproblem transfer of form discrimination in infants after reversal of positive and negative stimulus objects.

(Data from B. C. Ling, Form discrimination as a learning cue in infants. *Comparative Psychology Monographs,* 1941, *17,* 18, Table 2, subgroups I and II combined. By permission of the author and The Williams & Wilkins Co.)

matched for age. The experiment used a preference task, rather than learning, so comparisons could only be made in terms of general approach to the situation, manipulation, and reaction time. Form preferences were very similar for the two groups, which caused Ling to speculate that the effect of training was on *"attention* to form differences, rather than improvement in form discrimination capacity *per se* (p. 47)."

The transfer from task to task, evident as the experiment progressed, showed up as a kind of general adaptation when the behavior of infants in the experimental group was compared with that of the control group.

These infants were more amiable, interested and quiet, and were willing to work for a much longer period of time than untrained subjects. Second, they paid more immediate and selective attention to the stimulus pattern, both to the whole and to the parts. There was definite inhibition of extraneous bodily movement. Visual regard was of an anticipatory, "critical" and sustained type, and was directed to details often unnoticed by untrained subjects. Third, they showed a more direct and accurate motor approach to the units of the stimulus pattern. Having secured the block, their manipulative activities were more varied, and their visual-tactual examinations more minute. Finally, it has been repeatedly pointed out by their parents that these trained subjects developed a smoother adaptation to various "lay" situations within the home, implying a very *general* type of transfer (p. 56).

We infer then that even very specific training had a rather general effect, influencing selective attention and the strategy of exploratory behavior. Of very specific effects, which might have been revealed in the preference tests, there was little or no evidence.

PROLONGED EXPOSURE TO SPECIFIC FORMS IN RATS. Although discrimination training is not possible at a very early age, it is possible to introduce specific forms to the subject very early, to continue their presence for a prolonged period of exposure, and later to conduct discrimination training, comparing learning of an exposed group with learning of a control group to which the forms are novel. Gibson and Walk (1956) carried out a number of such experiments. The typical procedure began with rearing one group of rats in cages which had black cutout metal figures (circles and triangles) fastened to the wall and a control group in identical cages without the figures. At ninety days both groups were trained to discriminate between a black circle and a triangle painted on white backgrounds. In the first such experiment, the experimental group learned faster and made fewer errors, leading us to conclude that prolonged visual experience of the two figures facilitated learning the discrimination.

Subsequent experiments taught us to be very skeptical of how this result was to be interpreted. Replication of the experiment (Gibson, Walk, Pick, & Tighe, 1958) confirmed the findings, but the difference was not impressive. Furthermore, a group which learned to discriminate two different patterns (an isosceles triangle and an ellipse) showed equal facilitation, making us doubt the specificity of the effect. In another experiment (Walk, Gibson, Pick, & Tighe, 1958), only one of the two figures was hung on the wall previous to discrimination learning. Facilitation still occurred, and it made no difference whether the figure selected as positive had been the one exposed or not. In early trials, there was a significant preference for the figure that had not been exposed. Other replications (Gibson, Walk, & Tighe, 1959) designed to compare effects of early and later exposure to the patterns did not yield significant differences.

Two experiments which failed to replicate the original findings differed from the original in the mode of presentation of the figures during the rearing period. They were painted on a flat background, instead of cut out so as to provide depth differences at the edges. In a final experiment (Walk, Gibson, Pick, & Tighe, 1959) we made a direct comparison of the effectiveness of these two conditions. The decision was in favor of cutouts, but again differences were not impressive. Our interpretation of the effects of prolonged exposure to specific forms was in terms of drawing attention to visual cues later to be the basis for the learned discrimination. Cutout figures are more attention-getting because of edge depth. But on the whole, this kind of specific enrichment yielded nothing in the way of really specific effects.

Confirmation of the original result has been provided by other experimenters with variations which are consistent with the interpretation in terms of attention to appropriate cues (Kawachi, 1965). Meier and McGee (1959) compared effects of rearing with, first, solid blocks of different shapes inside the cage; second, only visual exposure to the same blocks; third, no blocks, but laboratory surroundings visible; and fourth, minimal visual experience. Discrimination learning involved crawling over the correct block. The maximally exposed group learned the discrimination fastest, the minimally exposed slowest, with no difference between the other two. It was concluded that the superior group had differentiated the objects during rearing, and so had only to learn later which one was rewarded when they were given the discrimination problem.

These results point to perceptual learning that is independent of differential reinforcement. Differentiation of distinctive features and selective attention to edges and corners was probably what was learned, rather than any specific identification, and this learning happened without differential reinforcement of any kind. In fact, when differential reinforcement was experimentally associated with early exposure (Walk et al., 1958), results were negative. Kerpelman (1965) argued that nondifferential reinforcement was involved, because the rats ate in the presence of the exposed figures, and that the figures at the beginning of discrimination training would be "at a higher level of excitatory tendency" than for the control group. I cannot think what this means except that the exposed animals would be more likely to pay attention to the figures, since there was no specifically associated response for them to excite.

The specific enrichment experiments just described have sometimes been compared to imprinting (Bateson, 1964). Shortly after hatching, Bateson placed chicks in pens painted with black and white vertical stripes, and after a week had them learn a discrimination between the black and white stripes and red and yellow horizontal stripes. The black and white stripes were made negative. They learned faster than a control group, and Bateson reported that they approached the familiar stimulus more often than the other during the first ten trials. However, as I noted above, a similar experiment of ours found just the opposite; during the first ten trials, rats approached the novel figure more often than the familiar one. It would thus be an error to infer from the imprinting comparison that perceptual learning for the rat consisted of imprinting on him an image of the exposed figure or figures, or that it could be reduced to a tendency to approach.

BIASED REARING

The experiments with specific augmentation approach what I have called rearing in a biased environment. This is one that has been altered in a systematic way, rendering it unrepresentative for the species. The argument behind such experiments, originally at least, was that normal behavior for the species should emerge, despite the abnormal environment during rearing, if the behavior was innate. If it did not so emerge, then normal behavior for the species must have to be learned.[3]

An experiment performed by Eckhard Hess (1949) is an example of such a method. He was interested in shadow as a depth cue, and speculated that its meaning might be learned on the basis of assumptions derived from the light source being normally overhead. He reared chicks for seven weeks in one of two environments: 1) all light from above, as if from the sun; 2) all light from a source below the transparent floor of the cage. He argued that if the learning hypothesis was correct chicks brought up in an environment where all light came from below should differ from normal chicks in their depth response to patterns of light and shade. The test was pecking at photographs of grain differing in the distribution of light and shadow depending on source of illumination, with, he hoped, no other cues for depth present. The photographs were presented upright, in a vertical position.

The chicks did, in fact, peck differentially. Control chicks pecked at the photograph taken under illumination from above and experimental chicks at the one illuminated from below. One is, nevertheless, very hesitant to jump to an innate or learned conclusion. That environmental conditions will interact with original nature in development is only to be expected on the basis of the experiments we have already reviewed. But what is a proper control for further inference? There cannot be a condition with no environment.

How the pecking preference could have been learned is mysterious, in view of the dissimilarity of the test to a real pecking situation. The chicks had not pecked at grain before (their diet during rearing was mash), nor seen grain casting shadows in this unusual position until the test; just before testing, real grain pasted on cardboard was presented in this position, and the chickens were allowed to eat some. Specific, reinforced cue learning might have occurred during this brief interval. But how a learned assumption about shadows as cues for depth could transfer to the test situation is not clear, nor is it clear that any perception of depth was involved. Parallax cues should indicate to the chick that the surface was flat, despite the pictured shadows. Once again, a rearing experiment failed to clarify the question of how perceptual learning occurs.

One of the most stringent ways of biasing the visual environment is to place transforming spectacles before the eyes, as in the experiments discussed in Chapter 10. Bishop (1959) asked whether such an abnormal transformation of the visual array present from the first visual experience

---

[3] The logic of this argument has been criticized by Lorenz (1965).

would result in deviation in perceptual development. Two groups of kittens were reared in the dark for eight weeks, and then fitted with a monocular eyepiece which held a prism for one group and a blank holder for the other. The second eye in each case was occluded. The prism reversed the up-down axis of the visual field. The total field of view was 19° and was the same for both groups. All visual experience occurred under these conditions for four weeks, at which time the optical devices were switched from one group to the other. Various tests were given both before and after the switch, such as obstacle and hole avoidance. Bishop concluded that the animals who wore prisms did not perform as well as nonprism wearers and that this argued for innateness. However, results of the various tests did not agree, nor is the logic of the argument clear.

I described earlier some experiments by Richard Walk and myself with dark-reared rats and cats tested on a visual cliff. Since rats reared in the dark for ninety days showed the same preference for the shallow side of the cliff as animals reared in the light, we concluded that discrimination of edge depth in this species was innate, in the sense that it developed without visual experience. Since that time, several experiments have been published showing that the rats' preference can be changed by rearing in a biased environment—in this case, over a void resembling the deep side of the cliff, or actually on the deep side of the cliff (Kaess & Wilson, 1964; Rosen & Ison, 1964; Carr & McGuigan, 1965). In two experiments the rats' preference shifted toward the deep side, and in one, there was no preference for either. In another experiment, chicks reared similarly shifted from a preference for the shallow side toward chance (Tallarico & Farrell, 1964). The latter authors concluded that the results cast doubt on whether chicks innately avoid a drop-off, but since newly hatched chicks do, the criticism appears unwarranted.

These experiments do not show that the specially reared subjects could not discriminate edge depth, but rather that habituation to a lack of optical support is possible. They show, I think, that behavior which normally occurs without previous experience in the presence of the appropriate releasing situation, will extinguish if the situation is repeatedly presented, a finding of which the ethologists have long been aware. To conclude, even behavior ready to go at birth will not necessarily be maintained without normal environmental conditions; and finding a change in behavior related to a specific environmental change is not proof that the behavior typical of the species depended on learning for its original appearance.

SUMMARY

We have reviewed a large number of experiments addressed to the question of how rearing conditions may influence perceptual development. Some of these can be described as depriving the young animal of normal sources of stimulation, and some as augmenting the normal sources. Some substitute an abnormal condition for an ordinary condition of the environment. Those studies which examined the effects of nonspecific deprivation or enrichment lead us to a nonspecific conclusion: environment makes a difference in development, but exactly how it affects perceptual development is not clarified. The experiments with more specific intervention in rearing conditions have told us little more. They do not tell us whether nature or nurture is more important but only that development depends on both. Since development must take place in some kind of environment, experiments with altered environments do not permit the deduction that changed behavior is evidence against innateness. The two-group design permits no such conclusion.

What do these experiments indicate for principles of perceptual development? They provide little, if any, support for specific neural integrations, or cell assemblies, or specific associational mechanisms, or copies, or image formation as the mechanism of perceptual learning. On the positive side, they suggest that impoverishment of stimulation in early life may result in a lack of perceptual curiosity, and an inability to sift out distinctive features from irrelevant stimulation; in short a maladaptive development of selective attention and perceptual motivation. A biased environment can extinguish attention to distinctive environmental variables, i.e., to stimulus information that would normally be differentiated and responded to. A careful program of training in perceptual differentiation, such as that of Ling, may result in advanced development of perceptual strategies, perceptual span, and selectivity with respect to critical differentiating properties of objects. The research required to follow up this guess would be laborious but rewarding.

These experiments have led us to the question of development of perception, as opposed to short-term learning. The following chapters will be devoted to the question of how perception develops, making both species comparisons and comparisons from age to age in the maturing organism.

13

The Phylogenesis of Perception: Taxonomy and Trends

In the preceding chapters, the term "learning" was used for modifications in perception that are due to experience or practice. The term "development" was used, particularly in the last chapter, when reference was made to modifications paralleling the individual's growth. Let us shift our emphasis now to the question of how perception develops. The ingredients producing developmental changes in what is perceived are complex and intricately interwoven; they include genetic factors, intraorganic factors, and environmental factors. Suppose my three-month-old kitten one day recognizes a mouse in the sense of demonstrating typical mouse-catching behavior. What factors have contributed to its perception of the mouse as prey? Certainly genetic factors are involved; a turtle or an anteater presented with the same object of prey would not under the most fantastic rearing conditions perceive it as something to be chased, caught, and eaten. Conditions for growth must also be right; the cat's eyes require a certain amount of light during development for visual discrimination of objects to develop normally. And there is evidence that environmental factors of a social nature—either opportunities to witness the mother mouse-hunting, or being reared with a mouse as a foster sibling—will determine whether the mouse is perceived as prey or partner.

In 1930 Kuo, a staunch environmentalist, investigated what he termed the "genesis of the cat's responses to the rat." In one of the earliest and most famous of rearing experiments he sought to determine how differently kittens would respond to rats when brought up under different controlled conditions. In one condition kittens were raised in isolation. They saw no rats nor any adult cats killing rats. They were tested every four days, from one week to four months of age, by putting a rat in the cage for one half hour. This could be an albino rat, a wild gray rat, or a dancing mouse. Of twenty kittens in the group, nine killed from one to three rats during these tests. A second group of kittens was reared in a rat-killing environment. Every four days they saw their mothers kill a rat and were tested immediately afterward. Of twenty-one kittens in the group, 18 killed one or more rats during the tests. The kittens always killed the kind of rat they had seen their mothers kill. In a third group, kittens were raised with rats as companions. Each kitten lived in a separate cage with one rat. Of 18 kittens in this group, only three killed rats during the tests, and in these cases the kind of rodent killed was not of the same breed as the cage-mate. Later on, Kuo put the kittens which had killed no rats through a training session, letting them see adult cats killing rats. Nine out of the eleven animals raised in isolation now became rat killers, but still only one kitten out of the group reared with rats as cage-mates killed a rat.

How shall we deal with these facts? Clearly it would be quite as unjustified to conclude that kittens must learn to perceive rats as prey, as to conclude that they do so instinctively. Environmental factors present during early rearing play a role; but so do genetic ones, as witness the kittens reared in isolation. The moral would seem to be that one must forego the urge to classify behavior as either innate or learned, and attempt instead to unravel the mysteries of development. The question is, how to pursue this goal? An appropriate beginning for the perception psychologist, it seems to me, is the cross species comparison of what is responded to. In making this comparison, I shall use the classification of stimulus information that I suggested in Chapter 1. Let us compare over a sample of species what kinds of stimulus information are perceived.

A PHYLOGENETIC COMPARISON OF WHAT IS PERCEIVED

Space

One class of stimulus sources is the spatial layout of the environment. All animals move around in space and somehow find their way about; this can vary from the simplest tropistic motion toward a light source to manned flight toward the moon. How do they find their way? The information for where to go is extracted from stimulation in innumerable ways, consonant with the animal's sensory structure and with his special environment. The stimulus control for choosing the path of locomotion is astonishingly varied, depending on the species. It would require an encyclopedia to do justice to the topic, so a few contrasting examples must suffice.

A lowly kind of directed locomotion can be found even in an animal having a single light-sensitive area, responding only to changes in intensity, such as the maggot larva. Locomotion occurs along an axis in line with the light source, but this is accomplished by symmetrical deviations of the head end, or of the whole organism. Deviation from side to side allows comparison of intensities, then body movement so as to equalize intensities, and finally movement toward or away from the place where the light comes from. The path is directed, but each step is merely a response to intensity change. An animal with two light receptors can orient directly toward or away from the source of stimulation and locomote in a more or less straight path.

Compare this simple behavior, called a taxis, with the navigation of birds over thousands of miles, perhaps from one hemisphere of the earth to another. Behavior is genetically determined in both cases, but the difference in complexity of stimulus control and of information pickup is dramatic. For instance, of 18 albatrosses taken from nests at Midway atoll in the Pacific and released from widely spaced points, 14 returned to the nest (Kenyon & Rice, 1958). The bird released at the greatest distance, 4,120 miles, returned in 32 days. How was the bird's flight guided? A variety of ingenious theories has been proposed to account for the stimulus information which could guide the so-called navigation of birds. Meyer (1964) has recently discussed the evidence for the four main theories: first, the sun-compass orientation hypothesis, which postulates the determination of directions by the sun regardless of time of day, and thus requires ability to correct for the sun's daily azimuth displacement; second, the star-navigation hypothesis, which assumes that nocturnal birds use the stars not only to determine a fixed compass direction but also to derive information, such as that relevant to the seasons, from the temporal shifts of the constellations; third, the sun-navigation hypotheses, involving determination of latitude and longitude from the sun's altitude, and determination of time by an internal clock; and, fourth, theories based on postulated sensitivity to geomagnetic fields. While a certain amount of evidence exists for all these theories (less convincing for the last), Meyer concludes that a general statement about the discriminative basis for bird navigation cannot be made at the present time. All three mechanisms based on discrimination of celestial cues may operate for different species. Whatever the ultimate conclusion, the stimulus information for bird navigation is not simple, nor is the ability integrated by association.

Orientation and locomotion in space are not controlled solely by visual information. Chemical sensitivity plays a role in the foraging of insects and in their return to the nest. Chemical trails are laid down by individual foragers which can be followed by other colony members, or used as guide lines for return to a food source. Chemical sensitivity is utilized for spatial orientation by mammals as well, in particular by dogs such as beagles and bloodhounds who have been bred for ability to follow odor trails. Trail-following and tracking by scent are not the only spatial behaviors in these animals, of course. Insects make use of visual cues for homing, and flying insects, in making a landing, must detect the flow patterns of visual motion-perspective just as the human aviator must detect them in landing a plane.

The avoidance of obstacles during locomotion by means of auditory information has been one of the most surprising discoveries in modern biology. Although an Italian naturalist, Spallanzani, had suggested in the eighteenth century that bats depended on hearing for their ability to fly between obstacles and to land accurately, clear proof of this guidance was given only in recent years when Griffin and Galambos (1941) were able to demonstrate that bats emitted ultrasonic squeaks, and that the auditory echoes from these sounds as reflected from obstacles were necessary for accurate flight. Bats with ears covered, or with mouths sealed with collodion, bumped into wires strung across a room, while bats with eyes covered did not. Echolocation, as Griffin (1958) termed this method of orientation in space, is an exploration or probing of the environment by sending out sounds and listening for echoes from objects lying in the path ahead.[1] The returning echoes not only serve to guide the bat around obstacles, but also aid it in locating and catching small insects in the dark. Directional localization depends primarily on very small temporal differences in the arrival of an echo at the two ears. Thus if an echo reaches one ear 0.1 msec. before the other, the two ears will receive differential stimulation. However the bat may utilize this available information, it is done with amazing effectiveness, for at least one variety consistently detects a 1 mm. wire at a distance of three to six feet (Griffin, p. 80).

Echolocation is not confined to the bat. Certain sea animals make underwater noises and may avoid collision by a method similar to the bat's. The porpoise, in particular, has been shown to perceive objects by reflected sound (Kellogg, 1958, 1961). The porpoise both emits and can receive underwater sounds which possess the necessary characteristics for echolocation such as short pulses. Experiments with bottlenose dolphins conducted by Kellogg demonstrated that these animals do in fact use this system for detecting obstacles. The noises emitted by the porpoise can be picked up by a hydrophone lowered into the water, listened to with special converting equipment, and recorded. When Kellogg threw a fish into the murky water, the dolphin typically emitted a burst of sound pulses and retrieved the fish within a few seconds. When approaching the target fish, the dolphin accompanied the sound bursts with oscillations of the head from right to left, behavior which would serve to optimize binaural localization. Control experiments in the dark showed that the dolphin was responding to auditory, not visual cues (Kellogg, 1958, 1961).

Dolphins have even been shown to differentiate types of food fish of variable size by echolocating. Kellogg speaks of "auditory scanning" to emphasize the active, exploratory quality of the system. The ability of the porpoise to swim an obstacle course without collision after the fourth trial (Kellogg, 1961) by beaming signals and reacting to the ensuing echoes is proof of its ability to get around in space by means of this astonishing kind of perception.

---

[1] See Chapter 1 for a discussion of echolocation in man.

The variety of strategies which different species have evolved for orientation and locomotion makes cross-species comparisons difficult when they do not depend on the same stimulus information. Yet one universal requirement holds for all terrestrial animals, the necessity to avoid falling from high places. A long fall means death. Whether the avoidance is learned or innate the animal must be able to respond as soon as he attains free locomotion unguided by a parent. He must be able to see a drop-off, a falling-off place. One hears stories of wild animals being driven over cliffs in a panic. The western Indians while hunting are said to have driven whole herds of buffalo over a cliff. But, on the whole, avoidance of cliffs appears to be the rule for terrestrial animals. It may perhaps be more pronounced and more universal in mountain-dwelling animals. But we can assume that information about depth downward at an edge exists in the light for any animal to pick up. If the information could be picked up at a distance by terrestrial animals the survival value would be obvious.

It is possible to make comparative studies of perception of depth at an edge by using the response of cliff avoidance in a controlled setting. Using a standard situation, with identical patterned surfaces below the glass of the shallow and deep sides, Walk and Gibson (1961) made comparative studies of cliff behavior in a number of species (see Fig. 13–1 for

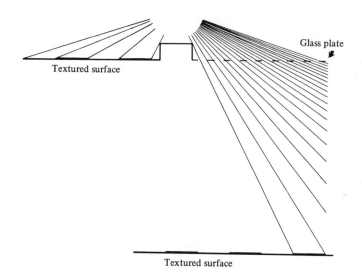

Glass plate

Textured surface

Textured surface

FIGURE 13–1. Cross-section of a visual cliff.

The diagram shows the pattern of light projected to the subject's eye from a textured surface at a shallow depth below his station point on the center runway and from an identical surface farther below. (From R. D. Walk & E. J. Gibson, A comparative and analytical study of visual depth perception. *Psychological Monographs*, 1961, *75*, 12. Copyright 1961 by the American Psychological Association, and reproduced by permission.)

diagram of a visual cliff). Those tested were hooded and albino rats (both infant and adult), chickens (both infant and adult), turtles, goats and sheep (both infant and adult), pigs, kittens, puppies, infant monkeys, and human infants. All of these species showed a preference for the shallow over the deep side. The predominant choice of the shallow side was least marked for the turtles, a result to be expected, since the variety tested was an aquatic animal (*Pseudemys scripta*) which normally spends time on land only for nesting and migration.

Infant monkeys from three to twenty days of age were tested on the cliff by Rosenblum and Cross (1963). They used the choice technique of Gibson and Walk, but they also observed each animal when it had been placed on the glass floor on the side with a textured surface just below and on the side with a textured surface *far* below. They recorded four types of behavior previously found to be indicative of emotional disturbance (crouching, vocalization, self-clasping, and rocking). There was a significantly higher frequency of disturbance when the monkey was not in visual contact with the surface of support. Although the animals were tested repeatedly for 18 days, there was no alleviation of the disturbance. In the choice trials, the shallow side was chosen significantly more frequently. The authors concluded that discrimination of depth was evident on the third day of life and showed no significant change thereafter, despite the fact that the neonatal monkey is normally carried by its mother during this period.

Other animals tested on a visual cliff include rabbits and ducklings (Walk, 1962, 1964). Rabbits chose the shallow side with perfect consistency, but ducklings waddled off carelessly in either direction. This behavior of the ducklings is not surprising if we assume that an aquatic animal would have less cause to avoid a cliff, in order to survive, than a terrestrial animal.

Routtenberg and Glickman (1964) have extended observations on the visual cliff to still other species. Three kinds of rodents, the gerbil, the African spiny mouse, and the golden hamster, showed highly consistent preferences for the shallow side of the cliff. Four species of aquatic turtle and two species of land turtle, when tested on the cliff, showed significant differences from one another in behavior. The land turtles descended from the center board with great consistency to the shallow side, but the aquatic turtles descended about as often to the deep side as to the shallow. Working in the Lincoln Park Zoo, Routtenberg and Glickman also tested eight infant cats, including two lions, two tigers, two jaguars, and two snow leopards. All the cats made their first descent to the shallow side. After the initial descent, some of the cats spent a certain amount of time exploring the glass floor over the deep side. But it is interesting to note that the snow leopards never did, even in later test sessions. These leopards are normally mountain dwelling animals and their behavior supports the notion that normal habitat is correlated with cliff behavior. The extremely consistent avoidance of the cliff in Gibson and Walk's experiments with sheep and goats also supports the notion, for the ancestors of these animals were mountain dwellers.

Do all species that avoid the visual cliff use the same visual information? Figure 13–1 shows a diagram of the apparatus in cross section. The texture of a surface produces a different optical texture in the light to the eye when it is far below the animal's eye than when it is near. This in itself could indicate a drop-off. Walk and Gibson (1961) investigated this possibility by testing animals on an apparatus having a textured surface directly under the glass on both sides, but with one texture finer in grain than the other. Would the finer texture then indicate a farther surface? Rats, both thirty-day-old animals and adults, preferred the coarse-textured side, although the preference was not as pronounced as it was in the standard situation. When a textured surface underlay the glass on one side of the center board and a relatively homogeneous gray surface underlay the other, a very strong preference was shown for the side with a textured floor. But other species (chicks and young goats) did not show a preference for the coarser of two textures when both textured surfaces underlay the glass. Chicks, in fact, exhibited a preference for a finer over a coarse texture (Schiffman & Walk, 1963) possibly because it resembled grain. The difference of texture density alone, therefore, does not determine avoidance behavior. If an animal does not show a preference for the coarser of two floor textures it might suggest that other information is present to specify that the two surfaces are actually at the same depth. Or it might mean that the texture difference alone was not sufficient to control the preference.

Another kind of information for the depth on the two sides of the center board is that usually called differential motion parallax. The slightest movement of the animal's head will yield different amounts of shearing motion of the texture at the two edges of the center board on which the animal is standing. The motion difference will occur despite a difference in the size of the texture elements, as long as there is some texture. Head movements vary from one species to another; the rat bobs its head up and down when looking over the cliff edge while the chick darts its head from side to side. This information seemed to be decisive in experiments with several species. In these experiments the optical texture was equated for the two sides of the apparatus by putting on the deep side a physical texture that was larger than that on the shallow side in proportion to the increased depth. Choice in this situation could thus not depend on texture density in the pattern projected to the eye. All species tested with this information, rats, sheep, goats, and chicks, showed a significant preference for the shallow side.

How important is the ability to see with two eyes? The behavior of monocular and binocular chicks was compared in the cliff situation by

Schiffman and Walk (1963). Monocular chicks had one eye occluded by collodion. Chicks about 1½ to 2 days old were tested on a standard apparatus as well as on one of the type described for isolating motion parallax, that is, with density of optical texture equated for the two sides. In both experiments the monocular as well as the binocular chicks preferred the shallow side. These results suggest that two eyes are not necessary and that motion parallax is sufficient information for cliff avoidance.

Monocular- and binocular-hooded rats were compared on an apparatus, both under standard conditions and with density equated, by Trychin and Walk (1964). As with the chicks, there was no difference between the monocular and binocular animals. Both groups descended to the shallow side significantly more often than to the deep, even with optical texture equal. Walk and Dodge (1962) also tested a monocular human infant on the cliff. One of the infant's eyes had been surgically removed; it had probably been sightless since birth. The child nevertheless performed on the cliff indistinguishably from binocular children. Thus, information for depth differences is obtained in this situation without binocular stimulation, and it was obtained by a species which probably has no binocular stereoscopic vision, the rat, and by another that certainly does have binocular stereoscopic vision, man. What both species have, and what probably all seeing animals have, is the ability to use motion as information for depth.

Events

The detection of events in the world, of happenings, is crucial for survival of an animal. Yet we know more about sensory thresholds for sound and light intensity in various species than we do about how events are perceived. Presumably, wild animals distinguish between the sounds of bubbling water and crackling twigs since the one may cause approach and the other flight, but who has studied such discriminatory behavior? (Pavlov actually did use the sound of bubbling water as a conditioned stimulus.) We know that forest animals respond instinctively to fire by flight; motion picture films have recorded evidence of wild animals fleeing in panic before a forest fire. But we have little idea of what the effective stimulation is. It could be multisensory and very complex; for some species, it might be highly specific and simple.

In recent years, ethologists have studied the responses of certain species (species-specific behavior) to highly specific stimulus situations which they term "releasers." An example is the releasing of sexual behavior in the female stickleback in response to special posturing movements of the male, the zig-zag dance. An example of aversive behavior to a specific releasing event is said to be the alarm reaction of ducks and geese to the simulation of a bird of prey in flight. Cardboard models of flying birds were displayed to various species of gallinaceous birds. Motion of the model combined with the form of the model was critical. When the model in Figure 13–2 was sailed to the right, it released escape reactions. But when it was sailed to the left, it provoked no such response. It was not the shape as such that elicited alarm behavior, but shape in relation to movement (Lorenz, 1939). More recent experiments with these birds (Rockett, 1955; Melzack, 1961) appear to demonstrate that the shape is in fact of little importance and that a dark shadow moving overhead is sufficient to evoke alarm.

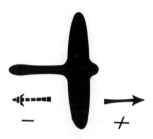

FIGURE 13–2.   Model of a bird of prey (Tinbergen, 1948).

It released no escape reactions when sailed to the left, but did when sailed to the right. (From *The Study of Instinct* by N. Tinbergen [Oxford: Clarendon Press, 1951].)

Analysis of the stimulating properties of events and comparison of the response to them by different species is rare. One such study has been performed by Schiff (1964). He studied the response of various animals, very young as well as adult, to a kind of optical-stimulus information that he called "looming." If a vehicle or even a small object such as a baseball is perceived as coming directly toward a person he ducks or dodges out of the way. Is such avoidance of collision automatic? If so, in what species? Schiff constructed an apparatus that simulated the approach of an object through the air. The optical information that specifies imminent collision is an accelerated magnification of a form in the field of view. According to Schiff it must be a radially symmetrical magnification of the form, with a rate of expansion that causes it to loom up at the end, that is, to fill the whole frontal visual field.

His apparatus was a shadow-casting device with a large translucent screen in front of the subject. The projected shadow on the screen could be made to undergo continuous magnification or, on the other hand, continuous minification. Magnification resulted in the visual experience of an object approaching; minification, in the experience of an object receding. The projected silhouette could be varied in form so as to compare, for instance, the effect of jagged contours with smooth ones, or meaningful silhouettes with meaningless ones. The subjects presented with this display were fiddler crabs, frogs, chicks, kittens, and humans.

All of the crabs responded to the magnification by running backwards, flinching, or flattening out. They did not respond at all to minification. Frogs were not quite as consistent, but jumped significantly more often and farther to simulated approach than to simulated recession. Chicks also responded more often to magnification than to minification by running, crouching, and hopping. Kittens tended to respond in the same way but the consistency of their behavior was not as marked as in the other species, and some did not respond at all, no matter what the stimulus. The kittens were young (28 days old) and it may be that their avoidance responses to looming mature late or even that they are learned. Other experiments gave evidence that crabs discriminate not only an object's approach but also its path of approach since they ran to the appropriate side when the magnification was not radially symmetrical. There was no effect of the form or meaning of the silhouette. Hayes and Saiff (1967) elicited alarm reactions to a looming shadow in turtles. The turtles' response was withdrawal of the head into the shell.

In an earlier experiment (Schiff, Caviness, & Gibson, 1962) rhesus monkeys, including eight infants five to eight months of age, were observed with this display under four stimulus conditions (expansion, contraction, lightening of the screen's illumination, and darkening of it). Both young and adult animals withdrew rapidly in response to the looming silhouette, leaping to the rear of the cage. Alarm cries frequently accompanied retreat in the younger animals. The contracting shadow caused responses which might be described as curiosity, but never retreat. Thus the merely optical representation of a rapidly approaching object elicits an avoidance response in several animal species, both vertebrate and invertebrate.

Objects

Schiff tried out different shapes in his looming experiments, as noted, but did not find that different apparent objects had much differential effect on avoidance. The accelerated magnification of any dark shadow sufficed. But much of an animal's behavior is controlled by objects. Food objects must be distinguished from the young, from nest materials, and so on. Objects such as food that are appropriate for one species are not necessarily so for another. Comparative studies of object perception, therefore, cannot profitably be conducted by comparing discrimination of the same set of objects by various species. The question is, how are objects that are relevant for a species identified? An egg is a highly relevant object for a bird and studies of what stimulus properties define "eggness" have been conducted. Lorenz and Tinbergen (1938) found, in the grey lag goose, that a rounded surface was a critical feature and that the bird responded by rolling such an object to its nest even when it was very much too large and could be manipulated only with difficulty. Ethologists have found several such cases of super-normal stimuli, in which some critical property of an object is exaggerated and the relevant behavior is elicited with normal or super-normal facility.

This example brings out the point that it is the distinctive features of objects that must be differentiated. In considering theories of perceptual learning, the question was, how do the distinctive features come to be detected? In considering the phylogeny of perception, we want to know what distinctive features of objects are responded to by different species; what properties of objects (if any) are universally responded to; and to what extent are these properties learned as a result of experience with sets of objects? It might be that some properties, such as curvature, straightness, and thickness, serve as distinctive features in many species and within many sets of objects. Other higher order properties might be relevant only as the result of rather specialized evolution, and detected only as a result of experience.

Few studies with nonhuman animals exist on the properties of objects which serve as distinctive features. As systematic as any is the experiment by Rheingold and Hess (1957) on the chick's preference for certain visual properties characteristic of water. They presented chicks with an array of six substances—water, and five others which possessed some but not all of the visual attributes of water. The substances were ordinary tap water, blue water, red water (both the latter transparent), a disc of metal, another of polished aluminum, mercury, and colorless transparent plastic. The experimenters judged that water possessed three visual properties: colorlessness, transparency, and a reflecting surface. In addition its fluidity renders it capable of motion. Thirsty chicks were placed on a platform with the six substances arranged in a semicircle. Six tests were made with different arrangements of stimuli. The chick was allowed to attempt to drink one of the substances on a given trial and was removed as soon as a response was made. The order of preference for three-day-old chicks inexperienced with food and water was mercury, plastic, blue water, water, metal, and red water. Three times as many chicks went to mercury as to water. Experienced chicks, seven days old, still preferred mercury to water. To test whether the motility of the mercury was its critical property, an experiment was run with two choices only, mercury and a piece of hammered metal mounted on a spring to maximize motion. The mercury was chosen twice as often as the metal. The experimenters concluded that brightness of the reflecting surface was the most critical attribute which attracted the chick, with a combination of brightness and movement providing a "still more powerful stimulus." The problem of analyzing the distinctive features of objects and testing their effective stimulus value for a given species is clearly one to which more attention should be given.

Daves and Boostrom (1964) compared certain properties of objects that might be effective in maintaining discrimination and preference behavior in cats. The experiments compared three object properties: surface texture (rough vs. smooth), outline shape (square vs. circular), and three-dimensional shape (pyramidal vs. hemispherical). A pair of training objects differed in all three properties. Later transfer tests varied these one at a time. The property most effective for maintaining the discrimination appeared to be outline, but all three properties were effective under some conditions. In a second experiment, outline and texture were varied, and a control group was run with photographs of the texture (rough or smooth) pasted on the objects to rule out tactile differences. Texture was just as effective when it was photographed as when there were differential tactile properties in addition to visual.

It appears that certain critical properties of objects (such as egg-shape for birds) are detected without specific experience in some animals. Fantz (1957) studied preferences in newly hatched chicks for pecking at stimulus objects differing in shape. The objects were small and the solid shapes were cylindrical, ovoid, pyramidal, cubed, etc. (see Fig. 13–3). They were covered with transparent plastic discs. There was a preference for rounded over angular forms, suggesting that the property of curvature as against angularity is differentiated very early. Fantz constructed a

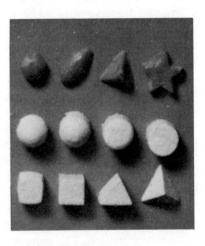

FIGURE 13–3. Stimulus objects of different shape compared for preference by newly hatched chicks.

(From R. L. Fantz, Form preference in newly hatched chicks. *Journal of Comparative and Physiological Psychology,* 1957, *50,* 423.)

"round-to-pointed" stimulus dimension with eight objects ranked on this dimension. Color, size, etc., were controlled, and chicks were kept in darkness and tested on their first visual experience. The roundness preference was exhibited during the first ten minutes of visual pecking experience. An attempt was made by Fantz to alter the roundness preference by feeding a group of chicks for four days on irregular angular bits of a mash preparation. After four days, the chicks' preference for round objects was less pronounced, but the initial preference was still apparent. Tests were also made to discover whether the roundness preference extended to flat forms as well as solid objects. The preference was still significant, but there was a higher percentage of pecks for a sphere than for a flat circle. Monocular as well as binocular chicks showed a higher degree of preference for solid spheres.

Differences in both surface and outline curvature are thus discriminated by chicks without learning. That simple relational properties of contours, such as straightness and convexity, are responded to in a unitary fashion has been shown by Maturana, Lettvin, Pitts, and McCulloch (1960) for frogs. Hubel and Wiesel (1962, 1963) recording from single fibers in the striate cortex with microelectrode techniques have shown that straight lines and edges presented to the receptive field in different orientations are specifically responded to by single neurons in cats and monkeys. Very young inexperienced kittens had adult-type receptive fields as regards these particular patterned stimuli (see Chapter 12). Higher order patterned features of objects may also be differentiated but perhaps they require experience or a more complex brain to be filtered from the total stimulus input. We shall return to this question.

Representations

Many properties of objects and of events can be artificially represented or reproduced as well as given in the natural environment. Photographs, drawings, and recordings are instances. The dog listening to "his master's voice" issuing from the horn-like speaker of an old-fashioned phonograph is a familiar example. Even without the master's physical presence, with its characteristic warmth, odor, look, and touch, the recorded sound is (presumably) adequate to arouse a differentiated attentive response in the dog. But has not something been lost? A key to understanding the effectiveness of representations as substitute stimuli, one may surmise, is their degree of fidelity of reproduction of the real object or event.

The most faithful visual representation is the image in a mirror. It is so faithful, in fact, that one wonders if all species with sufficiently developed visual acuity would not respond to it as if to the reality. Most of us have presented our own kitten with a mirror and watched it play and paw at the image. I once worked with goats, training them in an avoidance conditioning setup. In order to observe their behavior in a free situation they were left alone in a room and a one-way vision screen of the mirror variety was installed in a wall. The animal's behavior changed completely for several days; it disregarded the shock and devoted itself to licking its image in the mirror.

Not all animals, even social ones, make such responses to a mirror image, however. MacLean (1964) tested two varieties of squirrel monkeys with mirrors. One variety (called gothic) which typically displayed an erect phallus when another monkey appeared, displayed it consistently to its reflection in a mirror. The typical display pattern, accompanied by vocalization, could sometimes be elicited by a small mirror reflecting only one eye. But another variety (called roman) did not respond to its mirror image. Furthermore, when the monkeys were given a self-operated panel which opened to show either a mirrored reflection or another monkey, the gothic type operated the panel nearly as often to see its own reflection as to see another monkey. The roman type, on the other hand, would work only to see another monkey. MacLean speculated that there may have been some ancestral environmental difference in exposure to reflecting pools from overhanging boughs. But the interesting fact is that there should be discrimination, in one type, between the appearance of an animal which is actually one's own body and the appearance of an animal which is actually another animal. The difference in form is slight but it should be noted that the difference in movement is profound.

That mirror reflections should be effective carriers of stimulus information is not surprising; they accurately reproduce form, solidity, color, and motion. But what about photographs? One hears anecdotes from anthropologists to the effect that photographs are not recognized as representations of real things or people by members of a culture that lacks graphic art. The inference is that one must learn to recognize photographs as portrayals. But fidelity of the picture to the thing represented must be important, for there is ample evidence to show that various primate animals respond discriminatively to photographs. Köhler (1925) tested chimpanzees in a learning experiment where the ape was rewarded for choosing one of two photographs. The positive photograph could be of a full banana box, the negative of an empty one; or a photograph of a bunch of bananas could be positive, a pictured stone negative. The discriminations were learned but of course success in learning does not prove that the ape recognized the pictured bananas as bananas.

True recognition from a photograph was attested in the Hayes's observations of their home-reared chimp, Vicki (1951). Vicki not only enjoyed looking at pictures in magazines and picture books; her accompanying gestures gave evidence of identification, for instance when she put her ear to a magazine photograph of a watch.

The responsiveness of monkeys to motion pictures was studied by Klüver (1933) who found no behavioral evidence that a lemur and a java monkey were responding discriminatively to the films. But cebus monkeys seemed to be attending to the pictures and several showed evidence of fear when a python or a closeup of a lion appeared on the screen. Butler (1961) studied the responses of rhesus monkeys to motion pictures.[2] The displays were projected on a one-foot-square screen, from the rear. The monkey could open a spring-loaded door and look through the opening at the screen. The total number of door-opening responses in an experimental session and the total length of time the door was held open were recorded. The items displayed included a film of a male and female rhesus engaged in various activities (sex, eating, climbing); still pictures (colored slides) of similar behavior; homogeneous light; and four regular films, two of monkeys, one of snakes, and one an animated cartoon. The four latter films were presented half time in good focus and half the time out of focus. Significantly more time was spent looking at the film of the male and female monkey than at the color slides, or the homogeneously illuminated screen. For the two monkey films, every subject spent more time looking when the film was in focus than when it was out of focus. They were also more responsive to the animated cartoon when it was in focus. The animals responded in different ways to the snake film. One monkey was unresponsive, but two others opened the door more frequently when the film was in focus (shutting it again hurriedly). The evidence shows at least that rhesus monkeys are attentive to representations, that clear pictures are preferred to unclear ones, and that motion pictures are preferred to still pictures of the same subject matter. The aversive responses of two monkeys to the snake film suggest that the pictured objects were recognized as like the real ones.

Drawings, that is, outlines on paper or on a flat surface, do not have the fidelity of photographs. They not only lack solidity, they lack detail as well. We say that the portrayal is sketchy. Does this mean that the representation is less apt to be perceived as equivalent to the real object? We know from experiments with monkeys that solid objects (stereometric) make better cues in a discrimination experiment than drawings of the objects (planometric) (Harlow, 1945). They seem to have more attention value. But we should understand that a drawing or painting may have a greater or lesser degree of fidelity, and that the artist is free to emphasize any properties of the original he wishes, so that distinctive properties could even be enhanced in such a way as to facilitate recognition.

Pictorial recognition in infant rhesus monkeys has been studied by Zimmermann and Hochberg (1963) and Hochberg (1964, p. 85). In a

[2] See also other references to Butler in Chapter 7.

first experiment, three monkeys were trained to discriminate a three-inch drawn square from a three-inch raised square ⅝ inches deep, and were then transferred to photographs of the drawn and the raised square. Shadows were present in the latter. All three showed substantial savings. In a second experiment, eight infant monkeys were trained on the two squares as before, and then transferred to perspective line drawings of the two. Again there was significant transfer to the new pairs. In a third experiment, animals were trained first on perspective drawings of left- and right-hand views of a solid truncated pyramid. The transfer pairs were the corresponding real views of the actual solid object. There was some evidence of transfer, although the original learning with pictorial stimuli was very slow, consistent with earlier findings that so-called planometric stimuli require more trials in discrimination learning than stereometric. The experimenters concluded that lines drawn on a plane surface, if they corresponded to edges of a real object, would be responded to similarly. In other words, lines were perceived as surface edges without special associative training, and outline shapes were perceived as object edges, as they often are in human form perception. Zimmermann (1964) extended these experiments and concluded that object-discrimination learning facilitates the discrimination of pictures. Distinctive-feature differences are more easily picked up with a solid three-dimensional object and their surrogates in the drawings are thereby rendered more perceptible.[3]

Coded Items of Stimulation

There can be surrogates of actual objects and events that are not representations of them. They might be called surrogates without similarity. Such items I will call coded. The correspondence between a code item and an event may be quite arbitrary, discoverable only by reference to a code book. A code item must be differentiated from other items of the code, as words must be differentiated from each other, or letters. After this stage, the correspondences between code items and referents are learned, perhaps by an associative process like learning a foreign vocabulary. But the correspondence is sometimes inferred, too. Code symbols are not learned as set orders or strings, but are combined in many ways and orders. Orders new to the individual can usually be made and decoded. Skilled decoding is not, in most codes, a one-to-one, item-by-item translation for there is patterning in codes, and perception is facilitated by grouping into larger

[3] See also the discussion of experiments by Gibson and Walk in Chapter 12, showing cutout shapes to be more effective for discrimination than patterns painted on a flat surface.

units as in reading musical notation, where chords and other complex combinations are perceived as units.[4]

Do any animals but man perceive coded stimuli? Because codes have the purpose of communication, animals are sometimes said to possess them and examples are cited such as the language of bees. It involves signals which elicit responses and thus operates as an instrument of social control, but it is not clear that these signals can be fragmented and rearranged in newly invented patterns and the product then decoded as an original communication. Marler (1967) comments on the need for research on the question of whether elements are ever recombined in animal communication. "Such recombination could provide evidence for the occurrence in animals of that attribute most distinctive of man, an ability to make grammatical rearrangements of signals to generate new messages, with new meanings (p. 769)."

Perception of the phonemic patterns of human speech in all its complexity may be man's peculiar prerogative. Pet owners frequently claim that cats and dogs perceive and respond appropriately to words or commands, such as "lie down," or "where is Pat?" If these cases were to be established, it may still be true that perception is limited to a short string of phonemes of a set pattern, responded to as a unit signal. Often supporting stimuli, such as a given place or tone of voice, are needed to elicit the response, as in Thorndike's anecdote about his cats. Every day when he entered the laboratory, he announced, "I must feed those cats," and then fed them. The cats soon learned to respond and came running. When this behavior was well established, Thorndike entered the laboratory and announced, "My name is Edward Thorndike." But the same behavior ensued.

In the case of chimpanzees, there is evidence that short segments of human speech are occasionally differentiated and responded to as signals, if not symbols. The best documentation for this statement comes from the Hayes's experience in raising Vicki, a chimpanzee, in their home (1951). With much labor, they succeeded in teaching Vicki to utter three words ("Mama," "Papa," and "cup") more or less appropriately. One might suppose that her comprehension of human speech signals went far beyond this. Yet, it was only certain that Vicki obeyed a few well-rehearsed commands without the aid of supplementary cues ("Go to your room," "Put it back"). Despite more than eighteen months of coaching, Vicki did not learn to identify her nose, ears, eyes, hands, and feet by pointing. The verbal commands which she did learn to obey seem to have been, on the whole, set, unvaried, short phrases. They were probably generalized over at least two different voices. They could have been learned specifically for each one, though probably not for different tones of voice and intensities

[4] See discussion of higher order units in reception of Morse code in Chapter 9.

on different occasions, so Vicki may have perceived some phonemic invariants, without really breaking the code. Although Vicki was generally poor at comprehending words, she recognized, according to the experimenters, a surprising number of nonlanguage sounds—fizzing noises, barks, pops, and so on. Ability to discriminate sound patterns over time, therefore, was not lacking, but the coded aspect of verbal communication was not grasped.

An experiment with another chimpanzee, Washoe, is being carried on by Beatrice and Allen Gardner (Gardner & Gardner, 1967). Instead of trying to teach Washoe to utter or to comprehend human speech, they are attempting to communicate with the chimp in the American sign language for the deaf. After 22 months of training, Washoe responded appropriately to more than sixty signs, and emitted thirty or more of them appropriately (see Fig. 13–4). She combined strings of two or more (e.g., "gimme drink please") and spontaneously transferred signs to new referents.

FIGURE 13–4. The chimpanzeee Washoe signing "drink."

(Photograph courtesy of Dr. Allen and Dr. Beatrice Gardner.)

Summary

We can conclude that all species of animals extract information about the spatial environment from the impinging stimulus flux, though in different ways depending on the structure and habitat of the species. Events are in some sense perceived by all species, but with varying kinds of information pickup and with species-specific responses. The objects perceived by different species, and their properties, vary with the relevance of the objects for the animal's way of life, different distinctive features being critical for different animals. But all vertebrates, at least, perceive objects and some of their properties. It is much less certain that representations of objects and events are perceived below the mammalian level.

The real break in perceptual development over the animal series comes with coded stimuli. Registration of this class of stimuli in ordered and re-ordered sequences seems pretty well confined to man. Since there are cross-species differences in what information is extracted from stimulation, it seems appropriate to ask whether there are any trends observable over the evolution of species.

THE TREND TOWARD SPECIFICITY

Even the lowliest organisms, unicellular and without specialized sensory equipment, are to some degree responsive to changes in their surroundings. An amoeba is sensitive to changes in mechanical stimulation, chemicals, temperature, light, and electrical currents, although it has no differentiated receptor structures. But generalized response to change, without discrimination except between very weak and very strong stimuli, is the limit of its capacity for picking up information from the environment.

The direction of evolution in the discrimination of properties of the environment has been toward ever greater specificity. This parallels the trend of all evolution, a passage from homogeneity to heterogeneity. The trend shows itself in four ways. First, in the development of specialized receptors for different types of energy change. Multicellular animals developed organs containing sensory cells—receptors that were highly sensitive to one form of energy such as light or mechanical vibration. A second way was the development of distance receptors. From generalized crude chemical sensitivity in protozoa, for instance, there developed specialized proximate chemoreceptors and, at a later stage, in the insects, distance chemoreceptors, which seem to have reached their highest stage in some mammals such as the ungulates, which are said to detect the approach of an enemy, when the wind is right, as much as a mile away. Thirdly, there evolved more modes of sensitivity to the same type of energy change. In the case of mechanical stimulation, general responsiveness was followed, in the coelenterates, by primitive tactile receptors; in the insects, there are not only specialized tactile receptors but receptors (antennae) specialized for the detection of mechanical vibration and other, so-called kinaesthetic receptors for the reception of mechanical stimuli in joints and tendons. In the vertebrates as well as these, there are typically distance receptors, cells in the ear sensitive to vibratory stimuli. Within the auditory modality, evolutionary development has moved toward finer discrimination within stimulus dimensions, such as differential thresholds for tonal frequencies.

The phylogenetic trend towards specificity needs qualification, however. Differences in acuity and dimensional specificity in the sensory systems of animal species are related to the animal's habits and habitat—that is, to the kind of information he needs for his kind of life. In tracing the evolution of vision, for instance, one can point at first to the development of very simple eyes (pigment spots or light-sensitive body surfaces which indicate at best the intensity of light and its direction if the animal moves); then the great step to the complex eye, of which we can distinguish several types (the compound eye of the insect, the simple chambered eye with a lens, and finally the eye with a variable lens capable of producing good pattern vision). Beyond these steps, many specializations have taken place, such as foveal vision, the division of the receptors into rods and cones, and coordinated movement of foveal eyes so as to permit stereoscopic depth detection. But these latter specializations have not been an orderly march up the vertebrate ladder. They represent, rather, divergences correlated with life in trees or under the ground or on grassy plains.

Consider herbivorous, terrestrial mammals such as the ungulates. These animals are preyed on. Their safety depends on swiftness of flight. Vision, smell, and hearing have all developed so as to permit detection of danger quickly over a wide area. Vision is typically panoramic. Acuity is the same over a very wide area, sometimes enabling an animal to see nearly around its entire circumference at once. To accomplish this, the eyes are set out from the surface of the head and are laterally placed. The eyes may protrude increasingly with alarm, thereby increasing the circumference of vision at vital moments. The pupils are elongated and oval, so that the retina extends farther laterally. The absence of a fovea and the lateral placement require the sacrifice of binocular stereoscopic vision, but this loss is compensated for by the wide field of view and the use of other adequate information for the distance of objects, such as motion parallax.

Rodents as well are generally preyed-upon animals and their eyes are placed laterally. The optical axis in the eye of a hare diverges 85° from the axis of the body; there is little or no overlapping of the two binocular fields. (Sportsmen have been known to suggest that hares can be better approached from the front than from behind, having a certain amount of posterior binocular vision.) Rodents, living in burrows, typically have rather poor visual acuity in the light, with few if any cones, and there is no positive evidence of color discrimination.

The carnivores, in contrast to ungulates and rodents, are preying animals, with vision such that they can track and spring upon their victims. There is a smaller divergence of the visual axes and considerable overlapping of the fields of the two eyes. Good conjugate movements of the eyes and some convergence occur. Conjugate movements are used for pursuit (the cat follows the mouse with its eyes), and convergence movements, combined with a slightly concentrated *area centralis,* may make binocular stereopsis possible (the cat pounces on the mouse). No good behavioral evidence exists for stereoscopic depth discrimination, however, nor does it for color vision. Protective coloration of the animals upon whom the carnivores prey generally depends on patterning of light and shade which falls in with the background of their normal habitat (spectacular cases being the zebra and the giraffe).

Color vision seems to be associated especially with arboreal life, except in the case of man, but he presumably traces his descent from arboreal ancestors. The similarities in vision, especially color vision, between birds and primates is striking. Arboreal animals are all frugivorous and must distinguish between ripe and unripe fruits, alike in form and size but differing only in color. Brilliant coloration in many of these species is usually associated with sexual characteristics and phases of the reproductive cycle.

Binocular vision reached its highest stage of effectiveness in the primates, where it is coordinated with tactile prehension. Stereoscopic depth cues serve an obvious function in picking up small objects at fairly close range. The optic axes are nearly parallel, so that overlapping of the binocular fields is great. The presence of a fovea for fixation, and convergent eye movements provide the necessary conditions for utilization of stereoscopic depth cues. In the primates, panoramic vision is sacrificed in exchange for the conditions which make binocular fusion possible, but this loss is partly compensated for by good conjugate eye movements and, in man especially, free head movements. Compared to most of the mammals, man is a nearsighted creature, capable of detecting fine detail at close range. If this were not the case, his ability to learn to read would be even more amazing than it is.

In summary, sensory systems evolved from very general responsiveness to gross environmental change, through stages of specialization of receptors and their containing organs, to highly specific pickup of essential information in the environment. But in all stages of evolution, what is essential varies with the environment and way of life of the species and differentiation of perception has taken divergent courses.

THE TREND TOWARD DETECTION OF HIGHER ORDER RELATIONS

One might expect an important trend in the evolution of perception to be an increase in the ability to extract relations and structural properties from stimulation. But this does not mean that even "lower" organisms respond to a punctate stimulus, absolute and in isolation. Effective stimulation seems to be relational wherever the experiments have been done. A number of comparative studies of the perception of relational properties were performed by the Gestalt psychologists, beginning with Köhler's experiments demonstrating transposition in chickens and chimpanzees (Köhler, 1918, 1925). Chickens originally trained to discriminate two grays by choosing the lighter one and avoiding the darker were presented with the lighter gray and a still lighter one. Instead of choosing the originally positive stimulus, they chose the new positive stimulus. The same relationship existed in the two pairs, and the chickens were said to have responded to the perceived relationship rather than to the absolute stimulus value. Köhler carried out similar experiments with a chimpanzee and a human child three years of age, with comparable results. These subjects did not make more relational responses than the chickens, so that a structural property of this low order did not elicit evidence of species differences. Köhler also studied the choice responses to rectangles varying in size with two chimpanzees. Both transposed to new pairs. In another series of experiments, chimpanzees were trained to choose the bluer of two color patches containing blue and red and they transposed to other pairs containing the same relationship. Two other chimpanzees gave the same results with a yellow-red scale of five colors.

Extensive studies of the two-choice transposition problem were made by Klüver (1933) with monkeys. He studied transposition not only with the visual dimensions of size and brightness, but with sensory dimensions of audition and weight. Klüver pointed out that the mere statement that response is to a relation does not suffice. Monkeys sometimes responded relationally to changes on one dimension, such as size, even though changes were made in other dimensions, such as color or shape, at the same time. Two Java monkeys had been trained to the larger of two rectangles (300 sq. cm. as against 150 sq. cm.) by pulling in a box marked with the larger rectangle and securing food concealed within it. When the rectangles were changed to 150 sq. cm. vs. 75 sq. cm. or to 600 sq. cm. vs. 300 sq. cm., the monkeys continued to pull in the box marked with the larger rectangle. Even when the rectangles were replaced by figures of the same size but of different form (pairs of squares, circles, hexagons, or irregularly shaped figures), the larger figure was consistently responded to. In considering the implications of cases like the latter, Klüver said,

If a monkey reacts to stimuli which can be characterized as belonging to a large number of different "dimensions," and if in doing so he reacts consistently in terms of one relation, let us say, in terms of the "larger-than" relation, he may be said to "abstract." The fact that widely different stimulus situations may be equivalent can be understood only by assuming that one characteristic or set of characteristics is "abstracted" (p. 326).

While there is evidence of response to simple relational properties in species low in the evolutionary scale, it does not necessarily follow that the same information is being extracted as in "higher" species. For example, Hertz (1929) studied figural perception in bees. A square pane of glass was placed on a table near the hive. Under the glass was a sheet of white paper. For any given experiment, two small black figures of different shape were placed somewhere on the paper. A watch glass containing sugar water was located near one of these. The bees could swoop down and drink the sugar water. The size of the swarm descending toward the rewarded figure provided a rough measure of correctness of choice. After the swarm's departure, preparations for a new trial were made, cleaning the glass, refilling the container, and changing either the position of the black figures or the figures themselves. When a cross was made positive (next to the sugar water) and a circle negative, the swarm almost invariably chose correctly. Position and size were varied in tests, and the cross could be rotated without disturbing the preference. Correct transposition to larger pairs was possible. But though the bees distinguished easily between an articulated, open figure (such as the cross or a star or a wheel) and a closed one (a solid square or circle), they were unable to discriminate between simple closed forms such as a circle, triangle, and square. Visual units for the bee appeared to be differentiated on the basis of continuity or discontinuity of contour. It has been suggested that the differential responses shown were actually dependent on the detection of flicker, rather than on the detection of form. For a flying insect with a compound eye, movement toward a highly articulated open form might result in flickering light in the elements of the eye. Thus the bee might get information from the stimulus flow, from a temporal sequence, even though it is incapable of differentiating contour variables such as straight edges and curves.

Contour variables, however, are registered by some invertebrates. Sutherland's many studies of form discrimination in the octopus (Sutherland, 1962, 1963, 1964) demonstrate its capacity to choose consistently between various shapes, such as a square and a triangle, or a vertical and a horizontal rectangle, or a square and a cross. Sutherland speculated that instead of contour, the features detected by the octopus in differentiating shapes were their horizontal and vertical extents, which were presumably summed in some way and compared in controlling the discriminatory behavior. However this may be, the octopus can discriminate certain shapes, stationary as well as moving (though moving shapes are more easily discriminated). Furthermore, there is transfer of discrimination between a pair of shapes to the same pair in different sizes, suggesting that a summed vertical or horizontal extent cannot be the only feature detected in shape discrimination. Finally, Sutherland, Macintosh, and Macintosh (1963) have demonstrated transfer of a discrimination along a shape continuum in the octopus. The shapes varied from a square to an oblique parallelogram, with six shapes ordered along the continuum. Animals that were trained beginning with the maximally different pair, and were then shifted along the graded series to the most difficult pair, performed better on the difficult pair than animals trained on it from the outset. Animals trained on the most difficult pair improved their performance without further training when presented with the easier pair. Thus extraction of an invariant contrasting property seems to be possible in this invertebrate. The same type of transfer in rats and in humans was discussed in Chapter 6.

In birds, considerable behavioral evidence has accumulated that structural properties of the stimulus such as pattern and contour are discriminated. An experiment demonstrating selective response to the arrangement and grouping of objects is Hertz's study of figural perception in the jaybird. Hertz (translated by Ellis, 1938) used a sort of delayed response technique. The experimenter hid a bit of food under a flowerpot, with the bird watching. The bird was then allowed to approach, move the cover, and secure the food, which it did promptly when only one pot was present. The plan of the experiment was to arrange a number of pots in the bird's field of view, hiding the food under only one. The question was whether the bird's success in choosing would be related to the number and grouping of the pots. When three pots were arranged in a row, as in Figure 13–5, right,

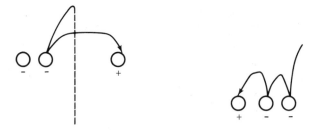

FIGURE 13–5. **Arrangements of flower pots used in Hertz's experiments with the jaybird.**

Food was concealed under the pot indicated with a +. When the baited pot was removed from the other two, as in the left figure, correct choices were made. (From W. D. Ellis, *A Source Book of Gestalt Psychology* [Routledge & Kegan Paul, Ltd., 1938].)

the bird chose in a completely random fashion. But when the pots were arranged as in the left figure, correct choice was possible. Other more elaborate arrangements which elicited correct choices are shown in Figure 13–6, where the nonbaited pots were arranged in a circle or an ellipse. But when they were arranged in a square, the bird made incorrect choices of the corners of the square before overturning the baited pot. Although it did not succeed in the problem, it exhibited orientation to a significant feature of the square.

Pastore (1958) found Pekin ducklings capable of learning to select a triangle as opposed to a trapezoid regardless of variations in area and altitude of the triangle and even when the base angles of the trapezoid were equal to the triangle. One bird learned to discriminate a triangle from a rectangle whatever its size, orientation, or placement on the background, except when the triangle was inverted and the squares were placed as

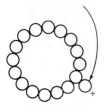  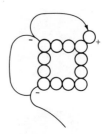

FIGURE 13–6.   Other arrangements of flower pots used by Hertz.

The bird chose the correct pot from the circular and the elliptical arrangement, but made incorrect choices of corners with the square arrangement.

diamonds. Pastore inferred that the bird was responding to the shape as a whole, a higher order structure than, say, a straight edge. Pastore also was able to demonstrate size constancy in the duckling. A bird trained to choose a two-inch square as opposed to a one-inch square continued to do so without error even when it was placed at four times the distance of the smaller object. Thus evidence exists that information for size invariance can be extracted from stimulation in this species.

A remarkable case of perceptual abstraction in the pigeon has been reported in an experiment by Herrnstein and Loveland (1964). The birds were trained to detect human figures in photographs. A very large number of photographic slides of natural settings—countryside, cities, water, etc.—were collected. For any one training session, eighty photographs were presented, half of them containing human beings and half not. The people portrayed varied in all possible ways—size, sex, number present, surroundings, etc. The pictures containing people were reinforced, the others were not. The pigeons learned to respond, with increasing frequency, to the pictures containing people, though the series presented was continually varied. One wonders how many mammalian species could match the trick.

That mammals discriminate features of visual contour and respond to certain formal relations is abundantly attested. Innumerable studies exist of the rat's ability to discriminate form, the best known being Lashley's brilliant series, "The Mechanism of Vision." Lashley invented the jumping stand as a method for testing pattern vision in the rat and demonstrated the animal's capacity to discriminate patterns varying in many properties. Some are illustrated in Figure 13–7, taken from Lashley (1930). Lashley pointed out that the nervous system is not a "neutral medium on which learning imposes any form of organization whatever (Lashley, 1949, p. 466, in Beach et al., 1960)." Certain stimulus patterns can be responded to as units, and the nervous system has some rules regarding the kinds of con-

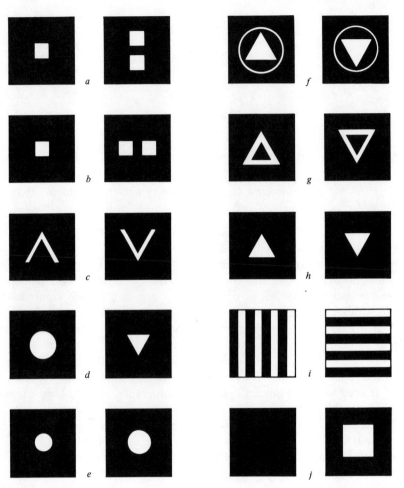

FIGURE 13–7. **Pairs of patterns between which rats were trained to discriminate.**

(From K. S. Lashley, The mechanism of vision: I. A method for rapid analysis of pattern-vision in the rat. *Journal of Genetic Psychology*, 1930, *37*, 456.)

straint which characterize these units. Lashley's example of two sets of dot arrangements is shown in Figure 13–8. Rats learned easily to distinguish the dots grouped as circle and triangle but failed to distinguish the random patterns after weeks of training.

Lashley showed in a long series of experiments on stimulus equivalence in the rat that the adequate stimulus was independent of particular

FIGURE 13–8. Structured and unstructured arrangements of dots.

Rats learned quickly to distinguish the dots arranged in the geometrical groupings on the left, but were unable to distinguish the groups of randomly scattered dots after many weeks of training. (From K. S. Lashley, Persistent problems in the evolution of mind. *Quarterly Review of Biology,* 1949, *24,* 31.)

receptors. The animal responded to a wide range of patterns as equivalent: transposition of size, reversal of brightness relations, and substitution of outlines for solid figures did not disturb a trained discrimination. What the equivalent patterns had in common, according to Lashley, was ratio of intensity, or proportion in spatial distribution. The animal, then, must be extracting some relational property in the stimulus and responding to it. According to Lashley, "The limits of capacity of each order of animals are set by the kinds of relations among objects that it can perceive (1949, p. 460, in Beach et al., 1960)."

Yet, systematic experimental evidence that response to relational properties increases in vertebrate evolution is not rich, since most studies have been directed at showing that a given species can achieve some perceptual performance. Size constancy, for instance, has been demonstrated in a number of vertebrates: the duckling (Pastore, 1958); the cat (Gunter, 1951; Koronakos & Freeman, 1967; Freeman, 1968); the monkey (Klüver, 1933); and the chimpanzee (Köhler, 1925). Other evidence is cited by Locke (1938) and by Walk (1965). Klüver (1933) pointed out that learning size discriminations with his pulling-in technique would be impossible were it not for size constancy. One very interesting difference between monkeys and man is revealed in an experiment on shape constancy by Zeigler and Leibowitz (1958). They trained rhesus monkeys to discriminate circles and ellipses on the basis of area and/or axis ratio. In testing for constancy, they made use of the fact that variations in the angle of tilt of a circle or ellipse will produce changes in the area and ratio of its retinal image. The test stimulus, after training, was presented at various degrees of tilt, paired with each of the training stimuli. For the monkeys, tilting the circular stimulus did not affect the responses established to it during training; their responses, in fact, were close to perfect constancy. But a group of human adults run through the same procedure showed responses correlated predominantly with the retinal image—the projected size and shape. The monkeys' responses seem, offhand, to be more relational than the humans'. But the human subjects were doing something which might be called analytical. A retinal match requires isolating a projected shape from the total situation, and is a sophisticated intellectual achievement.

Evidence for perception of the relational properties of similarity and difference has been found for chimpanzees. In a comparative study of matching, Lashley (1949) compared the learning behavior of a spider monkey and a chimpanzee. The animal was to choose either a red or a green square when a red or a green square was presented to him as a model. When the three squares were arranged equidistant, in a row as in a of Figure 13–9, the monkey never learned to perform above chance. But when the colored model was in any sort of visual contact with the correct

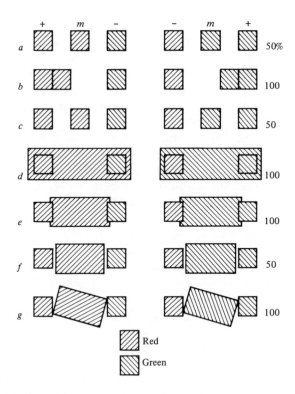

FIGURE 13–9. Arrangements of red and green squares presented to a spider monkey in a matching task.

The percentages given at the right represent the final level of accuracy attained in each of the seven situations. (From K. S. Lashley, Persistent problems in the evolution of mind. *Quarterly Review of Biology,* 1949, *24,* 35.)

square, as in lines *b, d, e,* and *g,* errorless choice occurred. The model apparently served as an indicator when it was in contact with the choice object, but then a colorless paper served to indicate the choice just as well. The relation of similarity of the colors was not grasped. The chimpanzee, on the other hand, performed the task readily without contact of the matching squares. The implication is that the chimpanzee, higher in the primate series, could respond to a relation in the stimulation that the monkey could not extract.

That the chimpanzee working on a matching-from-sample problem really is responding to similarity as a relation is confirmed by an experiment of Robinson's (1955). Six chimpanzees learned training problems in which a pair of identical objects (such as small cubes) was reinforced, as opposed to a pair of differing objects. Generalization tests were then given in which new objects as well as the training objects were presented. Both the training data and the generalization test scores gave evidence of the chimpanzee's ability to use "same" and "difference" relations as a basis for choice.

Response to the relation of oddity has been studied in various animals. When monkeys are presented with problems which require choice on the basis of single representation of a stimulus object as opposed to double (i.e., that object is correct which is different from the other two), they learn fairly quickly to respond correctly to the odd object. Furthermore, as Meyer and Harlow (1949) and others have shown, they can learn to respond successfully to a long series of transfer problems in which the stimulus objects are varied from problem to problem. Lashley tried, unsuccessfully, to train rats to perform an oddity problem. Wodinsky and Bitterman (1953) later reported that rats had learned to respond to the odd object and even transferred to a new set. A series of reversal oddity problems was given the animals. Each problem was learned more readily than its predecessor and after three or four problems there was evidence of somewhat better than chance performance on the first day of training. Boyd and Warren (1957), with similar training conditions, found that cats learned the oddity problem far more slowly than monkeys and showed no evidence of generalized response to the oddity principle. Successful transfer occurred only when the test stimuli were highly similar to the training stimuli.

Response to the oddity relation has been studied in birds as well. Pastore (1954) reported learning of an oddity problem by canaries, but it is not clear that the birds could transfer to a new set of stimulus objects. One did learn, however, with reversal of stimulus values on each trial from the outset of learning, which argues against mere association of the response to two separate stimulus configurations. Ginsburg (1957) compared pigeons on response to oddity (he referred to it as "non-matching") and matching. He found faster learning on oddity. No test of transfer to new stimuli was run for oddity, but transfer apparently occurred for matching. Both matching and oddity were possible when the three stimuli were presented successively, again arguing against the explanation that the animal had learned an association to a specific simultaneous stimulus configuration.

One other relational learning problem, the intermediate size problem, proved capable of solution by chimpanzees (Gonzalez, Gentry, & Bitterman, 1954). The problem is similar to ordinary size transposition, except that three objects varying in size are presented, the intermediate one being rewarded. When the absolute sizes of the objects were changed so that the one previously reinforced was no longer intermediate, the chimpanzee transferred its selection to the new intermediate object. This transfer is not explainable in terms of compounding positive and negative generalized responses to component discrete stimuli, as the two-choice transposition has been suggested to be (Spence, 1937). If transposition occurs, response must be to the relational stimulus.

The facts so far surveyed make it clear that all vertebrates at least perceive simple relations, with evidence of grasping of higher order relations for some primates. Except for Klüver's demonstration of transposition of weight and auditory discriminations in monkeys, the animal experiments have been mostly confined to visual perception. But the original example of transposability was the melodic pattern that remains invariant despite change of key and intensity. Do animals other than man hear invariant melodies or other invariants of sound patterns? One thinks at once of bird songs. Birds not only distinguish the songs of their own species from others; there is good evidence (Thorpe, 1961) that the songs of individual birds have slight idiosyncrasies that are recognizable and in fact serve as identification. The warning cry and the territorial song of the bird are not truly analogous to the coded stimuli of human speech, but still there must be perception of invariants of the pattern (over different birds, for instance) for them to function as signals or releasers for the flock.

Talking birds such as parrots or mynah birds which learn to imitate human speech may possibly be discriminating the invariant relations which distinguish one phoneme from another. But it is not self-evident that the production of these sounds means that the bird could respond discriminatively to them over different speakers and qualities of voices. Grosslight, Zaynor, and Lively (1964), working with six mynah birds, trained them to produce a "discriminated vocal operant" by reinforcing the vocal behavior in the presence of specific auditory stimulation ("Hello, Hello"). Other auditory stimuli ("I talk," and incidental sounds of the taperecorder without speech) were not reinforced. Since the birds learned the discrimination, it can be concluded that the mynah bird can discriminate one speech input from another and control his vocal behavior accordingly. But the discrimination might only be between specific stimulus patterns and not generalize to the critical invariant features of phonemes over different voices—that is, there might be no constancy of perception of these properties.

Dewson (1964) has shown that some discrimination of invariant phoneme features is possible in cats. He trained cats to discriminate between the speech sounds (u) and (i). The fundamental frequency of the test stimuli was then changed by changing from a male to a female speaker. Transfer was generally apparent after ten trials. Whether or not cats can learn to respond discriminatively to more complex invariant temporal patterns of phonemes as signals is a question with only anecdotal evidence. Differential response to phonemic contrasts, in any case, is not the same thing as perception of meaning of coded stimuli. As was clear in the case of Vicki, discriminative response seemed to be possible to only a limited number of set commands. The commands operated as signals, apparently, not surrogates. Vicki could respond to "get your bear," or "go to your room." But that is a different matter from perceiving the meaning of "I wonder if your bear is in your room," not an unusual feat for even a very young child.

Invariant relations which are common to more than one modality imply a high level of abstraction. In man, there is a good deal of evidence of the perception of amodal or intermodal invariant relations (see Chapter 11). The question arises whether such transfer is peculiar to man. Could it be that the amodal invariant is a very high-order relation not grasped by subhumans? Present evidence is inconclusive. Three experiments with monkeys by Ettlinger and his coworkers reported essentially negative results (Burton & Ettlinger, 1960; Ettlinger, 1960, 1961), with apparently no specific transfer between visual and tactual discriminations, or visual and auditory. Other studies (Wilson & Wilson, 1962; Wilson & Shaffer, 1963) yielded positive evidence of both general facilitation produced by a learning set and specific intermodal transfer in monkeys.

It seems obvious that specific transfer could only be expected to the extent that the two discrimination setups, original learning and transfer, have properties or stimulus dimensions in common and insofar as the original discrimination was actually based on this property and not some other property specific to only the first task. The point is illustrated in an experiment by Wegener (1963). Monkeys were taught a visual intensity discrimination (dim vs. bright illumination). They were then switched to an auditory discrimination (low- vs. high-intensity tone), with some animals reinforced for an intensity value similar to original learning and some the opposite. Presumably, positive transfer would occur for one group, negative for the other. Scores for the positive and negative animals did not differ significantly. However, other stimulus variables were present in both situations; the tones, for instance, differed not only in intensity

but in frequency, and the light sources in hue. The animals might therefore have learned the discrimination without regard to the intensity variable.

In an experiment which did yield positive results, Stepien and Cordeau (1960) gave monkeys discrimination training with differential frequencies of auditory clicks and tested these afterward with an analogous
intermittent light presentation. The auditory signals varied in frequency.
Two signals at the same frequency constituted a positive stimulus. Signals of different frequencies constituted the negative stimulus which was
sometimes a high-low sequence and sometimes low-high. Thus a signal of
a given frequency might be followed after several seconds by a duplicate
signal, making a positive stimulus, but it might also be followed by a signal of some different frequency, making an inhibitory stimulus. This discrimination required a very long training period before the monkeys mastered it to criterion (well over 4,000 trials in one case). But when the
intermittent light signals were introduced, the animals transferred completely and immediately. They were able to perform at criterion level with
visual signals by the end of the first test period. The authors quote Konor-
ski, from whom the technique was borrowed, as speculating that such
transfer phenomena involve a high level of neural activity whereby "the
rhythm is so to speak abstracted by the animal from the other characteristics of a given stimulus (p. 395)."

Another complex and interesting form of perceptual transfer is adaptation to an orderly transformation of the optic array. In man, great plasticity has been demonstrated in his ability to adjust to prismatic displacements, rotations, and even inversions of the optic array (see Chapter 10).
Evidence regarding such shifts in animals other than man is sparse, but as
far as it goes it indicates a distinct difference between mammals and lower
species. Foley (1940) fitted a rhesus monkey with a mask containing a
pair of inverting unit magnification telescopic spectacles, so that the visual
field was rotated 180°, that is, reversed in both vertical and horizontal
dimensions. The lenses were worn continually for a week. The subject
was kept in a restraining chair with a head holder at first, with restraint
gradually decreased. At first the subject remained passive and immobile,
but after several days his general activity increased. Interference effects
were pronounced, but by the seventh day, adaptation as revealed by overt
localizing responses was virtually complete. Interference effects were again
noted upon removal of the lenses, but quickly disappeared. The speed
of the monkey's shift in response to the spatial transform is remarkable
in view of its greatly reduced activity.

Bossom and Hamilton (1963) fitted 13° wedge prisms to one eye of
three male rhesus monkeys, keeping the other eye covered. The monkeys
had previously been subjected to split-brain surgery. They were kept in
primate chairs, but were allowed free use of both forelimbs and required
to feed themselves. Adaptation of reaching reportedly took place in two

to four days. One subject was returned to his cage with the prism still in place and was able to walk, climb, and retrieve food with accuracy. The changed coordination, furthermore, transferred to the eye which had been occluded.

Contrary to these results with monkeys, Hess (1956) found no correction of pecking errors in chickens after three days of wearing prismatic lenses which displaced the visual field 7° to the right or to the left. The chicks' pecks were scattered about a central point at first, as was the case with control chicks, but they were centered about a point 7° to the right or left of the target. After three days of wearing the prisms, the pecks were more closely clustered within a small area, again like controls, but this area was still displaced to the right or left of the target. Chicks maintained during the experiment in an environment where grain was loosely scattered over the floor showed signs of starvation, suggesting that differential reinforcement by pecking and missing or pecking and hitting had not altered their aim. It might be argued that three days was not a long enough period for adjustment to the displacement,[5] but the difference between chicks and primates is still impressive, since the monkeys of Bossom and Hamilton achieved complete adjustment within two to four days with a greater (13°) displacement.

Experiments by Sperry (summarized in Sperry, 1951) with frogs, salamanders, and teleost fishes, performed with a different but in some ways analogous technique, also suggest a phylogenetic break in perceptual plasticity. Sperry surgically rotated and replanted the eyeball on its optic axis through 180°, leaving the optic nerve intact. The eye healed so that the dorsal-ventral and nasal-temporal quadrants of the retina were exchanged in the orbit. The responses to visual spatial stimuli and to moving prey were ensuingly reversed and directed toward corresponding points in the opposite part of the visual field. These maladaptive responses persisted indefinitely without correction. Similar experiments were performed with transplantation of the eye so as to invert only one axis instead of both. The animals afterward behaved as if the visual field were inverted in only one dimension. Again, the visual-motor responses remained uncorrected. The inference is that these animals behaved as though responses to stimuli in the visual field were prewired to specific receptors in the retina instead of being made to the relational position in the field. Yet we know from the work of Maturana et al., referred to above, that even the frog responds differently to limited figural properties of visual stimuli such as moving edges and convexities.

---

[5] A very recent experiment by Rossi (1968) did find a reduction in the lateral displacement of pecking in chicks wearing 8.5° wedge prisms, and overcompensation in the direction opposite to the original displacement after eight days when the prisms were removed.

SUMMARY

This chapter has considered the development of perception in phylogeny. The question was what information animals at different levels in the evolutionary series take from their environment, and whether any trends can be observed. Several generalizations were made. All animals, however lowly, respond discriminatively in some degree to spatial information, to events, and to features of the objects around them. The mode of response and the dominant sensing process are more or less species specific, in keeping with the special environment of the animal and the receptor systems with which it is endowed. Discriminative response to representations of space, events, and objects appears to be less universal, depending on the fidelity of the representation to the reality, and on the extent to which the representation includes the critical features of the original object, event, or situation. Simulation offers a useful technique for studying perception, since the previous statement can be reversed; by experimenting with simulated events, one might determine from the character of the response what the critical features of the real event actually were.

Discriminative response to coded information requires the mapping of information from reality to a surrogate—a surrogate without similarity. It seems likely that only man is capable of perceiving the kind of specificity which is characteristic of a code, especially if transformation rules exist within the code. Insofar as domestic animals and pets respond discriminatively to speech, they appear to respond to a set signal rather than to a symbolic message.

In searching for overall trends, two have been examined. One is the increasing specificity of discrimination to stimulation. The evolution of specialized receptor structures and the refinement of dimensions of sensitivity are witness to the progressive differentiation of perception with respect to different kinds of stimulus energy. This trend, however, must be looked at in relation to the animal's adaptation, for differentiation can evolve, and has, along more than one line. There are differences among species not only in the amount and quality of stimulus information picked up but in the kinds which play dominant roles.

A second possible trend examined was the response to relational stimuli. A relation can be simple, such as on or off, or it can be complex, at different levels of structure. As Lashley said, an important difference among animals is in the kinds of relations which they can grasp. Even in the invertebrates there is a degree of response to stimulus relations, for useful information about the environment is not given in discrete punctiform stimulation. But the order of the relational property that can be detected probably increases with phylogenetic development.

14

Imprinting as a Type of
Perceptual Development

It has often been suggested that so-called lower species exhibit predominantly innate behavior (and by implication innate perception) and so-called higher species predominantly learned behavior and perception. This generalization is undoubtedly too simple, for it has been shown over the past two decades that even innate behavior, better referred to as species specific, frequently depends on a kind of perceptual development. This kind of development has been called imprinting. It seems to stand somewhere between innate perception and learned perception. Let us look for clarification of the phylogenetic development of perception in the perceptual development of instinctive or species-specific behavior.

INSTINCT AND PERCEPTION

Although the term "instinct" has been for some years in disrepute among psychologists, it has always been recognized that many behavior patterns develop spontaneously, are elicited at a highly predictable time in the animal's life span, and run their course in a highly predictable, relatively inflexible manner. They develop spontaneously in the sense that previous experience with a given stimulating situation is not essential for their appearance, nor is practice of the motor aspect of the behavior pattern necessary for its smooth running off. The temporal sequence of the pattern does not have to be learned, the sequence often following its course blindly to the end even when the environmental supports for it have been withdrawn. Such behavior as nest-building, the mating ceremony, care of the young, and the method of seizing prey is conveniently called instinctive, although calling it such in no way explains it. The weaving of the spider's web, for instance, is just as complex as any piece of learned behavior, and certainly is no less a problem for the psychologist because learning played a minor role, if any, in development. Neither, as Lashley pointed out, is the instinct more determined by heredity than is the habit. "Both," wrote Lashley, "are the expression of modes of the perception of relationships, and these modes are genetically determined (1949, p. 460)."

Naturalists have always been interested in instinctive behavior, and descriptions of it abound at all levels of scholarship. However, these have usually consisted of a mere description of a chain of reponses. As Lashley (1938) pointed out in his famous paper on the experimental analysis of instinctive behavior, the problem of the external stimulus control of such behavior was for many years largely neglected. It is manifest that stimulation emanating from specific objects or properties of objects elicits responses typical of a species. Eggs, for example, elicit typical responses from birds; young elicit typical responses from their parents. What are the effective stimulus properties? In the case of such maternal behavior as the retrieving of young the properties are known to be chemical, visual, auditory, and tactual. The critical properties, whatever they are, must be discriminated from the surrounding stimulation. Lashley believed that "eggness" was the property of roundedness, plus a quality of texture not absolutely specific but within some limited range. The work of Wiesner and Sheard (1933) on maternal behavior in rats revealed the fact of the stimulus control for retrieval of young along with the difficulty of defining it. A maternal animal would retrieve not only a young infant rat, but also an infant mouse, an infant rabbit, and they reported, even a chick. But a young rat past early infancy would not be retrieved. What is the invariant property of infancy that requires a certain range of objects to be accepted and others rejected?

Marler (1961) spoke of the "filtering of external stimuli during instinctive behavior," and contrasted examples of relatively simple sensory mechanisms with others that show sensitivity to a quite complex pattern of stimulation and must therefore involve a more elaborate central mechanism. Fly-catching behavior in frogs, for instance, is elicited by any small moving form within a certain range. The retinal receptive fields of the frog (Maturana et al., 1960) are of a size to take in a small object at a couple of inches distance. The frog's visual system is specifically sensitive to a moving edge and to contrast. But moving edge and contrast detectors cannot explain selective sensitivity to a unique bundle of features, such as that shown by chaffinches to owl-like objects. Chaffinches show unlearned mobbing responses to models portraying a set of owl-like features, including the general outline, the color, patterning, beak, and eyes (Hinde, 1954).

The discipline called ethology has specialized in the study of species-specific behavior. In studying such behavior, the ethologists have not confined themselves to observation and description of the motor aspect of behavior, but have also been concerned with the sensory aspect. They commonly employ the term "innate releaser" to refer to stimulation that typically and specifically excites a characteristic response sequence, such as feeding behavior, or mating. The term "releaser" carries the implication that the role of the stimulus is merely that of a trigger, of something that "touches off" the response chain, which then runs off automatically. This, of course, is the physiologist's concept of a stimulus. But stimulation, even for species-specific behavior, often appears to involve invariant relational information. The response of the finches to the set of distinctive features which together constitute "owlness" is a case in point. They respond to the visual information that usually specifies an owl, not simply to a visual stimulus.

The question has been asked by ethologists whether the components of releasing stimulation form an organized whole, a Gestalt, or whether, on the other hand, they simply sum additively. Weidman (1959) worked with the begging response of the black-headed gull chick. The chick begs for food by pecking at the bill of the adult. Weidman hatched chicks in incubators and then presented them with various colored cardboard models against a standard background. To release a maximum number of pecks, a model had to be moved, held near, low, and upright, and it had to be narrow, red, and dark, with a patch on the lower edge. Weidman tested the hypothesis of "heterogeneous summation," derived from stimulus-response theory. The hypothesis is that all the different stimuli of a complex releasing situation can elicit the response independently, and that each added stimulus only improves the releasing effect of the situation. Weidman tested various component features of the normal situation that elicits begging, compounded them in different ways, and concluded that his evidence favored additivity, though there was considerable variance in the results.

Hailman (1962) made a similar study with chicks of the laughing gull. He also used colored cardboard models, simulating the head of an adult gull to a greater or lesser extent. In one experiment he used a model of a standard relatively complete head, another of an irregularly shaped head, of a part head with a bill, of a bill only, and of a head without a bill. The standard head was best, and the head without a bill was almost totally ineffective. There was little support for heterogeneous summation, the bill appearing to be a highly critical feature. The presence of the head did improve the bill, but since the head without bill elicited nothing, it cannot be concluded that the two stimuli summed. The sum of responses to the head and the bill separately was less than the total response to the complete model. An enhanced bill (long and thin) did not prove, with this species, to be a "super-normal stimulus," but with another gull species (Tinbergen & Perdeck, 1950) it was.[1]

These two experiments by Weidman and Hailman do not solve the problem of whether or not stimuli summate in the release of instinctive behavior. It may turn out to be a false problem. The distinctive features of an adult gull, or of its head, are not easy to analyze, but surely they are not just stimuli. The theory of stimulus information and of the distinguishing features of a meaningful object is quite different from either the

[1] See Chapter 5 and Tinbergen (1953) for a discussion of the super-normal stimulus, or, as I would put it, the enhanced distinctive feature.

theory that a visual display is the sum of its parts (a "compound stimulus") or the theory that it is more than the sum of its parts. The isolation of the relevant stimulus information has very likely not been accomplished with these cardboard models. Discovery of a super-normally effective property of an object, by isolating and exaggerating it, would be evidence that the animal is responding selectively to a distinctive feature—relevant stimulus information.

IMPRINTING

Species-specific behavior cannot always be described as innate response to a releasing stimulus without the intervention of previous experience. A peculiar kind of perceptual learning can be observed in the neonatal animal of certain species. These young are capable of very early motility and are therefore called precocial. Young birds, for example, are often capable of independent locomotion immediately after hatching. These chicks will follow a moving parent-like object that goes away; this instinct presumably keeps the brood together. The peculiar learning is evidenced by the fact that some of the features of a nonparent object can be impressed on a chick who has performed this following behavior. The term "imprinting" (Prägung) was bestowed on this phenomenon by Lorenz (1935). It had been noted by earlier writers (e.g., Spalding, 1873; Heinroth, 1910) [2] that young animals of precocial species will follow a variety of moving objects, and will subsequently direct other kinds of behavior, mating for instance, rather specifically toward the kind of object first followed. The effect of the imprinting process after the first following behavior is apparently to increase the specificity of the response to the releasing object. This tendency presumably insures that the young animal will follow its parent in normal circumstances of hatching or birth, will stay with the brood or the herd, and will subsequently confine its social interactions to its own species.

Because this precocious learning is so clearly perceptual, I shall review its hypothesized characteristics—now the subject of much research. Imprinting is generally thought to take place only in a critical period, very early in life, after which avoidance responses rather than approaching responses will be elicited by novel objects. It was thought by Lorenz to be "irreversible" in that once a duckling was imprinted by a man, for example, it could never thereafter be imprinted by another duck. It takes place very rapidly. What gets imprinted appears to be the general features of the species, its class characteristics, not the distinguishing features of a specific individual such as the mother. In short imprinting seems to have

[2] For a detailed account of the early history of imprinting, see Gray (1963) and Sluckin (1965).

the function of securing, early and rapidly, a recognition of one's own kind without the need of any innate idea of one's own kind, or a specificity of responsiveness without the need of innate neural connections to certain stimuli.

The question has often been asked whether any object can be imprinted. The literature is full of anecdotes of young birds imprinted on their human caretaker to such an extent that they follow him in preference to other birds and even, when mature, show mating behavior in the presence of the caretaker but not in the presence of their own kind. The following response, on its first occurrence, is apparently elicitable by almost any moving object, but imprinting results in an increased specificity of the response to the visual stimuli that are normally furnished by a member of the animal's own species. Learning to recognize one's own parent is a later and slower process. So also is the recognizing of one's own young, or mate, or the place of other individuals in a dominance hierarchy.

The equipotentiality of objects for original imprinting is not complete. There is a prepotency of certain stimulus properties for any species. Certain kinds of sound and the visual quality of motion stand high in this hierarchy. Spalding thought, and this has since been corroborated, that young chicks would instinctively approach and follow the source of a clucking sound and, in the course of doing so, become imprinted to visual features of the object emitting the sound.

Analysis of the perceptual aspects of imprinting, of those features of an object that are most effective for imprinting, has been carried out in recent years in well-controlled laboratory experiments. The typical experiment employs newly hatched birds capable of leaving the nest and locomoting independently at birth or shortly thereafter, such as domestic chicks and ducklings. A runway or a circular track is provided. Suspended slightly above the track is an object of some sort. The chick is placed on the track, the object moves along the track in front of it, and the bird's behavior of following after is observed. In an apparatus designed by Hess (see Fig. 14–1), the decoy was fitted internally with a loud speaker and a heating element. The speaker emitted a recurrent sound ("gock, gock," recorded by a human speaker). Tests of the success of imprinting could be made in a later situation that involved a choice between approaching the same object or a different object in the same or a different runway.

Perceptual Aspects of Imprinting

It was originally supposed that motion of the object was essential for imprinting. But the term "motion" is unclear. A retreating mother would present a shrinking form in the field of view of the chick, so that following in response to this stimulation would be highly adaptive. Isolated stimulus

FIGURE 14–1. Apparatus for studying imprinting in newly hatched birds. (From E. H. Hess, Imprinting. *Science, 130,* 133–141, 17 July 1959.)

information of this sort (a diminishing shadow) has been shown to induce approach in chicks (Tronick, 1967). But this form would normally also fluctuate in some manner, since a living mother does not present an unchanging form in the field of view, and this change can also be called "motion." James (1959) and Abercrombie and James (1961) showed that a flickering light was effective in the imprinting situation. A stationary light placed at the end of a runway flashed on and off. Newly hatched chicks approached the light and stayed there. Another stationary object (a colored ball) was placed near the light for a number of trials, and the chicks learned to approach it when it was presented alone. Without the flickering light, the stationary lure was much less effective. Flicker or fluctuation was apparently equivalent to something in the ordinary stimulation arising from a moving mother. Motion thus has an attention-getting value before selective learning has taken place, and probably serves to orient the chick toward the appropriate object, such as the retreating mother or an active member of the flock. A bird acts in typical ways, pecking, strutting, cleaning itself, and all these are productive of motion in the visual array of the chick. Once oriented by the motion, there is opportunity for the chick to be imprinted by other features of the object.

In early observations of imprinting it was noted that color appeared to be an important feature of the object for young birds. Hess (1959) reported some systematic studies of the effectiveness of various colors in imprinting chicks at 13 to 16 hours of age. The object was a sphere seven inches in diameter colored in one of eight ways: red, orange, yellow, green, blue, near black, near white, or neutral grey. A chick was exposed to one of the spheres for about 17 minutes in an apparatus like that illustrated in Figure 14–1. The sphere moved a distance of forty feet. Twenty-four hours later, the chick was tested in a choice situation, with another colored sphere presented along with the imprinted one. In the original imprinting situation, following behavior was elicited in this order: blue, red, green, orange, grey, black, yellow, white. The same rank order was observed in the test period. The effectiveness of different colors in imprinting undoubtedly varies with the species of animal tested, and might interact with texture, shape, and other features. Results of Gray (1961) and Smith and Bird (1964), for instance, do not confirm Hess, but their testing conditions were different. Both the latter studies found red preferred, in terms of sustaining response, but Smith emphasized the point that motion in the object is so attractive as to mask differences in color values for eliciting following or approach. Klopfer (1967) found no difference in effectiveness between red and yellow for imprinting Pekin ducklings.

Hess also studied the effect of various shapes in imprinting chicks. The spheres used to study color preference were modified by adding head-like, tail-like, or wing-like appendages. Three different models were compared. The plain sphere was most effective; a sphere with wing- and tail-like features less so; and a sphere with wings, tail, and head least of all (see Fig. 14–2). A stuffed brown leghorn rooster was still poorer. Complexity of contour did not seem, in this experiment, to add to the effectiveness of imprinting. Color did, but not necessarily the color characteristic of the bird's own species.

Klopfer and Hailman (1964) have also studied the effectiveness of imprinting in domestic chicks by varying the visual properties of the model. The wooden models were mallard duck decoys, one simply painted flat white, and the other painted yellow and adorned with patches and stripes of red, green, blue, and brown. Each model carried a loudspeaker emitting a "kom-kom-kom" sound. During imprinting the chicks were exposed to one or the other moving model for twenty minutes. At testing time, 24 hours later, the chicks were exposed to both models simultaneously, each model being suspended from one arm of a T-shaped moving support. Approach time and following were measured. During the initial imprinting exposure chicks of the two groups followed their respective models with equal alacrity, but during the choice test, chicks of both groups preferred the varicolored model. Control chicks of the same age but without the earlier imprinting experience failed to follow either model strongly, so imprinting must have occurred in some degree for both experimental groups,

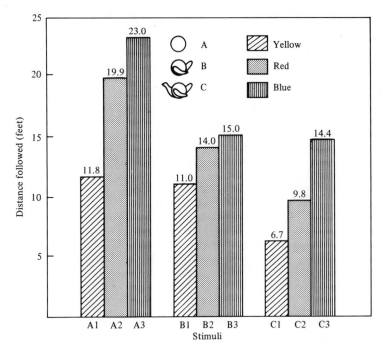

FIGURE 14–2. A comparison of the effectiveness of different models in eliciting the following reaction.

(From E. H. Hess, Imprinting. *Science, 130,* 133–141, 17 July 1959.)

even though the preference for one group was not consistent with the object used for imprinting. Klopfer (1965) repeated this experiment in all essentials, except that the two models were stationary during the choice test. The results did not replicate the first experiment; when the choice tests were conducted with stationary models, a preference for the training model, whichever it had been, was evident. A rotating motion (Klopfer, 1967) also elicited a preference for the varicolored model in the choice test, regardless of which object had been used for imprinting. Apparently, such features as color, texture, and motion can interact in eliciting an orienting response during and following imprinting.

The artificial models used in imprinting research have generally employed rigid motion, not necessarily the kind of motion characteristic of a live animal. It would be interesting to see whether rubbery or elastic motion of a model or decoy would be more effective for imprinting. There is evidence that jerky motion is superior to smooth motion, just as an intermittent, repetitive sound is more effective than a continuous one (Sluckin & Salzin, 1961). Deformation within the object, comparable to head-turning or wing-flapping, might be especially effective in eliciting following, as Fabricius (1951) suggested.

Further definition of the stimulus properties most effective in eliciting approach was attempted by Smith (1962), and Smith and Bird (1963), with some attention to forms of motion other than motion-away (a contracting silhouette in the field of view). For instance, a slowly rotating disc that also moved laterally across the field of view at a distance of five feet was found to be more effective than the same disc, not rotating, moving away. With a moderately distant intermittent light source, more approaches were made to a bright light than to a dim one, but colored filters (red, green, or white) before the light source made no difference. A rotating disc with contrasting sectors tended to be a stronger stimulus than an intermittent light in a choice situation, but not for initial approach when presented alone. Comparison of a more variegated disc (four black sectors) with a less variegated disc (one black sector), when both were slowly rotating (1.5 rev. per sec.), significantly favored the more variegated disc in a choice test of approach. Experiments with varied environmental contexts around the imprinting object did not reveal any effect of the contexts employed.

Bateson (1964, 1966) believed that "conspicuousness" of the stimulus was a crucial variable, and performed experiments to test the hypothesis that conspicuous static objects were more effective for imprinting than inconspicuous ones. Day-old chicks placed in the middle of a runway with colored panels at either end were observed for indications of preference as indicated by movement toward one end or the other. Three panels were compared: a grey one, a grey one with horizontal red stripes, and a white one with red stripes and red circles between the stripes. The chicks approached the last of the three significantly more often than the other two. They had been kept in the dark until the moment of testing, so this preference was presumably innate. But to say that the panel was conspicuous does not help in the analysis of the effective stimulus properties.

An important question is the extent to which imprinting increases selectivity; that is, how much does it narrow the range of positive responses and widen the range of avoidant responses? Imprinting is often described as acquired ability to discriminate the object to which an animal was first exposed at the critical period (Gray, 1957) or as development "from seeing of gross differences to the seeing of fine differences (Thorpe, 1956, p. 116)." Experiments investigating the extent of generalization or transfer of imprinting to other objects should help answer this question.

Generalization and Differentiation in Imprinting

Do mere repeated impressions of the same thing result in increased differentiation of the stimulus properties of an object? Does imprinting, whatever the mechanism, result in increased specificity of responsiveness? Ethologists have often emphasized the generality of imprinting. Hinde, Thorpe, and Vince (1956), working with coots and moorhens, found that the behavior of following one model did not necessarily prevent the later following of another. Moorhens trained on a black wooden model of a moorhen subsequently followed an object as different as a yellow football bladder. Sluckin and Salzen stated that the earliest effect of following something is very general, a mere priming, and that further experience is required to narrow the specificity of the imprinted object as a releaser of following behavior.

Is it true that the newly imprinted animal recognizes only general species characteristics and fails to discriminate the differences between members of the species? In an experimental situation, the answer to this kind of question would be expected to depend on the extent of the difference between the imprinting object and the test object. Ducklings imprinted to a facsimile of a male mallard discriminated later between a male and a female model (Ramsay & Hess, 1954). Baer and Gray (1960) imprinted chicks on a live black or white guinea pig, and found preferences for the imprinted animal in a later choice test. Gray and Howard (1957) made the claim that there was specific recognition of particular human beings by chicks imprinted on one or the other of two people. But human beings possess a very large number of stimulus properties, and we have no idea what properties the chicks were responding to in this experiment.

Jaynes (1956) studied the degree to which chicks imprinted by one object will also be imprinted on other objects in a laboratory situation. Chicks were presented with one of two receding objects, either a green seven-inch cardboard cube, or a red cylinder seven inches in diameter and length. Imprinting sessions were repeated once a day for the first four days of the chick's life. On days Three and Four, the objects were switched for a five-minute interval and a generalization test was given. All the birds showed a decrement in response to the strange moving object, although most did respond positively to it. In a choice test, all the birds trained to the green cube went to it, and all those trained to the red cylinder went to it. Imprinting did increase selectivity, therefore. How much the specificity appears to be increased depends on properties of both the imprinting object and the choice object (cf. Moltz, 1960; Cofoid & Honig, 1961). In Jaynes's experiment, the green cube was a better imprinting object than the red cylinder, but it did not increase specificity more than the cylinder. On the contrary, the green cylinder when presented as the strange object produced a much greater decrement in response, two of the chicks actually running from it in alarm. It had, evidently, some properties which were innately attention-getting and these rendered it particularly effective as an imprinting object at an early stage, and also as a strange object after imprinting to something else had occurred.

In a further experiment, Jaynes (1958) studied the course of generalization over the first four days of the chick's life. On each day, the chick was given thirty minutes exposure to the imprinting object, a red moving cylinder suspended above the run. After a short rest, the imprinting object was exchanged for another object, a different one each day. The strange object differed in color or shape or both (a pink pyramid, a yellow cube, a green cylinder, a white trapezohedron). The chick's approach and following behavior was recorded for five minutes. On the first day, there was no difference in following and approach behavior in response to the imprinting object and the strange object. But on the next three days, a reliable decrement in generalization developed, a response about 80 percent of that to the training object. When the chicks were given a choice test, on the fifth day, with two stimulus objects moving about the alley, they ran from one object to the other in the beginning, and again followed the strange object 80 percent as often as the red cylinder. But as the 45-minute period progressed, all the birds spent more and more time following the training object, and less following the strange object (see Fig. 14–3). As Jaynes put it, this was a learned adjustment in the ani-

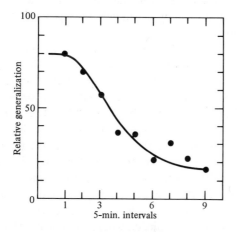

FIGURE 14–3. Development of discrimination in an imprinting situation.

Each point on the curve represents the ratio of the closeness of following the strange object to the closeness of following the training object. (From J. Jaynes, Imprinting: The interaction of learned and innate behavior: IV. Generalization and emergent discrimination. *Journal of Comparative and Physiological Psychology*, 1958, *51*, 241.)

mal's preference behavior occurring without external differential reinforcement, an "emergent discrimination." Gray (1961) criticized Jaynes's term "emergent discrimination" and suggested that the apparently increased specificity was rather a developmental shift in color preference. But this could hardly be true, since the increased specificity developed in the course of a short testing interval. It seems therefore that simultaneous presence of the two objects, presenting an opportunity for comparison and contrast of differences, was effective for increasing specificity.

A theory suggested to account for the increase of specificity during imprinting by Sluckin (1962) and also by Salzen (1962) is that accrual of impressions of the imprinting object over time is the sole process of importance. Sluckin (1965) uses the term "exposure learning." The learning is "purely a function of the time of exposure to any given stimulation (Sluckin, 1962, p. 194)," and the longer the animal experiences the pattern of stimuli, the more sharply it will discriminate it later from unfamiliar stimulus patterns. Impressions early in life "leave an imprint upon the passive mind." Repeated stimulus patterns serve to fashion a "neuronal model." "The more successfully the organism maintains the stimulus pattern input, the more determined and specific the model becomes and so in turn the more specific the stimulus input has to be in order not to set off the activities of moving, looking and listening (searching) that will continue until the perceptual model is matched or modified (Sluckin, 1962, p. 213)." Here is a kind of template-matching hypothesis to account for imprinting and its specificity.

Jaynes's results do not seem to me to fit this simple accrual or composite photograph hypothesis, and suggest, rather, the importance of contrasting properties of the imprinting object with another object or with properties of the background. A certain degree of specificity is present in the animal's behavior from the beginning, because some properties of stimulation such as flicker and intermittent sounds have an original high priority. Selectivity increases as the animal follows the moving and clucking object and observes whatever contrasts it presents with its surroundings. Further opportunity for differences to emerge comes with a single new object present (as Jaynes's experiment permitted in the generalization tests), but the main increase in specificity came as a result of the simultaneous presence of the two objects, where there was enhanced opportunity for observing their contrasting properties. Unlike passive stamping-in, this change seems to me analogous to the perceptual learning of distinctive features of things.

Imprinting and Reinforcement

Imprinting as it occurs in nature has been considered by ethologists to be independent of reinforcement (cf. Thorpe & Zangwill, 1961, p. 168). The filial animal follows the parental one whether or not it is fed or brooded. It is not motivated by hunger or thirst or any other metabolic need and imprinting is thus like perceptual learning. Its "irreversibility," as Lorenz put it, may also be analogous, if one takes irreversibility to mean that what is imprinted is not unlearned (though other things may be learned). Perceptual learning, as I pointed out earlier, does not seem to be subject to extinction, as an operant conditioned response would be.

I have repeatedly witnessed an infant goat, separated from its mother for several hours after parturition, make continuing and undiscouraged efforts to approach the mother despite being rejected by the most vicious butting. Kovach and Hess (1963) demonstrated that punishment administered during the imprinting process not only may not inhibit imprinting but can even strengthen it. Chicks were introduced to a circular runway with an imprinting object (a blue ball, emitting a "come-chick" sound) suspended in it. Electrical shocks were administered to half the chicks during the imprinting session. Chicks punished with shock at 18 hours of age followed the ball twice as far as controls of the same age; at later ages (32 and 48 hours) shock reduced following. In a second experiment, strength of shock and number of shocks delivered were varied. Very heavy, frequent shocks reduced following in chicks of 14, 18, and 32 hours of age. But moderate shocks increased following at 14 and 18 hours. Kovach and Hess concluded that there was an optimal intensity of excitation with which following is maximal at the critical period. Hess (1964) further interpreted these results as a proof that imprinting is not an associative-learning process. Since no reward need occur to maintain following, and even punishment does not inhibit it, the inference is inescapable that imprinting, insofar as perception increases in specificity, is perceptual learning without reinforcement via primary drives.

An experiment by Moltz, Rosenblum, and Halikas (1959) confirmed the above results. An experimental group of Pekin ducklings received shocks during a period of confinement in the test runway before following began. These ducklings were superior to control groups in the strength of the tendency to follow, suggesting to the authors that anxiety level during the period of exposure to the imprinting object has an important role in determining strength of following and also in maintaining it. Whether increased arousal has any effect on imprinting is another question, however.

Hess (1959) has argued that the amount of effort or energy expended in following is an important variable in strength of imprinting. He varied the distance travelled by ducklings, with exposure time during the imprinting period held constant. Groups of animals were run for zero, one, two, four, and eight turns in a ten-minute interval. Increasing the distance over which the duckling followed increased the strength of imprinting. There is, however, a confounding of intensity of stimulation by an object in motion here with the distance run. In a further experiment, Hess placed hurdles in the runway so that the ducklings had to scale them while following the moving object. Imprinting was stronger for these birds than for the control group.

Thompson and Dubanoski (1964) reported that early arousal produced by handling outside the test situation increased strength of imprinting. Increased activation and enhanced visual motion in the stimulus object could interact to strengthen imprinting. In a natural environment, they would be tied. If the parent bird begins to run, enhanced stimulus motion would result; so might anxiety in the infant, greater expenditure of effort, and heightened arousal.

Hess has performed a series of experiments to determine the interactive effect of differential reinforcement upon early preference for food objects. He argued that some innate preference for certain shapes of food object has been shown to exist (Fantz, 1957), and that the specificity of the releasing effect of the stimuli might be expected to increase in an early critical period in a fashion similar to the increase in specificity of following—the usual imprinting situation. It could be predicted then, he thought, that differential reinforcement should be most effective at some peak day, a critical period during which food reinforcement assists in fixing the innate preferences.

To investigate this hypothesis, Hess rewarded newly hatched chicks with food for pecking at normally nonpreferred shapes, while the preferred shape was not rewarded. Two stimuli were presented in a preference setup, a small white circle on a blue background, and a small white triangle on a green background. The chick would normally peck significantly more often at the circle. A hollow holder filled with grain was attached to the triangle so as to reward pecking at the nonpreferred object, but not the preferred one. The food reward was given six groups of chicks at different ages; at one, two, three, five, six, or seven days. Pecking at the triangle was rewarded for a two-hour period. For each of six days following, the chicks were tested for extinction with the same two stimulus objects present, but no food reward. The question was, would a preference established for the originally nonpreferred but rewarded stimulus extinguish at different rates, depending on the day when reward was delivered?

Food reward did in fact increase pecking at the triangle; and when the reward was delivered on Day Three, no extinction followed after its withdrawal. Reward given on any of the other days was followed by dropping off of the preference, supporting, Hess thought, his argument for a critical period for increasing the specificity of food preferences. Hess made the suggestion that there is a sort of maturation schedule of critical periods for three types of imprinting: imprinting to the parent (or species) on the first day; imprinting to the environment on the second day; and imprinting to food on the third day. This pronouncement has an almost biblical authority! If such a maturation sequence of three critical periods were a fact, the uniqueness of imprinting as a developmental process would be strongly supported. But a triangle and a circle are not food. How food is differentiated from other objects (such as parents) by stimulus variables has not been specified. Until it has, Hess's classification into parent, environment, and food stimulus sources can have little psychological validity.

The Critical Period for Imprinting

Hess's argument hinges on the notion of heightened impressionability at a critical period. Though his proposal that there are three sequenced critical periods is speculative, there is evidence that filial imprinting occurs most effectively during a peak interval during the precocial animal's first day of life. What is this critical period, and what brings it to an end? Is it some special kind of maturational magic or, as many investigators have suggested, does imprinting bring about its own end? Hess (1959a and b) has shown for chicks and for ducklings that the critical period for imprinting has a peak around 13 to 16 hours of age, declining thereafter to 36 hours. Imprintability presumably increases from birth up to the peak because the animal's strength and locomotor ability increases. What causes the decline thereafter?

The most popular theory to explain termination of the critical period is that there is a maturing fear response. With the onset of fear comes the end of imprintability (cf. Hess, 1959b). Strange objects elicit flight, thereafter. Hinde, Thorpe, and Vince (1956) found that in the coot, nearly all the decline of the following response could be attributed to growth of a tendency to flee. Decline of imprintability would not be due, therefore, to the waning of a special learning ability at the end of a critical period, but to cessation of the following response at the appearance of a novel object and its replacement with fear.

Whatever the motivational component of this sequence, there does seem to be a waning of imprintability correlated with an increase in specificity of behavior to a given stimulus object or environment. Might it be that the acquired specificity is the cause of the end of the critical period? Sluckin (1962) maintains that this is the case, saying "the closer the mind to the state of *tabula rasa,* the greater the impact of sensory stimulation, and the greater the facilitation of perceptual learning (p. 196)." Early impressions of the imprinting object serve to promote discrimination of it from other objects. It is this selectivity of response elicitation as a result of experience that brings about the end of the critical period, rather than sudden emergence of fear. Unfamiliar objects, after all, can be unfamiliar only as a result of familiarity with something else (Moltz, 1960; Sluckin & Salzen, 1961).

This hypothesis would predict that isolation, or a highly restricted environment should extend the length of the critical period. A certain amount of evidence for this statement is available. Guiton (1958) showed that chicks kept in isolation for the first three days after hatching were still responsive to a moving object, while birds reared socially were not. This finding was replicated by Sluckin and Salzen (1961) with birds isolated for six days. The implication is that the socially reared chicks were imprinted to each other, since they showed fear responses to the moving object whereas the isolated chicks followed it. Fear responses would occur, by this hypothesis, to strange (unfamiliar) objects—these latter being merely the objects to which they are not imprinted.

Hess (1964) has presented further evidence on the effects of early social experience as opposed to isolation. Control chicks remained in a dark room for periods up to 48 hours without visual or social experience. Experimental chicks were exposed to the company of other chicks for two hours prior to the imprinting experience. The control chicks followed the imprinting model (a blue ball emitting a "come-chick" sound) most strongly at 16 hours, with a steady decrease thereafter. The socialized chicks followed the model significantly more than the controls at all ages. In a second study (Polt & Hess, 1964), isolated and socialized groups of chicks were imprinted at 16 or 36 hours, isolated in a dark room for 24 hours more, and then tested for strength of imprinting by a choice procedure. Each animal during the test was placed in the imprinting apparatus between the imprinting model and a group of four chicks in a clear plastic enclosure. The only birds which gave evidence of imprinting to the model in this test were those in the 16-hour isolation group. The socialized chicks, despite having followed the model well during the imprinting session, were attracted to the other chicks during the test, rather than to the model. Hess concluded that they had already been imprinted to their siblings when they were first exposed to the model.

Hess (1964) reported similar experiments on ducklings, with more or less comparable results. Socialization did not prime the ducklings to follow the imprinting object, as it had the chicks, but the test scores for imprinting to the model were consistently lower than those for the 14- to 16-hours-old control ducklings that had had no chance to imprint to their siblings. Basically, Hess concluded, socialization lowers imprinting strength in both species, because the animals have already been imprinted to the first moving object in their environment.

Salzen (1962) also studied the effect of socialization on imprinting, relating it to development of fear responses and cessation of the critical period. Fear he considered a response to unfamiliar situations. Imprinting, being a process of familiarization with something, creates the possibility of unfamiliar objects or situations and thus fear responses. Socialized chicks showed fear of a moving cardboard cylinder when alone with it, at 24 hours of age. Isolated chicks, he said, responded "with pleasure" to it.

If birds are reared without the possibility of any visual familiarization, can the critical period be prolonged? If familiarization with consequent strangeness of new objects really causes the waning of the critical period, it should be possible to extend it indefinitely by deprivation of any exposure to visible, sounding objects. Moltz and Stettner (1961) tested this prediction with Pekin ducklings deprived of the opportunity to perceive visual forms prior to exposure to the imprinting object. Experimental ducklings were fitted with latex hoods immediately after hatching, so that only diffuse-light stimulation was available. Control subjects were reared with the typical patterned-light stimulation available in a lighted cage. All were reared in individual cages, but it is likely that they could hear other birds. Subgroups of birds were maintained under these conditions for 12, 24, 48, and 72 hours before the first imprinting experience. An imprinting trial consisted of 25 minutes in the presence of a green cardboard object that moved up and down a ten-foot wooden alley. Comparison of following scores at 12 hours of age revealed no difference between the control and experimental birds, but when the first imprinting experience was given at 24 or at 48 hours, the experimental (deprived) birds followed the test object significantly more than the control birds, suggesting that the period of imprintability was extended by curtailing their opportunity to perceive a visually structured environment. However, experimental birds given the initial imprinting trial at 72 hours did not follow. They differed from the control birds at 72 hours only in displaying a lesser tendency to avoid the test object. Although they stood quietly in the alley without following, no signs of fear or emotionality were given. It would seem that the critical period for imprinting can be extended within limits by deprivation of patterned light, but that termination of following is not contingent upon emotionality.

It would appear that the critical period has some exclusively maturational bases, whatever the contribution of posthatching experience. Klopfer and Gottlieb (1962a and b) have produced several lines of evidence to support the neurophysiological significance of the critical period. They found, as Gottlieb (1961) had suggested previously, that the critical period is best measured by the time elapsed since incubation, rather than time elapsed since hatching, which varies from bird to bird. Variable time since hatching should be more important if experience with stimulation from the external world is the important determinant of the critical period, but in their experiments a trend toward an interval of significantly high susceptibility to imprinting was evident only by counting from the onset of incubation. Furthermore, they discovered individual differences in ducklings in imprintability to auditory as contrasted with visual aspects of the stimulus object. The two susceptibilities were independent of each other; there was no correlation between incidence or strength of imprinting to these two aspects of the stimulus. This suggested to the authors an interpretation in terms of "genetic polymorphism." Finally, when testing for imprinting to auditory versus visual aspects of the stimulus object, Klopfer and Gottlieb found that those birds given imprinting experience on the first half of day 27 (after onset of incubation) exhibited more auditory imprinting, while imprinting to both aspects, with a shift in strength toward visual, occurred after this time. They thought that in this species of duckling the auditory component of stimulation functions mainly as an attention-getting signal, while imprinting resulting in later discrimination is related primarily to the visually perceived object. Other evidence (Smith & Bird, 1963, 1964) confirmed the primacy of the auditory stimulus with chicks and found responses to a combined auditory-visual stimulus best at all stages.

What can be concluded, at this time, about the critical period, the causes of its initiation, and its termination? There is, as in long-term perceptual development, an interplay of genetic and environmental factors. That there is some kind of maturational schedule, a developmental timetable, seems undeniable. Although the work of Moltz showed that the critical period can be extended by deprivation of stimulation, it cannot be extended indefinitely. On the other hand, the increase in perceptual specificity brought about by an animal's exposure to parental objects and other features of its environment contributes to the differentiation of newer objects and surroundings as unfamiliar, with resulting modification of behavior.

SUMMARY

As the earliest and most striking kind of perceptual development, imprinting has excited enormous interest among ethologists and psychologists alike, ethologists tending to emphasize its maturational or innate side, psychologists the fact that it is learning. It seems to be a kind of bridge between behavior so innately determined as to occur without any previous experience of the external environment and the long-term learning that occurs at later times during an animal's life.

Hess, in particular, has stressed the contrast between imprinting and association learning. He and others have pointed out that for imprinting to occur, there must be a class of potential stimuli (perhaps very wide) that acts as releaser for responses such as following, and that the class is narrowed as the stimuli actually displayed are responded to. Intermittent sounds and visual motion are prepotent features of stimulation for eliciting following, while the potency of other features such as color appears to be less. There is much work to be done in defining the critical stimuli in any imprinting situation. Convenient classifications of objects, such as parents, food, and home, are no substitute for the analysis of critical features of stimulation.

Exactly what degree of specificity is achieved in an imprinting situation is still a question, since few generalization experiments have been carried out. Are only rather vague species characteristics differentiated? Is a specific single feature, such as a red bill, or on the other hand a bundle of multiple features differentiated? The answers to these questions will not come easily, for it is hard to say where imprinting stops and discrimination learning with simultaneous or successive contrast of features begins. Jaynes has shown that the latter situation greatly increases the specificity of original imprinting, resulting in "emergent discrimination." In any case, perceptual learning has a vital function early in life, and it progresses from innate, rather gross selectiveness to greater specificity, without the intervention of external rewards or punishments. What ends the period of special susceptibility is not yet clear. It appears that both a maturational timetable and perceptual acquaintance with distinctive features of a parental or pseudo-parental object play a role.

15

The Development of Perception
in the Individual:
Methodological Considerations

INTRODUCTION

We have now considered the nature of perceptual learning, and the evolution of perception in the animal kingdom. The time has come to consider how perception develops in the growing individual. My criterion of perceptual learning is the achievement of greater specificity of correlation between stimulation and discrimination, increasing differentiation and pickup of invariant relations. In phylogeny as well, there is increasing differentiation and a progressive development of the capacity to detect higher order invariants in stimulus information.

It makes sense to look for evidence of these same trends in the development of the individual organism. One can cite the venerable slogan that "ontogeny recapitulates phylogeny," but I am more impressed by the likelihood that trends in learning and in development are similar. An instructive example comes from a classic study of prenatal development. Raney and Carmichael (1934), while investigating tactile stimulation in the foetal rat, found that the foetus' responses, as gestation age increased, became more and more precisely related to a smaller area of stimulation on the skin. This led Raney and Carmichael to propose:

From one point of view it may therefore be that the whole story of the development of adaptive, discriminative behavior, and thus of perception itself, may be considered as beginning in a condition of absolute non-specificity and gradually becoming, as described in this paper, more and more specific in relation to external stimulation as differential growth continues (p. 17).

The question we are asking follows the one just considered phylogenetically. What is it that can be perceptually discriminated at different age levels, and how does effective stimulation change with development? What features of his world, if any, are perceived by the neonate? What by the first grader? How has he changed? The facts of perceptual development will be organized around the classification of stimulation used in earlier chapters. But before attempting to review them, I think some consideration must be given to ways of studying perceptual development, for the store of facts is dependent on the methods available for the inquiry and on their validity. This chapter will consider the techniques of observation and experiment available for gathering data about perception in the infant and young child.

METHODS OF STUDYING PERCEPTUAL DEVELOPMENT

Tracing the development of locomotion from infancy on is relatively easy; one can photograph it and describe it quite objectively. But how does one find out what an infant perceives? The question poses the same problems as it does with animals but not quite the same problems; for one thing one cannot perform restrictive rearing experiments with human infants and, for another, after a few years the human child can speak, bringing about a radical change in the methods available.

Less than a decade ago, I wrote about methods of studying perceptual development in children (Gibson & Olum, 1960). But during the intervening time much effort has been expended on this area and real progress has resulted, especially in our knowledge of what young infants perceive.[1] Part of this advance has come from methodological wisdom, new apparatus, and ingenious substitutes for conventional scaling procedures, but much of it has come from what I will call ecological wisdom. If it is true that animals have evolved sensitivity in relation to their particular environments and ways of life, may it not prove that the infant's perceptual development also follows such a course? It seems wise to ask what his typical environment is like and what, if anything, he can do about it.

Consider three examples of behavior in human infants, looking, reaching, and crawling. At first the infant cannot do much except look. We ask, then, what there is to look at. His environment includes adult faces. Does he look at them? Does he discriminate them from other objects? From one another? After a while he can reach. What does he reach for? Does he reach accurately, revealing good spatial localization? After six or seven months he can crawl. Does he crawl over an edge, or does he perceive the depth at an edge and avoid the falling-off place? Does he avoid obstacles? Does he avoid things coming at him? The adaptive significance of things and places and events in the world should be considered in asking what the infant responds to. But it is not enough to point out adaptive significance; it is also essential to specify the stimulus information to which the young organism may (or may not) be responding.

[1] For a recent review of methods of studying visual perception in infants, see Vurpillot (1966).

Stimulus information refers to the stimuli that have "ecological validity," to use Brunswik's term.

Simulation of an Ecologically Significant Environment

Mere observation of behavior in a real world may result in interesting anecdotes, but seldom provides enough stimulus control. Ideally, therefore, a laboratory situation which simulates a typical situation in the infant's world should be used. The situation must be controllable so that the information can be analyzed and describable so that it can be replicated, but it should be natural. An example of simulation of an ecologically significant environment for which an adaptively relevant response exists is provided by the visual cliff (see Chapter 12). The cliff can be used not only for phylogenetic comparison of discrimination of depth-at-an-edge, but also for studying edge avoidance in the human infant. A cliff constructed for human infants is sketched in Figure 15–1. The center platform is raised only slightly above the glass, and is wide enough to hold the baby in creeping position. It is covered in a patterned material like the shallow side of the cliff and the floor below. The baby's mother stands alternately at either the deep or the shallow side, twirling a toy and calling to the baby to come to her (see Fig. 15–2). In the basic procedure (Walk & Gibson, 1961), each baby was given two minutes to respond before his mother changed sides, and two trials were given on each side.

Thirty-six infants, between the ages of 6½ and 14 months, were tested in the original experiment. Of this group, one quarter of the babies did not leave the center board, perhaps because they were still unable to crawl adequately. Of the babies that left the board, 24 out of 27 crawled to the mother when she called from the shallow side, but refused to come when she called from the deep side. Three babies crawled to their mothers over the glass of both sides. No baby crawled over the deep side only. It appears that the majority of infants, by the time independent locomotion is possible, perceive a drop-off and avoid it.

The cliff apparatus permits more than this rough assessment, however, since it is possible to vary systematically the optical array of stimulation provided, so as to study the stimulus control of this avoidance. Walk (1966) has reported several such experiments. In one, he placed a pattern with a very coarse texture under the glass of the deep side, and a similar pattern with a similar fine texture on the shallow side, so the projected size of the pattern elements at the infant's eye was approximately equal. Only 4 of 45 infants crossed over the deep side in this condition, while nearly all crawled to their mothers over the shallow side. Thus, it is not the stationary projected size of the pattern elements that control cliff

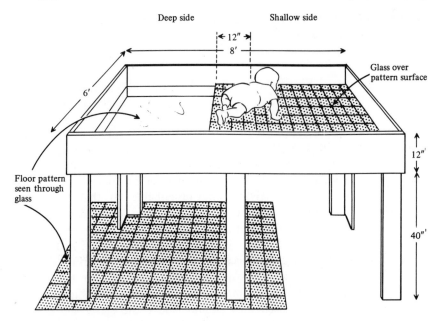

FIGURE 15–1. Drawing of a visual cliff for testing human infants.

(From E. J. Gibson, Development of perception: Discrimination of depth compared with discrimination of graphic symbols, in J. C. Wright & J. Kagan [Eds.], *Basic Cognitive Processes in Children*. The Society for Research in Child Development Monographs, Vol. 28, 1963, No. 2, p. 11.)

avoidance. The so-called relative size cue for distance was ineffective, suggesting that motion parallax at the edge is important information for the human infant as well as for animals (see Chapter 13).

On the other hand, texture of the surface does play an important role. There had to be a visible texture for normal crawling over the glass to take place. Walk compared the effect of a textured surface and a plain gray surface placed at increasing depths under the glass. For a given condition, the same texture was placed on both sides of the apparatus. The surface stayed at zero depth on one side, but was lowered from zero to 40 inches on the other side. This results essentially in a one-sided cliff. When the surface was patterned with checks ¾ in. square, a regular decrease was obtained for number of babies crawling to the mother on the variable side as the surface was lowered (see Table 15–1). But when the pattern was relatively textureless (gray masonite), the information for depth was less determinate. Only 50 percent of the babies would venture off the center board even when the masonite was directly under the glass, and still fewer when it was lowered, but there was no neat psychometric function as there was for the checkered surface. The different depths did not seem to be as distinguishable from one another. When the optical texture coming

FIGURE 15–2.   A baby looking at the visual cliff.

(Photograph courtesy of Dr. R. D. Walk.)

from the physical texture of a surface is such that the depth of the surface is ambiguous, crawling behavior no longer depends on depth. It should be remembered that the visual acuity of young babies is poor. Perhaps the texture of the smooth gray masonite could not be seen as such. Inhomogeneities in the light to an eye seem to be requisite for the detection of a surface, and locomotion seems to be controlled by the perception of the "surfaciness" of this array, that is, by the presence of visual support as distinguished from actual or tangible support. The infants rub the glass, and test the surface with the hands and even the mouth. But the surface has to look safe for locomotion, as well as feel solid.

TABLE 15–1

Comparison of Depth Avoidance of Textured and Untextured Surfaces

	Percent of Infants Crossing	
Depth in Inches	*Textured Surface (Checks)*	*Untextured Surface (Gray Masonite)*
0	89	50
10	38	32
20	27	35
40	8½	41

Data from R. D. Walk, The development of depth perception in animals and human infants. *The Society for Research in Child Development Monographs,* Vol. 31, 1966, No. 5, p. 97.

Innate Attentive Responses

In considering the orienting and following responses of a precocial animal to a mother-like object (Chapter 14), we found that young chicks and ducklings approach and follow objects having certain innately attention-getting properties in their first day of life. Motion, bright flashes of intermittent light, and intermittent sound all elicit approach and following. The newborn human infant is incapable of locomotion. Nevertheless, his behavior shows him not indifferent to what is happening around him. He looks at some things and not at others; he locates a sound and turns his eyes in the direction of it (Wertheimer, 1961). There is some discrimination of things and events immediately, as witnessed by gross but nevertheless observable differential orienting movements. The neonate, in fact, pays attention to some things more than others. There are various kinds of measurable indicator responses for such attention. One is the turning of the head or the eyes in a certain direction, another is the smiling response while looking at something, a third is a slowing of the heart rate, and a fourth the suppression of an ongoing activity such as sucking, all of which seem to indicate interest. At a later stage of development, reaching for something with the hand clearly indicates attention to it. Alternatively, one can measure the cessation of various indicators of attention to indicate habituation or loss of interest in something. All these methods are possible with infants without the necessity of training them in advance to make a learned discriminative response and of course without requiring a verbal discriminative judgment.

Fantz (1961) began his work in this now fashionable area of differential attention with a study of infant preferences for different visual patterns, measuring fixation time on each of a pair of patterns presented simultaneously in the field of view. Patterns were presented to an infant lying on his back. An observer noted to which pattern the infant first oriented and the duration of the fixation. In a typical experiment (Fantz, 1961), infants from 1 to 15 weeks old were exposed at weekly intervals to pairs of test patterns. The baby lay in a looking chamber (see Fig. 15-3) with its head facing up directly under the target station, one foot away. Its length of gaze at each target was recorded by an observer who watched through a small hole in the ceiling of the chamber. The criterion of looking was the superposition over the pupil of a tiny corneal reflection of the target. The targets were a bull's-eye paired with stripes; a checkerboard paired with a plain square; a cross paired with a circle; and a pair of triangles, one larger than the other. The bull's-eye was preferred over the stripes and the checkerboard over the square, but the other two pairs evoked no preference.

In another experiment, Fantz compared six test objects, but presented

FIGURE 15–3. **A looking chamber for measuring visual preferences in young infants.**

The baby is looking at objects hung from the ceiling, while an observer watches through a peephole and records the attention given each object. (From R. L. Fantz, Pattern vision in newborn infants, *Science, 140,* 296–297, April 19, 1963. Copyright 1963 by the American Association for the Advancement of Science.)

them one at a time in a random series, measuring fixation time on target for the first glance at each. There were three patterned circles (a schematic face, a patch of newspaper, a black and white bull's-eye) and three plain circles colored red, white, and yellow. The infants spent relatively twice as much time looking at patterned circles as at unpatterned ones. The face pattern was overwhelmingly the most interesting. These results with older infants (two to six months old) were essentially duplicated later with infants less than five days old (Fantz, 1963).

What can be concluded from these results? Certainly not that there is instinctive recognition of a human face, as we shall see later in considering work on infants' responses to faces and suitable control objects. But it would appear that the visual world of the neonate has some distinguishing properties, however gross; and that visual attention is attracted earlier to pattern than to color differences. Furthermore, it is of evolutionary significance that a face-like pattern appears to have stimulus characteristics (as yet to be defined) that attract attention at a very early age.

The skeptical scientist is tempted to look at this evidence and wonder about the validity of the measure. Have we any criterial test for inferring that the infant is actually seeing a face-like pattern? Of course the answer is no; but evidence for some perceptual differentiation is there, since there is differentiation of a figure from background and in some cases, one figure from another. Absence of indication of a preference does not mean that no discrimination is possible. Occurrence of a preference, furthermore, seldom gives firm evidence of exactly what it is that has attracted the infant's attention. Fortunately, other innate selective responses are available, so that by a procedure of what has been called converging operations there is a possibility of determining, eventually, what aspects of a visual display are discriminable at birth and how development subsequently occurs.

The procedure followed by Fantz has usually been a choice or preference situation. He compared priorities for attracting fixation, and took duration of fixation to be an index of the relative attention value of a display. It is difficult, with this technique, to infer whether or not specific features of a pattern are discriminated. But if an infant can move his eyes so as to track an edge, or lock on a corner, there would be evidence indicating that these formal properties are differentiated from background not merely as blobs of light or dark or heterogeneous texture, but as contour.

Exactly what dimension or property of a preferred display has attracted the infant's attention is a question of much interest. A patterned field is apparently preferred to a homogeneous one; but which of many possible variables of the pattern is the effective one? Brightness, texture, specific features, and structural relations are all possibilities. To be sure that an infant is responding to a dimensional feature of a display, such as brightness, several values of the dimension should be presented, as with any psychophysical technique, and evidence of differential response and of transitivity should be demonstrated along the dimension.

Two possibilities emerge for using visual fixation in such a way as to obtain more specific information. One is watching for orienting movements correlated with contour, or fixating on regions of special potential interest in a display; the other is looking for correlations between duration of fixation and value along some variable dimension of the displays.

Visual scanning movements in relation to a contour have been explored by Salapatek and Kesson (1966). The infant was placed in a head-restraining crib, with a stimulus display placed nine inches above its eyes. One of the baby's eyes was centered under a camera and photographed so as to obtain a running record of ocular orientation. An experimental group of neonates was presented with a black triangle on a white field. A control group was shown a homogeneous circular black field. Infrared marker lights in both displays permitted determination of ocular orientation by calculating deviation of the corneal reflections of the light from the center of the infant's pupil. Records of ocular postures were plotted and compared for the two groups. Ocular orientation among the control infants was widely distributed over the homogeneous field. But ocular orientations of the experimental group tended to cluster near the vertices of the triangle. Most infants tended to look at a single vertex, though not necessarily the same one on different trials. The effect of the triangle was not only to produce clustering of eye orientation at the vertices, but also to reduce overall dispersion of scanning and to reduce predominance of horizontal over vertical scanning.

These results suggest that at least one feature of a form, the vertex of a triangle, is specifically attended to shortly after birth. But the infants did not scan along edges of the triangle from one vertex to another. The inference might be made that the infant responds to a preferred feature in the visual display, and does not, at this age, respond to the figure as a whole. Kessen, Salapatek, and Haith (1965), with the same technique, investigated ocular response to a border or contour. A circular display was divided vertically into a lighter and a darker field, so as to produce a sharp contrast. Some of the three-day-old subjects showed a significant tendency to lock their gazes on the line between black and white.

The question of whether the newborn infant can detect dimensional differences in stimulation requires a psychophysical procedure in which an ordered set of samples are presented. If there is a correlated serially ordered set of responses, one might infer that the stimulus dimension can be perceived. Hershenson (1964) made this argument and ran an appropriate experiment with differing brightnesses, measuring fixation preference. He found transitivity of preferences among the samples (medium preferred over bright over dim) but not a monotonic gradient. The transitivity, however, argues for graded appreciation of brightness differences.

A combination of indicators of attention has been employed by Kagan and Lewis (1965) in an attempt to assess with greater accuracy what an infant is looking at, what aspects of a stimulus display attract his attention. In addition to visual fixation, they measured number of arm movements, vocalizations, and cardiac deceleration, comparing a number of visual and auditory presentations. These included projected pictures (colored photographs of a male and female human face, a black-white bull's-eye, a black-white checkerboard, a nursing bottle, and a panda bear); three patterns of blinking lights (a single blinking light, a blinking light moving across the horizontal field, and a blinking light that described a square helix); auditory stimuli, taped and played through a speaker (an intermittent tone, a bit of jazz music, and three human voices reading an identical paragraph, one male, one anonymous female, and the voice of the infant's mother). The infants were tested at 6 and 13 months. The displays are so varied that they permit no inferences about what stimulus attributes are actually being picked up by the infants, but the study is of methodological importance because of the interrelations of the response measures.

The four measures of attention showed convergence for some displays and correlated trends as opportunity was given for habituation. But there were differences, depending on the kind of display, age, and individual differences. For example, fixation time and vocalization were positively correlated for the pictures, being very high for photographs of human faces, whereas cardiac deceleration did not differentiate them significantly. But for blinking lights, fixation time and cardiac deceleration were significantly correlated, while vocalization did not differentiate. Realistic representations of human faces were preferred at 6 months but were not at 13 months, a schematic face then attracting more attention. As for individual differences, babies ranked high in attentiveness showed a significant positive relationship between long fixation times and cardiac deceleration, but no correlation resulted for minimally attentive infants.

Indicators of perceptual differentiation at a very early age are nonspecific. There are no one-to-one mappings to specific identifications; rather, the same response serves as an indication of differentiation or no differentiation, as it does in psychophysical operations of detection or recognition (see Chapter 9). As Fantz (1964) has pointed out, primates have few innate specific responses to specific stimuli, but have, rather, an innate capacity for selective visual exploration. Certain features or properties of stimulation attract and hold attention, but there are no identifying responses uniquely correlated with them. Experience and learning can change this state in two ways. First, experience modifies selective attention and further differentiates attention to distinctive features of things; and secondly, learning may result in specific identifying responses that get associated with specific classes of objects and events.

Before learning has taken place, one must rely entirely on nonspecific indicators of attention, but by two months slightly more specific selective responses begin to be available. The smiling response is one which has been widely exploited. It also is not very specific at first, but in combination with looking it may yield more subtle information about perceptual differentiation. Kagan (1965) found, for instance, that an infant at four months pays equal attention, as measured by visual fixation time, to a pictorial face with the features scrambled and to a face with its features in proper relationship. But he smiles at the latter and not at the former, thus indicating that they are discriminated. Learning plays a role in what is smiled at, but like looking, it happens spontaneously (Dennis, 1938) and shows some appropriate selectivity long before locomotion or reaching appears.

Reaching for an object is a potentially more specific response which develops around five months. It has often been assumed that the infant's perception of space depended on practice in reaching for things and that such perception is learned in the course of reaching as confirmed by touching and grasping. This assumption is obviously unjustified without supporting evidence, and requires in any case that the infant perceive the target as something to reach for. Early studies of reaching behavior, especially in Gesell's laboratory (cf. Halverson, 1932; Gesell, Thompson, and Amatruda, 1934) concentrated on a mere description of the motor act and its changes with age. Research is beginning to show more concern with visually directed reaching in relation to development of exploratory activity in perception.

Habituation

Habituation is in a sense the other side of the coin from attention. It also can be used as a method for telling us what a very young infant can discriminate. If continued exposure to a given stimulus source is accompanied by a decreased response in the infant and followed, in contrast, by an increased response when a new stimulus source is presented, we have evidence that some property of the two sources is differentiated, even though the attentive response is not specific to the stimulus. One limitation of the fixation-preference method is that failure to elicit a preference does not necessarily imply that no discrimination exists. An alternative test can be made when no preference is shown by exposing a new stimulus display following habituation to an original one. Another possible use of the method is to indicate the strength of a stimulus property for attracting attention, since data of Kagan and Lewis (1965) suggested that there is a positive correlation between attention value and delay of habituation.

Wagner Bridger (1961, 1962) used the tendency to habituate to a repeated stimulus in order to measure the discriminatory capacities of infants one to five days old. A pure tone of constant loudness was applied repetitively. Measurements of heart rate and behavior were taken. All the babies showed some behavioral habituation in the sense of cessation of gross startle responses to the tone as it was repeated. To measure discrimination, responses to one pure tone were habituated and then a tone of different pitch was produced. For example, when heart rate and behavioral responses to a repeated tone of 400 cycles had subsided, a tone of 1,000 cycles was substituted. Heart rate increased. One baby discriminated between tones of 200 and 250 cycles. Figure 15–4 shows changes in heart rate reflecting habituation to a tone, introduction of a novel tone, and reintroduction of the original one. According to Bridger, sensory habituation

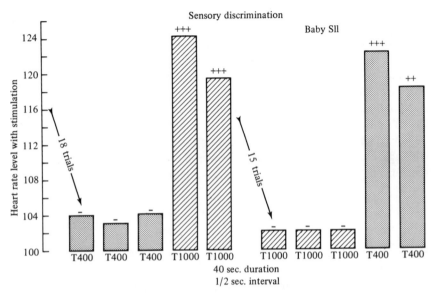

FIGURE 15–4. Habituation of a two-day-old infant to a pure tone, followed by increased heart rate to a tone of different pitch.

> After 18 trials, the level of the heart rate in response to sounding a tone of 400 cycles had fallen to the level prior to stimulation. When it was followed by a tone of 1,000 cycles, the heart rate rose. After 15 trials with the 1,000 cycle tone, response to this tone was habituated and the tone of 400 cycles again elicited an increase in heart rate. (From W. H. Bridger, Sensory habituation and discrimination in the human neonate. Reprinted from the *American Journal of Psychiatry*, Vol. 117, pp. 991–996, 1961.)

of this type is mediated by an inhibitory mechanism in the midbrain reticular system. That this is a primitive discriminatory mechanism is implied by the fact that decorticate animals have been shown to exhibit habituation and pitch discrimination by similar methods. Leventhal and Lipsitt (1964) did not succeed in replicating Bridger's evidence of pitch discrimination, using habituation and recovery of body movements and breathing in place of heart rate. But their method did produce evidence of sound localization in neonates.

A combination of response to novelty after habituation with a preference method was developed by Saayman, et al. (1964). Visual fixation of stimulus patterns of varied shape and color was studied, with an apparatus modeled after that of Fantz. But the procedure differed. A pair of stimulus cards was presented for two initial trials of 30 seconds each, and the infant's preference noted. Afterward, one of the displays was presented simultaneously in both card holders for a 4½ minute familiarization period. Finally, there were two more 30 second trials with the pair of patterns for a new determination of preference. The infants were between 6 and 16 weeks old. Stimulus patterns differed in: 1) form only (red cross and red circle); 2) color only (red circle and black circle); or 3) form and color (red cross and black circle). The method proved to be useful as a supplement to preference data alone. In all conditions there was a decline in time spent looking at the familiarized stimulus after familiarization, even when it had originally been the preferred one. Visual exploration declined as a function of time of exposure to a stimulus pattern. The results showed unequivocally that three-month-old infants discriminated circles from crosses, although fixation preference alone had previously failed to elicit this differentiation.

Reaction to novelty as indexed by suppression of ongoing sucking activity has been used by Soviet psychologists with interesting results (Bronshtein, et al., 1960). The infant's startle response (suppression of sucking) and its ability to habituate as indexed by resumption of sucking are connected with arousal mechanisms in the reticular activating system, and provide an opportunity for measuring simple sensory capacities shortly after birth.

Operant Conditioning

Discrimination-learning experiments can be carried out by a number of techniques in ambulatory children and animals, but work in the past gave few successes with ordinary training methods in the very young infant. Recently, however, operant conditioning (Lipsitt, 1963) has been successfully established in quite young infants and promises to increase our knowledge about discriminable features of the world in babies whose performatory abilities such as reaching and locomotion are still undeveloped.

An experiment by Bower (1964) illustrates an operant-conditioning method employed with infants between 70 and 85 days old. The operant response was a leftward rotation of the head. The child's head was clasped between two yielding pads, of which the left one contained a microswitch operating an event recorder. When the child's head turned to the left, the event recorder closed and reinforcement was administered. The reinforcement was provided by an experimenter who emerged into the infant's view and peek-a-booed at him—an ingenious and highly effective reinforcing event, showing that a baby will learn to do something to get a perception! The conditioned stimulus object was a white 12-inch paper cube at a distance of 3 feet in front of the subject. A discrimination was trained initially between cube present and cube absent. Then the negative stimulus was discontinued and head-turning to the cube was shaped to maintain a variable ratio schedule of one reinforcement to five responses for a period of one experimental hour.

At the end of training, generalization tests were introduced to probe the stimulus properties which were effective in eliciting the response. The displays were: 1) a 12-inch cube at 3 feet distance (the conditioned stimulus object); 2) a 12-inch cube at 9 feet distance; 3) a 36-inch cube at 3 feet distance; and 4) a 36-inch cube at 9 feet distance. Each was presented for 30 seconds and the baby's response rate was determined. Response was greatest to the training situation and least in Situation 4, where the cube was three times as far away and also three times as great, so that its projected retinal size was the same as in training. Since this situation was clearly discriminated from the training situation, the inference follows that the difference in either distance or size or both is detected. Situations 2 and 3 also elicited significantly fewer head turnings than the training situation, but the difference was not as great as in 4, where both size and distance of the cube were varied. It appears therefore that the infant picks up at least some of the stimulus variables specifying size and distance of an object before performatory actions such as reaching and locomotion have developed, so perceptual differentiation of some spatial properties of objects is not dependent on action in space. We shall return to the problem in Chapter 16.

Other responses, such as sucking (Lipsitt & Kaye, 1964), have been conditioned and are beginning to be used in studying perceptual development in infants.

Discrimination Learning

A child who has attained the age of controlled reaching and grasping, and later controlled locomotion, can be observed in the traditional discrimination-learning experiment, as we have known for many years. Classic experiments on form discrimination in the preverbal child are those of Gellerman (1933a, b) and Ling (1941). A choice between two simultaneously presented stimulus objects, with differential reward, was offered by Ling to infants six months old. Three-dimensional blocks differing in shape were presented on a board. The correct block was sweetened and could be lifted to the mouth, whereas the incorrect block was fixed to the board. Discrimination between various geometrical shapes (circle vs. ellipse, circle vs.

square, etc.) was demonstrated in this manner (see detailed description in Chapter 12). Gellerman worked with slightly older, but still preverbal children. The children (about 24 months old) were capable of locomotion and walked to the targets to make a choice. Transfer of learning with controlled stimulus changes can be used in this situation to determine equivalence of stimuli and thus tell us something about the stimulus properties that are critical for the child. Orientation of a shape, for instance, was found by Gellerman not to be critical. The children selected the rewarded shape despite its rotation, but rotated their heads correspondingly when observing it.

A currently popular method of collecting discrimination data on young children is the Wisconsin General Test Apparatus. Originally designed for use with other primates, it is easily adapted for children. Typically, a pair of stimulus objects is presented simultaneously to the subject, who chooses one and lifts it to disclose a food well underneath. If the object is the one chosen for reinforcement, candy or a token of some kind is found in the well. Otherwise, of course, it is unbaited. This procedure has been used extensively by Zeaman and House (1963) to study discrimination in retarded children. A table with a one-way screen, separating E from S, is furnished with a sliding tray for stimulus presentation. The tray is pulled out of sight behind the screen for baiting one of the food cups. Stimulus objects mounted over the food cups may be junk objects, or objects chosen so as to vary only along controlled stimulus dimensions (see Fig. 15–5).

Studies of retardates with mental ages between four and six years demonstrated that the number and kind of stimulus variables affected the rate of acquisition of the discrimination. Junk objects differing in many dimensions, such as pot lids and soap dishes, were discriminated in a median of 25 trials. Objects which differed in only two dimensions, color and form, were more difficult and training took about twice as long as with the junk objects. Objects which differed in only one dimension, form (e.g., triangle vs. circle) required a median of 100 trials, although the subjects had by this time considerable experience with the setup. Two objects differing only in color (e.g., red vs. green square) were extremely difficult; only 5 of 20 subjects learned the problem after 250 trials. A pattern-color-form discrimination was also difficult. This problem was like the color-form object discrimination, except that the three-dimensional objects were presented as two-dimensional flat portrayals (e.g., a painted red triangle vs. yellow cross). Only 8 out of 20 subjects learned the problem in the allotted 250 trials.

These experiments show that it is not merely attaching reinforcement to a response that matters in discrimination learning—the stamping-in of a single S-R link. Nor does the subject literally learn to see the difference between, say, red and green whereas he could not see it before. It is rather

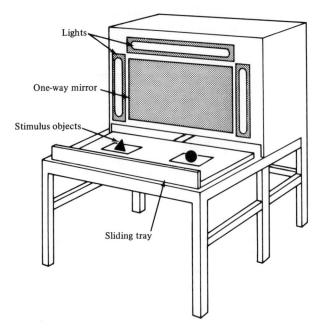

Lights

One-way mirror

Stimulus objects

Sliding tray

FIGURE 15–5. **Discrimination learning apparatus modified from Wisconsin General Test apparatus for use with children.**

(From D. Zeaman & B. J. House, The role of attention in retardate discrimination learning, from *The Handbook of Mental Deficiency,* edited by N. R. Ellis. Copyright © 1963 by McGraw-Hill, Inc. Used by permission of McGraw-Hill Book Company.)

a matter of learning to attend selectively to the relevant variables. When the stimulus objects differ in multiple ways, like the junk objects, there seems to be no problem, but when the difference is a matter of one variable to be isolated from all the properties of the object, difficulty is vastly increased. Zeaman and House plotted backward learning curves for the various problems, and found that the final portions of the curves rise very fast—almost vertically—to asymptote and are alike, no matter what the problem. It is the length of a prior stage, hovering near chance performance, that varies. Thus, attaching the response to the right cue is a trivial matter; it is discovering the critical differentiating feature that accounts for differences in difficulty between the problems. Because varying difficulty from problem to problem is not due to the association of a response, but rather to the relative difficulty of isolating a distinguishing feature of the stimulus objects, we can learn from this method something about pickup of distinctive features in children (in this case, retarded children), and the relative priority of features in children's perceptual exploration of the environment.

What properties of the world are perceived can be studied eventually with judgmental responses elicited by verbal instruction. We cannot expect perfect correlation between the results of verbal judgments and the foregoing methods for at least two reasons: first, the way the question is asked differs; and second, as more specific indicator responses become available, the organism is maturing and gradually changing.

An experiment by House (1964) shows some differences obtained by assessing psychophysical functions with oddity tests (using the Wisconsin General Test Apparatus) and with a verbal method. The oddity problem typically presents simultaneously three different stimulus objects, two exactly alike, except for position, and one different. The odd object is always correct. It may vary from the other two in value along one or more dimensions of difference. If a habit of choosing the odd (different) object is developed, not only can there be transfer to new values on the experienced dimensions of difference but there can also be transfer to new dimensions. House studied discrimination of visual size in retarded subjects who had already formed well-established oddity habits. The seven subjects ranged in MA from 44 to 60 months. In the Wisconsin General Test Apparatus, they were presented with three circles, two of identical diameter, and one different. There were ten sizes of circle. During a daily session, a standard circle was paired with the other nine circles in random order, sometimes as the odd member, sometimes as one of the two identical circles. Testing continued for twenty days, after which verbal tests were given the same subjects. Two of the circles used in the oddity experiment were presented side by side and the subject was asked by the experimenter to indicate which was bigger. The verbal trials also continued for twenty days.

When results for the two methods were compared, wide differences were revealed between the two functions for individual subjects. Two subjects, who had by no means performed perfectly with the oddity technique, discriminated all the differences presented without error when questioned. On the other hand, one subject performed better with oddity tests. One subject would not, or could not, perform under questioning at all. Four subjects (who did not start at 100 percent correct) improved from 74 percent correct on the first five days to 90 percent on the last five, despite the fact that they had apparently reached asymptote on the oddity problem before questioning began. The inference is plain that performance in a discrimination task depends on the method.

Judgmental Methods

With a caution in mind from the experiment just described, we can consider the value of the standard psychophysical methods of studying discrimination for developmental research. The methods depend on instructions. "Tell me whether it is the same or different," "Is it larger or smaller," and so on, are obviously the most efficient ways of getting useful data from verbal subjects, and as soon as children have a reasonable command of language, the experimenter thankfully proceeds to use them. Thankfully because they are more efficient; and also because developmental studies are only truly comparative when a common method can be used for all the subjects. But do the instructions in such an experiment have a common meaning for subjects of different ages? Words like "same" or "different" may not be equivalent at all ages, even after apparent verbal fluency has been attained (Cronin, 1967).

In Piaget's laboratory many developmental studies of perception have been conducted with subjects ranging from five years to adulthood with judgmental psychophysical methods (summarized in Piaget, 1961). A large proportion of these studies deals with illusions, many with size constancy, and others with dimensional properties of objects and line drawings such as size, angle, or distance.

It is easy to demonstrate that developmental psychophysical studies are fraught with problems and pitfalls. Lambercier (1946) has contributed a number of methodological studies of size constancy which will serve as an example of judgmental procedures combined with age comparisons. The same basic apparatus and display conditions were used in most of Piaget's and Lambercier's size constancy experiments, while methods of presentation, instructions, type of judgment, and age of the subjects were varied. The subject sat at the end of a long gray-surfaced table, with a homogeneous gray screen as background at the other end. Screens at the sides filled the rest of the field of view. The subject generally looked through a window or a slit, though this condition too might be varied. The objects to be compared for size were thin wire rods of variable height.

Lambercier found that many experimental variables affected a child's judgment of height of the rod. Among these conditions were 1) single comparison vs. comparison with a series of stimuli; 2) arrangement and scale level of the series (a central tendency may occur); 3) placing the standard nearer than the comparison object or placing it farther; 4) different types of stimulus objects (meaningful-meaningless, flat-solid, textured-untextured, etc.); 5) distance of the objects from one another and from the subject; 6) the background (size, nature of the visible surfaces, such as texture, whether objects are positioned on a ground surface, or whether they are seen in air against a vertical background, presence or absence of other objects); 7) the lateral and vertical displacement of the objects; 8) the subject's height of regard; 9) the method of comparison (distance can be constant and size varied or size can be constant and distance varied); 10) the subject's attitude (whether he is trying to match real, apparent, or projective size); 11) instructions; 12) repetition and practice; 13) treatment of results; and 14) the psychophysical method chosen. No wonder constancy experiments with children seem to present so many conflicting results! It is not only age that varies in developmental studies, but many other factors which may interact with age and confound the results.

Let us consider in some detail one of Lambercier's experiments which brings out the dependence of results on methodological differences. He compared a method of successive single presentation of the series of objects to be matched to the standard with two methods of simultaneous multiple presentation of a comparison series in order to determine the effect of the constitution of the series on size constancy. The standard object (a thin wire rod) was 10 cm. high and was placed a meter away from the subject. The variable rod (or rods) were four meters away and were from 3.5 to 21 cm. high, increasing in steps of 0.5 cm. In the method of single comparison, the variable rods were presented successively, one at a time, either in a regular order or by the concentric clinical method. The latter is a method favored in Piaget's laboratory for getting quick threshold determinations with children. The experimenter attempts to zero in on the child's match by alternating variables on either side of the true value, presenting extreme variables first and working in toward the limen.

One method of multiple presentation (fixed serial) presented an ordered comparison series of variable rods simultaneously (as many as 3, 7, 15, or 31 at once). The median height of this comparison set varied from trial to trial. The set was immobile for any one judgment. The subject chose the rod which seemed to him equal to the standard. The other method of multiple presentation (mobile serial) involved moving the comparison series progressively so as to expose a portion of the rods in a window before the subject until the whole series had been viewed. The fraction exposed in the window at any moment included 3, 7, or 15 rods. The subject judged when the middle rod of an exposed set matched the standard.

The results for single comparison and mobile serial comparison were similar and showed a small decrease in constant error with age (combined means were 11.6 cm. for the youngest age group and 10.3 cm. for adults). The precision of judgments increased markedly from the youngest children to the adults. That is, intrasubject variability of judgments decreased. The results for fixed serial comparisons were quite different. The precision was greatly increased, compared to the other techniques, for all ages. But the constant error for any series shifted with the level of the series revealing a central tendency effect. If the middle of the series was 10 cm., the same as the standard, perfect constancy resulted, but if the middle of the series was 8 cm., the mean judgment was lowered; if it was 12 cm., the mean judgment was raised accordingly. In other words, what is sometimes called over- or underconstancy occurred if the middle of the series of variables presented was under or over the standard. Lambercier felt that the absence of evidence for the increase of constancy with age found by certain experimenters might be explained by their use of a fixed series of comparison stimuli having a middle stimulus that was equal to the standard. The children were more susceptible than the adults to the central tendency effect. Figure 15–6 from Lambercier shows the wide variation in precision, depending on the method. Note the apparent precision with a fixed series of variables for comparison, especially series III 15, where the middle of the comparison series coincided in size with the standard. Note also the difference in variability (width of threshold) with age.

It would seem that one can (with Lambercier's setup) choose a series of variables of such composition, and presented by such a method, as to obtain almost any desired degree of constancy for any age group. But an experiment by Tanaka (1967) comparing a serial method with a method of single presentation did not find a central tendency effect, even with seven-year-old children. His experiment was performed outdoors. The objects to be judged were stakes from 20 to 170 cm. in height. Separation between the objects in the comparison series, size of the step in difference between them, the surface on which they were grounded (grass), and viewing conditions were all different from Lambercier's and yielded good objective matches, uninfluenced by the composition of the comparison series. The degree of size constancy was high for children as well as adults. Interaction of experimental variables with method is again apparent in determining developmental results.

Another methodological variable responsible for apparent over- or underconstancy is the location of the standard. Piaget and Lambercier (1943) investigated its effect for size constancy, with a method of adjustment rather than a constant method. In one condition the standard rod was placed 1 meter from the subject and the variable (raised and lowered until the subject judged it to be equal) at 4 meters. In another condition the positions of standard and variable were reversed. The measure of apparent constancy under these two conditions was different because of what Piaget terms the "'error of the standard." The standard tends to be overestimated; thus, if it is placed close at hand, the variable, farther away, will be made greater than the standard's 10 cm. and apparent underconstancy results. If the standard is farther away, the overestimation of it produces a trend toward overconstancy.

The problems produced by instructions in judgmental experiments with children are excellently illustrated by two experiments of Piaget and Lambercier (1951, 1956) comparing real size matches with projective ones at different age levels. They held the hypothesis that objective, real size matches were the result of learning to correct the projected size of an image on the retina. Since the learning would go on, presumably, with development, they thought younger children would make more accurate projective size matches than adults, who would have developed strong

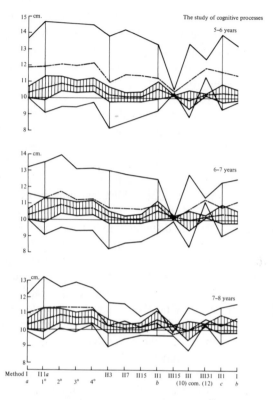

FIGURE 15–6. A comparison of three methods of measuring constancy.

The graphs show the upper and lower limits of the threshold (top and bottom line in each graph) and the median (dotted line) for three age groups (5 to 6 years, 6 to 7 years, and 7 to 8 years) and for adults (the crosshatched section in the center of the graph). The different methods of comparison are indicated below the horizontal axis in order of presentation. A key to the notation of methods follows:

I a. Single comparison, concentric clinical method.

II 1a. Single comparison, in regular order; 1st, 2nd, 3rd, and 4th indicate four successive repetitions.

II 3, II 7, and II 15. Mobile serial comparison; the arabic numbers indicate the number of elements presented simultaneously in a series.

II 1b. A repetition of II 1a.

III Fixed serial comparison: III 15 represents the result for a series of 15 elements, with its middle at 10 cm. (equal to the standard); III com. represents the overall (combined) result of all the fixed series; III 31 represents the result for a series of 31 elements, with its middle at 12 cm.

II 1c. A repetition of II 1a.

I b. A repetition of I a.

(From M. Lambercier, Recherche sur le développement des perceptions: VI. La constance des grandeurs en comparaisons sériales. *Archives de Psychologie Genève*, 1946, *31*, 195.)

habits of correcting the image for distance. But how to explain to a young child what a projective match is? It is hard enough to explain to an art student or a student in a psychology class. First they got real size matches from a group of subjects from six years of age up. This is comparatively easy, using their standard setup as described above (though one still wonders what the six year old is doing when told to choose the one that looks the same; that he is not always doing the same thing is suggested by the enormous variability). To get projective size matches required elaborate instruction, with examples and practice. The experimenter first taught S to make a perspective drawing of two lines at different distances. Then he questioned him to see if he understood the drawing. If he did not, he looked through a window behind which cartoon figures were placed at different distances. Behind the window were displayed two figures of the same height at different distances, and then two of such height that they projected on the window at the same level when one was farther away. Grids were used on the window and in front of the apparatus itself to have S indicate the projections of the cartoon figures and of the standard and variable which he chose during corrected practice. The youngest subjects able to perform this task were seven years old, and a number of this group had to be eliminated for inability to understand the instructions. The most striking fact about these results was the extraordinary inaccuracy of the projective matches at all age levels.

Judgmental methods are possible with verbal youngsters, then, but developmental comparisons are liable to ambiguity due to differences in comprehension of instructions. Modification of procedures to suit children is often necessary, but it can create problems of its own. Ingenuity in putting questions about what is perceived, at different age levels, is still an urgent need.

SUMMARY

A brief survey of ways of finding out what is perceived by the infant and young child has been presented. The reason for this is that the facts, to be considered in the next chapters, are not always entirely trustworthy because of methodological weaknesses. A decade ago, no one believed that a neonate discriminated such properties of form as edges and corners. And yet we now appear to have evidence that he does. Until recently, far more ingenuity was spent in devising methods of studying discrimination in animals than in children, but that is changing. Our problem now is going to be how to organize the information we have, how to proceed from cross-sectional studies of different ages to an understanding of the process of development, and how to ask the right questions about it. Some of the old questions that inspired quantities of research now seem wrong, such as "does the child see wholes or parts?" (It depends, among other things, on the task he is given.) Questions, as well as methods can be valid or invalid. I shall devote my last five chapters to answering the question of what information the child takes from the world of stimulation, and how this changes with development.

The Development of Perception
in the Individual:
Perceiving Objects

The next four chapters will consider the perceptual development of the human child. Following the classification of what is to be perceived in Chapter 1, we shall consider the perception of objects, of space, of events, the kind of perception arising from representations, and finally the kind of perception arising from symbols, that is, from the coded sources of stimulation produced by human beings. Perhaps the most direct of these types of perception is the observer's awareness of environmental objects, the concern of the present chapter.

There is always an interaction between potential stimulation and the exploratory activity, the searching and orienting responses, of the perceiving organism. The suggestion has often been made that young infants are stimulus bound, that is, are more dependent on outside events than on internal purposes. Relative to the human adult, there may be some truth in this statement, because exploratory strategy and the ability to ignore irrelevant information improves with age, as we shall see. There is some indication that early in life certain kinds of stimulation compel the attention of the infant, fix it so to speak, on something in its surroundings. Consider now what objects have been observed to have this effect, and how the perception of objects develops.

PRIMITIVE VISUAL ATTENTION TO CERTAIN PROPERTIES OF OBJECTS

The story of the development of object perception begins with evidence of automatic orienting to certain objects or their properties and goes on to evidence of more skillfully directed types of exploratory activity, such as tracking, systematic search, and scanning. Objects, I have been arguing, are distinguished by their bundles of features. The set of distinctive features that make any object or class of objects unique must be discovered in the course of exposure to other objects. But it appears that some features of objects command attention in the newborn infant in a rather compelling way.

The most primitive visual orientation is literally more of a fixation than an exploration. Pavlov's "orienting reflex" has been described as "unconditioned-reflex involuntary attention (Milerian, 1959)" and something like this happens in the human neonate. The infant orients to a feature of a display and tends to hold the orientation until habituation ensues or until the scene changes. Stechler (1965) refers to this behavior as "obligatory attention." It is best exemplified by relative suppression of other activity and pointing the eyes toward a visual target. Stechler presented black and white drawings of stylized faces and geometric forms and also presented living human faces to babies from about six days of age to three weeks. He studied their looking behavior as they grew older (see Fig. 16–1). Around the ninth or tenth day of age, attention to all objects was nearly 100 percent, he reported, and looking would continue for as much as 35 minutes on occasion. At a later age, however, when the infants looked away from the object the behavior began to have a "deliberate, volitional appearance." Immediate orientation to a new stimulus, with an increase in level of arousal, also appeared at this time. Stechler remarked that arousal with "pleasurable excitation" was more likely to occur to a live face than to a schematic face, or to a geometrical form. For some babies the arousal did not seem to be pleasurable, but nevertheless was strongly elicited by human forms, particularly real faces, even when they were unmoving.

The persistence and fixity of early orienting responses has also been noted by Ames and Silfen (1965) who found different patterns of looking in younger as compared with older babies. Their babies were older than Stechler's (seven weeks to 24 weeks), but the age difference showed the same trend. The younger infant, compared to the older, was more apt to hold his fixation on a single item for a long time, taking fewer but longer looks, and shifting his gaze (when he did) back to the same item. They found the same trend for moving as for stationary displays, but the difference was especially apparent when movement was present. They commented, "It appears to us that while the older infant may be capturing stimuli with his visual behavior, the young infant is being captured *by* the stimuli (p. 6)." The displays used by Ames and Silfen were checkerboard designs on canvas, either moving behind a window or stationary. It is possible that shifts of attention and voluntary sampling of the environment begin earlier for solid objects such as human faces than for flat forms if it be the case that some property of the former compels looking very early.

The notion of fixation dominance by stimulus features appears also in Piaget's theory of what he calls "centration." "Decentration" is an ability which, according to Piaget, only develops with age. Centration is

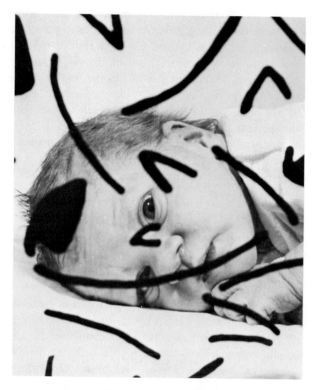

FIGURE 16–1. Four-day-old infant looking at line segments drawn on a sheet of transparent material.

(From G. Stechler, S. Bradford, & L. Levy, Attention in the newborn: Effect on motility and skin potential. *Science, 151,* 1246–1248, 11 March 1966. Copyright 1966 by the American Association for the Advancement of Science.)

a kind of compulsory fixing of attention upon some aspect of a stimulus display; it is thought to result frequently in distortion of perception, for example, overestimation in geometrical illusions (Piaget, 1961). Decrease of distortion with consequent correction of the illusion comes with age as the compensatory perceptual activity of decentration develops. Other forms of corrective perceptual activity are also thought by Piaget to develop with age, such as transport—a kind of visual comparison of one feature of a stimulus display with another. The point to be noted is the primitive tendency to center on a single striking feature of an object with rigidity of focusing instead of exploration.

Yet we know that mobility of the eyes begins very early. Visual pursuit of an object moving from left to right or right to left occurs soon after birth (Wolff & White, 1965). By one month, an object at the periphery of the field of vision elicits an orienting movement that brings its image to the fovea. A smooth tracking response of the eye in pursuit of a moving object develops somewhat later (White, Castle, & Held, 1964). It is interesting to note that exploration of the environment by the human infant begins with visual exploration; he first reaches out to the world with his eyes and the acts of reaching and manual grasping develop much later. The act of visual pursuit has been said to be a prolonging of contact with a selected portion of the environment (Wolff & White, 1965). It is notable that Piaget considers the pursuit movement of the eye to be essential for development of the concept of object permanence, that is, the realization that an object continues to exist when its retinal sensation ceases because the object has gone out of sight.

DISTINCTIVE FEATURES AND STRUCTURE

Primitive fixation followed by progressively more freely directed exploration, then, is characteristic of the growth of object perception. As exploratory eye movements develop so also can repertories of distinctive features differentiate, for contrasts between objects can be discovered only with such shifts of fixation between objects. Their distinctive features are relational. Eventually, what I have called higher order structures may also come to be perceived because of the development of exploratory movements. Is there some sort of progression from perceiving subordinate features to larger configurations?

One of the few developmental experiments dealing with real objects was done by Leuba (1940). Nursery school children 1½ to 5½ years old were shown an arrangement of small round pillboxes. The child was given a piece of candy to eat and shown how to open a pillbox. Then he watched the experimenter arrange the boxes in a pattern (circle, square, or triangle) and place a piece of chocolate in one of them. The child was told he could have the candy if he could find the right box without touching any of the others. The child's attention was diverted for a minute before he was allowed to choose. When the correct box was part of a pattern, the children had more trouble finding it than when it was placed just outside the pattern. But within the configuration, success was much greater when the correct box was at the end of a line or at the corner of a square or triangle. Distinctive features of the arrangement thus seemed to make a difference, while there was still evidence for perception of the arrangement as a unit. Yet, the experiment tells us little about perception of features and structure characterizing a unitary object.

There are several questions to be considered. Does an infant segregate figure from ground at birth? What is this figure? Is it a single property or feature of an object? Is it an object as a unitary thing? Is a vague figure of an object visually segregated, with only primitive differentiation of a feature or two? Are the distinctive features discovered over time and assembled as bundles so that given objects become unique? Are they merely bundles or collections at first and structured wholes later?

That some differentiation of figure from ground occurs in neonatal visual perception is obvious, since visual orienting would otherwise be impossible. In the work of Salapatek and Kessen (1965), Fantz (1961), Hershenson (1964), Stechler (1965), and others, we have seen that it happens. This work does not tell us to what extent the stimulus object is differentiated perceptually, nor whether an object is perceived as a whole. The indication is, however, that individual areas are singled out for attention, such as high contrast edges, vertices, spots, and moving parts. These early attention getters should not, in my opinion, be considered distinctive features. They are comparable to the display features that facilitate imprinting in young birds, as has often been suggested (Gray, 1958; Salzen, 1963). Distinctive features develop later out of these properties as contrasts are discovered and the specificity of discrimination is thereby increased (see Chapter 14). *Gestalten* or higher order structural units, I think, develop still later, as bundles of features are processed with greater simultaneity and relations between features are registered as units of structure.

In the chapter on imprinting the "law of heterogeneous summation (Seitz, 1942)" was discussed and experiments on the issue were reported. Some ethologists have held that, at least for animals low in the phylogenetic scale, the whole is literally equal to the sum of its parts. If a complex releasing stimulus is fragmented, the total number of responses released by these parts presented in isolation is said to be the same as the number released by the whole. Klopfer (1962), in reviewing the evidence on this principle, concluded that there is a shift in phylogeny (and perhaps in development) from responding to parts in isolation toward responding to a *Gestalt*. A recent experiment by Bower (1966) sought to discover whether such a shift occurs in the development of human infants.

The subjects of Bower's experiment were human infants aged 8 to 20 weeks. They were trained to make a leftward head movement as an operant conditioned response (see Chapter 15). On a translucent screen before the infant was projected a circular disc. Drawn within the disc was a cross and two black circles. This display served as the conditioned stimulus. After training with the complete display, generalization tests were carried out with the three parts in isolation (disc, cross, and circles), and the whole display was retested also. From 8 through 16 weeks, the strength of response to the individual parts when summed was equal to the strength of response to the whole. But at 20 weeks, the strength of response to the whole was far greater than the sum of response to the parts.

The circular disc was the most effective part when displayed in isolation as compared with the internal parts. But the internal parts progressed increasingly toward equal effectiveness with the disc, and had about caught up when the whole emerged as superior. The younger infants may have been responding to a cross, or a disc, or circles on any given trial, but not to all simultaneously, so no relation was perceived between the whole and the parts. Older infants could take them all in at once and discriminate the whole from a part.

The question of whether children perceive parts or wholes depends on what units are being considered, for there are subordinate and super-ordinate units in any display. It depends also on the amount of information in the display. If it cannot be taken in as a whole, what parts are perceived must depend on what features can be differentiated from the whole. The answer, also, will depend on whether we are really talking about the whole as a superordinate structure in which nothing is lost, or instead some large feature such as contour. Children's tendency to give more whole responses to Rorschach plates (Hemmendinger, 1953; Ames et al., 1953), for instance, may be contour related and is surely not a response to all the information in the picture. Many details get lost and go unnoticed, as they do in embedded figures. Some properties, such as contour, may have priority and thus leave other information unperceived and ineffective.

Ricciuti (1963) attempted to investigate this question by asking children for similarity judgments when the things to be judged differed in either contour (form) or some detail. The items to be judged were drawings of geometrical forms, such as squares and circles, with dots, protruding ears, bites out of the contour, etc., as details which could be alike or different. The children (three to eight years old) were shown a standard drawing and asked to choose from a group of four others the one "most like it." At all age levels, the children most often chose the form which was similar in contour rather than in a detail. Ricciuti thought this result was due to the simplicity and familiarity of the forms. The children were perfectly able to perceive the details, as second choices made clear, but the contour was given priority for classification as similar.

What features of objects stand out so as to cause them to be perceived as members of a set is an important question and one of educational significance if there should be a developmental trend. That contour has priority under some conditions was established in Ricciuti's experiments, but they were not made with solid objects or even pictures of solid objects. The only kind of natural object that has been widely used as a source of visual stimulation in perceptual studies with very young children is the human face. Let us see whether the questions raised so far—what distinctive features are attended to in the course of development, and whether a whole or merely an assemblage of features is perceived at an early stage—get an answer in these studies.

Development of Perception of the Human Face

Both of these questions have been studied in a number of experiments using the human face, or various features, or representations of it. An adult face in his field of view is a highly significant part of the infant's natural environment. These experiments therefore have considerable ecological validity. Furthermore, the face presents a complete and complex array of stimulus properties, including brightness contrast, shading, contour, shape, color, texture, motion, transformation, features in the literal sense of the term, the pattern of features, and even the motions of these features that constitute the facial expressions. The evidence will show that there is a developmental progression in the sensitivity of the infant to such properties of visual stimulation. Development seems to proceed from simple contours to differentiated features to structured relations or patterns to unique patterns of individual faces, and finally to higher order properties invariant over different individual faces.

Early studies of the smiling response in infants and of the approximations to a real human face that were adequate to release it suggested that the following properties were important: an oval frontal display was more effective than a profile view; a nodding motion was superior to no motion (Spitz & Wolf, 1946); and the presence of eyes was better than the absence of eyes (Kaila, 1932). But a multitude of recent experiments have been performed and the results are complicated and difficult to understand. In the effort to make them intelligible, I have summarized them in Table 16–1. Taken together, these experiments extend over an age period of about eight months. Fixation and smiling are the most frequent indicator responses. Differences in method from one study to another are great. The distance of the display from the infant's eyes, for instance, differs in different studies, and often is not reported. Sometimes the subjects are home-reared children and sometimes they are children reared in an institution, and this is a very important difference as regards the opportunity to become familiar with faces. The ages given for the children cannot be considered to be exact. Nevertheless, when the findings are compared at grossly separated age levels, some general trends emerge.

The table is divided into four sections, from the youngest to the oldest age groups. The first column states the nature of the stimulus display presented, the second gives the response indicator used and the degree of differentiation demonstrated, and the third column cites the author. The experiments include only those where no vocal or auditory stimuli accompanied the visual display. What is examined is the effectiveness of the various visual stimulus properties presented in eliciting a response of the infant.

TABLE 16-1

Studies of the Development of Effectiveness of the Human Face as a Stimulus Object

Nature of Stimulus Display	Nature of Response Indicator and Extent of Differentiation	Author
BIRTH TO ONE MONTH		
Cutout oval schematic face; scrambled oval schematic face	Neonates fixate both displays more than ovals of less complex pattern	Fantz (1963)
Cutout round schematic face	Neonates fixate more than bull's-eye, newsprint, homogeneous circle	Fantz (1963)
Real face, still and moving; drawn schematic and scrambled faces; geometric forms	Neonates show more arousal (EEG, heartrate, skin potential) and more attentive (fixation) behavior to real live face, even when motionless	Stechler (1965)
Realistic photo of face; distorted and scrambled versions	Neonates showed no consistent fixation preference	Hershenson (1965)
Real face	At 3½ weeks infant fixates eyes (eye-to-eye contact)	Wolff (1963)
Schematic oval drawing of face; checkerboard	Infants 2 weeks through 1 month fixated checkerboard more than face	Thomas (1965)
ONE TO TWO MONTHS		
Nodding face (real)	At 4 to 5 weeks, elicits smiling	Wolff (1963)
Eye-to-eye contact (real face)	5 weeks or so, elicits smiling	
Simple contrast and changes in brightness (lamps, light from window, oscillating human face, white cardboard with black sectors, oscillated)	At 7 to 8 weeks, brightness contrasts elicited smiling, face not preferred over nonhuman displays	Salzen (1963)
Dot arrangements, angles, on oval cutout; realistic drawn face; crossbar on oval cutout. Oval contour vs. round (with dots)	At 6 weeks, dot patterns most effective in eliciting smile; face becomes increasingly effective. Contour unimportant	Ahrens (1954)
Real face, unsmiling, immobile (presented at distance of 4 feet)	Smile appears circa 6 to 10 weeks (depending on home or institutional environment)	Ambrose (1961)

TWO TO FOUR MONTHS

Solid contoured model of head	Fixation preference for solid over flat cutout (2 mo.)	Fantz (1965)
Schematic drawings of regular face vs. scrambled face; eye pattern alone vs. off-center spots	More infants fixate regular in preference to scrambled; eye pattern in preference to off-center spots (3 mo.)	Fantz (1965)
Eye section of face realistically drawn on cutout face contour; dots for eyes; face cutout without eyes	Smiling is released effectively by eye section (with brows, etc.); realistic portrayal unnecessary, schematic suffices, but by 3 mo., realistic more effective; with increasing age, single features such as eyes begin to lose effectiveness; parts appear to be increasingly related by eye movements from feature to feature	Ahrens (1954)
Schematic portrayal; realistic portrayal; real face	All effective at 3–4 mo. but real face best, realistic portrayal next	Ahrens (1954)
Smiling vs. crying expression; smiling vs. indifferent (both pictures and real face)	Up to 5 mo., not differentiated by smiling response of infant	Ahrens (1954)
Presence or absence of mouth in pictured smiling face, full contour; face cut off above mouth, so contour changed	Up to 5 mo., absence of mouth indifferent, smiling response reliably occurs as long as contours unmutilated, but cutoff face produces turning away	Ahrens (1954)
Photographic vs. schematic representation of face; regular vs. scrambled feature arrangement	At 4 mo., longer fixation and more smiling to regular than to scrambled version. No difference between schematic representation and photo	Kagan et al. (1966)
3 dimensional, sculptured faces (regular, scrambled, no eyes, and blank)	At 4 mo., fixation and vocalization equal for regular and scrambled; presence of eyes elicited longer fixation than no eyes; longer fixation and smiling to eyeless face than to blank; more smiles to regular than to scrambled	Kagan et al. (1966)
Realistic photo of face, photo of cyclopean face, line drawing of face, scrambled line drawing	At 3 mo., both photos are equal in eliciting fixation and vocalization, and are preferred over line drawings; but realistic photo elicits more smiling	Lewis (1965)
3 different orientations of real and schematic (drawn) face, upright, 90° rotation, 180° rotation	From 8 to 14 weeks, role of orientation increases; at 8 weeks, no difference; at 14 weeks upright orientation elicits most smiling	Watson (1965)

　　　　　　　　　　　　　　　　　　　　　　Perceptual Learning

Nature of Stimulus Display	Nature of Response Indicator and Extent of Differentiation	Author
	TWO TO FOUR MONTHS (CONT'D)	
Life-size colored photo of face, with nodding motion, vs. real face, nodding	Beginning at 2 mo. 20 days to 3 mo. smiling occurs sooner, longer, and more strongly to real face; before this, photo equally effective	Polak, Emde, and Spitz (1964)
Approaching vs. receding face	At 3 mo., approaching face elicits preferential smiling	Polak, Emde, and Spitz (1964)
	FOUR TO SEVEN MONTHS	
Two different nonsmiling human faces (experimenter vs. mother figure)	Habituation of smiling response, decline beginning about 20 weeks, suggests discrimination between the two faces; later, with institutionalized infants	Ambrose (1961, 1963)
Real face, moving mouth (widening, pursing, or opening and closing)	By 5th mo., moving mouth is regarded, by 6th mo. is smiled at strongly; wide-drawn mouth has greatest salience; mouth-widening rather than real smile is important	Ahrens (1954)
Angry, wrinkled brows; painted and stylized eyes	From 5th mo. on, have negative effect; infant turns away, rather than smile	Ahrens (1954)
Drawn face of adult (realistic features and expression)	At 5 to 6 mo., infant quickly looks away from it or glance wanders between experimenter and picture, as if questioning	Ahrens (1954)
Plastic models of laughing and crying child's head compared with same faces, drawn (2 dimensional)	Plastic models only slightly better in releasing more than ephemeral affective reactions	Ahrens (1954)
To test animation, a live 4-mo.-old happy infant held over bed of another, so eyes could contact	Between 5 and 7 mo., the live baby is sometimes smiled at, arm reached out to touch him; life-likeness important, but does not suffice alone. Dummy faces with moving part (finger stuck through mouth) may still release smile, attention. Face schema requires no one single critical feature	Ahrens (1954)
Motionless drawing of face and plastic head of smiling child	From 5 to 7 mo. both equally ineffective in releasing affective response when compared to face of the experimenter; real face can be altered only slightly, by 5 mo., without reducing	Ahrens (1954)

FOUR TO SEVEN MONTHS (CONT'D)

Stimulus	Findings	Investigator
Motion of dummy faces	positive affective response. Total contour plays a role, but this Gestalt is not individualized. Yet an adult face is differentiated (by smiling response) from dummies and from another infant Increases effectiveness of dummies for releasing smile, especially if slow, rhythmical to-and-fro motion, but still not as effective as any real adult	Ahrens (1954)
Photographs of male face, female face, bull's-eye, checkerboard, nursing bottle, and panda bear	Faces at 6 mo. elicited most sustained attention (fixation and motor quieting); female face elicited more vocalization than male, suggesting a differentiation	Kagan and Lewis (1965)
Photos of face, cyclopean face, line drawing of face, scrambled line drawing	At 6 mo., fixation preference for regular photo over cyclopean; line drawings of regular face preferred over scrambled. Most smiling to regular photo	Lewis (1965)
3 different orientations of real or schematic face; upright, 90° rotation, 180° rotation	After 15 weeks, role of orientation wanes; face equally effective for fixation or smiling in all 3 orientations	Watson (1965)

Consider the studies reported in the first section of the table, from birth to one month. Neonates only two to six days old pay attention to a face or a face-like display, that is, fixate it or show an increase in arousal (Fantz, Stechler). What aspects of the displays were attracting attention, however, is by no means clear. A schematic face (Fantz) is fixated more than a less complex pattern. A real face yields more arousal than other displays (Stechler), but it differs from them in a great many dimensions of stimulation such as color and brightness and solidity and the shininess of the eyes. Hershenson found no fixation preference for a realistic photograph over a distorted picture and Thomas found that a checkerboard pattern was fixated more than a schematic face. Wolff reported that three-week infants fixated the eyes in a real face. What can we infer from such evidence? Only that there is information in the light from a human face, from a face-like display, and from other nonface-like displays that even a neonate attends to. What this information is we do not know. The emerging importance of the eyes at 3½ weeks, however, suggests the beginning of what might be called feature differentiation. Eyes are not only shiny but move independently of the face as a whole and this may explain why they are so effective in attracting primitive attention.

In the next section of the table, ages one to two months, we find that nodding and so-called eye-to-eye contact with a real face (being looked at) elicits a smile (Wolff). What stimulus coming from the eyes is the effective one? And are the eyes by now differentiated as a feature of the face? Probably not yet, for Salzen reported that smiling can be elicited at 7 to 8 weeks by almost any changes in brightness, including a moving human face to be sure, but also by flickering lamps, an oscillating cardboard disc with black sectors, and so on. Ahrens compared a number of dot arrangements, angles, and a rectangular bar drawn on a cardboard cutout with a realistically portrayed face and found that the dot patterns were in fact the most effective in eliciting a smile (see Fig. 16–2). The contour (oval vs. round) when the two black dots were present was not important.

After the age of two months there are indications that real facial features begin to be differentiated, starting with the eyes. Fantz (1966) found that an eye-pattern arrangement of dots is fixated more than an off-center arrangement, and a regular schematic drawing of a face more than a scrambled one. In the latter case, it may have been only the eye section, in its correct location, that mattered. This may also be the case for Watson's (1965) finding that at about three months a face presented in an upright orientation is smiled at more than one rotated 90° or 180°. The work of Ahrens especially supports the emergence of the eyes as a feature between two and three months. By three months, he found realistically portrayed eyes more effective than schematically drawn ones. The eyes remain a dominant feature in eliciting the smile for a rather long period (see Fig. 16–3), even when presented with an empty under-face. A mutilated face (cut off

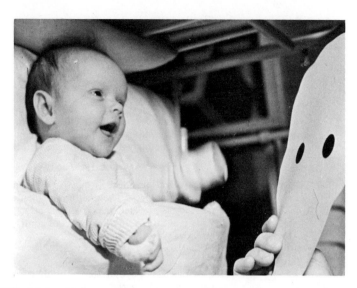

FIGURE 16–2.   Baby smiling at a pair of black dots on an oval cut from cardboard.

(From R. Ahrens, *Beiträge zur Entwicklung des Physiognomie—und Mimikerkennes*, 1954, p. 421.)

below the eyes) is noticed, however, and produces turning away. The mouth begins to be more important and differentiated as a feature around five months. Motion of the mouth increases attention to it. As the mouth is noticed more, a widely drawn mouth becomes progressively more effective.

Work by others (Kagan, 1965; Lewis, 1965; Kagan et al., 1965) with various response indicators provides evidence that by four months realistically portrayed sculptured faces are differentiated from scrambled portrayals or weird (e.g., cyclopean or eyeless) faces. But it is not unambiguously clear whether three-dimensional portrayals have priority over two-dimensional ones, or realistic representations (photographs) over scrambled ones. There are some indications that a real, live face gets more attention and elicits more smiles than a dummy, at least by five months, but a dummy still elicits smiling, especially if motion is included in the display. Pollak, Emde, and Spitz (1964) reported that latency and duration of smiling differentiated responses to a real face and to a life-size colored photograph at about three months. They interpret this difference as indicating the "first ability of the infant to perceive depth." But note the assumption here that the infant has depthless visual sensations just like the sensations aroused by a colored photograph and continues to have them

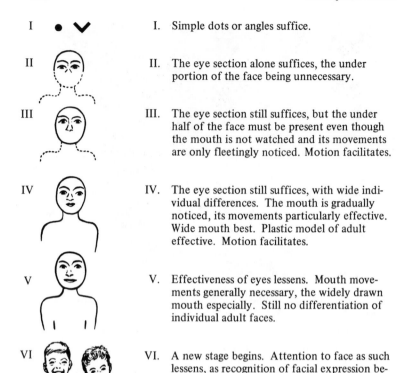

I. Simple dots or angles suffice.

II. The eye section alone suffices, the under portion of the face being unnecessary.

III. The eye section still suffices, but the under half of the face must be present even though the mouth is not watched and its movements are only fleetingly noticed. Motion facilitates.

IV. The eye section still suffices, with wide individual differences. The mouth is gradually noticed, its movements particularly effective. Wide mouth best. Plastic model of adult effective. Motion facilitates.

V. Effectiveness of eyes lessens. Mouth movements generally necessary, the widely drawn mouth especially. Still no differentiation of individual adult faces.

VI. A new stage begins. Attention to face as such lessens, as recognition of facial expression begins, and interest in other children. Progressive differentiation of individual faces.

FIGURE 16–3. **A developmental chart of stimulus conditions sufficient for visual elicitation of smiling.**

(From R. Ahrens, *Zeitschrift für experimentelle und angewandte Psychologie,* 1954, p. 445.)

until depth is added to the sensations by learning or maturation. This assumption, however traditional, is contrary to the evidence.

Sifting through all the evidence and taking into account the differences in indicator responses in different studies, it would seem possible to speculate that by five months several features of the human face have been perceptually differentiated: its plastic, solid surfaces; the eyes as features; the eyes in a characteristic orientation; the mouth as a feature; an oval head shape. But individual faces are not yet differentiated, nor are expressions (smiling vs. crying). Motion enhances attention, but until five months it is not clear that different kinds of motion are discriminated. Nodding the head is effective, but so are other motions, such as a wagging finger stuck through a dummy's mouth.

After five months, living or animate faces are clearly differentiated from solid dummies even when the latter are moving. Movements of mouth-widening are more effective than mouth-pursing or opening and closing the mouth. An angry brow begins to produce a negative response, and alterations of contour or feature arrangement are noted. At six months a female face is differentiated from a male (Kagan & Lewis, 1965). The uniqueness of individual faces is appreciated some time around six to seven months, showing perception of the structure characterizing a particular face whether it be still or moving or presented in one or another orientation. Persons, that is to say, are recognized. The perception of a smile considered as an abstract transformation that is invariant over any number of faces may begin with attention to the peculiar motion of the widely drawn mouth, but the differentiation of this motion from alternative motions is probably difficult and continues to develop for years.

After eight months, Ahrens found that differentiation of faces had become greatly refined and specified. No smile appeared in the infant without an expression on the face displayed to him appropriate for the response of a smile; familiar adults were distinguished from strangers; and negative expressions such as frowning were responded to negatively.

The approach to familiar persons and the avoidance of unfamiliar ones, at around eight months, has often been discussed, but seldom seriously studied. It seems to be true that the age of onset of a negative response to strangers varies with the child, beginning earlier in home-reared children with frequent parental contacts (Rheingold, 1961; Ambrose, 1961, 1963). At first, the critical stimulus property is probably not facial expression or highly specific recognition of a pattern of distinctive features but the more obvious presence in the array of any strange accoutrement, such as a hat or a beard. The negative response of infants to strangers has sometimes been compared to the fear or flight response in birds and some mammals following imprinting. There is even said to be an "eight-months anxiety" (Freedman, 1961). But, as we saw in the case of imprinting, there is no convincing reason to assume that the fear response, as such, suddenly matures and is released by some specific object which contrasts with a familiar one. The noticing of a strange face must develop reciprocally with the recognition of a familiar one. Development of behavioral specificity necessarily awaits this perceptual differentiation.

Morgan and Ricciuti (1965) have contributed one of the few empirical studies of the development of negative reactions to strangers in the first year of life. A large number of home-reared infants from four to thirteen months of age were observed in the laboratory in the mother's presence. Reactions to a strange (but smiling) face (and voice) and reactions to two masks were coded and recorded. The infant was either sitting on its mother's lap or in a seat four feet distant from her. The stranger's distance from the infant was also varied. In general, the younger infants in this experiment reacted positively to the stranger, smiling in return. Not until twelve months did infants exhibit more negative than positive responses, but there was an increasing decline in positive responses with age. The greatest frequency of smiling, cooing, and reaching out occurred in the four-months-old group. The drop from four to six months was very slight. The four- and six-month-old infants reacted just as positively to the stranger when they were separated from the mother as when they were on her lap, but the older infants reacted more negatively when separated. The response of the infants to the masks (a realistic woman's face and a distorted face) was positive at all ages. In fact, a number of the infants responded more positively to the masks than they had to the stranger on the last preceding run.

These observations support the conclusion that by six months of age, infants distinguish between a familiar and an unfamiliar smiling face and figure. It is likely that the older infants also perceived the masks as different, both from the familiar person and from the stranger. The fact that older infants who reacted negatively to the stranger sometimes smiled at the masks suggests that they were not only perceived as different, but even as funny.

Exactly what stimulus properties are crucial to these later discriminations can only be guessed at from these observations. Structural properties relating the features in a unique Gestalt or schema would not have to be picked up for many of the earlier differentiations to occur. The term "schema" has been used by Kagan (1965) and by Lewis (1965) to refer to a concept of a correctly structured face, and they believe that development of such a schema underlies differential response to real faces, distorted faces, and pictured faces. It is my thesis, however, that the schema does not underlie discrimination, but rather follows it. Development takes the course of first responding discriminatively with crude compulsory fixation on high contrast edges or spots in the field. Then follows gradual extraction of distinctive features of the oft-presented face object, differentiated as individual features only. Later comes noticing of invariant relations between features such as the two eyes in a given orientation in the head; later still, the array of features characterizing a real face as distinct from a dummy's or from schematic drawings is distinguished, with no one feature any longer dominant. Eventually, the unique feature pattern characterizing a particular face is selectively responded to.[1] This pattern is itself a structural characteristic of the face object, there to be grasped perceptually. A schematic concept of "face in general" would seem to follow, rather than to precede perceptual selectivity.

---

[1] Skill at recognizing different faces continues to develop for many years, even up to eighth grade, when recognition is tested with pictures (Goldstein & Chance, 1964).

FEATURES OR DIMENSIONS?

I have been proposing in the foregoing discussion that development of object perception begins with the discovery of distinctive features, progressing to grasping of higher order structure in the object. But what about dimensional properties of objects, such as color? Does discrimination of sensory dimensions precede feature differentiation? I think that simple feature contrasts are discriminated first, and that dimensions are abstracted much later. Ordering objects in a series by color, brightness, and the like was one of the tasks offered kindergarten children by Maria Montessori. She thought the exercise helped to develop abstraction and categorizing, as indeed it may. That discovery of a relevant dimension is an achievement related to mental development is supported by much experimental literature on discrimination learning, when reversal or other shifts within a dimension are required. Studying discrimination learning in retarded children, Zeaman and House (1963) found that their prolonged learning time was accounted for by difficulty in learning to attend to the relevant dimensional variable, not by attaching a response to the cue (see Chapter 15).

Perceptual development can be observed in discrimination of properties that can be ordered dimensionally, such as color. Color discrimination increases in precision through early childhood, to judge from the small amount of evidence available. Peters (1927) reported lowered differential thresholds with age, especially for saturation. Gilbert (1894) investigated discrimination of saturation by matching in school children between six and seventeen years old. Samples of cloth of different saturations of red were compared with a standard, and the child told to pick all the shades that were exactly like the standard. Younger children selected matches over a much wider range than older ones (9.6 were chosen as exactly alike at six years, but only 3.9 at seventeen). It seems, therefore, that abstraction of a dimension as something continuous and ordered develops with age, and at the same time, precision of discrimination within the dimension increases.

The same developmental trend can be illustrated by other properties of objects, for example, weight. Perception of weight as an abstract dimension is very slow in developing. Ordering weights is a difficult task for children, and weight is not easily separated from size or surface properties. A ball is not characterized for a child by so much weight; it is rather a unique object because of the bundle of features—roundness, bounciness, and so on—which distinguish it as an object.

Ohwaki (1953) investigated weight and size discrimination in young and retarded children. She presented them first with white boxes, exactly the same except for their weight. The majority of children below three years could not discriminate 3 from 15 grams, but 3 from 30 grams they could. Mentally retarded children (M.A. four to eleven and a half years) could arrange five objects, otherwise similar, in order of size. But only a quarter of them could arrange five otherwise similar objects in order of weight. When objects differed in both weight and size, most of these children, although supposedly comparing weight, arranged them in order of size.

The size-weight illusion has typically been found to increase with age, and to be absent or slight in the mentally defective (Jenkin & West, 1958). Why is this? Because size-weight contingencies must be learned? But such a view implies that they were first experienced in isolation, as separate experiences. If weight were completely abstracted from other object properties, one would expect, at the high end of the scale, a decrease in the illusion. Rey (1930) found an increase in the number of subjects showing the illusion from five to nine years, but after nine there was a decrease. A difficulty with almost all the experiments has been the doubt that children (especially defectives) knew what weight was when asked to judge it.

Robinson (1964) set out to study age trends in this illusion, and to relate them to skill in weight discrimination. Children aged two to ten years were subjects, and all were given preliminary training, to the same high criterion, in judging weight differences alone (see Fig. 16–4). Size was held constant and pairs of weights were compared which always differed by 90 grams but varied in absolute level from 15 to 125 grams. The two year olds, not surprisingly, required a mean of 134 training trials to reach criterion, while the five to six years olds required only 41. The younger subjects, therefore, needed much longer training to make discriminations of weight, even with size constant. But when they were tested for the illusion after reaching criterion, there were no age differences in number of subjects showing the illusion. The extent of the illusion, however, decreased with age. Robinson proceeded to train the two-year-old children to make finer discriminations of weight; one group was trained to discriminate a difference of 30 grams, and another a difference of 60 grams. The 30-gram difference was very difficult for these children and up to 320 trials were required before criterion was reached. But when the extent of the illusion was measured after training, it proved to be smaller for the group trained to make the finer discrimination. They were better able to isolate and attend to weight alone.

These findings bear out the statement that weight, as a dimension, is only gradually differentiated. Thresholds for weight discrimination drop as development proceeds, but they can in fact be lowered further with practice even in adults, probably because the average person seldom sets out to judge weight, by feel, in isolation. Training is if anything apt to be the other way round. A grocer asked to cut a pound of cheese estimates by eye rather than by hefting, before wielding the knife. It is not surprising,

FIGURE 16–4. A child putting a weight into a dummy clown's mouth as he learns to discriminate differences in weight.

(From H. B. Robinson, An experimental examination of the size-weight illusion in young children. *Child Development,* 1964, *35,* 96. By permission of The Society for Research in Child Development, Inc.)

therefore, that adults have not outgrown a size-weight illusion. Pure dimensional perception is a rarity in a world of objects bearing many kinds of information. It would seem to reach its asymptote of development only in the laboratory or with training in special skills requiring grading.

TACTUAL EXPLORATION AND DISCRIMINATION OF OBJECTS

Consideration of the weight of an object reminds us that common sense has generally taken for granted that the feel of an object is its most prominent testimony to objectivity. One thinks of Dr. Johnson's argument that the stone was real because he could kick it, that the solid object which can be struck and felt gives the ultimate meaning to visual percepts. That touch is the mother of the senses no longer seems so obvious, however, because we have seen in the new research on looking behavior in infants that the baby reaches out and "touches" things with his eyes long before he can do so with his limbs.

White, Castle, and Held (1964) have made a longitudinal study of visually directed reaching, starting with the very young infant. The normative sequence begins with tracking a moving object with head and eyes at a month to six weeks. An oscillating motion of the object (a brightly colored, fringed paper toy) secured the infant's initial regard and pursuit could then be induced by moving the toy slowly in a semicircular path in front of his eyes. Pursuit at this age consisted of jerky fixations that returned the image of the toy to the foveal area as it made its circuit and fell on the peripheral area.

Between six weeks and two months, they found, tracking begins to be continuous, the response appearing to anticipate the motion of the stimulus rather than lagging behind. By two to two and a half months, the infant begins looking at his own hand, holding it aloft to do so. When the test object is presented, he quickly fixates it and makes a swipe at it with the hand nearest it. The object may be struck, but not grasped, since the fist is closed. Sustained hand regard and swiping continue through three to three and a half months, with the introduction of glances from hand to object. Visual monitoring of the approach of one hand to the other or to an object increases until, between four and four and a half months, the glance follows the hand to the object, glancing back and forth between them. The object may be fumbled at and crudely grasped. At about five months, top level reaching appears, with rapid lifting of one hand out of the visual field to the object, and opening of the hand in anticipation of grasping.

Tactual exploration obviously can begin only after controlled manual contact with the object has been achieved. It is worth nothing that the face as an object has been quite well differentiated by this time, clearly not as a result of tactual exploration. Plastic dummies are already differentiated from two-dimensional representations, as are real heads from photographs. The ancient theory that the solid quality of a visual object is learned only through association with touching once again receives no support.

Development of touching and palpating with the hands and fingers, once visually directed grasping has been attained, is a good example of progress in exploratory skill, of increasing and optimizing the getting of information. Studies of the exploratory behavior of young children attempting to discriminate objects by touch have been made by Piaget and Inhelder (1956) and by a number of Russian psychologists. The trend, as in vision, is from a fixed grasp to orderly exploration. Piaget and Inhelder analyzed haptic perception into several developmental stages. Children were presented with familiar objects and cardboard cutouts of geometrical shapes of varying complexity with their hands behind a screen. Their exploratory hand movements were observed and their ability to identify the object or cutout noted. In an early stage (three and a half to four years) the children could identify familiar objects, although tactile exploration was global and relatively passive. Somewhat later, geometrical plane shapes which differed topologically by properties such as open, closed, and intertwined began to be distinguished and explored tactually. After this came progression to crude differentiation of linear from curvilinear shapes, but no differentiation within these classes, followed by progressive differentiation of shapes according to angles and dimensions, and some tactile search for clues. Finally, from six years on, there was methodical exploration and search for distinctive features with ability to distinguish between complex forms such as star, cross, and rhombus. Page (1959) confirmed these observations and reported that after exploratory handling common objects were the first that could be selected correctly from a visual display, followed by forms differing by topological transformations and, last, Euclidean forms. He also emphasized the development with age of exploratory handling and search for distinguishing features.

Zinchenko (see Pick, 1963; Zaporozhets, 1965) and his coworkers have performed a series of experiments on the development of active touch, looking, and intermodal transfer from one to the other. In a typical experiment children were given cutout geometrical shapes for tactual exploration. A standard shape was to be explored and then matched to one of a group of three shapes by tactual search alone. The task was too difficult for three year olds to perform at all, and was still difficult for seven year olds. Exploratory hand movements were slow and clumsy in the four year olds and did not trace the contour of the figure. In the older children, contour-tracing became expert; one finger often dominated the exploration, while the hand grasped the whole, and salient features were the basis for comparison. Measurement of extents came much later than the detection of salient features.

That the haptic parallel to visual search is very much later in maturing is supported by evidence from older children as well. Lobb (1965) compared vision and active touch in form learning in eighth grade children and found vision vastly superior to touch. A set of four random shapes, cut out of masonite, was presented to the subject one shape at a time, for examination either visually or tactually, and a name was given each shape. After five learning trials, a test trial was given in which the subject had to pick out a designated shape. The test trial might be conducted either tactually or visually. However it was conducted, there was a very significant superiority of visual learning over tactual. Greatest superiority showed up when both learning and test were conducted visually, next when learning was visual, followed by tactual learning with visual test, and last the tactual-tactual condition.

Another experiment, by Zinchenko and Ruzskaya (see Zaporozhets, 1965) provided children of different ages (three to seven) with different means of acquainting themselves with objects (flat wooden figures of irregular forms), and then asked them to recognize them visually by dis-

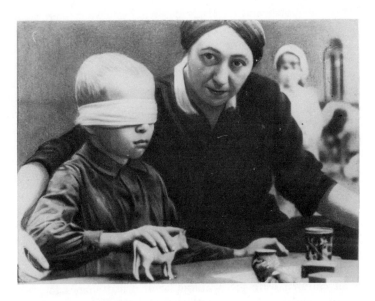

FIGURE 16–5. A blindfolded child feeling a toy animal as he tries to identify it.

(From A. V. Zaporozhets, The Development of perception in the pre-school child, in Paul Henry Mussen [Ed.], *European Research in Cognitive Development,* Monographs of the Society for Research in Child Development, 1965, *30,* No. 100, p. 86.)

tinguishing them from new figures. The four ways of acquainting themselves were: 1) by looking at them only; 2) touching them only; 3) both looking at and touching them; and 4) inserting them into corresponding holes in a form board. Over all the ages, touching only was poorest and the fourth way, fitting the shapes into corresponding holes, best. Fitting the piece undoubtedly calls attention to its distinctive features.

Despite the superiority of vision for shape discrimination, transfer to tactual recognition or vice versa does occur. Once the child's hands are under control, the natural mode of exploring an object would be simultaneous visual and manual examination, the two supplementing one another. From this it is reasonable to expect some amodal invariant properties of objects to emerge—sharpness, jaggedness, curviness, and so on. It is these, I have argued (see Chapter 9) that would carry inter-modal transfer of object recognition. Amodal, invariant properties of objects are relatively more abstract and high order, structurally, than subordinate distinctive features. As higher order structural properties of objects are differentiated either visually or haptically, inter-modal transfer might be expected to increase.

PERCEIVED CONSTANCY OF OBJECTS

Under what optical stimulus transformations and displacements is an object perceived as the same object by a young child? One of the most persistent problems since experimental psychologists began studying perception has been that of the perceived constancy of objects and one of the most persistent controversies has been that over its development. Does it develop? If it does, is the development accounted for by learning? If so, what kind? The literature is voluminous, but many apparent contradictions exist. Animals, even stupid ones like hens, exhibit size constancy; yet, in the opinion of Piaget, it is learned by the human child in the course of development, his perception shifting from retinal matches toward objective ones.

Fortunately, recent years have shown a real breakthrough in techniques for studying perception in infants, and we can dismiss some of the confusion over the constancy issue by pointing to new experimental results with very young babies. These results speak for themselves; babies do exhibit a high degree of object constancy. They do not respond first to the absolute properties of a retinal image such as its size or shape, but appear to respond to invariant features of the object as early as two or three months. On the other hand, it must be said that changes in constancy measurements do occur with age; but these are highly dependent on variations in experimental conditions (Lambercier, 1946, reported in Chapter 15).

Consider first some ingenious experiments that demonstrate constancy in infants. Recall the experiment of Bower (1964), described in the preceding chapter. Bower (1965a) replicated and extended this experiment with infants between forty and sixty days of age. An infant was trained to turn the head when a white paper cube 30 cm. square was presented at a distance of 1 meter from its eyes. Then generalization tests were performed comparing the training condition with a second condition in which the same cube was placed at a distance of 3 meters; a third condition with a 90-cm. cube placed 1 meter away; and a fourth with a 90-cm. cube placed 3 meters away. It will be noted that the size of the visual angle projected by the cube differs in conditions II and III from the training condition. These were differentiated from the training condition by the infants, probability of response falling to nearly half the original level. But one cannot conclude that the babies were responding to isolated size of a retinal projection of the box, because in Condition IV, where retinal projected size was identical with the training condition, differentiation was even more marked, responses falling to about a fifth of the original level. The inference follows that the babies could (and did) detect both a change in spatial position of the object and a change in real, objective size.

Bower included two other conditions in this experiment. A second group of babies went through the same experimental conditions, except that they wore an eye patch to prevent binocular viewing. Essentially the same results followed, so the information for distance is not necessarily given by binocular parallax. Could it be given by perspective cues in the array? Bower's third group was designed to investigate the possibility. The infants were trained and tested monocularly, like group two. But the conditioned stimulus was a projection of the cube on a translucent screen, placed so that visual angles, luminance, and so on were the same as for the other two groups. The same four conditions were duplicated in discrimination tests, except that all were projections on the screen rather than a solid cube at different distances. The results were in contrast with the first experiment. Conditions II and III, in which projected size was not the same as in Condition I, were differentiated from it. But Condition IV, in which projected size was the same, was not differentiated, despite the fact that good pictorial cues were present in the projection to give information for the different distance. The pictorial cues were therefore insufficient to enable these infants to discriminate size at a distance. Bower concluded that the size constancy exhibited in his first experiment depended upon information from motion parallax about changes in distances of an object, since binocular parallax could be eliminated, and since the pictorial cues alone were ineffective at this age.

Bower (1966) studied slant perception and shape constancy in infants fifty to sixty days old. A conditioned operant response was used again as indicator. The discriminated stimulus was a wooden board placed on a turntable and turned at an angle of 45° to the infant's fronto-parallel plane. After conditioning to the board in this orientation, generalization testing was begun with four stimulus conditions: 1) the board (conditioned stimulus) in its original 45° setting; 2) the same board in the fronto-parallel plane; 3) a board in the fronto-parallel plane cut in the form of a trapezoid so that its retinal projection was the same as that of the conditioned stimulus at 45°; and 4) the trapezoid set at an angle of 45° on the turntable. Condition I, the same as training, elicited most responses. Condition II, where objective shape was the same but orientation different, was only slightly lower. Condition III, where projected shape was identical but objective shape different, was significantly lower. Condition IV where both objective shape and projective shape were different elicited fewest responses. The infants therefore were not responding to a projective or retinal shape but to an objective shape which was recognized in a new orientation. In other words, they exhibited shape constancy, ability to detect an invariant shape under rotational transformation in the third dimension. Further experiments of Bower's led to the conclusion that while the infants responded discriminatively to an object in space, it was difficult for them to respond in isolation to change in a single dimensional variable, such as orientation. Infants do not learn to compute real shape from projective shape × orientation, but rather develop toward the differentiation of single variables.

Nevertheless, it has often been urged by previous authorities, Brunswik (1956) for one, that constancy of shape and size are acquired by slow learning of associated variables and thereafter by inference from these. How can the differences be reconciled? Early experiments of Klimpfinger (1933) reported that shape constancy increased between three and fourteen years. This does not necessarily contradict Bower's result, for it might be present at two months and still increase, but differences in method are a more likely explanation of the difference. A judgmental, matching technique such as Klimpfinger used is notoriously suspect with three year olds, since the instructions are hard to get across.

Meneghini and Leibowitz (1966) investigated the effect of age on shape constancy at distances of 3 and 15 feet. The subjects ranged from children of four years to adults. The standard test object was a white circle, cut out of plastic, 1.2 inches in diameter, viewed through a small (2 × 3 in.) window 12 inches in front of it. The circle was tilted at angles of 10, 28, 45, and 90°. The comparison objects were 19 ellipses with axis ratios of .114 to 1.302, also cut from white plastic. They were mounted on the perimeter of a rotating disc which was viewed through a window like the test object. Only one ellipse could be viewed at a time. Rotation of the disc was controlled by the subject as he selected a match for the test object. The subject was told to look at the shape of the test object and then to find a matching shape in the comparison series, which was always 3 feet from him and to his left. When the test object was 3 feet away, the youngest children manifested almost perfect constancy. But as age increased, the tendency toward constancy decreased. When the test object was 15 feet away, the matches were very near a so-called retinal match for all ages. Considering the very small size of the standard and the manner of viewing it, this is not surprising. But why at the near distance, did the older children and adults depart from the perfect constancy of the youngest children?

As several investigators have pointed out (Klimpfinger, 1933; Guignot, Mace, Savigny, & Vurpillot, 1963), the subject's attitude—that is, whether he is trying to make an objective match or a projective match—makes an enormous difference in the results obtained in a constancy experiment, the objective attitude of course being associated with greater constancy. But the projective attitude is a very sophisticated one; it is associated with age and ability to abstract, and with special training, such as the artist's. Adults have been found to be able to adopt one or the other at will (Brault, 1962) and even to shift between the two attitudes (Guignot, et al.), no matter what the instructions. But a five-year-old child would not have attained the level of abstraction required by the projective attitude and would be likely to match on a purely objective basis—the only kind of match he would understand.

Evidence from results with monkeys (Zeigler & Leibowitz, 1958) reinforce this point. Monkeys would hardly be expected to isolate shape from slant, as. a projective match requires, and indeed they do not. They strongly manifest shape constancy. High intelligence might also be expected to be associated with lowered shape constancy (projective matches), if an analytical, abstracting process is involved, and such is the case (Leibowitz, Waskow, Loeffler, & Glaser, 1959). Four groups of subjects were run in an experimental setup similar to that of Meneghini and Leibowitz, described above. They included mental defectives, slow learners from a public school, and average and superior college students. They were asked to choose the ellipse which "looks the most like the disc," an instruction which permits the subject to adopt either attitude, depending on his interpretation and his ability to separate shape and slant as dimensions. The most intelligent subjects tended to produce a projective match. The mental defectives, on the other hand, produced matches closest to shape constancy.

It is thus well established that constancy is the rule for perceived shape of an object in the young, naive organism. But what of size? While Bower found convincing evidence of size constancy in very young infants, the literature is replete with claims of development of size constancy in the direction of greater constancy. How can these claims be understood? Does shift in attitude with age affect size judgments, as well as judgments of shape?

Sifting through and comparing all the experiments would be extraordinarily tedious. Let me therefore summarize what I believe to be the proper interpretation.[2] I think, as is the case with perceived shape, that an object tends to be perceived in its true size very early in development, not because the organism has learned to correct for distance, but because he sees the object as such, not its projected size or its distance abstracted from it. As with projected shape, isolation of either projected size or distance as a dimension is the sophisticated, learned accomplishment. When special objective instructions are given, older subjects overcompensate for the analytical attitude and the actual trend in development of size constancy is not toward veridicality but toward so-called overconstancy (Wohlwill, 1963).

That attitude affects judgments obtained in an experiment on size constancy was demonstrated by Gilinsky (1955). Her subjects were high school students and they were able to assume either the objective or the projective attitude upon instruction. When asked to make a retinal match, the subjects judged fairly close to the projected size of the object (though

---

[2] The reader interested in more detail can consult the summary of the research by Piaget and Lambercier in Piaget's *Les Mécanismes Perceptifs* (1961); also, Gibson and Olum (1960); and Wohlwill (1960).

it was still always overestimated); when asked to make an objective match, they judged the object to be even larger than it actually was. Because most of the experiments on size constancy, especially the ones seeking developmental trends, do not vary the instructions as Gilinsky did but simply give one rather equivocal instruction, such as "choose the one that looks most like it," there is ample range for different interpretations on the part of different subjects, and in fact there could even be an age trend based on changing understanding of the instructions.

Age trends in developmental studies of constancy vary with many methodological variables, as I have already pointed out (Chapter 15). Judgmental studies such as those of Lambercier (1946) and Cohen et al. (1958) with ages from five years up, have typically found a decrease in variability with age, and an increase in the constant error in the direction of overconstancy. Many studies find a slight underconstancy at age five. Wohlwill (1963, p. 277) has averaged together results of Piaget and Lambercier to yield a constant error of −4.1 percent in a five-year-old group, less than 1 percent between six and eight, and as high as 17 percent in adults. What trend, if any, exists between infancy and five years is hard to say, since no one as yet has employed nonjudgmental methods over this age range. Judgmental methods are clearly unsuitable below five years and perhaps then, when one considers the enormous variability of children's judgments.

That cognitive development, in the sense of increased intelligence, is not responsible for development of size constancy (in the sense of accurate objective judgments of size, not of overconstancy), was shown in experiments by Jenkins and Feallock (1960) and by Leibowitz (1961). Jenkin and Feallock compared judgments of size as a function of distance in mentally deficient subjects (mean M.A. of 8.2 years, mean C.A. of 15.10 years) and in normal subjects of three age groups, children (mean C.A. of 8.3), adolescents (mean C.A. of 13.7), and adults. The stimulus objects to be judged were white cardboard squares, the standard 4 inches on a side. Differences for the three age groups of normal subjects were small but significant, the mean size of the matches increasing from 3.80 inches for the children to 4.47 for the adults. The retarded group had a mean match of 4.1 inches, the most accurate of any group. Leibowitz compared defective subjects (mean M.A. of 8.7 years, mean C.A. of 21.3) with college students (C.A. of 21.2 years). Performance of the two groups was accurate and indistinguishable, except at the farthest distance, where the college students tended more toward overconstancy.

To conclude this discussion of the perceived constancy of objects, it would seem that the major developmental change is not the acquisition of constancy, but rather the abstraction of independent dimensions from earlier perceptions of an unanalyzed object. Any changes in the direction of error, for both shape and size, appear to be related to the coming in of a sophisticated analytic attitude that affects the judgmental process in a laboratory setup.

SUMMARY

We have considered in this chapter how the perception of objects develops, beginning with an analysis of the effectiveness of the human face as a stimulus object during the first year of life. The newborn infant attends, visually, to high-contrast spots, edges, and corners within his view; but he does this in a way that has been referred to as obligatory or compulsory. As his attention becomes more exploratory, so does it become more selective, responses such as smiling and vocalizing developing to critical features of objects in the environment. Differentiation of features of the face object begins with the eyes. Then the eyes in a given setting become important; and later the mouth, especially when it is moving. Mouth-widening movements are particularly attractive. A realistic head is discriminated from unrealistic dummies by five months or so. But only after the first half year does the infant discriminate the high-order invariants of unique faces and different facial expressions.

Dimensional properties, as well as higher order structure, are abstracted later than distinctive features of objects. Abstraction of some dimensions, such as weight, or isolation of them from the object, as in the case of size, is a sophisticated achievement. Constancy of the object is primitive; discrimination within separate dimensions is not and it develops slowly. Many of the puzzles that have plagued us with respect to the development of constancy arise from the fact that it probably is not constancy that develops.

Touching and reaching are exploratory, like vision, only developing later. But as systematic exploration of objects with the hands becomes possible, new intermodal invariants can be extracted. As control over body movements increases, space can be explored and objects can be moved around making possible the discovery of invariants. Development of space perception follows closely upon object perception, and will be the subject of the next chapter.

17

The Development of Perception
in the Individual:
Perceiving Space and Events

PERCEIVING SPACE

In the last chapter, we considered the fact that objects are, or come to be, perceived as the same object, despite their translation, rotation, approach toward or recession from the perceiver. They have constancy of size and of shape (as well as other properties) despite transformations in the image they project to the retina caused by change of their position in space. We infer from this relationship of an object to its place in the visible spatial layout that as object constancy develops, so must perceptual differentiation of the space in which the object resides.

Because maintenance of object constancy implies appreciation of the spatial relationships over which the transformations occur, it has often been assumed that the child first learns the dimensions of space, like near, far, up, down; that he conceives some kind of metric for quantifying displacement of an object along the spatial axes; and then, when an object appears, plugs into an equation in his head the size of the retinal image projected by the object and some values for the spatial parameters, thereby correcting the retinal image and achieving constancy. As I argued in the last chapter, this is an outlandish hypothesis, for dimensions of things are not abstracted as dimensions (let alone quantified) until well after object constancy can be demonstrated.

Constancy develops, I think, as the child has the opportunity to watch events. The face appears in the doorway and then looms toward him; after a bit, it recedes. The continuous transformation that the infant witnesses, of this object and of others, provides direct stimulus information for an invariant. The fact that size or shape constancy is tested experimentally with a static object by no means permits the conclusion that it is learned that way.

The object that looms toward the infant or recedes from him is a figure on a background—a spatial background—and as constancy develops it is reasonable that the background should be differentiated too; not in the abstract, or as isolated dimensions, but as the informative features of the spatial layout that, if perceived, will allow accurate seizing, avoiding, and locomotion. What are the informative features of the spatial layout? The surfaces which can be walked on and that things can rest on; the edges that are information for a gap, or an occlusion, or a corner, or a falling-off place; the gradients over surfaces that are information for near or far, whether something can be reached or not; and the multimodal stimulus information for ground and sky. What is the developmental history of the child's responsiveness to these spatial aspects of the world?

The Perception of Surfaces

Does a child distinguish surfaces, respond to them selectively, and perceive them as something which objects (and himself) rest on? This question is a basic one in the development of space perception, although I can answer it with little but anecdote.

The texture of a surface—both how it looks and feels—is appreciated very early. This would be granted by everyone who has ever watched a baby pat surfaces, or cling to a soft blanket. If objective evidence be needed, we can refer to Harlow's studies of the infant monkey who not only felt but saw the difference between a wire mother and a cloth mother at a couple of weeks or earlier. In this case, "wireness" and "clothness" are object properties. What about surfaces of the world that contain the objects? I think a floor, as a surface on which things stand, is perceived as soon as (and probably before) objects are manipulated. I have never seen a baby try to put an object on a wall, or in the air—though I have often seen an infant throw toys out of his crib to the floor with obvious glee. It seemed unmistakable that he knew where they were going to land.

I watched a little girl about 14 months old playing with a new toy—a shoe house which held an old lady and all her many children. The family were of sculptured more or less cylindrical shapes, and varied sizes. When they had all been released from the shoe (by the baby's mother) the child could try to put them back through small doors and windows where they might or might not fit. The little girl tried for some time to put them in, but matching for size and shape was not yet well developed and she gave up. Then she picked them up, one at a time, and stood them with remarkable care on their bases, in a row on the floor. Not one fell over and they were all placed neatly on their bottoms. This performance was a convincing demonstration of appreciation of "floorness"—a surface with a typical relation to gravity.

There have been few developmental studies of surface perception even with older children. One relating the nature of surface texture to perceived distance can be cited. Wohlwill (1960) speculated that the young child needs "a greater variety of cues than the adult to maintain invariance in his perception." He performed an experiment (Wohlwill, 1963) in which he predicted an interaction between age and cue redundancy. Judgments of bisection of distance on a surface extending away from the subject—a "floor"—were obtained from kindergarten, grade school, and high school children. The surface to be bisected could be covered with panels textured in various ways; a blank one, three randomly textured ones with varying densities of elements, and two with more regular arrangements of elements. An object (toy cow) was to be placed at the midway point. Wohlwill expected that the high density, very regular texture would assist the judgments of the younger children toward veridicality. A slight age interaction was found, but it was the two oldest groups, rather than the youngest that were affected by this kind of cue redundancy. The highly regular texture was associated in them with a reduction in error compared to the other conditions. The older age groups were actually less accurate overall than the younger ones (a phenomenon related to overconstancy in Wohlwill's opinion). But it is clear that regularity of texture was of use only to older children, not to younger.

Two points come out of these results. First, that regular arrangements which assist a metric judgment on a specified dimension are not necessary for perceiving a surface and where an object is located on it. And second, that younger children do not require more information, in the sense of cue redundancy; they do not use it.

Depth at an Edge

Studies of human infants in response to a visual cliff were described in Chapter 15, and the point made that an infant is reluctant to crawl on a perfectly safe, heavy glass surface that can be touched and tested, if it does not look safe. If the material directly under the glass is untextured gray masonite, only half the infants will venture forth, despite maternal coaxing. But if it has a checkerboard texture, nearly all will. A surface, to look safe for locomotion, must have a visible texture. The masonite used in Walk's (1966) experiment had some texture, of course, but it was so fine grained that it was probably hard for many infants to detect. Walk found that the age of the infant made a difference in this situation. Of the babies less than 300 days old, 52 percent ventured onto the glass when the gray masonite was 40 inches beneath it. But only 29 percent of the babies over 300 days old did. The older infants with better acuity could presumably detect the depth of the surface and so differentiate between the two sides of the apparatus.

A clearer choice was offered the infants in another experiment of

Walk's (1966). The apparatus was prepared with a gray masonite surface 40 inches below the glass on the other side, and with a textured (checkered) surface directly below the glass on the outside. The baby was placed at one end of the center board and its mother stood at the opposite end of the board. To get to her, the baby could crawl over the shallow, textured side, could straddle the narrow center board, or could crawl over the deep, gray-surfaced side. Ninety percent of the infants crawled over the shallow, textured side, a few straddled, and a very few crawled over the gray side. There was no age difference. Walk also found that avoidance of the deep side, when it was 40 inches below the glass and the visible substratum conspicuously textured, was equivalent for younger and older infants.

Perception of contact with a supporting surface is a very primitive kind of detection for all terrestrial animals. A cat even after neodecortication continues to avoid the deep side of a visual cliff (Meyer, 1963; Meyer et al., 1966). This is a kind of discrimination of depth downward. It is basic in space perception and in at least some animals does not depend on association of visual stimulation from the substratum with successful loco-motion over it. Human infants, of course, have had some opportunity for such association before they are testable on the cliff. It should be noted that there are two kinds of depth at an edge to be perceived; depth down-ward (a falling-off place) and depth forward (as at a corner).

What stimulus information is picked up in discriminating depth at an edge? A jump in the density of optical texture, and a step in the gradient of motion parallax might well be involved. Bower's experiments (see chap-ters 15 and 16), as well as work with the visual cliff, suggest that differ-ential motion parallax is responded to very early. When binocular parallax becomes effective, we do not really know, except that it probably is by two years (Johnson & Beck, 1941). In any case, we can suspect that this kind of stereo vision is redundant in the detection of edge depth. It is not neces-sary (Walk & Dodge, 1962) and may not be used in the young or primitive organism as it is not in animals having no binocular overlap, like the goat. Accommodation (blur cues) is apparently not relevant to cliff perform-ance (Palen, 1965); and pictorial cues may become effective only after depth at an edge has already been shown to be discriminated. So re-dundant information is not a requirement for early effective perception. Motion parallax—shearing at an edge—is probably detected first.

Depth Considered as Solidity of the Object

Does the optical information provided by the motion of the observer's head also give usable differential stimulation about depth of a solid object, its plasticity? There is Bower's (1966) experiment in which slant of a board was discriminated under monocular as well as binocular viewing conditions. There is also evidence (Fantz, 1966) that infants, after two months, show fixation preferences for a sphere over a circle. The preference held with monocular vision as well as binocular. No difference appeared unless the objects were well textured and illuminated from one side, which suggests pickup of shadows. But well-differentiated texture is also a necessary condition for motion parallax, so the latter could have been a critical stimulus difference.

Fantz found that infants under two months fixated a two-dimensional head model more than a solid one, but after two months the solid, sculptured head was preferred. He thought that early preference for the two-dimensional model may have been due to higher reflectance from it than from the solid model with shadows; the change to appreciation of solid molding occurred under monocular as well as binocular viewing conditions.

Studies of depth judgments made by older children and adults of various degrees of curvature of a cylindrical surface behind a window (Smith & Smith, 1966) indicated the importance of binocular parallax in detecting curvature. However, under the conditions of their experiment, even with binocular vision the judgments were quite inaccurate, except for the case of no curvature at all. The subjects were children from five years up and adults, and no consistent effect of age on the accuracy of judgments was found. The inaccuracy of judgments in this task may seem odd in view of the apparently early discrimination of solidity. But the judgment asked for was a difficult one—matching a test curvature to a comparison set of 15 different degrees of curvature after turning the head 90° from the test object—and the measure was the percentage of correct judgments.

Binocular parallax may differ in importance relative to motion parallax depending on the situation. In view of the redundancy of the kinds of information for depth, distance, solidity, edge depth, curvature depth, and corner depth, it would not be surprising if selective dependence on different kinds of information occurred with differences in the situation, with the nature of the judgment called for, and with age. The Smiths (1966) performed a factorial study of depth and distance judgments in a large number of tasks and found evidence of considerable specificity for the different tasks. The tasks varied widely in amount of information presented in the display, in viewing conditions, and in the judgment called for (matching, reproduction, relative judgments, and absolute judgments, both natural and metric). No interesting age dependencies appeared in their study, perhaps because the subjects were all school age or over.

Location of Objects in Space

Localizing objects in space has been thought of by empiricists as an achievement of sensory-motor learning; assuming that the child learns to perceive where each object is by having reached for it or walked to it, and thus associated the stimulation elicited by the object with a specific action in response to it. Carr's theory of space perception was of this type. Piaget (Piaget & Inhelder, 1956) conceives of the development of space perception as depending on the construction of sensory-motor schemata. Space is perceived by the child only in relation to himself and to his own activity. In the earliest stage, space is simply a collection of unrelated schemata, each assembled around an individual sensory-motor activity. It progressively becomes more objective, externalized, continuous, and unitary. For Piaget, it is really a concept of space that is developing, not the perception of the environment. Space expands in the course of development. Near space, reachable space, is cognized first, but as the child's activities push out, so does his phenomenal space enlarge.

For the Russian psychologists, as for Piaget, action in space is essential for development of the perception of space, but the notion of an intellectual construction of a unitary space relating the self and objects is pretty much unique to Piaget. Ananiev (1957), discussing the basis of spatial discrimination, says "space and time are basic forms of the existence of matter, reflected (and not constructed) by the activity of the brain (p. 144)." As with the perception of objects, space perception for the Russian psychologists evolves from activity which copies the world, beginning with orienting activity, which has the character of a "motor-tactual investigation" of the situation (Zaporozhets, 1957). In discussing maze behavior in a child, for instance, Zaporozhets describes the child as initially performing haphazard touching movements, unconnected with one another and not corresponding adequately to the maze. But eventually a system of touching movements is built up which corresponds to the configurations of the maze, one section of the path signaling the next. Just as the maze is mirrored by action, by a system of conditioned reflexes, so also, insofar as a man knows it, is the world.

I think it quite likely that both Piaget and the Russians are right in one respect, in that space becomes better differentiated with practice and with the extension of a child's sphere of activities. But I do not believe that the perception of the continuity of the ground and the adjacency of other surfaces to the ground has to be gradually pieced together. It seems to me that available stimulation for perceiving continuous surfaces—and for the sky, as well—is present from birth on, and that learning consists of differentiating and making more specific areas and locations on the surfaces of the world.

Metric space, in the sense of judgment of a quantity of distance from here to there, either from the observer to a target or from one object to another, is probably learned in connection with activity, and is refined still further when the child learns about conventional units of measurement, which is a symbolic achievement. A small child riding a tricycle for the first time will sometimes try to squeeze his vehicle through an aperture too narrow to admit it, but such errors are soon eliminated.

Does perceived space stretch out with growth and a widening sphere of activity? Gilinsky (1960) in an experiment on five children (five to eleven years old) and two adults, concluded that with increasing age there was an increase in the apparent depth of environmental visual space, and that this was attributable to growth in stature and in interpupillary distance. Harway (1963) conducted an experiment with sixty subjects ranging in age from four years and nine months to thirty years. The experiment took place out-of-doors in a level, grassy field, free of deliberate markers for at least 65 feet. The subjects stood at one end of the field and directed the experimenter to mark off successive one-foot intervals. There was a ruler one foot long at the subject's feet which he was told to consider his unit of measurement. A marker (a yellow pencil) was placed on the ground where the subject directed, and a pointer (a long rod) was then moved to the spot indicated by him as marking off the next one-foot unit. After this distance was measured, the marker was moved further and the judgment was repeated. This was continued for twenty judgments. Judgments were with the standing observer at his normal height, and also either from a platform adjusted to raise the children's height to a uniform five feet six inches, or in the case of adults from a kneeling posture.

The results indicated, on the average, a constant error of underestimation which increased as the marker receded from the subject. This increasing underestimation was significantly smaller for the twelve year olds and for adults than for the younger children. Comparison of the two series made it evident that the smaller constant error was not a function of the difference in height of the subjects. Practice, however, produced an improvement in accuracy of all groups except the adults, an improvement that did not depend on knowledge of results, suggesting that repeated exposure to the task promoted perceptual differentiation.

This experiment is hard to interpret for two reasons. First, the error is steadily compounded with succeeding judgments, for the subject is probably shifting his standard, using the last stretch judged as his unit rather than the ruler at his feet. But more important is the great variability of judgment in the younger children. The most veridical of the 5½-year olds performed better on the first series than all but one of the older subjects. So, just as in the constancy experiments, variable error decreases steadily with age, and more consistently than does constant error (see Chapter 15). And, as in the constancy experiments, it seems that changes in judgmental processes are playing an important but poorly understood role. Though it may sound plausible that the phenomenal dimensions of space should increase in scale with increased perceptual differentiation, it is not clear that this happens except as some complex judgmental process develops.

Perception of Direction

I have been emphasizing the importance of surfaces in the spaces between and under things. Even for the young infant, a surface below the level of support is differentiated from a surface at its feet. The up-down dimension of space is not only fundamental because it is rooted in gravity; it is also specified visually by the horizon, by the difference in the optic array between sky and ground. Up and down is implicit in the perception of surfaces, and of the top and bottom of an object, as in the case of the child who can stand small objects upright on the floor. It may be a related fact that a child can copy accurately a linear pattern of objects in a row such as blocks much earlier when the blocks are vertically rather than horizontally arranged (Huttenlocher, 1966). Distinguishing what is up and what is down is a primitive accomplishment.

The other axis in space, right and left on the horizontal plane, notoriously results in more confusions than does up and down. The right-left symmetry of the body and the lack of the equivalent of gravitational force pulling in one direction obviously has something to do with this. Nevertheless, the horizontal axis of visual space provides a better anchor than do lines inclined diagonally between the vertical and horizontal; it coincides with the horizon, as the word implies, and bears an invariant relation to upright posture.

Most of the developmental research with children on discrimination of direction has, unfortunately I think, been performed with lines drawn on paper, and may not be at all representative of discrimination in the actual environment. I will take up this point in the next chapter in discussing perception of representations and symbols. Meanwhile, two examples which investigated children's relative attention to tops and bottoms of drawings can be cited. In an experiment by Kerpelman and Pollack (1964), children from three and a half through seven years were asked to discriminate five irregular black pentagons from one another by a matching-to-sample procedure. The children's errors and successes were analyzed on seven stimulus dimensions, and high and low confusions for each figure were related to differences in these dimensions. The results led to the conclusion that four- and five-year-old children discriminated mainly on the basis of differences in the bottoms of the forms. In the older children, top-to-bottom scanning appeared to play a progressively greater role, as others have suggested (Ghent, 1963). It seems likely that this change comes in as the child is taught to read. The saliency of the bottom for the younger children was clear, though generality of the finding cannot be inferred from the experiment.

Discrimination of the direction of lines was studied in children by Rudel and Teuber (1963), using vertical, horizontal, or oblique lines, and U shapes with the opening in varied orientations. The figures were made of plastic strips ¹⁄₁₆ inch thick, pasted on Plexiglas plaques. The task was discrimination learning, with two figures presented simultaneously, one right and the other wrong. The children went through four pairs of discriminanda: 1) vertical vs. horizontal, 2) two diagonals, 3) two U's open top vs. bottom; and 4) two U's open R vs. L (see Fig. 17–1). Discrimina-

FIGURE 17–1. Pairs of figures presented to children for discrimination tests.

(From R. G. Rudel & H. L. Teuber, Discrimination of direction of line in children. *Journal of Comparative and Physiological Psychology,* 1963, *56,* 893.)

tion was quite easy for all the children (3½ to 8½ years old) for 1 and 3, with hardly any failures. Discrimination of right-left oriented U figures was difficult, and hardly any children younger than 6½ managed to discriminate the two diagonals. Children, it would seem, are like the octopus (Sutherland, 1957) in finding the two diagonals difficult to discriminate, while a vertical and a horizontal line are easily distinguished. However, if the child's task is detection (find the one diagonal in an array that is oriented the same way as a standard) instead of learning to identify, four-year-old children can perform quite well (Over & Over, 1967). Up from down was more easily distinguished than right from left (the U figure). However, horizontal U figures are easier to discriminate when they are not presented as a mirror-image reflection of one another, but one above the other, as Huttenlocher (1967) and Sekuler and Rosenblith (1964) have shown.

The reference axes of up-down and right-left, the frame of reference of vertical and horizontal, are characteristic of both the environment and the stimulus array of light to the eyes of the observer. The saliency of the invariant position of the horizon in the visual array and of the up-down axis which is contingent with upright posture has often led psychologists to ask whether postural space and visual space were progressively coordinated through experience or whether a primordial unity was progressively analyzed and differentiated. Developmental data on the relationship between the postural and the visual vertical were collected by Witkin et al. (1954). Their method, essentially, was to put the two kinds of reference axis in conflict, as regards the normal invariant relationship, and to test whether one or the other axis dominated judgments of orientation.

Two such tests were given to children ranging in age from eight through seventeen and to adults. One, called the tilting-room–tilting-chair test, required the subject to adjust his own body position to upright. The subject sat in a tiltable chair inside a specially constructed room which could itself be tilted. Room and chair were initially tilted to the same side and then to opposite sides, as the subject tried to adjust his position. In another, the chair and room were tilted and the subject attempted to set the room upright. (See Fig. 17–2.) In both tests, error (measured as deviation from the true gravitational upright) decreased from age eight to age seventeen, though even at seventeen (and a bit more in adults), there was some tendency to be influenced by the tilted visual framework, shifted from its usual correspondence with gravity. To respond correctly, the subject had to disregard the erroneous visual directional axes of the room and discriminate on the basis of gravitational stimulation in isolation. (This is not always an adaptive criterion, if one considers the task of flying a plane, where the visual vertical is the correct one.)

The other task was called the rod-and-frame test. The subject was placed in a darkened room, facing a luminous frame which surrounded a movable luminous rod. With the frame tilted at various angles, the subject was required to bring the movable rod to an upright position, in line with the gravitational pull on his body. This meant isolating the rod from its tilted background and relying on gravitational cues. In this test, as in the others, the degree of error in setting the rod away from the gravitational vertical in the direction of the visual vertical decreased progressively with age, though there was a slight rise again for adults over 17 years olds.

Witkin et al. describe the subject who is free of error in these tasks as "field-independent," meaning that he has the ability to differentiate himself from the environment. I think it might better be described as ability to differentiate gravitational cues—vestibular, kinaesthetic, and skin pressure—from visual-directional stimulation, a highly analytical performance, as the subjects testified. It is also a highly artificial discrimination, for the two kinds of information do not normally conflict.

An experiment by Liebert and Rudel (1959) found similar results with subjects who were tilted in a chair to the right or left and asked to judge the auditory midline of a sound moved in an arc around the head. The subjects ranged from five to seventeen years old. Error of estimating the upright body position, as such, decreased with age. But there was increasing displacement of the estimated auditory midline toward the side opposite the body's tilt. Thus, the more accurately the tilt was felt, the more

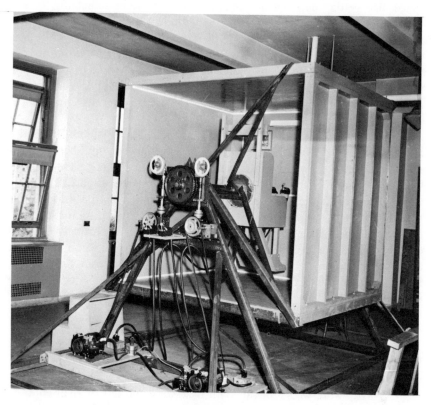

FIGURE 17–2.   Tilting-room–tilting-chair test.

    The subject sits in a chair which can be tilted from the upright, surrounded by a lighted "room" bordered with white stripes so as to provide horizontal and vertical lines. The chair, the room, or both can be tilted to the same or opposite sides. The subject is required to set himself upright in the chair despite conflicting visual information from the room. (From H. A. Witkin, H. B. Lewis, M. Hertzman, K. Machover, P. B. Meissner, & S. Wapner, *Personality Through Perception,* New York: Harper, 1954, p. 28.)

it was compensated for. With isolation of gravitational cues, overcorrection for tilt (analogous to overconstancy) developed.

Multimodal Invariants

    In Chapter 10, I described a number of experiments in which spatial information from one sensory input was put in conflict with that from another, and made the argument that perceptual monitoring of behavior in space, like getting up from a reclining posture to seize something, or setting a picture straight, is generally correspondent with, and dependent on multimodal invariant stimulation. The visual directional axes and their correlation with gravity are a good example. Breaking up the normal invariant relation and producing conflict, so that one source of stimulation must be relied on and the other ignored, causes perceptual conflict and demands recalibration, learning of a new invariant relation of multimodal stimulus information.

Recorrelation with reversed visual feedback was studied by Smith and Greene (1963) in a visual-motor task. The subjects, boys between 9½ and 13½ years, drew dots in a matrix, wrote letters, and drew triangles while watching their performance through a television display. The view was 1) normal, 2) reversed right-to-left, 3) inverted up-down, or 4) inverted both right-left and up-down. Children under twelve years generally failed to reorient their responses so that they appeared normally oriented on the screen. There appeared to be an abrupt developmental change at about twelve years, boys over that age learning to perform successfully. Smith and Greene concluded that there was a "critical period" for development of this type of space-organized compensatory behavior, maturation rather than learning being responsible for the change.

Does learning occur if opportunities for practice are given in tasks where the usual intermodal or sensory-motor relations are tampered with? Pick and Hay (1966) performed a developmental study of adaptation to prismatic visual displacement. The subjects (eight, twelve, and sixteen years of age) wore wedge prisms with bases oriented left or right so as to displace the apparent location of objects laterally. After fifteen minutes of activity while wearing the prisms, all the subjects manifested adaptation to an approximately equal degree. It is interesting to consider why there were no age differences in this task, whereas there have been in other studies. In the task used by Witkin et al., the subject had to isolate gravitational cues from visual cues and disregard the visual ones.[1] Disregarding irrelevant information is very definitely age-related, as we know from anecdote ("children are most distractible") and also from experiments which will be reported in a later chapter. In prismatic spectacle-wearing, the subject has to learn a new visual-kinaesthetic invariant for monitoring movements in space, such as touching together the index fingers of the two hands, walking around the world, and avoiding obstacles. Successful performance requires not so much disregard of one channel as recalibration of the intermodal monitoring system.

Visual-haptic monitoring of behavior in space commonly involves information from a number of input channels—the visual, vestibular,

[1] Other developmental studies of experimentally induced intersensory conflict requiring suppression of visual information have found similar results (see Pick, Pick, & Klein, 1967).

muscle, and joint senses. Multimodal invariants of a high order are consequently required for skillfully directed action. Monitoring action by attending to one channel and suppressing another, as these experiments with displacement of the visual array so often require in early stages of compensation, means isolation of part of a normally interlocking perceptual system and this is not easy, as any subject will report. The integration of originally separate systems is not the way of development; it seems more likely that the systems did not originate as independent single channels; and that independence is a learned achievement rather than interdependence.

PERCEIVING EVENTS

An event happens over time, and generally speaking over space as well. An event is unified or integrated over time by some invariant stimulus property which gives it continuity, be it long or short. When an event involves an object moving in space, that object must have constancy and permanence. It must be the same object, or we could not perceive an event. A ball rolling across the floor is a simple example of an event. The ball, if it is rolling toward us, projects to the eyes a retinal image ever changing in size, but size constancy holds and we do not see a series of balls of different sizes, nor do we see the ball as growing in size. It is the same ball, changing its position in space. If the ball has a picture on one side of it but not on the other, the picture will be occluded during the roll when it is not on the momentarily leading hemisphere, but we do not see a different ball each time it completes a revolution and the picture returns. It has what Piaget terms "object permanence."

Object permanence and perception of an event are reciprocal phenomena. One quite literally implies the other. If the ball rolls behind a chair, is temporarily occluded, and then rolls out again, we do not see it as a different ball and a new event. But if we did see it as a different ball, we should also perceive a new event. A fragmentary succession of unrelated happenings is not the way we perceive the world; the retinal image may be transitory and ever changing (in constant motion, actually, as we move about) and yet we see a world containing permanent objects. The water poured from the pitcher into a glass appears to be the same water while it is being poured, and water being poured is a unified event.

Does an infant have to learn to integrate over time to perceive an event? Does it perhaps detect only very short happenings at first and gradually develop so as to take in longer event sequences? We know too little about perception of dynamic aspects of the world (especially how it develops), but these are interesting questions. Perhaps the infant detects some invariants over time from the outset.

Motion and Velocity

It is a long while since any psychologist held the belief that perception of motion involves an act of integrating successive still pictures over time and space. In fact, no one believes that one must learn to perceive motion. And yet it is rather commonly believed that the persistence of an object and hence the unity of an event must be learned. Fortunately, we do know a little about perception of motion in infants.

Perception of the human face by infants is greatly influenced by motion, as we saw. Motion attracts fixation, much as it releases following in precocial birds. Furthermore, motion parallax seems to be used effectively as information for depth at a very early age. Differential motion parallax is effective as information, obviously, only over a time span, so there must be pickup of invariance over time in an event-like fashion.

That infants perceive stroboscopic motion without opportunity for learning has recently been demonstrated (Tauber & Koffler, 1966). The experiment took advantage of the fact that an infant reacts innately to a continuously moving striped field with optokinetic nystagmus, that is, by pursuit movements. A stationary cylinder was prepared containing a columnar device flashing stroboscopically so as to simulate rotation of the cylinder without any actual movement of the image across the retina. Of nineteen neonatal subjects, eleven responded positively with sustained optokinetic nystagmus appropriate to the direction of the apparent movement. When the columns were lit but stationary, the nystagmus did not occur, or if it did occur, it was not correlated in direction or speed as it was with the stroboscopic flashing. It appears that continuous (real) optical motion and stroboscopic optical motion give equivalent information.

Perception of stroboscopic motion in older children (five to twelve years old) was studied by Meili and Tobler (1931) and comparison was made with adults. They varied time intervals between projected figures so as to produce percepts that varied from succession to optimal motion and then to simultaneity. A real movement was projected below the stroboscopic movement, in the opposite direction. For a movement response to be scored, the observer had to say that the apparent and real movement looked the same, except for direction. Thresholds were determined at which succession gave way to motion with decreasing time intervals. Stroboscopic motion was seen by children as by adults, and with longer time intervals; that is, children saw motion at some intervals when adults saw succession. Greater integration over time, therefore, did not progress with age, but was more characteristic of the children.

A similar experiment, in the same age range, was performed by Gantenbein (1952). She confirmed the finding that the younger the subject the more easily perception of motion was produced, and that children experienced motion over a larger range in the scale between the extremes of succession and simultaneity than do adults. Thus children develop the ability to perceive discontinuity, not motion; temporal acuity, in other words, improves with age.

In superficial contradiction to these results is an experiment by Carpenter and Carpenter (1958) in which thresholds for perceiving real motion were determined with a moving belt behind a window, using a method of limits. The subjects were two children (81 and 101 months old), two chimpanzees, and adults. A training situation with reward was used with the chimpanzees and children. The thresholds were apparently lowered with maturity. It seems likely that the phenomenon of paying attention was responsible for this trend. The observer's criterion plays a very important role with a method of limits—much more so than in a matching situation of the kind used in the two previous studies.

Discrimination of velocity (speed of movement) was studied in 4½ and 5½ year olds by Fraisse and Vautrey (1952). Velocity is presumably a more difficult or more abstract judgment than simple motion. If a child watches two toy cyclists moving on a track perpendicular to his line of regard at different rates, will he perceive their relative speeds of movement directly, or will he make judgments on the basis of specific events such as passing and time of arrival? Fraisse and Vautrey varied the courses of two such cyclists in a number of ways, so that they could observe the influence of amount of space covered, time of arrival, witnessing or not witnessing arrival at a station point, overtaking, and so on. Passing or preceding during the run were associated with those errors that occurred, but of a group of children aged 4½ to 5½ years, nearly 75 percent generally judged correctly which cyclist was going faster, even when the greater speed did not correspond with passing. It was concluded that there was "direct perception of velocity."

Piaget considers perception of speed to be elementary in the sense that it is not a calculation derived from estimations of space covered in relation to time, but he hypothesizes that there is not absolute perception of speed of movement, only perception of one speed relative to another. Experiments were performed by Piaget, Feller, and McNear (1958) to investigate this hypothesis, using films of two objects, one projected above the other, manipulating relative speeds and passing. Contrast effects were observed with passing (the object passed appeared to slow down and the passer, relatively, to speed up). The observations led to the conclusion that comparison of changing separations between the two mobile objects was crucial to the judgment—i.e., the distance separating them was observed as a variable distance between two points constantly changing position, a perceptual activity of transport being the basic process in the comparison of the distances. Results for children (five to six) were similar to those for adults, but contrast effects were less pronounced in the adults. The main conclusion we can draw from these experiments is that children perceive motion, and discriminate relative speed of motion very well at least as early as four years.

Continuous Optical Magnification or Looming

The experiments just reported pertained to perception of movements of translation across the field. What about the perception of an approaching object? Experiments on the optical stimulus of looming with animals were discussed in Chapter 13. These experiments demonstrated that a variety of animals flinch, duck, or indicate by some appropriate response that continuously accelerating magnification of a shadow on a screen is perceived as rapid approach. In human adults, not only is the event of approach perceived, but time to collision can be accurately judged, so that rate of approach is perceived as well.

The perception of accelerated optical magnification in human infants can be inferred from the time of development of a blink to a visually approaching object. Burton White (1963) studied development of blinking in ten infants from one month through five months of age. The infant lay on its back in a crib, with a circular bull's-eye target, painted in red and white concentric rings, suspended above it. The target was dropped toward the infant's eyes with a range of drop of 2⅝ to 12½ inches. Air currents were controlled by an intervening shield of transparent plastic. The median age of onset of blinking was two months. The maximum target drop was necessary to elicit the response at that age and the blinks were slow and incomplete. By 3½ months, rapid and complete blinks were the rule, and a target drop of 2⅝ inches was sufficient to elicit them. The blinks were accompanied by apparent startle in many cases.

We do not know the mechanism for this development; perhaps there is avoidance conditioning with air pressure as the unconditioned stimulus (though not in the testing situation). The approach movement would have to be detected for conditioning to occur, since the stationary red and white target and the target receding were not effective in eliciting the blink. Thus, magnification and minification are differentiated as events by the time an infant is two months old.

Object Permanence

A still higher order kind of perception that involves invariance over time is what Piaget refers to as object permanence. In Piaget's thinking, there is no perception of an object, a thing with permanence, until a number of properties of the object are combined and until the sensory-motor schemata are coordinated, and even then, intellectual activity is involved in achieving a concept of permanence. This view has been neatly summarized by Tuddenham: "During this period (the first two years) the various sensory spaces, of vision, touch, and the rest, are coordinated into a single space and objects evolve from their separate sensory properties into *things* with multiple properties, permanence, and spatial relationships to other objects (1966, p. 215)."

A concept of permanence would indeed be an intellectual achievement, but invariants over time in a stimulus sequence may provide a basis for the perception of an object's permanence (like the ball rolling behind a chair and out again). Piaget's observations of his own children's behavior when he displaced or hid an object formed the principal basis for his theory of development of object permanence. A toy or some other object was covered or put out of sight and the child was watched for indications of searching for it. If he did not appear to search, he was presumably unaware that it still existed. Bower (1966) questioned whether or not the behavior required of the infant might not have been too complex, and devised a simpler method of observing its response when an object was hidden. The measure used was heart rate, and the infants tested were 20, 40, 80, and 100 days old. At the beginning of a trial, a box placed in the infant's field of view was lighted within and an object displayed. There was a screen at the extreme right of the box which, after 10 seconds, began to move so as to occlude the object. It continued to hide the object for 1.5, 3.0, 7.5, or 15 seconds, and then moved off. In half the trials, the object was again revealed, but in the other half, the object had been removed while the screen was covering it. Bower reasoned that if the infants continued to believe in the existence of the object when it was behind the screen, they should be more startled when the object failed to be revealed than when it was revealed. The evidence of startle would be a change in heart rate.

The results showed that infants of all four age groups were startled by failure of the object to be revealed after the shortest occlusion duration, but only the oldest age group was startled by this failure after all occlusion durations. The youngest group showed a change in heart rate when the object reappeared after the two longer occlusion durations. Bower concluded that there was not a qualitative jump to development of a belief in object permanence, but rather a quantitative shift in memory capacity.

A second experiment was performed to investigate this hypothesis. Four stimulus objects were used—a red sphere, a red cube, a green sphere, and a green cube. Four event sequences could be presented: 1) occlusion followed by failure to be revealed; 2) occlusion followed by the revealing of an object differing in color; 3) occlusion followed by the revealing of an object differing in shape; and 4) occlusion followed by the revealing of an object differing in both color and shape. For example, in event sequence 2, a red sphere might be displayed first in the viewing box; the screen would then glide in to cover it, pause, and move away to reveal a green sphere. The subjects tested with these four sequences were 70, 98, and 126 days old. Bower reasoned that if the development studied was a quantitative change in storage capacity, fewer changes in the occluded object should suffice to elicit startle as age increased.

What happened was as follows. The youngest group tested was not startled by any change of the object, but only by failure of an object to be revealed at all. The intermediate group was startled by a shape plus color change and by change of shape alone, in addition to failure of any object to reappear. The oldest group showed startle to all of the changes. It does not seem to me that these age differences are best explained either as increase in memory capacity or as acquisition of an intellectual concept of object permanence; rather they show progress in specificity of differentiation of event sequences. It is not duration of the event sequence that is making the difference here, but rather the constitution of the event. A big change in the component structure is noted early, a slight change is not.

Later experiments of Bower's (1967) on object permanence (also referred to as "existence constancy") varied other structural properties of the event witnessed by the infants. An operant conditioning technique (interruption of conditioned nonnutritive sucking) rather than heart rate was chosen as indicator response, since Bower thought its interpretation less ambiguous. The conditioned stimulus (a red and white sphere) was occluded by a screen at varying rates and with varying transformations at the margin where contour was being occluded. When the screen occluded the sphere gradually so as to permit edge information (progressive contour transformations) for disappearance, there was evidence of perceived existence constancy in infants as young as 7 weeks. A developmental change noted by Bower was a steady increase in the rate of occlusion necessary to elicit constancy behavior. He speculated that existence constancy as a perceptual phenomenon appears very early, but that conceptual constancy, a "prediction about objects rather than events," comes later.

The reader can convince himself of the fact of perceived object permanence in a five-month-old infant in a very simple way—a game of peek-a-boo. Sudden appearance, disappearance, and reappearance of a human face is viewed with fascination and glee by the infant. Can anyone believe that the object is not believed to exist while it has been temporarily hidden? This sequence is surely perceived as an event, for it is only the succession of appearance, disappearance, and reappearance that brings the response. Infants even learn to play this game themselves at a very early age. Kleeman (1967) has reported such an instance at 22 weeks.

What happens, perceptually, when an object is occluded temporarily and is then revealed? If the occlusion is brief, we can infer that the phenomenal object is not lost by even a young infant, on the basis of Bower's

FIGURE 17–3. Infant playing peek-a-boo.

(From the New York *Times,* March 10, 1968.)

first experiment. A similar experiment of displaying an object moving in a given direction, disappearing behind a screen, and reappearing from behind the other edge of the screen is often referred to as the tunnel phenomenon; it has been investigated principally by Michotte (Michotte et al., 1964), who considers it a case of "amodal perception." The fact is that the object is perceived to exist while it is hidden even though it is not represented during the interval by a specifiable sensory impression. This phenomenon would seem to be an example of event perception—a unified happening over time, with sequential patterning but without moment-to-moment correlation with sensory data. The grasping of longer sequential structures and more complexly embedded ones should increase with age and with evolution.[2] Lashley (1951) called our attention to sequential structure in "The Problem of Serial Order in Behavior." We shall return

---

[2] That animals perceive events over time seems fairly evident from common-sense observations of stalking prey, specific responses to courtship dances, a dog running to catch a flying stick, and so on.

to it in Chapter 19 when we consider development of the perception of language.

Conservation

Closely related to the perception of an event is what Piaget has named and brought to our attention as "conservation." Conservation may apply to an object—i.e., its permanence—and also to the properties of an object, such as mass, quantity, or volume. Transformation of moment-to-moment phenomenal features such as apparent shape or apparent size during the course of an event may prevent conservation of the invariant properties of an object if the event is not perceived as a unitary happening. In my opinion, conservation is invariance over time and over an event sequence; it is analogous to size and shape constancy over simple motions of the object and simple changes of the observer's point of view.

Piaget has taught us to think of conservation as an intellectual achievement, and in its more conceptual modes it surely is. Comprehension of the conservation of matter and energy in the world is an intellectual achievement, but it is not reached by a sudden qualitative jump in development or even education. When a child watches a quantity of water being poured from a rather squat tumbler into a tall narrow beaker he will perceive the column of water as taller than before. If he asserts that there is more water in the beaker than there was in the tumbler he has failed, in Piaget's terminology, to conserve volume. Volume, as a concept, is abstract, and its acquisition comes late. But I should maintain that perceiving the event of the water being poured and perceiving the sameness of the water while it flows through a shape transformation from one vessel to another are fundamental to acquiring the concept of volume, rather than the other way round. Logical and verbal explanation of the physical principle of conservation is possible. But we may suspect that protoscientists had to perceive physical events in many simpler manifestations before the conceptual principle could be stated. It is unfortunate that perception of invariant properties over the transformations of an event sequence has received so little study by developmental psychologists.

Piaget's explanation of the development of conservation is a theory of stages, the child moving from one stage to another. In Stage 1, the child attends to one isolated static property of the display, such as height. In Stage 2, he substitutes a centration on another property, such as width. In Stage 3, he may alternate between the two, bringing them into conjunction, a sort of joint apprehension of both properties without a clear coordination.[3] In Stage 4, attention shifts to the transformations which lead from one state to another, and conservation (and transitivity) are manifest.

[3] See Flavell, pp. 246 ff.

The child may also be intellectually capable of compensation—a multiplying of relations, such as lesser height and greater width.

This is a plausible description. To some extent the young child is aware of prominent features such as height in a static display and this may explain his misperception. He does not automatically and immediately appreciate the invariants over the whole event. Consider an experiment by Frank (cited by Bruner, 1964; Bruner et al., 1966). She filled two standard beakers so that the watching child pronounced them equally filled with water. Then a wider beaker of the same height was introduced and a screen placed before them so that only the tops were visible. Then the experimenter poured the water from one of the filled beakers into the wider one, and the child judged whether the two quantities of water were equal or not, without seeing the beakers, but only the act of pouring. Equality judgments rose from a level of 0 to 50 percent for four year olds, from 20 to 90 percent for five year olds, and from 50 to 100 percent for six year olds. The act of pouring was perceived as a unified event and the water was perceived as the same water. But when the screen was removed and the static display of beakers revealed, the four year olds changed their minds. A new judgment of quantity based on a static display was made. The older children stuck to their judgments—the wide beaker was perceived as containing the same water that had undergone the transformation and thus a longer event span had been attained, with perceived invariance over a complex transformation.

To what extent is this an idea, rather than perception of an event sequence over a triple transformation? Bruner, in commenting on the experiment, says, "It is plain that if a child is to succeed in the conservation task, he must have some internalized verbal formula that shields him from the overpowering appearance of the visual displays . . . (1964, p. 7)." I wonder if this is really true. It is certainly true that a verbal formula or rule is a powerful intellectual tool, reducing uncertainty in a most useful way. But I doubt that teaching the verbal formula without letting the child watch the transformation would be very effective. It is the static appearance that is overpowering. The perception of sameness over change is what is critical and it must be at least coordinate with the successful use of a verbal formula, if not necessary and preliminary to it.

Shifts from no conservation to conservation are seldom accompanied by a coherently stated logical formula, as Flavell (1963, pp. 373 ff.) points out. Wohlwill and Lowe (1962) gave children various kinds of nonverbal experience relevant to conservation of number (e.g., shortening and lengthening of rows containing the same number of objects). They improved on a nonverbal measure of conservation, but not on a traditional verbal one. Exactly what improved in this experiment is hard to state, except the ability to disregard irrelevant transformations, but improvement was surely not due to acquisition of a verbal formula.

Perception of Causality

As perception of invariance over time—sameness despite change—is possible, so also is perception of a real change. Suppose a balloon, for instance, is blown up and bursts, something is obviously perceived as changed. Suppose an object emerges from contact with another object moving at a faster rate than it did before? Is a cause perceived for these changes, or is some intellectual rationalization called upon? Michotte began research in this area, studying the perception of causality, which he believed to be directly perceptible despite its being in a sense amodal, there being no analyzable elementary sensory experience to correspond to it.

An experimental setup of Michotte's for the investigation of perception of causality is shown in Figure 17–4. Two spirals are drawn in the disk, one in black and one in red. The disk is rotated behind a screen with a narrow horizontal slot. As it rotates, the subject sees two small rectangles, one black and one red, moving from left to right. With proper rate and timing of movement, the subject typically sees the black object bump the

FIGURE 17–4. **Michotte apparatus designed to study the perception of causality.**

The rotating disk is pictured on the left. The subject's view is on the right, with the disk behind a screen. When the disk is rotated, he sees two small rectangles, one black and one red, moving from one side to the other. Under certain conditions of rate and rapprochement, an adult observer will perceive one object bumping the other and causing it to move. (From E. J. Gibson & V. Olum, Experimental methods of studying perception in children, Ch. 8, in P. H. Mussen [Ed.], *Handbook of Research Methods in Child Development*. New York: John Wiley & Sons, 1960, p. 323. Permission granted by John Wiley & Sons, Inc.)

red object and set it in motion—i.e., cause it to move. Olum (1956) compared adults and seven-year-old children in this situation. The subjects were simply asked to describe what they saw. The children sometimes gave causal and noncausal responses under the same conditions that elicited these in adults, but they also sometimes reported passing or mutual approach when adults reported causality.

In another experiment, however, Olum (1958) gave the subjects more specific instructions, teaching the children labels for causal and noncausal responses ("shove" and "tag"). Now no passing or mutual approach responses were given and the children gave more causal responses than adults.

Piaget (1961) has argued for an analogy between perception of causality and the perceptual constancies. To quote him:

> Perceptual impressions of causality . . . seem to us to belong in the category of perceptual constancy. Perceptual constancy is identified by three characteristics: conservation of a perceived property despite the transformation of other properties of the object or figure; "phenomenal doubling" permitting simultaneous perception of the invariant properties and those which are transformed; and compensation with respect to inverse transformations of the inconstant properties. These three characteristics are found in the perception of causality. . . .
>
> In the case of perception of causality, what is conserved is not the property of a single object but a property transmitted from a first object (A) to another (B): a movement passing from A to B (pp. 297 ff., my translation).

Compensation, for Piaget, is illustrated in perception of causality by the fact of perceived resistance; his schema for one object striking another goes as follows: 1) There is perceived loss of speed of the agent A, following an impact; 2) there is an impression of a *push* exerted by A; 3) the passive B is perceived as modified by the impact and gains speed; 4) B's gain in speed does not always compensate completely for A's loss; one perceives, therefore, resistance of the passive B. It is perceived as put in motion more or less easily by A.

Piaget attributes perception of causality not to a "simple field effect" but to "complex perceptual activities" of a compensatory, regulatory kind. One reason for this is a difference found by him and Lambercier (1958) in the perception of causality by children and by adults. Children, while they exihibit a wider threshold for the perception of contacts, do not perceive an object as set in motion from a distance, without contact, for instance, by compression or across a gap. Piaget attributed the coincidence of the impression of contact with perception of causality to the growth of visually perceived causality from a tactile-kinaesthetic impression of causality—a sort of intermodal translation of it. It is another case, for him, of integration of schemata of two modalities.

For Michotte, this point of view would be unacceptable, since the perception of causality is amodal, a spatio-temporal organization. An interesting experiment by Piaget and Maroun (1958) attempted to get at intermodal effects in the perception of causality, comparing adults with children. The judgment concerned the localization of impact when the subject pushed a box with a small rake. There was a series of boxes of different weight spaced along a slide or track. Resistance, when the first box was touched, was felt at the end of the rake; but when the first box struck the second, the feeling of impact might be delegated to the extremity of the first box, then to the second when it struck the third, and so on. The experiment was performed with eyes open and with eyes closed. In this study, impressions of the delegation of impact increased with age. For both the children and the adults, delegation of impact was facilitated by performing the task with eyes open. Thus visual perception of causality influences and facilitates tactile-kinaesthetic impressions of causality. This is an interesting intermodal effect, for which Piaget argues a sort of conversion and correspondence of perceived causality between the two modes. But it is equally likely that the perception of causality is not sensory or modality specific and that no activity of conversion or conservation is required. In this experiment, it was again the length of span of the event, with greater differentiation of the agents, that distinguished the perception of adults from children.

SUMMARY

The perception of space and events has been considered in relation to object perception. Objects are located in space and their perceived invariance of size, shape, and other features as they are moved about (or the observer moves) implies discrimination of the spatial layout, of surfaces, edges, drop-offs, and the difference between ground and sky or floor and ceiling. Space perception does not begin as the abstracting of dimensional axes and the learning of a metric for them, as old explanations of constancy often imply; it begins rather as perception of objects relative to surfaces and edges, relative to one another, and relative to the observer. Differentiation of these relations may begin as rather gross, and become refined as the child's exploration of the environment and objects expands with looking, reaching, and locomotion. These activities provide the opportunity for detection of invariant properties of objects, as they undergo perspective transformations in space, and also the opportunity for the detection of the multimodal invariant stimulation which monitors or guides reaching or locomotion toward a target in the spatial layout.

Just as perspective transformations of the light projected from objects exist in a spatial layout, so do continuous perspective transformations occur over time with motion and locomotion. It is important to remember that a temporal flow is implied as well as a spatial layout. Invariants over continuous transformations in time are the basis for perception of an event, a unitary occurrence in time. Perceptual development with regard to events consists in detecting invariants of gradually higher order, over a more diverse set of transformations and a longer time span. Perception of sameness of an object property such as a quantity of fluid, as the fluid is poured from one container to another undergoing continuous nonrigid shape transformations, is such a case. Perception of causality within an event sequence is another.

Perception of sequential information, as Lashley (1951) so eloquently pointed out, is at once the height of human accomplishment and the least understood problem in psychology. Despite our ignorance, I think we can conclude that an invariant property of a sequence, such as a constant object in the case of an event, or a superordinate structure, as in a melody or speech, must be detected for a unitary event to be perceived. The alternative—associative integration of every stimulus sequence that comes to be perceived as a unit—seems hardly possible of accomplishment in an individual lifetime.

18

The Development of Perception in the Individual: Perceiving by Means of Representations

PERCEPTION OF REPRESENTATIONS OF OBJECTS

Is the perceiving of pictured objects learned? Pictures provide for a kind of mediated perception of real things, an indirect way of getting information about objects, the space they are located in, and even events. They are only tracings or pigments on a surface and yet something may be perceived which is more than marks on paper. Pictures can be perceived as surrogates for real objects and scenes. How does this perception of an object via its surrogate come about? It has been claimed not infrequently by anthropologists that people belonging to tribes unacquainted with western pictorial art and photography do not recognize a photograph of a face of a friend or relative for what it is; that they turn the photograph over and over in bewilderment. The inference has been drawn, even by psychologists, that man must therefore learn to see pictures of things as the objects represented. I think it should be clear that this can only be true in two rather special senses. In the first place, if the representation has fidelity to the object or scene which it simulates, then one might well have to learn that it differs, and how it differs, from the reality. The anthropologists' naive subject is probably struck by the incongruity of his perception. The similarity of the optic array to the real face is apparent, but so is the difference—the flatness of the object, the sharp rectangular edges surrounding it, the lack of color, the lack of motion, the absence of the back of the head. No wonder he turns it over with puzzled looks. A western, educated man can be fooled by the *trompe l'oeil* art of the eighteenth century and must often explore to find out how it differs from the reality. In the second place, a different kind of learning may be required when the representation has little fidelity to the simulated scene. Highly stylized or idiosyncratic drawings, or pictures accompanied by a great deal of noise, such as a bad picture on a television screen, might require instruction or practice for apprehension of the intended meaning to occur. But I do not believe that instruction or interpretation or learning are required to see that a representation with high fidelity is similar to the real thing.

Why should this question about pictorial perception be brought up in considering how perception develops? It is necessary, first, because of all the experiments on perceptual development that use pictures and drawings on paper rather than natural scenes and objects. Perhaps there is some special attitude—the pictorial attitude—which the observer adopts when looking at pictures and drawings. If there is, how far can we generalize to perception from results obtained with pictures? It is important, second, because there is a range of variation from highly representational portrayals to portrayals of shapes like geometrical forms, not copied from nature but abstracted from it, and this leads us down the path taken by the evolution of writing and the perceiving of meaning by means of graphic symbols.

In short, there is a profound difference between all kinds of pictures, representative or nonrepresentative, and the objects pictured. Drawings are not things, and their man-made character is usually evident. When it comes to the special kind of drawings that constitute the geometric illusions (the happy hunting ground for experiments in visual perception) the difference is still more profound. Nevertheless, they have in common with pictures the two-dimensional quality of made drawings—a different class of things from actual objects located in a three-dimensional space with floors, gravity, and differential occlusion and transformation as the observer moves.

Objects vs. Pictures in Learning Experiments

It has often been shown that the above difference is of consequence in controlling the behavior of animals and children in learning experiments. Harlow (1945) demonstrated many years ago that monkeys solved discrimination problems with greater facility when the discriminanda were objects instead of figures painted on cards. Stevenson and McBee (1958) compared differences in learning rate with young children when the discriminanda were solid objects (cubes), planometric objects (cardboard cutouts), and patterns (squares) painted on pieces of cardboard. Children of four and six learned to make size discriminations with triads constructed from one of the different materials. Those trained with solid objects performed significantly better than the ones trained with the other two materials. The planometric figures were no more effective overall than the painted patterns. But for the most difficult problem (that with the intermediate size correct), those children who were able to learn were successful with both solid and planometric figures, but not at all with painted patterns.

Why should the solid objects be more effective for learning a size discrimination? Presumably they provided more redundant information, since the children handled them besides looking at them, that is, they picked them up to uncover a reward. One would expect size differences for the cubes in particular to be thereby enhanced. It is also likely that an attentional factor is operating. Remember that Fantz (1966) found fixation preferences in infants for spheres over circles. If a solid shape is selected for visual inspection over a flat counterpart, distinctive features of the object would have a better opportunity of being differentiated.

House and Zeaman (1960) invoked an attention hypothesis for the interpretation of an experiment showing transfer of discrimination from objects to patterns. Retarded children were trained in color-form object discriminations and color-form pattern discriminations. The former were easily learned, but the latter proved very difficult. However, when the easy object discrimination was learned first, the difficult pattern discrimination could be mastered, presumably because attention was now focused on the relevant dimension. The transfer in this case was really to a representation, since the color-form pattern was a flat representation of the objective situation just previously experienced.

Mentally retarded children were again the subjects in an experiment comparing object with picture discrimination by Iscoe and Semler (1964). Objects and pictures of the same objects were employed as stimulus materials in a paired associate learning task. The objects were common articles, and they were paired so as to emphasize or to avoid categorical similarity within the pair, for instance, banana-orange in one case and banana-shoe in another. There was a difference between learning with objects and learning with their pictures, the objects being easier. But there was no interaction between the type of material and retardation. These authors refer to their photographic material as "abstract." But a photograph of high fidelity is not so very abstract. It is important to consider how it really does differ from the thing it portrays. Depth information from binocular and motion parallax is not available, but good fidelity in other respects can be achieved.

In contrast to the above results, an experiment by de Haan and Wischner (1963) found no difference between objects and colored slides of the objects in the formation of learning sets by retarded children. The objects were "laboratory-fabricated three-dimensional objects" varying in multiple dimensions. This is a departure from studies that used familiar articles, and has the effect of making the object and the picture equally strange. The photographs of the objects were color transparencies, projected on a screen.

In this study, why did not the objects favor formation of learning sets over the photographic slides? Is it because the photographs were better and had more cues than those used in the previous study? Dornbush and

Winnick (1966) investigated the role of perspective information in learning to discriminate drawings, and compared the results with discrimination of solid objects. In one experiment, five- and seven-year-old children learned to discriminate between a cube and a parallelopiped, or else between a square and a rectangle. The discrimination between the two solids was learned faster. In another experiment, discrimination between two-dimensional perspective drawings of the cube and the parallelopiped was compared with discrimination between the square and the rectangle. Discrimination of the perspective drawings was faster, and comparable to that for the solids.

Perspective drawings do, therefore, carry some information for children of five and seven. But they are not confused with the real object, even though they may be recognized as similar. Absence of some characteristic information from the solid object (motion parallax, for instance) may lead to a special attitude toward pictures. Consider the performance of a child about six years old who has been handed a piece of paper and asked to draw a picture of a box which sits before him. He sees a flat piece of paper —and a box which is not flat. Typically, a child does not draw something which looks to us much like the box in front of him—he may even, in fact, draw a flattened-out box, as in Figure 18–1. Does this mean that a correct

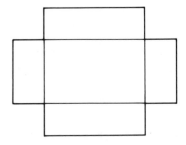

FIGURE 18–1.   Schematic drawing of a flattened-out box.

Children occasionally will draw something which looks more like this than a box seen in perspective. Such a production is indication of the child's development of a pictorial attitude.

drawing of a box in perspective would not be recognized as a box, and that the child must learn to recognize it as such? Not at all—it means that he sees the difference between something in real space and lines on a piece of paper and may adopt an attitude seemingly appropriate to the flatness of the paper—as the flattened-out box in a way is. We shall return to this question.

Recognition and Differentiation of Pictured Objects in Very Young Children

Recall the experiments on babies' responses to human faces, described in Chapter 16. At the earliest ages, the babies responded with apparently equal attention to cardboard cutout displays and real faces, as long as the displays provided certain favored stimulus properties produced by real or simulated eye patterns and certain types of movement. Features, both real and simulated, were gradually differentiated. And, somewhere along the course of this development, the real face began to be differentiated from the simulated one, the process bearing a relationship to the fidelity of a given representation to the real face. When the representation lacked critical properties of the real object—for instance, when it was flat, cut off short, without symmetry, without movement, or had randomly arranged features —evidence of differential response was found by the end of three or four months of life.

I do not mean to imply by this that the human face is perceived differentially and meaningfully at the start, whereas a dummy is not. A real face must be differentiated from nonface objects and recognition is gained with experience as its distinctive features are discovered. It is the possessing of distinctive facial features by the representation that determines its effectiveness as a surrogate for the object, not simply the number of identical elements in common. As we saw in Chapter 6, a caricature can be more effective than a high-quality photograph for both adults and children. It may even have super fidelity because the distinctive features are enhanced and the irrelevant details omitted.

A still picture lacks one of the most salient forms of information that stimulation from the real world provides; that is, the continuous transformations over time that permit detection of invariants over an event. And motion of an object, as we saw, attracts attention in the youngest infant. Motion pictures can provide this information, and one might expect the availability of many developmental studies of children's perception of events and objects moving, or portrayed from a continuously moving camera. But they do not exist. The techniques of Butler and his collaborators (see Chapter 13) developed with monkeys—measuring amount of looking in relation to goodness of focus, for instance—could be used. One somewhat comparable experiment (Wilcox & Clayton, 1968) was performed with five-month-old infants. Their visual fixations of facial displays were measured. Silent, colored motion pictures of a model portraying various facial expressions were used. Amount of movement of the model's facial musculature, as well as expression, was varied. Unpatterned white light was also compared with the pictures. The white light elicited minimal fixation, as compared with any picture, but moving pictures elicited much more looking than pictures low in movement. There was no difference between facial expressions, however.

Common observation tells us that quite young children enjoy not only motion pictures of real people, but cartoon movies as well. Donald Duck and Woody Woodpecker are sure-fire entertainment at a birthday party for four year olds. It appears to the observing adult that it is the events in these films that are so interesting to the child, but no research has been done.

I infer from the available evidence that differentiation of pictured objects is learned at the same time that distinctive features of the real object are learned. That is, the features will also be recognized when they are present in pictures. Is this learning transferred only to realistic copies or to well-drawn cartoons? What about outline drawings or silhouettes, representations of objects which omit features inside the object? Must they be learned as paired associate matches or codings for the real object, as a kind of language?

In an investigation of this question, Hochberg and Brooks (1962) conducted a study for 19 months with a child who learned his vocabulary by reference to solid objects alone and had absolutely no instruction or training as to pictorial meaning. He saw no pictures close at hand and heard no reference to pictured content. He was taught the names of a variety of toys, his relatives, and common objects, all presented only in their natural, solid forms and environment. Tests were made at 19 months by presenting pictures, both photographs and outline drawings, of a number of these objects to the child (see Fig. 18–2). The pictures were handed to the child, one at a time, and his verbal responses were recorded on tape. The tapes were scored (blind) by two judges. The line drawings were shown the child before the photographs. The judges agreed that the child's identification of the line drawings was significantly better than chance. The results appear conclusive that this child was able to recognize both photographs and outline drawings of familiar objects without specific training. Recognizing a picture as a representation of an object is not, therefore, a case of learning a code by simultaneous association of the two, given reasonable fidelity of features or contours.

How is it that outline drawings do not have to be learned as a language is learned? Hochberg (1962) offers the proposition that "if an understanding of outline drawings is learned at all, this must occur not as a separate process but in the normal course of whatever learning may be involved in seeing the edges of objects in the world (p. 32)." Perception of edges is essential for perceiving contour and form. As we saw in Chapter 15, fixation on an edge, corresponding to a luminous discontinuity in the optic array, appears in a compelling fashion in the neonate. Scanning along edges develops later, but the edges of objects or of surfaces seem to be

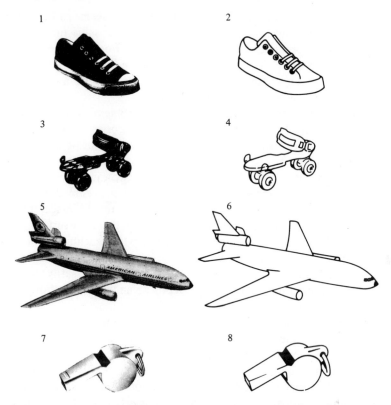

FIGURE 18–2. Photographs and outline drawings like those named correctly by a young child who had no previous experience in associating pictured objects with their names (Hochberg, 1962).

(Redrawn from *Audio-Visual Communication Review*.)

foci for perception from birth on. The evolution of man's retinal and neural structures must be in great part responsible for this. But scanning of edges with the resulting detection of features and structural relations is a developmental contribution—a learning process. According to Hochberg, outline drawings (and silhouettes) are "surrogates for edges," not by a process of association, but by transfer from perception of objects, whether the latter kind of perception be learned or unlearned.

Depth in Pictures

I have been emphasizing the point that perception of distinctive features displayed in a representation is learned in the same way and to the same degree that perception of distinctive features of objects is learned, and that no specific associative process linking them to objects seems to be required. But pictures are flat, and the real world is not. At the same time a picture can give us an impression of depth and solidity. For example, a photograph, properly viewed, can yield fairly accurate judgments of distance stretches and size at a distance (Gibson, 1947), as well as shape constancy (Buytendyk & van Rotingen, 1949).

How we see depth in a picture has been a problem for much speculation and has resulted in two radically opposed theories. One of them, in its most extreme form, says that we start with two-dimensional form perception and, through learned association with touch and action, build up the third dimension. On this theory, whatever two-dimensional stimulus information has been learned as a cue to depth can presumably occur in a picture as well as in a retinal image. The very term retinal image, it will be noted, seems to imply such a notion. But another theory asserts that perception of depth is not learned by association with reaching or walking; that it is perceived in the objects and surfaces of the real world very early, and that pictorially represented depth is not necessarily conveyed by the same information that conveys depth at an edge or solidity of an object in the world.

That depth at an edge is perceived by human infants by the time they can crawl, and by some animals at birth, has been demonstrated with the visual cliff. The information arising from differential motion parallax at the edge appears to be important in this perception. It will be remembered (see Chapter 16) that Bower (1965), in a demonstration of size constancy in two-month-old human infants, concluded likewise that information from motion parallax made the discrimination possible. He then went on to show that pictorially available cues to depth (in a static projection that excluded parallax) did not suffice at two months as information for the same judgment. This finding suggests that such pictorially available cues as linear perspective are secondary to the information about size, depth, and distance that is available with real objects and a moving observer. The pictorial cues could be learned by their association with such information, and they could function mainly in limited situations where an observer is set to use them.

Such a situation would be the pictorial one, where the flatness of the surface of the picture is clearly revealed by information from binocular and motion parallax. The discrepancy between the cues for depth and the information for flatness is apparent, and the sophisticated viewer has presumably learned to attend to the former and to ignore the latter—the cues that give the plane of the picture. Eliminating the edges of a picture, so that head movements do not reveal them against the background, should enhance the effectiveness of perspective and size cues within the picture. Indeed it does, as anyone knows who has looked at a photographic slide with the naked eye and then within a viewer.

Is there reason to think that the pictorial cues for depth are learned?

Bower's study suggests that they are not used at the age of two months, and children do not draw in perspective without some instruction. But this is not evidence, necessarily, that they are merely conventions. Plane projections of the edges of objects and surfaces to a given station point, recorded accurately on a piece of paper or traced on glass, do have an isomorphic correspondence with the real edges and contours, rather than an arbitrary mapping like a code. There is, therefore, some common invariant information shared by the two stimulus sources.

Hudson (1952) investigated the role of education in spatial judgments of pictured scenes, taking as his subjects Bantus and other Africans, both white and black, of varied ages. It was his opinion that pictorial representation of a three-dimensional scene depends on the acceptance by artist and viewer of certain artistic and graphic conventions observed in Western culture but not by Africans. Outline drawings and a photograph were prepared, the drawings incorporating relative size differences, superposition, and perspective, either combined or in isolation (see Fig. 18–3). The subjects were asked such questions as: What do you see? What is the man doing? Which is nearer the man, elephant, or antelope? If the subject reported the antelope to be nearer than the elephant, his response was classified as three dimensional.

All subjects generally identified the pictured objects correctly, the only exceptions occurring when the insertion of a depth cue had the effect of obscuring a contour. There were, however, differences in responses classified as three dimensional, the differences being associated with educational level. The school-going subjects reported depth more frequently than illiterates or subjects living in greater isolation from the school-dominated culture. It is interesting that the cue of overlap or superposition was the most effective, and that linear perspective was the least. The perspective lines have a particularly artificial appearance in the drawings. But the illiterate subjects did not perceive depth more readily in the photograph than in the drawing, so it is not only realistic portrayal that matters. It seems rather that judging depth in pictures depends on learned attitudes and habits of attending to graphic information on the picture plane and ignoring the compelling information given by parallax.

Does this mean that pictorial depth perception is learned? It does, in the sense that habits of selective attention to one kind of information and exclusion of another kind are involved. The elephant and the antelope in the picture are equally near the observer, in a literal sense. He has to forget that, and play the experimenter's game to give answers classified as three dimensional.

Further evidence for differences in judging depth in pictured and real situations was provided by Wohlwill (1965). He obtained judgments of distance bisection in a three-dimensional viewing display, the ground of the viewing box being covered with textures varying in degree of regularity

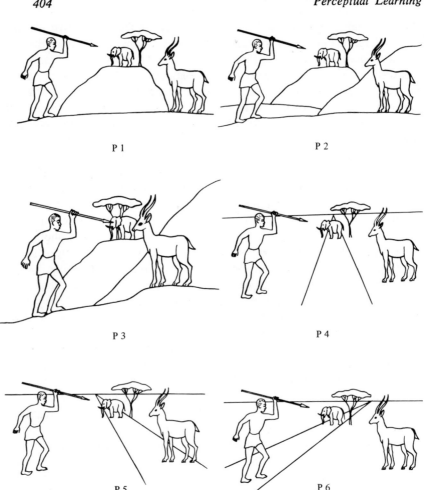

P 1

P 2

P 3

P 4

P 5

P 6

FIGURE 18–3. Drawings used by Hudson in a study of pictorial depth perception in subcultural groups in Africa.

(From W. Hudson, Pictorial depth perception in sub-cultural groups in Africa. *Journal of Social Psychology,* 1960, *52,* 186.)

and number of elements (see Chapter 17). Texture played a minimal role, information from parallax and cues other than texture apparently determining the judgments. But texture variables might play a role when distance judgments had to be made from two-dimensional photographic displays, eliminating potential information from parallax, convergence, etc., as regards the judgments to be made. Sets of photographic slides were made with different backgrounds varying in density and regularity of texture (see Fig. 18–4). A miniature toy model of a cow, a horse, and a fence

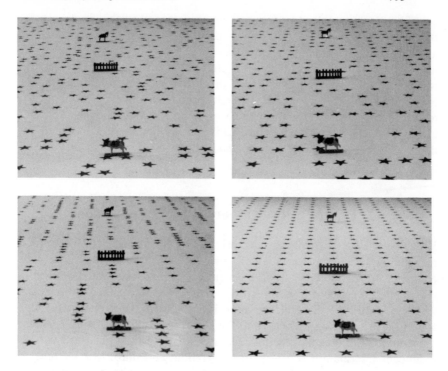

FIGURE 18–4. Pictured grounds varying in regularity of texture.

(From J. F. Wohlwill, Texture of the stimulus field and age as variables in the perception of relative distance in photographic slides. *Journal of Experimental Child Psychology,* 1965, *2,* 166.)

were positioned on the field with the cow in the foreground, the horse in the background, and the fence somewhere in between (position varied over nine equal-angle steps). The subjects viewed the projected slides through an eyepiece that restricted vision to a circular area containing cow, fence, and ground, but cut out the borders of the screen so as to reduce information about the picture plane. The subject made judgments of whether the cow or the horse was closer to the fence.

Adults and children from first, fourth, and eighth grades were subjects. Even the youngest children made quite consistent judgments of relative distance in the photograph. For all age groups there was a constant error of displacement of the apparent midpoint toward the front (underconstancy). When the three-dimensional viewing box was used, the error was in the other direction. Results in this study also differed in the effect of texture. There was an overall decrease in constant error as texture density increased. Regularity of texture was less influential, reducing error only in the most regular example (where counting of elements might conceivably play a role). Age was not an important variable in the study, the eighth grade subjects exhibiting the largest constant error, and no age and texture interaction appearing.

In our society, it would seem, children in first grade judge relative distance in drawings much as adults do. When viewing conditions reduce the cues for the flat picture plane (thereby reducing conflict of information), texture density plays a significant role in judgment, even though it did not in the three-dimensional situation. Children do not depend more on redundancy or regularity of texture than adults do in judging distance in pictures.

Picture Recognition and Picture Completion

It has been said that children and primitive men are deficient in pictorial recognition because pictures are impoverished sources of stimulation as compared to real objects and that experience is therefore required to fill in the picture, to enrich it by adding imagery or knowledge gained in the actual situation portrayed. Several presuppositions underlie this statement. One is that fidelity of a representation to the object is insufficient for it to arouse a perception without the addition of associated information; another, that redundant information is a help to recognition; and third, that learning to recognize pictures is a different process from learning to differentiate objects.

Experiments on the recognition of incomplete pictures stress the second of the above propositions, implying that children need more information to recognize an incomplete picture than do adults. The Street figures (1931) are well-known demonstrations of fragmentary pictures; probably no one is surprised that a child tends to take longer to identify the objects in these displays than does an adult. There could be many explanations. The set of pictured objects and their names would be less available to the child. As for filling in the gaps in an outline, there is evidence that continuity of line is important to younger children in following a contour, and that dashed-line patterns are not so easily recognized (Piaget & von Albertini, 1954). The objects represented in the Street figures have been better differentiated from one another by adults than by children. Insofar as they have been differentiated and insofar as the incomplete pictures retain the distinctive features of the objects, success should follow.

Gollin (1960, 1961, 1962) performed a number of experiments with children and adults on the recognition of objects from incomplete pictures. The procedure began by showing the subject complete representations of pictured objects and asking him to identify them. Later incomplete line drawings prepared from the original pictures were presented. There were four degrees of fragmentation, presumably done at random. On the whole, adults recognized the pictured object at a greater degree of fragmentation than the children. Previous practice in identifying the pictures decreased the amount of detailed representation required for recognizing the incomplete pictures, especially when the training was given with pictures that were themselves partially incomplete. This procedure would provide the subject with knowledge (and names) of the set of objects pictured, and it would also instruct him to look for distinctive features other than contour (e.g., tails, fins, legs, parallel lines in upper left quadrant, etc.).

In the most fragmented displays of Gollin's experiment, few distinctive features were preserved. Even adults, after going through many graded practice series beginning with the complete picture, could identify only 7.5 out of 20 of the most fragmented ones. The children, four to five years old, could recognize only one out of 20. This poor performance does not mean that picture recognition depends on abundant detail, since there is evidence that both adults and children find it easier to identify caricatures with few lines than photographs or detailed drawings of the same objects with many lines (see Chapter 6). But caricatures are not random fragmentations. They are the result of careful effort to eliminate the irrelevant and excess information while preserving the distinctive features.

It might be objected that caricatures are not as described, that they depend on graphic conventions, that they are symbols for something of general social knowledge, like the picture of Uncle Sam. Newspaper caricatures of The Capitalist and The Communist are sometimes of this kind. But these are stereotypes, not representations of a real person with a real set of distinctive features or of a valid type of person with the distinctive features of his class.

Children's comic books of the kind enjoyed by a four year old exploit the distinctive features of a type of animal human. Mickey Mouse and Porky Pig enjoy enough mouse-like and pig-like features to make it easy to distinguish the mouse from the pig, whatever else has been added. But of course they are more than just animals.

Geometrical Illusions

It has long been known that judgments of certain geometrical illusions change with age, and also with exposure or practice.[1] Binet (1895) showed that the amount of the Muller-Lyer illusion decreased with age, and many studies have demonstrated that it diminishes with prolonged exposure (e.g., Köhler & Fishback, 1950). Some developmental psychologists, in particular Piaget, have found this change intriguing and have expected it to throw considerable light on perceptual development. Man has developed the

[1] For a detailed discussion of various illusions and changes in perception of them with development, see Wohlwill (1960), and Vurpillot (1963).

ability to distinguish fine differences in the structure of graphic material in addition to differences in the structure of solid objects in his environment. Because the geometrical illusions are two-dimensional graphic designs, it has been the hope that investigation of the geometric illusions would reveal in exaggerated form the normal perceptual process. But it may be the case that one can only generalize from these illusions to the perception of other two-dimensional drawings.

Piaget has made an elaborate experimental analysis of geometrical illusions, with the help of many collaborators.[2] He makes use of the same concepts he employs in analyzing other perceptual phenomena. These include centration, transport, exploration, comparison, coupling, transposition, in short, perceptual activities, which are sensory-motor and which build a schema, a generalized structure to which new equivalent situations are assimilated.

Piaget divides perceptual schematization into four categories, distinguishing first "empirical" schemata from "geometrical" schemata. The empirical schemata are derived from real objects, such as hands, faces, animals, vegetables, etc., whereas the geometric forms are, by definition, schematic, general, categorical. All schemata, whether empirical or geometric, may bear certain distorting aspects (leading to errors), or they may be compensatory, compensating for the distortion and leading to good forms.

Empirical schemata, for Piaget, are the rule in everyday perception. They are the result of the action of earlier perceptions on later ones, perceptions of objects that are conceptually categorized (Piaget, 1961, pp. 244 ff.). They are the product of perceptual activities of transport and temporal transformation, and the number of repetitions plays a role, as well as the interests of the observer. They give rise to perceptual expectations which may or may not be right.

Geometrical schemata have similar properties, but the distinction between distortion and compensation is particularly important. A geometrical schema is generally compensatory. Equivalences, and symmetry characterizing them, result in an evening up of comparisons and couplings and thus compensate for momentary errors due to centration. But sometimes geometric schemata can be a source of systematic distortion. The perceptual activities, by relating elements not primarily related in a single field and moment of fixation, can give rise to secondary deformations. Arising as a product of structuring, they result in heterogeneous centrations without compensation. Schematization thus marks the achievement of structure, but on the other hand, it may end in distortion.

Piaget divides the geometrical illusions into three categories. First is the class of primary illusions. They depend on field effects occurring

2 The work is summarized in *Les Mécanismes Perceptifs* (Piaget, 1961). See also Vurpillot (1959) for a description of Piaget's system of dealing with illusions.

in a single glance or instant of fixation, and can thus be demonstrated with tachistoscopic exposure. They occur prior to the perceptual activity of exploration as a result of centration alone and can be interpreted in terms of over- and underestimation of elements of the display. Systematic distortion results from overestimation of fixated elements. These include most of the familiar geometric illusions, such as the Muller-Lyer, the Delboeuf, and illusions of angles. These illusions tend to diminish with age as decentration and perceptual activities increase, but qualitatively they remain the same and yield the same curves of error as proportions of component lines are manipulated.

The class of secondary illusions is subdivided into two, but Piaget contrasts them generally with primary illusions because they depend, not on simultaneous, momentary field effects, but on perceptual activities of exploration, comparison, putting in a frame of reference, and so on. These activities increase in number and importance with age. In general they serve to diminish the primary errors, but they sometimes give rise to secondary deformations, of the kind discussed above with reference to geometric schemata. These secondary illusions increase with development; some increase continuously or to asymptote, and some increase to a point and then diminish slightly. An example of an illusion classified by Piaget as secondary is the so-called Oppel-Kundt illusion (a divided line compared to an undivided one of the same length is overestimated). This illusion begins, according to Piaget, as a primary illusion but it increases with age as exploratory activities are added to the original centration with its accompanying field effects and reinforce the error.

Piaget's classification of illusions, with his speculations as to perceptual development and inference as to the role of perceptual activities, has a certain post hoc quality about it. The elaborate detail of both description and reasoning defies coming to terms with it, and few American psychologists, even those who are interested in studying illusions developmentally, have made much use of it.[3] I am left with a stronger impression than ever that the geometric illusions are a far cry from perception of real things and pictures of real things, and that one should be cautious in generalizing from them to development of perception of ecologically valid sources of stimulation.

---

[3] See for instance Spitz (1965). Spitz rejects Piaget's classification as arbitrary and cites developmental data (for the Muller-Lyer illusion, for instance) showing that the situation is not as simple as the classification implies. He substitutes classifications of his own—"physiological illusions" and "experiential illusions"—and cites his own work comparing retardates to normals, finding that retardates are less susceptible to physiological illusions, but equally so to experiential illusions. Pollack (1966, and Pollack & Silver, 1967) makes a similar distinction; illusions of Piaget's primary type are considered to change with age along with physiological changes, while illusions of the secondary type develop on the basis of cognitive factors.

Eye Movements and Pictures

There is one perceptual activity that can be objectively observed and measured—the movements of the eyes. Here is a promising technique for studying perception; the pictorial display helps in defining and limiting what can be looked at, and techniques have been invented for superposing a photographic record of eye movements while looking at a picture on the actual picture being looked at (Mackworth, 1967). Vinh-bang (reported in Piaget, 1961), in Piaget's laboratory, compared eye movements of adults and six-year-old children who were asked to look at pairs of lines and judge which was longer. He found that the children's eye movements had a wider dispersion with considerable oscillation, shorter fixation times with much more shifting of the regard, and fewer actual comparisons ("transports") of the lines to be judged. Visual exploration, in short, was less systematic and directed.

Mackworth and Bruner (1966) photographed eye movements of children and adults during attempts of a subject to recognize a picture. A picture, for example of a fire hydrant, was presented out of focus while the subject searched the display for details which would assist him in identifying what was represented. The children made more short eye movements than adults, and they tended to look at less informative areas. There was less use of peripheral scanning leading to rejection of these areas. Furthermore, the children tended to be trapped by a detail, returning again and again to it, and to restrict themselves to a very small field. In general, children's search techniques in examining pictures were piecemeal and less successful than adults'. They were also highly variable from one another and within themselves.

Mackworth's photographic technique was also used by Vurpillot (1968) in a developmental study of judgment of visual similarity. Children were presented with a pair of drawings, either identical or different, and required to decide if they were the same. Eye movements were recorded in order to study which areas were fixated and the sequence of fixations. The children were between five and nine years old. The displays were pairs of schematically drawn houses. On each house were drawn six windows always placed in two columns, but for any house the windows varied in one or more features; for instance, one had blinds, one had curtains, one a bird cage hanging in it. One pair of houses had one different window, one had three different, and one five. Three other pairs were identical.

Even at five years, more than 90 percent of the judgments were correct. But the younger children made some errors when judging nonidentical houses, especially the pair that had only one difference. These children made fewer fixations on distinct windows and did not make a systematic sequence of paired comparisons, which would be the optimal strategy. They tended to make a judgment on the basis of a too small sampling; they looked at about the same number of windows no matter how many differences there were. A systematic plan of scanning, starting at the top, and comparing window pairs, was not adopted by the youngest group.

These three studies agree in telling us, not surprisingly, that children as young as five and six are still relatively unskilled in visual exploratory behavior; they scan, but they do not scan systematically, fixate accurately, or sample as widely as the task often requires. Accuracy of perceptual differentiation must surely increase with the development of scanning skill and strategy. Vurpillot concluded that the limited scope of the scan is due to the children's limited ability to handle information; that they stop before taxing their processing capacity. But direction of the search for distinctive features in picture recognition would be expected to improve with age in strategy and adaptiveness. We will return to this point in the last chapter.

From Pictures to Symbols

Pictorial representation began as long as 30,000 years ago when Stone Age man began painting the animals of his environment on the walls of caves. Many thousands of years elapsed before the invention of writing, and even writing began as pictographs. The history of writing (Moorhouse, 1953) is a history of the sending of messages, beginning as representations and only gradually evolving toward a conventional set of graphic symbols. Invention of the alphabet—graphic symbols coded to a set of phonological units—may have happened only once (Gelb, 1963), but the transition from picture to symbol can be plainly seen in the history of writing.

In spite of the fact that pictures are much more like real objects than abstract geometric forms are, much perceptual work with children has made use of circles, triangles, squares, and so on. Interest in the experiments centered for a decade or more on questions raised by the Gestalt psychologists, such as principles of organization of good forms. Do good forms have symmetry, wholeness or closure, simplicity; do children exhibit a primitive tendency to reorganize forms in these directions?

These questions have never been answered satisfactorily, perhaps because they were the wrong questions. Most of the studies have depended on inference from children's drawings. Consider as an example a study by Graham, Berman, and Ernhart (1960). Children ranging in age from two and a half to five years were presented with 18 designs to copy, including a single line, circle, triangle, square, diamond, cross, and others. Some unclosed designs were included. The children's productions were rated from two points of view: first, on their accuracy, in terms of curvature-linearity, number of parts, correct relationship of parts, orientation on background, size relationships; and second, on whether the reproductions were more primitive than the original designs. Primitive reproductions were supposed to manifest the figural changes (autonomous organization tendencies) that Gestalt psychology postulated. It was asked whether the reproduction was more closed than the original, whether it was simpler, and whether it was more symmetrical. Simpler was defined as more uniform, homogeneous as to parts, less complex.

Children's drawings of forms are notoriously hard to rate, but two judges rating independently achieved reliability coefficients of .81 to .88 for more openness or more closure. Figure 18–5 gives some samples of the children's drawings, and the ratings with respect to change in simplicity, closure, and symmetry. On the whole, the predictions of Gestalt psychology were not confirmed. Simplification and closure were more common in the reproductions of younger children than older ones, but so were their opposites—complication and opening. Increasing rather than decreasing symmetry was more common in only one age group, the 3½ year olds. But accuracy of the reproductions increased steadily with age for each of the characteristics judged. The nature of the design was related to its difficulty, especially the number of its parts, or turns (often used as a measure of complexity), and a sharp discontinuity or change in direction. Nonchange in direction—linearity—seems to be the simplest perceptual feature for children, if one takes accuracy of reproduction as a criterion.

The copying of designs entails a kind of motor ability as well as the ability to perceive. We expect children of 5½ to discriminate graphic patterns so that they can learn to read. What is the evolution of this graphic ability, when discrimination alone, without graphic production, is in question? An experiment by Gibson, Gibson, Pick, and Osser (1962) sought to trace the development of discrimination of letter-like forms in children four to nine years old, paying special attention to the kinds of transformation that were easy and hard to discriminate at different age levels. They began by constructing a set of graphic forms comparable to printed Roman capitals in that they followed, insofar as possible, the same rules that govern the formation of those letters. The forms consisted of joined lines, both straight and curved, none of more than four strokes. Some were open, some were closed, some were symmetrical, some not. From twelve such forms chosen as standards, twelve variants on each were constructed to yield specifiable transformations. There were three transformations of line to curve or curve to line; five transformations of rotation or reversal; two perspective transformations (a slant left and a slant back, comparable to the deformations produced in tipping a book to the left, or tipping it away from the direct line of sight); and two topological changes, a break and a close. The entire set of forms is shown in Figure 18–6.

The master drawings were copied photographically on small cards, and these were covered with plastic so that they could be handled without

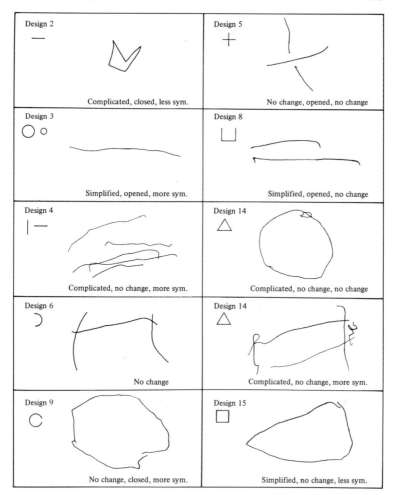

FIGURE 18–5. Children's reproductions of designs, with types of error indicated.

(From F. K. Graham, P. W. Berman, & C. B. Ernhart, Development in preschool children of the ability to copy forms. *Child Development,* 1960, *31,* 344. By permission of The Society for Research in Child Development, Inc.)

soiling. The task given the children was to compare the standard with all its variants and to select and hand to the experimenter only exact copies of it. The cards were presented on a lectern-shaped stand containing five slotted rows. The standard was centered in the top row. All transformations of a given standard were randomly arranged in one row, accompanied by one or more identical copies. Each child matched

S	L to C 1	L to C 2	L to C 3	45° R	90° R	R-L Rev.	U-D Rev.	180° R	Perspective Trs. Slant L Tilt back	Close	Break

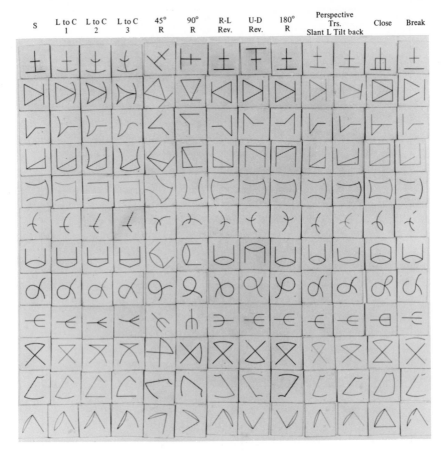

FIGURE 18–6. Twelve letter-like forms (in the far left column) and twelve transformations of each of them.

The types of transformation are indicated across the top row. (From E. J. Gibson, J. J. Gibson, A. D. Pick, & H. Osser, A developmental study of the discrimination of letter-like forms. *Journal of Comparative and Physiological Psychology*, 1962, *55*, 898.)

all 12 standards. An error consisted of choosing as "same" an item that did not exactly match the standard. The number of errors was obtained for each child, and the errors were classified according to type of transformation.

Errors decreased from age four through eight, but rate of decline was quite different for different types of transformation. Figure 18–8 shows curves of decline with age for four transformation types. Data have been combined for each of the four types—that is, all the rotation and reversal transformations have been pooled, and likewise for the other types.

Errors for break and close started low and dropped to near zero by

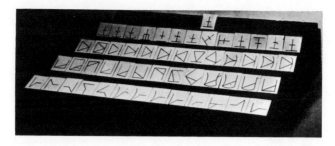

FIGURE 18–7. **Stand for displaying forms in a matching task.**

(From E. J. Gibson, J. J. Gibson, A. D. Pick, & H. Osser, A developmental study of the discrimination of letter-like forms. *Journal of Comparative and Physiological Psychology*, 1962, *55*, 899.)

eight years. Errors for perspective transformations started high and remained high at eight years. Errors for rotations and reversals started high, but declined swiftly, few occurring by seven years. Line to curve transformations (especially if there was only one change) were productive of many errors at four years, but of only a very small number by eight years.

Can we account for the differences in error rate between the earliest age of testing, before schooling has begun, and after the child has received instruction in reading? We concluded earlier that the child transfers to a line drawing some of his knowledge of distinctive features of objects of the world. Positive transfer in discrimination might be expected to occur when the transformation of standard to variable happens to be a critical one for distinguishing solid objects in the child's environment from one another. But there should be no transfer, and more false "same" judgments would be expected, when the transformation is of the kind experienced as continuous and as accompanying the slanting or tilting of things. Shape constancy is maintained despite such transformation.

Considering the four types of transformation, we can speculate as follows. Errors with break and close should be few initially, because these changes are critical for object identification. There are no transitions from break to close in rigid objects. Such a difference is discriminated early with solid objects (Piaget & Inhelder, 1956) and presumably this carries over to drawings. Objects usually do not develop holes where none were before, or fill in ones that were there. Such differences constitute permanent differentiating features and they are learned as such early, so there is little error to reduce after four years.

Transformations of rotation and reversal, on the other hand, do not serve as distinctive features of objects. An object is seen to remain the same object if it is turned over or walked around, and what the child learns (if learning is necessary) is to perceive its permanence despite change in position. It is not surprising, therefore, that reversed and rotated forms

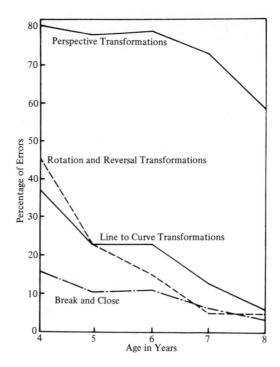

FIGURE 18–8. Developmental error curves as a function of type of trans-formation.

(From E. J. Gibson, J. J. Gibson, A. D. Pick, & H. Osser, A develop-mental study of the discrimination of letter-like forms. *Journal of Comparative and Physiological Psychology,* 1962, *55,* 901.)

are so often matched as identical by young children. But when children are exposed to our writing system, they suddenly discover that a number of letters are rotations or reversals of others and yet are actually unique. However, it is clear from the fast decline in the error curve that a child of six is perfectly capable of learning this distinction. He can, in fact, see it if the question is put "show me which way the triangle points" or "show me the way the E faces" (Robinson & Higgins, 1967).

Perspective transformations, like rotation and reversal, do not identify objects as different or unique. They indicate a change in orientation in the third dimension—a tilt or slant and shape constancy is strong in young children, as we have seen. There is only a small drop in error with age, furthermore, since such transformations are not critical for identifying letters, either. In fact, books are held at many different angles, producing such transformations in stimulation projected from the printed page. The reader tolerates such change.

Line to curve transformations are a particularly interesting case. They are distinguishing features for rigid objects—a round ball does not transform into a square cube or vice versa. On the other hand, live plastic objects do undergo such transformations. Take the case of facial expressions, and the rubbery changes from a dead pan to a smile, for instance. They indicate different states of the same object, a permanent one. A change of only one line or curve elicits many errors at four years, but three such changes are easily differentiated. Straight vs. curve is an important distinction in letter differentiation, and children soon learn to attend to it and eliminate most errors.

We have come all the way from pictures to letter-like forms of the kind used as symbols in the writing system. Although the latter do not portray actual objects,[4] they must be differentiated from one another, as objects are, and there seems to be some carry-over from differential perception of real objects when the child is learning that letter forms constitute a special set with its own common and distinctive features. He has to learn that each of these drawings is unique, and how it varies from others of the set, quite aside from its status as a symbol, its coded meaning. Does it have any meaning before coding? I think so, insofar as it is distinguished as different from others of its set. But symbols are arbitrary and have another kind of meaning. Let us consider in the next chapter how they differ from ordinary drawings and pictures.

SUMMARY

In this chapter, we left the material world of objects and events as sources of stimulation and turned to the perception of representations of things and events, to a kind of mediated perception. But the development of perception for pictures and other representations is not very different from the development of perception of objects, as long as the representations have fidelity. Caricatures can even have super fidelity, by articulating and stressing distinctive features and playing down noisy and irrelevant ones. Perception of space and depth as it is represented in pictures is necessarily dependent on different information than in a real scene, but there is some common information. Transfer of differentiation of distinctive features from objects to representations and even to more arbitrary graphic patterns has been demonstrated. Perceptual learning, beyond what is accomplished in the natural ecological surroundings, is probably only required for perceiving the meaning of representations that employ special conventions or distortions, ones that are peculiar to the requirements of the graphic act or to the artist.

---

[4] Actually, in the Semitic alphabet from which ours derived there are a few characters which may have been retained from earlier pictograms.

The Development of Perception in the Individual: Perceiving by Means of Symbols

SYMBOLS CONTRASTED WITH PICTURES

We have just considered a kind of mediated perception, perceiving by means of representations of things and events. Representations are surrogates for things and events, and they can convey information about the world at the same time that they carry stimulus information about themselves. How does perceiving symbols differ from perceiving representations? In the first place, the meaning of the representation, if it is a reasonably faithful one, is simply transferable from the object. If the object pictured has been differentiated from other objects, so is the picture differentiated from pictures of those other objects. It became clear in the preceding discussion of pictures that one does not have to associate names, for instance, with pictures in order to identify them as representations of familiar objects.

The shadow of a tree is, in a sense, a representation of the tree; it stands in a projective correspondence with the tree, a relationship which does not require associative learning to be perceived. The word "tree" corresponds to the tree as well, but the mapping in this case is an arbitrary one, determined by convention, and it must be learned (see Gibson, 1966, chapter 11, "The Structuring of Light by Artifice"). In considering development of the perception of objects, space, events, and representations of them, the concepts of differentiation and detection of distinctive features and relations were emphasized, and we found little need for the concept of association. The information, in these cases, is there in the stimulation and whether he extracts it or not is a matter of the observer's attention, interest, and opportunity for exploratory and filtering activity.

For symbols the case is different. The meaning of the word "pretty" is not carried unequivocally in the light to the eye. It must be associated with the word, and it could be associated just as well with *"belle"* or *"hubsch."* Likewise, the graphic character p means "say /p/" in our alphabet, but it means "say /r/" in the Cyrillic alphabet. The correspondence is there, but it is coded, determined by the conventions of a given society. The symbol itself—letter, word, or whatever—must first be differentiated from the other members of its set. But the code meaning must thereafter be associated with it.

Graphic symbols were introduced in the last chapter because we were considering how forms—pictorial, geometric, and letter-like—are differentiated in development. The spoken word is also a symbol, and it has priority over the graphic symbol, since writing certainly developed later than speech as a surrogate for it. Some linguists think human speech must have evolved from animal cries and the development of writing from pictograms might be somewhat analogous. The animal cry needs no associative coding by another animal of the same species. We know from studies of birds reared in isolation (Thorpe, 1961) that territorial songs typical of a species are produced without opportunity to copy, with the essential pattern and distinctive features of the song though without the embellishment and personalized features that might be imitated, given exposure to other birds. The human infant in any culture produces spontaneous sounds that are interpreted by the adult as indicating some inner emotional state, but predication about things, symbolized in speech, is coded and varies from one language to another.

One learns the meaning of a word. Has this anything to do with perceptual learning, or is it entirely a matter of associating a name with a referent? The question is too broad to examine here in detail and would take us far afield, but I want to make two points about learning words. One is that words, like things, must be differentiated from one another. Young children confuse homophones, and infants may fail to differentiate an utterance at all except by inflection. As adults, we hear speech as differentiated and segmented, but this is an achievement that takes time. Meanings of words, at a later stage, become more finely differentiated too, but this process would seem to take place on a more conceptual level.

Once segmented, how is a word mapped to a thing or an event? Concrete nouns and adjectives designate things and properties of things. Verbs denote events and prepositions denote relations, like "up," "down" or "under." The order in which these classes of words are learned and used appropriately may bear some relation to the kind of stimulus information referred to, but their use as early as 24 months or so attests to the child's pickup of the stimulus information that is being mapped. It must itself be differentiated before it can be associated with a word, if the word gains meaning by reference. Perhaps the relation between the object or event and the word is itself differentiated, dissected as a unit from the total stimulus flux.

SYMBOLS AND SEQUENCE

A second way in which perception with symbols differs from perception with pictures lies in the fact that the information given by symbols is nearly always presented sequentially in a string, and perception must somehow take account of order as well as items. Of course pictures can also be presented in a sequence, as in a movie or a comic strip, but the sequence still lacks something that sequential presentation of symbols usually has—a grammar, that is, internal structural rules for combining elements. Order in a movie replicates the order of natural events, giving segmentation into units automatically, by way of transfer from the actual events. But in a language, segmentation is given by rule. The structural constraints are the unit formers and thus, when perceived, permit processing the information in chunks. They also permit transfer to new cases of similarly ordered components when practice has allowed them to become functional.

Perception of sequences of symbols and the information in the order seems to be a distinguishing mark of human symbolic behavior. Research with animals has suggested that other primates than man may respond to a single learned stimulus as a symbol, but response to order in a string of symbols and to new orders of the same items after fragmentation does seem peculiar to man. There is some evidence that chimpanzees might be able to learn a manual sign language with grammatical rules (see Chapter 13). If this can be done, even in a rudimentary way, it would not only be remarkable but would have the advantage of giving us a new means of studying the beginnings of sequential symbolic perception.

We know little about perception of sequences, both when the sequences are natural events and when they are made by man. Music, speech, information on ticker tapes, strings of letters, manual language watched or felt on the skin are all cases in which information is presented in a sequence that has order and structure which the perceiver must discern if he is to get the message. How does he do it? Perception of the structure in a sequence of symbols is only beginning to be looked at by the developmental psychologist. Lashley pointed out the importance of the problem of serial order in behavior, which he equated with the "problem of syntax," in 1951. He argued that the individual items of sequentially perceived events like speech did not have a temporal tag for their associative connections with other elements but that order was given by a general pattern or plan (Lashley, 1951).

Inspired by their concern with the development of speech perception in hearing children, as compared with deaf children who must learn speech in a formal rather than a self-regulated way, Furth and his collaborators have studied learning of sequences in both groups (Furth, 1964; Furth & Pufall, 1966; Furth & Youniss, 1967). They conducted a number of experiments on paired associate learning of sequences that required responding to the sequence per se rather than to the discrete items combined in it. The task was thought of as analogous to learning different responses to different sequences of the same letters, such as APT, PAT, or TAP. In a typical experiment, deaf and hearing children seven and ten years old learned visual sequences of random shapes as first members of paired associates. Two such shapes were elements of a sequence of three items (of the form ABB or BAB, for example). The subject responded to a given sequence by pressing a response button arbitrarily designated as correct. Beginning with a couple of pairs, more pairs with sequences of the same elements were progressively added, up to six, each sequence paired with a different button. The sequenced shapes were presented simultaneously in one condition and successively in another. The number of different sequences that he could learn to associate correctly with their designated responses was determined for each child.

Age comparisons showed developmental improvement in this number, but the task was difficult. Simultaneous presentation was generally easier than successive, but the difference was small.

An auditory sequence task analogous to the visual one was compared with the successive visual condition. The sequences were constructed again from two elements, white noise and an organ tone (which could be distinguished, with amplification, by the deaf subjects). Age effects were again apparent. The auditory sequences were easier to associate with responses than visual ones for young hearing children but not for the older children or for the deaf children.

A study of errors for visual sequences revealed effects of symmetry and reversal of order. A symmetrical sequence was more often confused with another symmetrical system and an asymmetrical sequence with another asymmetrical sequence. Most errors were made to asymmetrical sequences which had element reversals of another sequence, showing that the structure was perceived as the same; elements were confused rather than ordering. Thus, although there was no syntax built into these sequences, structural features were playing a role in perception.

Furth and Youniss (1967) concluded that the difficulty in learning to respond to sequences is not due to "memory load" but to what they termed their "combinative" aspect. The tendency to reduce the information in combinations of discrete items by use of structure is strong, but there were no rules relating structure of the sequences in this task that could help in associating unique responses with each one.

Suppose the elements within sequences of items presented to a child were rule governed, that there was structure in the sense of combinatory rules determining the order in which items could appear (as would be the case in a natural language). Experiments with both adults and children (Miller, 1958; Bogartz & Carterette, 1963; Braine, 1963b; Smith, 1966; Reber, 1967) have compared free recall or recognition of sequences of items (such as letter strings) structured according to a simple grammar, with unstructured sequences of the same items. Let us consider two examples in which children were subjects.

Strings of letters or digits were prepared by Bogartz and Carterette (1963) so as to yield two kinds of sequence: one, where the sequence had structure in that order of constituent items was constrained by rules; and the other, where the constituent items were randomly assigned. The same constituent symbols were used in both random and ordered strings, and the strings varied in length from four to seven symbols. The subjects were children from the fourth, fifth, and sixth grades. A subject was shown either randomly ordered strings or constrained strings, either all digits or all letters. The constraining rules were the same. After a list of nine strings had been presented, the child was asked to recall as many strings as he could. Repetitions of the list and recall followed. The mean number of letter or digit strings correctly recalled was greater for the constrained sequences in all three grades, and the mean number of constrained strings recalled increased with grade. The difference in number of random strings recalled did not increase significantly with grade. Constraints in the strings were learned reasonably well, though not as well as the same constraints were learned by adults (Miller, 1958). When new strings with the same constraints were given the children after ten trials, recall was as good as when the identical lists were repeated. Thus, structure—the sequential constraints within and between the strings of symbols—is an important determiner of the kind of learning tested here.

Consider one more experiment, in which the subject is given the opportunity to recognize or create a sequence of items which was not presented to him during learning trials, but is generated by the same rules. Smith (1966) asked subjects to recall a set of letter pairs that conformed to the rules of a very simple generative grammar. There were two classes of letters (five in each) which were constrained as to order, in that letters of one class always preceded letters of the other class. The subjects included adults and children from the fourth, fifth, and sixth grades. Pairs of letters were shown the subject, with the instruction that he was to remember as many as possible of the pairs in a later recall test. Of all the possible letter pairs generated by the grammar, only 80 percent were shown. The subjects erroneously recalled significantly more items which had not been shown but were generated by the grammar than would be expected if such intrusions were random combinations of letters appearing in the presented pairs. The subjects—both adults and children—had learned something about the structure of the presented pairs and generalized it.

It may well be true, therefore, that it is the combinative aspect of sequentially presented information that makes for difficulty, but it is equally true that when there is order in sets of sequences it will be picked up and used. We shall turn now to the symbols that constitute real, natural language and consider how perception of them develops.

PERCEPTION OF SPEECH

Discrimination of Phonological Features of Speech

Sequential information appears at many levels in language—within sentences, within words, and within even smaller units. Is simple order, like a rising inflection, perceived first, or are the smallest units discriminated first and then integrated into sequences? Do infants have to learn to perceive the distinctive features of the phonemes of their language?

Experimental studies of the development of discrimination of phonological contrasts are so scarce that the broadest questions, let alone the more precise ones, are as yet unanswered. Most psycholinguists believe that the phonemic contrasts characteristic of any given language are learned, not only their production but also their perception, and that they are furthermore learned in a given order. It should be said, however, that there are nativists who question this position, linguists who accept the notion that the infant has the capacity for detecting all phonemic contrasts without learning and that he need only find out the vocabulary of the ones that characterize the language his parents are speaking.

Such evidence as bears on this question comes mainly from studies of production of contrasts, not perception. The method has been biographical study of the development of a single child. There are few even of these studies, for the observer must be a trained linguist, and he must have some linguistic theory to organize his observations. The theory which has received some confirmation is that of Roman Jakobson. It holds that phonemic elements of speech are distinguished by bundles of distinctive features and that differentiation of feature contrasts proceeds in an orderly hierarchical fashion (see Chapter 5).

Studies by Leopold (1953, 1954) and by Velten (1943) seem to support Jakobson's hypothesis of the acquisition of features, although it is important to remember that inference is made only from production, and from a small number of cases. Everyday observation of young children tells us quite convincingly that speech discrimination at all levels is apt to be ahead of production. Ervin and Miller (1963) report a Russian study by Shvarkin in which he taught children between 11 and 25 months to discriminate words differing in only one phoneme at a time, and organized his results according to the features distinguishing classes of phonemes. He found that the children could distinguish all the phonemes of Russian by the end of the second year, a time considerably earlier than that at which they could produce all phonemes. Furthermore, the phonemic features were said to be learned in a given order, with vowel distinction first, followed by vowel-consonant distinction, and then orderly differentiation of consonant features.

Evidence from the diaries of speech production suggests that there is an across-the-board acquisition of features in contrast pairs, instead of a one-by-one gradual acquisition of the phonetic vocabulary. For instance, when a child learns a feature contrast such as voiced-voiceless it can be applied to a whole class of phonemes at once, and this automatically doubles the number of available phonemes. Ervin and Miller (1963) summarize the evidence from the diaries in a few hypotheses which they consider tenable, though as yet imperfectly substantiated.

(a) The vowel-consonant contrast is one of the earliest, if not the earliest, contrast for all the children. (b) A stop-continuant contrast is quite early for all children. The continuant is either a fricative (e.g., /f/) or a nasal (e.g., /m/). (c) When two consonants, differing in place of articulation but identical in manner of articulation exist, the contrast is labial vs. dental (e.g., /p/ vs. /t/, /m/ vs. /n/). (d) Contrasts in place of articulation precede voicing contrasts. (e) Affricates (ch, j) and liquids (l, r) do not appear in the early systems. (f) In the vowels, a contrast between low and high (e.g., /a/ and /i/) precedes front vs. back (e.g., /i/ and /u/). (g) Consonant clusters such as /st/ and /tr/ are generally late. In regard to contrasts at different positions within the word, certain tendencies are observed. Children normally acquire initial consonants before final or medial consonants, and consonantal contrasts often apply to initial position before other positions (pp. 113–14).

The linguists who made the observations leading to these generalizations were not concerned with psychological questions of how this orderly development comes about, but we are. Is it possible, as Chomsky suggests (1959) that "ability to select out of the complex auditory input those features that are phonologically relevant may develop largely independent of reinforcement, through genetically determined maturation?" It is certainly hard to conceive how external reinforcement could play any role, if perceptual differentiation precedes articulatory production.

Does it? This is a really crucial question. If traditional learning theory invoking external reinforcement is to apply at all, production must come first. Liberman (1957) and his associates at the Haskins laboratory introduced such a view, that acquired distinctiveness of phonemic contrasts follows from cues supplied by articulation. As Liberman put it, "The articulatory movements and their sensory effects mediate between the acoustic stimulus and the event we call perception." In a more recent paper (Liberman et al., 1967) this idea has been revised to incorporate the notion of a speech code. These researchers have been unable to locate a segment of phonemic size within the acoustic signal that is invariant with perception of a phoneme. Because no segment smaller than the syllable will map to perception with invariance, and yet phonemes are discriminated, they assume that phoneme perception requires a special decoding process. The presumed invariants in this process are neural signals referred to as "motor commands." These motor commands control phonemic production, signalling a given pattern of articulatory gesture. It is then assumed that speech is perceived by processes that are also involved in its production—the motor commands—so that there is only one decoding language for both perception and production. Perception, they feel, mirrors articulation more closely than it does the acoustic signal. How does the listener find his way back from the acoustic signal to the articulatory gestures that produced perception? This is still a problem, even if it be conceded that the invariant for both perception and production is the motor command.

This hypothesis is similar to one called "analysis-by-synthesis" proposed by Stevens and Halle (1967). In their model (a computer model) the acoustic input goes to an auditory mechanism to yield auditory patterns. These go to an abstract representation which has rules for articulation. The rules in turn lead to instructions for articulation in speech production. There is assumed to be a close correspondence between auditory patterns and articulatory instructions; the abstract features of the representation are presumed to be related in a direct way to both the auditory patterns and the articulatory instructions. The listener makes a preliminary hypothesis from the auditory pattern concerning the abstract representation of the utterance. The hypothesis is then tried out as a pattern of motor commands. An auditory pattern derived from these commands is then matched with the pattern yielded by the acoustic signal. If there is agreement, the original pattern is perceived as correct. How the auditory pattern signals even approximate representation and thus the correct motor commands is not clear, but if there is a learning process, this model would seem to have to base it on production.

Certainly it makes sense that there should be a coincidence between hearing distinctive features of speech and producing them. But the question of genesis is not thereby answered. Ordinary observation tells us that a child practices sound production very early; by 2½ years, as Ruth Weir has shown us (1962), he is practicing in what appears to be a highly controlled and purposeful way, alone and unimpelled by adult example or reinforcement. Such practice gives opportunity for matching auditory feedback with articulation. But could not selection go the other way? That is to say, the child could select the articulatory pattern that gives him the best auditory contrast.

There is evidence from another source to support the latter view. This evidence, collected by Lenneberg (1964, 1967) stems from the study of sensory deficits in relation to speech perception and production. He pointed out that the congenitally deaf, however artfully trained to shape sounds with appropriate articulation, never learn to produce speech that sounds like that of the normal hearing person. Correction by matching to an auditory criterion is essential. Proprioception, as Lenneberg put it, cannot take the place of auditory control. Even more convincing is the case of a child with a congenital defect in speech production. The child was literally speechless, but he understood speech and executed complicated commands. The capacity for making speech sounds was not necessary for the development of perceptual skill.

Further evidence that the child makes distinctions not yet evident in his speech has been presented by Shipley, Smith, and Gleitman. They observed children's responses to simple commands and to commands containing nonsense. Evidence of discrimination did seem to precede performance and also to vary with linguistic maturity in other respects.

Students of speech development generally emphasize that the child first distinguishes only the coarsest contrasts, and proceeds gradually to appreciation of finer ones. Leopold (1953–1954) says, for instance, that the child learns to distinguish low from high vowels first, then the mid vowels, and eventually the breakdown of these three major levels into still more refined subdivisions. The phonemic classification is not built up, but rather differentiated by division; this, of course, is a good biological principle.

In this connection, one might ask whether another phonological aspect of language, the intonation patterns, is not perceived before the phonemic contrasts. It seems, from ordinary observation, that this is the case, and Lewis (1951, 1963) cites observations to show that the infant before nine months discriminates among different patterns of expressive intonations. Ruth Weir (1966) reported some evidence that babies of Chinese and American English-speaking parents had different intonation patterns in babbling (around five to eight months) before phoneme differentiation had begun; the Chinese infants could be identified by distinct pitch patterns. It seems reasonable that this more primitive communicative aspect of language should be appreciated earlier than phonemic contrasts, which are only useful for communication when they are combined in complex sequential patterns. To quote an expert,

The linguistic development of utterances does not seem to begin by a composition of individual, independently movable items but as a whole tonal pattern. With further development, this whole becomes differentiated into component parts: primitive phonemes appear which consist of very large classes of sounds that contrast with each other. . . .

Perceptually, the child reacts also to whole patterns rather than to segments, and so the intonation pattern of a sentence is the more immediate input rather than individual phonemes (Lenneberg, 1967, p. 279).

Perception of Grammatical Structure

As Lashley, Hebb, Furth, and others have pointed out, strings of varied combinations of the same phonemes must be recognized as different by the human perceiver in communication. Lenneberg (1964) expresses thus the apparent magnitude of this achievement.

A sentence of 10 words contains an enormous amount of detail. It might consist of a sequence of some 60 phonemes, each one characterized by 9 to 12 distinctive features; each word in the sentence has well-defined intonation and stress characteristics; the sentence as a whole is the product of a male or female organ and bears acoustic peculiarities of age and idiosyncrasies of the speaker. "Blind" reproduction of all of this material, or even of the essentials, should be impossible, seeing that our memory is not even capable of reproducing a train of 10 random digits (p. 123).

Words can be segmented into their subordinate phonemic constituents, but they are themselves the constituents of higher order units defined by the rules of grammar. Research on the perception of speech with units larger than minimal phonological ones has converged to show us that predictability by rules is operating in the hearing of human speech. One of the major psycholinguistic generalizations which we are able to offer (Diebold, 1965, p. 226) is that speech recognition increases directly with the increase in redundancy. Redundancy in speech can be characterized in a number of ways, but its grammatical structure is the most obvious one. Speech recognition increases with increasing redundancy, yes; but how is the redundancy detected? Few would believe that a child is born with a knowledge of grammar, though all children are born with the capacity for learning it.

As is the case with development of phonological aspects of language, our knowledge about grammatical development is mainly on the side of production. How a child comes to perceive grammatical patterns in the speech of adults around him has to be inferred, for the most part, from order in the speech that he emits. But although even two-word sentences are rare before a child is two years old, we can be sure that he is already taking advantage of syntactical order in the speech he hears. While he utters only one-word sentences, he has what Ervin and Miller (1963, p. 118) call a "passive grammatical system, rules for decoding or understanding many adult grammatical patterns." A child responds appropriately to such adult statements as "Danny give Mommy the doll" and clearly does not expect Mommy to give it to Danny. But intonation and situation are all part of the stimulation and the exact extent to which a child has become sensitive to grammatical structure at an early age we do not know. When he invents analogical forms such as "bended" for "bent," around three years, we know that he is responding to patterning in language but he may have heard it sooner than that.

An experiment by Fraser, Bellugi, and Brown (1963) compared production and comprehension of grammatical contrasts in the speech of children three years old. They prepared two pictures each for ten grammatical contrasts, such as singular-plural. The contrasting pictures each had an appropriate partner sentence, such as "the boy draws" or "the boys draw." The picture in one case presented one boy drawing, in the other, two. The child was required to point to the picture that corresponded to one of the two sentences. To test production, on the other hand, the child was shown a picture and asked to say the corresponding sentence. Performance on the test of comprehension exceeded that on production for all the grammatical contrasts tested in these children, so the anecdotal (but generally accepted) evidence was supported for comprehension before production of order and morphology.

How the child discerns the order in adult discourse is the great unsolved problem. Since the advent of information theory, a popular explanation has been that the properties of sequential messages are learned by association as sequential dependencies. A theory of this sort stressing probabilistic sequential dependencies and associative hierarchies was presented by Osgood (1963), and research exists to demonstrate that presence of sequential dependencies in word chains does enhance recall (Miller & Selfridge, 1950). But the limitations of a probabilistic associative model for learning language have been pointed out many times (cf. Miller et al., *Plans and the Structure of Behavior,* 1960). Life would simply not be long enough to learn language this way; equivalence of sentence transforms (e.g., active to passive) is not taken into account, nor is the child's ability to invent new sentences accounted for.

Studies of the child's learning of grammatical structures have proceeded in recent years primarily by the method of recording on tape all of a given child's utterances for a period of an hour or so at frequent intervals, beginning before the first two-word combination is produced, at about the second birthday. Miller and Ervin (1964) reported a longitudinal study testing 25 children in this manner, five of them studied more intensively. The grammar of the two-word sentences was by no means identical with that of the adult, but grammar there was. The children tended to omit the so-called function words while including those carrying the most information. As Miller and Ervin point out, a child's two-word sentences can often be translated into an adult utterance by the addition of function words. For instance, "Sweater on" expands correctly to "Put my sweater on."

The children in Miller and Ervin's sample tended to use a few high-frequency words in a given position in a sentence in such a way that they were classed as "operators." They were precursors of function words, which characterized a later phase of development. One child, for instance, used "no" in this manner: a statement beginning with an accented "no" was followed by a noun, such as "toy," and meant she did not want the toy. Obviously the child was not simply repeating an adult statement which had been heard frequently. There was in these two-word sentences a relatively systematic arrangement of word classes even though it was a much simpler system than the complex one of adults. Braine (1963a) also found two-word classes at a similar stage, which he termed "pivot class" and "open class."

Eventually the child's word classes could be identified by markers as well as by order. A verb, for instance, might be marked by suffixes or auxiliaries. Mistakes at this point are apt to be indications that the child has learned a morphological rule, such as "finded" for "found," "foots" for "feet." One child began correcting himself at two years and nine months, indicating that certain sentences were judged ungrammatical and proving that he had a formal grammatical system. Generalizations were learned and used for transfer, such as the plural-singular contrast and certain verb transformations. Once learned, they could soon be applied and generalized with no specific practice or training of an associational type. The pattern of acquisition of the singular-plural contrast went in a regular sequence: no contrast, to acquisition of particular familiar instances of contrast, to generalization a few months later, and finally to correction and differentiation of irregular forms (e.g., "feet" for "feets" or "foots").

Another detailed study of the natural speech production of very young children was performed by Brown and Fraser (1964). The grammar of a child of two, as they analyzed it, did not generate adult English sentences. The child omitted certain morphemes and abbreviated, achieving what they termed a "telegraphic" reduction of adult grammar. Furthermore, a group of children reduced sentences in a similar fashion under experimental conditions. When they were asked to repeat a sentence given them by the experimenter, some words were retained and some were dropped, but the omissions were not random or specific to the child. The most informative words were retained, such as reference-making forms and morphemes relatively unpredictable from the context. The ones most likely to be dropped were, for example, intermediate terms and ones predictable from context and thus carrying little information. At this early stage of reduction of adult speech, a child might have no construction rules and be performing by selective imitation. But from the reduced speech he presumably induces rules that are revised and supplemented as more details of adult speech are registered. The fact that the imitation (if present) is selective means that the child is doing perceptual learning, reducing the total information and taking in that which is most distinctive.

Research by Berko (1958) employed invented linguistic materials to show that children, after four years or so, have rules of morphology. Nonsense syllables such as "wug" were applied to pictures of animal-like cartoons, and inflections were elicited from the child. ("This is a wug. There are two of them. Now there are two —." The child, hearing a question in the investigator's voice, supplied the implied plural, "wugs.") Any inflections given by the child are evidence that he possesses construction rules, since he could not have copied specific models with made-up words. Berko's materials provided a complete inventory of the English inflectional system, including plural and possessive endings on nouns, the past tense, the third person present indicative, and the progressive, and the comparative and superlative for adjectives. Children generalized the regular inflections very consistently, first graders more so than preschoolers, but even the latter had formed and applied many rules. Adults were much more apt to produce irregular formations, such as "heaves" for the plural of "heaf," than were the children. Berko concluded that the children's performance exhibited consistency and regularity. New words were not treated idiosyncratically, especially when forms with few variants were appropriate.

Brown and Berko (1960) performed a somewhat similar experiment with nonsense words in an attempt to investigate children's command of syntactical rules. The subjects were asked to construct sentences using the nonsense words given them by the experimenter. Children in first, second, and third grade could construct grammatically correct sentences, their ability to do so increasing with age.

The influence of Noam Chomsky is much felt these days in discussions of the development of grammatical structures in children. He pointed out (1964) that the child's utterances are not perfect mirrors of the structures he has actually internalized and mastered, and that it is these latter we should be concerned with, whether or not they are utilized in practice.

There is surely no doubt that the child's achievements in systematizing linguistic data, at every stage, go well beyond what he actually produces in normal speech. Thus it is striking that advances are generally "across the board." A child who does not produce initial s + consonant clusters may begin to produce them all, at approximately the same time, thus distinguishing for the first time between "cool" and "school," etc.—but characteristically will do this in just the right words, indicating that the correct phonemic representation of these words was present to the mind even at the stage where it did not appear in speech (p. 39, 1964).

He is impressed too with the likelihood that hardly anything is acquired by imitation; that the child is always hearing new sentences formed by adults and producing new ones himself. He composes by means of rules and a lexicon.

Chomsky's points underline the importance of the problem of how higher order structure is detected and generalized. Grammatical structures are somehow perceived or induced through listening and eventually applied as rules for production. Braine (1963b) proposed that a child learns a temporal tag for word orders. But he could not learn a location for every word in every sentence. The hypothesis requires patching in order to work. One would need to assume that there is generalization between words belonging to the same form classes, but if true, this in itself would need explanation. We are so far from an answer at present that the suggestion has been seriously made that grammatical categories are universal and part of the child's innate endowment. The role of such a universal hierarchy would be "to direct the child's discovery of the classes of English (McNeill, 1966, p. 35)." McNeill discusses in detail the possibility of a universal hierarchy of grammatical rules, and states the hypothesis that "the basic grammatical relations are also part of innate linguistic capacity (p. 45)."

If one eschews the easy solution of appealing to innate endowment, the magnitude of the problem is evident, but the failure of well-worn associationist concepts to handle it is not thereby alleviated. Fodor compares the child's learning of his native language to the behavior of a scientist.

The similarities between the child's problem and normal problems of scientific induction are thus very striking. Like the scientist, the child finds himself with a finite body of observations, some of which are almost certain to be unsystematic. His problem is to discover regularities in these data that, at very least, can be relied upon to hold however much additional data is added (Fodor, 1966, p. 109).

Learning of artificial grammars, described earlier in the chapter, has been likened to perceptual learning and abstraction at a primitive level (Smith, 1966; Reber, 1967). We can go this far at least with development of perception of natural languages. Both perception and eventually conception or abstraction must be involved. Perception is involved because the child must detect the structure—the regularities and the order—in the ongoing flow of language that enters his ears. This order is present in the stimulation. It is not invented by the infant but filtered out of what the world of speakers presents to him. He has a motive to filter it out, to extract it from noise and complexity, because the order reduces information, allows processing more of what might otherwise be unusable chaos or "cognitive clutter" to borrow McNeill's phrase. As samples of a once-detected type of order recur, the infant begins to recognize the syntax, despite its being embedded in new contexts and exemplified by different levels and tokens of stimulation and represented by different voices. He can then begin to abstract the rules from the sample patterns, to pull the invariant relations out of the variable contexts. When he has some grasp on a rule, he can himself invent new sentences. He does not invent new orders—he uses the ones presented to him by his linguistic environment, so he must detect them before sentence invention begins. The problem of how the child detects structure in sequences of symbols will come up again in the acquisition of reading skill, to which we now turn.

READING: THE PERCEPTION OF WRITTEN SYMBOLS

The acquisition of reading skill might be expected to parallel, in some ways, the acquisition of language, but its development comes much later and presents special problems of its own. Let us begin with an analysis of what it is that is learned.

Analysis of Reading Skill

Reading is not simply a matter of discriminating graphic symbols from one another and decoding them one at a time. Like the acquisition of language, it has more than one aspect to be considered. Discrimination of graphemes is analogous to discrimination of phonemes. Like phonemes, graphemes are perceived sequentially, and the combining rules for sequencing give the basis for apprehending units larger than the grapheme. But the analogy of reading to understanding speech is not perfect, since writing decodes to speech and thence to things rather than directly to things. It has been suggested (Liberman et al., 1967) that it is a different kind of code than the speech code, which is not like an alphabet. And it is clear that every human child learns to speak without special tuition, whereas reading must be taught and even so not everyone learns readily.

An analysis of how reading skill is acquired leads us to recognize that there are several subskills and that certain subskills are logical prerequisites for others. First comes the skill of learning to speak the language. The child has been learning this for six years before coming to school, and will continue to perfect his language skills for many years. But fairly expert perception of speech is essential before it is feasible to begin learning to decode another symbol system to it. It is not enough to comprehend the meaning of a spoken message; the child must be able to perceive its segmentation and combinatory order.

The second skill is learning to discriminate visually the letters of the alphabet, which we have already discussed.[1] Most children start doing this between five and six years, and can name some letters at this stage. Many have trouble after entering first grade, however, and may be able to discriminate and name only a few letters after several months. For these children a good program of training could be very important, but there has been no systematic research on the problem. Should one begin by presenting letters with the biggest contrasts and the least complexity, such as I and O?

[1] See the discussion in Chapter 18 and the discussion of distinctive features of letters in Chapter 5.

Should one proceed by introducing gradually greater complexity and more distinctive feature differences? Or should, on the other hand, all possible contrasts be introduced early in the training, so that the child will not learn to disregard any potentially distinctive feature as irrelevant?

A third skill in learning to read is the decoding phase, learning to read out in units of the spoken language what is directed by the graphic units. Superficially, it sounds so simple; just a matter of learning paired associates. But this is far from the case, as we shall see. What should the child decode as a unit? A letter? A word? A whole phrase?

Whatever the first units chosen for decoding, the child must move toward a fourth skill, whose perfecting continues for many years. This is the skill of learning to read in terms of higher order units, to read in chunks, to improve his strategies by using all the structural regularities in the written language, as well as those provided by correspondences with speech. One could add further superordinate skills, such as learning to bypass the vocal-auditory speech units and to go more directly from the printed page to the apprehension of things and events—a kind of shortcircuiting of the mediating speech. This bypass would presumably add to reading speed, but the other skills are more essential for pickup of information from messages coded in graphic symbols.

Decoding Graphic Units to Speech

The units of writing must in some way correspond to the units of speech, but deciding on the relevant unit is not an easy problem in either case. On first thought it might seem that one should start with elementary units of each system, and teach a child to associate an element of one with an element of the other. The elementary unit of the writing system, a letter, should correspond with an elementary unit of speech, a phoneme. Unfortunately, things are not that simple for the elements are not building blocks. As Liberman et al. (1967) have shown, there is no segment of the acoustic stream as small as a phoneme that maps to it with invariance. Context influences phonemic units to make them different. And even if this were not so, English spelling does not have one sound per letter. The context or combinations of written letters influences the way they are to be sounded out.

Consider the word as a unit, then. Does not a written word correspond to a predictable pronunciation? On the whole, yes. Why not, in that case, simply teach the child to pronounce words and not bother with the letters at all? The whole-word system, very popular not long ago, had this kind of reasoning behind it and some merit. A word was supposed to be a total gestalt. But note what this theory of teaching implies; it expects a child to learn separately, by rote, to decode every word in the language. That would mean losing the advantages of an alphabetic writing system.

What are the advantages of an alphabetic system for reading? In theory, knowledge of the component relationships of letters within the word makes possible transfer to the reading of new words never previously encountered. That is, if a new written word can be subvocally pronounced it may turn out to be an old word of the vocal-auditory language. This theory was tested in an experiment by Bishop (1964). She used college students as subjects, but simulated the situation of a child learning to read by using wholly novel (Arabic) letters and hence unfamiliar letter-to-sound correspondences. A three-stage transfer design was employed. Each of the 12 Arabic characters had a one-to-one letter-sound correspondence. There were eight consonants and four vowels, which were combined to form two sets of eight Arabic words. The twelve letters appeared at least once in both sets of words. A native speaker of the language recorded on tape the twelve letter sounds and the two sets of words. The graphic form of each letter or word was printed on a card.

The subjects were divided into three groups—the letter training group (L), the whole-word training group (W), and a control group (C). Stage I of the experiment was identical for all groups. The subjects learned to pronounce the set of words (transfer set) which would appear visually in Stage III by listening to the recording and repeating the words. Stage II varied. Group L listened to and repeated the 12 letter sounds and then learned to associate the individual graphic shapes with their sounds. Group W followed the same procedure, except that eight written words were given them to learn, rather than letters. Group C spent the same time interval on an unrelated task. Stage III was identical for the three groups. All subjects learned to read the set of words they had heard in Stage I, responding to the presentation of a word on a card by pronouncing it. This was the transfer stage on which the three groups were compared.

At the close of Stage III, all subjects were tested on their ability to give the correct letter sound following the presentation of each printed letter.

Figure 19–1 shows the learning curves of each group on the transfer task. Learning took place in fewest trials for the letter group and next fewest for the word group, so letter training had more transfer value than word training. Then Bishop looked at the knowledge of component letter-sound relationships for the three groups. The subjects of Group L who had learned letters in Stage II knew, as one would expect, more letter-sound pairs on the average than the other groups, but there were individuals in Group W who knew all 12. When these individuals were separated from the others in Group W and learning curves were drawn for the subgroups, it was clear that all the transfer for the group that learned whole words was accounted for by the subjects who had, without instruction or separate presentation of single letters, nevertheless learned the component correspondences. The subjects who had not learned the component letter-sound correspondences learned the words, but there was no transfer to new words.

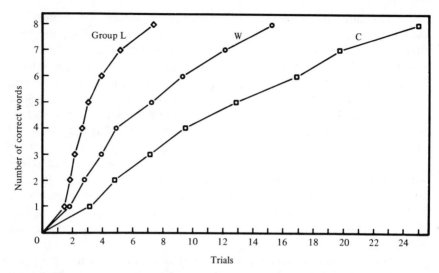

FIGURE 19–1. Learning curves on a transfer task for a group trained originally with whole words (W), a group trained with single letters (L), and a
control group (C).

(After Bishop, 1964; from E. J. Gibson, Learning to Read. *Science, 148,*
1066–1072, 21 May 1965. Copyright 1965 by the American Association
for the Advancement of Science.)

An experiment modeled on Bishop's was performed by Jeffrey and
Samuels (1967) with kindergarten children. Six artificial graphemes were
designed and assigned to six letter sounds. One group had original training
with pairs of graphemes and learned a word for the pair. Another group
had original training with individual graphemes and their sounds. A control group had no pretraining with graphemes and their sounds. All
groups learned new transfer words, pairs made of different combinations
of graphemes already presented to the two experimental groups. The children given letter training made some correct responses on the first transfer
trial, and reached the criterion significantly faster than both the other
groups. The word training group did not differ from the control group.

It seems, then, that the child must somehow learn the component
letter-to-sound correspondences if he is going to be able to transfer what
he has learned in reading familiar words to reading unfamiliar words. But
the answer to how this should be accomplished is not simple, for English
orthography does not decode one letter to one sound with regularity. This
is what advocates of spelling reform and the revising of the alphabet are
fond of pointing out.

The advocates of ITA (the Initial Teaching Alphabet) would have
the schools simplify the child's decoding problem so that a unique graphic

symbol is available for each speech sound. There has been devised an alphabet of 42 characters for this purpose (Downing, 1962). This expedient might take care of the problem of the reading difficulty which many children now experience if a complete change of English orthography could be legislated, but that is not at all likely. Moreover, there is order within the orthographic system to be taken into account. We must ask what this is, and what correspondences actually exist between our present writing system and sound. The correspondences exist on a higher level than that of the single letter. This fact has been demonstrated in detail (Venezky, 1967).

Higher Order Units

We have known for many years, since the work of Cattell in 1885, that an adult reader, with a tachistoscopic exposure of one tenth of a second, can pick up a string of at most four unrelated letters, but that he can in the same exposure pick up a long word of many more letters than that, and all the letters of several words if they form a sentence. In short we perceive graphic symbols in larger units than that of a single letter. We see them in chunks as Miller (1956) has recently called them. In the older terminology, the span of perception of discrete items gets larger as the items are increasingly more related to one another, or more organized. The letter chunks are not available at once to the beginning reader, and we know very little about how he attains skill at grasping them. An early study of learning the telegraphic code of dot-dash combinations (Bryan & Harter, 1899) showed a shift, after long practice in receiving single symbols, to the receiving of longer symbol units as a whole, but that study did not tell us how it happens. Are larger units for reading formed because there is structure to be detected in the writing system itself? Do they form because the system maps to speech and eventually the speech units create segments in the orthography, that is, transfer their structure to it? Are there perhaps correspondence rules relating the writing system to the speech system which dictate the grouping principles?

The second of these three alternative hypotheses, that higher units in reading are simply mapped backward from higher units in the speech system, seems too simple. Sequential reading is not the same as hearing speech sequentially because the act of reading is self-determined by the reader. Words are presented in adjacent order from left to right across the page and from the top down. The act of reading is sequential, but the reader does not always proceed in the adjacent order presented on the page. He can jump ahead or go back and look again. He can also adapt his speed to the semantic aspects of the text, that is, change his pace. In short, he does not read as he listens to speech.

There is plenty of evidence to show that the adult reader does not read a word by identifying each letter, one at a time, decoding it to a separate response in a left-to-right sequence. A letter is read in its context and is not responded to in isolation. It is a well-known fact that when the eye jumps from one fixation to another in reading, it takes in a whole group of letters during each fixation period. Experiments by Newman (1966) and by Kolers and Katzman (1966) demonstrated that when letters forming a familiar word are exposed successively in the same place, it is almost impossible to read the word.

The question is, what are the grouping principles or structure that yield larger units than the letter in reading? Sequential dependencies of letters within the word—the probability that one letter will follow another—have been suggested as a type of constraint that might facilitate perception of units larger than the single letter. Tachistoscopic experiments testing perception of strings of letters of varying degrees of approximation to English (Miller, Bruner, & Postman, 1954; Wallach, 1963) lend support to the view. Wallach ran his experiment with children, and found that relative facilitation by this statistical resemblance to English was significantly correlated with spelling achievement. Miller (1958) has also shown that redundant strings of letters (structured) as opposed to random ones have an advantage in recall of the strings. The structure in the redundant strings was generated by rules devised for purposes of the experiment. If structure exists in English orthography, we can expect it to be used to reduce the amount of information processed in reading. Spelling patterns are structure in much the same sense that the term was used in Miller's experiment on redundant letter strings. For instance, certain clusters of letters can begin a word (e.g., QU or CR) but may not end it; others may end it but not begin it (e.g., CK). These are rules stating a redundancy of a special sort found in English spelling. Fries (1963) has provided a useful discussion of patterns of English spelling. Venezky (1967) has analyzed both the internal structure of English orthography and the set of patterns that relate spelling to sound.

A question of importance is whether or not these structural constraints can be demonstrated to facilitate perception. An experiment by Gibson, Pick, Osser, and Hammond (1962) was designed to answer the question. Two sets of pseudo-words were constructed, one set containing strings of letters (four to ten letters in length) which conformed to English spelling patterns, although they were not real words. These strings were pronounceable (verified by a rating scale) and were referred to as the pronounceable words. An example of a pronounceable string is GLURCK. A second set of letter strings which did not conform to rules of English orthography was formed by permutation of the order of letters in the pronounceable strings. Initial and final consonant clusters were reversed, but the vowel cluster in the middle was left unchanged. For example, GLURCK became CKURGL. The pronounceable strings were chosen so that change of initial and final clusters would render the pseudo-word orthographically impossible, and at the same time unpronounceable as an English word.

The two lists of 25 words each were presented to subjects tachisto-scopically in random order, in five successive presentations with an exposure time beginning at 50 ms. and progressing up to 250 ms. The subjects (college students) wrote what they saw as each group of letters was projected. The mean percentage of pronounceable words correctly perceived was consistently and significantly greater at all exposure times. Replication of the experiment with a different judgment (matching) gave the same result. We can conclude, therefore, that skilled readers are more apt to perceive correctly letter strings which follow the rules of English orthography and spelling-to-sound correspondence.

These results were obtained with adult subjects. How are structural constraints within words picked up by the child learning to read? The question is somewhat analogous to one we have considered, how does the child learn grammatical rules? An obvious way to make a first attack on the problem was to collect some developmental data on how early beginning readers make use of simple orthographic rules. Gibson, Osser, and Pick (1963) investigated the question, comparing children at the end of first and third grades. Three-letter words, pronounceable trigrams, and unpronounceable trigrams were exposed tachistoscopically as in the previous experiment. The three-letter words were taken from the first-grade reading list. Each word chosen was rearranged to form a meaningless but pronounceable trigram and a meaningless unpronounceable one (for example, RAN, NAR, RNA). Some longer pseudo-words (four and five letters) taken from the previous experiment were included as well. The first graders perceived most accurately the familiar three-letter words. The unpronounceable trigrams resulted in most errors, and the pronounceable trigrams were intermediate. The longer pseudo-words were seldom perceived accurately by first graders and the pronounceable ones fared no better than the unpronounceable ones. By the end of third grade, many children perceived all the three-letter combinations with high and nearly equal accuracy, but differentiated the longer pseudo-words, the pronounceable ones now being perceived correctly significantly more often than their unpronounceable counterparts.

These results suggest that a child in the early stages of development of reading skill reads in short units, but is already beginning to generalize certain regularities of spelling and spelling-to-sound correspondences. A further question which arose as we contemplated the meaning of this finding was the role of the sound correspondences in perception of the letters and in abstracting the spelling patterns. Do invariant mappings of a visually perceived spelling pattern (itself an abstraction) enhance the generalized unit, dissect it, so to speak, from varying contexts? An invariant auditory accompaniment of the regular spelling patterns would be a further regularity that might promote abstraction of the patterns and thus facilitate formation of higher units. It seemed that deaf subjects should be handicapped compared to hearing ones if this were the case. The experiment with pronounceable and unpronounceable pseudo-words was therefore repeated with students at a college for the deaf (Gibson, Shurcliff, & Yonas, 1966). The subjects selected were congenitally deaf, or else had lost their hearing very early, long before learning to read. When the number of pseudo-words correctly read by these subjects was compared with the number read by hearing subjects of comparable age and education, the deaf subjects read fewer. But there was, nevertheless, a similar difference between the potentially pronounceable pseudo-words and the unpronounceable ones. The deaf students had picked up a knowledge of English spelling patterns and were using it to process strings of letters in chunks, even though they had never heard the sounds to which the letters mapped.

The spelling patterns per se, therefore, provide regularities that are used. Our term "pronounceable" was perhaps misleading, since the spelling rules can function independently of pronunciation. But the hearing subjects did read more words, on the average, and so it is likely that redundant invariant sound correspondences can be facilitating when they are available to the learner.

How children pick up the spelling patterns is a problem of great importance. They must perceive recurrent clusters so as to treat them as units; they must detect positional constraints; and they must abstract the patterns from varying contexts. It seems as though a kind of learning to notice and abstract spelling regularities develops in the young reader, and, at some stage, permits transcendence of rote learning of individual words and transfer of regularities found in them to the perceiving of new words. Easy-to-notice clusters which appear frequently in a given position might be abstracted first, such as a double vowel in the middle of a word (e.g., moon, toot, spook), and only much later would a more general pattern be noticed such as the marker "e" at the end of a word preceded by a vowel and a consonant, which determines the value of the vowel (e.g., duke, late, cede, dope, tribe). The even more general contrast with the markerless string and its rule for mapping to sound (e.g., hop *vs.* hope, at *vs.* ate, cut *vs.* cute) might come still later.

Detection of structure in orthography seems to me a kind of perceptual learning akin to learning syntax in spoken language, which we considered earlier in the chapter. The structure is there to be detected and must be extracted as a kind of invariant in order to be generalized to new instances. Overgeneralization, of the kind found in morphological errors (e.g., "bended"), occurs as evidenced by both reading and spelling errors. A child may pronounce an unfamiliar word incorrectly when it is first encountered, on the basis of rules he has mastered that might have applied to it. He might pronounce "great" as if it rhymed with "treat"; or he might in going from sound to spelling, spell "dream" as if it followed the same rule as "seem." It is interesting that the deaf subjects in the experiment of Gibson et al. (1966), made no spelling errors in writing answers to some questions given them. Cross-modal correspondences which often lead to spelling errors in hearing students were not available to them.

This brings us back to the question of the kinds of regularities actually detected and used in reading units larger than single letters. Certainly orthographic (spelling) patterns are used, and the hearing child probably uses the correlated speech sounds as an auxiliary regularity in discovering the spelling patterns. The situation is a little like a concept formation experiment in which a redundant dimension is provided for defining all the positive instances. It has generally been found to facilitate learning. But is a cross-modal redundancy facilitating? That it is used by some readers seems indicated by the spelling errors attributable to spelling-to-sound correspondences, but the problem needs study.

That properties of the spoken language, with all its patterns of segmentation and syntax, carry over to reading beyond the limits of spelling-to-sound correspondences within the word seems indubitable. The deaf student is not handicapped in learning to spell, but he is badly handicapped in learning to read at all in the first place, and in learning to read with speed and fluency at a later stage. Going beyond the word, there is good reason to suppose that still higher levels of structure facilitate reading. Meaningful context and syntax are structural principles that might operate to permit chunking. Phrase structure and punctuation indicating stress patterns could determine holistic perception of several words at a time. The hearing child brings knowledge of the rules of phrase structure to the reading situation. Does it transfer to it and generate word chains which are treated as functional units?

There is evidence that chains of several words or more are treated as units in reading, and that the units are correlated with phrase structure. The influence of context on speed of reading has often been emphasized (Tinker, 1958; Morton, 1964). It is conceivable that a skilled reader takes in more at a glance simply because practice has stretched his span of apperception, or the extent to which he can use peripheral vision in a single fixation. Remedial courses for retarded readers have often operated on such a notion. But it is also possible that structural features of the material are correlated with the word chains grouped into a unit, and that they have a causal role in creating units. Levin and Turner (1966) and Levin and Kaplan (1966) have investigated this hypothesis in several experiments on the eye-voice span, showing the correlation of phrase structure and syntax with the pickup of super-word units.

The eye-voice span is the distance that the eye gets ahead of the voice in reading aloud. It can be measured by turning off the illumination at some point in the reader's delivery and seeing how far he can continue when the print is no longer visible. This is a measure, presumably, of how far ahead his last glance had been directed and thus where he stopped perceiving the words. The optical input can be stopped when the reader reaches a phrase boundary or at any point before or after it. Does the eye reach for the end of a phrase, a structural unit of syntax, as a new fixation begins? The reaching hypothesis is a plausible one, because we suspect that peripheral vision contributes to skilled reading, although we do not know exactly how. When a reader is forced to depend on foveal vision alone (for instance, by wearing spectacles which occlude all but a small central portion of the field), he is greatly hampered. It seems as if visual input to the corner of the eye, however poor the acuity of reception, is determining where the next glance is directed.

Here are some of the findings for the eye-voice span. It is significantly longer for structured sentences than for unstructured word lists. It increases, in general, with school grade. It is longer before the verb in a passive sentence and longer after the verb in an active one. The number of times a subject reads to the end of a phrase unit, corrected for his modal eye-voice span, is significantly greater than zero. There is a tendency to read to phrase boundaries rather than to nonboundary positions, and older subjects do this significantly more often than children just learning to read.

This evidence supports the hypothesis that we tend to read in phrase units and that the span for a fixation in reading is not a constant of so many words or so many centimeters of print, but rather shrinks or expands so as to accommodate to phrase boundaries, fluctuating with the degree of structural constraint. It can be argued that the eye-voice span is not entirely a matter of what is perceived in a visual fixation, but is dependent also on the subject's ability to guess what would come next. The more constrained a chain of words, the better he should be able to predict what he has not yet seen. The paradigm of this experiment does not allow us to settle the argument, and predictability might well play a role. But it seems unlikely that it accounts for all the findings. Suppose one reads such a sentence as "Although the boy was eating taffy, he accepted a pickle." Now suppose the light is turned off just before the reader speaks the word "taffy." One could predict that a noun and in fact a noun indicating food of some kind might come next, but the predictability of "taffy" is very low. If the phrase can be delivered as a unit here, it is evident that the reader's fixation extended to the phrase boundary. Recognition tests administered in the Levin and Kaplan study supported the view that the words were perceived and not merely guessed at.

The point is that knowledge of the structure of language, in combination with peripheral reaching, directs the eye ahead in the sentence so as to take in the structural unit presented in stimulation. Here again is proof that skilled perception takes advantage of higher order structure in the interest of good cognitive strategy.

SUMMARY

Perceiving by means of symbols was compared with perceiving by means of representations. It is mediated perception too, but a different kind, because the mapping of a symbol to the thing or event symbolized is arbitrary and conventional, not naturally given. Learning enters into the perception of symbols in three important ways. First, the symbols themselves, such as speech sounds and letters, must be perceptually differentiated from one another. Second, invariants of mapping from the symbol set to the set symbolized must be learned. This may be a matter of paired associate learning of a code, but it is also possible that the correspondences are abstracted from the stimulus flux. A letter-sound correspondence, for instance, may be induced from a larger context where a recurrent regularity can be detected. Third, a set of symbols has rules for how they may be put together in a sequence. These rules constitute structure and man must learn to perceive the structural constraints in the sequence for the information in even the simplest sentence to be transmitted.

Trends in
Perceptual Development

The time has come, the author said,
To sum up many things:
Of features learned for face and space
And rules for letter strings—
Of structure found and noise reduced
That reinforcement brings.

(Apologies to Lewis Carroll)

In my last chapter I do not so much want to summarize the facts that have emerged about perceptual development, as to point out some general trends observable from a vantage point that lets us view the course from birth to maturity; and to consider how they fit with and illuminate the conception of perceptual learning that I have presented.

There are always left over from the past some credos or clichés implying the priority of certain issues, and we might do well to get these out of the way first. Let us scrutinize them briefly, and then go on to a fresher formulation.

LAST THOUGHTS ON SOME CLASSIC
FALSE ISSUES

Learning or Maturation?

This issue was examined in Chapter 12, where we considered rearing experiments and the light they throw on perceptual development. It seems clear that as a dilemma it can be buried, for concurrent processes of both maturation and learning can be demonstrated. As for learning, children (and animals) learn to attend to distinctive features of things, to invariants that lead to perceptual constancy and permanence, and to higher order structures and rules. The latter may be best observed in human skills such as speech and reading, but perception of invariance over transformations, such as a ball being seen to roll behind a screen and out again, can be demonstrated to develop in a cat.

It was also demonstrated that all the progress witnessed in these accomplishments is not solely a matter of learning. Experiments on the visual cliff with animals of different ages, species, and rearing histories show that maturation has a role in depth perception. The effects of special rearing conditions also made it clear that maturation assumes an environment ecologically normal for the species, and that abilities already mature require it for their maintenance. The trends in perceptual development emerge as the product of both experience with an environment and the maturing powers of an individual. There is no either-or issue.

Perception and Production

The question of which comes first, perception or action, is like the question of which comes first, the hen or the egg. The currently fashionable predilection for motor theories of perception would seem to imply that action has priority, but we know, on the other hand, that production often follows after discriminatory achievements. We considered this fact in the chapter on perception of symbolic stimuli, for speech is a case in point where discrimination often procedes production. Another interesting case is the drawing of a diagonal line (see Chapter 8). A child can draw an acceptable circle at three, a square at four, a triangle at five, but a diamond only later still, at seven. This is an interesting progression in itself, but it becomes still more interesting when one learns that the diagonals of the triangle and the diamond can be discriminated considerably earlier than they can be drawn (Maccoby & Bee, 1965; Olson, 1968). It is not the motor performance as such that is wanting, for training in executing the movement does not facilitate accurate production, while training in discrimination does (Maccoby, 1968).

Leaving visible tracings on paper with a tool, trace making, is an interesting event to children, as J. J. Gibson and Patricia Yonas (in preparation) have shown, whereas the motor act without the tracings, as with a pencil that leaves no marks, is not interesting. Even watching the tracings being made, although the child himself is not the direct executor, is interesting. I observed children at an exhibition of kinetic sculpture by the artist Tingueley. One of the exhibits was a complicated machine which held a pencil. When activated the pencil made random marks on a piece of paper—scribbles. The machine was provided with pads of paper and colored marking pens which a child could put in place. Crowds of children were waiting for a turn at this machine. So there is a strong motivation merely to observe marks being made on paper, and it is not the motor act as such, the feel of it, that is responsible. There is no particular reason, therefore, why the ability to produce a given pattern and the ability to discriminate it should emerge at the same time. Motor schemata there may be, and response-produced stimulation as well. But perception is an activity in its own right—an exploratory activity, not a performatory activity. Performatory acts have a developmental history, but so do exploratory acts, and the histories are not the same.

Which comes first, perception or production? The question is a red herring that leads us off the scent. Perception and production serve different purposes. Adaptiveness of behavior is served by exploratory perceptual activity that provides information about the environment prior to performance. Exploratory activity begins early, yielding informative stimulation with the first eye movements. We would not call these eye movements production, but they are a kind of activity. Performatory action, like seizing a proffered rattle, or banging a spoon on a tin plate, appears later than looking at the object. But when it comes about, there is informative feedback from this action, too, which takes on a role in monitoring behavior. I have tried to indicate this relationship in the chart on page 161.

The Part or the Whole?

Another "which comes first" question that has bewildered developmental psychologists is the part-whole controversy. It has been the contention of many child psychologists that children begin by perceiving globally, and progressively analyze or differentiate out the details. But just as many have taken the opposite view, that the young child begins by noticing only details in isolation and gradually, through a learning process, integrates them into a whole.

This issue was considered in Chapter 16, on the perception of objects. It is another false issue. Children learn to perceive distinctive features of objects, and so one might be inclined to say that these are parts and that they are being differentiated from a whole. But what kind of whole? Not a whole with intricate structure, certainly. It is equally true that the pickup of structure characterizes development, in fact progressively higher order levels of structure, and this sounds like progress toward a whole. But the very notion of parts and wholes in perception is mistaken; objects are differentiated by distinctive features which must be discriminated, and objects are also characterized by structure. Higher order structure creates new units by grouping subordinate units, enabling more information to be handled while reducing uncertainty. Enlarging the chunks might be considered integration of parts into wholes, but we must not forget that there is also progress toward discovery of the most economical and critical set of distinctive features. Which of these two equally adaptive kinds of change characterizes behavior will depend upon the task and the stimulus information, and both may even occur at once.

From Perception to Inference

It is often asserted that the young child is stimulus bound, enslaved by the surrounding milieu, dependent on the present sensory information, and that perceptual development is a process of liberation from the constraints of stimulation. Another way of putting this has been to say that he is misled by perceptual factors and must make inferences. A related statement is that cognitive development consists in "going beyond the information given" (Bruner, 1957).

One cannot doubt that the child's conceptual life expands as he matures and gains experience. Concepts and generalized rules can have a guiding and directing effect on perception, just as labels and verbal instructions can have. I have discussed this in chapters 7 and 8. Labels or instructions can direct attention to distinctive parts of a display, and concepts, especially rule-like ones, can help to reveal structure not easily or automatically detected perceptually. But this is not to say that perception is left behind in favor of inference as we grow up, nor is it even to say that perception develops by making use of inference.

What is wrong with saying that the young child is stimulus bound, and that cognitive development is a liberation from these bonds by the operations of intelligence? This is Piaget's opinion. One must admit its popularity and its persuasiveness, for a neonate's attention does seem to be captured by a few kinds of events in its environment. But the developmental change is not one of doing without stimulus information; it is one of seeking stimulus information in a directed, systematic fashion. Does perception mislead us, whereas conception and generalization lead to truth and reality? Concepts and generalizations can sometimes themselves mislead us; we speak of biased observation. It is then not perception that is misleading. We are misled by the failure to grasp the invariants in the stimulus flux. When the invariants occur over a temporal sequence of transformations, as in an event like the pouring of water from one container to another, they may or may not be detected. A still shot of a filled container at one moment of stimulation can be misleading, like a single frame from a motion picture, for invariants occur that can be discovered only over variation and transformation.

Does the child need more information in stimulation, or more redundancy in stimulation, than adults do because his concepts are immature? One kind of evidence cited for this conclusion is drawn from experiments with incomplete figures (Gollin, 1960, 1961). Children can fill in the figures and recognize them better as age increases. To quote Wohlwill,

"Compared to the adult the young child requires more redundancy in a pattern to perceive it correctly; thus both incomplete and very complex patterns will be difficult for him (1960, p. 281)." They may be more difficult but not, I suggest, because "the younger child requires a greater amount of surplus information." He cannot handle more information than an adult, and is far less adept at seeing and using redundancy in stimulation when it is present. Distinctive features of objects do have to be learned, however, and an increased knowledge of them would be expected to aid in rcognizing incomplete pictures.

Bruner, also, has claimed that "less redundancy is needed as we grow older" (Bruner, Olver, Greenfield, et al., 1966, p. 23), using again the evidence from recognition of incomplete pictures. The reasoning is that perception is based on representations, on a constructed model of reality against which the input is tested. As this model grows richer, he suggests, the child uses it to fill in details that are not given in stimulation.

As the reader knows by now, I disagree with this interpretation of perception and perceptual development. Perception is not a process of matching to a representation in the head, but one of extracting the invariants in stimulus information. Constraints in stimulation can be useful, and adaptive development depends on more effective pickup of this information rather than less dependence upon it. Although our concepts increase in number, richness, and complexity as we grow older, it does not follow that our percepts become more and more reflections of our concepts. We do not perceive less because we conceive more. If we did, it would be maladaptive for getting information about what is going on in the world around us.

Stages or Transitions?

The manifestations of change over time are a fascinating problem for the dramatist, the archaeologist, and the biologist alike. Shakespeare celebrated the seven ages of man, wondering how the mewling infant could possibly be identified with the whining schoolboy, the lover, and the "lean and slippered pantaloon." Yet, dramatic as these contrasts are, there is some identity over the ages of man. Are these different stages arbitrarily chosen from a sequence that really proceeds in continuous fashion, or are there times in the sequence when the transition is abrupt and a quite new organization follows? Biologically, there is no clear-cut answer to this question. One can point to the insects where there is a metamorphosis in development, with a radical shift in structure and manner of adapting to the environment, but one can also point to cases of continuous growth where the transformation is spectacular only if it is speeded up, as if in a time-lapse motion picture that emphasizes the change.

This chapter is concerned with trends. But the identifying of psychological trends is difficult. Does a trend imply a gradual transition in a kind of behavior, maintaining identity while exhibiting progress toward some biological adaptation? If so, how do we describe the changed behavior and still recognize the identity? Or does a trend imply not gradual transitions but stages of behavior, with abrupt changes in organization comparable to metamorphosis in insects?

Human growth, after birth, does not display metamorphosis. The closest thing to it is the speeded-up change at adolescence, and perhaps the heightened responsiveness occurring at so-called critical periods during infancy. We are aware of the great docility of the human organism, and the extent to which its behavior can be shaped by programmed schedules of training. The contribution of the environment is so great that the appearance of stages might result from the program that the culture has provided for the child's education.

I want to look for trends in development, but I am very dubious about stages. Instead of the child study psychologists of fifty years ago, who thought of the child as almost a distinct species, or even the more recent experimental child psychologists, let us try to be developmental psychologists. Let us examine developmental studies of perceptual activity, hoping to discover generalizations that will reveal the laws of behavior and its adaptation to ongoing events. We look for a progressive sequence which spans the activity from birth to maturity.

It is a hazardous undertaking, but I am going to propose, and summarize evidence for, certain trends in perceptual development. To repeat, trends do not imply stages in each of which a radically new process emerges, nor do they imply maturation in which a new direction exclusive of learning is created.

THREE TRENDS IN PERCEPTUAL DEVELOPMENT

Increasing Specificity of Discrimination

In earlier chapters, it was shown that perceptual learning is characterized by a progressive increase in the specificity of discrimination to stimulus information. In Chapter 9, I described the effects of practice on acuity judgments, on differential limens, and on absolute estimations along a stimulus dimension; all showed this kind of change—a narrowing of the band of stimulus values eliciting any given response value within the continuum. The same trend, though complicated by species-specific methods of adaptation, appears in phylogenetic development. With evolution, specialized receptors proliferated, along with distinct modes of sensitivity to different types of energy change.

The evidence cited in preceding chapters showed that the human infant differentiates properties of things and events to some degree quite early. Nevertheless, a developmental trend toward specificity can be demonstrated in the ways described below.

DECREASE IN STIMULUS GENERALIZATION. The experimental measurement of what is called stimulus generalization affords a method of comparing the size of the class of different stimulus events that will elicit the same response at various age levels. It is a method in the strict stimulus-response tradition of psychology. The generalization gradient around a stimulus to which a given response has been associated does in fact steepen between infancy and maturity; the amount of generalization decreases. One example is an experiment by Riess (1946), in which subjects of four age groups, ranging from seven years to eighteen and a half, had an electrodermal response conditioned to a word for which a homophone, an antonym, and a synonym existed, and then were tested for generalization to these. The youngest group generalized most to homophones. Generalization to synonyms increased with age, relative to the other words, if only the three older groups were compared. But the youngest group generalized more to all words, regardless of the particular relationship of the words. Properties that relate or distinguish words were not yet effectively dif-

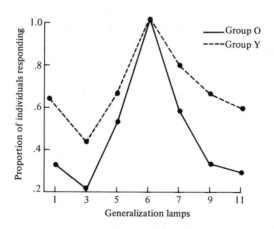

FIGURE 20–1. Comparison of stimulus generalization for older (Group O) and younger (Group Y) children.

The gradients are steeper for the older group. (From S. A. Mednick & L. E. Lehtinen, Stimulus generalization as a function of age in children. *Journal of Experimental Psychology*, 1957, *53*, 182.)

ferentiated and merely the appearance of a word elicited the conditioned response.

A second illustration is provided by Mednick and Lehtinen (1957), who compared stimulus generalization in children of various ages, the youngest seven years old. A horizontal row of eleven lamps was arranged on a curved plywood panel, spaced 9° apart. The subject had a reaction key, and was told to react as quickly as possible when the center lamp was lit. He was told that the other lamps would be lighted occasionally, but not to respond to them. False responses to lamps other than the center one were considered cases of generalization, and they occurred significantly less often as the children tested were older. Adults, too, make a certain number of false responses in this situation, the number increasing as the lamp is nearer the center, but the task of ignoring lamps other than that designated and responding selectively to it is much harder for children. This result seems less due to inexperience or lack of opportunity to learn differentiating features than to immature strategies of attention, a problem we shall return to shortly.

An experiment comparing the breadth of generalization at different age levels (Gibson & Gibson, 1955) was reported in Chapter 5. This experiment required the subject to distinguish between specially constructed scribbles by matching to a standard scribble designated and shown in advance of the series. The size of the class of scribbles that were called "same" by adults was small at the start (three), and with practice was reduced to one. The size of the class called "same" by the younger children was more than four times as great, and most of these children, even with practice, could not attain perfect specificity, although the "same" class was significantly reduced. A set of distinctive features characterized these scribbles and various combinations of them rendered each one unique. The younger children were unable, in the course of the experiment, to master the set of features and thereby to discover the uniqueness of each scribble but, as greater specificity was achieved, verbal comments spontaneously occurred indicating that some of the distinctive features were being detected and used.

REDUCTION OF VARIABILITY. In Chapter 9 many cases were cited showing reduction with practice of the variable error in a psychophysical experiment. Decrease in this kind of error is also characteristic of development with age. The experiments of Piaget and his collaborators on perception provide many demonstrations. Figure 20–2 drawn from one of the studies of the change in size constancy with age shows the striking decrease in variability of size matches (for the height of a rod) from five years to an asymptote at about twelve years. This is a drop in the variability of judgments made by each child, not by different children, so it is a genuine

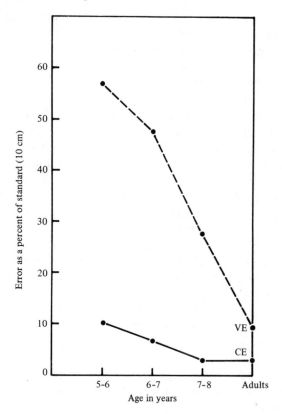

FIGURE 20–2. Decrease with age of variable and constant error in size matches.

The upper curve shows the drop in variability of size judgments with age. It represents, in percent of the standard, the median width of the area of uncertainty, or upper and lower limits of the threshold. The lower curve shows a drop in the constant error, as represented by the median judgment. (Drawn from data of M. Lambercier, Recherche sur le développement des perceptions: VI. La constance des grandeurs en comparaisons sériales. *Archives de Psychologie,* 1946, *31,* 170.)

increase in the precision and consistency of their discrimination. The constant error, plotted on the same graph, also changes with age but remarkably little as compared to the variable error. The youngest age group accepts as equivalent in height to a standard rod a group of rods varying over more than half the height of the standard. The width of the area of uncertainty—the variable error—is about six times as great as the mean constant error, and it narrows progressively with age.

We have seen in earlier chapters many examples of differential thresholds becoming smaller with age, of improved discrimination for such properties as pitch, color, the two-point limen, and weight.[1] For pure tones as well as for more complex acoustic properties such as rhythm the well-known Seashore tests have provided evidence for the development of more precise discrimination with age.

In discussing the perception of objects we considered weight in some detail, and it is worth recalling how slowly this is abstracted by children as a dimension of objects. This usual developmental history is only made more obvious by Robinson's (1964) feat of training a two year old, by heroic methods continuing over months, to distinguish objects differing only in weight, and bringing the just noticeable difference down to 30 grams. There is also the developmental study of the size-weight illusion by Pick and Pick (1967) with subjects ranging from four year olds to adults. The notable finding in their experiment was the progressive lowering of the interval of uncertainty with age although, after six years, there was no decrease in the magnitude of the illusion. To repeat, it is the variable error, typically, that lessens with age.

REDUCTION IN DISCRIMINATION TIME.   Psychologists have known for many years that the reaction time required for making different responses to different objects that are suddenly presented increases with the similarity of the objects (Merkel, 1885; Lemmon, 1927). The latency corresponds, in other words, with their discriminability. It is interesting, therefore, to find that the reaction time for discriminating between objects decreases with age.

The disjunctive reaction time experiment by Yonas and Gibson, described in Chapter 7, is an example. The subject pushed a lever in one direction if a letter exposed on a small screen before him was a letter that had been designated by the experimenter; he pushed it in the other direction if it was any other letter. The class of letters used was limited. Children from second grade, from fourth grade, and college students took part in the experiment. The curves in Figure 20–3 reveal the differences between the age groups.

Could it be that the younger children simply do not understand the task, or are not always paying attention? The latter explanation is possible but it is not sufficient, for the latencies of reaction reflect the influence of similarities and differences between stimulus displays much as do the adults'. In an experiment with same-different judgments, a confusion matrix for a set of letters was obtained (see Chapter 5). The latencies for discrimination correspond to the tendency to confuse the letters very well; for example, discriminating E and F has an extremely long latency and the letters are frequently confused, while discriminating C and M has a very

---

[1] See Gibson and Olum (1960) for further references.

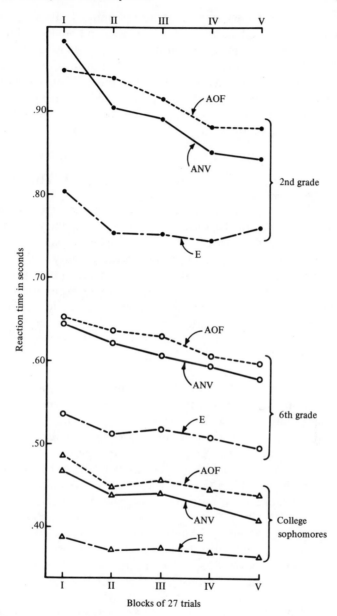

FIGURE 20–3. Comparison of age groups in a disjunctive reaction-time experiment by Yonas and Gibson (1967).

much shorter one and they are almost never confused. These differences appear in the data of both seven-year-old children and adults, although the children's reaction times for any given pair are up to twice as long as the adults'. There may be a shift with age in the set of distinctive features used in discrimination that accounts for the shorter time; either a reduction of the set to a more economical one, or a pickup of tied features (higher order structures) [2] that reduces the number of comparisons required for discrimination as same or different.

The Optimization of Attention

The second trend in perceptual development I shall call the optimization of attention. We refer to the selective aspect of perception as attention, implying activity on the part of the perceiver. Now I want to point out that there are changes in the strategy of this exploratory activity, which are in fact correlated with other developmental changes in perception. They are, first, the tendency for attention to become more exploratory and less captive; second, the tendency for the exploratory search to become more systematic and less random; third, the tendency for attention to become more selective; and fourth, the inverse tendency for attention to become more exclusive.

FROM CAPTURE TO ACTIVITY. The aim of perception is to get information from the environment. But from the vast array of potential stimulation arriving at receptor surfaces at any instant, selection must occur. There seems to be some mechanism for selection very early in life. Precocial animals at birth will follow instinctively a moving, shining, clucking object; they will in fact become imprinted by it. A human infant is incapable of running bodily after a moving thing but he will pursue it with his eyes, demonstrating his attention by prolonged fixation, as Fantz (1965), Ames and Silfen (1965), Salapatek and Kessen (1966), and others have shown us. But, as Ames and Silfen pointed out, the young infant is not so much himself selecting the bright corner or the dancing sunbeam to attend to, as it is capturing his attention. Others have referred to this kind of attention as "obligatory" (Stechler & Latz, 1966) or "involuntary." William James, who was not afraid to use the word "voluntary," said: "This reflex and passive character of the attention which, as a French writer says, makes the child seem to belong less to himself than to every object which happens to catch his notice, is the first thing which the teacher must overcome (1890, p. 417)."

Along the same lines, Piaget speaks of centration, meaning that the

[2] For example, no roman capital containing a straight line also contains an open curve.

young child is caught by what he calls Gestalt-like structural features of the stimulus array, from which he is later able to release himself by letting his intelligence take over. I do not like to make this distinction between perception and intelligence, for I think there is intelligent perception. I cannot doubt, however, that perception becomes more active. Periods of fixation become shorter and visual exploration of the world increases.

How attention becomes voluntary, we cannot say, but we can describe some ways in which it changes from being captured to being exploratory; from being wandering and mobile to being sustained; and from being random and repetitive to being systematic; in short, toward optimizing the active search for information in the world of stimulation.

STRATEGIES OF SEARCH. How is the search for information optimized? We have noted some characteristics of the early development of visual exploration in the chapter on object perception—how the infant reaches out to the world visually, with stationary fixations and pursuit fixations of his eyes, long before he can grasp objects with his hands. Zinchenko et al. (1963) studied the child's method of visually familiarizing himself with an object and the way the method changes from three years to six. They photographed the eye movements of a child while he was examining an unfamiliar design to be remembered. The three year olds kept their eyes fixed on a single spot longer than did the older children, did not seek out distinctive features, and stayed within the area of the figure rather than following the contour. The visual exploration of the six year old was quite different, as Figure 20–4 shows. Fixed gazes were of briefer duration, the

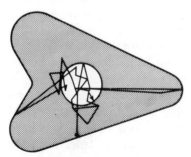

Trajectory of eye movements of three year old in familiarization with figure (20 seconds)

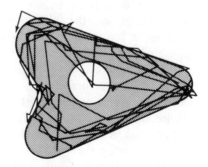

Trajectory of eye movements of six year old in familiarization with figure (20 seconds)

FIGURE 20–4. Path of eye movements of three- and six-year-old children examining an unfamiliar design.

(From V. P. Zinchenko, van Chzhi-Tsin, & V. V. Tarakonov, The formation and development of perceptual activity. *Soviet Psychology and Psychiatry*, 1963, *2*, 3–12.)

number of movements was much greater, there were movements along contour, and there was orientation to distinctive features. This was not due to mere loosening up of the eye muscles, for Zinchenko showed that children of three could pursue a lighted moving target following the same contour very accurately. What was lacking at three years was locating the distinctive features and singling them out from the total display. Zinchenko also compared the eye movements during the later act of recognition of the picture previously given for familiarization. The three year olds who had not adequately searched were poor at recognition and now made many more eye movements than they had originally; but the six year olds showed a different strategy. There was a diminution of the number of movements, an economical eye-movement trajectory, examination of a few key features, and a passing over of the redundant information, such as much of the outline.

A study of eye movements during a same-or-different comparison was made by Vurpillot (1968) with children between five and nine (see Chapter 18). The child had to look back and forth between the items to be compared. Vurpillot showed that skill in scanning systematically and in sampling the relevant features increases during this age period. The sequencing of eye movements so as to guarantee the necessary comparisons, without either repetition or skipping, improved greatly. We have found in our laboratory that a visual search task requiring an orderly scan of a column of letters from the top down is not feasible for children under about seven, and that search time decreases greatly after that (Gibson & Yonas, 1966).

The ordered sequencing of exploratory eye movements is of course very much determined by the conventions of written text, and this special skill develops once the child has begun school; for English text the scanning sequence of left to right and top to bottom becomes fixed and habitual for a page of print. But this special type of scanning is not the best exploratory strategy in most everyday situations where visual information is sought; the higher order structure of the scene, or the unfamiliar distinctive feature of the object, might not be registered if a rigid adherence to the reading sequence were to be adopted. There is probably an appropriate strategy of looking that is different for different visual situations such as reading a map or crossing the street on the way to school. In the latter case, the appropriate strategy (outside of England) is "look left, then right." The child's ability to adopt the appropriate strategy of ocular scanning for the various environmental situations he encounters probably increases with experience, although it has not yet been investigated experimentally.

The most economical method of perceptual exploration is sought and this, of course, depends on the perceptual task. Consider the haptic exploration of objects by the hands, already treated in Chapter 16. Abravanel (1968) studied this active touching in children between three and fourteen years on several tasks requiring a comparison of something felt with something seen. For example, the subject was given a wooden bar to handle, without seeing it, and asked to tell how long it was by having the experimenter extend a variable white line until it looked the same length as the bar felt. Needless to say, accuracy in making these judgments increased with age, and variability of judgments decreased. But notably this shift toward precision was accompanied by changes in haptic exploration, changes toward more mature forms of exploration. Clutching with the entire hand, or palpation of the bar as if trying to determine its shape rather than its length, was characteristic of the three- and four-year-old subjects. But by five years most children held the bar by its ends, generally with the fingers or fingertips of the two hands, occasionally pressing it at both ends. By nine years, no subjects used the palms for exploration; they relied on finger activity, often spanning the bar with the opposed finger and thumb of one hand and running a finger along the bar with the other. This is an efficient method for detecting length (Gibson, 1966, pp. 119 ff.).

Attention develops, then, from a relatively fixed or forced activity to an exploratory activity, which in turn progresses toward selective, systematic, and flexible patterns of search that are adapted to the task. This activity cannot be described in terms of a chain of stimuli and responses, or in terms of a sequence of sensations. In writing about active touch, Gibson (1962) pointed out the complexity of the stimulation to which the subject intentionally exposes himself when he moves his fingers over the object in a variety of ways; he does so in order to get the information from the flux of stimulation. He is actively selecting the information or maximizing it.

SELECTIVE PICKUP OF INFORMATION. Selective attention, focusing on the wanted information, seems to mature developmentally. People working with disadvantaged children who make little progress in school describe their lack of attentiveness as the outstanding quality marking them off from children who make satisfactory progress. But until recently we have had little other than anecdotal evidence to show that the ability to attend selectively in a sustained and directed manner grows with age. We now have some experimental evidence. Eleanor Maccoby has modified Broadbent's technique of "selective listening" to ask whether children's ability to attend to one kind of message and filter it out from the total auditory input increases with age (Maccoby & Konrad, 1966; Maccoby, 1967). The method involves presenting the subject with two messages concurrently, coming over a loudspeaker or through earphones. When children listened to a man's voice and a woman's voice speaking words at the same time, with instructions to report what only one of the voices was saying, the number of correct reports of the word spoken by the specified voice increased with age. Conversely, the number of intrusive errors, that is, reports of words spoken by the nonspecified voice, decreased progressively. There was improvement in the ability to select the wanted stimulus information.

Since Maccoby was interested in locating factors underlying this improvement, she proceeded to manipulate various conditions of stimulus presentation, on the alert for a possible interaction with age. One of these was separating the sources of the messages by placing two loudspeakers at different places in the room, with one voice coming over each speaker. This separated presentation was easier, and about equally so for all ages. If two messages must be kept separate, it can be done more easily when each comes from a different location, but the spatial information helps equally at all ages to separate the verbal information. Ability to use binaural cues for localizing sound sources is not responsible for the improvement with age in selective listening. The external activity of listening by orienting the head to a sound source is a primitive ability. It is the internal act of selective listening, a neural filtering in Broadbent's sense, that improves with age.

Does the growing child really improve in his ability to filter the relevant from the irrelevant, to select what is wanted and discard what is unwanted before final perception occurs? Or does he, perhaps, sense both messages equally and only remember better the message that was designated as relevant? This is a debatable question at present. Experiments with a preparatory set (telling the child before the messages which voice to listen for, rather than after) indicated that perception is truly selective, for a prior set to listen to one voice improved the report as compared to an immediately subsequent instruction about which voice to report. The advantage was present, Maccoby found, to as great an extent in the younger subjects as the older.

Another factor which Maccoby varied was length of the words spoken by the two voices. Some of the words were monosyllabic, while others contained two or three syllables. There was an advantage for the longer words, and the advantage was relatively greater for the older children. Maccoby interpreted this superiority as due to the older children's greater ability to use the redundancies in the multisyllabic words. A related interaction with age was turned up when Maccoby introduced phrases of two words which varied in sequential probability, or something like grammaticality, since some made a phrase unit while others did not (e.g., "dark night" vs. "night only"). The phrases were equated for familiarity of words and length, the same words appearing in different presentations in high- and low-probability phrases. The high-probability phrases were more easily heard, and their advantage increased with age. Grouping items into a single, longer unit made it easier to extract them from the complex presentation, and the ability to use the kind of redundancy present in the phrases was greater for the older children. It is interesting that a higher level of familiarity of the stimulus words was of no greater advantage to the older children than the younger; it is the ability to use the structure present in the phrase units that increases with age.

These experiments, especially the one investigating the role of pre-paratory set, demonstrate that six-year-old children do have the ability to select wanted information from a complex stimulus display, though they do so less efficiently than older children.

IGNORING IRRELEVANT INFORMATION.   If a component is to be selected from a complex of ongoing stimulation, then the rest—all that is irrelevant—must be discarded. The opposite of attention to something is inattention to something else. Is it the ability to ignore what is unwanted that develops with age? Is it, perhaps, the ability not to attend that increases?

The so-called incidental learning experiment seems to be an appropriate paradigm for this question. Do both incidental learning and intentional learning become more effective as a child grows older or, on the other hand, does the task set progressively enable a child to shut out stimulation that does not aid him in achieving the assigned end? In an unpublished experiment on learning to identify letters, Sharon Shepela and I found that five-year-old preschool children noticed and remembered characteristics of the letters which did not distinguish them uniquely and were not needed for the identification. The task was simply to learn the names of nine roman capital letters of the alphabet. The letters presented were colored, three of them red, three blue, and three yellow. After a number of practice sessions, the children were asked to identify the same nine forms but uncolored; they were now black. As expected, if a child had learned to identify correctly (say) five or six of the colored letters he could do about as well with the black letters. We then asked the child if he remembered what color each letter had been, showing him the black letters one at a time. To our surprise, these children remembered correctly as many or more colors as they did letter names, although the former were incidental and irrelevant. Correct responses of the two sorts did not necessarily coincide. Confusion errors during learning were influenced by sharing a color, further evidence that the colors had been noticed and remembered.

We now asked whether older subjects would do the same thing. Adults can use color as a differentiating feature in paired associate learning of nonsense syllables when given the opportunity, as shown by Weiss and Margolius (1954), but in these experiments the color was a useful feature; since it was unique for each syllable it could, in fact, be substituted for the syllable. In our letter identification experiment this was not the case. We repeated the above experiment as nearly as possible with nine-year-old children, but used unfamiliar artificial graphemes instead of familiar letters. Arbitrary names of seven or eight of the colored graphemes were learned in about six trials, and the names transferred to the black copies. But the number of colors correctly remembered was at chance level. Some nine year olds did not even remember what colors had been present. In short, there was no incidental learning. Color may have a strong attention-getting value for five-year-old children, and since younger children find it harder to shift criteria in learning a discrimination (Kofsky & Osler, 1967), the preference could be playing a role. But the explanation is insufficient, since a similar developmental trend appears when color is relevant and a pattern is irrelevant.

Maccoby and Hagen (1965) carried out a developmental study of incidental learning in a short-term recall task. The material was an array of six picture cards, each with a distinctively colored background. A set of cards drawn from the array was placed before the child. He was told to notice the order of the colors. Then the cards were turned over and a color sample presented that matched the now-concealed background color of one of the cards. The subject was to point to the card that matched the sample. After repeated trials with subsets of the cards, the child was asked to identify the picture that had consistently appeared on each one of the background colors. Children from the first through the fifth grade recalled the correct picture significantly more often than older children, although recall on the main task increased steadily with age. Maccoby and Hagen concluded that somewhere between the fifth and seventh grade, children begin to ignore task-irrelevant aspects of the stimulus complex. But it is evident from the younger ages of the children in our experiment that there is no critical age for this attentional strategy to appear. Filtering out irrelevancies is related to the task. It may be that the more the task is centered on discrimination, as it is in the experiments reported just previously, the sooner filtering of useful information will occur.

Adding to the number of potentially useful cues may not in fact facilitate the learning of a simple discrimination task for young children. Hyman (1967) found that increasing the number of features that could be used to differentiate two stimulus patterns only made the task harder for retarded children. Attention wandered over the increased number of stimulus properties and detection of a sufficient, minimal contrast was less efficient.

It can be concluded that changes in ability to focus on wanted information and shut out the irrelevant do occur with age. As the child matures, he is better able to select out and use those properties that serve to distinguish things from one another and are adapted to his task, and to disregard nonessential properties. This improved filtering ability is itself evidence of increasing economy in information pickup, my third trend.

Increasing Economy of Information Pickup, and the Search for Invariance

The third trend in perceptual development that I identified at the outset of the chapter is progressive economy in the extraction of information from stimulation. I think of extraction as usually being a search for and discovery of invariants in the stimulus flux. Ways in which economy is achieved are by the detection of distinctive features of things, by the extraction of invariants over time, and by the processing of larger units of structure.

DISTINCTIVE FEATURES.   It is highly economical to discriminate the objects of the world by means of the minimal set of features that will serve to distinguish them. As my husband put it, "Those features of a thing are noticed which distinguish it from other things that it is not—but not *all* the features that distinguish it from *everything* that it is not (Gibson, 1966, p. 286)." Many illustrations, both anecdotal and experimental, were given in the preceding chapters to show that children do learn such sets, and learn to assign priorities to critical features in the course of development. Caricature in art is a case of enhancing that which serves to distinguish and omitting that which does not. There is a minimal feature set that makes the caricatured object unique, and the good cartoonist has left out of his drawing that which is redundant or nondistinguishing. Children appreciate caricatures astonishingly early, as all publishers of comic books know. They can learn to perceive objects on the basis of sparse details, as long as they are essential details.

In Chapter 7 I described an experiment by Albert Yonas and myself in which both children and adults learned to abstract a single feature in order to discriminate two subsets of stimulus figures. With practice there was increasing use of an optimal strategy. Figure 20–3 shows the practice curves for three age groups. While the reaction times of the children were very much longer than the adults', the same trend was found. Discrimination time was faster with only one letter in the positive set. But when a single feature could be extracted from a positive set of three letters and used for differentiation, the curve fell faster with practice than in a control condition.

An interesting example of economical extraction of a single differentiating feature occurs in a developmental study by Vurpillot et al. (1966). The experiment is ostensibly a study of concept identification, since the aim was to compare two theories of how concepts are identified when common dimensions are perceptually present in the instances given. When positive instances presented to a child contain several common features, does the child learn a concept by abstracting all these features and representing them schematically, or does he simply learn to differentiate the positive from the negative instances on the basis of the fewest criteria that will suffice?

Vurpillot designed a transfer experiment to test this idea, using children aged six and a half to ten and adults. The positive instances of the concept all contained four specified values of features of a cartoon drawing of a bird (a round tail, lined eye, two chevrons on the wing, and spots on the chest), while the negative instances contained different values of these features (e.g., square tail, three chevrons on the wing, etc.). They were assigned, however, so that a single feature difference would suffice to separate the two sets. After sorting the examples to learn which ones were positive instances and had the name designated for the concept, the subjects were given a number of new instances in a transfer series, to see what was generalized as a positive instance.

The new instances presented in the transfer task were chosen so that the subject could generalize to only those instances carrying all four of the common features, or to all the instances carrying a single feature that sufficed to differentiate the sets in Task I. In the transfer task, no subject chose only the cards which contained all four of the common features of the concept. They chose, instead, all the cards which had just one feature that sufficed, the one they had selected as criterial for sorting.

The interesting thing here is that four features, all common to the positive instances, were uniformly reinforced, but what was learned and generalized was only a single distinctive feature that was sufficient for differentiation. This demonstrates remarkable economy in learning, and it is especially interesting to note that the children behaved in essentially the same way as the adults.

INVARIANTS. The search for an invariant—the relation that remains constant over change—is the essence of object perception. The stimulus invariant that keeps its identity despite the transformations of stimulation caused by a motion of the object or a movement of the observer is the basis for perception of that object. Let me give an example from an experiment by Gibson and Gibson (1957). A pattern, which might be regular or irregular, was mounted on a transparent sheet of plastic. The shadow of this pattern was projected on a translucent screen by a point source of light. The observer sat on the other side of the screen and observed the shadow. The shadow caster was supported on a turntable which could rotate through an angle of 90° away from the plane parallel to the screen. Thus a continuous slant transformation of the shadow could be produced. A given pattern was presented while turning back and forth in a cycle, the degree of the excursion being varied from 15° to 70° on different presentations. The subject was asked to judge how much rotation he saw, if any, of an object as he watched the shadow being transformed on the screen. Potentially, he might perceive a two-dimensional shape undergoing compression, or any of a whole set of different two-dimensional shapes, but what he did perceive was a rigid shape turning toward and away from him—a constant object undergoing a change of slant. The subjects could estimate the angle of this change of slant with great accuracy, even when the shape was unfamiliar and irregular. A continuous sequence of perspective transformations led to the perception of an invariant object.

Does the child progress from experiencing a succession of ever-changing retinal images at birth toward the perceiving of a moving object of this sort as he grows older? Such has been the assumption of the empiricists in philosophy and psychology for centuries, but there is no evidence for it. What kind of progress might the child make in the perceiving of objects? I believe it is progress in the search for invariants under transformations. If this is true, some of the invariant properties in the stimulus flux are picked up by the infant, and other more complex invariants are only detected later, but at no time does the child, young or old, experience the stimulus flux as a flow of changing sensations. Observation of the stimulus flux, perception over time, is necessary for progress in detecting invariants because it permits the invariants to be extracted, not because it permits associating of separate sensations. The child seems to have built-in propensities for teaching himself about the permanent aspects of the world. One device is observing his own hands, bringing them together, rotating them, moving them toward or away from himself; and later grasping objects and manipulating them. The invariants over the resulting perspective transformations give him the information for shape and size constancy. Another propensity for self-teaching is dropping things, or throwing them from a crib or a high chair, or spilling milk. These are wonderful ways learn about properties like rigidity, elasticity, and fluidity, and the child tries most of them.

The conservation experiment has frequently been offered as evidence that permanent properties of objects such as mass are appreciated only when logical thinking is attained and intellectual concepts such as length, number, and mass have evolved. The prelogical child, according to Piaget, does not conserve because he does not follow logical rules, but rather judges on the basis of an isolated instance of perception. But it may be that the child who fails to perceive the same amount of water when it has been poured from a squat container into a tall container has simply not had enough opportunity to look for the invariant stimulus properties under the transformations shown him. Although a simple transformation like the changing slant of an object is perceived as an event by infants, extracting the invariant over the shape transformation imposed by different containers is a high-level achievement.

Gelman (1967) trained children of five to attend to length and to number under various transformations and tested the effect on standard conservation problems. A discrimination-learning set procedure was employed. A pretest of conservation was given first, so as to select subjects who failed initially to conserve. Two days of training followed. On each day, 16 problems were given, with six trials on each one. A typical training problem presented varying irrelevant properties over the six trials, while one property, the relevant one (length or number), remained invariant. The child had to learn, within a single problem and over a series of them, to make a judgment on the basis of the constant, relevant variable. For example, the child might be shown three sticks, two of equal lengths and one different, and asked to choose the two that were the same. He was corrected if he made an error. Over problems the sticks were presented in ways that changed various properties of the display such as initial arrangement, size, and color. Within a problem, the arrangement was changed from trial to trial so as to introduce properties that might distract the child from selecting the constant length; for instance, two sticks of different length might be aligned in a row, leaving the matching stick isolated below. In short, the training led the child to ignore the many varying aspects of the presentations that were unrelated to length or quantity and to attend to the feature that was constant over the trials and problems. A posttest following training evaluated the extent to which training induced conservation. Specific transfer was tested with length and number problems; nonspecific transfer was tested with mass and liquid problems. Nearly 100 percent of the subjects responded correctly on length and number tests of conservation after the training. Well over half responded correctly on mass and liquid tests of conservation, whereas no one did in a control condition.

It would seem, therefore, that training in looking for the invariant property and ignoring changing irrelevant ones can be effective in inducing adequate responses in the conservation experiment, even when a new set of stimulus objects is introduced. Paying attention to the invariant and learning to look for it is a prime way of developing cognitive economy.

HIGHER ORDER STRUCTURE. Does the span of perception stretch with age? Does the ability to process a lot of things simultaneously increase? The length of a perceptual span does seem to distinguish the perception of adults from that of children, but I believe it is the ability to find the structure, the embedded relations constituting subordinate units or clusters, that makes the difference. It is not just a stretching out but a making of one unit out of many smaller units.

A familiar example of a memory experiment where the packaging of smaller units occurs is the test of so-called free recall of the items in a list of words. If they do not have to be recalled in sequential order, they can be clustered or grouped in meaningful categories. There is evidence to show that younger children do not make much use of the properties inherent in a list that reduce the amount of information to be handled or processed in performing the task. Rossi (1964) gave children twenty-word lists with five words from each of four different categories for recall. The children ranged from five to eleven. Clustering was a linear function of age, with very little in the five year olds but a great increase by eleven years. Retarded subjects show less clustering than normal ones, but presenting the words to them by categories, or telling them to look for categories, facilitates clustering and improves recall (Blount, 1968).

The visual grouping principles embodied in Wertheimer's laws of figural perception, the law of proximity, of similarity, of good continuation, and of common fate, are relations that structure units for perception. There is reason to believe that the laws of similarity do not function as well to structure larger units early in development as it does later, or in backward children compared to bright ones. Honkavaara (1958) gave a sorting task to backward and bright children five to eight years old. In one task they were shown 24 cards of four different shapes scattered over a table and were asked to sort them into piles. The normal older children instantly sorted them into four piles, but the younger and retarded children put them in rows without matching, or left them in disorder. In another test, they were given cards on which were drawn dot patterns embedded among different shapes. When asked to find a pattern matching a model, the older children surpassed the younger and the bright surpassed the backward children of the same age. Rush (1937) made developmental comparisons of the effectiveness of several Gestalt principles on perceptual grouping within drawn patterns and found that the effectiveness of similarity increased with age.

Detecting similarities is basic to finding structure, as the principles of geometry show us. The perceptual pickup of all forms of redundancy [3] and structural regularity has recently become of considerable interest to developmental psychologists. Manipulations of repetition, symmetry, and the regularities in a display have been tried out using various perceptual tasks and subjects of different ages.

Symmetry is clearly one of the principles for structuring a unit. Is it equally effective, perceptually, at all age levels? Spitz (1964) studied perception of dot patterns by retardates and normal children of equivalent mental age and found that symmetrical patterns were reproduced as well by the retardates as by the normal children, whereas with what he called "random" patterns they were inferior. Some of the patterns which differentiated the two groups were four-dot patterns like those shown in Figure 20–5. A so-called random pattern does have a structure, although not a simple one, and the normal children were able in most cases to distinguish it. But the asymmetrical nonlinear patterns were hard for the retarded children to perceive as units.

House (1966) also found that individual differences in ability to perceive order are related to differences in I.Q. She compared discrimination of symmetrical, asymmetrical, and repetitive dot patterns. Symmetry was more effective than repetition but other factors, such as distinctive

[3] The meaning of redundancy is ambiguous, since it can be viewed as varying in form as well as amount (Garner, 1962), or as a mere surplus as opposed to increased constraint (Evans, 1967). We will not worry here about technical definitions of the term, but consider some forms of redundancy that have been manipulated in experiments on perceptual development.

SYMMETRICAL   RANDOM

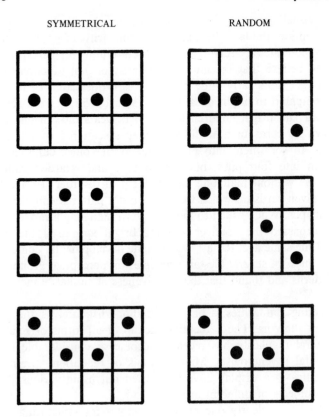

FIGURE 20–5. Symmetrical and random dot patterns.

(From H. H. Spitz, Effects of symmetry on the reproduction of dot patterns by mental retardates and equal MA normals. *American Journal of Mental Deficiency,* 1964, *69,* 103. By permission of The American Journal of Mental Deficiency.)

clusters and continuity of line, were also important. House concluded that failure of discrimination was due to a perceptual deficit, that is, an inability to perceive the pattern differences as described by these features.

An experiment of Munsinger's (1967) illustrates the effect of symmetry and repetitiveness on perception at different ages. The subjects were presented with an 8 × 8 matrix, like the one in Figure 20–6. It was divided into four submatrices, each of which had one or more of its cells filled with a black tile. The submatrices might be randomly related to one another, repetitions of one another, or symmetrical with one another. The subject looked at the matrix for five seconds and then was asked to reproduce it on a tile board. The redundant matrices (especially the symmetrical

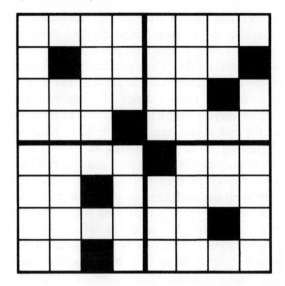

FIGURE 20–6. An 8 × 8 matrix with two symmetrical submatrices.

(From H. L. Munsinger, Developing perception and memory for stimulus redundancy. *Journal of Experimental Child Psychology*, 1967, *5*, 41.)

ones) were reproduced better than the random ones. In a separate experimental condition, the redundant matrices were filled with blue tiles to call attention to the symmetry or repetition. This color coding facilitated the performance of adults, whereas it interfered with the performance of both second- and sixth-grade children, who did not perceive the conditional relationship between the presence of color and the presence of order and appeared, in fact, to be distracted by the color.

The value of order for the ability to extract a visual signal from a background of visual noise was demonstrated by Munsinger and Gummerman (1967). The ability was shown to improve with development. Black angular shapes were presented tachistoscopically against a grid of dense lines, the lines being spaced randomly over a set of coordinates in one experimental condition but spaced systematically in another condition. The subjects (second- and fifth-grade children and college students) matched the tachistoscopically exposed shape to one of a set of sample shapes. Accuracy increased with age, as might be expected, and also with systematic noise, as opposed to random noise. There was a significant interaction with age; the children displayed less difference between the two conditions with different kinds of noise and were relatively less facilitated by order. However, they improved during a training session with systematic noise, so we may conclude that the efficient use of order or regularity increased with experience as well as with age.

The examples just quoted were chosen to illustrate the pickup of structure considered as a perceptual economy that develops with age and experience. The abstracting of common features or dimensions over time also increases developmentally. The literature of discrimination learning provides examples of the latter. One of these is the oddity problem. The requirement is as follows. Over a series of single problems with varying stimulus objects, or varying properties of similar objects, the subject must learn to choose the odd object from a set of three, whatever the nature of the variation. Then he must perform without error on a new problem. Instead of treating each problem as a new and independent one, in which a specific S-R connection must be learned, the subject must operate with a rule which covers all the problems, despite change in absolute properties of stimuli. A rule does not mean a verbalized rule, for a monkey can solve the general oddity problem (Meyer & Harlow, 1949; Moon & Harlow, 1955). Children may verbalize the rule, but they need not, as House (1964) has shown. In any case, learning of a three-position oddity problem by human children improves from kindergarten to third grade (Lipsitt & Serunian, 1963). Perceptual enhancement of the odd item by increasing the number of identical items facilitates solution for kindergarten children, but does not help preschool children, who still fail to reach criterion (Gollin, Saravo, & Salten, 1967).

Two other classical discrimination-learning experiments show related changes with age. One is the reversal-learning experiment, which asks whether, having learned that a tall cylinder is "right" and a short cylinder is "wrong," it is easier to learn the reverse than it is to learn that a black cylinder is "right" and a white cylinder is "wrong." Younger children typically have more difficulty with reversal shifts than older ones (Kelleher, 1956; Kendler & Kendler, 1959). Certain kinds of preparatory training serve to reduce the age difference, such as perceptual training in abstracting the relevant dimensional stimulus variable (Tighe, 1965). The age difference appears to be due to the propensity of younger children to respond to specific stimulus compounds (e.g., the tall black cylinder) instead of abstracting a single dimension from the complex of variables and reducing the information to one simple relation (Jeffrey, 1965).

The conditional discrimination problem, invented by Lashley, illustrates a higher order constraint that is definitely age related. The problem requires the subject to respond appropriately to joint values of two or more stimulus variables. Gollin and Liss (1962) compared learning of a simple discrimination, a reversal discrimination problem, and a conditional discrimination in children between 3½ years and 6 years old. There was no difference between the age groups in learning a simple discrimination. Some developmental differences appeared when reversal training was introduced, and marked differences were apparent when complex conditional discrimination was tested. The conditional discrimination problem required the subject to respond positively to a circle or a triangle presented alternatively on a black or a striped background and also to shift the relationship on odd and even trials. Thus, the relation to be discovered was a given shape (e.g., circle), when presented on a given background (e.g., stripes) and in a given sequential order; this complex relation was too difficult for 4½ and 5 year olds, although they had all reached criterion in the reversal task.

This doubly tied relationship is still less complex than the order found in spelling patterns. In the last chapter, I discussed perception of higher order structure in letter strings, and presented evidence that patterns and clusters of letters within words are perceived as units by adults, and that there is developmental progress in detecting the kind of structure found in orthography and in spelling-to-sound correspondences. Rules come to be used as learning progresses, despite the fact that the user could not explain the rules and that the order in the constraints has only recently been penetrated by trained linguists.

Psychology has not gone far enough in investigating the growth of ability to detect regularity, order, and structure. This ability is basic for cognition. The detection of similarity, equality, symmetry, transitivity, and congruence is essential for learning mathematics, and the good teacher does his best to make them perceptible by clearing away the superfluous details and baring the skeleton. Here is a last example, taken from Wertheimer's book on *Productive Thinking* (1945). He taught a child of 5½ how to find the area of a rectangle by drawing it for him, filling it with small squares, and counting them in various ways. Then he presented him with a parallelogram and asked if he could find its area. After some moments of puzzled staring at the new figure, the child asked, "Do we have a pair of scissors?" They were produced and he proceeded to snip a triangle off one end of the parallelogram and fit it neatly on the other, thus converting it into a rectangle. Then he said, "Now I can do it." He had literally perceived the solution.

EPILOGUE

I have set forth as positively as I can the nature of perceptual learning, first what is learned, and then what I believe to be some of its laws. They are laws of differentiation and filtering, not laws of association; and laws of the reduction of uncertainty, not laws of external reinforcement. Finally, I have described the developmental trends in perceptual functioning— progressive specificity, optimization of attention, and progressive economy in information pickup. Now I must admit how much remains unanswered. We do not know how the distinctive features are discovered. We do not know how attention functions to filter out the irrelevant and preserve the critical information. I think we are still a pretty long way from knowing.

It cheers one up a bit, however, to know that mysteries remain even in the older sciences, to judge from this paragraph by the Nobel-prize-winning physicist Feynman:

The biggest mystery of physics is where the laws are known, but we don't know exactly what's going on. We don't know the strategy in the middle game. We know castling, or how the different pieces move, and we know a little bit about the end game, but nothing in the middle.

We get reports from the experimentalists, the watchers of the chess game, and we try to analyze the information. We may even suggest a new experiment. But we're still waiting and hoping for the big strategy. Then maybe we'll really understand how wonderful is nature.[4]

So goes the psychology of perception and its development. We know something about the laws, and what experiments we can be doing to improve our knowledge of them, but the "strategy in the middle" leaves us a great deal to think about.

[4] *New York Times Magazine,* October 8, 1967.

References

Abercrombie, B. & James, H. The stability of the chick's response to visual flicker. *Animal Behaviour*, 1961, *9*, 205–212.

Abravanel, E. The development of intersensory patterning with regard to selected spatial dimensions. *Monogr. Soc. Res. Child Develpm.*, 1968, *33*, Serial No. 118.

Ahrens, R. Beiträge zur Entwicklung des Physiognomie–und Mimikerkennes. *Z. f. Exp. u. angew. Psychol.*, 1954, *2*, 412–454, 599–633.

Allan, M. D. Training in perceptual skills. *Occup. Psychol.*, 1957, *31*, 113–119.

Allan, M. D. A pattern recognition method of learning Morse code. *Brit. J. Psychol.*, 1958, *49*, 59–64.

Allport, G. W. & Pettigrew, T. F. Cultural influence on the perception of movement: The trapezoidal illusion among Zulus. *J. abnorm. soc. Psychol.*, 1957, *55*, 104–113.

Ambrose, J. A. The development of the smiling response in early infancy. In B. M. Foss (Ed.), *Determinants of infant behavior*. New York: Wiley, 1961. Pp. 179–196.

Ambrose, J. A. The concept of a critical period for the development of social responsiveness in early human infancy. In B. M. Foss (Ed.), *Determinants of infant behavior, II*. New York: Wiley, 1963. Pp. 201–225.

Ames, E. W. & Silfen, C. K. Methodological issues in the study of age differences in infant's attention to stimuli varying in movement and complexity. Paper presented at the meeting of the Society for Research in Child Development, Minneapolis, Minn., 1965.

Ames, L. B., Learned, J., Metraux, R., & Walker, R. Development of perception in the young child as observed in responses to the Rorschach test blots. *J. genet. Psychol.*, 1953, *82*, 183–204.

Ammons, C. H., Worchel, P., & Dallenbach, K. M. "Facial Vision": The perception of obstacles out of doors by blindfolded and blindfolded-deafened subjects. *Amer. J. Psychol.*, 1953, *66*, 519–553.

Ananiev, B. G. The basis of spatial discrimination. In B. Simon (Ed.), *Psychology in the Soviet Union*. Stanford, Calif.: Stanford University Press, 1957. Pp. 131–151.

Arnoult, M. D. Transfer of predifferentiation training in simple and multiple shape discrimination. *J. exp. Psychol.*, 1953, *45*, 401–409.

Atkinson, R. C. The observing response in discrimination learning. *J. exp. Psychol.*, 1961, *62*, 253–262.

Attneave, F. Transfer of experience with a class-schema to identification-learning of patterns and shapes. *J. exp. Psychol.*, 1957, *54*, 81–88.

Attneave, F. & Arnoult, M. D. The quantitative study of shape and pattern recognition. *Psychol. Bull.*, 1956, *53*, 452–471.

Axelrod, S. *Effects of early blindness: Performance of blind and sighted children on tactile and auditory tasks.* No. 7, Research series, 1959, American Foundation for the Blind, New York.

Baer, D. M. & Gray, P. H. Imprinting to a different species without overt following. *Percept. Mot. Skills*, 1960, *10*, 171–174.

Bain, A. *The senses and the intellect.* (1st ed.) London, 1855.

Baker, C. H. & Young, P. Feedback during training and retention of motor skills. *Canad. J. Psychol.*, 1960, *14*, 257–264.

Baker, E. J. & Alluisi, E. A. Information handling aspects of visual and auditory form perception. *J. eng. Psychol.*, 1962, *1*, 159–179.

Baker, R. A. & Osgood, S. W. Discrimination transfer along a pitch continuum. *J. exp. Psychol.*, 1954, *48*, 241–246.

Barch, A. W. & Levine, J. R. Stimulus factors in auditory identification learning. *Psychon. Sci.*, 1965, *3*, 147–148.

Bartlett, F. C. *Remembering.* Cambridge: Cambridge University Press, 1932.

Bateson, P. P. G. Relation between conspicuousness of stimuli and their effectiveness in the imprinting situation. *J. comp. physiol. Psychol.*, 1964, *58*, 407–411.

Bateson, P. P. G. The characteristics and context of imprinting. *Biol. Rev.*, 1966, *41*, 177–220.

Beach, F. A., Hebb, D. O., Morgan, C. T., & Nissen, H. W. *The neuropsychology of Lashley.* New York: McGraw-Hill, 1960.

Beatty, F. S., Dameron, L. E., & Greene, J. E. An investigation of the effects of reward and punishment on visual perception. *J. Psychol.*, 1959, *47*, 267–276.

Békésy, G. von. Sensations on the skin similar to directional hearing, beats, and harmonics of the ear. *J. acoust. soc. Amer.*, 1957, *29*, 489–501.

Békésy, G. von. Similarities between hearing and skin sensations. *Psychol. Rev.*, 1959, *66*, 1–22.

Bellugi, U. & Brown, R. The acquisition of language. *Monogr. Soc. Res. Child Develpm.*, 1964, *29*, No. 1.

Berkeley, G. *An essay towards a new theory of vision.* 1709 (see any modern edition).

Berko, J. The child's learning of English morphology. *Word*, 1958, *14*, 150–177.

Berko, J. & Brown, R. Psycholinguistic research methods. In P. Mussen (Ed.), *Handbook of research methods in child development.* New York: Wiley, 1960.

Berlyne, D. E. Curiosity and exploration. *Science*, 1966, *153*, 25–33.

Bevan, W. & Saugstad, P. Breadth of experience, ease of discrimination and efficiency of generalization. *Brit. J. Psychol.*, 1955, *66*, 13–19.

Bexton, W. H., Heron, W., & Scott, T. H. Effects of decreased variation in the sensory environment. *Canad. J. Psychol.*, 1954, *8*, 70–76.

Binet, A. La mesure des illusions visuelles chez les enfants. *Rev. philos. de la France et de l'Étranger*, 1895, *40*, 11–25.

Binns, H. A comparison between the judgments of individuals skilled in the textile trade and the natural judgments of untrained adults and children. *J. Textile Institute,* 1926, *17,* 1615–1641.

Binns, H. Visual and tactual 'judgment' as illustrated in a practical experiment. *Brit. J. Psychol.,* 1936, *27,* 404–410.

Birch, H. G. & Lefford, A. Intersensory development in children. *Monogr. Soc. Res. Child Develpm.,* 1963, *28,* No. 5, Serial No. 89.

Bishop, C. H. Transfer effects of word and letter training in reading. *J. verb. learn. verb. Behav.,* 1964, *3,* 215–221.

Bishop, H. E. Innateness and learning in the visual perception of direction. Unpublished doctoral dissertation, University of Chicago, 1959.

Björkman, M. Predictive behavior: Some aspects based on an ecological orientation. *Scand. J. Psychol.,* 1966, *7,* 43–57.

Björkman, M., Garvill, J., & Molander, B. Cross-modal transfer as a function of preparatory set and distinctiveness of stimulus aspects. *Reports from the Psychological Laboratories, Univ. of Stockholm,* 1965, No. 186.

Björkman, M. & Ottander, C. Improvement of discriminative ability by training. *Reports from the Psychol. Lab., Univ. of Stockholm,* 1959, No. 66.

Blackwell, H. R. *Psychological thresholds.* University of Michigan Engng. Res. Inst. Bull. No. 36, Ann Arbor, 1953.

Blake, R. B. & Ramsey, G. V. *Perception: An approach to personality.* New York: Ronald Press, 1951.

Blank, M. & Bridger, W. H. Cross modal transfer in nursery school children. *J. comp. physiol. Psychol.,* 1964, *58,* 272–282.

Blount, W. R. Concept usage research with the mentally retarded. *Psychol. Bull.,* 1968, *69,* 281–294.

Bogartz, R. S. & Carterette, E. C. Free recall of redundant strings of symbols by children. *J. exp. Psychol.,* 1963, *66,* 399–408.

Boneau, C. A., Holland, M. K., & Baker, W. M. Color-discrimination performance of pigeons: Effects of reward. *Science,* 1965, *149,* 1113–1114.

Boring, E. G. The control of attitude in psychophysical experiments. *Psychol. Rev.,* 1920, *27,* 440–452.

Boring, E. G. A new ambiguous figure. *Amer. J. Psychol.,* 1930, *42,* 444–445.

Boring, E. G. *Sensation and perception in the history of experimental psychology.* New York: Appleton, 1942.

Bossom, J. & Hamilton, C. R. Interocular transfer of prism-altered coordinations in split-brain monkeys. *J. comp. physiol. Psychol.,* 1963, *56,* 769–774.

Bower, T. G. R. Discrimination of depth in premotor infants. *Psychon. Sci.,* 1964, *1,* 368.

Bower, T. G. R. The parameters of performance of two perceptual tasks. Unpublished doctoral dissertation, Cornell University, 1965.

Bower, T. G. R. Stimulus variables determining space perception in infants. *Science,* 1965, *149,* 88–89.

Bower, T. G. R. Heterogeneous summation in human infants. *Animal Behav.,* 1966, *14,* 395–398. (a)

Bower, T. G. R. Slant perception and shape constancy in infants. *Science,* 1966, *151,* 832–834. (b)

Bower, T. G. R. The visual world of infants. *Scient. Amer.*, 1966, *215*, 80–92. (c)

Bower, T. G. R. Object-permanence and short-term memory in the human infant. Manuscript, 1966. (d)

Bower, T. G. R. The development of object-permanence: Some studies of existence constancy. *Percept. and Psychophysics*, 1967, *2*, 411–418.

Boyd, B. O. & Warren, J. M. Solution of oddity problems by cats. *J. comp. physiol. Psychol.*, 1957, *50*, 258–260.

Braine, M. D. S. On learning the grammatical order of words. *Psychol. Rev.*, 1963, *70*, 323–348. (a)

Braine, M. D. S. The ontogeny of English phrase structure: The first phase. *Language*, 1963, *39*, 1–13. (b)

Braly, K. W. The influence of past experience in visual perception. *J. exp. Psychol.*, 1933, *16*, 613–643.

Brault, H. Étude génétique de la constance des formes. *Psychol. franç.*, 1962, *7*, 270–282.

Bray, C. W. Transfer of learning. *J. exp. Psychol.*, 1928, *11*, 443–467.

Bridger, W. H. Sensory habituation and discrimination in the human neonate. *Amer. J. Psychiat.*, 1961, *117*, 991–996.

Bridger, W. H. Sensory discrimination and autonomic function in the newborn. *Amer. Acad. Child Psychiat.*, 1962, *1*, 67–82.

Broadbent, D. E. A mechanical model for human attention and immediate memory. *Psychol. Rev.*, 1957, *64*, 205–215.

Broadbent, D. E. *Perception and communication.* New York: Pergamon Press, 1958.

Bronshtein, A. I., Antonova, T. G., Kamentskaya, A. G., Luppova, N. N., & Sytova, V. A. On the development of the functions of analysers in infants and some animals at the early stage of ontogenesis. In *Problems of evolution of physiological functions.* Office of Technical Service, U. S. Dept. of Commerce, Washington, D. C. Report No. 60-51066, 1960 (Tr. from the Russian). Pp. 106–116.

Brown, J. S., Bilodeau, E. A., & Baron, M. R. Bidirectional gradients in the strength of a generalized voluntary response to stimuli on a visual-spatial dimension. *J. exp. Psychol.*, 1951, *41*, 52–61.

Brown, R. W. & Berko, J. Word association and the acquisition of grammar. *Child Develpm.*, 1960, *31*, 1–14.

Brown, R. & Fraser, C. The acquisition of syntax. In U. Bellugi & R. Brown (Eds.), *The acquisition of language.* Mongr. Soc. Res. Child Develpm., 1964, *29*, No. 92. Pp. 43–79.

Brown, R. & Hildum, D. C. Expectancy and the perception of symbols. *Language*, 1956, *32*, 411–419.

Brown, R. W. & Lenneberg, E. H. A study in language and cognition. *J. abnorm. soc. Psychol.*, 1954, *49*, 454–462.

Bruce, R. H. & Low, F. N. The effect of practice with brief-exposure techniques upon central and peripheral visual acuity and a search for a brief test of peripheral acuity. *J. exp. Psychol.*, 1951, *41*, 275–280.

Bruner, J. S. Personality dynamics and the process of perceiving. In R. R.

Blake & G. V. Ramsey (Eds.), *Perception: An approach to personality.* New York: Ronald Press, 1951. Pp. 121–147.

Bruner, J. S. Going beyond the information given. In *Contemporary approaches to cognition.* Cambridge, Mass.: Harvard University Press, 1957. (a)

Bruner, J. S. On perceptual readiness. *Psychol. Rev.,* 1957, *64,* 123–152. (b)

Bruner, J. S. The course of cognitive growth. *Amer. Psychol.,* 1964, *19,* 1–15.

Bruner, J. S. & Goodman, C. C. Value and need as organizing factors in perception. *J. abnorm. soc. Psychol.,* 1947, *42,* 33–44.

Bruner, J. S., Miller, G. A., & Zimmerman, C. Discriminative skill and discriminative matching in perceptual recognition. *J. exp. Psychol.,* 1955, *49,* 187–192.

Bruner, J. S., Olver, R. R., Greenfield, P. M., et al. *Studies in cognitive growth.* New York: Wiley, 1966.

Bruner, J. S. & Postman, L. Emotional selectivity in perception and reaction. *J. Pers.,* 1947, *16,* 69–77.

Bruner, J. S. & Postman, L. Perception, cognition, and behavior. *J. Pers.,* 1949, *18,* 14–31.

Bruner, J. S. & Potter, M. C. Interference in visual recognition. *Science,* 1964, *144,* 424–425.

Brunswik, E. Representative design and probabilistic theory in a functional psychology. *Psychol. Rev.,* 1955, *62,* 193–217. (a)

Brunswik, E. In defense of probabilistic functionalism: A reply. *Psychol. Rev.,* 1955, *62,* 236–242. (b)

Brunswik, E. *Perception and the representative design of psychological experiments.* Berkeley, Calif.: University of California Press, 1956.

Brunswik, E. & Herma, H. Probability learning of perceptual cues in the establishment of a weight illusion. *J. exp. Psychol.,* 1951, *41,* 281–290.

Bryan, W. L. & Harter, N. Studies on the telegraphic language. *Psych. Rev.,* 1899, *6,* 345–375.

Burton, D. & Ettlinger, G. Cross-modal transfer of training in monkeys. *Nature,* 1960, *186,* 1071–1072.

Bush, R. R., Galanter, E., & Luce, R. D. Characterization and classification of choice experiments. In R. D. Luce, R. R. Bush, & E. Galanter (Eds.), *Handbook of mathematical psychology.* Vol. 1. New York: Wiley, 1963. Pp. 77–102.

Butler, R. A. Discrimination learning by rhesus monkeys to visual exploration motivation. *J. comp. physiol. Psychol.,* 1953, *46,* 95–98.

Butler, R. A. Incentive conditions which influence visual exploration. *J. exp. Psychol.,* 1954, *48,* 19–23.

Butler, R. A. The responsiveness of rhesus monkeys to motion pictures. *J. genet. Psychol.,* 1961, *98,* 239–245.

Butler, R. A. & Woolpy, J. H. Visual attention in the rhesus monkey. *J. comp. physiol. Psychol.,* 1963, *56,* 324–328.

Buytendijk, F. J. J. & van Ratingen, J. R. M. La constance de la forme d'une ellipse. *L'Année Psychol.,* 1949, *50,* 371–377.

Campbell, R. A. & Small, A. M., Jr. Effect of practice and feedback on frequency discrimination. *J. acoust. soc. Amer.,* 1963, *35,* 1511–1514.

Campbell, V. & Freeman, J. T. Some functions of experimentally-induced language in perceptual learning. *Percept. Mot. Skills,* 1955, *5,* 71–79.

Cantor, G. N. Effects of three types of pretraining on discrimination learning in school children. *J. exp. Psychol.,* 1955, *49,* 339–342.

Cantor, J. H. Transfer of stimulus pretraining to motor paired-associate and discrimination learning tasks. In L. P. Lipsitt & C. C. Spiker (Eds.), *Advances in child development and behavior.* Vol. II. New York: Academic Press, 1965. Pp. 19–58.

Carpenter, B. & Carpenter, J. T. The perception of movement by young chimpanzees and human children. *J. comp. physiol. Psychol.,* 1958, *51,* 782–784.

Carr, H. A. *An introduction to space perception.* New York: Longmans Green, 1935.

Carr, W. J. & McGuigan, D. I. The stimulus basis and modification of visual cliff performance in the rat. *Animal Behav.,* 1965, *13,* 25–29.

Cattell, J. McK. Ueber die zeit der erkennung und bennenung von schriftzeichen, bildern und farben. *Phil. Stud.,* 1885, *2,* 635–650.

Caviness, J. A. Visual and tactual perception of solid shape. Unpublished doctoral dissertation, Cornell University, 1964.

Chapanis, A. *Man-machine engineering.* Belmont, Calif.: Wadsworth, 1965.

Chapman, D. W. Relative effects of determinate and indeterminate *Aufgaben.* *Amer. J. Psychol.,* 1932, *44,* 163–174.

Cherry, C. *On human communication.* New York: Tech. Press of M.I.T. and Wiley, 1957.

Chomsky, N. Review of B. F. Skinner, *Verbal behavior. Language,* 1959, *35,* 26–58.

Chomsky, N. Formal discussion. In U. Bellugi & R. Brown (Eds.), *The acquisition of language.* Monogr. Soc. Res. Child Develpm., 1964, *29,* No. 1. Pp. 35–39.

Chow, K. L. & Nissen, H. W. Interocular transfer of learning in visually naive and experienced chimpanzees. *J. comp. physiol. Psychol.,* 1955, *48,* 229–237.

Cofoid, D. A. & Honig, W. K. Stimulus generalization of imprinting. *Science,* 1961, *134,* 1692–1694.

Cohen, W., Hershkowitz, A., & Chodak, M. Size judgment at different distances as a function of age level. *Child Develpm.,* 1958, *29,* 473–479.

Cole, M., Chorover, S. L., & Ettlinger, G. Cross-modal transfer in man. *Nature,* 1961, *191,* 1225–1226.

Cooper, F. S., Liberman, A. M., & Borst, J. M. The interconversion of audible and visible patterns as a basis for research in the perception of speech. *Proc. Nat. Acad. Sci.,* 1951, *37,* 318–325.

Cramaussel, E. Ce que voient des yeux d'enfants. *J. Psychol.,* 1924, *21,* 161–170.

Cronin, V. Mirror-image reversal discrimination in kindergarten and first-grade children. *J. exp. child Psychol.,* 1967, *5,* 577–585.

Daves, W. F. & Boostrum, E. Object properties mediating visual object discrimination in the cat. *Percept. Mot. Skills,* 1964, *19,* 343–350.

de Haan, H. J. & Wischner, G. J. Three-dimensional objects vs. projected color photographs of objects as stimuli in learning-set formation by retarded children. *J. comp. physiol. Psychol.,* 1963, *56,* 440–444.

Dennis, W. Infant development under conditions of restricted practice and of minimum social stimulation: A preliminary report. *J. genet. Psychol.*, 1938, *53*, 149–158.

Dennis, W. Causes of retardation among institutional children: Iran. *J. genet. Psychol.*, 1960, *96*, 47–59.

Dennis, W. & Sayegh, Y. The effect of supplementary experiences upon the behavioral development of infants in institutions. *Child Develpm.*, 1965, *36*, 81–90.

DeRivera, J. Some conditions governing the use of the cue-producing response as an explanatory device. *J. exp. Psychol.*, 1959, *57*, 299–304.

Deutsch, J. A. & Deutsch, D. Attention: Some theoretical considerations. *Psychol. Rev.*, 1963, *70*, 80–90.

Dewey, J. *How we think*. Boston: Heath, 1910.

Dewson, J. H. Speech sound discrimination by cats. *Science*, 1964, *144*, 555–556.

Dibble, F. N. A study of the process of stimulus discrimination in relation to serial learning. Unpublished master's dissertation, Smith College, 1948.

Diebold, A. R. A survey of psycholinguistic research, 1954–1964. In C. E. Osgood & T. A. Sebeok (Eds.), *Psycholinguistics: A survey of theory and research problems*. Bloomington, Ind.: Indiana University Press, 1965.

Djang, S. The role of past experience in the visual apprehension of masked forms. *J. exp. Psychol.*, 1937, *20*, 29–59.

Dollard, J. & Miller, N. E. *Personality and psychotherapy*. New York: McGraw-Hill, 1950.

Donderi, D. C. & Kane, E. Perceptual learning produced by common responses to different stimuli. *Canad. J. Psychol.*, 1965, *19*, 15–30.

Dornbush, R. L. & Winnick, W. A. The relative effectiveness of stereometric and pattern stimuli in discrimination learning in children. *Psychon. Sci.*, 1966, *5*, 301–302.

Downing, J. A. The relationship between reading attainment and the inconsistency of English spelling at the infant's school stage. *Brit. J. educ. Psychol.*, 1962, *32*, 166–177.

Dresslar, F. B. Studies in the psychology of touch. *Amer. J. Psychol.*, 1894, *6*, 313–368.

Drever, J. Early learning and the perception of space. *Amer. J. Psychol.*, 1955, *68*, 605–614.

Drever, J. Perceptual learning. *Ann. Rev. Psychol.*, 1960, *11*, 131–160.

Eagle, M. N. & Klein, G. S. Fragmentation phenomena with the use of the stabilized retinal image. *Percept. Mot. Skills*, 1962, *15*, 579–582.

Edmonds, E. M. & Mueller, M. R. Effects of incidental training and reinforcement on mixed schema learning. *Psychon. Sci.*, 1968, *10*, 75–76.

Edmonds, E. M., Mueller, M. R., & Evans, S. H. Effects of knowledge of results on mixed schema discrimination. *Psychon. Sci.*, 1966, *6*, 377–378.

Egeth, H. Selective attention. *Psychol. Bull.*, 1967, *67*, 41–57.

Egeth, H. & Smith, E. Selective tuning of visual perception. *J. exp. Psychol.*, 1967, *74*, 543–549.

Egger, M. D. & Miller, N. E. Secondary reinforcement in rats as a function of information value and reliability of the stimulus. *J. exp. Psychol.*, 1962, *64*, 97–104.

Egger, M. D. & Miller, N. E. When is a reward reinforcing?: An experimental study of the information hypothesis. *J. comp. physiol. Psychol.*, 1963, *56*, 132–137.

Elkonin, D. B. The physiology of higher nervous activity and child psychology. In B. Simon (Ed.), *Psychology in the Soviet Union*. Palo Alto: Stanford University Press, 1957.

Ellis, H. C., Bessemer, D. W., Devine, J. V., & Trafton, C. L. Recognition of random tactual shapes following predifferentiation training. *Percept. Mot. Skills*, 1962, *10*, 99–102.

Ellis, H. C., Fuege, R. L., Long, K. K., & Pegram, V. G. Evidence for acquired equivalence of cues in a perceptual task. *Percept. Mot. Skills*, 1964, *19*, 159–162.

Ellis, H. C. & Muller, D. G. Transfer in perceptual learning following stimulus predifferentiation. *J. exp. Psychol.*, 1964, *68*, 388–395.

Ellis, W. D. *A source book of Gestalt psychology*. New York: Harcourt, Brace, 1938.

Engen, T. Effect of practice and instruction on olfactory thresholds. *Percept. Mot. Skills*, 1960, *10*, 195–198.

Engen, T. Identification of odors. *Amer. Perfumer*, 1961, *76*, 43–47.

Engen, T., Lipsitt, L. P., & Kaye, H. Olfactory responses and adaptation in the human neonate. *J. comp. physiol. Psychol.*, 1963, *56*, 73–77.

Englund, S. A. J. & Lundberg, I. Discriminative learning: Some restricting criteria and illustrative experiments. *Reports from the Psych. Lab., Univ. of Stockholm*, 1963, No. 142.

Eriksen, C. W. Effects of practice with or without correction on discrimination learning. *Amer. J. Psychol.*, 1958, *71*, 350–358.

Eriksen, C. W. & Doroz, L. Role of awareness in learning and use of correlated extraneous cues on perceptual tasks. *J. exp. Psychol.*, 1963, *66*, 601–608.

Eriksen, C. W. & Hake, H. W. Multidimensional stimulus difference and accuracy of discrimination. *J. exp. Psychol.*, 1955, *50*, 153–160.

Ervin, S. M. & Miller, W. R. Language development. Ch. III in H. W. Stevenson (Ed.), *Child psychology: The sixty-second yearbook of the National Society for the Study of Education*. Chicago: University of Chicago Press, 1963. Pp. 108–143.

Ettlinger, G. Cross-modal transfer of training in monkeys. *Behaviour.*, 1960, *16*, 56–65.

Ettlinger, G. Learning in two sense-modalities. *Nature*, 1961, *191*, 308.

Evans, S. H. Redundancy as a variable in pattern perception. *Psychol. Bull.*, 1967, *67*, 104–113.

Ewert, P. H. A study of the effect of inverted retinal stimulation upon spatially coordinated behavior. *Genet. Psychol. Monogr.*, 1930, *7*, 177–363.

Fabricius, E. Zur Ethologie junger Anatiden. *Acta zool. fenn.*, 1951, *68*, 1–175.

Fantz, R. L. Form preferences in newly hatched chicks. *J. comp. physiol. Psychol.*, 1957, *50*, 422–430.

Fantz, R. L. The origin of form perception. *Scient. Amer.*, 1961, *204*, 66–72.

Fantz, R. L. Pattern vision in newborn infants. *Science*, 1963, *140*, 296–297.

Fantz, R. L. Ontogeny of perception. In A. M. Schrier, H. F. Harlow, & F. Stollnitz (Eds.), *Behavior of nonhuman primates.* New York: Academic Press, 1965. Pp. 365–403.

Fantz, R. L. Pattern discrimination and selective attention as determinants of perceptual development from birth. In A. H. Kidd & J. L. Rivoire (Eds.), *Perceptual development in children.* New York: Int. University Press, 1966.

Fantz, R. L. Visual perception and experience in early infancy: A look at the hidden side of behavior development. In H. W. Stevenson, E. H. Hess, & H. L. Rheingold (Eds.), *Early behavior: Comparative and developmental approaches.* New York: Wiley, 1967. Pp. 181–224.

Fantz, R. L., Ordy, J. M., & Udelf, M. S. Maturation of pattern vision in infants during the first six months. *J. comp. physiol. Psychol.,* 1962, *55,* 907–917.

Feigenbaum, E. A. & Simon, H. A. Generalization of an elementary perceiving and memorizing machine. *Proc. IFIP Congress,* 1962, Munich. Pp. 401–406.

Feigenbaum, E. A. & Simon, H. A. Performance of a reading task by an elementary perceiving and memorizing program. *Behavioral Science,* 1963, *8,* 72–76.

Fernberger, S. W. The effect of practice in its initial stages in lifted weight experiments and its bearing upon anthropomorphic measurements. *Amer. J. Psychol.,* 1916, *27,* 261–272.

Fieandt, K. von. Dressurversuche an der Farbenwahrnehmung. *Arch. ges. Psychol.,* 1936, *96,* 467–495.

Fitts, P. M., Weinstein, M., Rappaport, M., Anderson, N., & Leonard, J. A. Stimulus correlates of visual pattern-recognition: A probability approach. *J. exp. Psychol.,* 1956, *51,* 1–11.

Flavell, J. H. *The developmental psychology of Jean Piaget.* Princeton, N. J.: Van Nostrand, 1963.

Fodor, J. A. How to learn to talk: Some simple ways. In F. Smith & G. A. Miller (Eds.), *The genesis of language, a psycholinguistic approach.* Cambridge, Mass.: M.I.T. Press, 1966. Pp. 105–122.

Foley, J. E. Perceptual adaptation to size and distance transformation. Mimeographed paper, June, 1965.

Foley, J. P. An experimental investigation of the effect of prolonged inversion of the visual field in the rhesus monkey (Macaca mulatta). *J. genet. Psychol.,* 1940, *56,* 21–51.

Forgays, D. G. & Forgays, J. W. The nature of the effect of free-environmental experience in the rat. *J. comp. physiol. Psychol.,* 1952, *45,* 322–328.

Forgays, D. G. & Read, J. M. Crucial periods for free-environmental experience in the rat. *J. comp. physiol. Psychol.,* 1962, *55,* 816–818.

Forgus, R. H. The effect of early perceptual learning on the behavior organization of adult rats. *J. comp. physiol. Psychol.,* 1954, *47,* 331–336.

Forgus, R. H. Early visual and motor experience as determiners of complex maze learning ability under rich and reduced stimulation. *J. comp. physiol. Psychol.,* 1955, *48,* 215–220.

Fowler, W. Longitudinal study of early stimulation in the emergence of cognitive processes. Paper given at conference on Intervention in Preschool Education, SSRC, Chicago, 1966.

Fraisse, P. & Elkin, E. H. Étude génétique de l'influence des modes de présentation sur le seuil de reconnaissance d'objets familiers. *L'Année Psychol.,* 1963, *63,* 1–12.

Fraisse, P. & Vautrey, P. La perception de l'espace, de la vitesse, et du temps chez l'enfant de cinq ans. *Enfance,* 1952, *5,* 1–20.

Francès, R. *La perception de la musique.* Paris: Librairie J. Vrin, 1958.

Francès, R. L'apprentissage de la ségrégation perceptive. *Psychol. franç.,* 1963, *8,* 16–27.

Fraser, C., Bellugi, U., & Brown, R. Control of grammar in imitation, comprehension, and production. *J. verb. learn. verb. Behav.,* 1963, *2,* 121–135.

Freedman, D. G. The infant's fear of strangers and the flight response. *J. child Psychiat.,* 1961, *2,* 242–248.

Freeman, R. B., Jr. Perspective determinants of visual size constancy in binocular and monocular cats. *Amer. J. Psychol.,* 1968, *81,* 67–73.

Frenkel-Brunswik, E. Intolerance of ambiguity as an emotional and perceptual personality variable. *J. Pers.,* 1949, *18,* 108–143.

Friedlander, B. Z. Effects of stimulus content, reinforcement contingency and age on preschool children's performance of an operant for pictorial reward. Unpublished doctoral dissertation, Western Reserve University, Cleveland, 1962.

Fries, C. C. *Linguistics and reading.* New York: Holt, 1963.

Fritz, J. J. The effect of over-training and method of stimulus presentation on reversal shifts. Unpublished master's dissertation, Cornell University, 1966.

Furth, H. G. The influence of language on the development of concept formation in deaf children. *J. abnorm. soc. Psychol.,* 1961, *63,* 386–389.

Furth, H. G. Sequence learning in aphasic and deaf children. *J. speech hearing Disorders,* 1964, *29,* 171–177.

Furth, H. G. & Pufall, P. B. Visual and auditory sequence learning in hearing-impaired children. *J. Speech Hear. Res.,* 1966, *9,* 441–449.

Furth, H. G. & Youniss, J. Sequence learning: Perceptual implications in the acquisition of language. In W. Wathen-Dunn (Ed.), *Models for the perception of speech and visual form.* Cambridge, Mass.: M.I.T. Press, 1967. Pp. 344–353.

Gagné, R. M. & Baker, K. E. Transfer of discrimination training to a motor task. *J. exp. Psychol.,* 1950, *40,* 314–328.

Gagné, R. & Gibson, J. J. Research on the recognition of aircraft. Ch. 7 in J. J. Gibson (Ed.), *Motion picture training and research.* Report No. 7, Army Air Force Aviation Psychology Program, Research Reports, U. S. Gov. Printing Office, Washington, D. C., 1947.

Ganz, L. & Riesen, A. H. Stimulus generalization to hue in the dark-reared macaque. *J. comp. physiol. Psychol.,* 1962, *55,* 92–99.

Ganz, L. & Wilson, P. D. Innate generalization of a form discrimination without contouring eye-movements. *J. comp. physiol. Psychol.,* 1967, *63,* 258–269.

Gardner, B. T. & Wallach, L. Shapes of figures identified as a baby's head. *Percept. Mot. Skills,* 1965, *20,* 135–142.

Gardner, R. A. & Gardner, B. T. Teaching sign language to a chimpanzee. Part I. Methodology and preliminary results. Report presented at meeting of Psychonomic Society, Chicago, October, 1967.

Garner, W. R. *Uncertainty and structure as psychological concepts.* New York: Wiley, 1962.

Gaydos, H. F. Intersensory transfer in the discrimination of forms. *Amer. J. Psychol.,* 1956, *69,* 107–110.

Gebhard, J. W. & Mowbray, G. H. On discriminating the rate of visual flicker and auditory flutter. *Amer. J. Psychol.,* 1959, *72,* 521–529.

Gelb, I. J. *A study of writing.* Chicago: University of Chicago Press, 1963.

Gellermann, L. W. Form discrimination in chimpanzees and two-year-old children. I. Form (triangularity) per se. *J. genet. Psychol.,* 1933, *42,* 3–29.

Gellermann, L. W. Form discrimination in chimpanzees and two-year-old children. II. Form vs. background. *J. genet. Psychol.,* 1933, *42,* 29–50.

Gelman, R. Conservation, attention and discrimination. Unpublished doctoral dissertation, University of California at Los Angeles, 1967.

Gesell, A., Ilg, F. I., & Bullis, G. E. *Vision: Its development in infant and child.* New York: Paul Hoeber, 1949.

Gesell, A., Thompson, H., & Amatruda, C. S. *Infant behavior: Its genesis and growth.* New York: McGraw-Hill, 1934.

Ghent, L. Perception of overlapping and embedded figures by children of different ages. *Amer. J. Psychol.,* 1956, *69,* 575–587.

Ghent, L. Form and its orientation: A child's eye view. *Amer. J. Psychol.,* 1961, *74,* 177–190.

Gibson, E. J. Sensory generalization with voluntary reactions. *J. exp. Psychol.,* 1939, *24,* 237–253.

Gibson, E. J. A systematic application of the concepts of generalization and differentiation to verbal learning. *Psychol. Rev.,* 1940, *47,* 196–229.

Gibson, E. J. Retroactive inhibition as a function of degree of generalization between tasks. *J. exp. Psychol.,* 1941, *28,* 93–115.

Gibson, E. J. Intra-list generalization as a factor in verbal learning. *J. exp. Psychol.,* 1942, *30,* 185–200.

Gibson, E. J. Improvement in perceptual judgments as a function of controlled practice or training. *Psychol. Bull.,* 1953, *50,* 401–431.

Gibson, E. J. A re-examination of generalization. *Psychol. Rev.,* 1959, *66,* 340–342.

Gibson, E. J. Development of perception: Discrimination of depth compared with discrimination of graphic symbols. In J. C. Wright & J. Kagan (Eds.), *Basic cognitive processes in children.* Monogr. Soc. Res. Child Develpm., 1963, *28,* No. 1. Pp. 5–24.

Gibson, E. J. Perceptual Development. Ch. IV in H. W. Stevenson, J. Kagan, & C. Spiker (Eds.), *Child Psychology,* Sixty-second Yearbook Nat. Soc. Stud. Ed., 1963. Pp. 144–195.

Gibson, E. J. Learning to read. *Science,* 1965, *148,* 1066–1072.

Gibson, E. J. & Bergman, R. The effect of training on absolute estimation of distance over the ground. *J. exp. Psychol.,* 1954, *48,* 473–482.

Gibson, E. J., Gibson, J. J., Pick, A. D., & Osser, H. A developmental study of the discrimination of letter-like forms. *J. comp. physiol. Psychol.,* 1962, *55,* 897–906.

Gibson, E. J., Gibson, J. J., Smith, O. W., & Flock, H. Motion parallax as a determinant of perceived depth. *J. exp. Psychol.,* 1959, *58,* 40–51.

Gibson, E. J. & Olum, V. Experimental methods of studying perception in children. In P. H. Mussen (Ed.), *Handbook of research in child development.* New York: Wiley, 1960. Pp. 311–373.

Gibson, E. J., Osser, H., & Pick, A. D. A study in the development of grapheme-phoneme correspondences. *J. verb. learn. verb. Behav.*, 1963, *2*, 142–146.

Gibson, E. J., Osser, H., Schiff, W., & Smith, J. An analysis of critical features of letters, tested by a confusion matrix. In *A basic research program on reading.* Cooperative Research Project No. 639, U. S. Office of Education.

Gibson, E. J., Pick, A., Osser, H., & Hammond, M. The role of grapheme-phoneme correspondence in the perception of words. *Amer. J. Psychol.*, 1962, *75*, 554–570.

Gibson, E. J., Shurcliff, A., & Yonas, A. The role of pronounceability in perception of pseudo-words by hearing and deaf subjects. *Project Literacy Reports*, 1966, No. 7, 62–72.

Gibson, E. J. & Walk, R. D. The effect of prolonged exposure to visually presented patterns on learning to discriminate them. *J. comp. physiol. Psychol.*, 1956, *49*, 239–242.

Gibson, E. J. & Walk, R. D. The "visual cliff." *Scient. Amer.*, 1960, *202*, 64–71.

Gibson, E. J., Walk, R. D., Pick, H. L., & Tighe, T. J. The effect of prolonged exposure to visual patterns on learning to discriminate similar and different patterns. *J. comp. physiol. Psychol.*, 1958, *51*, 584–587.

Gibson, E. J., Walk, R. D., & Tighe, T. J. Enhancement and deprivation of visual stimulation during rearing as factors in visual discrimination learning. *J. comp. physiol. Psychol.*, 1959, *52*, 74–81.

Gibson, E. J. & Yonas, A. A developmental study of the effects of visual and auditory interference on a visual scanning task. *Psychon. Sci.*, 1966, *5*, 163–164.

Gibson, E. J. & Yonas, A. A developmental study of visual search behavior. *Percept. and Psychophys.*, 1966, *1*, 169–171.

Gibson, J. J. Adaptation, after-effect and contrast in the perception of curved lines. *J. exp. Psychol.*, 1933, *16*, 1–31.

Gibson, J. J. Adaptation with negative after-effect. *Psychol. Rev.*, 1937, *44*, 222–244.

Gibson, J. J. (Ed.), *Motion picture testing and research.* Report No. 7, AAF Aviation Psychology Research Reports. Washington: U. S. Gov. Printing Office, 1947.

Gibson, J. J. The information contained in light. *Acta Psychologica*, 1960, *17*, 23–30.

Gibson, J. J. Ecological optics. *Vision Res.*, 1961, *1*, 253–262.

Gibson, J. J. Observations on active touch. *Psychol. Rev.*, 1962, *69*, 477–491.

Gibson, J. J. The problem of temporal order in stimulation and perception. *J. Psychol.*, 1966, *62*, 141–149.

Gibson, J. J. The senses considered as perceptual systems. Boston: Houghton-Mifflin, 1966.

Gibson, J. J. & Gibson, E. J. Perceptual learning: Differentiation or enrichment? *Psychol. Rev.*, 1955, *62*, 32–41.

Gibson, J. J. & Gibson, E. J. Continuous perspective transformations and the perception of rigid motion. *J. exp. Psychol.*, 1957, *54*, 129–138.

Gibson, J. J., Olum, P., & Rosenblatt, F. Parallax and perspective during aircraft landings. *Amer. J. Psychol.*, 1955, *68*, 372–385.

Gibson, J. J. & Yonas, P. A new theory of scribbling and drawing in children. Manuscript in preparation.

Gilbert, J. A. Researches on the mental and physical development of school children. *Stud. Yale Psychol. Lab.*, 1894, *2*, 40–100.

Gilinsky, A. S. The effect of attitude upon the perception of size. *Amer. J. Psychol.*, 1955, *68*, 173–192.

Gilinsky, A. S. The effect of growth on the perception of visual space. Paper read at the meeting of the Eastern Psychological Association, New York City, April, 1960.

Ginsburg, N. Matching in pigeons. *J. comp. physiol. Psychol.*, 1957, *50*, 261–263.

Goldstein, A. G. & Chance, J. E. Recognition of children's faces. *Child Develpm.*, 1964, *35*, 129–136.

Gollin, E. S. Developmental studies of visual recognition of incomplete objects. *Percept. Mot. Skills*, 1960, *11*, 289–298.

Gollin, E. S. Observations on method in child psychology. *Merrill-Palmer Quarterly of Behavior*, 1960, *6*, 250–260.

Gollin, E. S. Tactual form discrimination: A developmental comparison under conditions of spatial interference. *J. exp. Psychol.*, 1960, *60*, 126–129.

Gollin, E. S. Further studies of visual recognition of incomplete objects. *Percept. Mot. Skills*, 1961, *13*, 307–314.

Gollin, E. S. Tactual form discrimination: Developmental differences in the effects of training under conditions of spatial interference. *J. Psychol.*, 1961, *51*, 131–140.

Gollin, E. S. Factors affecting the visual recognition of incomplete objects: A comparative investigation of children and adults. *Percept. Mot. Skills*, 1962, *15*, 583–590.

Gollin, E. S. & Liss, P. Conditional discrimination in children. *J. comp. physiol. Psychol.*, 1962, *55*, 850–855.

Gollin, E. S., Saravo, A., & Salten, C. Perceptual distinctiveness and oddity-problem solving in children. *J. exp. child Psychol.*, 1967, *5*, 586–596.

Gonzalez, R. C., Gentry, G. V., & Bitterman, M. E. Relational discrimination of intermediate size in the chimpanzee. *J. comp. physiol. Psychol.*, 1954, *47*, 385–388.

Goodenough, F. *Developmental psychology: An introduction to the study of human behavior.* New York: Appleton, 1934.

Goss, A. E. Transfer as a function of type and amount of preliminary experience with the task stimuli. *J. exp. Psychol.*, 1953, *46*, 419–428.

Goss A. E. & Greenfield, N. Transfer to a motor task as influenced by conditions and degree of prior discrimination training. *J. exp. Psychol.*, 1958, *55*, 258–269.

Gottlieb, G. Developmental age as a baseline for determination of the critical period in imprinting. *J. comp. physiol. Psychol.*, 1961, *54*, 422–427.

Gottschaldt, K. Ueber den Einfluss gehäufter Einprägung auf die Wahrnehmung von Figuren: I. Ueber den Einfluss gahäufter Einprägung von Figuren auf ihre Sichtbarkeit in umfassenden Konfigurationen. *Psychol. Forsch.*, 1926,

8, 261–318. Or see translation, Gestalt factors in repetition, pp. 109–135, in W. D. Ellis (Ed.), *A source book of Gestalt psychology,* New York: Humanities Press, 1938.

Graham, F. K., Berman, P. W., & Ernhart, C. B. Development in preschool children of the ability to copy forms. *Child Develpm.,* 1960, *31*, 339–359.

Gray, P. H. Theory and evidence of imprinting in human infants. *J. Psychol.,* 1958, *46*, 155–166.

Gray, P. H. The releasers of imprinting: Differential reactions to color as a function of maturation. *J. comp. physiol. Psychol.,* 1961, *54*, 597–601.

Gray, P. H. The descriptive study of imprinting in birds from 1873 to 1953. *J. gen. Psychol.,* 1963, *68*, 333–346.

Gray, P. H. & Howard, K. I. Specific recognition of humans in imprinted chicks. *Percept. Mot. Skills,* 1957, *7*, 301–304.

Gregory, R. L. & Wallace, J. G. Recovery from early blindness: A case study. *Exp. Psych. Soc. Monogr.,* 1963, No. 2, Cambridge.

Grice, G. R. Investigation of response-mediated generalization. In D. I. Mosotof-sky (Ed.), *Stimulus generalization.* Stanford, Calif.: Stanford University Press, 1965. Pp. 373–382.

Griffin, D. R. *Listening in the dark.* New Haven: Yale University Press, 1958.

Griffin, D. R. & Galambos, R. The sensory basis of obstacle avoidance by flying bats. *J. exp. Zool.,* 1941, *86*, 481–506.

Griffith, B. C., Spitz, H. H., & Lipman, R. S. Verbal mediation and concept formation in retarded and normal subjects. *J. exp. Psychol.,* 1959, *58*, 247–251.

Grosslight, J. M., Zaynor, W. C., & Lively, B. L. Speech as a stimulus for differential vocal behavior in the Mynah bird (Gracula religiosa). *Psychon. Sci.,* 1964, *1*, 7–8.

Guignot, E., Mace, H., Savigny, M., & Vurpillot, E. Influence de la consigne sur une mésure de constance de forme. *Bull. de Psychologie,* 1963, *16*, 11–12.

Guiton, P. The effect of isolation on the following response of brown leghorn chicks. *Proc. roy. phys. Soc. Edinb.,* 1958, *27*, 9–14.

Gunter, R. Visual size constancy in the cat. *Brit. J. Psychol.,* 1951, *42*, 288–293.

Guttman, N. Laws of behavior and facts of perception. In S. Koch (Ed.), *Psychology: A study of a science.* Vol. V. New York: McGraw-Hill, 1963. Pp. 114–178.

Hailman, J. P. Pecking of laughing gull chicks to models of the parental head. *Auk,* 1962, *79*, 89–98.

Haire, M. A note concerning McCulloch's discussion of discrimination habits. *Psychol. Rev.,* 1939, *46*, 298–303.

Hake, H. W. & Eriksen, C. W. Effect of number of permissible response categories on learning of a constant number of visual stimuli. *J. exp. Psychol.,* 1955, *50*, 161–167.

Hake, H. W. & Eriksen, C. W. Role of response variables in recognition and identification of complex visual forms. *J. exp. Psychol.,* 1956, *52*, 235–243.

Halsey, R. M. & Chapanis, A. On the number of absolutely identifiable spectral hues. *J. opt. Soc. Amer.,* 1951, *41*, 1057–1058.

Halverson, H. M. An experimental study of prehension in infants by means of systematic cinema records. *Genet. Psychol. Monogr.,* 1932, *10*, 110–286.

Hamilton, C. R. Intermanual transfer of adaptation to prisms. *Amer. J. Psychol.,* 1964, *77,* 457–462.

Hanawalt, N. G. The effect of practice upon the perception of simple designs masked by more complex designs. *J. exp. Psychol.,* 1942, *31,* 134–148.

Hanes, R. M. & Rhoades, M. V. Color identification as a function of extended practice. *J. opt. soc. Amer.,* 1959, *49,* 1060–1064.

Harlow, H. F. Studies in discrimination learning by monkeys. III. Factors influencing the facility of solution of discrimination problems by rhesus monkeys. *J. genet. Psychol.,* 1945, *32,* 213–227.

Harlow, H. F. Primate learning. Ch. 7 in C. P. Stone (Ed.), *Comparative psychology.* (3rd ed.) Englewood Cliffs, N. J.: Prentice-Hall, 1951.

Harlow, H. F., Harlow, M. K., & Meyer, D. R. Learning movitated by a manipulation drive. *J. exp. Psychol.,* 1950, *40,* 228–234.

Harrington, T. L. Adaptation of humans to colored split-field glasses. *Psychon. Sci.,* 1965, *3,* 71–72.

Harris, C. S. Adaptation to displaced vision: Visual, motor or proprioceptive change? *Science,* 1963, *140,* 812–813.

Harris, C. S. & Haber, R. N. Selective attention and coding in visual perception. *J. exp. Psychol.,* 1963, *65,* 328–333.

Harway, N. I. Judgment of distance in children and adults. *J. exp. Psychol.,* 1963, *65,* 385–390.

Hay, J. C. & Pick, H. L., Jr. Gaze-contingent adaptation and prism orientation. *J. exp. Psychol.,* 1966, *72,* 640–648.

Hay, J. C., Pick, H. L., Jr., & Rosser, E. Adaptation to chromatic aberration in the human visual system. *Science,* 1963, *141,* 167–169.

Hayek, F. A. *The sensory order.* Chicago, Ill.: University of Chicago Press, 1952.

Hayes, C. *The ape in our house.* New York: Harper, 1951.

Hayes, W. N. & Saiff, E. I. Visual alarm reactions in turtles. *Anim. Behav.,* 1967, *15,* 102–106.

Haynes, H., White, B. L., & Held, R. Visual accommodation in human infants. *Science,* 1965, *148,* 528–530.

Hebb, D. O. The innate organization of visual activity: I. Perception of figures by rats reared in total darkness. *J. genet. Psychol.,* 1937, *51,* 101–126.

Hebb, D. O. *The organization of behavior: A neuropsychological theory.* New York: Wiley, 1949.

Hebb, D. O. *A textbook of psychology.* Philadelphia: Saunders, 1958.

Hebb, D. O. The semiautonomous process: Its nature and nurture. *Amer. Psychol.,* 1963, *18,* 16–27.

Heimer, W. I. & Tatz, S. J. Practice effects, knowledge of results and transfer in pitch discrimination. Technical Report: Navtradevcen IH-52, Port Washington, N. Y., 1966.

Hein, A. & Held, R. Dissociation of the visual placing response into elicited and guided components. *Science,* 1967, *158,* 390–391.

Heinroth, O. Beiträge zur Biologie, namentlich Ethologie und Physiologie der Anatiden. *Vehrl. 5 Int. Orn. Kongr.,* 1910, 589–702.

Held, R. Shifts in binaural localization after prolonged exposures to atypical combinations of stimuli. *Amer. J. Psychol.,* 1955, *68,* 526–548.

Held, R. Exposure history as a factor in maintaining stability of perception and coordination. *J. nerv. ment. Dis.,* 1961, *132,* 26–32.

Held, R. Adaptation to rearrangement and visual-spatial aftereffects. *Psychol. Beit.*, 1962, *6*, 439–450.

Held, R. Plasticity in human sensori-motor control. *Science*, 1963, *142*, 455–462.

Held, R. M. Our understanding of perception. *Tech. Rev., M.I.T.*, 1964, *67*, 1–3.

Held, R. Plasticity in sensory-motor systems. *Scient. Amer.*, 1965, *213*, 84–94.

Held, R. & Bauer, J. A. Visually guided reaching in infant monkeys after restricted rearing. *Science*, 1967, *155*, 718–720.

Held, R. & Bossom, J. Neonatal deprivation and adult rearrangement: Complementary techniques for analyzing plastic sensori-motor coordinations. *J. comp. physiol. Psychol.*, 1961, *54*, 33–37.

Held, R. & Hein, A. V. Adaptation of disarranged eye-hand coordination contingent upon re-afferent stimulation. *Percept. Mot. Skills*, 1958, *8*, 87–90.

Held, R. & Hein, A. Movement produced stimulation in the development of visually guided behavior. *J. comp. physiol. Psychol.*, 1963, *56*, 872–876.

Helmholtz, H. v. *Handbook of physiological optics*, Vol. III. Tr. by J. P. C. Southall. New York: Optical Society of America, 1925.

Hemmendinger, L. Perceptual organization and development as reflected in the structure of Rorschach test responses. *J. proj. Tech.*, 1953, *17*, 162–170.

Hendrickson, L. N. & Muehl, S. The effect of attention and motor response pretraining on learning to discriminate B and D in kindergarten children. *J. educ. Psychol.*, 1962, *53*, 236–241.

Henle, M. An experimental investigation of past experience as a determinant of visual form perception. *J. exp. Psychol.*, 1942, *30*, 1–22.

Hernandez-Peon, R., Scherrer, H., & Jouvet, M. Modification of electrical activity in cochlear nucleus during "attention" in unanaesthetized cats. *Science*, 1956, *123*, 331–332.

Heron, W. Perception of retinal locus and attention. *Amer. J. Psychol.*, 1957, *70*, 38–48.

Hershenson, M. Visual discrimination in the human newborn. *J. comp. physiol. Psychol.*, 1964, *58*, 270–276.

Hershenson, M. Form perception in the human newborn. Paper presented at the Second Annual Symposium, Center for Visual Science, University of Rochester, June, 1965.

Hertz, M. Figural perception in the Jay bird. In W. D. Ellis (Ed.), *A source book of Gestalt psychology*. New York: Harcourt, 1938. Pp. 238–252.

Hertz, M. Figural perception in bees. In W. D. Ellis (Ed.), *A source book of Gestalt psychology*. New York: Harcourt, 1938. Pp. 253–263.

Hess, E. H. Development of the chick's responses to light and shade cues of depth. *J. comp. physiol. Psychol.*, 1950, *43*, 112-122.

Hess, E. H. Space perception in the chick. *Scient. Amer.*, 1956, *195*, 71–80.

Hess, E. H. Imprinting. *Science*, 1959, *130*, 133–141. (a)

Hess, E. H. Two conditions limiting critical age for imprinting. *J. comp. physiol. Psychol.*, 1959, *52*, 515–518. (b)

Hess, E. H. Imprinting in birds. *Science*, 1964, *146*, 1128–1139.

Hinde, R. A. Factors governing the changes in strength of a partially inborn response, as shown by the mobbing behavior of the Chaffinch (Fringilla collebs). I and II. *Proc. Roy. Soc.*, B, 1954, *142*, 306–331, 331–358.

Hinde, R. A. The establishment of the parent-offspring relation in birds, with some mammalian analogies. Ch. VII in W. H. Thorpe & O. L. Zangwill

(Eds.), *Current problems in animal behavior.* Cambridge: Cambridge University Press, 1961. Pp. 175–193.

Hinde, R. A., Thorpe, W. H., & Vince, M. A. The following response of young coots and moorhens. *Behaviour,* 1956, *9,* 214–242.

Hochberg, J. E. Nativism and empiricism in perception. In L. Postman (Ed.), *Psychology in the making.* New York: Knopf, 1962. Pp. 255–330. (a)

Hochberg, J. E. The psychophysics of pictorial perception. *Audio-vis. comm. Rev.,* 1962, *10,* 22–54. (b)

Hochberg, J. E. *Perception.* Englewood Cliffs, N. J.: Prentice-Hall, 1964.

Hochberg, J. E. & Brooks, V. Effects of previously associated annoying stimuli (auditory) on visual recognition thresholds. *J. exp. Psychol.,* 1958, *55,* 490–491.

Hochberg, J. E. & Brooks, V. Pictorial recognition as an unlearned ability: A study of one child's performance. *Amer. J. Psychol.,* 1962, *75,* 624–628.

Holmgren, G. L., Arnoult, M. D., & Manning, W. H. Intermodal transfer in a paired-associates learning task. *J. exp. Psychol.,* 1966, *71,* 254–259.

Holst, E. v. Relations between the central nervous system and the peripheral organs. *Brit. J. anim. Behav.,* 1954, *2,* 89–94.

Honig, W. K. & Day, R. W. Discrimination and generalization on a dimension of stimulus difference. *Science,* 1962, *141,* 29–31.

Honkavaara, S. Organization processes in perception as a measure of intelligence. *J. Psychol.,* 1958, *46,* 3–12.

House, B. J. Oddity performance in retardates. I. Size discrimination functions from oddity and verbal methods. *Child Develpm.,* 1964, *35,* 645–651.

House, B. J. Discrimination of symmetrical and asymmetrical dot patterns by retardates. *J. exp. child Psychol.,* 1966, *3,* 377–389.

House, B. J. & Zeaman, D. Transfer of a discrimination from objects to patterns. *J. exp. Psychol.,* 1960, *59,* 298–302.

House, B. J. & Zeaman, D. Reversal and nonreversal shifts in discrimination learning in retardates. *J. exp. Psychol.,* 1962, *63,* 444–451.

Hovland, C. I. Comments on Littman's "Conditioned generalization of the galvanic skin reaction to tones." *J. exp. Psychol.,* 1949, *39,* 892–896.

Howard, I. P., Craske, B., & Templeton, W. B. Visuomotor adaptation to discordant exafferent stimulation. *J. exp. Psychol.,* 1965, *70,* 189–191.

Howard, I. P. & Templeton, W. B. *Human spatial orientation.* New York: Wiley, 1966.

Hubel, D. H. & Wiesel, T. N. Receptive fields of single neurons in the cat's striate cortex. *J. Physiol.,* 1959, *148,* 574–591.

Hubel, D. H. & Wiesel, T. N. Receptive fields, binocular interaction and functional architecture in the cat's visual cortex. *J. Physiol.,* 1962, *160,* 106–154.

Hubel, D. H. & Wiesel, T. N. Receptive fields of cells in striate cortex of very young, visually inexperienced kittens. *J. Neurophysiol.,* 1963, *26,* 994–1002.

Hubel, D. H. & Wiesel, T. N. Receptive fields and functional architecture in two nonstriate visual areas (18 and 19) of the cat. *J. Neurophysiol.,* 1965, *28,* 229–289. (a)

Hubel, D. H. & Wiesel, T. N. Binocular interaction in striate cortex of kittens reared with artificial squint. *J. Neurophysiol.,* 1965, *28,* 1041–1059. (b)

Hudson, W. Pictorial depth perception in sub-cultural groups in Africa. *J. soc. Psychol.*, 1960, *52*, 183–208.

Hull, C. L. *Principles of behavior*. New York: Appleton, 1943.

Hunt, J. McV. Motivation inherent in information processing and action. Ch. 3 in O. J. Harvey (Ed.), *Motivation and social interaction*. New York: Ronald Press, 1963.

Huttenlocher, J. Children's ability to orient and order objects. *Child Develpm.*, 1967, *38*, 1169–1176.

Huttenlocher, J. Discrimination of figure orientation: Effects of relative position. *J. comp. physiol. Psychol.*, 1967, *63*, 359–361.

Hyman, L. M. The effect of redundant patterns on retardate discrimination learning. *Psychon. Sci.*, 1967, *9*, 195–196.

Hymovitch, B. The effects of experimental variations on problem solving in the rat. *J. comp. physiol. Psychol.*, 1952, *45*, 313–321.

Iscoe, I. & Semler, I. Paired-associate learning in normal and mentally retarded children as a function of four conditions. *J. comp. physiol. Psychol.*, 1964, *57*, 387–392.

Ittelson, W. H. The constancies in perceptual theory. *Psychol. Rev.*, 1951, *58*, 285–294.

Ittelson, W. H. *The Ames demonstrations in perception*. Princeton, N. J.: Princeton University Press, 1952.

Ittelson, W. H. Perception and transactional psychology. In S. Koch (Ed.), *Psychology: A study of a science*. Vol. IV. New York: McGraw-Hill, 1962. Pp. 660–704.

Jackson, D. N. A further examination of the role of autism in a visual figure-ground relationship. *J. Psychol.*, 1954, *38*, 339–357.

Jakobson, R. About the relation between visual and auditory signs. In W. Wathen-Dunn (Ed.), *Models for the perception of speech and visual form*. Cambridge, Mass.: M.I.T. Press, 1967. Pp. 1–7.

Jakobson, R. & Halle, M. *Fundamentals of language*. The Hague: Mouton, 1956.

James, H. Flicker: An unconditioned stimulus for imprinting. *Canad. J. Psychol.*, 1959, *13*, 59–67.

James, H. Imprinting with visual flicker: Evidence for a critical period. *Canad. J. Psychol.*, 1960, *14*, 13–20

James, W. *Principles of psychology*. New York: Holt, 1890.

Jaynes, J. Imprinting: The interaction of learned and innate behavior: I. Development and generalization. *J. comp. physiol. Psychol.*, 1956, *49*, 201–206.

Jaynes, J. Imprinting: The interaction of learned and innate behavior: II. The critical period. *J. comp. physiol. Psychol.*, 1957, *50*, 6–10.

Jaynes, J. Imprinting: The interaction of learned and innate behavior: IV. Generalization and emergent discrimination. *J. comp. physiol. Psychol.*, 1958, *51*, 238–242.

Jeffrey, W. E. The effects of verbal and nonverbal responses in mediating an instrumental act. *J. exp. Psychol.*, 1953, *45*, 327–333.

Jeffrey, W. E. Variables affecting reversal-shifts in young children. *Amer. J. Psychol.*, 1965, *78*, 589–595.

Jeffrey, W. E. & Samuels, S. J. Effect of method of reading training on initial learning and transfer. *J. verb. learn. verb. Behav.*, 1967, *6*, 354–358.

Jenkin, N. & Feallock, S. M. Developmental and intellectual processes in size-distance judgment. *Amer. J. Psychol.*, 1960, *73*, 268–273.

Jenkin, N. & West, N. Perception in organic mental defectives: An exploratory study. I. The size-weight illusion. *Training Sch. Bull.*, 1958, *55*, 5–10.

Johansson, G. *Configurations in event perception.* Uppsala: Almkvist and Wiksell, 1950.

Johnson, B. & Beck, L. F. The development of space perception: I. Stereoscopic vision in pre-school children. *J. genet. Psychol.*, 1941, *58*, 247–254.

Johnson, M. L. Observer error: Its bearing on teaching. *Lancet*, 1955, ii, 422.

Jones, A. Information deprivation in humans. In B. Maher (Ed.), *Progress in experimental personality research.* Vol. III. New York: Academic Press, 1966. Pp. 241–307.

Kaess, D. W. & Wilson, J. P. Modification of the rat's avoidance of visual depth. *J. comp. physiol. Psychol.*, 1964, *58*, 151–152.

Kagan, J. The growth of the "face" schema: Theoretical significance and methodological issues. Paper presented at meetings of the American Psychological Association, Chicago, September, 1965.

Kagan, J., Henker, B. A., Hen-Tov, A., Levine, J., & Lewis, M. Infant's differential reactions to familiar and distorted faces. *Child Develpm.*, 1966, *37*, 519–532.

Kagan, J. & Lewis, M. Studies of attention in the human infant. *Merrill-Palmer Quarterly of Behavior and Development*, 1965, *11*, 95–127.

Kaila, E. Die Reaktionen des Säuglings auf das menschliche Gesicht. *Annales Univ. Aboensis*, Ser. B. Bd. 17, 1932.

Kalish, H. L. The relationship between discriminability and generalization: A re-evaluation. *J. exp. Psychol.*, 1958, *55*, 637–644.

Kaplan, G., Yonas, A., & Shurcliff, A. Visual and acoustic confusability in a visual search task. *Percept. and Psychophysics*, 1966, *1*, 172–174.

Kaplan, I. T. & Carvellas, T. Scanning for multiple targets. *Percept. Mot. Skills*, 1965, *21*, 239–243.

Kaspar, J. C. & Schulman, J. L. The explication and solution of a specific error in copying diamonds. *J. exp. child Psychol.*, 1964, *1*, 311–315.

Katz, P. A. Effects of labels on children's perception and discrimination learning. *J. exp. Psychol.*, 1963, *66*, 423–428.

Kawachi, J. Effect of previous perceptual experience of specific three-dimensional objects on later visual discrimination behavior in rats. *Jap. Psychol. Res.*, 1965, *7*, 20–27.

Kelleher, R. T. Discrimination learning as a function of reversal and nonreversal shifts. *J. exp. Psychol.*, 1956, *51*, 379–384.

Keller, F. S. & Schoenfeld, W. N. Studies in International Morse code. III. The efficiency of the code as related to errors made during learning. *J. appl. Psychol.*, 1944, *28*, 254–266.

Keller, F. S. & Taubman, R. E. Studies in International Morse code. II. Errors made in code reception. *J. appl. Psychol.*, 1943, *27*, 504–509.

Kellogg, W. N. Echo ranging in the Porpoise. *Science*, 1958, *128*, 982–988.

Kellogg, W. N. *Porpoises and sonar.* Chicago: University of Chicago Press, 1961.

Kellogg, W. N. Sonar system of the blind. *Science*, 1962, *137*, 399–404.

Kelvin, R. P. Discrimination of size by sight and touch. *Quart. J. exp. Psychol.,* 1954, *6,* 23–34.

Kelvin, R. P. & Mulik, A. Discrimination of length by sight and touch. *Quart. J. exp. Psychol.,* 1958, *10,* 187–192.

Kendler, H. H. The concept of the concept. In A. W. Melton (Ed.), *Categories of human learning.* New York: Academic Press, 1964. Pp. 212–236.

Kendler, H. H., Glucksberg, S., & Keston, R. Perception and mediation in concept learning. *J. exp. Psychol.,* 1961, *61,* 186–191.

Kendler, T. S. & Kendler, H. H. Reversal and non-reversal shifts in kindergarten children. *J. exp. Psychol.,* 1959, *58,* 56–60.

Kenyon, K. W. & Rice, T. W. Homing of the Layson Albatross. *Condor,* 1958, *60,* 3–6.

Kerpelman, L. C. Preexposure to visually presented forms and nondifferential reinforcement in perceptual learning. *J. exp. Psychol.,* 1965, *69,* 257–262.

Kerpelman, L. C. & Pollack, R. H. Developmental changes in the location of form discrimination cues. *Percept. Mot. Skills,* 1964, *19,* 375–382.

Kesson, W., Salapatek, P., & Haith, M. M. The ocular orientation of newborn infants to visual contours. Paper presented at the meeting of the Psychonomic Society, Chicago, October, 1965.

Kilpatrick, F. P. Two processes in perceptual learning. *J. exp. Psychol.,* 1954, *47,* 362–370.

Kilpatrick, F. P. *Explorations in transactional psychology.* New York: New York University Press, 1961.

Kinney, J. S. Discrimination in auditory and visual patterns. *Amer. J. Psychol.,* 1961, *74,* 529–541.

Kleeman, J. A. The peek-a-boo game: Part 1. Its origins, meanings, and related phenomena in the first year. *The Psychoanalytic Study of the Child,* 1967, *22,* 239–273.

Klimpfinger, S. Die Entwicklung der Gestaltkonstanz vom Kind zum Erwachsenen. *Arch. ges. Psychol.,* 1933, *88,* 599–628. (a)

Klimpfinger, S. Ueber den Einfluss von intentionaler Einstellung und Uebung auf die Gestalt-konstanz. *Arch. ges. Psychol.,* 1933, *88,* 551–598. (b)

Klopfer, P. H. *Behavioral aspects of ethology.* Englewood Cliffs, N. J.: Prentice-Hall, 1962.

Klopfer, P. H. Imprinting: A reassessment. *Science,* 1965, *147,* 302–303.

Klopfer, P. H. Stimulus preferences and imprinting. *Science,* 1967, *156,* 1394–1396.

Klopfer, P. H. & Gottlieb, G. Imprinting and behavioral polymorphism: Auditory and visual imprinting in domestic ducks (Anas platyrhinchos) and the involvement of the critical period. *J. comp. physiol. Psychol.,* 1962, *55,* 126–130. (a)

Klopfer, P. H. & Gottlieb, G. The relation of developmental age to auditory and visual imprinting. *J. comp. physiol. Psychol.,* 1962, *55,* 821–826. (b)

Klopfer, P. H. & Hailman, J. P. Perceptual preferences and imprinting in chicks. *Science,* 1964, *145,* 1333–1334.

Klüver, H. *Behavior mechanisms in monkeys.* Chicago: University of Chicago Press, 1933.

Koffka, K. *The growth of the mind.* (2nd ed.) New York: Harcourt, 1931.

Koffka, K. *Principles of Gestalt psychology.* New York: Harcourt, 1935.

Kofsky, E. & Osler, S. Free classification in children. *Child Develpm.,* 1967, *38,* 927–937.

Kohler, I. Über Aufbau und Wandlungen der Wahrnehmungswelt, insbesondere über 'bedingte' empfindungen. Vienna: Rohrer, 1951.

Kohler, I. Experiments with goggles. *Scient. Amer.,* 1962, *206,* 62–72.

Kohler, I. The formation and transformation of the perceptual world. *Psychological Issues,* Vol. III, No. 4, Int. Univ. Press, 1964.

Köhler, W. Nachweis einfacher Structurfunktionen beim Shimpansen und beim Haushuhn. Über eine neue Methode zur Untersuchung des bunte Farbensystems. *Abh. d. Königl. Preuss. Ak. d. Wissen,* Jahrg. 1918, Phys-Math. Klasse, Nr. 2, pp. 1–101.

Köhler, W. *The mentality of apes.* (Tr. by Ella Winter). New York: Harcourt, 1925.

Köhler, W. & Fishback, J. The destruction of the Müller-Lyer illusion in repeated trials: I. An examination of two theories. *J. exp. Psychol.,* 1950, *40,* 267–281.

Kolers, P. A. Some aspects of problem-solving: I. Method and materials. WADD Technical Report 60-2, Project No. 7183, Task No. 71618, Wright-Patterson Air Force Base, Ohio, 1960.

Kolers, P. A. & Katzman, M. T. Naming sequentially presented letters and words. *Language and Speech,* 1966, *9,* 84–95.

Kolers, P. A. & Zink, D. L. Some aspects of problem solving: Sequential analysis of the detection of embedded patterns. Technical Documentary Report No. AMRL-TDR-62-148, Project No. 7183, Task No. 718303, Wright-Patterson Air Force Base, Ohio, 1962.

Koronakos, C. & Freeman, R. B. Visual size constancy in cats following dimensional discrimination training. *J. comp. physiol. Psychol.,* 1967, *64,* 290–294.

Kottenhoff, H. Situational and personal influences on space perception with experimental spectacles. *Acta Psychol.,* 1957, *13,* 79–97 (Part I), 151–161 (Part II).

Kovach, J. K. & Hess, E. H. Imprinting: Effects of painful stimulation upon the following response. *J. comp. physiol. Psychol.,* 1963, *56,* 461–464.

Külpe, O. Versuche über Abstraction. *Ber. I Kongr. exp. Psychol.,* 1904, 56–68.

Kuo, Z. Y. The genesis of the cat's responses to the rat. *J. comp. Psychol.,* 1930, *11,* 1–35.

Lambercier, M. Recherche sur le développement des perceptions: VI. La constance des grandeurs en comparaisons sériales. *Arch. Psychol. Genève.,* 1946, *31,* 79–282.

Lashley, K. S. The mechanism of vision: I. A method for rapid analysis of pattern-vision in the rat. *J. genet. Psychol.,* 1930, *37,* 453–460.

Lashley, K. S. Experimental analysis of instinctive behavior. *Psychol. Rev.,* 1938, *45,* 445–471.

Lashley, K. S. The problem of serial order in behavior. In L. A. Jeffress (Ed.), *Cerebral mechanisms in behavior.* New York: Wiley, 1951. Pp. 112–136.

Lashley, K. S. Persistent problems in the evolution of mind. *Quart. Rev. Biol.*, 1949, *24*, 28–42. Reprinted in F. A. Beach et al. (Eds.), *The neuropsychology of Lashley*. New York: McGraw-Hill, 1960. Pp. 455–477.

Lashley, K. S. & Russell, J. T. The mechanism of vision. XI. A preliminary test of innate organization. *J. genet. Psychol.*, 1934, *45*, 136–144.

Lashley, K. S. & Wade, M. The Pavlovian theory of generalization. *Psychol. Rev.*, 1946, *53*, 72–87.

Lawrence, D. H. The transfer of discrimination along a continuum. *J. comp. physiol. Psychol.*, 1952, *45*, 511–516.

Lawrence, D. H. & Coles, G. R. Accuracy of recognition with alternatives before and after the stimuli. *J. exp. Psychol.*, 1954, *47*, 208–214.

Leeper, R. A study of a neglected portion of the field of learning—the development of sensory organization. *J. genet. Psychol.*, 1935, *46*, 41–75.

Leibowitz, H. Apparent visual size as a function of distance for mentally deficient subjects. *Amer. J. Psychol.*, 1961, *74*, 98–100.

Leibowitz, H., Waskow, I., Loeffler, N., & Glaser, F. Intelligence level as a variable in the perception of shape. *Quart. J. exp. Psychol.*, 1959, *11*, 108–112.

Lemmon, V. W. The relation of reaction time to measures of intelligence, memory, and learning. *Arch. Psychol.*, 1927, *15*, No. 94.

Lenneberg, E. H. Color naming, color recognition, color discrimination: A re-appraisal. *Percept. Mot. Skills*, 1961, *12*, 375–382.

Lenneberg, E. H. The relationship of language to the formation of concepts. *Synthèse*, 1962, *14*, 103–109.

Lenneberg, E. H. Speech as a motor skill with special reference to non-aphasic disorders. In U. Bellugi & R. Brown (Eds.), *The acquisition of language*. Monogr. Soc. Res. Child Develpm., 1964, *29*, No. 1. Ch. 5.

Lenneberg, E. H. *Biological foundations of language*. New York: Wiley, 1967.

Leontiev, A. N. The nature and formation of human psychic properties. In B. Simon (Ed.), *Psychology in the Soviet Union*. Stanford: Stanford University Press, 1957. Pp. 226–232.

Leopold, W. F. Patterning in children's language learning. *Language Learning*, 1953–54, *5*, 1–14. Reprinted in S. Saporta & J. R. Bastian (Eds.), *Psycholinguistics: A book of readings*. New York: Holt, 1961. Pp. 350–358.

Leuba, C. Children's reactions to elements of simple geometric patterns. *Amer. J. Psychol.*, 1940, *53*, 575–578.

Leventhal, A. S. & Lipsitt, L. P. Adaptation, pitch discrimination, and sound localization in the neonate. *Child Develpm.*, 1964, *35*, 759–767.

Levin, H. & Kaplan, E. The eye-voice span for active and passive sentences. *Language and Speech*, in press.

Levin, H. & Turner, E. A. Sentence structure and the eye-voice span. *Project Literacy Reports*, September, 1966, No. 7, 79–87.

Lewis, M. M. *Infant speech*. New York: Humanities Press, 1951.

Lewis, M. M. *Language, thought and personality in infancy and childhood*. New York: Basic Books, 1963.

Lewis, M. Exploratory studies in the development of a face schema. Paper presented at the meeting of the American Psychological Association, Chicago, September, 1965.

Liberman, A. M. Some results of research on speech perception. *J. acoust. soc. Amer.*, 1957, *29*, 117–123.

Liberman, A. M., Cooper, F. S., Harris, K. S., & MacNeilage, P. F. A motor theory of speech perception. Paper presented at the Speech Communication Seminar, Stockholm, September, 1962.

Liberman, A. M., Cooper, F. S., Shankweiler, D. P., & Studdert-Kennedy, M. Perception of the speech code. *Psychol. Rev.*, 1967, *74*, 431–461.

Liberman, A. M., Harris, K. S., Horrman, S. H., & Griffiths, B. C. The discrimination of speech sounds within and across phoneme boundaries. *J. exp. Psychol.*, 1957, *54*, 358–368.

Liberman, A. M., Harris, K. S., Kinney, J., & Lane, H. The discrimination of relative onset-time of the components of certain speech and non-speech patterns. *J. exp. Psychol.*, 1961, *61*, 379–388.

Liebert, R. S. & Rudel, R. G. Auditory localization and adaptation to body tilt: A developmental study. *Child Develpm.*, 1959, *30*, 81–90.

Ling, B. C. Form discrimination as a learning cue in infants. *Comp. Psychol. Monogr.*, 1941, *17*, No. 2 (Whole No. 86).

Lipsitt, L. P. Learning in the first year of life. In L. P. Lipsitt & C. C. Spiker (Ed.), *Advances in child development and behavior*. New York: Academic Press, 1963. Pp. 147–195.

Lipsitt, L. P. & Kaye, H. Conditioned sucking in the human newborn. *Psychon. Sci.*, 1964, *1*, 29–30.

Lipsitt, L. P. & Serunian, S. A. Oddity-problem learning in young children. *Child Develpm.*, 1963, *34*, 201–206.

Littman, R. A. Conditioned generalization of the galvanic skin reaction to tones. *J. exp. Psychol.*, 1949, *39*, 868–882.

Lobb, H. Vision versus touch in form discrimination. *Canad. J. Psychol.*, 1965, *19*, 175–187.

Locke, N. M. Perception and intelligence: Their phylogenetic relation. *Psychol. Rev.*, 1938, *45*, 335–345.

Lorenz, K. Der Kumpan in der Umwelt des Vögels. *J. f. Orn.*, 1935, *83*, 137–214, 289–413.

Lorenz, K. Vergleichende Verhaltensforschung. *Zool. Anz. Suppl. Bd.*, 1939, *12*, 69–102.

Lorenz, K. *Evolution and modification of behavior*. Chicago: University of Chicago Press, 1965.

Lorenz, K. & Tinbergen, N. Taxis und Instinkthandlung in der Eirollbewegung der Graugans I. *Zeitsch. Tierpsychol.*, 1938, *2*, 1–29.

Low, F. N. *Effect of training on acuity of peripheral vision*. CAA Division of Research Report No. 68, 1946. (a)

Low, F. N. Some characteristics of peripheral visual performance. *Amer. J. Physiol.*, 1946, *146*, 573–584. (b)

Lunn, J. H. Chick sexing. *American Scientist*, 1948, *36*, 280–287.

Maccoby, E. E. Selective auditory attention in children. In L. P. Lipsitt & C. C. Spiker (Eds.), *Recent advances in child development and behavior*. Vol. 3. New York: Academic Press, 1967. Pp. 99–124.

Maccoby, E. E. What copying requires. *Ontario J. Ed. Res.*, 1968, *10*, 163–170.

Maccoby, E. E. & Bee, H. Some speculations concerning the lag between perceiving and performing. *Child Develpm.*, 1965, *36*, 367–378.

Maccoby, E. E. & Hagen, J. W. Effects of distraction upon central versus incidental recall: Developmental trends. *J. exp. child Psychol.*, 1965, *2*, 280–289.

MacLean, P. D. Mirror display in the squirrel monkey, Saimiri Sciureus. *Science*, 1964, *146*, 950–952.

Mackworth, N. A stand camera for line-of-sight recording. *Percept. and Psychophys.*, 1967, *2*, 119–127.

Mackworth, N. H. & Bruner, J. S. Selecting visual information during recognition by adults and children. Center for Cognitive Studies, Harvard, 1966. Unpublished report.

Maier, G. W. & McGee, R. K. A re-evaluation of the effect of early perceptual experience on discrimination performance during adulthood. *J. comp. physiol. Psychol.*, 1959, *52*, 390–395.

Mangan, G. L. The role of punishment in figure-ground reorganization. *J. exp. Psychol.*, 1959, *58*, 369–375.

Mangan, G. L. Retention of figure-ground reorganization occurring under electric-shock punishment. *Percept. mot. Skills*, 1961, *12*, 151–154.

Marler, P. The filtering of external stimuli during instinctive behavior. In W. H. Thorpe & O. L. Zangwill (Eds.), *Current problems in animal behavior*. Cambridge: Cambridge University Press, 1961. Ch. VI.

Marler, P. Animal communication signals. *Science*, 1967, *157*, 769–774.

Maturana, H. R., Lettvin, J. Y., McCulloch, W. S., & Pitts, W. H. Anatomy and physiology of vision in the frog (Rana pipiens). *J. gen. Physiol.*, 1960, *43*, 129–175.

McCleary, R. A. & Longfellow, L. A. Interocular transfer of pattern discrimination without prior binocular experience. *Science*, 1961, *134*, 1418–1419.

McCollough, C. The conditioning of color-perception. *Amer. J. Psychol.*, 1965, *78*, 362–368.

McCurdy, H. G. Coin perception studies and the concept of schemata. *Psychol. Rev.*, 1956, *63*, 160–168.

McFadden, H. B. *Visual acuity*. Duncan, Okla.: Optometric Extension Program, 1940.

McGinnies, E. Emotionality and perceptual defense. *Psychol. Rev.*, 1949, *56*, 244–251.

McKinney, J. P. Disappearance of luminous designs. *Science*, 1963, *140*, 403–404.

McNeill, D. Developmental psycholinguistics. In F. Smith & G. A. Miller (Eds.), *The genesis of language, a psycholinguistic approach*. Cambridge, Mass.: M.I.T. Press, 1966. Pp. 15–84.

Mednick, S. A. & Lehtinen, L. E. Stimulus generalization as a function of age in children. *J. exp. Psychol.*, 1957, *53*, 180–183.

Meili, R. Les perceptions des enfants et la psychologie de la Gestalt. *Arch. Psychol. Genève*, 1931, *23*, 131–156.

Meili, R. & Tobler, E. Les mouvements stroboscopiques chez les enfants. *Arch. Psychol. Genève*, 1931, *23*, 131–157.

Melzack, R. On the survival of mallard ducks after "habituation" to the hawk-shaped figure. *Behavior*, 1961, *17*, 9–16.

Melzack, R. Effects of early perceptual restriction on simple visual discrimination. *Science*, 1962, *137*, 978–979.

Meneghini, K. A. & Leibowitz, H. W. The effect of stimulus distance and age on shape constancy. *J. exp. Psychol.*, 1967, *74*, 241–248.

Menzel, E. W., Davenport, R. K., & Rogers, C. M. The effects of environmental restriction upon the chimpanzee's responsiveness to objects. *J. comp. physiol. Psychol.*, 1963, *56*, 78–85.

Merkel, J. Die zeitlichen Verhältnisse der Willensthätigkeit. *Philos. Stud.* (Wundt), 1885, *2*, 73–127.

Meyer, D. R. & Harlow, H. F. The development of transfer of response to patterning by monkeys. *J. comp. physiol. Psychol.*, 1949, *42*, 454–462.

Meyer, M. E. Stimulus control for bird orientation. *Psychol. Bull.*, 1964, *62*, 165–179.

Meyer, P. M. Analysis of visual behavior in cats with extensive neocortical ablations. *J. comp. physiol. Psychol.*, 1963, *56*, 397–401.

Meyer, P. M., Anderson, R. A., & Braun, M. G. Visual cliff preferences following lesions of the visual neocortex in cats and rats. *Psychon. Sci.*, 1966, *4*, 269–270.

Meyers, B. Discrimination of visual movement in perceptually deprived cats. *J. comp. physiol. Psychol.*, 1964, *57*, 152–153.

Meyers, B. & McCleary, R. A. Interocular transfer of a pattern discrimination in pattern deprived cats. *J. comp. physiol. Psychol.*, 1964, *57*, 16–21.

Michotte, A., Thinès, G., & Crabbé, G. *Les compléments amodaux des structures perceptives.* Louvain, Belgium: Publications U. Louvain, 1964.

Milerian, E. A. Involuntary and voluntary attention. In B. Simon (Ed.), *Psychology in the Soviet Union.* Stanford: Stanford University Press, 1957. Pp. 84–91.

Miller, G. A. The magical number seven, plus or minus two: Some limits on our capacity for processing information. *Psychol. Rev.*, 1956, *63*, 81–97.

Miller, G. A. Free recall of redundant strings of letters. *J. exp. Psychol.*, 1958, *56*, 484–491.

Miller, G. A., Bruner, J. S., & Postman, L. Familiarity of letter sequences and tachistoscopic identification. *J. gen. Psychol.*, 1954, *50*, 129–139.

Miller, G. A., Galanter, E., & Pribram, K. H. *Plans and the structure of behavior.* New York: Holt, 1960.

Miller, G. A. & Selfridge, J. A. Verbal context and the recall of meaningful material. *Amer. J. Psychol.*, 1950, *63*, 176–185.

Miller, N. E. Theory and experiment relating psychoanalytic displacement to stimulus-response generalization. *J. abn. soc. Psychol.*, 1948, *43*, 155–178.

Miller, N. E. & Dollard, J. *Social learning and imitation.* New Haven: Yale University Press, 1941.

Miller, W. & Ervin, S. The development of grammar in child language. Ch. 2 in U. Bellugi & R. Brown (Eds.), *The acquisition of language.* Monogr. Soc. Res. Child Develpm., 1964, *29*, No. 1.

Minsky, M. Steps toward artificial intelligence. *Proc. Inst. Radio Engrs.*, 1961, *49*, 8–30.

Mishkin, M. & Forgays, D. G. Word recognition as a function of retinal locus. *J. exp. Psychol.*, 1952, *43*, 43–48.

Moltz, H. Imprinting: Empirical basis and theoretical significance. *Psychol. Bull.*, 1960, *57*, 291–314.

Moltz, H., Rosenblum, L. A., & Halikas, N. Imprinting and level of anxiety. *J. comp. physiol. Psychol.*, 1959, *52*, 240–244.

Moltz, H., Rosenblum, L., & Stettner, L. J. Some parameters of imprinting effectiveness. *J. comp. physiol. Psychol.*, 1960, *53*, 297–301.

Moltz, H. & Stettner, L. J. The influence of patterned light deprivation on the critical period for imprinting. *J. comp. physiol. Psychol.*, 1961, *54*, 279–283.

Montessori, M. *The Montessori method.* New York: Frederick A. Stokes, 1912.

Moon, L. E. & Harlow, H. F. Analysis of oddity learning by rhesus monkeys. *J. comp. physiol. Psychol.*, 1955, *48*, 188–195.

Moorhouse, A. C. *The triumph of the alphabet: A history of writing.* New York: Henry Schuman, 1953.

Morgan, G. A. & Ricciuti, H. W. Infants' responses to strangers during the first year. In B. M. Foss (Ed.), *Determinants of infant behavior IV.* London: Methuen; New York: Wiley, 1969, in press.

Morton, J. The effects of context upon speed of reading, eye-movements and eye-voice span. *Quart. J. exp. Psychol.*, 1964, *16*, 340–354.

Mukherjee, K. C. The duration of cutaneous sensation (I) and the improvement of its sensible discrimination by practice (II). *J. exp. Psychol.*, 1933, *16*, 339–342.

Munsinger, H. Tachistoscopic recognition of stimulus variability. *J. exp. child Psychol.*, 1965, *2*, 186–191.

Munsinger, H. Developing perception and memory for stimulus redundancy. *J. exp. child Psychol.*, 1967, *5*, 39–49

Munsinger, H. & Gummerman, K. The identification of form in patterns of visual noise. *J. exp. Psychol.*, 1967, *72*, 75–81.

Munsinger, H. & Kesson, W. Stimulus variability and cognitive change. *Psychol. Rev.*, 1966, *73*, 164–178. (a)

Munsinger, H. & Kesson, W. Structure, variability and development. *J. exp. child Psychol.*, 1966, *4*, 20–49. (b)

Murdock, B. B. Effects of task difficulty, stimulus similarity, and type of response on stimulus predifferentiation. *J. exp. Psychol.*, 1958, *55*, 167–172.

Nealy, S. M. & Edwards, B. J. "Depth perception" in rats without pattern vision experience. *J. comp. physiol. Psychol.*, 1960, *53*, 468–469.

Nealy, S. M. & Riley, D. A. Loss and recovery of discrimination of visual depth in dark-reared rats. *Amer. J. Psychol.*, 1963, *76*, 329–332.

Neisser, U. Decision-time without reaction-time: Experiments in visual scanning. *Amer. J. Psychol.*, 1963, *76*, 376–385.

Neisser, U. Visual search. *Scient. Amer.*, 1964, *210*, 94–101.

Neisser, U., Novick, R., & Lazar, R. Searching for ten targets simultaneously. *Percept. mot. Skills*, 1963, *17*, 955–961.

Newman, E. B. Speed of reading when the span of letters is restricted. *Amer. J. Psychol.*, 1966, *79*, 272–278.

Nickerson, R. S. Response times for "same-different" judgments. *Percept. mot. Skills*, 1965, *20*, 15–18.

Norcross, K. J. The effects on discrimination performance of the similarity of previously acquired stimulus names. *J. exp. Psychol.*, 1958, *56*, 305–309.

Norcross, K. J. & Spiker, C. C. The effects of type of stimulus pre-training on discrimination performance in preschool children. *Child Develpm.*, 1957, *28*, 79–84.

Nunnally, J. C. Amplification of stimulation: A principle concerning the effects of reward-value on perception and memory. Mimeographed mss., 1964.

Ohwaki, S. A developmental study of weight perception, especially on Charpentier's illusion. *Tohoku Psychol. Fol.*, 1953, *13*, 120–142.

Oldfield, R. C. Memory mechanisms and the theory of schemata. *Brit. J. Psychol.*, 1954, *45*, 14–23.

Oldfield, R. C. & Zangwill, O. L. Head's concept of the schema and its application in contemporary British psychology. *Brit. J. Psychol.*, 1942, *32*, 267–286 (I); 1942, *33*, 58–64 (II).

Olson, D. From perceiving to performing the diagonal. *Ontario J. Ed. Res.*, 1968, *10*, 171–179.

Olum, V. Developmental differences in the perception of causality. *Amer. J. Psychol.*, 1956, *69*, 417–423.

Olum, V. Developmental differences in the perception of causality under conditions of specific instructions. *Vita Humana*, 1958, *1*, 191–203.

Osgood, C. E. Psycholinguistics. In S. Koch (Ed.), *Psychology: A study of a science*, Vol. 6. New York: McGraw-Hill, 1963. Pp. 244–316.

Over, R. & Over, J. Detection and recognition of mirror-image obliques by young children. *J. comp. physiol. Psychol.*, 1967, *64*, 467–470.

Page, E. Haptic perception: A consideration of one of the investigations of Piaget and Inhelder. *Educ. Rev.*, 1959, *II*, 115–124.

Palen, G. F. Focusing cues in the visual cliff behavior of day-old chicks. *J. comp. physiol. Psychol.*, 1965, *59*, 452–454.

Pastore, N. Discrimination learning in the canary. *J. comp. physiol. Psychol.*, 1954, *47*, 389–390.

Pastore, N. Form perception and size constancy in the duckling. *J. Psychol.*, 1958, *45*, 259–261.

Pavlov, I. P. *Conditioned reflexes: An investigation of the physiological activity of the cerebral cortex.* Tr. by G. V. Anrep. London: Oxford University Press, 1927.

Pearson, R. G. & Hauty, G. T. Adaptive processes determining proprioceptive perception of verticality. *J. exp. Psychol.*, 1959, *57*, 367–371.

Pearson, R. G. & Hauty, G. T. Role of postural experiences in proprioceptive perception of verticality. *J. exp. Psychol.*, 1960, *59*, 425–428.

Peters, W. Die Entwicklung von Wahrnemungsleistungen beim Kind. *Z. Psychol. Physiol. Sinnesorg.*, 1927, *103*, 129–184.

Peterson, J. & Peterson, J. K. Does practice with inverting lenses make vision normal? *Psychol. Monogr.*, 1938, *50*, No. 5, 12–37.

Pfafflin, S. M. Stimulus meaning in stimulus predifferentiation. *J. exp. Psychol.*, 1960, *59*, 269–274.

Piaget, J. *The construction of reality in the child.* New York: Basic Books, 1954.

Piaget, J. Développement et apprentissage perceptif. In *Proc. Sixteenth International Congress of Psychology*, Bonn, 1960. Pp. 323–325.

Piaget, J. *Les mécanismes perceptifs.* Paris: Presses Universitaires de France, 1961.

Piaget, J. Le développement des perceptions en fonction de l'age. In *Traité de psychologie expérimentale. VI. La perception.* Paris: Presses Universitaires de France, 1963.

Piaget, J. & v. Albertini, B. Recherches sur le développement des perceptions. XIX. Observations sur la perception des bonnes formes chez l'enfant par actualisation des lignes virtuelles. *Arch. Psychol. Genève,* 1954, *34,* 203–243.

Piaget, J., Feller, Y., & McNear, E. Essai sur la perception des vitesses chez l'enfant et chez l'adulte. *Arch. Psychol. Genève,* 1958, *36,* 253–327.

Piaget, J. & Inhelder, B. *The child's conception of space.* New York: Humanities Press, 1956.

Piaget, J. & Lambercier, M. Recherches sur le développement des perceptions. III. Le problème de la comparaison visuelle en profondeur et l'erreur systématique de l'étalon. *Arch. Psychol. Genève,* 1943, *29,* 205–308.

Piaget, J. & Lambercier, M. Recherches sur le développement des perceptions. XII. La comparaison des grandeurs projectives chez l'enfant et chez l'adulte. *Arch. Psychol. Genève,* 1951, *33,* 81–130.

Piaget, J. & Lambercier, M. Recherches sur le développment des perceptions. XXIX. Grandeurs projectives et grandeurs réeles avec étalon éloigné. *Arch. Psychol. Genève.,* 1956, *35,* 257–280.

Piaget, J. & Lambercier, M. Recherches sur le développement des perceptions. XXXIII. La causalité perceptive visuelle chez l'enfant et chez l'adulte. *Arch. Psychol. Genève,* 1958, *36,* 77–202.

Piaget, J. & Maroun, J. Recherches sur la développement des perceptions. XXXIV. La localisation des impressions d'impact dans la causalité perceptive tactilo-kinaesthésique. *Arch. Psychol. Genève,* 1958, *36,* 202–236.

Pick, A. D. Improvement of visual and tactual form discrimination. *J. exp. Psychol.,* 1965, *69,* 331–339.

Pick, A. D., Pick, H. L., & Thomas, M. L. Cross-modal transfer and improvement of form discrimination. *J. exp. child Psychol.,* 1966, *3,* 279–288.

Pick, H. Some Soviet research on learning and perception in children. In J. C. Wright & J. Kagan (Eds.), *Basic cognitive processes in children.* Monogr. Soc. Res. Child Develpm., 1963, 28, No. 86. Pp. 185–190.

Pick, H. L. Perception in Soviet psychology. *Psychol. Bull.,* 1964, *62,* 21–35.

Pick, H. L. & Hay, J. C. Adaptation to prismatic distortion. *Psychon. Sci.,* 1964, *1,* 199–200.

Pick, H. L. & Hay, J. C. Gaze-contingent adaptation to prismatic spectacles. *Amer. J. Psychol.,* 1966, *79,* 443–450. (a)

Pick, H. L. & Hay, J. C. Visual and proprioceptive adaptation to optical displacement in children. In *Perceptual development: Its relation to theories of intelligence and cognition.* Bethesda, Md.: National Institute of Health, 1966. Pp. 174–187. (b)

Pick, H. L., Hay, J. C., & Willoughby, R. H. Interocular transfer of adaptation to prismatic distortion. *Percept. mot. Skills,* 1966, *23,* 131–135.

Pick, H. L. & Pick, A. D. A developmental and analytic study of the size-weight illusion. *J. exp. child Psychol.,* 1967, *5,* 362–371.

Pick, H. L., Pick, A. D., & Klein, R. E. Perceptual integration in children. In L. P. Lipsitt & C. C. Spiker (Eds.), *Advances in child development and behavior.* Vol. 3. New York: Academic Press, 1967. Pp. 191–223.

Piéron, Mme. H. Contribution expérimentale a l'étude des phénomènes de transfert sensoriel. *Année Psychol.,* 1922, *23,* 76–122.

Plotkin, L. Stimulus generalization in Morse code learning. *Arch. Psychol.,* 1943, *40,* No. 287.

Polak, P. R., Emde, R. N., & Spitz, R. A. The smiling response to the human face. I. Methodology, quantification and natural history. *J. Nerv. Ment. Dis.,* 1964, *139,* 103–109. (a)

Polak, P. R., Emde, R. N., & Spitz, R. A. The smiling response to the human face. II. Visual discrimination and the onset of depth perception. *J. Nerv. Ment. Dis.,* 1964, *139,* 407–415. (b)

Pollack, R. H. Temporal range of apparent movement as a function of age and intelligence. *Psychon. Sci.,* 1966, *5,* 243–244.

Pollack, R. H. & Silver, S. D. Magnitude of the Mueller-Lyer illusion in children as a function of pigmentation of the Fundus oculi. *Psychon. Sci.,* 1967, *8,* 83–84.

Polt, J. M. & Hess, E. H. Following and imprinting: Effects of light and social experience. *Science,* 1964, *143,* 1185–1187.

Postman, L. Association theory and perceptual learning. *Psychol. Rev.,* 1955, *62,* 438–446.

Postman, L. Perception and learning. In S. Koch (Ed.), *Psychology: A study of a science.* Vol. 5. New York: McGraw-Hill, 1963. Pp. 30–113.

Postman, L. & Tolman, E. C. Brunswik's probabilistic functionalism. In S. Koch (Ed.), *Psychology: A study of a science.* Vol. I. New York: McGraw-Hill, 1959. Pp. 502–564.

Pritchard, R. M., Heron, W., & Hebb, D. O. Visual perception approached by the method of stabilized images. *Canad. J. Psychol.,* 1960, *14,* 67–77.

Pustell, T. E. The experimental induction of perceptual vigilance and defense. *J. Pers.,* 1957, *25,* 425–438.

Putnam, V., Iscoe, I., & Young, R. K. Verbal learning in the deaf. *J. comp. physiol. Psychol.,* 1962, *55,* 843–846.

Rabbitt, P. M. Learning to ignore irrelevant information. *Amer. J. Psychol.,* 1967, *80,* 1–13.

Ramo-Wooldridge. Technical Report, Part II, on Word Searching Device, C 117-1U14. Canoga Park, Calif., 1961.

Ramsay, A. O. & Hess, E. H. A laboratory approach to the study of imprinting. *Wilson Bull.,* 1954, *66,* 196–206.

Raney, E. & Carmichael, L. Localizing responses to tactual stimuli in the foetal rat in relation to the psychological problem of space perception. *J. genet. Psychol.,* 1934, *45,* 3–21.

Ranken, H. B. Effects of name learning on serial learning, position learning, and recognition learning with random shapes. *Psychol. Reports.,* 1963, *13,* 663–678.

Rasch, E., Swift, H., Riesen, A. H., & Chow, K. L. Altered structure and composition of retinal cells in dark-reared mammals. *Exp. Cell Research,* 1961, *25,* 348–363.

Razran, G. Semantic and phonetographic generalizations of salivary conditioning to verbal stimuli. *J. exp. Psychol.*, 1949, *39*, 642–652.

Reber, A. S. Implicit learning of artificial grammars. *J. verb. learn. verb. Behav.*, 1967, *6*, 855–863.

Reinhold, D. B. & Perkins, C. C., Jr. Stimulus generalization following different methods of training. *J. exp. Psychol.*, 1955, *49*, 423–427.

Replogle, A. The effect of similarity on the behavior of perceived figures in a stabilized retinal image. Paper read at the meeting of the Eastern Psychological Association, Atlantic City, April, 1962.

Rey, A. Contribution a l'étude de poids chez les anormaux. *Arch. Psychol. Genève*, 1930, *22*, 285–297.

Rheingold, H. L. The effect of environmental stimulation upon social and exploratory behaviour in the human infant. In B. M. Foss (Ed.), *Determinants of infant behavior*. New York: Wiley, 1961. Pp. 143–171.

Rheingold, H. L. & Hess, E. H. The chick's "preference" for some visual properties of water. *J. comp. physiol. Psychol.*, 1957, *50*, 417–421.

Ricciuti, H. N. Geometric form and detail as determinants of comparative similarity judgments in young children. In *A basic research program on reading*. Final Report, Cooperative Research Project No. 639, U. S. Office of Education, 1963. Pp. 1–48.

Rice, C. E. Human echo perception. *Science,* 1967, *155*, 656–664.

Riesen, A. H. The development of visual perception in man and chimpanzee. *Science,* 1947, *106*, 107–108.

Riesen, A. H. Stimulation as a requirement for growth and function in behavioral development. In D. W. Fiske & S. R. Maddi (Eds.), *Functions of varied experience*. Homewood, Ill.: Dorsey Press, 1961. Pp. 57–80.

Riesen, A. H. & Aarons, L. Visual movement and intensity discrimination in cats after early deprivation of pattern vision. *J. comp. physiol. Psychol.*, 1959, *52*, 142–149.

Riesen, A. H., Kurke, M. I., & Mellinger, J. C. Interocular transfer of habits learned monocularly in visually naive and visually experienced cats. *J. comp. physiol. Psychol.*, 1953, *46*, 166–172.

Riesen, A. H., Ramsay, R. L., & Wilson, P. D. Development of visual acuity in Rhesus monkeys deprived of patterned light during early infancy. *Psychon. Sci.*, 1964, *1*, 33–34.

Riess, B. F. Genetic changes in semantic conditioning. *J. exp. Psychol.*, 1946, *36*, 143–152.

Robinson, H. An experimental examination of the size-weight illusion in young children. *Child Develpm.*, 1964, *35*, 91–107.

Robinson, J. S. The effect of learning verbal labels for stimuli on their later discrimination. *J. exp. Psychol.*, 1955, *49*, 112–115. (a)

Robinson, J. S. The sameness-difference discrimination problem in chimpanzee. *J. comp. physiol. Psychol.*, 1955, *48*, 195–197. (b)

Robinson, J. S., Brown, L. T., & Hayes, W. H. A test of the effect of past experience on perception. *Percept. mot. Skills*, 1964, *18*, 953–956.

Robinson, J. S. & Higgins, K. E. The young child's ability to see a difference between mirror-image forms. *Percept. mot. Skills*, 1967, *25*, 893–897.

Rock, I. *The nature of perceptual adaptation*. New York: Basic Books, 1966.

Rock, I. & Fleck, F. S. A re-examination of the effect of monetary reward and punishment in figure-ground perception. *J. exp. Psychol.*, 1950, *40*, 766–776.

Rockett, F. C. A note on "an experimental test of an alleged sign-stimulus" by Hirsch, Lindley, and Tolman. *Percept. mot. Skills*, 1955, *5*, 155–156.

Rosen, A. J. & Ison, J. R. Effects of deprivation level, reinforcement conditions, and continued testing on visual cliff performance. *J. comp. physiol. Psychol.*, 1964, *57*, 471–472.

Rosenblatt, F. The perceptron: A probabilistic model for information storage and organization in the brain. *Psychol. Rev.*, 1958, *65*, 386–408. (a)

Rosenblatt, F. The design of an intelligent automaton. *Research Reviews*, 1958, 5–13. (O.N.R., Washington, D. C.) (b)

Rosenblatt, F. Analytic techniques for the study of neural nets. *Proc. American Inst. Elec. Eng. Joint Automatic Control Conference*, 1962.

Rosenblum, L. A. & Cross, H. A. Performance of neonatal monkeys on the visual cliff-situation. *Amer. J. Psychol.*, 1963, *76*, 318–320.

Rossi, E. Development of classificatory behavior. *Child Develpm.*, 1964, *35*, 137–142.

Rossi, P. J. Adaptation and negative aftereffect to lateral optical displacement in newly hatched chicks. *Science*, 1968, *160*, 430–432.

Rossman, I. L. & Goss, A. E. The acquired distinctiveness of cues: The role of discriminative verbal responses in facilitating the acquisition of discriminative motor responses. *J. exp. Psychol.*, 1951, *42*, 173–182.

Rothkopf, E. Z. A measure of stimulus similarity and errors in some paired-associate learning tasks. *J. exp. Psychol.*, 1957, *53*, 94–101.

Rothkopf, E. Z. Stimulus similarity and sequence of stimulus presentation in paired-associate learning. *J. exp. Psychol.*, 1958, *56*, 114–122.

Routtenberg, A. & Glickman, S. E. Visual cliff behavior in undomesticated rodents, land and aquatic turtles, and cats (panthera). *J. comp. physiol. Psychol.*, 1964, *58*, 143–146.

Rudel, R. G. & Teuber, H. L. Decrement of visual and haptic Müller-Lyer illusion on repeated trials: A study of crossmodal transfer. *Quart. J. exp. Psychol.*, 1963, *15*, 125–131. (a)

Rudel, R. G. & Teuber, H. L. Discrimination of direction of line in children. *J. comp. physiol. Psychol.*, 1963, *56*, 892–898. (b)

Rudel, R. G. & Teuber, H. L. Crossmodal transfer of shape discrimination by children. *Neuropsychologia*, 1964, *2*, 1–8.

Rush, G. P. Visual grouping in relation to age. *Archives Psychol.*, N. Y., 1937, *31*, Whole No. 217.

Ryan, T. A. Interrelations of the sensory systems in perception. *Psychol. Bull.*, 1940, *37*, 659–698.

Ryan, T. A. & Schwartz, C. B. Speed of perception as a function of mode of representations. *Amer. J. Psychol.*, 1956, *69*, 60–69.

Saayman, G., Ames, E. W., & Moffett, A. Response to novelty as an indicator of visual discrimination in the human infant. *J. exp. child Psychol.*, 1964, *1*, 189–198.

Salapatek, P. & Kesson, W. Visual scanning of triangles by the human newborn. *J. exp. child Psychol.*, 1966, *3*, 155–167.

Salzen, E. A. Imprinting and fear. *Symp. Zool. Soc. Lond.*, 1962, *8*, 199–217.

Salzen, E. A. Visual stimuli eliciting the smiling response in the human infant. *J. genet. Psychol.*, 1963, *102*, 51–54.

Santos, J. F. & Garvin, E. A. A further examination of the Schafer-Murphy effect. *Amer. J. Psychol.*, 1962, *75*, 259–264.

Schafer, R. & Murphy, G. The role of autism in a visual figure-ground relationship. *J. exp. Psychol.*, 1943, *32*, 335–343.

Schiff, W. The perception of impending collision: A study of visually directed avoidant behavior. *Psychol. Monogr.*, 1965, *79*, Whole No. 604.

Schiff, W., Caviness, J. A., & Gibson, J. J. Persistent fear responses in rhesus monkeys to the optical stimulus of "looming." *Science*, 1962, *136*, 982–983.

Schiffman, H. R. & Walk, R. D. Behavior on the visual cliff of monocular as compared to binocular chicks. *J. comp. physiol. Psychol.*, 1963, *56*, 1064–1068.

Seashore, H. & Bavelas, A. The functioning of knowledge of results in Thorndike's line-drawing experiment. *Psychol. Rev.*, 1941, *48*, 155–164.

Seashore, H. & Kurtz, A. K. Analysis of errors in copying code. Office of Scientific Research and Development, Report No. 4010, 1944.

Segal, E. M. Demonstration of acquired distinctiveness of cues using a paired-associate learning task. *J. exp. Psychol.*, 1964, *67*, 587–590.

Segall, M. H., Campbell, D. T., & Herskovits, M. J. *The influence of culture on visual perception*. Indianapolis: Bobbs-Merrill, 1966.

Seitz, E. Die paarbildung bei einigen Cichliden. *Z. Tierpsychol.*, 1942, *5*, 74–101.

Sekuler, R. W. & Rosenblith, J. F. Discrimination of direction of line and the effect of stimulus alignment. *Psychon. Sci.*, 1964, *1*, 143–144.

Selfridge, O. G. & Neisser, U. Pattern recognition by machine. *Scient. Amer.*, 1960, *203*, 60–68.

Senden, M. von. *Space and sight: The perception of space and shape in the congenitally blind before and after operation*. Tr. by P. Heath. London: Methuen, 1960.

Seymour, W. D. Experiments on the acquisition of industrial skills (Part 3). *Occup. Psychol.*, 1956, *30*, 94–104.

Shepard, R. N. Analysis of proximities as a technique for the study of information processing in man. *Human Factors*, 1963, *5*, 33–48.

Shipley, E. F., Smith, C. S., & Gleitman, L. R. A study in the acquisition of language: Free responses to commands. Technical Report VIII, Grant # MH 07990, The acquisition of linguistic structure, Eastern Pennsylvania Psychiatric Institute.

Shvarts, L. A. Raising the sensitivity of the visual analyser. In B. Simon (Ed.), *Psychology in the Soviet Union*. Stanford: Stanford University Press, 1957. Pp. 100–107.

Siegel, A. I. Deprivation of visual form definition in the Ring Dove. I. Discriminatory learning. *J. comp. physiol. Psychol.*, 1953, *46*, 115–119. (a)

Siegel, A. I. Deprivation of visual form definition in the Ring Dove. II. Perceptual-motor transfer. *J. comp. physiol. Psychol.*, 1953, *46*, 249–252. (b)

Siipola, E. M. Studies in mirror drawing. *Psychol. Monogr.*, 1935, *46*, No. 6, 66–77.

Sluckin, W. Perceptual and associative learning. *Symp. Zool. Soc. Lond.,* 1962, *8,* 193–198.

Sluckin, W. *Imprinting and early learning.* Chicago, Ill.: Aldine, 1965.

Sluckin, W. & Salzin, E. A. Imprinting and perceptual learning. *Quart. J. exp. Psychol.,* 1961, *13,* 65–77.

Smedslund, J. The utilization of probabilistic cues after 1100 and 4800 stimulus presentations. *Acta Psychol.,* 1961, *18,* 383–386.

Smith, D. E. P. & Hochberg, J. E. The effect of "punishment" (electric shock) on figure-ground perception. *J. Psychol.,* 1954, *38,* 83–87.

Smith, F. V. Perceptual aspects of imprinting. *Symp. Zool. Soc. Lond.,* 1962, *8,* 171–191.

Smith, F. V. & Bird, M. W. The relative attraction for the domestic chick of combinations of stimuli in different sensory modalities. *Anim. Behav.,* 1963, *11,* 300–305.

Smith, F. V. & Bird, M. W. The sustained approach of the domestic chick to coloured stimuli. *Anim. Behav.,* 1964, *12,* 60–63. (a)

Smith, F. V. & Bird, M. W. The approach response of chicks in groups in relation to the strength of the stimulus. *Anim. Behav.,* 1964, *12,* 252–258. (b)

Smith, F. V. & Bird, M. W. The correlation of responsiveness to visual and auditory stimuli in the domestic chick. *Anim. Behav.,* 1964, *12,* 259–263. (c)

Smith, K. H. Grammatical intrusions in the free recall of structured letter pairs. *J. verb. learn. verb. Behav.,* 1966, *5,* 447–454.

Smith, K. U. & Greene, P. A critical period in maturation of performance with space-displaced vision. *Percept. mot. Skills,* 1963, *17,* 627–639.

Smith, K. U. & Smith, W. M. *Perception and motion: An analysis of space-structured behavior.* London: Saunders, 1962.

Smith, M. P. & Means, J. R. Effects of type of stimulus pretraining on discrimination learning in mentally retarded. *Amer. J. Mental Deficiency,* 1961, *66,* 259–265.

Smith, O. W. & Smith, P. C. Developmental studies of spatial judgments by children and adults. *Percept. mot. Skills,* 1966, *22,* 3–73.

Smith, S. L. & Goss, A. E. The role of the acquired distinctiveness of cues in the acquisition of a motor skill in children. *J. genet. Psychol.,* 1955, *87,* 11–24.

Snyder, F. W. & Pronko, N. H. *Vision with spatial inversion.* Wichita: University of Wichita Press, 1952.

Snyder, F. W. & Snyder, C. W., Vision with spatial inversion: A follow-up study. *Psychol. Rec.,* 1957, *17,* 20–31.

Sokolov, E. N. Higher nervous activity and the problem of perception. In B. Simon (Ed.), *Psychology in the Soviet Union.* Stanford: Stanford University Press, 1957. Pp. 92–99.

Solley, C. M. Reduction of error with practice in perception of the postural vertical. *J. exp. Psychol.,* 1956, *52,* 329–333.

Solley, C. M. & Long, J. Perceptual learning vs. response set learning. *Percept. mot. Skills,* 1958, *8,* 235–240.

Solley, C. M. & Murphy, G. *Development of the perceptual world.* New York: Basic Books, 1960.

Solley, C. M. & Sommer, R. Perceptual autism in children. *J. gen. Psychol.,* 1957, *56,* 3–11.

Solomon, R. L. & Lessac, M. S. A control group design for experimental studies of developmental processes. *Psychol. Bull.,* 1968, *70,* 145–150.

Spaulding, D. Instinct, with original observations on young animals. *MacMillan's Magazine,* 1873, *27,* 282–293.

Spence, K. W. The differential response in animals to stimuli varying within a single dimension. *Psychol. Rev.,* 1937, *44,* 430–444.

Sperry, R. W. Mechanisms of neural maturation. In S. S. Stevens (Ed.), *Handbook of experimental psychology.* New York: Wiley, 1951. Pp. 236–280.

Spiker, C. C. Verbal factors in the discrimination learning of children. In J. C. Wright & J. Kagan (Eds.), *Basic cognitive processes in children.* Monogr. Soc. Res. Child Develpm., 1963, *28,* No. 2, 53–69.

Spitz, H. H. Effects of symmetry on the reproduction of dot patterns by mental retardates and equal MA normals. *Amer. J. Ment. Defic.,* 1964, *69,* 101–106.

Spitz, H. H. Perceptual testing of retardates: Methodological problems, with some results using illusions. Paper presented at APA Symposium on "Perception, intelligence, and educability," Chicago, September, 1965.

Spitz, R. A. Hospitalism: An inquiry into the genesis of psychiatric conditions in early childhood. Part I. *Psychoanal. Stud. Child,* 1945, *1,* 53–74.

Spitz, R. A. & Wolf, K. M. The smiling response: A contribution to the ontogenesis of social relations. *Genet. Psychol. Monogr.,* 1946, *34,* 57–125.

Spragg, S. D. S. The relative difficulty of Morse code characters learned by the whole method. *J. exp. Psychol.,* 1943, *33,* 108–114.

Stechler, G., Bradford, S., & Levy, L. Attention in the newborn: Effect on motility and skin potential. *Science,* 1966, *151,* 1246–1248.

Stechler, G. & Latz, E. Some observations on attention and arousal in the human infant. *J. Amer. Acad. Child Psychiat.,* 1966, *5,* 517–525.

Stepien, L. S. & Cordeau, J. P. Memory in monkeys for compound stimuli. *Amer. J. Psychol.,* 1960, *73,* 388–395.

Sternberg, S. Two operations in character recognition: Some evidence from reaction-time measurements. *Percept. and Psychophysics,* 1967, *2,* 45–53.

Stevens, J. C., Mack, J. D., & Stevens, S. S. Growth of sensation on seven continua as measured by force of hand-grip. *J. exp. Psychol.,* 1960, *59,* 60–67.

Stevens, K. N. & Halle, M. Remarks on analysis by synthesis and distinctive features. In W. Wathen-Dunn (Ed.), *Models for the perception of speech and form.* Cambridge, Mass.: M.I.T. Press, 1967. Pp. 88–102.

Stevenson, H. W. & McBee, G. The learning of object and pattern discrimination by children. *J. comp. physiol. Psychol.,* 1958, *51,* 752–754.

Stratton, G. M. Some preliminary experiments in vision without inversion of the retinal image. *Psychol. Rev.,* 1896, *3,* 611–617.

Stratton, G. M. Vision without inversion of the retinal image. *Psychol. Rev.,* 1897, *4,* 341–360, 463–481.

Street, R. F. *A Gestalt completion test.* New York: Teachers College, Columbia University, 1931.

Supa, M., Cotzin, M., & Dallenbach, K. M. "Facial vision": The perception of obstacles by the blind. *Amer. J. Psychol.*, 1944, *57*, 133–183.

Sutherland, N. S. Visual discrimination of orientation by *Octopus. Brit. J. Psychol.*, 1957, *48*, 55–71.

Sutherland, N. S. Visual discrimination of shape by *Octopus:* Squares and crosses. *J. comp. physiol. Psychol.*, 1962, *55*, 939–943.

Sutherland, N. S. The shape-discrimination of stationary shapes by Octopuses. *Amer. J. Psychol.*, 1963, *76*, 177–190. (a)

Sutherland, N. S. Shape discrimination and receptive fields. *Nature*, 1963, *197*, 118–122. (b)

Sutherland, N. S. Visual discrimination in animals. *Brit. Med. Bull.*, 1964, *20*, 54–59.

Sutherland, N. S., Mackintosh, N. J., & Mackintosh, J. Simultaneous discrimination training of *Octopus* and transfer of discrimination along a continuum. *J. comp. physiol. Psychol.*, 1963, *56*, 150–156.

Swets, J. A. Is there a sensory threshold? *Science*, 1961, *134*, 168–177.

Swets, J. A., Harris, J. R., McElroy, L. S., & Rudloe, H. Computer-aided instruction in perceptual identification. *Behav. Science*, 1966, *11*, 98–101.

Swets, J. A., Millman, S. H., Fletcher, W. E., & Green, D. M. Learning to identify nonverbal sounds: An application of a computer as a teaching machine. *J. acoust. Soc. Amer.*, 1962, *34*, 928–935.

Tallarico, R. B. & Farrell, W. M. Studies of visual depth perception: An effect of early experience on chicks on a visual cliff. *J. comp. physiol. Psychol.*, 1964, *57*, 94–96.

Tanaka, K. Developmental studies on size constancy. In Y. Akishige (Ed.), Experimental researches on the structure of the perceptual space. *Kyushu Psychological Studies*, 1967, *IV*, Fukuoka, Japan. Pp. 98–128.

Tauber, E. S. & Koffler, S. Optomotor response in human infants to apparent motion: Evidence of innateness. *Science*, 1966, *152*, 382–383.

Tawney, G. Ueber die Wahrnehmung zweier Punkte mittelst des Tastsinnes, mit Rücksicht auf die Frage der Uebung. *Phil. Stud.*, 1897, *13*, 163–222.

Taylor, D. W. The learning of radio-telegraphic code. *Amer. J. Psychol.*, 1943, *56*, 319–353.

Taylor, J. G. What is learned in perceptual learning. In *Proc. Sixteenth Intern. Congress of Psychol.*, Bonn, 1960. Pp. 339–340.

Taylor, J. G. *The behavioral basis of perception*. New Haven: Yale University Press, 1962.

Taylor, J. G. The behavioural basis of perceived size and distance. *Canad. J. Psychol.*, 1965, *19*, 1–14.

Terman, M. Improvement of absolute pitch naming. *Psychon. Sci.*, 1965, *3*, 243–244.

Thomas, H. Visual-fixation responses of infants to stimuli of varying complexity. *Child Develpm.*, 1965, *36*, 629–638.

Thompson, W. R. & Dubanovski, R. A. Early arousal and imprinting in chicks. *Science*, 1964, *143*, 1187–1189.

Thompson, W. R. & Heron, W. The effects of restricting early experience on the problem-solving capacity of dogs. *Canad. J. Psychol.*, 1954, *8*, 17–31.

Thorndike, E. L. *The fundamentals of learning.* New York: Teachers College, Columbia University, Bureau of Publications, 1932.

Thorpe, W. H. *Learning and instinct in animals.* Cambridge, Mass.: Harvard University Press, 1956.

Thorpe, W. H. *Bird-song: The biology of vocal communication and expression in birds.* (Cambridge Monographs in Experimental Biology, No. 12.) Cambridge: Cambridge University Press, 1961.

Thorpe, W. H. & Zangwill, O. L. (Eds.). *Current problems in animal behaviour.* Cambridge: Cambridge University Press, 1961.

Tighe, L. S. The effect of perceptual pretraining on reversal and nonreversal shifts. *J. exp. Psychol.,* 1965, *70,* 379–385.

Tighe, L. S. & Tighe, T. J. Discrimination learning: Two views in historical perspective. *Psychol. Bull.,* 1966, *66,* 353–370.

Tikofsky, R. S. & McInish, J. R. Consonant discrimination by seven year olds: A pilot study. *Psychon. Sci.,* 1968, *10,* 61–62.

Tinbergen, N. *The study of instinct.* Oxford: Clarendon Press, 1951.

Tinbergen, N. *The herring gull's world: A study of the social behavior of birds.* London: Collins, 1953.

Tinbergen, N. & Perdeck, A. C. On the stimulus situation releasing the begging response in the newly hatched Herring Gull chick (Larus argentatus argentatus Pont.). *Behav.,* 1950, *3,* 1–39.

Tinker, M. A. Recent studies of eye-movements in reading. *Psychol. Bull.,* 1958, *55,* 215–231.

Titchener, E. B. *A text-book of psychology.* New York: Macmillan, 1909–1910.

Tolman, E. C. Cognitive maps in rats and men. *Psychol. Rev.,* 1948, *55,* 189–208.

Tolman, E. C. There is more than one kind of learning. *Psychol. Rev.,* 1949, *56,* 144–155.

Trabasso, T. R. Stimulus emphasis and all-or-none learning in concept identification. *J. exp. Psychol.,* 1963, *65,* 398–406.

Trabasso, T., Deutsch, J. A., & Gelman, R. Attention in discrimination learning of young children. *J. exp. child Psychol.,* 1966, *4,* 9–19.

Treisman, A. M. Selective attention in man. *Brit. Med. Bull.,* 1960, *20,* 12–16.

Tronick, E. Approach response of domestic chicks to an optical display. *J. comp. physiol. Psychol.,* 1967, *64,* 529–531.

Trychin, S. & Walk, R. D. A study of the depth perception of monocular hooded rats on the visual cliff. *Psychon. Sci.,* 1964, *1,* 53–54.

Tucker, A. F. The effect of early light and form deprivation on the visual behaviors of the chicken. Unpublished doctoral dissertation, University of Chicago, 1957.

Tuddenham, R. D. Jean Piaget and the world of the child. *Amer. Psychol.,* 1966, *21,* 207–217.

Turnure, C. & Wallach, L. Influence of contextual variation on the differentiation of parts from wholes. *Amer. J. Psychol.,* 1965, *78,* 481–485.

Uhr, L. Intelligence in computers: The psychology of perception in people and in machines. *Behav. Sci.,* 1960, *5,* 177–182.

Uhr, L. "Pattern recognition" computers as models for form perception. *Psychol. Bull.,* 1963, *60,* 40–73.

Uhr, L., Vossler, C., & Uleman, J. Pattern recognition over distortions, by human subjects and by a computer simulation of a model for human form perception. *J. exp. Psychol.*, 1962, *63*, 227–234.

Urban, F. M. Der Einfluss der Uebung bei Gewichtsversuchen. *Arch. f.d. ges. Psychol.*, 1913, *29*, 271–311.

Vanderplas, J. M. Relations of learning to form perception. Paper presented at meetings of the Southern Society for Philosophy and Psychology, Biloxi, Miss., April, 1960.

Vanderplas, J. M. Associative processes and task relations in perceptual learning. *Percept. mot. Skills*, 1963, *16*, 501–509.

Vanderplas, J. M. & Garvin, E. A. Complexity, association value, and practice as factors in shape recognition following paired-associates training. *J. exp. Psychol.*, 1959, *57*, 155–163.

Velten, H. V. The growth of phonemic and lexical patterns in infant language. *Language*, 1943, *19*, 281–292.

Venezky, R. L. English orthography: Its graphical structure and its relation to sound. *Reading Res. Quart.*, 1967, *2*, 75–105.

Venezky, R. & Weir, R. A study of selected spelling-to-sound correspondence patterns. Cooperative Research Project No. 3090 with the U. S. Office of Education. Stanford, 1966.

Vernon, M. D. *A further study of visual perception.* Cambridge: Cambridge University Press, 1954.

Vernon, M. D. The functions of schemata in perceiving. *Psychol. Rev.*, 1955, *62*, 180–192.

Vernon, M. D. Cognitive inference in perceptual activity. *Brit. J. Psychol.*, 1957, *48*, 35–47.

Volkmann, A. W. Über den Einfluss der Uebung. *Leipzig Berichte. Math.-phys. Classe*, 1858, *10*, 38–69.

Vurpillot, E. Piaget's law of relative centrations. *Acta Psych.*, 1959, *16*, 403–430.

Vurpillot, E. L'organisation perceptive: Son rôle dans l'évolution des illusions optico-géométriques. *Études de Psychol. et de Philos.*, 1963, XVI, Paris.

Vurpillot, E. Données expérimentales récentes sur le développement des perceptions visuelles chez le nourrisson. *Année Psychologique*, 1966, *66*, 213–239.

Vurpillot, E. The development of scanning strategies and their relation to visual differentiation. *J. exp. child Psychol.*, 1968, *6*, 622–650.

Vurpillot, E. & Brault, H. Étude expérimentale sur la formation des schèmes empiriques. *L'Année Psychol.*, 1959, *59*, 381–394.

Vurpillot, E., Lacoursière, A., de Schonen, S., & Werck, C. Apprentissage de concepts et différenciation. *Bulletin de Psychologie*, 1966, *252*, XX, 1–7.

Walk, R. D. "Visual" and "visual-motor" experience: A replication. *J. comp. physiol. Psychol.*, 1958, *51*, 785–787.

Walk, R. D. Can the duckling respond adequately to depth? Paper presented at the 33rd meeting of the Eastern Psychological Association, Atlantic City, 1962.

Walk, R. D. Class demonstration of visual depth perception with the albino rabbit. *Percept. mot. Skills*, 1964, *18*, 219–224.

Walk, R. D. The study of visual depth and distance perception in animals. In D. Lehrmann (Ed.), *Advances in the study of behavior.* New York: Academic Press, 1965. Pp. 99–154. (a)

Walk, R. D. Tactual and visual learning of forms differing in degree of symmetry. *Psychon. Sci.,* 1965, *2,* 93–94. (b)

Walk, R. D. The development of depth perception in animals and human infants. *Monogr. Soc. Res. Child Develpm.,* 1966, *31,* 82–108.

Walk, R. D. & Dodge, S. H. Visual depth perception of a 10-month-old monocular human infant. *Science,* 1962, *137,* 529–530.

Walk, R. D. & Gibson, E. J. A comparative and analytical study of visual depth perception. *Psychol. Monogr.,* 1961, *75,* No. 15.

Walk, R. D., Gibson, E. J., Pick, H. L., & Tighe, T. J. Further experiments on prolonged exposure to visual forms: The effect of single stimuli and prior reinforcement. *J. comp. physiol. Psychol.,* 1958, *51,* 483–487.

Walk, R. D., Gibson, E. J., Pick, H. L., & Tighe, T. J. The effectiveness of prolonged exposure to cutouts vs. painted patterns for facilitation of discrimination. *J. comp. physiol. Psychol.,* 1959, *52,* 519–521.

Walk, R. D., Gibson, E. J., & Tighe, T. J. Behavior of light- and dark-reared rats on a visual cliff. *Science,* 1957, *126,* 80–81.

Wallach, H. & Karsh, E. B. Why the modification of stereoscopic depth-perception is so rapid. *Amer. J. Psychol.,* 1963, *76,* 413–420.

Wallach, H. & Karsh, E. B. The modification of stereoscopic depth-perception and the kinetic depth-effect. *Amer. J. Psychol.,* 1963, *76,* 429–435.

Wallach, H. & Kravitz, J. H. The measurement of the constancy of visual direction and of its adaptation. *Psychon. Sci.,* 1965, *2,* 217–218.

Wallach, H., Kravitz, J. H., & Lindauer, J. A passive condition for rapid adaptation to displaced visual direction. *Amer. J. Psychol.,* 1963, *76,* 568–578.

Wallach, H. & Moore, M. E. Modification of stereoscopic depth-perception. *Amer. J. Psychol.,* 1963, *76,* 191–204.

Wallach, M. A. Perceptual recognition of approximations to English in relation to spelling achievement. *J. ed. Psychol.,* 1963, *54,* 57–62.

Warren, H. C. *A history of the association psychology.* New York: Scribner's, 1921.

Watson, J. S. Orientation-specific age changes in responsiveness to the face stimulus in young infants. Paper presented at the meeting of the American Psychological Association, Chicago, September, 1965.

Wedell, C. H. The nature of the absolute judgments of pitch. *J. exp. Psychol.,* 1934, *17,* 485–503.

Wegener, J. G. Cross-modal transfer in monkeys: A review and some new data. Paper read at symposium on cross-modal transfer, American Psychological Association, Philadelphia, September, 1963.

Weidmann, U. The begging response of the black-headed gull chick. Paper read to Sixth International Ethological Congress, 1959.

Weiner, M. Perceptual development in a distorted room: A phenomenological study. *Psychol. Monogr.,* 1956, *70,* No. 16.

Weinstein, B. Matching-from-sample by Rhesus monkeys and by children. *J. comp. physiol. Psychol.,* 1941, *31,* 195–213.

Weinstein, S., Sersen, E. A., Fisher, L., & Weisinger, M. Is reafference necessary for visual adaptation? *Percept. mot. Skills,* 1964, *18,* 641–648.

Weir, R. H. *Language in the crib.* The Hague: Mouton, 1962.

Weir, R. H. Some questions on the child's learning of phonology. In F. Smith & G. E. Miller (Eds.), *The genesis of language: A psycholinguistic approach.* Cambridge, Mass.: M.I.T. Press, 1966. Pp. 153–168.

Weiss, W. & Margolius, G. The effect of context stimuli on learning and retention. *J. exp. Psychol.,* 1954, *48,* 318–322.

Werner, H. Musical "micro-scales" and "micro-melodies." *J. Psychol.,* 1940, *10,* 149–156.

Werner, H. *Comparative psychology of mental development.* (Rev. ed.) New York: Science Editions, 1961.

Wertheimer, M. *Productive thinking.* New York: Harper, 1945.

Wertheimer, M. Psychomotor coordination of auditory and visual space at birth. *Science,* 1961, *134,* 1692.

White, B. L. The development of perception during the first six months of life. Paper presented at the meeting of the A.A.A.S., Cleveland, December, 1963.

White, B. L. Informal education during the first months of life. Paper presented at the Social Science Research Council Conference on Preschool Education, Chicago, February, 1966.

White, B. L. An experimental approach to the effects of experience on early human behavior. In J. Hill (Ed.), *Minnesota symposium on child psychology.* Vol. 1. Minneapolis: University of Minnesota Press, 1968.

White, B. L., Castle, P., & Held, R. Observations on the development of visually-directed reaching. *Child Develpm.,* 1964, *35,* 349–364.

White, B. L. & Held, R. Plasticity of sensorimotor development in the human infant. In J. F. Rosenblith & W. Allinsmith (Eds.), *The causes of behavior: Readings in child development and educational psychology.* Boston: Allyn and Bacon, 1966. Pp. 60–70.

Whorf, B. Science and linguistics. In S. Saporta (Ed.), *Psycholinguistics.* New York: Holt, 1961. Pp. 460–468. (Reprinted from *Language, thought and reality,* edited by J. B. Carroll. New York: Wiley, 1956.)

Wiesner, P. B. & Sheard, N. M. *Maternal behavior in the rat.* Edinburgh: Oliver and Boyd, 1933.

Wilcocks, R. W. An examination of Külpe's experiments on abstraction. *Amer. J. Psychol.,* 1925, *36,* 324–341.

Wilcox, B. M. & Clayton, F. L. Infant visual fixation on motion pictures of the human face. *J. exp. child Psychol.,* 1968, *6,* 22–32.

Wilcox, W. W. An interpretation of the relation between visual acuity and light intensity. *J. gen. Psychol.,* 1936, *15,* 405–435.

Willey, C. F., Inglis, E., & Pearce, C. H. Reversal of auditory localization. *J. exp. Psychol.,* 1937, *20,* 114–130.

Wilson, M. Cross-modal transfer effects in monkeys. Paper read at the Symposium on Cross-modal Transfer, American Psychological Association, Philadelphia, September, 1963.

Wilson, M. & Wilson, W. A., Jr. Intersensory facilitation of learning sets in normal and brain operated monkeys. *J. comp. physiol. Psychol.,* 1962, *55,* 931–934.

Wilson, P. D. & Riesen, A. H. Visual development in rhesus monkeys neonatally deprived of patterned light. *J. comp. physiol. Psychol.*, 1966, *61*, 87–95.

Wilson, W. A., Jr. & Shaffer, O. Intermodality transfer of specific discriminations in the monkey. *Nature*, 1963, *197*, 107.

Witkin, H. A. Individual differences in the ease of perception of embedded figures. *J. Pers.*, 1950, *19*, 1–15.

Witkin, H. A., Lewis, H. B., Hertzman, M., Machover, K., Meissner, P. B., & Wapner, S. *Personality through perception*. New York: Harper, 1954.

Wodinsky, J. & Bitterman, M. E. The solution of oddity-problems by the rat. *Amer. J. Psychol.*, 1953, *66*, 137–140.

Wohlwill, J. F. The definition and analysis of perceptual learning. *Psychol. Rev.*, 1958, *65*, 283–295.

Wohlwill, J. F. Developmental studies of perception. *Psychol. Bull.*, 1960, *57*, 249–288.

Wohlwill, J. F. From perception to inference: A dimension of cognitive development. In W. Kesson & C. Kuhlman (Eds.), *Thought in the young child*. Monogr. Soc. Res. Child Develpm., 1962, *27*, No. 2. Pp. 87–112. (a)

Wohlwill, J. F. The perspective illusion: Perceived size and distance in fields varying in suggested depth, in children and adults. *J. exp. Psychol.*, 1962, *64*, 300–310. (b)

Wohlwill, J. F. The development of "overconstancy" in space perception. In L. P. Lipsitt & C. C. Spiker (Eds.), *Advances in child development and behavior*. Vol. 1. New York: Academic Press, 1963. Pp. 265–312.

Wohlwill, J. F. Changes in distance judgments as a function of corrected and noncorrected practice. *Percept. mot. Skills*, 1964, *19*, 403–413.

Wohlwill, J. F. Texture of the stimulus field and age as variables in the perception of relative distance in photographic slides. *J. exp. child Psychol.*, 1965, *2*, 163–177.

Wohlwill, J. F. Perceptual learning. *Ann. Rev. Psychol.*, 1966, *17*, 201–232.

Wohlwill, J. F. & Lowe, R. C. An experimental analysis of the development of the concept of number. *Child Develpm.*, 1962, *33*, 153–167.

Wolff, P. H. Observations on the early development of smiling. In B. M. Foss (Ed.), *Determinants of infant behavior*, II. New York: Wiley, 1963. Pp. 113–134.

Wolff, P. H. & White, B. L. Visual pursuit and attention in young infants. *J. amer. acad. child Psychiat.*, 1965, *4*, 473–484.

Woodworth, R. S. *Experimental psychology*. New York: Holt, 1938.

Woodworth, R. S. Reënforcement of perception. *Amer. J. Psychol.*, 1947, *60*, 119–124.

Wooster, M. Certain factors in the development of a new spatial co-ordination *Psychol. Monogr.*, 1923, *32*, No. 4.

Wyatt, R. F. Improvability of pitch discrimination. *Psychol. Monogr.*, 1945, *58*, No. 2 (Whole No. 267).

Wyckoff, L. B., Jr. The role of observing responses in discrimination learning. Part I. *Psychol. Rev.*, 1952, *59*, 431–442.

Yonas, A. & Gibson, E. J. A developmental study of feature-processing strategies in letter discrimination. Paper presented at Eastern Psychological Association, Boston, April, 1967.

Young, P. T. Auditory localization with acoustical transposition of the ears. *J. exp. Psychol.*, 1928, *11*, 399–429.

Zaporozhets, A. V. The development of voluntary movements. In B. Simon (Ed.), *Psychology in the Soviet Union*. Stanford: Stanford University Press, 1957. Pp. 108–114.

Zaporozhets, A. V. On the reflectory origin of visual perception of objects. In *Proc. Sixteenth Int. Contress of Psychology*, Bonn, 1960. Pp. 326–330.

Zaporozhets, A. V. The development of perception in the preschool child. In P. H. Mussen (Ed.), *European research in child development*. Monogr. Soc. Res. Child Develpm., 1965, *30*, Serial No. 100. Pp. 82–101.

Zeaman, D. & House, B. J. The role of attention in retardate discrimination learning. In *Handbook of mental deficiency*. New York: McGraw-Hill, 1963. Pp. 159–223.

Zeigler, H. P. & Leibowitz, H. A methodological study of "shape constancy" in the rhesus monkey. *J. comp. physiol. Psychol.*, 1958, *51*, 155–160.

Zimmermann, R. The facilitation of picture discrimination after object discrimination learning in the neonatal monkey and probably vice versa. Paper read at the meeting of the Psychonomics Society, Niagara Falls, 1964.

Zimmermann, R. & Hochberg, J. E. Pictorial recognition in the infant monkey. Proceedings of the Psychonomics Society, Bryn Mawr, 1963, p. 46 (abstract).

Zinchenko, V. P. Perception as action. In volume on *Perception and action*, Symposium 30, Proceedings 18th Int. Congress of Psychology, Moscow, 1966. Pp. 64–73.

Zinchenko, V. P., van Chzhi-Tsin, & Tarakanov, V. V. The formation and development of perceptual activity. *Sov. Psychol. and Psychiat.*, 1963, *2*, 3–12.

Zuckerman, C. B. & Rock, I. An appraisal of the roles of past experience and innate organizing processes in visual perception. *Psychol. Bull.*, 1957, *54*, 269–296.

Zwislocki, J., Maire, F., Feldman, A. S., & Rubin, H. On the effect of practice and motivation on the threshold of audibility. *J. acous. Soc. Amer.*, 1958, *30*, 254–262.

Name Index

Aarons, L., 248
Abercrombie, B., 302
Abravanel, E., 458–459
Ahrens, R., 348, 349, 350, 351, 352, 353, 354, 355
Albertini, B. von, 406
Allan, M. D., 189
Allinsmith, W., 254–255
Allport, G. W., 132
Alluisi, E. A., 222
Amatruda, C. S., 327
Ambrose, J. A., 348, 350, 355
Ames, A., 41, 42, 51
Ames, E. W., 342–343, 456
Ames, L. B., 346
Ammons, C. H., 10
Ananiev, B. G., 54, 374
Arnoult, M. D., 62, 65, 70, 172, 225–226
Atkinson, R. C., 115, 116
Attneave, F., 70, 153, 172
Axelrod, S., 229

Baer, D. M., 306
Bain, A., 53
Baker, C. H., 137
Baker, E. J., 222
Baker, K. E., 63
Baker, R. A., 177
Baker, W. M., 136
Barch, A. W., 189
Baron, M. R., 176
Bartlett, F. C., 46, 52, 153
Bateson, P. P. G., 259, 305
Bauer, J. A., 250–251
Bavelas, A., 136–137
Beach, F. A., 289
Beatty, F. S., 135
Beck, F. L., 372
Bee, H., 148, 446
Békésy, G. von, 218
Bellugi, U., 429
Bergman, R., 137, 183–185
Berkeley, Bishop, 1, 19, 27, 216

Berko, J., 151, 430–431
Berlyne, D. E., 125–127
Berman, P. W., 411–412, 413
Bessemer, D. W., 69–70
Bevan, W., 178
Bexton, W. H., 127
Bilodeau, E. A., 176
Binet, A., 407
Binns, H. A., 6
Birch, H. B., 228
Bird, M. W., 303, 305, 314
Bishop, C. H., 435–436
Bishop, H. E., 260–261
Bitterman, M. E., 291, 292
Björkman, M., 15, 176, 227
Blackwell, H. R., 167
Blake, R. B., 130
Blank, M., 229–230
Blount, W. R., 466
Bogartz, R. S., 423
Boneau, C. A., 136
Boostrom, E., 274
Boring, E. G., 20, 166
Borst, J. M., 111, 221
Bossom, J., 138, 211, 294, 295
Bower, T. G. R., 122–123, 329–330, 345, 363–365, 366, 372, 385–386, 402–403
Boyd, B. O., 291
Bradford, S., 343
Braine, M. D. S., 423, 430, 431–432
Braly, K. W., 33
Brault, H., 104, 365
Bray, C. W., 210
Bridger, W. H., 230, 327–328
Broadbent, D. E., 112–114, 459, 460
Bronshtein, A. I., 329
Brooks, V., 400
Brown, J. S., 176
Brown, L. T., 33
Brown, R. W., 84–85, 102, 151, 158–159, 429, 430, 431
Bruce, R. H., 165
Bruner, J. S., 49–51, 52, 131, 389, 410, 438, 448, 449

Brunswik, E., 14, 37–41, 42, 45, 128, 319, 365
Bryan, W. L., 189, 437
Bullis, G. E., 27
Burton, D., 229, 293
Bush, R. R., 164, 180
Butler, R. A., 125, 126, 399
Buytendyk, F. J. J., 402

Campbell, D. T., 132
Campbell, R. A., 178
Campbell, V., 69
Canfield, T. H., 7
Cantor, G. N., 65
Cantor, J. H., 66
Cantril, H., 41, 51
Carmichael, L., 317
Carpenter, B., 383
Carpenter, J. T., 383
Carr, H. A., 2, 25, 26, 200, 374
Carr, W. J., 261
Carterette, E. C., 423
Carvellas, T., 171
Castle, P., 344, 359–360
Cattell, J. McK., 437
Caviness, J. A., 226–227, 272
Chance, J. E., 356
Chapanis, A., 87, 186
Chapman, D. W., 121
Cherry, C., 83–84
Chomsky, N., 425–431
Chorover, S. L., 221
Chow, K. L., 245, 247
Clayton, F. L., 399–400
Cofoid, D. A., 306
Cohen, W., 367
Cole, M., 221
Coles, G. R., 121
Cooper, F. S., 56, 111, 221
Cordeau, J. P., 229, 294
Cotzin, M., 10
Crabbé, G., 218–219
Craske, B., 211
Cronin, V., 334
Cross, H. A., 268

Dallenbach, K. M., 10
Dameron, L. E., 135
Davenport, R. K., 238
Daves, W. F., 274
Day, R. W., 110
de Haan, H. J., 397
Dennis, W., 236, 327
De Rivera, J., 67, 69
Deutsch, D., 114
Deutsch, J. A., 114
Devine, J. V., 69–70
Dewey, J., 2, 49

Dewson, J. H., 293
Dibble, F. N., 62–63
Dickinson, E., 215
Diebold, A. R., 428
Djang, S., 33
Dodge, S. H., 270, 372
Dollard, J., 63–64, 176
Dominis, J., 11
Donderi, D. C., 72
Dornbush, R. L., 397–398
Doroz, L., 40
Downing, J. A., 437
Dresslar, F. B., 166
Drever, J., 45, 229
Dubanovski, R. A., 310

Eagle, M. N., 60
Edmonds, E. M., 180
Edwards, B. J., 239
Egeth, H., 122
Egger, M. D., 129, 140
Elkin, E. H., 103
Elkonin, D. B., 151
Ellis, H. C., 69–71
Ellis, N. R., 332
Ellis, W. D., 32, 218, 286
Emde, R. N., 350
Engen, T., 168, 182–183
Englund, S. A. J., 164, 178
Eriksen, C. W., 40, 66–67, 69, 137, 184
Erismann, T., 199
Ernhart, C. B., 411–412, 413
Ervin, S. M., 424–425, 428, 429–430
Ettlinger, G., 221, 229, 293
Evans, S. H., 180, 467
Ewert, P. H., 198

Fabricius, E., 304
Fantz, R. L., 241, 242–244, 274–275, 310, 322–324, 329, 345, 348, 349, 352, 373, 397, 456
Farrell, W. M., 261
Feallock, S. M., 367
Feigenbaum, E. A., 93–94, 146, 154
Feller, Y., 383–384
Fernberger, S. W., 80, 176
Feugue, R. L., 71
Fishback, J., 407
Fitts, P. M., 179–180
Flavell, J. H., 47, 388, 389
Fleck, F. S., 134
Fletcher, W. E., 187
Flock, H., 39
Fodor, J. A., 432
Foley, J. E., 205–206
Foley, J. P., 294
Forgays, D. G., 59, 252, 253
Forgays, J. W., 252

Forgus, R. H., 252–253
Fowler, W., 233, 234
Fraisse, P., 103, 383
Francès, R. L., 81, 111–113
Fraser, C., 429, 430
Freedman, D. G., 355
Freeman, J. T., 69
Freeman, R. B., 289
Frenkel-Brunswik, E., 130
Friedlander, B. Z., 125
Fries, C. C., 438
Fritz, J. J., 109
Furth, H. G., 157, 422, 428

Gagné, R. M., 63, 83, 99, 146–148
Galambos, R., 266
Galanter, E., 2, 164, 180
Gantenbein, M. M., 382–383
Ganz, L., 245
Gardner, B. T., 104, 280
Gardner, R. A., 280
Garner, W. R., 2, 124, 184, 467
Garvill, J., 227
Garvin, E. A., 69, 70, 134
Gaydos, H. F., 225, 229
Gebhard, J. W., 221
Gelb, I. J., 411
Gellerman, L. W., 330–331
Gelman, R., 465–466
Gentry, G. V., 292
Gesell, A., 27, 36, 327
Ghent, L., 376
Gibson, E. J., 16, 39, 61, 62, 71, 77–79,
    86, 88, 106–107, 137, 139–140, 142–
    143, 144, 163, 169–170, 175, 176, 179,
    181, 183–185, 190, 234, 239–241, 242–
    243, 258–259, 267–269, 278, 318, 319,
    320, 366, 390, 412–417, 436, 438–439,
    440, 441, 452, 454–456, 458, 464
Gibson, J. J., 4, 6, 8, 13, 14, 16, 39, 61,
    77–79, 83, 88, 99, 105, 115, 146–148,
    179, 194, 195, 200, 201, 210, 219, 223,
    226, 272, 402, 412–417, 419, 446, 452,
    459, 463, 464
Gibson, Jean, 193
Gilbert, J. A., 357
Gilinsky, A. S., 366–367, 375
Ginsburg, N., 291–292
Glaser, F., 366
Gleitman, L. R., 427
Glickman, S. E., 268
Glucksberg, S., 156
Goldstein, A. G., 356
Gollin, E. S., 104–105, 148–149, 406–407,
    448, 470
Gonzalez, R. C., 292
Goodenough, F., 26
Goodman, C. C., 131

Goss, A. E., 64–65
Gottlieb, G., 313
Gottschaldt, K., 31, 33, 34, 111–113, 130,
    171
Graham, F. K., 411–412, 413
Gray, P. H., 300, 303, 305, 306, 307–308,
    345
Green, D. M., 187
Greene, J. E., 135
Greene, P., 380
Greenfield, N., 65
Greenfield, P. M., 449
Gregory, R. L., 216–217, 220, 234
Grice, G. R., 72
Griffin, D. R., 10, 266
Grosslight, J. M., 292–293
Guignot, E., 365–366
Guiton, P., 311–312
Gummerman, K., 469
Gunter, R., 289
Guttman, N., 175

Haber, R. N., 122
Hagen, J. W., 462
Hailman, J. P., 299, 303–304
Haire, M., 100
Haith, M. M., 325
Hake, H. W., 66–67, 69, 184
Halikas, N., 309
Halle, M., 83–86, 426
Halsey, R. M., 186
Halverson, H. M., 327
Hamilton, C. R., 211, 294, 295
Hammond, M., 438–439
Hanawalt, N. G., 33, 171
Hanes, R. M., 186
Harlow, H. F., 125, 157, 277, 291, 370,
    396, 470
Harrington, T. L., 205
Harris, C. S., 122, 139, 211
Harris, K. S., 72
Harter, N., 189, 437
Harway, N. I., 375
Hauty, G. T., 137
Hay, J. C., 201–204, 205, 380
Hayek, F. A., 217–218
Hayes, C., 276, 279–280
Hayes, W. H., 33
Hayes, W. N., 272
Hebb, D. O., 58–61, 89, 216, 233, 237,
    239, 246, 251, 252, 428
Heimer, W. I., 177
Hein, A. V., 211, 249–250, 251
Heinroth, O., 300
Held, R., 138–139, 194, 208–209, 210–
    211, 249–251, 253–255, 344, 359–360
Helmholtz, H. von, 21, 24, 35, 37, 51,
    124, 200

Hemmendinger, L., 346
Hendrickson, L. N., 68
Henle, M., 33
Hering, E., 22
Herma, H., 39, 41
Hernandez-Peon, R., 114
Heron, W., 89, 127, 236–237
Herrnstein, R. J., 287
Hershenson, M., 325, 345, 348, 352
Herskovits, M. J., 132
Hertz, M., 284–285, 286–287
Hertzman, M., 379
Hess, E. H., 260, 273–274, 295, 301, 302, 303–304, 306, 309, 310, 311, 312, 314
Higgins, K. E., 416
Hildum, D. C., 84, 102
Hinde, R. A., 298, 305–306
Hobbes, T., 19
Hochberg, J. E., 20, 135, 277–278, 400–401
Holland, M. K., 136
Holmgren, G. L., 225–226
Holst, E. von, 138, 249
Honig, W. K., 110, 306
Honkavaara, S., 467
Hornbostel, E. M. von, 218
House, B. J., 115–116, 331–333, 357, 397, 467–468, 470
Hovland, C. I., 175
Howard, I. P., 59, 106, 138, 195, 211
Howard, K. I., 306
Hubel, D. H., 2, 88, 89, 234, 247, 275
Hudson, W., 403–404
Hull, C. L., 1, 57, 176
Hume, D., 19
Hunt, J. McV., 125
Huttenlocher, J., 376, 377
Hyman, L. M., 462
Hymovitch, B., 252

Ilg, F. I., 27
Inglis, E., 208
Inhelder, B., 88, 142, 150–151, 230, 360–361, 374, 415
Iscoe, I., 72, 397
Ison, J. R., 261
Ittelson, W. H., 41, 42, 45, 51

Jackson, D. N., 134
Jakobson, R., 83–86, 424
James, H., 302
James, W., 4, 10, 23–25, 108–109, 119, 124, 132, 215, 456
Jaynes, J., 306–308, 315
Jeffrey, W. E., 66, 436, 470
Jenkin, N., 358, 367
Johannson, G., 16
Johnson, B., 372

Johnson, M. L., 9
Jones, A., 127–128

Kaess, D. W., 261
Kagan, J., 320, 325–326, 327, 349, 351, 353, 355, 356
Kaila, E., 347
Kalish, H. L., 175
Kane, E., 72
Kant, I., 22, 36
Kaplan, E., 441–442
Kaplan, G., 169
Kaplan, I. T., 171
Karsh, E. B., 206–208
Kaspar, J. C., 148
Katz, P. A., 71
Katzman, M. T., 438
Kawachi, J., 259
Kaye, H., 330
Kelleher, R. T., 470
Keller, F. S., 189
Kellogg, W. N., 10, 266
Kelvin, R. P., 220
Kendler, H. H., 156, 470
Kendler, T. S., 470
Kenyon, K. W., 265
Kerpelman, L. C., 259, 376
Kessen, W., 123, 325, 345, 456
Keston, R., 156
Kilpatrick, I. F. P., 43, 44
Kinney, J. S., 72, 221–222
Kleeman, J. A., 386
Klein, G., 130
Klein, G. S., 60
Klein, R. E., 229, 380
Klimpfinger, S., 38, 365
Klopfer, P. H., 303–305, 313, 345
Klüver, H., 277, 284, 289, 292
Koch, S., 86
Koffka, K., 28, 29, 31, 32, 33
Koffler, S., 382
Kofsky, E., 462
Kohler, I., 195, 199–200, 201, 202–205, 209
Köhler, W., 29, 110, 276, 283–284, 289, 407
Kolers, P. A., 171–174, 438
Koronakos, C., 289
Kottenhoff, H., 200
Kovach, J. K., 309
Kravitz, J. H., 139, 206
Külpe, O., 121–122
Kuo, Z. Y., 263–264
Kurke, M. I., 246
Kurtz, A. K., 189

Lambercier, M., 13, 334–338, 363, 366, 367, 391, 453

Lane, H., 72
Lashley, K. S., 175–176, 239, 287–289, 290, 291, 296, 297, 298, 387, 393, 421, 428, 470
Latz, E., 456
Lawrence, D. H., 100–101, 108, 109, 121
Lazar, R., 170
Leeper, R., 29, 30, 31
Lefford, A., 228
Lehtinen, L. E., 451–452
Leibowitz, H. W., 9, 289, 365, 366, 367
Lemmon, V. W., 454
Lenneberg, E. H., 156–157, 158–160, 426–427, 428
Leontiev, A. N., 53, 54, 56, 228–229
Leopold, W. F., 424, 427
Lessac, M. S., 234–235
Lesser, R., 106
Lettvin, J. Y., 88, 275
Leuba, C., 344
Leventhal, A. S., 328
Levin, H., 441–442
Levine, J. R., 189
Levy, L., 343
Lewis, H. B., 379
Lewis, M., 325, 327, 349, 351, 353, 355, 356
Lewis, M. M., 427
Liberman, A. M., 56, 72, 86, 111, 221, 425, 433, 434
Liebert, R. S., 378–379
Liddell, H. S., 129
Lindauer, J., 139
Ling, B. C., 255–258, 262, 330
Lipsitt, L. P., 328, 329, 330, 470
Liss, P., 470
Littman, R. A., 175
Lively, B. L., 292–293
Lobb, H., 361
Locke, J., 12, 20, 23, 24, 216
Locke, N. M., 289
Loeffler, N., 366
Long, J., 134
Long, K. K., 71
Longfellow, L. A., 247–248
Lorenz, K., 260, 271, 273, 300, 308–309
Low, F. N., 102, 165
Lowe, R. C., 389
Luce, R. D., 164, 180
Lundberg, I., 164, 178
Lunn, J. H., 6

Maccoby, E. E., 148, 446, 459–461, 462
Mace, H., 365–366
Machover, K., 379
Mack, J. D., 220
Mackintosh, J., 285

Mackintosh, N. J., 285
Mackworth, N. H., 410–411
MacLean, P. D., 276
Maier, G. W., 259
Mangan, G. L., 135
Manning, W. H., 225–226
Margolius, G., 461
Marler, P., 279, 298
Maroun, J., 392
Maturana, H. R., 2, 88, 275, 295, 298
McBee, G., 396
McCleary, R. A., 247–248
McCulloch, W. S., 88, 275
McCullough, C., 205
McCurdy, H. G., 135
McFadden, H. B., 165
McGee, R. K., 259
McGinnies, E., 131
McGuigan, D. I., 261
McInish, J. R., 85
McKinney, J. P., 60
McNear, E., 383–384
McNeill, D., 432
Means, J. R., 69
Mednick, S. A., 451–452
Meili, R., 382
Meissner, P. B., 379
Mellinger, J. C., 246
Melzack, R., 237, 271
Meneghini, K. A., 365, 366
Menzel, E. W., 238
Merkel, J., 454
Merrill, M. A., 149
Meyer, D. R., 291, 470
Meyer, M. E., 265
Meyer, P. M., 372
Meyers, B., 247, 248–249
Michotte, A., 16, 218–219, 387, 390, 391–392
Milerian, E. A., 342
Miller, G. A., 2, 50, 141, 181, 423, 429, 437, 438
Miller, J. G., 130
Miller, N. E., 63–64, 129, 140, 176
Miller, W. R., 424–425, 428, 429–430
Millman, S. H., 187
Minsky, M., 91–92
Mishkin, M., 59
Molander, B., 227
Moltz, H., 306, 309, 311, 313, 314
Molyneux, 12, 20, 216
Montessori, M., 234, 357
Moon, L. E., 470
Moore, M. E., 206
Moorhouse, A. C., 411
Morgan, G. A., 355–356
Morton, J., 441
Mowbray, G. H., 221

Muehl, S., 68
Mueller, M. R., 180
Mukherjee, K. C., 166
Mulik, A., 220
Muller, D. G., 70–71
Müller, J., 22
Munsinger, H. L., 123, 139, 468–469
Murdock, B. B., 66
Murphy, G., 132, 133–134
Mussen, P. H., 362, 390

Nealy, S. M., 239
Neisser, U., 87, 92, 169–171
Newman, E. B., 438
Nissen, H. W., 247
Norcross, K. J., 65, 66
Novick, R., 170
Nunnally, J. C., 131

Ohwaki, S., 357–358
Oldfield, R. C., 46, 152–153
Olson, D., 446
Olum, P., 8
Olum, V., 318, 366, 390–391, 454
Olver, R. R., 449
Osgood, C. E., 429
Osgood, S. W., 177
Osler, S., 462
Osser, H., 86, 88, 412–417, 438–440
Ottander, C., 176
Over, J., 377
Over, R., 377

Page, E., 361
Palen, G. F., 372
Pastore, N., 286–287, 289, 291
Pavlov, I. P., 54, 61, 99–100, 124, 175,
    270, 342
Pearce, C. H., 208
Pearson, R. G., 137
Pegram, V. G., 71
Perdeck, A. C., 299
Peters, W., 357
Peterson, J., 199
Peterson, J. K., 199
Pettigrew, T. F., 132
Pfafflin, S. M., 69
Piaget, J., 13, 22, 47–48, 52, 88–89, 116,
    142, 150–151, 152, 161, 230, 334, 335,
    336, 342–343, 344, 360–361, 363, 366,
    367, 374, 381, 383–384, 388–389, 391,
    392, 406, 407–409, 410, 415, 448, 452,
    456–457
Pick, A. D., 88, 96–99, 105, 146, 179,
    227–228, 229, 380, 412–417, 438–440,
    454
Pick, H. L., 55, 56, 154, 201–204, 205,
    227–228, 228–229, 258–259, 361, 380,
    454

Pieron, Mme. H., 220
Pitts, W. H., 88, 275
Plato, 75
Plotkin, L., 189
Polak, P. R., 350
Pollack, R. H., 376, 409
Polt, J. M., 312
Postman, L., 34, 37, 50, 61, 86, 131, 438
Potter, M. C., 50
Pribram, K. H., 2
Pritchard, R. M., 89
Pronko, N. H., 199
Proust, M., 151
Pufall, P. B., 422
Pustell, T. E., 135
Putnam, V., 72

Rabbitt, P. M., 190–191
Ramsay, A. O., 306
Ramsay, R. L., 244
Ramsey, G. V., 130
Raney, E., 317
Ranken, H. B., 69
Rasch, E., 245
Read, J. M., 253
Reber, A. S., 423, 432
Replogle, A., 72
Rey, A., 358
Rheingold, H. L., 273–274, 355
Rhoades, M. V., 186
Ricciuti, H. N., 346, 355–356
Rice, C. E., 11
Rice, T. W., 265
Riesen, A. H., 234, 244–245, 246–247,
    248
Riess, B. F., 451–452
Riley, D. A., 239
Robinson, H. B., 358–359, 454
Robinson, J. S., 33, 67, 69, 157, 178–179,
    291, 416
Rock, I., 33, 134, 195
Rockett, F. C., 271
Rogers, C. M., 238
Rosen, A. J., 261
Rosenblatt, F., 8, 50, 92
Rosenblith, J. F., 254, 255, 377
Rosenblum, L., 309
Rosenblum, L. A., 268
Rosser, E., 205
Rossi, E., 466
Rossi, P. J., 295
Rossman, I. L., 64
Rothkopf, E. Z., 189
Routtenberg, A., 268
Rudel, R. G., 148, 223–224, 228, 377,
    378–379
Rush, G. P., 467
Russell, B., 102

Russell, J. T., 239
Ryan, T. A., 102–103, 219

Saayman, G., 329
Saiff, E. I., 272
Salapatek, P., 325, 345, 456
Salten, C., 470
Salzen, E. A., 304, 306, 308, 311–312, 345, 348, 352
Samuels, S. J., 436
Santos, J. F., 134
Saravo, A., 470
Saugstad, P., 178
Savigny, M., 365–366
Sayegh, Y., 236
Schafer, R., 133–134
Schiff, W., 16, 86, 271–272
Schiffman, H. R., 269–270
Schoenfeld, W. N., 189
Schulman, J. L., 148
Schwartz, C. B., 102–103
Scott, T. H., 127
Scott, Moncrieff, C. K., 151
Seashore, H., 136–137, 189
Segal, E. M., 69
Segall, M. H., 132
Seitz, E., 345
Sekuler, R. W., 377
Selfridge, J. A., 429
Selfridge, O. G., 87, 92
Semler, I., 397
Senden, M. von, 12, 216, 234
Serunian, S. A., 470
Seymour, W. D., 6
Shaffer, O., 229, 293
Sheard, N. M., 298
Shepard, R. N., 189–190
Shepela, S., 461–462
Shipley, E. F., 427
Shurcliff, A., 440
Shvarts, L. A., 165
Siegel, A. I., 242
Siipola, E. M., 210
Silfen, C. K., 342–343, 456
Silver, S. D., 409
Simon, H. A., 93–94, 146, 154
Sluckin, W., 300, 304, 306, 308, 311, 312
Small, A. M., 178
Smedslund, J., 40
Smith, C. S., 427
Smith, D. E. P., 135
Smith, E., 122
Smith, F. V., 303, 305, 314
Smith, J., 86
Smith, K. H., 423, 432
Smith, K. U., 195, 380
Smith, M. P., 69
Smith, O. W., 39, 373

Smith, P. C., 373
Smith, S. L., 65
Smith, W. M., 195
Snyder, C. W., 199
Snyder, F. W., 199
Sokolov, E. N., 54
Solley, C. M., 132, 133, 134, 137
Solomon, R. L., 234–235
Spalding, D., 300, 301
Spence, K. W., 292
Spencer, H., 119
Sperry, R. W., 295
Spiker, C. C., 65–66
Spitz, H. H., 409, 467, 468
Spitz, R. A., 236, 347, 350
Spragg, S. D. S., 189
Stechler, G., 342–343, 345, 348, 352, 456
Stepien, L. S., 229, 294
Sternberg, S., 143
Stettner, L. J., 313
Stevens, J. C., 220
Stevens, K. N., 426
Stevens, S. S., 220
Stevenson, H. W., 244, 396
Stratton, G. M., 25, 196–198, 212
Street, R. F., 29, 30, 31, 406–407
Supa, M., 10
Sutherland, N. S., 89, 285, 377
Swets, J. A., 167, 187
Swift, H., 245

Tallarico, R. B., 261
Tanaka, K., 336
Tatz, S. J., 177
Tauber, E. S., 382
Taubman, R. E., 189
Tawney, G., 166
Taylor, D. W., 189
Taylor, J. G., 57, 209, 212
Templeton, W. B., 59, 106, 195, 211
Terman, L. M., 149, 181–182
Teuber, H. L., 148, 223–224, 228, 377
Thines, G., 218–219
Thomas, H., 348, 352
Thomas, M. L., 227–228
Thompson, H., 327
Thompson, W. R., 236–237, 310
Thorndike, E. L., 1, 2, 29, 136, 279
Thorpe, W. H., 221, 292, 305–306, 308, 311, 420
Tighe, L. S., 116, 470
Tighe, T. J., 116, 234, 239–241, 258–259
Tikofsky, R. S., 85
Tinbergen, N., 104, 271, 273, 299
Tinker, M. A., 441
Titchener, E. B., 23, 26, 35
Tobler, E., 382
Tolman, E. C., 1, 37, 135

Torgerson, W., 90
Trabasso, T. R., 99
Trafton, C. L., 69–70
Treisman, A. M., 114
Tronick, E., 302
Trychin, S., 270
Tuddenham, R. D., 385
Turner, E. A., 441
Turnure, C., 109

Uhr, L., 51, 87, 92
Uleman, J., 51
Urban, F. M., 80, 176

Vanderplas, J. M., 65, 69, 70
van Ratingen, J. R. M., 402
Vautrey, P., 383
Velten, H. V., 424
Venezky, R. L., 437, 438
Vernon, M. D., 9, 46, 47, 52
Vince, M. A., 306, 311
Volkmann, A. W., 165–167
Vossler, C., 51
Vurpillot, E., 104, 318, 365–366, 407,
    408, 410–411, 458, 463–464

Wade, M., 175–176
Walk, R. D., 6, 8, 16, 222, 234, 239–
    241, 242, 243, 253, 258–259, 267–270,
    278, 289, 319–321, 371–372
Wallace, J. G., 216–217, 234
Wallach, H., 139, 206–208, 209
Wallach, L., 104, 109
Wallach, M. A., 438
Wapner, S., 379
Warren, J. M., 291
Waskow, I., 366
Watson, J. B., 1
Watson, J. S., 349, 351, 352
Wedell, C. H., 181
Wegener, J. G., 293–294
Weidmann, U., 299
Weiner, M., 44, 45
Weinstein, B., 157
Weinstein, S., 138
Weir, R. H., 85, 426–427
Weiss, W., 461
Werner, H., 34, 35, 36, 80–81, 108
Wertheimer, M., 322, 467, 471
West, N., 358
White, B. L., 253–255, 343–344, 359–360,
    384

Whorf, B., 158 ff.
Wiesel, T. N., 2, 88, 89, 234, 247, 275
Wiesner, P. B., 298
Wilcocks, R. W., 122
Wilcox, B. M., 399–400
Wilcox, W. W., 165
Willey, C. F., 208
Willoughby, R. H., 204, 205
Wilson, J. P., 261
Wilson, M., 293
Wilson, P. D., 244, 245
Wilson, W. A., Jr., 229, 293
Winnick, W. A., 398
Wischner, G. J., 397
Witkin, H. A., 378–379, 380
Wodinsky, J., 291
Wohlwill, J. F., 47, 62, 137, 181, 366, 367,
    370–371, 389, 403–406, 407, 448–449
Wolf, K. M., 347
Wolff, P. H., 343–344, 348
Woodworth, R. S., 124–125, 146, 155,
    166, 169
Woolpy, J. H., 125
Wooster, M., 26, 200
Worchel, P., 10
Wright, J. C., 320
Wyatt, R. F., 154, 176–177
Wyckoff, L. B., 115, 116

Yonas, A., 71, 90, 142–143, 144, 169–
    170, 190, 440, 454–456, 458, 463
Yonas, P., 446
Young, P., 137
Young, P. T., 208
Young, R. K., 72
Youniss, J., 422

Zangwill, O. L., 46, 308
Zaporozhets, A. V., 53, 54, 55, 361–362,
    374
Zaynor, W. C., 292–293
Zeaman, D., 115–116, 331–333, 357, 397
Zeigler, H. P., 289, 366
Zimmerman, C., 50
Zimmerman, R., 277–278
Zinchenko, V. P., 55, 141–142, 229, 361–
    362, 457–459
Zink, D. L., 171–173
Zuckerman, C. B., 33
Zwislocki, J., 167, 178

Subject Index

Abstraction, of dimensional differences, 325, 357–359
of distinctive features, 109
Accommodation, 372
Accretion, in discrimination, 24
Acuity, effect of practice, 164–167
temporal, and motion perception, 383
visual, evolutionary trends, 282–283
in visual cliff avoidance, 321, 371
Adaptation, conditional (gaze contingent), 202–205, 212
to environment, 13, 20, 251–252, 296
measurement of, 195 ff.
with negative aftereffect, 194
to surgically rotated eyes, 295
to transformed stimulus arrays, 5–6, 25, 26, 57, 138–139, 194, 196–200, 201–205, 208–212, 294–295, 380; see also Chapter 10
Aftereffects, and color, 205
measurement of adaptation, 195 ff.
negative, 194, 197, 201, 204
situational, 202–204, 209
Aircraft, landing, 7
recognition, 83, 99, 140, 146–148, 165
Alarm reaction, see Response(s), fear
Ames demonstrations, 42–43
Amodal perception, 218–219, 293, 362, 387, 390, 392; see also Michotte, A. (Name Index)
Analysis, in absolute estimation of multidimensional stimuli, 187–188
and memory for form, 146
in shape discrimination, 89
Analysis-by-synthesis, 426
Aphasia, 85–86
Articulation, of distinctive features, and recognition, 146
of figures, and past experience, 31–32
in Gestalt theory, 28
and pitch discrimination, 56
role in speech perception, 425–426
Association, in Brunswikian perception, 15, 38

and concept formation, 156
and context theory of perception, 23
and correspondence of writing with speech, 434
and cross-modal equivalence, 224–225
and depth perception, 372, 402
in development of perceptual constancies, 13, 360, 365
in discrimination, 86, 175, 331–332, 419–420
in Helmholtzian theory, 22
in imprinting, 309, 314
and intermodal transfer, 215, 217
and James' theory of perception, 23–25, 109
and language, 86, 419–420, 429, 430
laws, 19, 20, 35
of local signs, 98
and localization of objects in space, 374
and oddity response, 291–292
in schema theory of preceptual learning, 47
theory of perception, 1, 61, 92
Attention, and channeling by culture, 132
and conservation, 388
to cutout figures, 259
to dimensions of stimulation, and discrimination, 357
and direction of perception, 121
and discriminating objects vs. pictures, 397
and early development of object perception, 341–344
effect on generalization, 452
facilitation by massive stimulation, 253–255
facilitation by verbal labels, 155–156
following visual deprivation, 242–244, 246
in human infant, 256–258, 322–327, 352
and imprinting, 302
in James' theory of discrimination, 25

Attention (*cont.*)
  and memory for form, 146
  and "new look," 130–131
  obligatory, 342, 456
  peripheral mechanisms, 114–116
  selective, 33, 115, 160, 227, 237, 238, 332, 403, 459–461
  trend toward optimization, 456–462
Attitude, in Bruner's theory of perception, 50
  and direction of perceptual search, 129–132
  effect on constancy judgments, 365–366
  and perception of pictures, 398
  in transactional theory of perception, 41, 45
Aufgabe experiments, 121–122
Augmentation, of environmental stimulation, 233–235, 252–261
Autism(-istic) factors in perceptual selection, 129–132
Avoidance, of depth at an edge, *see* Visual cliff
  of novel objects, and imprinting, 300
  of obstacles, 243, 245, 265–266
  of strangers by human infant, 355–356

Bantus, 403–404
Begging response (gulls), 299–300
Behaviorism, and acquired distinctiveness/equivalence, 63–73
  enrichment vs. differentiation theories of perceptual development, 61
  explanation of deprivation experiments, 248
  explanation of visual cliff behavior, 242
  impact on perception, 25
  view of concept learning, 156
  view of motivation, 124
Bias, cultural, 129–132
  in rearing, 234, 259–261
  response, 80, 131, 134–136
  of stimulus information, 194–195
Binocular disparity, 199–200, 206–208; *see also* Depth perception; Information, depth
Blind, perceptual capabilities, 4–5, 10–12, 229
  restored to sight, 12, 216–217, 234
Blindness, after visual deprivation, 245

Caricature, 17, 102–103, 217, 399, 407, 463
Categorization, in Bruner's theory of perception, 49, 50

and detection of higher order structure, 466
and disjunctive reaction time, 190–191
in problem-solving theory of perception, 52
Causal texture, of environment, 128, 129
Causality, perception of, 16, 390–392
Causation, law of, in Helmholtzian perception, 22
Central tendency effect, 336
Centration (Piaget), 342, 388, 408–409, 456–457
Child psychology, 26–27, 36
Chunking, 141, 421, 434, 437, 440, 447
Classification, and acquired equivalence, 71
  of geometric illusions, 408–409
  of intermodal relations, 219–220
  of perceptual learning experiments, 164
  of theories of perceptual learning, 73–74
Cocktail party phenomenon, 111, 112–113; *see also* Filtering
Coding, in Bruner's theory of perception, 49
  and cross-modal transfer, 227, 230
  and discrimination of colors, 158–160
  and language, 425–426, 433, 434–437
  of multidimensional stimuli, 187
  phylogenetic comparison of perception of coded stimuli, 278–280
  and representations, 8, 400, 417
  of stimulation, 17
  of structure, 469
Cognition, and detection of structure, 471
  development, 28, 39–41, 47, 157, 160–161
  and development of phenomenal space, 374
  and perceptual learning, *see* Chapter 8
  in Soviet theory of perceptual development, 54
Color, aftereffect, 205
  discrimination, 158–160, 357
  effect on imprinting, 302–305, 307–308
  fringes, with wedge prisms, 200, 201, 205
  generalization, after visual deprivation, 245
  identification of, 186–187
Color vision, in blind restored to sight, 12, 216–217
  evolutionary trends, 282–283
  in human neonate, 324, 329
  Gestalt theory, 28

Communication, by animals, 278–280, 420, 421

Communication theory, *see* Information, theory of

Compensation, in Piaget's theory, 389, 391

Computer(s), models for pattern recognition, 91–94

Concentric clinical method, 335, 337

Concept(s), in cognitive development, 153–154, 161
  cross-modal, 230
  formation, and abstraction of distinctive features, 99, 109, 463–464
  formation, dependence on language, 156–157, 158
  and inference in perception, 448
  of space, 374

Conditioning, in adaptation to transformed stimulus arrays, 212
  and age differences in generalization, 451–452
  and avoidance of looming, 384
  classical, 53, 54–56, 57, 76, 129, 139
  differential, 72–73, 99
  and interocular transfer, 247
  operant, in human neonates, 329–330, 345, 363–365, 386
  in Soviet theory of perceptual development, 54–56
  in Taylor's theory of perceptual development, 57
  see also Association, Behaviorism

Confusion, of fingerprints, and effect of practice, 179
  of form, 55, 181, 376
  and labelling, 71, 156
  of letters (graphemes), 86, 89–91, 461–462
  matrix, 90, 91, 101–102, 122–123, 454–456
  in Morse code learning, 189–190
  of phonemes, 84
  in predifferentiation experiment, 139
  and reduction in generalization, 80
  and transfer of form discrimination, 97–99
  of words, 85

Conservation, 388–389, 391, 465–466

Constancy, brightness, 38 ff.
  in Brunswikian perception, 38
  in distorted rooms, 43–44
  and event perception, 381 ff.
  existence, *see* Object(s), permanence
  with inverting lens system, 197
  maturation vs. learning, 445–446
  object, 12–13, 16, 42, 48, 58, 363–367, 369, 415–416

and perception of invariants, 464–466
  relation to causality, 391
  shape, 256, 289, 363–365
  size, 201–202, 205, 287, 289, 334–338, 402
  and transformations, 86, 415–416; *see also* Constancy, object, size

Context, theory of perception, 23, 25, 26, 28, 35

Continuity-discontinuity controversy, 100

Contract, method of, 99–100

Correction, *see* Knowledge of results

Criterion, and motion thresholds, 383
  and perceptual learning, 167 ff.

Critical periods, 233, 246, 300, 305, 310, 311–314, 380, 450

Cross-modal transfer, *see* Chapter 11

Cue(s), acquired distinctiveness, 63–73, 99, 156
  acquired equivalence, 26, 64, 68–72, 190
  in Bruner's theory of perception, 49, 50
  in Brunswik's theory of perception, 15, 38
  concepts, as, 156
  conflicting, 207, 378–379
  depth, 206 ff., 260, 402
  irrelevant, 461–462
  in learning experiments, 39–41
  probabilistic, learning, 37–41, 51
  reinforcing, 129
  response produced, 64, 71 ff., 73, 425–426
  validity, 39–41, 207–208

Cue-family hierarchy, 38

Culture, influence on perception, 132, 152 ff.

Curiosity, as motive, 125–126

Dark-rearing, 238–246

Deaf, concept formation in, 157
  perception of sequential information by, 422
  speech production in, 426–427
  spelling and pronounceability of words, 439–440
  word discrimination, 72

Deprivation, environmental, 233–252, 263–264, 311–314
  sensory, 3, 10–12, 59, 127–129

Depth, at an edge, *see* Visual cliff
  Gestalt notion, 28
  information for, 206, 260, 370–371, 372, 397
  motion in, 16
  and object solidity, 372–373

Depth (*cont.*)
  in pictures, 397, 401–406
  size relation, 320, 330
Depth perception, age differences, 375
  and dark rearing, 239–243
  evolutionary trends, 282–283
  factor analysis, 373
  of infant, 27, 330, 353–354; *see also*
    Visual cliff
  monocular vs. binocular vision, 269–
    270
  and probabilistic cue-learning, 39–40
  with transformed stimulus array, 198–
    200
Detection, of direction by children, 377
  experiments on perceptual learning,
    164–174
Differentiation, in cognitive development,
    160–161
  of color, following visual deprivation,
    245
  of features, 150, 156, 259, 314, 346,
    348–350
  figure-ground, 324, 344–345
  following passive vs. active motion,
    249–250
  of forms, 181, 216–217
  and Gestalt theory of perceptual de-
    velopment, 28, 29, 76
  of gravitational and visual cues to
    verticality, 378
  in imprinting, 305–308, 314
  of Morse code signals, 189
  of nonsense items (scribbles), 77–79
  of phonemes, 85, 424 ff., 427
  and picture perception, 399–401, 406,
    411, 419
  vs. production of visual patterns, 148–
    151
  of representations of faces, and de-
    velopment of reaching, 360
  and reproduction of melodies, 151
  retinal images, and object constancy in
    human infants, 363–364
  theory, contrasted with enrichment
    theories, 61
  of schema, in Piaget's view of per-
    ceptual development, 48
  and spatial localization, 374
  of spatial properties of objects, 330,
    360–362, 397, 419
  of symbols, and association of mean-
    ing, 420, 451–452
  of weight, as a dimension, 357–359
Werner's theory of perceptual devel-
    opment, 34–35, 76
Discrimination, in Bruner's theory of
    perception, 50

conditional, and detection of higher
    order structure, 470–471
cross-modal, 221–224
definition, 174
of depth, *see* Depth, Depth perception
and developmental changes in disjunc-
    tive reaction time, 454–456
effect of knowledge of results, 136, 139
effect of predifferentiation, 73, 100–
    108
effect of redundant cues, 462
effect of varying object properties, 274
in EPAM model for perception, 93
experiments on perceptual learning,
    99, 174–179
following restricted rearing, 237, 238,
    241–242, 243–245
of form, 96–99, 252–253, 255–259
of higher order properties, evolution-
    ary trends, 283–295
in imprinting, 305 ff.
James' theory, 4, 23–24
and labelling, 64–69, 158–160
in language, 72, 85, 86, 110, 151, 292–
    293, 412–417, 424–427, 433–434
learning, in children, 330–333, 357–
    358
of linguistic symbols, 86
of motion, 248–249
net, 93, 146, 154; *see also* Feature(s),
    Hierarchy
and observing responses, 115–116
of odors, and distinctive features, 168
of part vs. whole relations, 345–346,
    447–448
of pitch, 56, 154
vs. preference, in human neonate, 324
vs. production, 149–152, 154
and response mediation, 53, 73
representation vs. object, 277–278
shape, 10–11, 89
spatial, motor copy theory, 374
of spatial direction, development, 376–
    379
tactual, 98, 104–105, 359–362
task dependence, in children, 333
test, as control in identification experi-
    ments, 181
theories of perceptual development,
    61–73
transfer, 61, 62–63, 219–220, 224–228,
    230, 246–248
trend toward specificity, 450–456
of velocity, 383–384
Displacement, of auditory stimulation,
    208–209
Dissociation, 108–109

Distinctive features, abstraction, 108–111, 139, 153–154, 160
and acquired distinctiveness of cues, 64
and acquired equivalence, 71
in amodal perception, 218–219, 225
cross-modal, 222–223, 230
detection, 4, 82–91, 150, 169–171, 259, 341 ff.
and developmental changes in perceptual activity, 344–346, 454, 456, 457 ff.
and discrimination, 168, 209, 332
and economy in perception, 463–464
enhanced, 99, 146–150, 152, 217, 299
faces, 107, 155, 355, 356, 399
of forms, 64, 69, 361 ff.
in imprinting, 314
of language, 86–91, 142–143, 144, 424 ff., 426–427
learning, as medical skill, 8–9
learning, of nonsense items (scribbles), 77–79, 452
learning, and visual deprivation, 243–244
and learning objects vs. pictures, 397, 400
and memory images, 150
number, and errors of recognition, 79
and perceptual strategies, 122–123
in picture perception, 406–407, 411
potential, in discrimination nets, 94
in predifferentiation, 33, 73, 100–108
and priority of part vs. whole perception, 447
and recognition, 146–148, 179
and reduction of information processed, 129
for rigid objects, 417
shared, and categorization, 190
and species-specific response, 272–275, 298
and thresholds, 165
of water, 273–274
Distorted rooms, 42, 43
Distortion, adaptation to, 5–6, 57, 194, 200–201, 211; *see also* Chapter 10
in Ames demonstrations, 42 ff.
with conflicting depth cues, 206–208
of patterns, and recognition, 51
of perception, and centration, 342–34⁊
in schemata, and geometric illusions, 408–409
types, 195
Drawing(s), by children, Gestalt analysis, 411–412, 413
compared to photographs, 102–103

effect of orientation on form, 106–107
forms, 148–151
from memory, and distinctive features, 146–148
neonate attention to, 352 ff.
production vs. discrimination priority, 446–447
and projective size, 338
recognition by animals, 277–278
similarity judgments by children, 346
Drive(s), 120, 124–125

Echoes, 10–12, 16, 265–266; *see also* Blind, Facial vision, Sonar
Ecological validity, 38, 319
Ecology, in Brunswik's theory of perception, 15, 37 ff., 42
and perception, 13, 132
Embedded figures, *see* Figure(s), embedded
Empiricism, and associationist theory of perception, 19, 20
nativism-empiricism controversy, 19–21
view of effects of experience, 119
Enhancement, 102–105, 252–255; *see also* Augmentation
Enrichment, of stimulus environment, theories of perceptual development, 61, 75, 215; *see also* Augmentation
EPAM (Elementary Perceiving and Memorizing Machine), 93–94
Equivalence, acquired, of cues, 26, 64, 68–72
binocular, 246
cross-modal, 1, 6, 12, 196–197, 220–224, 227, 230, 331
in geometric schemata, 408
of responses, and categorization, 190
of sentence transforms, 429
and shared features, 71
transformations, in computer models for pattern recognition, 92
Error(s), confusion, forms, 181
constant, age differences, 405–406, 453
constant, in absolute judgments, 182–184
constant, in children's size judgments, 334–335
constant, in depth judgments, 375
constant, in drawing aircraft, 148
constant, effect of knowledge of results, 136–137
constant, in object constancy judgments, 367
in discrimination of letter-like forms, age differences, 414–417
in judgment of uprightness, 378

Error(s) (*cont.*)
in learning sequential material, 422
localizing, with prism spectacles, 138
matching, and spatial directions, 376
matrix, 86–87, 89–91; *see also* Confusion
in Morse code learning, 189–190, 222
reading and spelling and overgeneralization of orthographic structure, 440–441
in scanning tasks, 171
in selective listening, developmental differences, 459–460
of the standard (Piaget), 336
variable, in absolute judgments, 183–184
variable, age differences in depth judgments, 371, 375
variable, decrease with practice, 80
variable, in discrimination, 175
variable, effect of knowledge of results, 136–137
variable, reduction in perceptual development, 452–454
Ethology, 13, 298–299; *see also* Chapters 13, 14
Event(s), and conservation, 388
distal, in Brunswik's theory of perception, 15
invariants, 13, 193 ff., 399
motion pictures as representations, 17
and object constancy, 369
ontogeny of perception, 381–392
as sources of stimulation, 15, 16
phylogeny of perception, 270–272
properties of, in unidimensional stimulation, 178
Evolution, 20, 281–283; *see also* Chapter 13
Exploration, auditory, in dolphins, 266
and cross-modal invariants, 223
developmental changes, 456–459
facilitation by massive stimulation, 253–255
and formation of schema, 152
and geometric illusions, 408–409
and habituation in human neonates, 329
motive, 125–126
in motor copy theory, 229
and ontogeny of object perception, 344
in Piaget's view of perception, 48
priority of features, and discrimination by children, 332
reflexes, 54–55
and schema formation, 230
and selective perception, 121
sense organ adjustment, 115, 116

tactual, 55–56, 359–362
termination of perceptual, 133–143
Extinction, 139–140, 261, 308–309, 310
Eye movements, in detection of embedded figures, 174
evolutionary trends, 282–283
as feature of human faces, 352
Gesell's observations, 27
in Hebb's theory of perceptual development, 58, 59–60, 216
in human neonate, 325, 360, 382
and ontogeny of perception, 343–344, 457–459
in perception of visual direction, 198
in picture perception, 410–411
in Soviet theory of perceptual development, 54–55
after visual deprivation, 234, 246
Eye-voice span, 441–442

Face(s), distinctive features, and naming, 155, 156
drawings, 104, 106–107
expressions, 217, 347 ff.
infant perception, 318, 322–324, 326–327, 342–343, 347 ff., 360, 373, 382, 399
Facial vision, 10, 11
Familiarity, effect in imprinting, 308, 311, 312–313
of faces, 355–356
of features, and discrimination, 105–108
and habituation in human neonates, 329
and similarity judgments by children, 346
of stimulus materials, in transfer experiments, 225
of words, effect in listening experiments with children, 460
Feature(s), attended to by human neonate, 324, 325, 329 ff., 342–343
in computer models for pattern recognition, 93–94
exaggeration, 217, 273
of faces, 347–356, 399; *see also* Face(s)
familiarity, and discrimination, 105–108
in imprinting, 300–301, 304, 314, 345
intermodal, 217, 227
invariant, of objects, pick-up by infant, 363
linearity as, in children's drawings, 412
and memorial representation, 150
patterns, 82–83

in perception of language, 84, 86–89, 292–293, 424–427
priority, in discrimination, 332, 346
priority in ontogeny of object perception, 357–359
redundant, effect on discrimination, 462
relational, 2, 188, 345; *see also* Distinctive features
sampling, and developmental changes in search strategies, 458
and the schema, 153
of spatial layout, 370
task utility, and perceptual strategy, 122, 123
Feedback, and absolute estimation of multidimensional stimuli, 187
and adaptation to transformed stimulus arrays, 195, 210–211, 380
auditory, 10–12, 426–427
in cognitive development, 160–161
effect on pitch differential limen, 176–177
effect of restricted, 248–251
and kinetic depth effect, 207
in Morse code learning, 189
from production to discrimination, 154
from self-produced movements, 137–139
in Soviet theory of perceptual development, 55
see also Knowledge of results; Punishment; Reinforcement; Stimulation, response-produced
Field independence, 378
Figure(s), ambiguous, 30, 31, 130, 133–134, 135
articulation, and experience, 31–32
constrained, 179–180, 222
copying, by children, 148–151
embedded, 31, 32, 33, 109, 111–113, 115, 135, 171–174, 346
and eye-movement, 55
incomplete, 29, 30, 448–449
learning of planometric vs. stereometric, 396
metric, 179–180, 222
perception by animals, 284–287
perception by birds, 286–287
Figure-ground, differentiation, 324, 344–345, 369–370
in Hebb's theory of perceptual development, 58
reversal, 130
Filtering, developmental changes, 459–461
by environmentally deprived animals, 237

of external stimuli, and "instinctive" behavior, 298
and incidental learning, 461–462
of irrelevant stimulation, 111–114
in scanning tasks, 171
Fingerprints, 66, 67, 178–179
Fixation, and developmental changes in attention, 456–458
after environmental deprivation, 234, 242
and eye movements, in picture perception, 410
and geometric illusions, 409
in infants, 27, 322–325, 329, 342–344, 356, 360, 373, 382, 399–401
in reading, 438, 442
and stabilized images, 60
Following response, 301, 304, 306, 307, 314
Form(s), confusion, 181
discrimination, by children, 148–151, 330–331, 346, 412–417
discrimination, and dark-rearing, 239–241
discrimination, and enhanced stimulus environment, 252–253
discrimination, interocular transfer, 247–248
discrimination, and labelling experiments, 68–71
discrimination, and prolonged visual experience, 258–259
discrimination, tactile, 98
effect of deprivation on imprinting, 313
effect of orientation in drawings, 106–107
graphic, 179
and looking behavior in human neonates, 255–258, 325, 329, 342–343
in looming experiments, 271–272
memory for, 146
perception, criticism of Soviet theory, 56–57
perception, cross-modal, 222–224, 226–228
perception, past experience and, 31–34
Freudian psychology, 124
Functional psychology, 36
and James' theory, 24
theory of perception, 25–26
theory of perceptual development, 21

Generalization, in absolute pitch estimation, 182
and acquired equivalence of cues, 64, 73
in concept formation, 464

Generalization (*cont.*)
    to continuum of difference, 110
    in discrimination theories of perceptual
        learning, 61
    in imprinting, 305–308, 314
    and inference in perception, 448
    and intermediate size relation, 292
    as inverse of discrimination, 175–176
    and law of heterogeneous summation,
        345
    and method of contrasts, 99–100
    of morphological rules by children,
        430–431
    and predifferentiation, 62, 139–140
    reduction, 64, 80, 94, 451–452
    and response-produced cue, 71
    of same-different relation, 291
    secondary, 64; *see also* Cue(s), ac-
        quired equivalence
    in spelling, 439–440
    of structure in letter sequences, 423
    test for object constancy in human
        neonates, 330, 363
    after visual deprivation, 245–246
Gestalt psychology, 36
    and amodal perception, 218
    analysis of drawings, 411–412, 413
    as descendant of Kantian theory, 22
    and Gottschaldt's experiments, 171
    perceptual grouping, 467
    relational perception in animals, 283–
        284
    theory of perceptual development, 21,
        28–34
Grammar, 421, 423, 428–432, 460
Grapheme(s), 86–91, 102, 179, 216–217,
    412–417, 433, 461–462; *see also* Let-
    ter(s), Writing
Gravity, 370, 376–379

Habituation, 5, 160, 327–329, 342; *see
    also* Adaptation
Hand regard, 251, 253–254, 360, 465
Handwriting, *see* Writing
Heterogeneous summation, 299–300, 345
Hierarchy, associative, and sequential
        dependencies in speech, 429
    cognitive, 151–152
    in differentiation of phoneme contrasts,
        424 ff.
    feature, for letters, 88
Homeostasis, and reinforcement, 120
Hospitalism, 236

Identification, definition, 180
    experiments on perceptual learning,
        180–191

tactual, development in children, 360–
        362
Illusions, 130, 132, 228, 407–409
Image(s), 150–154
    body, with inverting lens system, 197
    -building, in EPAM model of percep-
        tion, 93
    in cognitive development, 161
    displacement, with prisms, 200–201
    in form discrimination, 98–99
    memory, 146, 150–151
    mirror, animals' reactions, 275–276
    retinal, 25, 196–200, 241, 248–249,
        289, 363–364, 402
    stabilized, 59–60, 72, 89, 246
Imprinting, 233, 259, 345, 456; *see also*
    Chapter 14
Incidental learning, 461–462
Industry, perceptual learning in, 6–7
Inference, in Bruner's theory of percep-
        tion, 49
    in development of perception, 132,
        365, 448–449
    in problem-solving theory of percep-
        tion, 52
    unconscious, 21–22, 35, 51
Information, conflict, 208, 378–379
    about distortion, and adaptation, 211
    depth, 206–207, 267 ff., 270, 320–321,
        372, 402
    extraction, 3, 4, 120, 122
    feedback, *see* Knowledge of results
    for human face, 352
    hypothesis, of reinforcement, 129
    invariant, and transformations in
        space, 369
    irrelevant, attention to, 461–462
    lack of, as a motive, 126, 128
    meaning of term, 140
    in mirror reflections, 276
    modality specific, and transfer, 230
    for motion, 248, 382
    in motion pictures, 399–400
    for object permanence, 386
    in optic array, 14
    overload, 128
    potential, 12, 14, 17, 75–77, 129
    processing, 127, 411, 449
    reduction, 4, 140, 422, 430, 432, 438,
        466
    relational, and prism spectacles, 195
    for representations, 397, 398, 402–405
    in representations, 104, 397, 398, 403–
        405, 419
    selection, under sensory deprivation,
        128–129, 238–248
    in selective listening, 113–114

sensory, in Piaget's view of perceptual development, 47

sequential, and event perception, 381, 393

sequential, and symbol perception, 421–424

spatial properties, 10–13, 264–266, 370–371, 372–373

in stimulation, 129

in stimulation, and amodal perception, 219

in stimulation, correspondence with events, 15

in stimulation, differentiation theory, 94

in stimulation, for distal sources, 14

in stimulation, temporal properties, 13

stimulus, biased, 194–195

stimulus, correspondence with perception, 163

stimulus, differences as, 110

in stimulus flow, 285

stimulus, and heterogeneous summation, 299–300

stimulus, and inference in perception, 448–449

stimulus, and mapping to words, 420

stimulus, and part-whole problem, 346

stimulus, and transactionalist demonstrations, 45

theory of, 2, 429

transmitted, 123, 137, 183, 184–187, 188

trend toward economy in pick-up, 458, 461–471

Inhibition, and adaptation to transformed stimulus arrays, 197, 199, 210–211

of conflicting information, 207, 208, 380, 381

differential, in predifferentiation experiment, 139

and habituation, 328, 329

and obligatory attention, 342

of vision, in occluded eye, 247

Initial Teaching Alphabet, 436–437

Insight, 29

Instinct, 297–300

Instructions, *see* Task effects in perception

Integration, associative, 1, 53, 58

by blind restored to sight, 12

and development of sensory systems, 381

in enrichment theories of perceptual development, 75

in event perception, 381

intersensory, 228–229

in schema theory of perception, 46, 47

of schemata, and perception of causality, 391

Soviet theory of perceptual development, 54

of spatial properties, and object permanence, 385

in Werner's differentiation theory, 34

Intelligence, and detection of higher order structure, 466, 467–468

and discrimination by children, 333

effect of environmental deprivation, 236–237

effect on object constancy judgments, 366–367

effect of stimulus environment enhancement, 252 ff.

in Piaget's view of perceptual development, 48

Interval of uncertainty, *see* Uncertainty

Invariant(s), amodal, 230, 362

and auditory directional localization, 208

in bird song, 292

body axes and spatial directions, 376–379

common to objects and pictures, 403

and conservation, 388–389

description in perceptual learning experiments, 163

in differentiation theory, 94

over events, 13, 16, 193 ff., 381, 399

extraction, 16, 142, 160–161, 285

in flow patterns, 7

of human faces, 347, 355, 356

multimodal, 204, 210–213, 224, 293–294

of objects, pick-up by infant, 363

in perception of letters, 86

in spatial perception, 208, 210, 369, 376–379

of speech, 84, 111, 432

over transformations, 13, 84, 355, 369, 446

trend toward economy in search for, 462–471

Isolation, *see* Deprivation

Judgment, absolute estimation along dimensions, 181–184

in perception by children, 333–338

theories of perception, 45 ff.

Kinetic depth effect, 206–208

Knowledge of results, and cross-modal transfer, 228

and depth judgments, 375

and improvement in acuity, 165

Knowledge of results (*cont.*)
and improvement of discrimination, 178
and perceptual learning, 136–140
see also Feedback, Punishment, Reinforcement

Labelling, in cognitive development, 161
colors, and memory, 159–160
and discrimination learning, 64–69, 99, 158–160
of metric figures, and recognition, 180
and perception of causality, 391
verbal, role in perceptual learning, 154–160
see also Naming
Language, facilitation of perceptual learning, 155–157
mediation in transfer, 225, 229–230
in ontogenetic study of perception, 334
and phoneme features, 83–85
sequential structure, 421 ff.
statistical approximation, 438, 460
see also Grapheme(s), Phoneme(s), Speech, Word(s), Writing
Letter(s), categorization, 190–191
detection, effect of practice, 169–171
discrimination, 110, 433
distinctive features, 86–88, 142–144;
see also Grapheme(s), Symbols, Writing
identification, 188, 461–462
learning sequences and structure, 423
recognition, by blind restored to sight, 216–217
Light, deprivation, 238–248
direction, as depth cue, 260
effect on imprinting, 302
sensitivity, evolutionary trends, 281–283
Listening, 112–114, 178, 459–461
Local signs, 22, 25, 198
Localization, and adaptation to transformed optical array, 138, 197, 198, 200, 201, 211, 294
auditory, 208 ff., 266, 322, 328, 460
movements of, 25, 26, 197–198
of objects in space, 48, 318, 373–376
Locomotion, 197, 248, 264 ff., 300, 318, 319, 321
Looking, developmental changes, 27, 458
effect of movement, 399–400
in infants, 318, 342
and intermodal transfer, 359–362
in monkeys, 125, 277
see also Scanning
Looming, 16, 141, 249, 271–272, 384

Magnification, 205–206, 271–272, 384;
see also Looming
Manipulation, as drive in monkeys, 125
effect of massive stimulation, 253–254
following discrimination training in infants, 257
in perceptual development, 27, 458–459
in Soviet theory of perceptual development, 54
and visually directed reaching, 360–361
Mapping, of information to source, 17, 296
in language, 420, 426, 434, 437
of objects to representations, 403, 419
of one language into another, 158
Matching, cross-modal, 220–224, 226–227, 458, 459
of letter-like forms by children, 413–414
to memorial representations, 154, 449
phylogenetic comparisons, 290, 291
vs. production, 148–149
projective vs. objective, 336–338, 363, 366–367
template (prototype), 50–51, 91–92, 146
tests for object constancy, 365–366
and transfer of discrimination, 96–99
Maturation, and critical periods for imprinting, 310–311, 313, 314
in Gesell's theory of perceptual development, 27
vs. learning in perceptual development, 445–446
Meaning, in context theory of perception, 23
of percepts, with transformed stimulus arrays, 213
in representations, 417, 419
visual, through touch, 359
Mediation, additive, 61
verbal, 225, 227, 229–230, 389, 470
Medicine, perceptual learning in, 8, 9
Melodies, and perceptual learning, 80–82, 151
Micro-melodies, 35, 80
Memory, in *Aufgabe* experiments, 121–122
and codability (labelling), 155–156, 158–160
for form, 146 ff.
and object permanence, 385
representations, 148–150
schema theories, 152–154
Migration, of birds, 265

Military, perceptual learning in, 7–8, 10, 11
Minification, 205–206, 271–272, 384
Mirror image, perception in animals, 276
Morse code, 17, 188–190, 222, 279, 437
Motion, discrimination, 248–249
  in imprinting, 301–302, 303–305, 314
  and neonate attention, 352, 354–355, 360
  ontogeny of perception, 382–384
  passive vs. active, 249–251
  perceived, in depth, 16
  receptive fields (frog), 298
  relative, and depth judgment, 39–40
  as releasing stimulus, 271
Motion pictures, 17, 277, 399–400
Motivation, in direction of perceptual search, 124–129
  and imprinting, 308–311
  and priority of production vs. perception, 446–447
  after restricted rearing, 237–238
  see also Drive(s)
Motor commands, in speech perception, 426
Motor copy theory of perceptual development, 53 ff., 74
  and cross-modal transfer, 229
  and feedback from overt action, 138
  Hebb's theory, 58–61
  and localization of objects in space, 374
  and Piaget's view of perceptual development, 47
  and priority of production vs. perception, 446
  and reduction of uncertainty, 141
  Soviet theory of perception, 53–57, 151
  Taylor's theory, 57
Movement(s), and abstraction of shape, 150–151
  and adaptation to transformed stimulus arrays, 194, 197, 212
  articulatory, in learning phonemic contrasts, 425–426
  and detection of invariants by infants, 142
  effects of restricted, 248–251
  exploratory, 54–55, 229, 344, 360–362
  eye, see Eye movements
  feedback, and perceptual development, 138–139
  head, 269–270, 329–330
  and looking behavior in human neonates, 322, 342–343, 352, 354–355, 399–400
  in Soviet theory of perceptual development, 54–56

Naming, and acquired distinctiveness of cues, 64, 155
  and acquired equivalence of cues, 64, 68–72
  in cognitive development, 160–161
  in James' theory of discrimination, 24
  and memory for colors, 158–160
  in schema theory of perception, 46
  see also Labelling
Nativism, 19–21, 35, 233, 251, 263–264, 424, 432; see also Empiricism
Nature-nurture problem, 20, 233, 251, 263–264; see also Empiricism, Nativism
Normalization, 92, 194
Nystagmus, 234, 241, 382

Object(s), constancy, see Constancy
  ontogeny of perception, see Chapter 16
  permanence, 344, 381, 384–388
  phylogeny of perception, 272–275
  vs. pictures in learning experiments, 396–398
Occlusion, and object permanence, 16, 218, 381, 385–387
Oddity problem, 157, 291–292, 470
Odor, see Smell
Order, cross-modal similarities, 229
  detecting higher order structure, 467–469, 471
  in English orthography, 436–440
  perception by child, 14
  in speech, 428, 432
Organization, in children's drawings, 412
  in Gestalt theory of perception, 29–30, 76
  influence of habit on, 30–31
  in Werner's differentiation theory, 34
Orientation, in animals, 264 ff.
  effect on discrimination by children, 106–107, 331, 376–377
  and motor copy theory of perceptual development, 54–56, 374
  ocular, in human neonate, 325, 352
  in ontogeny of object perception, 345, 364, 416
  postural-visual relation, 378–379
  reflex, 54–56, 342
  after visual deprivation, 242, 243
Orthography, 436–441, 471

Parallax, binocular, 270, 364, 372, 373
  motion, 39–40, 269–270, 364, 372, 373, 402
  in object vs. picture perception, 402, 404
Parallel processing, 170; see also Template matching

Pattern(s), auditory, in production of articulation, 426
and avoidance on visual cliff, 319–320
cross-modal equivalence, 221–222, 225–226
detection, 81–82, 287–289
detection of higher order structure in, 467–468
differentiation by children, 148–151, 344
of features, 82–83
fragmentation of, stabilized image, 59–60
in Gestalt theory, 28
graphic, 412–417
and looking in human neonate, 322–324, 329, 342–343, 352–356
machine recognition, 50–51, 91–94
perception in language, 84, 279–280, 427, 438–441, 471
playback, 111, 154, 221–222
and restricted rearing, 238–248
tactual discrimination, 104–105
Perceptron, 50–51, 92
Perceptual defense, 131
Personality, in Bruner's theory of perception, 49 ff.
influence on perception, 130–132
in Transactional theory of perception, 41, 45
Phenomenal doubling, 391
Phoneme(s), 72, 83–86, 110, 155, 279–280, 292–293, 424–427
Photograph(s), aerial, interpretation of, 8
compared to other representations, 102–103, 397–398
human neonate attention to, 353
recognition by animals, 276–277, 287
Physiognomic perception, 34, 107
Picture(s), information in, 104; *see also* Depth
perception, 395–396, 403–404, 406–407
as sources of stimulation, 17; *see also* Caricature, Motion pictures, Photograph(s), Representation(s)
Pitch perception, 176–178, 181–182, 327–328
Predifferentiation, 62–63, 73, 99, 139–140, 179, 181
Prisms, adaptation, 26, 57, 138–139, 193, 195, 199–204, 260–261, 294–295, 380; *see also* Adaptation; Chapter 10
Problem-solving in perception, 45 ff., 49–52
Production, as cognitive process, 148–152, 161

priority in perception, 446–447
in speech development, 424–425, 428, 430
Pseudophones, 208–209
Psychophysics, methods for studying perceptual learning, 164 ff., 333–338
Punishment, 132, 133–136, 165, 309

Reaching, development, 318, 327, 344, 360
effect of massive stimulation, 253–254
Reaction time, 90, 142–143, 190–191, 452, 454–456, 463
Reading, 59, 169, 412–417, 433–442, 458
Reafference, 249–251; *see also* Feedback
Receptive fields, 89
in cats, 235
in frogs, 298
Receptors, evolution, 281–283
Recognition, definition, 179
of faces, 355–356
and imprinting, 301, 306–308
and perceptual learning, 145–148, 179–180
of representations, 275–278, 399–401, 406–407
Redundancy, developmental changes in effect, 371, 448–449, 458, 467 ff.
intermodal, 218, 219, 362
in language, 428, 438, 440–441
and learning of objects vs. pictures, 397
and Transactionalist demonstrations, 45
Reflection theory, *see* Motor copy theory of perceptual development
Reflex(es), exploratory, 54–56, 342, 374; *see also* Orientation
Reinforcement, and absolute judgments of multidimensional stimuli, 187
and adaptation to transformed optical array in animals, 295
and categorization, 191
and discrimination by children, 331–332
effect on threshold judgments, 165, 167–168
and imprinting, 308–311, 315
and intrinsic cognitive motivation, 124
and learning phonemes, 425, 426
in Morse code learning, 189
negative, and autistic perception, 132
of observing responses, 115–116
of operant conditioning, in human neonate, 330
of perception, 4, 120, 124–125, 133
and termination of perceptual search, 133 ff.; *see also* Punishment

and visual cliff performance, 242

Releaser, *see* Stimulus, releasing

Representation(s), comparison of modes of, 102–103
and concepts, 153
in ethological research, 104, 303–304
of faces, and neonate attention, 353–354
memorial, 146–148, 150, 151–152, 449
ontogeny of perception, 161; *see also* Chapter 18
phonemic, 431
phylogeny of perception, 275–278
and transfer, 154
as sources of stimulation, 17

Representative design of experiments, in Bruner's theory of perception, 50
in Brunswik's theory of perception, 42
in development of spatial directions, 376
and geometric illusions, 409
in sensory deprivation studies, 128
in Transactional theory of perception, 45
and verticality judgments, 378

Response(s), bias, *see* Bias
confounded with perceptual learning, 134–136, 163–164, 180–181, 188, 226
fear, 237–238, 270–271, 272, 277, 311, 312–313, 355–356
indicator, 174, 180, 322, 325–327, 347
localizing, *see* Localization, Orientation
mediation, 53, 57
observing, 115–116
-oriented theories of perceptual learning, 74; *see also* Chapter 4

Retarded, perception in, 236, 331–333, 357–358, 366–367, 397, 409, 462, 466, 467–468

Retrieving in rats, 298

Reversal learning, 109, 256, 291, 470

Reward, *see* Feedback, Knowledge of results, Punishment, Reinforcement

Rod and frame test, 378

Rorschach test, 130, 346

Same-different judgments, 33, 65, 71, 85, 91, 105, 122, 151, 174, 178, 189, 227, 290–291, 294, 301, 334, 346, 357, 382, 410, 454–456, 458

Scanning, auditory, 10, 266
developmental changes, 376, 410, 458
effect of practice, 169–171
in human neonate, 325, 400–401
in letter perception, 89

Schema, in Bruner's theory of perception, 49
in cognitive development, 161
and geometric illusions, 408–409
and localization of objects in space, 374
and memory, 152–154, 155
and object permanence, 385
and perception of causality, 391
and perception of faces, 356
in Piaget's view of perceptual development, 47–48, 52, 152, 230
theory of perception, 46–47, 52, 74

Scribbles (nonsense items), 77–78, 145–146, 155–156, 179, 446, 452

Search, perceptual, 169–171, 457–459; *see also* Chapter 7

Sensation(s), in theories of perception, 22, 46, 75

Sequential processing, 170; *see also* Discrimination, net

Set, in Attneave's schema theory, 153
for discrimination, 33, 175
effect on perception, 121–124, 460
learning, 255–258, 293, 397–398, 465–466
see also *Aufgabe* experiments

Shape, construction through movement, 48
discrimination, 10–11, 89, 222–224, 225, 274, 285, 330 ff., 360–362
effect on imprinting, 303–304
preferences, in neonate animals, 274–275
see also Figure(s), Form(s)

Sign language, 72, 280, 421

Size-weight illusion, 357–358, 454

Slant perception, 364, 366, 372, 464

Smell, 4–5, 168, 182–183, 265

Sonar, 10, 11; *see also* Echoes

Sound spectrograph, 111, 221–222

Soviet theory of perception, *see* Motor copy theory of perceptual development

Space, and development of object permanence, 385
judgments in pictures, 403–404
ontogeny of perception, *see* Chapter 17
in perceptual theories, 21, 25, 26, 43
phylogeny of perception, 264–270
and search for invariants, 210
as source of stimulation, 16

Species specific behavior, stimulation for, 298–299, 309–310, 314; *see also* Stimulus, releasing

Specific nerve energies, 217, 228 ff.

Spectacles, adaptation to, 5–6, 204–205, 294

Spectacles (*cont.*)
  see also Prisms
Speech, as coded stimulation, 17, 420
  filtering in, 112–114
  invariants, 111
  perception, 279–280, 292–293, 424–432
  priority of production vs. discrimination, 446
  in relation to reading, 433 ff.
  see also Language, Phoneme(s)
Spontaneous recovery, 139–140
Stabilized images, 59–60, 72, 89, 246
Stimulation, correspondence with perception, 15, 76, 77, 95
  distal sources, 14, 15–17, 38
  impoverished, 406
  modality specific, 222, 227
  multidimensional, 163, 168–174, 178–179, 184–190, 223, 331–333
  multimodal, in space perception, 379–381
  potential, 4, 14, 75–76, 77, 115, 314, 341; *see also* Information
  proximal, 14, 15, 43, 45
  punctate, 2, 20, 22, 37
  relational, 208–209, 210, 283–284, 289, 290–291, 296
  response-produced, 61, 211, 229
Stimulus, compound, 300
  flow, information in, 285
  -oriented theory of perceptual learning, 74; *see also* chapters on differentiation theory
  releasing, 3, 16, 104, 261, 270–271, 298–299, 306, 314, 345
  supernormal, 104, 273 ff., 299
  transformations, *see* Transformation(s)
Street figures, 29, 30, 406–407
Structuralism, *see* Context, theory of perception
Structure, of coded stimulation, 17
  in differentiation theory, 94
  evolutionary trends, in perception, 283 ff.
  as factor in form perception, 33
  and geometric illusions, 408
  in Gestalt theory, 28
  higher order, 82, 91, 161, 188, 189, 273, 286–287, 437–442, 456, 466–471
  in language, 421–422, 428–432, 433, 434, 437, 440–442, 460; *see also* Grammar, Orthography
  in multidimensional stimuli, 187
  in ontogeny of object perception, 344, 346
  and part vs. whole perception, 447

  and reading, 433 ff., 437–442; *see also* Grammar, Orthography, Structure, in language
  and reduction of information, 141
  sequential, 422–423, 433 ff., 437–442; *see also* Grammar, Order, Orthography, Structure, in language
  in stimulation, assumptions, 13–14
Summation, heterogeneous, 299–300, 345
Surfaces, 370–371
Symbols, and coding, 278–279
  compared with pictorial representations, 411–417, 419–420
  discrimination, 86; *see also* Grapheme(s), Letter(s), Word(s), Writing
  and reading, 433–442
Syntax, 17, 421, 428, 432
Synthesis, 24, 150, 426

Tabula rasa, 311
Task effects in perception, 121–124, 336–338, 366–367, 458–459
Taxonomy, perceptual, 15–17
Telestereoscope, 206–208
Template-matching, 50–51, 91–94, 146, 308
Texture, 269, 274, 320–321, 370–372, 373, 403–406
Thinking, in perceptual learning, 45 ff.
Threshold(s), absolute, 167–168, 178
  auditory, 56
  determination with children, 335
  differential, 56, 176–179, 357
  effect of practice, *see* Chapter 9
  effect of reward and punishment, 135
  for motion, 382–383
  for phoneme boundaries, 72
  for recognition of drawings vs. photographs, 102–104
  for weight discrimination, developmental trends, 358–359
  two-point, on skin, 25, 165–167
Tilting-room–tilting-chair test, 378–379
Transactional psychology, 2, 41–45, 51, 132
Transfer, and abstraction of distinctive features, 100–110, 463–464
  and abstraction of invariants, 466
  of adaptation to transformed stimulus arrays, 198, 204, 209, 211–212
  in concept-learning, 99, 463–464
  as control in identification experiments, 181
  of discrimination, 61, 62–63, 242, 274, 278, 285, 331, 397, 414–416
  following discrimination training in infants, 257–258

and distinctive labels, 66–67
between distorted rooms, 44–45
and filtering, 111–113
in form perception, 33, 68, 96–99, 179
by imaginal representation, 154
of improved auditory thresholds, 167, 177–178
of intermediate size relation, 292
intermodal, 12, 293–294, 361–362, 392; *see also* Chapter 11
interocular, 204, 242, 246–248
and language, 190–191, 430, 435–436
of objects to representations, 278, 397, 401, 419
of oddity response, 291–292
of practice on detection of embedded figures, 171, 173
of stabilized image pattern perception, following visual deprivation, 246
of telestereoscope training, 207
of two-point limen reduction, 165–166
Transformation(s), and conservation, 388–389
and cross-modal transfer of discrimination, 227–228, 361
and differentiation of facial expressions, 355
imposed, 260–261, 294–295; *see also* Chapter 10
invariants over, 13, 84, 464 ff.; *see also* Invariant(s)
in language, 86, 292–293, 429
and object permanence, 386
and perception of causality, 391
and perception of forms, 96–99, 412–417
in space, 48, 369
Transitivity, 324, 325, 388
Transport, 383–384, 407–409
Transposition, 408
learning, 109–110, 245, 256, 283–285

of intermediate size relation, 292
of melody, 28, 80–82, 151, 292
Tunnel effect, 218

Uncertainty, interval, 80, 175, 176, 453–454
reduction, 120, 126–127, 129, 140–143, 389, 447
in sensory deprivation experiments, 128

Velocity, perception, 382–384
Verticality, 378–379
Visual cliff, frontispiece, 16, 60, 239–243, 249, 261, 267–270, 319–321, 371–372, 402, 446

Weight, perception, 39, 80, 176, 178, 357–359, 454
Weighting of experience, 42, 132
Whorfian hypothesis, 158–160
Wine tasting, 4, 6–7, 8, 24
Wisconsin General Test Apparatus, 331–333
Wool grading, 6
Word(s), as corresponding units in writing and speech, 434–436
frequency, 131, 429–430
generalization, 451–452
perception by animals, 279–280
as symbols, *see* Chapter 19
taboo, and perceptual defense, 131
Writing, 17, 86, 87, 411, 434–437; *see also* Grammar, Grapheme(s), Language, Letter(s), Orthography

X-ray plate reading, 8, 9

Zuni Indians, 159–160